The
Routledge Guide to
Music Technology

The
Routledge Guide to
Music Technology

Edited by Thom Holmes

Routledge
Taylor & Francis Group
New York London

Routledge is an imprint of the
Taylor & Francis Group, an informa business

Published in 2006 by
Routledge
Taylor & Francis Group
270 Madison Avenue
New York, NY 10016

Published in Great Britain by
Routledge
Taylor & Francis Group
2 Park Square
Milton Park, Abingdon
Oxon OX14 4RN

Printed in the United States of America on acid-free paper
10 9 8 7 6 5 4 3 2 1

International Standard Book Number-10: 0-415-97323-6 (Hardcover) 0-415-97324-4 (Softcover)
International Standard Book Number-13: 978-0-415-97323-6 (Hardcover) 978-0-415-97324-3 (Softcover)
Library of Congress Card Number 2005030642

Library of Congress Cataloging-in-Publication Data

The Routledge guide to music technology / edited by Thom Holmes.
    p. cm. -- (Routledge guides)
  Includes bibliographical references and indexes.
  ISBN 0-415-97323-6 (hb) -- ISBN 0-415-97324-4 (pb)
  1. Sound--Recording and reproducing--Dictionaries. 2. Sound recording industry--Dictionaries. 3. Music and technology. 4. Sound recordings--History. I. Holmes, Thom. II. Series.

ML102.S67.R68 2006
621.389'303--dc22
          2005030642

Taylor & Francis Group
is the Academic Division of Informa plc.

Visit the Taylor & Francis Web site at
http://www.taylorandfrancis.com

and the Routledge Web site at
http://www.routledge-ny.com

Contents

Contributors

Dr. Garth Alper is an associate professor in jazz piano and is coordinator of the Music Media Division at the University of Louisiana in Lafayette. An active composer and arranger, he performs regularly with the Garth Alper Trio.

Frank Andrews is an English collector and writer who has authored more than 100 articles about acoustic-era labels and phonograph history, including histories of Aeolian-Vocalion, Edison Bell, Imperial, Zonophone, and Homophone. He served as contributing editor for the first edition of the *Encyclopedia of Recorded Sound*.

Rev. Claude G. Arnold, C.S.B., is Associate professor, Department of English, at St. Michael's College, University of Toronto in Ontario, Canada.

William Ashbrook is a contributing editor for *Opera Quarterly*. He is a distinguished professor emeritus at Indiana State University in Terre Haute.

Carl Benson is the editor of *The Bob Dylan Companion* and writes on pop, rock, and folk music as well as music history.

Garrett Bowles, music librarian, University of California—San Diego, is the past president of the Association for Recorded Sound Collections.

George Brock-Nannestad, for seven years with the School of Conservation of the Royal Danish Academy of Fine Arts, Copenhagen, Denmark, has specialized in early sound recording technology.

Tim Brooks, currently vice president, research at the USA cable network in New York is the past president of the Association for Recorded Sound Collections and a contributing editor to its journal. He is the author of *Complete Directory to Prime Time Network TV Shows* and numerous articles.

E. T. Bryant was a city librarian in England. His memory is honored annually through the E. T. Bryant Prize given by the International Association of Music Libraries (IAML) and the Music Libraries Trust for a significant contribution to the literature of music librarianship by a library and information science student. It recognizes the enormous contribution Bryant made to the field of professional music librarianship.

Craig Bunch, library coordinator, Coldspring Independent School District, Coldspring, Texas, has contributed articles on the arts to *The St. James Encyclopedia of Popular Culture* and *The Dictionary of American History*.

Richard C. Burns, audio engineer, Packburn Electronics, Inc., Dewitt, New York was formerly an audio engineer, Syracuse University School of Music in Syracuse, New York, and producer of Overtone Records in the 1950s.

John Case is the owner of Priority/Anomaly Records in Fort Worth, Texas.

B. Lee Cooper, provost and vice president for Academic Affairs at Newman University in Wichita, Kansas, is the author of numerous scholarly articles and monographs relating to popular music recordings.

Ranjita (Anji) Kalita Cornette has over fifteen years of experience with sound engineering and preservation. She is director of the Sound Preservation Laboratory at the Cutting Corporation in Bethesda, Maryland (www.cuttingarchives.com). Her work and staff was featured in the documentary *Save Our History/Save Our Sounds*, which premiered on the History Channel on December 26, 2002.

Martin Elste, curator, Musikinstrumenten-Museum, Staatliches Institut für Musikforschung PK, Berlin, is the author of, among many other books and articles, *Kleines Tonträger-Lexikon, Modern Harpsichord Music: A Discography*, and *Meilensteine der Bach-Interpretation 1750–2000*, which won the Association for Recorded Sound Collections (ARSC) Award for Excellence in Historical Recorded Sound Research, 2001. Having been a record reviewer for *Die Zeit, Fono Forum, Klassik heute*, and *Fanfare*, he has served on the panel of the German Record Critics' Award since 1983 and was elected president of it in 2000.

Howard Ferstler, formerly librarian for Florida State University in Tallahassee, is the author of *High Fidelity Audio-Video Systems, High Definition Compact Disc Recordings, The Home Theater Companion*, and *The Digital Audio Music List*.

Paul Fischer, associate professor of recording industry at Middle Tennessee State University in Murfreesboro, studies the origins and development of recording technologies and the careers of inventors. He writes on the application of literacy and cultural theory to popular culture and American popular music, among other subjects.

Doug Gelbert, in addition to writing on issues relating to popular music, is the author of a series of guides on hiking.

Gerald D. Gibson is head, Curatorial Section, Motion Picture, Broadcasting and Recorded Sound Division at the Library of Congress in Washington, D.C. He is past President of the Association for Recorded Sound Collections.

Michael H. Gray, researcher, Voice of America in Washington, D.C., is past president of the Association for Recorded Sound.

Bruce D. Hall is music coordinator/reference librarian of the Newton Gresham Library at Sam Houston State University in Huntsville, Texas.

Val Hicks is a retired music educator, vocal arranger, songwriter, music historian, and veteran member (fifty-two years) of the Barbershop Quartet Society, which is part of the Society for the Preservation and Encouragement of Barbershop Quartet Singing in America (SPEBSQSA). Dr. Hicks just completed a book titled *The Six Roots of Barbershop Harmony*.

Brad Hill is a writer, musician, and computer expert. He has worked in the online field since 1992 and is the best-selling author of many books including *MIDI for Musicians, The Digital Songstream*, and numerous articles on digital technology and music. His website is www.bradhill.com.

Frank Hoffmann is professor of library science at Sam Houston State University in Huntsville, Texas. He has written over thirty-five books and many articles, including *Popular American Recording Pioneers: 1895-1925* with Tim Gracyk and CHOICE book award winner *The Literature of Rock* with B. Lee Cooper.

Thom Holmes, a musicologist, composer, and performer of electronic music, has been active in the field of electronic music for over thirty years. He recently published a second edition of *Electronic and Experimental Music*. His website is www.thomholmes.com.

Geoffrey Hull is professor of recording industry and coordinator of the music business program at Middle Tennessee State University in Murfreesboro.

Edgar Hutto, Jr., was formerly principal member, Advanced Technology Laboratories, at Radio Corporation of America (RCA).

Warren Rex Isom (1910–2003) was formerly chief engineer, RCA Records and engineer, RCA Applied Research.

Paul T. Jackson is the initiator, a founding member, former vice president, and contributing editor of ARSC. A retired librarian, he is the owner of Trescott Research, which does information and library development consulting. He is also a writer and editor of the *Plateau Area Writers' Association's Quarterly*, a choral musician and timpanist for Renton Community Concert Band, and president and timpanist for the Gateway Concert Band, all in Washington State.

Allen Koenigsberg teaches ancient history and classics at Brooklyn College in New York City, and is the author of *Edison Cylinder Records, 1889–1912* and *The Patent History of the Phonograph*. For many years, he was the editor and publisher of *The Antique Phonograph Monthly*. His research website is located at www.phono-books.com.

Dave Mandl is a writer and photographer. His weekly radio show "World of Echo" can be heard on WFMU in New York City and Resonance FM in London.

Martin Manning, research librarian for the U.S. Department of State in Washington, D.C., has degrees from Boston College (B.S.) and Catholic University of America (M.S.L.S.). He has been a federal librarian and archivist for thirty years, and he has contributed to several reference books. His book, *Historical Dictionary of American Propaganda*, will be published by Greenwood at the end of 2004.

R. Dale McIntosh is associate professor and chair, arts in education, at the University of Victoria, Victoria, British Columbia. Formerly, he was director of performing arts for the Province of Alberta.

Chuck Miller is the author of *Warman's American Records*, soon to come out in a second edition. He also writes extensively on music and animation.

Kurt Nauck is the owner of Nauck's Vintage Records in Spring, Texas (www.78rpm.com), and author of the *American Record Label Image Encyclopedia*.

Susan Nelson teaches instrumental music at Bemidji State University, Bemidji, Minnesota, where she has also worked as a music librarian.

Robert J. O'Brien is professor of English at West Virginia Wesleyan College in Buckhannon, West Virginia. A long-time member of the Association of Recorded Sound Collections, he has an extensive collection of literary recordings, especially of Shakespeare's works, and has delivered many presentations on recordings of Shakespeare.

Ian Peel, producer and writer, has contributed to the *Virgin Encyclopedia of Popular Music*, the *New Grove Dictionary of Music and Musicians*, and other reference works as well as being the author of *Music & The Internet (Future, 1995), The Unknown Paul McCartney (Reynolds & Hearn, 2003),* and numerous reviews and interviews.

Steven Permut is senior music cataloger at the Library of Congress in Washington, D.C. Formerly, he worked as music cataloger and reference librarian at the University of Maryland.

Jeffrey Place is archivist, Ralph Rinzler Archives at the Center for Folklife Programs and Cultural Studies at the Smithsonian Institution in Washington, D.C. He is the producer and annotator of over two dozen recordings of American music for the Smithsonian.

Robert C. Reinehr is professor of psychology, Southwestern University, Georgetown, Texas, and the co-author of *Handbook of Old-Time Radio: A Comprehensive Guide to Golden Age Radio Listening and Collecting* with Jon D. Swartz.

Brian Rust is an independent scholar and collector who lives in England. He formerly served as a librarian at the British Broadcasting Corporation (BBC) Gramophone Library.

William Schurk is sound recordings archivist for the Jerome Library at Bowling Green State University, Bowling Green, Ohio.

Julia Scott is a journalist in San Francisco. She teaches at DeAnza College in Cupertino, California.

Gerald Seaman is professor of music, University of Auckland in Auckland, New Zealand.

James Smart is a former reference librarian, Music Division, at the Library of Congress in Washington, D.C.

Ron Streicher is proprietor of Pacific Audio-Visual Enterprises in Pasadena, California, and current president of the Audio Engineering Society. During the summer months, he also is the director of audio production for the Aspen Music Festival and School. His book, *The New Stereo Soundbook*, has become a reference standard of the audio industry.

Jon D. Swartz is a psychologist, formerly associate dean for Libraries and Learning Resources, as well as professor of education and psychology at Southwestern University in Georgetown, Texas. He is the author, with Robert C. Reinehr, of *Handbook of Old-Time Radio: A Comprehensive Guide to Golden Age Radio Listening and Collecting.*

Susan Garretson Swartzburg (1938–1996) was preservation specialist and assistant librarian for Collection Management at the Rutgers University Libraries in New Brunswick, New Jersey.

James L. Van Roekel, director of academic instructional technology and distance learning at Sam Houston State University in Huntsville, Texas, is a part-time musician, audio engineer, and sound designer.

Sara Velez is librarian, Rodgers & Hammerstein Archives of Recorded Sound, at the New York Public Library in New York City.

A

AAC · *See* ADVANCED AUDIO CODING.

A/B Comparison · Typically done between audio components as a way to ascertain if one is superior to the other, or if they are either essentially identical or different sounding. A refinement is the ABX testing device. The latter works by allowing known A and B components to be compared to an unknown X, which may be either A or B, depending on which listening trial is taking place, it allows for an easy-to-enforce, double-blind protocol to minimize participant prejudices. *See also* CLARK, DAVID.—Howard Ferstler

A & B Switch · A control in a stereo amplifier that is used to channel the signal from a monaural record into both speakers, for greater sound spread. It also removes one cause of rumble and noise in the playback by canceling the vertical response of the cartridge.

A Side · The two sides of a double-sided disc are usually identified as A and B, with the A side being the featured selection. This term was applied to 78s, 45s, and LPs, but is no longer appropriate for CDs, which feature digitally programmable selections on what is, in essence, one playable side.

AC-3 · *See* DOLBY DIGITAL.

Academy Curve · Formalized in 1938, it is the name of the standard motion picture optical-audio track, which has been around since sound first appeared in film. Not exactly high in fidelity by modern standards, the response is only flat between 100 Hz and 1600 Hz. In the bass range, the response is down 7 dB at 40 Hz (making it utterly useless for killer-sound action movies), and in the treble, it is down 10 dB at 5 kHz and 18 dB at 8 kHz. The extreme attenuation of the higher frequencies was designed to hide the high-frequency artifacts in early film sound production.— Howard Ferstler

Acetate Disc · *See* LACQUER DISC.

Acoustic · The name given to a recording made without electrical technology. As extensive electrical recording began in 1925, the period up to that time is usually identified as the acoustic era. *See also* ACOUSTIC RECORDING.

Acoustic Compensator · A device in a binaural sound system that adjusts the signal path lengths so that they are properly matched.

Acoustic Feedback · A recording situation where the sound from speaker system is picked up by the microphone feeding it, re-amplified to the same loudspeaker, picked up by the microphone again, and so forth. With each complete cycle, the signal becomes larger until the loop rapidly runs wild and produces the squeal often accidentally heard during programs that feature sound reinforcement.—Howard Ferstler

Acoustic Generator · A transducer that converts electrical, mechanical, or other energy into sound.

Acoustic Horn · *See* HORN I.

Acoustic Recording · Also known as mechanical recording. It is the method of recording in which all energy comes from the sound waves themselves; it was used from the earliest days of Edison and Berliner until the onset of electrical recording in 1925. Sounds to be recorded were sung, played, or spoken into a horn (see also HORN I), which activated a diaphragm attached to a stylus. The stylus transferred the vibration patterns to the surface of a cylinder or a disc. To concentrate this acoustic energy sufficiently for the stylus to etch a usable pattern it was necessary for singers and performers to direct their vibrations into a large collecting horn; this requirement favored strong sound producers, and worked against inclusion of weaker vessels like string instruments (*see also* STROH VIOLIN.) Great ingenuity was applied in the acoustic recording studio to overcome these inherent obstacles. Horns were varied in diameter for different sound sources; they were wrapped with tapes to counter their own resonance; they might be used in clusters, running to a single tube that moved the diaphragm. For a few recordings, Edison used one brass recording horn 125 feet long, five feet in diameter at the bell. Different thicknesses of diaphragm were used depending on the volume of sound being handled—thinner for weak sounds, thicker for heavy sounds.

As there was no volume control device to regulate acoustic recording, artists had to be positioned in the studio in ways that would bring their contributions to the diaphragm in proper balance. Brasses were placed at some distance from the recording horns, and French hornists had to play with their backs to the conductor to put their tones on the right track to the horn. Bass drums did not record well, and were usually omitted; tubas typically played the parts written for double basses. (The string bass can be heard on early jazz recordings, however, such as Victors of 1917 and dance band discs.)

A recording orchestra in the acoustic studio had to squeeze into a tight formation around one or more horns, a requirement that mitigated against large ensembles; thus, an orchestra of 60 musicians might be reduced to 30 for the recording session. Military bands often recorded with a group of about 15 of their membership. Problems of blend and balance were dealt with by moving the musicians here and there, now closer and now farther from the sound collector. Cellos were mounted on movable platforms.

For an experienced musical listener, the resulting reproduction of a familiar work could be embellished by memory and imagination —techniques used even in later sophisticated eras of recording to achieve "concert hall realism." For the many persons who listened to orchestras only on cylinder or disc, the impression gained of the symphonic world of music must have been as imprecise as that of Queen Victoria's appearance derived from one of the pioneer postage stamps.

Acoustic Suspension · The principle was developed by Edgar Villchur in 1953 (patented in 1956) in his effort to reduce the most common problem with speakers of the day: excessive bass distortion. The first commercial product to use this system was the Acoustic Research model AR-1, introduced in October 1954. In simplest terms, the acoustic-suspension speaker uses the elastic body of air in a sealed speaker enclosure as the primary "restoring force" for the speaker cone, instead of the mechanical suspension of the speaker itself. It resembles the principle of a vacuum, where the outward movement of the cone reduces pressure and the inward movement increases pressure against the speaker cone. The entrapped air is linear for this small change in pressure, and the result is greatly improved linearity and reduced harmonic distortion. A secondary dividend is that the enclosure must be relatively small to work properly, and this made the small acoustic-suspension bookshelf speaker commercially acceptable for most households. *See also* BASS REFLEX SYSTEM; LOUDSPEAKER.—Howard Ferstler

Acoustical Elements · Parameters in an acoustical system that are analogous to electrical elements. *See also* MECHANICAL-ELECTRICAL ANALOGIES.

Acoustical Labyrinth · A kind of loudspeaker enclosure in which a maze-like folded passage is added behind the speaker to improve its bass response without promoting unwanted resonance of the enclosure.

Acoustics · The science or physics of sound. Often the term is used in a narrow sense, to describe the sound qualities of a room or auditorium. *See also* ACOUSTIC; AUDIO FREQUENCY; HEARING; PITCH I.

Accordion Recordings

Early recordings of the instrument were made by John J. Kimmel on Zonophone (1904) and Edison (1906) cylinders. Victor recorded Kimmel in August 1907, and later engaged several other accordionists; in their 1917 catalog, there were about 70 accordion items, by Guido Deiro, Pietro Deiro ("Pietro"), and Pietro Frosini, as well as Kimmel. Many of the early accordion recordings were made either by Italian or Irish immigrants; Kimmel, who was actually of German extraction, was famous for his performances of Irish dance music.

In the later 78-rpm era, the accordion was heard primarily in dance orchestras, particularly in tango and polka numbers. It was also a typical member of ensembles playing French popular music. Charles Magnante was a soloist who recorded for Columbia in the 1940s (set no. C-53), performing arrangements of pieces like the "Blue Danube Waltz" and "Two Guitars." Anthony Galla-Rini was Victor artist of the time who performed a similar repertoire.

Dick Contino was a well-known soloist in the 1940s.

In the post-World War II era, the accordion fell into somewhat of an eclipse, associated with the kitschy music of Lawrence Welk and other older-styled bands. With the emergence of world music in the 1980s and 1990s, however, the accordion has returned both in traditional settings and in bands that are more experimental. As in earlier decades, Irish musicians have led the way, including noted players like Joe Burke (recording for Shanachie and Green Linnet labels). Scottish revivalist Phil Cunningham has helped repopularize the piano accordion both in the folk-rock group Silly Wizard and on his own. Eclectic performing groups like Brave Combo include accordion in their mix of instruments performing Mideastern, Eastern European, and other musical styles.

A few artists, such as Yuri Kazakov, Robert Young McMahana, Julia Haines, and William Schimmel, have explored the limited classical repertoire for the instrument. Pauline Oliveros has composed and performed several works for accordion. Her composition, "The Wanderer," was recorded for the Lovely Music label (no. 1902) by the Springfield Accordion Orchestra.—Rev. Carl Benson

Aczel, Peter, May 30, 1926– · Born in Budapest, Hungary, and immigrating to the United States in 1939, Aczel is a graduate of Columbia College of Columbia University, where he studied physics and mathematics as well as the liberal arts. He also did some postgraduate work at Middlebury College in Vermont and the Sorbonne in Paris. He came to the world of audio via Madison Avenue, where he had been a copywriter and creative director for two decades, with at least 25% of his accounts in audio at all times (e.g., Fisher, Garrard, and Pioneer, among others). At the end of 1976 he left the advertising business to start *The Audio Critic*, a strictly objectivist audio journal devoted to measurements in depth and blind listening tests. Between 1981 and 1987 he put *The Audi Critic* on a back burner to start Fourier Systems, the first loudspeaker manufacturing operation to use fully computerized protocols for the design of crossover networks and bass enclosures. The company was ahead of its time in many ways, but still went out of business after 5½ years. Having resumed publication of *The Audio Critic* at the end of 1987, Aczel continues to publish it to this day, albeit somewhat irregularly. He is a Life Member of the Audio Engineering Society.—Howard Ferstler

ADT · *See* AUTOMATIC DOUBLE TRACKING.

Advanced Audio Coding · A data compression scheme intended for audio systems and in wide use with portable digital music players such as Apple's iPod. AAC was first specified in 1997 as part of the MPEG-2 family of international standards known formally as ISO/IEC 13818-7. It is noted for providing better playback than MP3 files for audio frequencies above 16 kHz and having more robust coding efficiency for both stationary and transient signals. This translates to slightly better audio reproduction than MP3 and faster access times for music playback and recovery. A secure version of ACC—"Protected ACC"—is used to provide file downloads from Apple's iTunes music store, and protect against the copying of copyrighted music files. *See also* WINDOWS MEDIA AUDIO. —Thom Holmes

AF · *See* AUDIO FREQUENCY.

AGC · *See* AUTOMATIC GAIN CONTROL.

Air Suspension · *See* ACOUSTIC SUSPENSION.

Album · Originally, the name of the holder for two or more 78s or, by extension, for the actual discs. Later, the term was applied to a single 33 1/3-rpm LP in a sleeve. The modern compact disc, DVD-A disc and DVD music disc as installed in a jewel or snap case, would not normally be called an album, and multi-disc compendiums are usually called "sets," so the term is rapidly becoming archaic. *See also* DVD-A; LONG-PLAYING (LP) RECORD.

Album Cover · A term loosely applied to all packaging for discs, whether singles or parts of album sets, with particular reference to the graphic art involved. Most 78 singles were offered in plain wrappers, possibly with advertising of the label's other records; 78 albums often had portraits of the performers or composers, or reproductions of art works. LP popular and jazz albums began to show livelier scenes, including psychedelic art on rock covers, and eventually there emerged the notion of the cover as an "artistic statement." With the *Sgt. Pepper's Lonely Hearts Club Band* album by the Beatles (1967) the cover was said to be "as important as the recorded material itself. The Beatles extended the theme of the album to the cover, and the 'total-package' idea was born." On popular albums, this idea often led to controversy, with nudity or representations of violence bringing organized opposition. In the 1980s, offensive graphics became scarcer. In the classical field, album art has remained limited to artist portraits, evocative photographs, pictures of the instruments, and representations of paintings. An exhibition of the album cover as art, said to be the first of its kind, was presented at the Galerie Beaumont, Luxembourg, in 1989. Many audiophiles have complained that since the beginning of the CD era, reissued album graphics have been significantly "shrunk" to fit the dimensions of the jewel case, losing the "grandeur" of the presentation found on the original LPs.

Album Number · The number assigned to an album (set) of discs by the manufacturer.

ALC · *See* AUTOMATIC LEVEL CONTROL.

Aliasing (Digital) · In digital-audio recording systems, this phenomenon involves the problem of unwanted frequencies created when sampling a signal of a frequency higher than half the sampling rate. When the sample interval is too large, the spectrum copies overlap, the signals are not recognized correctly, and a low-pass filter cannot recover the signal exactly. In other words, aliasing will occur when the sample rate is smaller than twice the signal bandwidth. Consequently, aliasing is a form of distortion. *See also* OVERSAMPLING.—Howard Ferstler

Alignment · In a tape recorder, the position of the tape head with respect to the tape. If alignment is imprecise, there will be distortion or reduced output; this is more critical with cassette decks than with reel-to-reel recorders because of the narrow recording tracks on a cassette tape. Some cassette decks have built-in alignment equipment. Test tapes are used to check accuracy of alignment.

Allison, Roy, May 6, 1927– · Noted speaker designer, writer, and researcher. He became involved with electronic matters during U.S. Navy service and later at the University of Connecticut's school of Electrical Engineering. Early in his audio career, Allison was editor of *Radio Communication*, *TV and Radio Engineering*, and *Communication Engineering* magazines, audio editor of *High Fidelity* magazine, and editor of *Audiocraft* magazine.

In 1959, he joined Acoustic Research, Inc. He became chief engineer in 1962 and plant manager in 1964. In 1967, he became vice president in charge of research and development. In 1974, after leaving AR, he helped to found Allison Acoustics, RDL, and RA Labs. He has published numerous professional-level and hobby-related articles and wrote a book, *High Fidelity Systems*. He has been a Fellow of the Audio Engineering Society since 1973.

His most important later articles, published in both technical and consumer-oriented journals, deal with speaker/room interactions. He is responsible for defining the "Allison Effect," which involves mid-bass cancellation artifacts between loudspeaker systems and room boundaries, and is also responsible for some highly regarded speaker driver and loudspeaker system designs. *See also* ROOM ACOUSTICS; BOUNDARY EFFECTS; LOUDSPEAKER, 9.—Howard Ferstler

Amberol · A new cylinder material, and label of the same name, introduced in the United States by Thomas Edison in November 1908, that could play four minutes of music (as opposed to the earlier two). The material was a waxlike metallic soap compound, fragile, and quick to wear. A special sapphire point reproducer was used to play the records; this was incorporated in the Amberola phonograph. The name Amberol was selected from several alternatives, despite the lack of amber in the record, because it was thought to suggest the popular amber products of the day —notable for their beauty and quality.

In 1912, Edison improved on the formula and offered the much more effective Blue Amberol. It is said to be unbreakable and playable for 3,000 or more times with no wear. Its exterior was a rich glossy blue. Run at 160 rpm, a Blue Amberol cylinder played for four minutes or longer. The Amberola phonograph was fitted with a diamond point reproducer for these new records, and the acoustic results were excellent. Record slips, giving information about the artist, the music, and advertising for other records, were included from 1912 to 1914. Blue Amberols sold for .50¢.

Competition from discs was mounting, and after a few years, the primary product for Edison had become the Edison Diamond Disc. Nevertheless, $2.5 million came in as late as 1920 from Amberola and Blue Amberol sales, most of the customers being in rural areas. In 1913, there were a million cylinder players in use in America. Until 1914, all Blue Amberol cylinders were direct live recordings; but in December of that year, transfers were introduced via dubbing from discs. Dubbing became the standard recording process in 1915. Cylinder sales fell drastically after 1922, due to competition from radio, and dealers began to drop their Edison franchises. Total sales for the period 1911 to 1929 were impressive: 21,400,000 records and 356,000 players; but in the years 1927 and 1928 operating losses were posted. The last Blue Amberol catalog appeared in 1927, the final Amberolas were made in 1928, and cylinder production ceased in 1929 with Edison's abandonment of phonographs and entertainment records in all formats, with the exception of Edison School Records.

Ambiance (also Ambience) · In sound recording, the environment in the recording studio or hall, and likewise the acoustic conditions in the playback room. Ambiance, in contrast to ambient sounds, may be incorporated (intentionally or not) in the recorded program. *See also* REVERBERATION; SURROUND SOUND.—Howard Ferstler

Ambiance Extraction · Used in some home-based surround-sound processors, it involves removing out-of-phase information from a two-channel soundtrack and converting it for use in the surround channels. In the early 1960s, David Hafler developed one of the original extraction systems, a passive, unamplified hookup for a group of four loudspeakers hooked up to a two-channel amplifier, which steered out-of-phase components in a stereo recording to a set of rear loudspeakers, which were themselves wired to deliver a kind of ersatz stereo effect. This process, called Dynaquad, was marketed as a product by Hafler's Dynaco company. In the late 1960s, Peter Scheiber, at that time a professional bassoonist, filed a U.S. patent for an encoder/decoder matrix system that would turn out to be a major competing format for quadraphonic sound in the early 1970s. Later, Dolby Laboratories cited many of Scheiber's patents in the creation of the Dolby Surround system. *See also* HAFLER CIRCUIT.—Howard Ferstler

Ambiance Synthesis · Used in some home-based surround-sound processors, particularly those that employ digital circuitry, it involves synthesizing new ambiance from the in-phase information on a two-channel soundtrack and sending it to the surround channels. It differs from ambiance extraction by not making primary use of the recorded ambiance on a recording, except in the front speakers.—Howard Ferstler

Ambiophonics · An effective, but primarily sweet-spot-oriented, surround-sound technique developed by Ralph Glasgal that involves a highly refined degree of two-channel cross talk cancellation, coupled with surround-channel ambiance synthesis.—Howard Ferstler

American Engineering Standards Committee · *See* AMERICAN NATIONAL STANDARDS INSTITUTE (ANSI).

American National Standards Institute (ANSI) [website: www.ansi.org] · A private, nonprofit organization with offices located in New York City and Washington, D.C., ANSI was first established in 1918 as the American Engineering Standards Committee. Later, it was called the American Standards Association (1928), and still later the United States of America Standards Institute (1966). It took its present name in 1969. One of its purposes is to act as clearinghouse for norms and specifications developed voluntarily by organizations in the safety, engineering, and industrial fields. Another is to enhance both the global competitiveness of U.S. businesses and the quality of life in the United States by promoting and facilitating voluntary consensus standards and conformity assessment systems, and safeguarding their integrity. It also represents the United States in international standardization work. There were over 1,000 members in 2000, with an annual operating budget of approximately $16 million.—Rev. by Howard Ferstler

Amet, Edward H., 1860–1948 · Inventor of a spring motor for Edison's phonograph (Class M) in 1894; he was the first to receive any patent (U.S. no. 462,228; filed January 28, 1891; granted November 3, 1891) for a spring-driven phonograph motor. Later he introduced double-mainspring models, and portable two- or four-mainspring coin-ops. He also developed the Metaphone ("Meta" being an anagram for Amet's name; it was later called the Echophone) in 1895; it was the first cylinder phonograph with a distinct tone arm. It sold for only $5 (Edison and Columbia machines were then sold for

$30 to $40). Amet had to suspend manufacture of his player after only a few months, however, because of court action taken by American Graphophone Co. He was also a pioneer in early sound motion pictures, using Lambert cylinders synchronized with the film. He received 11 U.S. patents in the sound recording field.

Ampex Corp. [website: www.ampex.com] · An American electronics firm, located in Redwood City, California. Established in 1944 by Alexander M. Poniatoff in San Carlos, California, it pioneered high-quality tape recorders and related equipment in the United States in the late 1940s and early 1950s, and maintained its preeminence for several decades. The Ampex 300 series was widely found in recording and broadcast studios, and the ATR-102 tape deck became recognized as the state of the art in analog magnetic recording technology. The company's many firsts include: the first multitrack audio recorder, introduced in 1954, the first videotape recorder in 1956, and the first broadcast-quality color video recorder in 1964. Ampex was also a pioneer producer of magnetic tape. Since the mid-1960s, the company has increasingly focused on high-end products for broadcasters, recording, and more recently digital storage.

Amplification · The process or mechanism that increases signal magnitude. The effectiveness of amplification is a dimensionless ratio known as Gain. In electrical systems, it is the ratio of the output voltage or power to the input voltage or power. Non-electrical amplification is possible in playback machines. Edison achieved this with a type of mechanical advantage device, using a lever and a floating weight principle in his phonograph reproducers. The idea was to increase the pressure of the stylus on the record and thus to increase diaphragm movement amplitude. *See also* AMPLIFIER; HIGHAM AMPLIFIER; OPEN LOOP GAIN.

Amplifier · An electronic device that increases the strength of a signal input, drawing the necessary power from a source other than the signal itself. The signal may be received from a tuner (in a radio), a cartridge (in a phonograph), a tape deck, a microphone, a digital source, or a preamplifier. Signal strength may be increased hundreds or even thousands of times. Because a standard audio amplifier provides the necessary power to operate the loudspeaker, it is also called a power amplifier. Where there is a separate preamplifier, or voltage amplifier, its function is to magnify the signal voltage from the source and pass it to the amplifier for further enhancement as needed to drive the loudspeaker. The more recent commercial amplifiers incorporate the preamplifier function into one unit, the integrated amplifier. Modern amplifiers are often combined with input devices into receivers, which are integrated amplifiers with tuners.

Lee De Forest invented the electronic amplifier in 1907. His device was a three-electrode vacuum tube, which he named the "audion." Later, amplifiers used triodes, pentodes, or beam-power tubes; the design effort has been directed toward high efficiency and low distortion. Distortion could be practically eliminated by use of beam-power tubes in a push-pull circuit and the application of negative feedback.

Most modern amplifiers are tubeless, solid-state (transistor) devices. When they appeared in the 1960s, these newer designs demonstrated superiority over tube amplifiers, and over the next few decades, they eclipsed what tubes had to offer. Solid state offered low measured distortion in combination with much higher power output, greater reliability, and cooler operation. Whereas typical tube amplifiers at the beginning of the solid-state era had 20- to 75-watt output norms, solid-state devices of the middle 1970s had already surpassed 200 watts per channel. Manufacturers such as CM Labs, Dynaco, Kenwood, Marantz, and McIntosh competed in the power race, which peaked around 1971 with the Carver 350 watt/channel Phase Linear Model 700. In the last two decades, the number of companies making amps of even greater power, including some with as many as five 200-watt channels for home-theater use, has proliferated. From the mid-1990s on, A/V receivers with power outputs of more than 100 watts in each of five channels were available in medium price ranges.

Another advantage of solid state was in its use of differential circuits. These had been found in tube amplifiers also, but they functioned better in the stable thermal environment of solid state. By converting differential output to a single output, with the so-called current mirror, extra gain was achieved and thus more feedback was possible. Concerns over the type of feedback that offered the most pleasing result developed in the 1970s and continued through the 1980s: for the issues. *See also* FEEDBACK.

Recent systems have operated successfully to reduce distortion further, among them cascoding and Class A. The cascode is a pair of transistors acting together; one provides high voltage gain while shielding the other from voltage changes; the second provides voltage and current gain. Giving high gain, high linearity, and broad bandwidth, the cascode system has found a place in contemporary amplifiers.

Class A operation originated in tube systems, and was carried into transistor systems around 1968, and still can be found in some designs. It removes switching distortion in transistors, while keeping the transistors thermally stable; it leads to a strong output power. High cost has kept Class A devices out of the mass market, and their sonic advantages are of more interest to high-strung big spenders than to knowledgeable music lovers and engineers who realize that amplifiers are essentially appliances and not mystery devices.

In the late 1970s, Sony and others marketed pulse-width modulation amplifiers, also known as digital amplifiers or Class D amplifiers, with moderate success, and some subwoofer systems use amps of this kind. "Current dumping" designs have been more widely accepted; they have been made by Nakamichi, Quad, Technics, and Threshold. In the late 1980s, "high current" amplifier design became a topic of discussion and experiment, beginning with the work of the Finnish audio engineer Matti Otala. This design orientation is most useful in connection with electrostatic, instead of dynamic, loudspeakers; most contemporary amplifiers have enough current to drive common speaker loads to high volume levels in normal sized rooms.

Many amplifiers have no controls at all, other than maybe an on/off switch. Controls on an integrated amplifier or receiver may include: balance control, filter switch, input selector, loudness compensation, mode selector, monitor, phase reverse control (phasing switch), tone control, and volume control. Receivers designed for home-theater use will have even more controls. Amplifiers are compared with respect to their channel separation, frequency response, hum, distortion, bandwidth power output (in watts), and signal-to-noise ratio. Distortion is specified as a percent at given power output, frequency, and load impedance (e.g., 0.1% at 100 watts, at 1 kHz, and driving an 8-ohm load), and comparisons must be made at equal power outputs, frequency range, and load impedance to be meaningful. A 30-watt power output per channel is sufficient for most musical purposes with typical speaker systems (particularly if we are talking about five-channel surround-sound systems), but more power is desirable for playback at very high volume levels (definitely possible with home-theater use), or in unusually large rooms, or if the speakers are unusually inefficient. The effect of the amplifier's power output is related to the impedance of the loudspeaker(s) attached to it; in general, the lower impedance, the more current it draws from the amplifier. Under some conditions, low-impedance loads may cause some solid-state amplifiers to run too hot or generate excessive distortion.

The most common measurement of amplifiers involves the continuous output into a given load, over a given bandwidth, at specific impedance. The amount of extra power delivered by an amplifier on musical peaks is its dynamic headroom, and the importance of this with musical playback will depend upon just how much power an amp can deliver at a steady state. If steady-state power is already adequate, the headroom issue is academic. A proper audio amplifier will exhibit a frequency response of 20 to 20,000 Hz, with only a fraction of a dB variation over that range, although some units have a considerably wider bandwidth. Channel separation will typically be in excess of 50 dB, which, because 30 dB is more than adequate for musical or home-theater situations, means that most amps are subjectively perfect in this area. A good amp will have intermodulation distortion levels of less than 0.5%; it will have a signal-to-noise ratio of at least 65 dB or, possibly, considerably more.—Rev. by Howard Ferstler

Amplitude · In a vibratory movement, the distance from the equilibrium position to either point of maximum displacement is called the amplitude of the vibration. One cycle includes movements to both displacement points and back. The amplitude determines the intensity of a sound.

Amplitude/Frequency Distortion · *See* DISTORTION, II.

Analog Recording · The process using an electronic signal with a continuously varying waveform resembles that of the original sound. An analog recording pattern may be the cuts in the groove of a disc, or the arrangement of magnetized particles on a tape. *See also* DIGITAL RECORDING; DISC; ELECTRICAL RECORDING; MAGNETIC RECORDING; RECORDING PRACTICE.

Ando, Yoichi, 1939– · A noted audio researcher and expert on acoustics, professor Ando is currently a member of The Department of Global and Human Environmental Science, Graduate School of Science and Technology, Kobe University, Japan. At Kobe, he has been studying room acoustics, in particular the forecasting of subjective impressions based upon binaural acoustic measurements, and the relationship with evoked potentials of the brain stem and the acoustic planning of buildings. Among other publications, Dr. Ando authored the book, *Concert Hall Acoustics.*—Howard Ferstler

Anechoic Environment · Literally, without echo. An anechoic situation exists with acoustic signals produced by a source are not reflected back to it. Because the ground is reflective, true anechoic conditions would only exist outdoors and at a somewhat high altitude. Anechoic chambers that have special acoustic materials on the walls to absorb reflections are only that way down to lower-midrange frequencies.—Howard Ferstler

ANSI · *See* AMERICAN NATIONAL STANDARDS INSTITUTE (ANSI).

Apple iPod · *See* IPOD.

Armature · The movable part in an electronic device; the vibrating element in a magnetic cartridge.

Armstrong, Edwin Howard, December 18, 1890–February 1, 1954 · One of the pioneers of wireless transmissions, Arm-

strong started his career by building an amateur radio station when only 15 years old. Later, while at Columbia University, he studied under the physicist Michael Pupin, and he was eventually appointed to the same teaching and research position that had been occupied by the great physicist. During his career, he earned three different doctor of science degrees, and received more than a dozen awards for outstanding achievement. During his career, Armstrong developed the superheterodyne circuit that is the basis of almost all modern radio receiving and radar equipment, and went on to formulate the principles of radio frequency modulation in the 1930s. This contribution resulted in the development of FM radio.—Frank Hoffmann

Atkinson, John, June 12, 1948– (Born in Hertfordshire, United Kingdom) · Atkinson was educated in the sciences (B.S., London, 1972) and trained as a teacher, worked for awhile as a research scientist and as a professional musician (bass guitar), before joining *Hi-Fi News & Record Review* magazine (United Kingdom) in 1976 as news editor. He became the editor of *Hi-Fi News* in October 1982 before immigrating to the United States in May 1986 to become editor of *Stereophile*, a position he still occupies. In addition to editing the magazine and writing reviews and articles, he has produced, engineered, and played instruments on more than 40 commercial recordings. Atkinson is a member of the Audio Engineering Society, National Academy of the Recording Arts & Sciences, and Associate Member of the Institute of Electrical and Electronics Engineers.—Howard Ferstler

Atmosphere Microphone · A microphone placed at some distance from the performers in order to include environmental ambience in the recording.

Attenuation · A reduction of voltage, intensity, amplitude, or loudness; the opposite of amplification.

Attenuation Distortion · See DISTORTION, 2.

Audible Frequency Range · See AUDIO FREQUENCY.

Audio (I) · A general term pertaining to hearing or sound, from the Latin *audire*, to hear; often used as a modifier to identify a system designed to record or reproduce sound, or an element of such a system.

Audio (II) · The sound portion of a film or television program.

Audio Bandwidth · Typically stated as being from 20 Hz to 20 kHz, these are the acoustic signals that normal humans supposedly can be said to "hear" reasonably well. In older individuals, the low end may still be 20 Hz, or even a bit lower, but the high end often drops to 15 kHz, 10 kHz, or even lower, depending on both heredity and lifetime environmental factors. The musical significance of signals above about 15 kHz or even sometimes above 12 kHz is debatable.—Howard Ferstler

Audio Cables, Wires, and Hardware: Audio Interconnect · The shielded cables that are used to connect disc players and recording devices to preamplifiers or receivers and preamplifiers to power amps. Premium versions (some of which are very expensive) are often more durable than cheaper designs, but rarely sound better than anything but defective items.

  Connectors. Connectors allow cables to be connected to inputs and outputs. In consumer audio, they vary from balanced and more common RCA types, which are used on line-level inputs, to banana, spade, and pin connectors, which are used on typical speaker-level inputs.

  Fiber Optic. Cables that are used for digital connections between players and digital processors. They have the advantage of being immune to RF or electrical interference.

  Microphone. The shielded cables that connect microphones to mixers or measuring equipment.

  Speaker. The typical unshielded leads that are used between power amplifiers and loudspeaker systems. Even lamp cord is sometimes adequate for this use, provided the run is not extremely long. Some speaker wires are outrageously expensive, but those esoteric designs have no proven advantage over more mundane versions, provided the latter are large enough to keep signal losses to a minimum.—Howard Ferstler

Audio Cartridge · See CARTRIDGE.

Audio Cassette · See CASSETTE.

Audio Compression · See COMPRESSED AUDIO FILES.

Audio Engineering Society · Begun in 1948, in New York, it is the only professional society devoted exclusively to audio technology. Among its 10,000+ members are specialists in most branches of recorded sound: designers of equipment, installers and operators, journalists, teachers, salespersons, and technicians. In recent years, its membership of leading engineers, scientists, and other authorities has increased dramatically throughout the world, greatly boosting the society's stature and that of its members in a truly symbiotic relationship. The Technical Council and its technical committees respond to the interests of the membership by providing technical information at an appropriate level via conferences, conventions, workshops, and publications. They work on developing tutorial information of practical use to the members and concentrate on tracking and reporting the very latest advances in technology and applications. This activity is under the direction of the AES Technical Council and its Committees. AES Sections serve members in 47 concentrated geographic areas throughout the world.—Howard Ferstler

Audio Frequency · One of the frequencies within the range of sound frequencies audible to humans, from about 15 to 20,000 cycles per second (or Hz). Acoustic recording achieved coverage of about 1,000 to 2,000 or 3,000 Hz. With the emergence of electrical recording in 1925, manufacturers could claim coverage of 100 to 8,000 Hz. The frequency range of notes playable on certain instruments is encompassed by the capabilities of early electrical recording (e.g., all the high brasses and winds, the violin, and the viola). Female voices and higher male voices could also be reproduced with all fundamental frequencies. One reason that realistic reproduction did not occur was that a sounding note produces not only a fundamental frequency but also an entire series of overtones, or harmonics, and it is these elements that give color and distinctiveness to the sound of an instrument or a voice. Some instruments, especially the percussions, also produce "transient tones," heard on initialization of a tone and then subject to quick fading. The audio experience of record listeners in the 1920s is often suggested today when loudspeakers of limited range are heard—for example in elevators or in small portable radios. The effect is one of blurred identity for instruments and voices. Outside the audio frequency range, humans perceive vibrations as feelings, not sounds. *See also* HEARING.

Audion · The three-element vacuum tube invented by Lee De Forest. *See also* AMPLIFIER.

Audiophile · An individual who is extremely interested in high-fidelity sound reproduction, particularly as it relates to equipment designed for home-listening situations.—Howard Ferstler

Audiophile Recording · A concept begun in 1960s to produce recordings of exceptional quality, which uses very careful techniques and equipment. Production techniques included half-speed mastering, improved vinyl, and even direct-to-disc methods, whereby the LP record was cut directly during the musical session, instead of by a tape feed later on. (Sheffield Records was one of the pioneers in direct-disc LP recording.) The idea was to achieve better instrumental definition, better sound-staging, improved channel separation, and greater frequency range.

In the digital era, both small and large companies have endeavored to capitalize on the love some audiophiles have for ultra-high-quality recordings, and assorted systems have been devised to enhance the performance of the compact disc. The most recent audiophile recordings have made use of SACD and DVD-A technologies, with many of those involving more than the usual two channels.—Howard Ferstler

Audio Spectrum · *See* AUDIO FREQUENCY.

Audio Tape · *See* TAPE.

Auger, Robert, 1928–December 12, 1998 · An important recording engineer, Auger proved that an independent artist could succeed in major recording projects, and that leading performers would prefer to work with him, because of his skills. Working with Robert Fine, Auger's first recording at Mercury Records was Barbirolli conducting Vaughan Williams *Symphony Number 8*, in 1956. He worked for Pye Records when they were exploring stereo, and in 1959, he made historic recordings of

Handel's *Fireworks* and later Janáček's *Sinfonietta*, both with Charles Mackerras. In 1969, he set up Granada Recordings, and in 1974, he became a freelance engineer. In later years, he made historic CBS and RCA recordings with artists such as Bernstein, Maazel, Stokowski, Leinsdorf, and Boulez. Clients included Unicorn and later CRD.—Howard Ferstler

Augspurger, George, July 9, 1929– · George Augspurger is currently best known in the audio industry as an expert in studio design through his consulting firm, Perception Inc. Many of North America's most prestigious studios proudly boast of having "Augspurger designed" rooms and monitors. Before striking out as an independent consultant, Augspurger spent over a decade with JBL starting in 1958. He began as JBL's Technical Service Manager and was later responsible for establishing and managing the Professional Products Division. In 1968, he became Technical Director for JBL, a position he held for two years before deciding to move on to independent consulting.—Howard Ferstler

Aural Exciter · A device used by radio stations to improve the broadcast signal, and in record production for the enhancement of clarity and presence.

Auto-locate · Also known as automatic search. The feature in a tape recorder or tape deck that allows rapid location of a chosen point on the tape.

Automatic Dialog Replacement (ADR) · A motion-picture film post-production term used to indicate the process whereby dialogue that is not taped during production or that needs to be redone is recorded and synchronized to the picture. It is commonly used with music videos as well as in film.—Howard Ferstler

Automatic Double Tracking (ADT) · *See* DOUBLE TRACKING.

Automatic Level Control (ALC) · A circuit used to maintain a recording level despite changes in the amplitude of the signal. In playback, extremes of volume are evened out to a middle ground (e.g., presenting ffff as ff).

Automatic Microphone Mixer · First patented by Dan Dugan, this is a specialized, multi-feed mixer that is optimized for solving the problems of multiple inputs operating together as a system. Voice activated, the device controls the live-feed microphones by temporarily turning the proper unit up when someone is talking, and turning down any that are not used. At the same time, the arrangement must adapt to changing background noise conditions. A good automatic mixer must be able to make rapid and dramatic changes in the levels of the various inputs while giving the impression that nothing out of the ordinary is happening. This is especially important when such systems are used in recording and broadcasting.—Howard Ferstler

Automatic Record Changer · *See* RECORD CHANGER.

Automatic Replay · A system that allows repeated playbacks of a recorded program without user intervention. It operates on a signal within the recording, or can be activated by a preset mechanical device. *See also* AUTOMATIC REVERSE; TALKING DOLLS.

Automatic Reverse · In a magnetic tape recorder, a system that begins playback of the second tape track upon completion of the first track. The reversal is achieved by a foil sensing tape at the proper point on the magnetic tape, or by means of a signal on the tape. In earlier cassette devices, there was a mechanism to turn the cassette over for playback of the second track. The foil sensing or signal systems require two playback heads, one for each direction. *See also* AUTOMATIC REPLAY.

Automatic Search · A system in a tape recorder for rapid movement of the tape to a desired point, for playback of selected material.

Automatic Sequence · *See* MANUAL SEQUENCE.

Automatic Shutoff · A device that turns off the motor of all or part of an audio system when playback of a recording has concluded.

Automatic Stop · Beginning around 1911 or earlier, many inventions were introduced for bringing a turntable to a stop at the end of a disc; the reason was to avoid the noise made by the needle as it reached the tail groove. Earliest advertisers in *Talking*

Automobile Sound Systems

The first generally marketed cars to be radio equipped appeared in the United States in 1930. Equipment was rudimentary and results were poor. No serious attention to the problem of overcoming the auto's hostile environment was given until the hi-fi revolution of the 1950s. Then audio manufacturers began to deal with the need for miniaturization (to fit into the relatively small space available), for amplification to counter road and engine noise, and for physical toughness of components to withstand vibration and extremes of temperature. Those problems notwithstanding, favorable factors are present in the automobile, which are not usually found in a home audio environment. The listeners are located in fixed positions; reverberation time is short; and there is greater discrimination against ambient sounds because the loudspeaker(s) and the listeners are so close to each other.

FM radio was the first major breakthrough; it became available in American cars in the 1950s. The 4-track and 8-track tape cartridge appeared in the mid-1960s, gradually giving way to the cassette in the late 1970s. Noise reduction systems were added, and electronic tuning, followed by computerized controls in certain "high-end" installations like the Blaupunkt TQR-07 Berlin, or the Polk 12-speaker, 160 watt, H700 system; these were selling for around $1,500 in 1990. Although these complexities have tended to take more and more of the space in the driver area—at a time when other gadgetry was also crowding into the dashboard—some success has been achieved in space saving. Cassette/receivers with built-in multichannel amplifiers can power all the speakers; and CD changers can be mounted in the trunk.

Compact disc changers for automobiles became available in the United States in 1988, made by Alpine, Pioneer, Sony, and Technics. Ten- and 12-disc models by Clarion, Concord, and Kenwood were brought out in 1989. Alpine, Clarion, JVC, and Kenwood marketed DAT players for automobiles in 1988. Lincoln Continental and Cadillac Fleetwood offered DAT as a factory-installed option. Single-band parametric equalizers came into use in these players, to improve fidelity of the bass frequencies in both front and rear speakers. Optical fiber technology is applied to the elimination of interference by removing the analog signals from long cables. In fall 2001, Mazda introduced a limited-edition MP-3 Protégé that featured a built-in MP3 player in the dash. *See* DAT.

During the mid-to-late 1990s, two firms, Sirius and XM, introduced satellite radio systems. Some automakers are beginning to offer one or the other of these systems in their vehicles.

Machine World were Sonora and Condon-Autostop Co. The latter's Autostop device required adjustment for each disc, but in 1912, Condon offered the Altobrake, which was self-adjusting. Simplex was the name of a 1912 device by Standard Gramophone Appliance Co.; it could stop the turntable and restart it for a repeat of the record. Edison's Diamond Disc Phonograph had a Duncan Automatic Stop in models offered from April 1917 to mid-1918 (described and illustrated in Paul 1988). Several similar devices appeared in the next few years, and the Columbia Grafonola player of 1920 had one built in.

Automatic Turntable · *See* TURNTABLE.

Automatic Volume Control · *See* AUTOMATIC LEVEL CONTROL.

Auxiliary Input · An audio device, usually found on a tuner or amplifier, which allows receipt of a signal from an outside source. For example, a turntable or a radio tuner may be attached, via a cable, plug, and jack, to an amplifier. Connecting components should be matched in impedance and voltage level, for optimum performance.

Aylsworth, Jonas Walter, Ca. 1868–1916 · A chemist with Thomas Edison from ca. 1890. After his retirement in 1903, he remained as a consultant in the West Orange laboratories. His inventions included the commercial nickel-iron alkaline storage battery and various cylinder-molding processes. He was known particularly for the Edison gold molded cylinder. He also improved the cast solid-wax cylinder that could be shaved and reused. The brittleness of the 1908 black-wax Amberol led him into research on materials for disc records (*see also* EDISON DIAMOND DISC). Aylsworth held, alone or jointly, 38 patents for audio-related inventions, the last of which was filed in June 1911.

Azimuth · In a tape recorder, the angle between the gap in the tape head and the longitudinal axis of the tape. It should be 90°. *See also* GAP ALIGNMENT.

B

B Side · The reverse side of a double-sided disc, the side with the less featured material. It is also known as the flip side. *See also* A SIDE.

Back Coating · The addition of a conductive material to the back of a magnetic tape to eliminate static buildup and improve winding characteristics.

Back Cueing · A means of starting a disc so that the music begins exactly on cue. The stylus is placed at the point of the first recorded sound, and then the disc is backed up slightly with the stylus left in the groove. The idea is for the first note to encounter the stylus as the turntable reaches proper speed. This technique is commonly used by disc jockeys. Experts are divided on the question of damage to cartridge or disc that may result from frequent back cueing, such as would take place at a radio station.

Back Spinning · A technique used by hip-hop deejays. By rapidly and rhythmically reversing directions of the turntable while a record is being played, a skilled deejay can create a stuttering sound, or rapidly repeat a key vocal, melodic, or rhythmic phrase so as to emphasize it.

Back Tracking · The technique of composite recording in which a new live sound is combined with a previously recorded track (the backing track). In this process, the performer listens through headphones to the backing track and adds a new solo part to it. The resulting composite track may be used as the backing track for other new parts.

Backing · *See* BASE.

Badische Anilin Und Soda Fabrik · *See* BASF AG.

Baffle · A loudspeaker enclosure, or a rigid surface encircling the loudspeaker rim, or a board on which a speaker is mounted, intended to prevent interference between the sound waves created simultaneously on both sides of the speaker's diaphragm. *See also* BASS REFLEX SYSTEM; INFINITE BAFFLE.

Bailey, A. R. · *See* LOUDSPEAKER, 5.

Balance · The characteristic of a stereo sound system that describes the relative volume of playback signal emanating from several loudspeakers.

Balance Control · A device in a stereo sound system that adjusts the relative loudness of the channels to obtain an accurate reproduction of the input sound.

Band · Also known as a cut. The portion of the recorded surface of a disc that is separated from adjacent bands by a marker space or scroll. It usually contains one song, or one movement of a larger work.

Bandwidth · The characteristic of an amplifier or receiver that expresses its frequency range (e.g., 20 Hz–20,000 Hz). It is

Backmasking

Also called backward masking, the term is used to describe reversal of recorded sound or speech. Such sounds were used in *musique concrète* compositions of the 1950s; later the Beatles, beginning with the single "Rain" (April 1966), used backmasking as an expressive tool (see, for example, the guitar in the Beatles' "I'm Only Sleeping," 1966). Because of the "Paul is dead" rumors from 1969 to 1970, however, some fans believed that the Beatles deliberately concealed secret backward messages in their songs (e.g., the repeated "number nine" from "Revolution 9" [1968] became "Turn me on, dead man" when reversed).

In the 1970s and 1980s, religious fundamentalists claimed that backward messages (usually of an occult nature) were encoded in rock lyrics, either by simple tape reversal or by carefully constructed lyrics that would yield different statements when played in reverse [Aranza 1984]. Led Zeppelin's "Stairway to Heaven" (1971), for example, was widely alleged to contain satanic references—speculation fueled largely by guitarist Jimmy Page's interest in the occult. According to Evan Olcott, such coincidental (and anecdotal) instances are examples of "phonetic reversal" [Olcott 2001]. Outcomes of reversible messages are hard to predict, and there is little evidence that they are understood when played forward.

Nevertheless, in response to this controversy, some musicians have "planted" backward messages in some of their songs. For example, the Electric Light Orchestra's "Fire on High" (1976) contained a reversed spoken message: "The music is reversible, but time is not. Turn back! Turn back!" Pink Floyd added a barely audible reversed message to the beginning of "Empty Spaces" (1979) that begins, "Congratulations! You've just discovered the secret message." Prince's salacious "Darling Nikki" (1984) concludes with a backmasked Christian message. Olcott has labeled such deliberate instances "engineered reversal." For a detailed objective account of backmasking, see Poundstone 1983.—Kevin Holm-Hudson

stated for given output levels and distortion percentages.

Bar Automatico · The name given to phonograph parlors in Italy, around the turn of the century. Customers could listen to cylinder recordings of opera or popular music for 10 centesimi.

Barron, Michael, September 6, 1945– · Born in England and a noted researcher in large-room acoustics, Barron attended the University of Cambridge from 1964 through 1967, taking a B.A. at the end of his studies. He went on to receive a Ph.D. from the University of Southampton in 1974. Since 1987, he has been a partner in Fleming & Barron (acoustic consultants) and has since 1989 been Senior Lecturer (now part time) at the University of Bath Department of Architecture and Civil Engineering. In 1988, he was awarded the Tyndall Medal by the British Institute of Acoustics. Dr. Barron has published papers in the *Journal of the Acoustical Society of America*, *Acustica/Acta Acustica*, *Journal of Sound and Vibration*, and *Applied Acoustics*, and in 1993 he published *Auditorium Acoustics and Architectural Design* (Routledge and Spon Press).—Howard Ferstler

Base · Also known as backing. The material of which a magnetic tape is made; that is, the carrier of the magnetizable coating that holds the pattern representing the signal. Acetate (lacquer) and polyester bases have predominated, with a thickness of 1/2 mil,

Banjo Recordings

The five-string "American" banjo was the most popular instrument on early records; its acoustic qualities were well suited to the possibilities of recording equipment, and there were a number of outstanding artists available. The first banjo music to be heard was on Edison North American cylinders in 1889, performed by Will Lyle; "Banjo Jingles" was the earliest noted in the Edison "Musical Cylinder Accounts"— the date was September 30, 1889. Lyle performed in nine sessions that year. W. S. Grinsted made Edison cylinders on October 22, 1891.

Columbia cylinders initiated their banjo catalog in ca. 1893, with the "Banjo King" Vess Ossman and two lesser known players named Cullen and Collins. Steph Clement made a seven-inch Berliner disc, "Mittoam Gallop," on October 18, 1896. Ossman made 11 records for Bettini in 1898. Ruby Brooks made Edison cylinders from before 1900 (e.g., "Belle of Columbia," no. 2636) until he died in 1906. Fred Van Eps was the star performer later on; he began with Edison in 1901 and recorded until 1922. Van Eps, Ossman, and F. J. Bacon were the artists listed in the Victor 1917 catalog, which carried 40 banjo titles. Popular performers on the four string or tenor banjo during the 1920s were "Blackface" Eddie Ross and fleet-fingered guitarist Roy Smeck. British banjoists included Alfred Cammeyer, Emile Grimshaw, Joe Morley, Olly Oakley, John Pidoux, and Charlie Rogers.

The first women to make banjo records were also British: Bessie and Rose Skinner, in 1903 for Zonophone in London. Helen Sealy was the first woman on HMV ("Kettledrums," no. B648). Shirley Spaulding was the first American woman to make a banjo record: it was "Royal Tourist—March Novelette" (Edison Diamond Disc no. 80625; 1921). The five-string banjo declined in popularity during the 1930s and 1940s. Jazz and ragtime groups preferred the four-string tenor banjo, and only a few artists remained with the five-string instrument, notably Uncle Dave Macon and Grandpa Jones, and Bill Monroe's Bluegrass Boys. Pete Seeger, who played a major role in popularizing the instrument as part of the post-World War II folk revival, also used the banjo in much of his recorded work.

Bluegrass music also enjoyed a boom in the 1950s and 1960s, led by Earl Scruggs (one of the Bluegrass Boys) and Lester Flatt. A popular American television show, *Beverly Hillbillies*, premiered in 1962 with a bluegrass theme song played by Scruggs. On the four-string or tenor banjo, Eddie Peabody made several hit LP albums on the Dot label in 1958. The Banjo Kings, John Cali (who had recorded for Grey Gull in the 1920s), Joe Maphis, and Jad Paul were among the other successful tenor-banjo artists of the 1950s. Five-string banjo music received a boost with the filming of *Bonnie and Clyde* (1966); it had a Grammy-winning bluegrass score by Charles Strouse. *Dueling Banjos*, from the soundtrack to *Deliverance*, was a popular album in 1973 (Warner no. 7659).

Since the 1970s, the five-string banjo has continued to appear on country music recordings, with a resurgence of bluegrass styles since the 1980s "new country" movement began. Bela Fleck has been the most popular solo artist on the instrument, expanding its use into jazz, funk, and electronica styles. With the new country revival movement of the mid-1980s, the banjo returned to a prominent place on many country recordings. The tenor banjo has been most prominent in the hands of traditional Irish music revivalists, such as Mick Moloney.—Rev. by Carl Benson

1 mil, or one and 1/2 mil. Tapes of greater thickness are less liable to print-through.

BASF AG [website: www.basf.de/basf/html/rampe/home_e.htm] · A German firm, presently located in Ludwigshafen. It is one of the world's largest chemical manufacturers, with over 90,000 employees worldwide and sales (2001) of 32.5 billion euros (approximately $29 billion). Among its many products are audio- and videotapes.

The firm was founded in 1865 as the Badische Anilin und Soda Fabrik by Friedrich Engelhorn. It was successful in producing synthetic dyes, and diversified into various petrochemical products. Experiments with magnetic tape in the 1930s led to the cellulose acetate tape, coated with ferric oxide, used in the Magnetophon. Easy breakage and brittleness with age were its defects. In 1976, the firm introduced the Unisette cassette, with tape 1/4-inch wide; it was similar to the Elcaset.

Basic Amplifier · *See* POWER AMPLIFIER.

Bass · The lower range of the audible musical spectrum, usually considered to be from 18–20 Hz on up to about 300–400 Hz. The driver element in a loudspeaker system that is designed to reproduce bass sounds is called a woofer. *See also* SUBWOOFER.—Howard Ferstler

Bass Reflex System · A speaker-box design that makes use of a port or drone (unpowered) cone, in addition to a powered woofer driver that, according to parameters outlined by Neville Thiele and Richard Small more than twenty years ago, allows the rear radiation of a woofer cone to reinforce the output of the front, extending and smoothing low-range response. At frequencies below the reinforcement range, there will be a sharp attenuation of the system output, as the port signal goes back out of phase with the radiation from the front of the cone. *See also* ACOUSTIC SUSPENSION; LOUDSPEAKER.—Howard Ferstler

Bass Trap · An acoustical device used in multi-track recording to minimize the reflection of sound from one instrument to the microphone of an adjacent instrument. It is built into the floor beneath each performer, and by means of its absorbent surface, it draws much of the sound down into its interior, which is filled with spaced fiberglass panels. The same principle can be applied to walls and ceilings to avoid reflected signals.

Batchelor, Charles, December 21, 1845–January 1, 1910 · British/American inventor, born in Dalston, near London. He went to the United States around 1870 as a representative of J. P. Coates, the Manchester thread manufacturer. He decided to remain in America, working for Thomas Edison from 1871 as a machinist and laboratory associate. He and Edison worked closely in telegraphy experiments during 1874 to 1875, then in developing the "electric pen" (mimeograph machine). The Edison establishment at Menlo Park, New Jersey, was planned by Batchelor and Edison, and Batchelor became the "keeper of notes and designer of prototypes" there. In 1877, the first project was the telephone, which was greatly improved beyond the stage reached by Alexander Graham Bell—the Menlo Park work made the modern Bell System possible, and created the mode for long-distance calling.

Batchelor's connection with the phonograph began with the first working model; he and John Kruesi made it together on Edison's plan in November 1877. Probably Batchelor was responsible for "constructing the phonets [reproducer] and provided the mechanisms for the fine adjustments necessary for successful operation."

Later, he and Edison made thousands of experiments with filaments and carbonization methods to perfect the incandescent lamp—succeeding finally in October 1879. Batchelor extended the electrical work to the design of dynamos for the Pearl Street station in New York, where operations began in May 1882. At the same time, he planned the Edison exhibit for the Paris Electrical Exposition of 1881, displaying a complete lighting system that won the highest awards. Remaining most of four years in Europe, he organized electrical installations in France and elsewhere.

Kruesi and Batchelor ran the great Edison operation in Schenectady, New York. In 1889, when the Edison interests were sold and a new firm, Edison General Electric Co., was formed, Batchelor was named to the board of directors. He was able to work on a small scale as well, inventing the talking doll in 1888; this was based on a tiny phonograph with an automatic return motion. The Edison Toy Phonograph Co. was formed, and by February 1889 425 dolls had been shipped to New York City for sale.

Batchelor produced artificial sapphire for use in recording styli, and filed a patent application for it in May 1890. It was this sapphire that was used by Eldridge Johnson in making disc masters and remained in use through the LP era for cutting lacquer masters. After 1890, he spent little time on the phonograph or other key inventions, having been detoured by Edison into iron ore research, one of the master's less inspired projects. He did develop a "belt-type ore concentrator" in late 1889, but this area of experiment proved unsatisfying and exhausting. The ore business failed, and the effort was converted in time to the production of Portland cement. Batchelor left regular employment with Edison in 1893, and after 1899, he devoted himself to travel with his family. He died in New York. In the world of the early phonograph, he was regarded as the second most important inventor, after Edison.

Battelle Memorial Institute [website: www.battelle.org] · A research and development firm located in Columbus, Ohio, said to be the world's largest non-profit scientific institute. George Battelle, whose family made its fortune in the steel business, founded it in 1929. Xerography was developed there, and titanium for aerospace applications. In audio history, Battelle is noted for participation in wire recorder development during World War II. The institute also did key early research in digital sound recording during the 1970s that lead to the development of the compact disc. The organization has research establishments in the state of Washington, Geneva, Switzerland, and Frankfurt, Germany, and operates several other scientific research centers, including the Brook Haven and Oak Ridge National Laboratories.

Bauer, Ben, June 26, 1913–March 31, 1979 · An important figure in the history of audio and recording, Bauer did notable research in microphone and other audio technologies, including quadraphonic technologies. One of his more notable achievements occurred in 1938, when, while working for Shure Brothers, he engineered a single microphone element to produce a cardioid pickup pattern. The resulting product was called the Unidyne Model 55, and the basic design later became the basis for the well-known SM57 and SM58 microphones that were used by performers to good effect for many years. Bauer later went to work for CBS, and in the late 1960s, he was influenced by Peter Scheiber's four-channel research. He worked on his own variant of the matrix encode/decode (record/playback) technique, and the result was called "SQ" for Stereo-Quad. This matrix rejected the specific phase and amplitude parameters of the Scheiber proposal (which would only yield 3dB adjacent channel separation) and was claimed to be fully stereo and mono compatible. Bauer was president of the Audio Engineering Society in 1969, having received the Society's John H. Potts award in 1963, and was made a life member in 1972. In 1978, he received the Acoustical Society of America's Silver Medal. *See also* TONE ARM; MICROPHONE, 3; AMBIANCE EXTRACTION.—Howard Ferstler

Baxandall, Peter J., 1921–1995 · Known primarily for his analog circuit designs, after attending King's College School, in England, Baxandall went on to study electrical engineering at Cardiff Technical College, receiving a degree in 1942. After helping with research in radar during the war, he joined Royal Signals and Radar Establishment, where he remained until his retirement in 1971. At that time, he became a freelance electroacoustical consultant. Baxandall had already published a description of his widely used tone-control circuit in 1952, but after 1971, he also researched and helped to further develop other technologies, including audio-frequency transformers, radio-frequency carrier microphones, powered loudspeakers, dipole and electrostatic loudspeakers, motional-feedback circuits for loudspeakers, bandbass loudspeakers, line-source loudspeakers, oscillators, high-speed tape-duplicating equipment, and microphone-calibration methods. He also published numerous papers on amplifier design and electrostatic loudspeaker systems, and was known for his guarded antipathy toward members of audio's lunatic fringe. In 1980, Baxandall became a Fellow of the Audio Engineering Society, and in 1993, he won the Society's Silver Medal.—Howard Ferstler

BBC · *See* BRITISH BROADCASTING CORP (BBC).

Belfer Audio Library and Archive [website: libwww.syr.edu/information/belfer/main.htm] · Originally known as the Syracuse Audio Archive, and housed in the Syracuse (New York) University Library,

the Belfer Audio Library and Archive was founded in 1963, with the Library's acquisition of the Joseph and Max Bell Collection of 150,000 early sound recordings. It is the third largest audio archive in the United States. Collections now number more than 300,000 recordings in all formats, including cylinders, discs, and magnetic tapes. Particular strengths line in the Archive's holdings of late 19th and early 20th century commercially released cylinders and phonodiscs of classical and popular performances. Although the majority of its holdings comprise music recordings, the Archive also contains early radio broadcasts, as well as thousands of spoken word recordings covering a wide range of personalities. Voices include Amelia Earhart, Thomas Edison, Albert Einstein, Lenin, and Oscar Wilde, among others. In addition, the Archive contains an exhibit gallery for visitor education that houses a collection of early recording and reproducing equipment, on loan through the generosity of the Charles Edison. In 1998, the Archive began a project to digitize large portions of its collection for web access. It has also conducted sound preservation workshops throughout New York State as part of its educational mission. Walter L. Welch was the archive's first curator, serving until 1991 when Susan Stinson replaced him.

Bell, Alexander Graham, March 3, 1847–August 2, 1922 · Scottish/American inventor most famous for his development of the telephone, but one who was also active in early sound recording. He was born in Edinburgh, the son of Alexander Melville Bell, a specialist in vocal physiology. From 1868 to 1870, he worked with his father in London, and studied anatomy and physiology at University College, developing a keen interest in education of the deaf. When his family moved to Canada in 1870, Bell went on to Boston where he taught teachers of the deaf. During 1873–1876, he experimented with the phonautograph and the telegraph, developing the theory of the "speaking telegraph" or telephone in 1874. In 1876, he transmitted the first intelligible telephonic message. In 1877, he organized the Bell Telephone Co. to produce and market the telephone, and after considerable patent litigation the U.S. Supreme Court upheld his rights to the invention.

Bell married Mabel G. Hubbard in 1877, a woman who had been deaf from childhood, and settled in Washington, D.C., taking U.S. citizenship in 1882. He gave some ideas, as well as financial support, to his cousin Chichester Bell, who worked with Charles Sumner Tainter on the graphophone cylinder player. His own voice was presumably used to make one of the first wax cylinder recordings, in 1881. (Sealed in the Smithsonian in 1881, this recording was supposedly played in public for the first time in 1937, but clear documentation is lacking for the event.) Bell (or, as some have said, Tainter) was then heard to say "There are more things in heaven and earth, Horatio, than are dreamed of in your philosophy. I am a graphophone, and my mother was a phonograph." Bell also invented the Photophone system of recording by light rays, and experimented with binaural sound.

He had set up a laboratory in Washington in 1879, with Tainter employed as engineer; in 1881, he established the Volta Laboratory. From 1896 to 1904, Bell was president of the National Geographic Society. After 1897, he turned to aviation research and experimentation. He died in Nova Scotia.

Bell, Chichester A., 1848–1924 · Cousin of Alexander Graham Bell, and a prominent inventor. In the Volta Laboratory in Washington, he and Charles Sumner Tainter worked in the early 1880s on improvements in cylinder recording and on transmitting sound through light (the Photophone). In place of tinfoil coating on cylinders, they used beeswax, and they applied the same

surface to cardboard discs. Another area of novel experimentation may have been in magnetic recording. They made both lateral recordings and vertical-cut discs, and they approached the problem of angular versus linear velocity in disc players. The landmark product of their association was the 1886 graphophone, a wax-covered cylinder device (though cylinder is not mentioned in the application, nor the word graphophone), for "recording and reproducing speech and other sounds," primarily a dictating machine. This patent was the center of legal controversy in the industry for many years. The Edison Speaking Phonograph Co. refused to buy the patent, so it remained with Volta, and later American Graphophone Co., until the patent expired in 1903. Edison had to be licensed to use the wax-cutting method of recording. Chichester Bell left Volta in 1885 to work in Europe.

Bell Telephone Laboratories [website: www.bell-labs.com] · A research organization established in 1925 as a unit of AT & T (American Telephone and Telegraph Corporation). Many discoveries have issued from the Laboratories, including the transistor, solar battery, laser beams, transoceanic radiotelephone, the first communications satellite, and microwave radio relay systems. More than 25,000 patents have been acquired. Bell was the first major organization to conduct research in electrical recording, commencing in 1915; Joseph P. Maxfield and Henry C. Harrison were the investigators. An electrical system was developed by 1924.

In 1926, the Laboratories created the Vitaphone records for motion picture soundtracks. These were the first 33 1/3-rpm discs. There were a number of projects in the area of recorded sound during the 1930s. In March 1932, a team of scientists led by Arthur Charles Keller experimented with stereophonic sound, using two microphones to create discs with two parallel tracks. The records, of the Philadelphia Orchestra, were demonstrated at the Chicago Century of Progress Exposition in 1933. In 1933, an extended range vertical-cut disc recording system was announced; it covered up to 10,000 Hz in both recording and reproduction, and as high as 15,000 Hz in recording alone. In 1937, the Laboratories patented a precursor to stereo: a vertical-lateral disc system in which one sound channel was carried by motion 45° to the right and the other channel 45° to the left of vertical, producing a balanced effect. Also in 1937, engineer C. N. Hickman demonstrated a steel-tape recorder that operated at the slow speed of 16 inches per second; the tape was made of Vicalloy.

In 1947, Bell Labs developed the first solid-state transistor, which would quickly replace the vacuum tube in radios, home audio equipment, and all other sound reproducing equipment. This allowed for the revolution of the portable radio in the 1950s, which in turn allowed teenagers to take their music with them "on the road," fueling the growth of R&B and rock and roll. Over the following decades, Bell Labs has continued to work in sound technologies, during the 1990s and early 21st century focusing primarily on wireless communication and speech-recognition technologies. The Labs became part of Lucent Technologies in 1996 as part of a spin-off of AT&T companies.

Beranek, Leo, September 15, 1914– · A noted researcher in acoustics and architectural acoustics, Dr. Beranek has an undergraduate degree from Cornell and earned a D.Sc. degree from Harvard in 1940. After graduation, he formed and directed Harvard's first World War II research laboratory to study electroacoustics, followed in 1943 by formation of the Systems Research Laboratory for redesigning ships to fight the Japanese Kamikaze aircraft. In 1948, he received the Presidential Certificate of

Merit for his war-research contributions, notably advances in shoring up the ship's radar defenses. That same year, he helped found Bolt, Beranek, and Newman, an acoustics-engineering firm that has been responsible for the design of several notable concert halls. Under his presidency, BBN shifted its emphasis from acoustics to computer science and built the ARPANET, the predecessor to the Internet. A founder and former president of WCVB-TV Channel 5, Boston, Dr. Beranek has also long been active in civic organizations, serving as Chairman of the board of trustees of the Boston Symphony Orchestra, member of the Harvard Board of Overseers, and president of the World Affairs Council of Boston. From 1989 to 1994, he was president of the American Academy of Arts and Sciences.

Beranek has written several important books, including *Acoustic Measurements*; *Acoustics*; *Music, Acoustics, and Architecture*; and *Concert and Opera Halls*, and has completed writing an entirely new book on Concert Halls and Opera Houses. He has received gold medal awards from the Acoustical Society of America, the Audio Engineering Society, and the American Academy of Arts and Sciences, in addition to five honorary degrees.—Howard Ferstler

Berger, Ivan, 1939– · Journalist and writer. Born in Brooklyn, New York, Berger was introduced to high fidelity by his high-school chemistry teacher, and started assembling his first component system while an undergraduate at Yale. His journalistic career was launched when a friend who knew of his ambition to be an audio writer showed him a magazine advertisement for just that kind of work. One thing led to another and he ended up spending the next 16 years writing for *Saturday Review*'s music section. In addition, he contributed regularly to *High Fidelity*, *Hi-Fi/Stereo Review* (now *Sound & Vision*),

Audio, Popular Science, the *Los Angeles Times,* and several other publications. For most of this period, however, his primary work involved writing ad copy for audio and photo equipment and even for precision scientific microscopes.

In 1972, Berger joined *Popular Mechanics* as Electronics and Photography Editor, moving in 1977 to a post as Senior Editor at *Popular Electronics.* In 1980, he joined with Lancelot Braithwaite to form Berger-Braithwaite Labs, with Braithwaite serving jointly with him as Technical Editor of *Video Magazine.* From 1982 to early 2000, Berger was Technical Editor at *Audio;* since it ceased publication, he has been writing manuals and white papers for commercial clients and contributing articles on audio and other topics for *The New York Times, Home Theater, The Audio Critic, Sound & Vision, Mobile Entertainment,* CNET. Com, and others. In 1983, he published *New Sound of Stereo,* a book he felt would have served him well when he was just getting started in the hobby. His works have appeared in about 200 magazines, newspapers, and websites and have been translated into at least seven foreign languages. Berger is also (like surprisingly many technically oriented journalists) a published poet.—Howard Ferstler

Berliner, Emile, May 20, 1851–August 3, 1929 · Inventor of the gramophone. Born in Hanover, Germany, son of a Talmudic scholar, fourth of 11 children. His given name was Emil, to which he later added the final "e" in the United States. His formal education, in Wolfenbåttel, ended at age 14, and gave no indication of special talent. After working for a printer and as a sales-clerk, he immigrated to America in 1870, settling in Washington, D.C. For three years, he clerked in the dry goods store of a friend of the family before moving on to New York. There he taught himself electricity and acoustics while employed in menial occupations. He returned to Washington in 1876, set up a home laboratory for experimenting with electrical communication, and patented a telephone transmitter that utilized a principle basic to the development of the microphone. Bell Telephone purchased the patent from him in 1878, establishing a professional relationship between Bell and Berliner that allowed him to work on the problems of sound recording. In 1881, he married Cora Adler, by whom he had eight children.

Experimenting with sound recording, he tried cylinders first, influenced by the phonautograph he had seen in the Smithsonian Institution, then in 1887 invented the lateral (i.e., side-to-side) method of recording on a flat zinc disc. Pressings were on glass at first, then on celluloid, then—as mass production began in 1894—on hard rubber. On May 16, 1888, Berliner demonstrated his device at the Franklin Institute in Philadelphia. It consisted of a recording machine and a reproducing machine (both illustrated in Chew 1981). On a visit to Germany in the following year he made another important demonstration, at the Elektrotechnische Verein, and arranged for the first commercialization of his invention: a toy gramophone manufactured by Kammer und Reinhardt of Waltershausen. (By coincidence, Edison was at the same time marketing his talking doll in America.) He also devised a duplicating system to make records from a master.

In 1890, Berliner returned to the United States and set up a structure for his gramophone work. He established the American Gramophone Co. in Washington in April 1891, and in the building that housed that firm he made the first seven-inch disc records (June 1892); these were issued beginning in late 1894 by the successor company to American Gramophone, the United States Gramophone Co. (established April 1893). That firm also made and sold gramophones. The discs—about 90 of them by the end of 1894—were made of black celluloid at first, then of hard rubber, from zinc masters. The label was not a paste-on piece of paper, but an actual engraving into the record surface; it read "E. Berliner's Gramophone" and gave the Berliner patent dates of Nov 8, 1887, and May 15, 1888.

In the following year, the Berliner Gramophone Co. was formed in Philadelphia; in 1896, the National Gramophone Co. was set up in New York by Frank Seaman to take care of Berliner advertising and sales. Another piece of the Berliner enterprise resided in Camden, New Jersey, across the Delaware River from Philadelphia: there inventor Eldridge Johnson contributed numerous improvements to the gramophone, including a spring motor (the first machines were hand cranked). Johnson also replaced the zinc master with a disc of wax. Johnson had powerful entrepreneurial impulses, which were matched by those of Frank Seaman, who headed the National Gramophone Co. Johnson's version of the disc player, named the Improved Gramophone, which included a new sound box he had developed with the assistance of Alfred Clark. This machine appeared in the famous Nipper painting (1899), and Seaman marketed it in 1898 under the trade name Zonophone. Seaman's firm was sued by American Graphophone Co., with a claim for priority of the Chichester Bell and Charles Sumner Tainter patents, which dealt with recording processes using the method of cutting into wax (whether disc or cylinder). There were years of litigation over patents in the recording industry, but by 1902, Berliner (Victor) and American Graphophone (Columbia) had taken control of the lateral disc market, and retained it until electrical recording and expiration of patents brought forth new competitors. Berliner himself received 12 U.S. patents in the sound recording field.

In Europe, Berliner worked toward the establishment of the Deutsche Grammophon Gesellschaft—headed by his brother Joseph Berliner—in Hanover; and the Gramophone Co. in London, developed by William Barry Owen. Both firms were set up in 1898: pressing was done in Hanover, and recording in London. Berliner himself took a less active part in the gramophone business after the demise of his Philadelphia firm; he retained a financial connection with Victor, and with the Montreal company, acting as a consultant for them. Most of his time, however, was devoted to various other interests after 1900: He was active in an educational campaign about the risks of drinking raw milk (this following the illness of a daughter); he studied aeronautics, and guided his son, Henry, in the development of a successful helicopter (1919). Research in sound waves led to the invention of Sonar, used for submarine detection during World War II. He invented a practical acoustic tile for theaters and halls. According to a story in *Talking Machine World*, January 1918, he was also inventor of a "flying torpedo." He died August 3, 1929 of a cerebral hemorrhage, at home in Washington. A few weeks before his death, he received the Benjamin Franklin Medal for scientific achievement.

Berliner Gramophone Co. · A firm established in Philadelphia, on October 8, 1895, by Emile Berliner, to manufacture discs and disc players under patents held by the United States Gramophone Co.

In 1897, the company opened a London office under William Barry Owen (to become the Gramophone Co. in April 1898), and in 1899, the firm was established in Canada as "E. Berliner, Montreal." About 43,000 gramophones were sold by April 1900. Litigations quickly caused difficulties for the company, however. In 1900, Johnson acquired the patents and even the Nipper trademark that Berliner had registered in July of that year. The Berliner Gramophone Co. shut down in September 1900, and the gramophone passed to the Consolidated Talking Machine Co. In 1901, the gramophone was then passed to its successor firm, the Victor Talking Machine Co. Berliner himself retained a one-third interest in Victor.

Berliner, Joseph, 1858–1938 · German engineer, brother of Emile Berliner and founder with him of the J. Berliner Telephon-Fabrik in Hanover (Kniestrasse 18) on August 3, 1881. The firm had branches in Berlin, Vienna, Budapest, Paris, and London. This company introduced the telephone into Germany. In 1898, he and his brothers Emile and Jacob established Deutsche Grammophon Gesellschaft at the same Hanover address, and ran it until the takeover by the Gramophone Co. in 1900; it had several European branches. When Berliner retired in 1930, he donated 70,000 marks to the workers in his factory.

Bettini, Gianni, 1860–1938 · Italian army officer, born in Novarra. He immigrated to the United States in the mid-1880s, marrying an American socialite, Daisy Abbott of Stamford, Connecticut. Although he had no scientific training, he experimented in sound recording, attempting to improve on Thomas Edison's cylinder reproducer. On August 13, 1889, he received three U.S. patents for a "spider," an attachment that connected a mica diaphragm to a stylus with a view to capturing more vibrations. The actual effect of the spider was to shift the response downward, strengthening the bass and weakening the treble; it improved the rendition of the female singing voice. Eventually, in 1902, Edison bought the patent from him. Bettini also patented reproducing devices for copying cylinders, and received 14 U.S. patents in the sound recording field.

In 1891 or 1892, he went into business as the Bettini Phonograph Laboratory in New York, making cylinders called Micro-Phonograph "Excelsior" Records. Due to the social position of his wife, he met the great singers of the day—Enrico Caruso, Nellie Melba, Victor Maurel, Mario Ancona, Giuseppe Campanari, Pol Planáon, and others, as well as Lily Langtree, Ellen Terry, Sarah Bernhardt, and Mark Twain—and engaged them to record for him. He also personally recorded the voices of Pope Leo XIII and ex-President Benjamin Harrison. His sales were good: In 1897, he was able to produce a 12-page catalog, which grew to 32 pages in the next year. He offered more than 200 items of serious music, copied to order (at relatively high prices, $2–$6 each; competitors were selling at .50¢) without mass production. These records are very rare today because most of the inventory was destroyed in France during World War II. Bettini also sold his micro-diaphragm, which was available in 1899 in models suitable for the Edison Home or Standard phonograph, as well as for the Columbia graphophone.

Bettini established his name in France in 1898 by selling French rights to the Compagnie Microphonographes Bettini. In 1901, he moved to Paris, setting up the Société des Micro-phonographes Bettini, and leaving the New York firm under new management; his successors used the name Bettini Phonograph Co. That firm sold a German disc machine called the Hymnophone, the first to have an inside horn (anticipating the Victrola). Five years later, he abandoned the record business. Bettini lost most of his fortune in the stock market crash of 1929, but continued to experiment, working on various projects including television and games. He died in San Remo, Italy, on February 27, 1938.

Beveridge, Harold N., July 13, 1914 –June 24, 1996 · Born in Upper Sackville in New Brunswick, Canada, Beveridge worked summers in the wilds of Quebec, supplying firefighting outposts with radio equipment to raise money for his tuition at McGill University. Described by colleagues as a consummate engineer, inventor, and businessman who had a knack for recruiting top talent, he was instrumental in developing radar technology during and after World War II for the U.S. and Canadian navies. Some of his radar innovations are still in use on vessels around the world.

Beveridge worked for Raytheon and Arrow Physics before starting his own company, Defense Research Corporation, in 1960. Although a serious designer of high-tech industrial goods, Beveridge had also long been interested in loudspeakers. He opened a shop in downtown Santa Barbara, California, and from 1972 to 1980 sold about 600 pairs of $9,000 speaker systems that some knowledgeable enthusiasts believe were the best line-source designs ever made. About two-thirds of his legendary speakers were sold overseas for as much as $27,000 a pair.—Howard Ferstler

Biamping · A technique whereby the woofer and tweeter (or tweeter/midrange) in a speaker system are driven by separate amplifiers. By dividing the audio frequency spectrum between two amplifiers, the effective output headroom of the system is increased. There may also be better damping control over cone motion if an electronic crossover is used, and there may be adjustment-flexibility advantages with an electronic crossover. Disadvantages of these systems are the increased cost and bulk that result from having a second power amplifier and possibly an electronic crossover network. It is also possible to "tri-amp," which involves separate amplification for the woofer, midrange, and tweeter.—Howard Ferstler

Bias · In tape recording, a high-frequency alternating current, usually between 75 kHz and 100 kHz, applied to the tape record head along with the audio signal with the purpose of reducing distortion and enhancing signal-to-noise ratio. The reason for applying bias is the non-linearity of the magnetic recording medium.

Various tape types (*see also* CASSETTE) require different amounts of bias. No absolute standards for bias or equalization have been established, which leads to problems of compatibility between tapes and equipment. "Biasing" is also achieved by superimposing a magnetic field on the signal magnetic field during recording.

Bias Trap · A low-pass filter in a tape relay circuit, intended to reduce any excessive high frequency bias present.

Biasing · *See* BIAS.

Bill, Edward Lyman, June 5, 1862–January 1, 1916 · Born in Lyme, Connecticut, Bill served in the Dakota State Militia, and was said to have served with Teddy Roosevelt's Rough Riders. Apparently based on this military service, Bill took to calling himself "Colonel E. L. Bill" by the time he came to prominence in New York City life in the early 1900s. Bill served as President of the Police Board (noted in a 1903 article in *the New York Times*) and, in 1904, was treasurer of the New York State Commission to the St. Louis World's Fair. Bill was the founder, editor, and proprietor of the journal *Talking Machine World*, from 1905 to 1916, which he developed out of the earlier Music Trade Review, which he purchased sometime earlier. His son, Raymond Bill, was also an editor of *Talking Machine World*. Bill also published books on industry topics, including a guide to piano tuning. He had a large estate in Larchmont, New York, which his son, Edward Jr., converted into the Bonnie Briar Country Club in 1921. Bill died in New Rochelle, New York.—Rev. by Carl Benson

Binaural Recording · *See* STEREOPHONIC RECORDING.

Binaural Sound · Two-channel sound in which each ear receives only one of the channels. To record binaurally, microphones are mounted on a dummy head, possibly with actual models of human ears on it. Ideally, playback is through headphones at the same respective sound levels that were received by the microphones. One of the early experimenters was Alexander Graham Bell (in ca. 1881). During World War I a binaural apparatus consisting of two receiving trumpets spaced several feet apart, connected by rubber tubes to the ears of an operator, was used to locate enemy airplanes. The principle was applied in World War II in underwater submarine detection. Radio use of binaural sound began experimentally in Germany in 1925, in broadcasts from the Berlin Opera House. In the same year, there were binaural transmissions from New Haven, Connecticut, on station WPAJ. Listeners used two radio sets, tuned to slightly different frequencies, each attached to a tube going to one ear. The need for two radio sets was a deterrent to progress and binaural work was soon abandoned, despite the attractive results that had been achieved.

At the Chicago Century of Progress Exposition in 1933, General Electric engineers demonstrated a binaurally equipped dummy named Oscar (originally displayed in 1932 at the Academy of Music in Philadelphia). Oscar's two microphones picked up sounds from various parts of the room, which could be precisely located by listeners with binaural headphones. With the rise of stereo tape recording in the 1950s, the term binaural became confused with stereo, and because stereo did not require special headphones, the binaural systems faded from sight for two decades.

In the 1970s, some experimental discs were made in Japan that provided remarkable environmental realism, but problems inherent in the system remain to be solved. For example, a sound source moving perpendicularly across the front of the dummy head will produce in the listener the effect of a source describing an arc instead of a straight line, and a circle around the microphones becomes an oval to the listener. Experiments of the 1980s have included Hugo Zuccarelli's "holophonics"—a digital system based on the way we perceive (instead of receive) sound. A firm called Optimax III has made "total dimensional" sound systems for motion pictures and television, using individual stereo headsets. *See also* STEREOPHONIC RECORDING; SURROUND SOUND.

Binder · A glue used to fasten magnetic particles to the base material on a tape. Thickness in use for open-reel tape is 0.56 mil; for cassette tape, it is 0.24 mil. In preparation of the tape, the coating is mixed with the binder—both wet—so that the magnetic particles are evenly dispersed. The binder when dry has to remain flexible, and it must adhere firmly to the base without attaching itself to adjacent layers when the tape is tightly wound.

Birnbaum, Theodore B., February 27, 1865–March 19, 1914 · British recording industry executive, born in Islington, London. He and his brother went into the importing business, and evidently included talking machines among their stock. In 1898, he became associated with William Barry Owen, who was establishing the Berliner interests in London in what was to be the Gramophone Co. When that firm took over the International Zonophone Co. of Berlin in 1903, Birnbaum was made director there. Birnbaum became managing director of the Gramophone Co. in April 1904, remaining with the organization until 1910, when he returned to the import business.

Biscuit · The plastic material from which a commercial disc is pressed. *See also* DISC.

Bishop, Michael, June 14, 1951– · Bishop has been engineering award-winning recordings since the 1970s. He was awarded the 1997 Grammy Award for Best-Engineered Classical Recording, received two Grammy nominations in 1999, and again for 2000 in the same category, and is a member of AES, MPGA, NARAS, ASCAP, AQHA, and NRHA. As part of the engineering and production team at Telarc Records, he has recorded many major orchestral, jazz, blues, and pop recordings. Having worked on pop quadraphonic mixes in the early 1970s, he has applied that early experience to produce some of Telarc's most notable surround-sound releases. He currently lives in Burton, Ohio, with his wife, country music singer Wendy Bishop, and their two daughters.—Howard Ferstler

Blackmer, David E., January 11, 1927– March 21, 2002 · Born in Urbana, Ohio, Blackmer graduated from High Mowing School in Wilton, New Hampshire, studied radar electronics while in the U.S. Navy, and went on to do formal studies at both MIT and Harvard University. After graduation, he worked as an engineer for a number of companies, including Lafayette Radio, Trans-Radio Recording Studio, Epsco, HiCon Eastern, and Raytheon, and was involved in the design of the telemetry systems for the Mercury space program. An inventor by nature, he held many patents, and went on to found three different audio electronics companies: DBX, Kintek, and Earthworks, with the first of the three being responsible for a number of major recording-technology breakthroughs. He was also a co-founder of Instrumentation Laboratory, a medical-electronics company. A hands-on engineering generalist with a love for precision sound recording and reproduction technologies, he was a longtime Fellow of the Audio Engineering Society and a life member of the Institute of Electrical and Electronics Engineers.— Howard Ferstler

Blauert, Jens, June 20, 1938– · Born in Hamburg, Germany, Blauert attended elementary and secondary schools in Dresden and Hamburg, and went on to study communication engineering at Aachen, where he received a Doctor of Engineering degree in 1969. In college, he concentrated in signal theory, electro-acoustics, and psychoacoustics, and since 1974, he has held a chair in electrical engineering and acoustics at the Institute of Communication Acoustics of the Ruhr-Universität at Bochum. His major fields of current interest are binaural technology, models of binaural hearing, architectural acoustics, noise engineering, product-sound design, speech technology, and virtual environments. He has authored or coauthored more than 130 monographs, including the highly regarded *Spatial Hearing: The Psychophysics of Human Sound Localization*, and has been awarded several patents. Blauert has also been awarded an honorary Doctorate from the University of Aalborg, is a former chairman of the ITG committee on electroacoustics, was former dean of the Faculty of Electrical Engineering and Computer Science at Bochum, is a former chairman of the board of the European Acoustics Association, and is currently the president of the German Acoustical Society. In addition to being a member of several other European scientific organizations, committees, and societies, Blauert is also a fellow of the Acoustical Society of America, the Institute of Electrical and Electronics Engineers, and the Audio Engineering Society. His list of major awards and commendations is too extensive to list here.—Howard Ferstler

Blend Control · A device in a stereo amplifier that mixes small portions of the signals coming from both channels. The purpose is to create a smoother sound front across the two speakers.

Blesser, Barry, April 3, 1943–· Blesser has been providing consulting services for 35 years in a wide range of fields, with specialization in digital signal processing for audio. He received his S.B, S.M, and Ph.D. degrees from MIT in the fields of electrical engineering communications and was an Associate Professor of Electrical Engineering and Computer science at that school from 1969 to 1978. During that time, he helped to found Lexicon (1970), and in 1976, he invented the first commercially available, all-digital delay line, which was marketed as the EMT-250 in West Germany in 1978.

Since 1978, he has been providing product development for more than 50 companies, and has been a principle in several start-up companies and has numerous patents and published papers. Dr. Blesser was President of the Audio Engineering Society in 1980 (he co-chaired the first AES conference on digital audio that same year), and has been on the organization's editorial review board since 1975. His landmark paper on digital audio, first published in 1978, is still being distributed, and he has been awarded numerous patents. Dr. Blesser provides both technology development services as well as management of complex hardware and software projects. He has received the AES Bronze Medal, Board of Governors Award, as well as publications awards, and in 1981, the Society awarded him its Silver Medal award for his accomplishments in audio and digital audio research.—Howard Ferstler

Blue Amberol · *See* AMBEROL.

Blumlein, Alan Dower, 1903–June 7, 1942 · British electroacoustics engineer; one of the research team at Columbia Graphophone Co., Ltd., in London from 1929. He and H. E. Holman developed a moving coil microphone, known as the EMI type HB-1. They patented this device as well as a single turn moving coil cut-

ting head; however, he is best known for his pioneering research into stereophonic recording, having demonstrated stereo discs in the early 1930s that illustrated the same principles employed commercially a quarter century later. He designed and patented a stereo system in 1931, and directed a recording of the London Philharmonic, under Thomas Beecham, partly in stereo, on January 19, 1934. He also made a successful stereo motion picture soundtrack (1935). His death came in the crash of a Halifax bomber.

Blumlein Stereo Recording · A variant of the coincident recording technique, it involves the use of two dipolar microphones located very close together and aimed 90° apart, meaning that sounds reaching them are primarily intensity controlled, instead of controlled by time-of-arrival clues. First described by Alan Blumlein in 1931, and sometimes known as stereosonic, it was modified and applied by EMI during the early days of the stereo LP in England. Because the microphones are bidirectional, sounds coming from the audience area are recorded out of phase from those up front. *See also* MICROPHONE; COINCIDENT STEREO RECORDING .—Howard Ferstler

Bongiorno, James, April 2, 1943–· Educated at Westfield Academy and Central, as well as Deveaux School, and graduating in 1961, Bongiorno initially went to work for the Wurlitzer Organ Company. From there, his interest in all aspects of audio sound reproduction resulted in his working for a large variety of top-tier audio and audio-related companies. He also founded several companies of his own, including GAS, Sumo, and Spread Spectrum Technologies, and worked as a consultant for Harmon-Kardon. During this time, he was responsible, or in part responsible, for the design of several notable products including: the Marantz Model 15 power

Boombox

Slang name given to large, portable stereo cassette/radios that were popular during the 1980s in the days before the introduction of the Walkman. Webster's dictionary dated the term to 1981, although the first commercial machines appear to have been made around 1976, combining high-quality speakers with AM/FM radios and cassette players. These machines were larger and better quality machines than typical portable units, but not as bulky as home systems. They were also pejoratively called "ghetto blasters" because of their popularity among black teenagers, who would walk urban streets carrying these players perched on one shoulder, with the music blaring out for all to hear. Sony was a major manufacturer of these units, which by the 1990s also featured CD players. By that time, however, portable radio/players with headphones had been introduced, and boomboxes were gradually replaced by all-in-one units designed for placing on bookshelves at home. —Carl Benson

amplifier; the Dynaco Stereo 400 power amplifier and AF-6 tuner; several SAE, Sumo, and GAS amplifiers, preamps, and tuners (including the renowned Ampzilla); the redesigned Harmon-Kardon Citation 23 tuner; and several Crown Radio of Japan amplifiers and an electronic crossover. Over the years, Bongiorno has written a number of articles for *Popular Electronics*, *Audio*, *Radio-Electronics*, and *Audio Amateur*, and was also winner of the *Stereo Sound* "State of the Art of the World" award in both 1976 and 1980. He is a member of the American Federation of Musicians, the Audio Engineering Society, and ASCAP, and is listed in *Who's Who in America*.—Howard Ferstler

Borwick, John, June 2, 1924–· Born in Edinburgh, Borwick obtained a B.S. degree in physics from Edinburgh University. He later served in the Royal Air Force as a Signals Officer, mostly in India and Sri Lanka, before entering the British Broadcasting Corporation as a program engineer in 1947. He balanced and supervised the recording and broadcasting of music programs of all types, and later taught at the BBC Engineering Training School, writing the BBC's internal instruction manual *Programme Operations Handbook*. After leaving the BBC, he became a frequent broadcaster on audio/recording and has written or edited a number of books including *Microphones: Technology and Technique* (1990), *Sound Recording* Practice (4th ed., 1994), and *Loudspeaker and Headphone Handbook* (3rd ed., 2001).

Borwick was for many years Secretary of the Association of Professional Recording Services and is now an Honorary Member. He is a Fellow and Life Member of the Audio Engineering Society, has served as the Society's Vice President in Europe, and helped to set up the British AES Section in 1970, serving as its first Secretary. He helped to formulate the unique 4-year bachelor of music (Tonmeister) degree course at the University of Surrey in 1971 and was Senior Lecturer (Recording Techniques) for about 10 years. He has acted as a consultant to a number of bodies, including British Phonograph Industry and the Advertising Standards Authority, and is on the Law Society register of expert witnesses. He received an Award from the Federation of British Audio in 1986 "for outstanding service to the industry." Borwick joined *Gramophone* magazine in 1964 as Audio Editor/Director and contributed to the magazine's audio pages in practically every issue until the company was bought out 36 years later.—Howard Ferstler

Bose, Amar, November 2, 1929–· Bose has S.B., S.M., and Sc.D. degrees in electrical engineering from Massachusetts Institute of Technology, with the latter degree earned in 1956. From 1957 to 1960, he was an assistant professor at the institution, becoming an associate professor in 1960, and a full professor in 1966. From 1958 until 1964, he worked as a consultant for Epsco, Edgerton Germeshausen and Grier, and Standard Oil. In 1964, he founded the Bose Corporation, one of the largest and most successful audio-equipment manufacturers in the world. He is currently Chairman of the Board and Technical Director of that company.

Bose holds numerous patents in the fields of acoustics, electronics, nonlinear systems, and communication theory, and his research in those areas led to the formation of the company that bears his name. Before the company entering the consumer-audio field, Dr. Bose's electronic patents formed the basis of the research and development that Bose secured with the armed forces, NASA, the DOT, and the AEC.

He is a Fellow of the Institute of Electrical and Electronics Engineers, and a member of the Audio Engineering Society, and has an honorary Doctorate of Music degree from the Berklee College of Music (1994) and an honorary Doctorate of Science degree from Framingham State College (1990). Numerous other honors and awards include the Western Electric Fund Award (N.E. Section), the Baker Memorial Award for Outstanding Teacher (MIT), membership in The Audio Hall of Fame, membership in the National Academy of Engineering, membership in the American Academy of Arts and Sciences, membership in the Radio Hall of Fame, and listings in *Who's Who in the World* and *American Men and Women of Science*. Dr. Bose has also published numerous articles in *MIT Research Laboratory of Electronics, Technology Review, International Symposium on Circuit and Information Theory*, and other journals and conference reports, and

coauthored *Introductory Network Theory* with Kenneth Stevens (Harper and Row, 1965).—Howard Ferstler

Bose Corporation [website: www.bose. com] · American audio manufacturer, located in Framingham, Massachusetts, founded by Amar Bose, a professor at MIT, in 1964. The company's first products were high-power amplifiers produced under contract to the U.S. military. Proprietary technology created for those units has since been used by Bose in a variety of consumer products—now the foundation of the corporation's success. Bose is best known for creating products that combine high technology with simplicity and small size. The highly successful—and since imitated—Wave radio and Bose home theater products are examples of the company's philosophy: music, not equipment is considered the ultimate benefit.

Over the years, Bose products and technologies evolved. The company introduced the world's first factory-installed, acoustically customized music system for automobiles, pioneered active noise-cancellation technology employed in their pilot and consumer headsets, and are also installed in sports arenas, performing arts centers and other professional venues. With this diversification, Bose is now one of the premier audio-product manufacturers in the world, and annual sales in 2001 exceeded $1.1 billion. The corporation has operations across the world, including the United States, Europe, Canada, Australia, Japan, and India.

Among audio enthusiasts, however, the company may still be mainly identified by its first marketable system, the 901 loudspeaker, which was introduced in 1968 and still makes use of nine small and same-sized, full-bandwidth speaker drivers. Eight of the drivers faced the front wall of the room, with only one facing outward into the listening area, in contrast to more conventional, forward-facing woofer/midrange/tweeter designs being designed by most other manufacturers. The idea was to simulate the direct/reflecting nature of typical concert halls. The 901 had no cross-over at all, and to compensate for power-response losses in the bass and treble, the system utilized active equalization. Shortly after it was introduced, the system was lauded by *Stereo Review's* Julian Hirsch as being superb for realistic reproduction in home-listening situations, and this helped to launch the company into the main-stream, where it has remained to this day. The model 901 system has gone through many alterations since its introduction, and remains a controversial design in audio circles. Some enthusiasts still consider it a reference standard.—Howard Ferstler

Boston Audio Society [website: www.bostonaudiosociety.org] · Founded in the Boston area, in 1972, by Alvin Foster, with the help of Peter Mitchell, Richard Goldwater, and James Brinton, it is the country's old-est, still-active audio-hobby club. Initially, it was tied in with the radio program, *Shop Talk*, on WBUR. The club was influential beyond its often-modest membership size (there are members in areas far removed from Boston), and many individuals who later became influential audio journalists or were (or would become) important in the audio manufacturing business were, and continue to be, members of the BAS. The club publishes a small newsletter, the *BAS Speaker*, which continues to be read by notables in the audio community.—Howard Ferstler

Bottom · A term for the bass response of a sound system.

Bottom Radius · *See* GROOVE.

Boundary Effects · Important in both recording situations and during playback in home-listening rooms, boundary effects involve wave cancellations and reinforce-ments that exist when audio signals inter-act with a room, its larger furnishings, and even a speaker cabinet itself. Perhaps the most audible manifestation involves mul-tiple-boundary effects, which are called standing waves.—Howard Ferstler

Bowers, John, 1922–December 20, 1987 · Born near Worthing on the south coast of England, Bowers spent the war years as a special operations executive in clandestine radio contact with allied resistance opera-tives in occupied Europe. He specialized in electronics and radio-transmission, and after the war, he opened a retail hi-fi store in Worthing with his business partner Roy Wilkins. In 1966, he decided to go into the loudspeaker manufacturing business on his own, and formed B&W Electronics, later renamed B&W Loudspeakers, with his friend John Hayward. (Wilkins may not have been involved with the new manufac-turing operation, and it remains a mystery why the company was not called B&H.) The company thrived under his leadership, in part because of his emphasis on serious research and development, and it eventu-ally became one of the powerhouses of the audio industry.—Howard Ferstler

Bozak, Rudolph Thomas, 1910–1981 · A noted speaker designer and former owner of Bozak Loudspeakers, Bozak was born in Uniontown, Pennsylvania, and stud-ied at the Milwaukee School of Engineer-ing. He went to work for Allen-Brady as a designer in 1933, moved to Cinaudagrph in 1935 (Bozak helped to set up the company's speakers in a huge PA system at the World's Fair in 1939), joined the Dinion Coil Com-pany during the war years, and trans-ferred to Wurlitzer in 1948. After leaving Wurlitzer later that same year, he went on to found his own speaker company in 1952, and, working at times with people like Lin-coln Walsh and Emory Cook, created some of the most prestigious, visually imposing speaker systems of the 1950s. In 1965, the

Audio Engineering Society awarded him a Fellowship, and in 1970 it presented him with its prestigious John H. Potts Award (later to become the Gold Medal). *See also* LOUDSPEAKER, 2.—Howard Ferstler.

Bridging · The process of connecting two channels in a stereo amplifier to play back a monophonic signal; also called strapping.

Briggs, Gilbert A., 1890–January 11, 1978 · Briggs had an early career that had nothing to do with audio or recording technology at all, being a world-traveling textile agent, operating from his home in Yorkshire, England. During the depression, however, his business went sour and he gravitated toward another interest: building custom-made loudspeaker systems. Ultimately, this resulted in him founding Warfedale Wireless Works, in 1933, and the establishment of a brand name that eventually became known worldwide. Briggs was an excellent writer, as well as speaker designer, and between 1948 and his death he published over 20 books on topics as varied as pianos and other musical instruments (he was a fine piano player), amplifiers, loudspeakers, antennas, and audiology. Besides his loudspeaker systems and writings, Briggs, assisted by Raymond Cooke and Peter Walker, may best be known for a series of live-vs.-recorded demonstrations involving his speaker systems, a technique that was also utilized a number of years later by Edgar Villchur.—Howard Ferstler

British Broadcasting Corp (BBC) · A firm established in London, in November 1922, as the British Broadcasting Co. The BBC began broadcasting on November 14, 1922 (following some experimental transmissions in the previous year). At first, the company held a monopoly on sales of radio sets in Britain (1922–1925), and it kept exclusive rights to broadcast on radio and television until 1955. In 1927, the company became a corporation.

Research and development activities were prominent from the early days, and in 1990 were the responsibility of 215 workers. Over the years, important research has been done in loudspeaker design, microphones, diaphragms, and studio design. BBC pioneered in magnetic recording in 1930. One of the world's principal libraries of sound recordings (dating from 1933) has been assembled in Broadcasting House, the BBC's main building since 1932. The archival collection was stored in a coal mine during World War II; other records were moved out of London. The collection includes more than 1 million discs, cylinders, and tapes.

Christopher Stone was radio's first "disk jockey," playing records on a regularly scheduled series of broadcasts. The BBC Symphony Orchestra was created in 1928, and under conductor Adrian Boult, it became one of the leading symphonic ensembles of its time.

Brociner, Victor, 1911–1977 · A graduate of Columbia University, with both bachelor's and master's degrees, and considered to be one of the founders of the modern hi-fi industry, Brociner developed what could be considered the first real hi-fi system in the 1930s. The package included a broadband AM receiver, a low tracking force (for the time) record player, and component-style speaker systems. A version of that system has been displayed in the Smithsonian Institution. In 1937, along with Avery Fisher, he founded the Philharmonic Radio Club. After World War II, he founded Brociner Electronics and in the early 1950s, he produced one of the first fully integrated hi-fi amplifiers, the first practical Williamson circuit amplifier, and some of the first high-fidelity components utilizing printed-circuit boards.

The company eventually failed, and for a while, Brociner joined University Loudspeakers. Later on, in the 1960s, he signed on with the H. H. Scott Company, which at that time was one of the biggest names in the hi-fi business. At Scott, he helped to improve the company line of amplifiers, receivers, tuners, and speakers. In 1972, he left Scott and joined the Avid Corporation. While there, he helped to build Avid into one of the industry's most respected speaker-building companies.

Brociner published extensively, and was a member of several professional societies, including the Audio Engineering Society, the Institute of Electrical and Electronics Engineers, and the Acoustical Society of America.—Howard Ferstler

Brunswick-Balke-Collender Co. · A firm established in 1845, with varied interests (furniture, carriages, equipment for games), that entered the phonograph business in 1916. It appears that the firm entered into an agreement with Pathé to sell only its discs in the United States in exchange for Pathé's undertaking to stay out of the American talking machine market; Brunswick did sell Pathé records from 1916 to 1920. Brunswick records were sold in Canada from 1916; however, this arrangement did not endure beyond 1919, when Brunswick records came to the United States and Pathé began to advertise its phonographs in the American national magazines.

In 1924, the firm acquired Vocalion records from Aeolian Co., and a year later announced a technological breakthrough: the Panatrope all-electric phonograph and the Pallotrope system of electrical recording developed with General Electric. The "light ray" recording process used a microphone (called a "palatrope"), a crystal mirror, a light source, and a photoelectric cell. Despite these advances, and despite the gathering of an international star roster of artists on the Brunswick label, sales peaked in 1926 and dropped $2 million to $27 million in 1927. Brunswick joined the radio manufacturers in 1928, and then in April 1930, sold out both radio and phonograph interests to Warner Brothers.

Buchla, Don, April 17, 1937– · Buchla is recognized as one of the most progressive and visionary electronic instrument builders. He and Robert Moog worked independently during the 1960s to build the first voltage-controlled analog synthesizers—collections of devices, such as oscillators and filters that could be flexibly interconnected by the user with patch cables. Buchla responded to the suggestions of Morton Subotnick and Ramon Sender at the San Francisco Tape Music Center and built the Buchla Modular Electronic Music System, supported by a grant from the Rockefeller Foundation.

Buchla went into business building electronic instruments. The 100 Series (1963) included innovations such as touch-sensitive plates, a random voltage source, and the first sequencer. Morton Subotnick used this system in the composition of "Silver Apples of the Moon" (Nonesuch H71174; 1967), the first work to be commissioned expressly for the long-playing record format. CBS/Fender manufactured the instruments for a while. The 200 Series (1970) introduced new techniques for polyphonic signal generation, dynamic spectral and timbral modification, complex pattern generation, quadraphonic control of spatial location, and had digital connections to interface with computers. Its touch plates (the "Kinesthetic Input Port") explored control by the amount of fingertip surface contact. In contrast to Moog systems, Buchla's systems differentiated between control voltages (accessed with banana plugs) and audio signals (via mini-phone jacks). This made it easy to patch audio in and out of the system at any point at standard line level, so that tape loops, radios, microphones, and other devices could be incorporated. Any number of control inputs could be connected to a single output by merely stacking connectors.

The designs that followed moved increasingly toward greater digital control, as well as the use of digital oscillators. The 300 series was a computer, peripherals, and interfaces, and a patch programming language designed for flexible real-time control of 200 series modules, with function generators and tables taking the place of the earlier sequencer modules. The Buchla 400 was an integrated instrument with digital oscillators and analog filters, which could be augmented with 200 series modules. Its operational language combined a piano roll style graphic score editor with an instrument definer.

Minicomputers became more affordable, and the 500 Series (1971) became the first digitally controlled analog synthesizer. This was followed by the Music Easel (1972), a portable analog performance instrument that accepted patch cards, which were small circuit boards that were precursors of digital preset memory. Although most of Buchla's instruments are not meant to be played with conventional technique using organ type controllers, the Touché (1978) was designed with David Rosenboom for technically skilled keyboard players. The 400 series (1982) anticipated changes in music technology of the next decade with its three computers, graphics display, storage cards, score editing, frequency modulation, and SMPTE capability. The 700 (1987) had yet another computer, three MIDI ports, and a number of expressive performance controls among its facilities.

In 1990, Buchla and Associates shifted their attention to alternative controllers. First came Thunder (1990), a tactile surface with 36 elements that transmit MIDI messages in response to the touch of human hands, followed by Lightning (1991), which reacts to the position and movement of handheld wands.

In addition to electronic and acoustic instrument design, Buchla has been involved with space biophysics research, multimedia composition, and the performance of avant-garde and traditional music. As a Guggenheim fellow, he performed research in interactive performance-oriented computer music languages, and as an NEA fellow designed instrumentation and music for a hundred piece electronic orchestra. Although the majority of instrument manufacturers have gone in and out of business, he survived by producing a smaller number of advanced alternative systems, working out of his home in Berkeley, California.—Robert Willey

Bulk Eraser · A device used to erase the signal from a recorded magnetic tape (cassette or reel-to-reel). It operates by producing a strong magnetic field; when it is passed over the tape in a circular motion it cancels the extant signal. Metal tapes are difficult to erase in this manner.

Bump · "To bump" on a tape means to reduce the number of tracks (e.g., four to two) to make space for new material. Also known as JUMP.

Burnishing Facet · *See* STYLUS.

Butterfly Head · In a tape recorder, a multi-track head with a flared guard band; it provides protection against crosstalk.

Byte · (Digital) The number of digital bits necessary to encode on character of information in any given computer system, including digital audio and digital video systems.—Howard Ferstler

C

C/S · Cycles per second. It is usually expressed as Hertz (Hz).

Cage, John, September 5, 1912–August 12, 1992 · Experimental composer and one of the 20th century's most important musical "inventors." Born in Los Angeles in 1912, Cage spent a childhood fascinated by both early radio and Grieg and nineteenth century piano music. He is best known for *4'33"*, a piece that he first performed in 1952. In this, Cage took music to its most challenging, most questioning conclusion by instructing the performer to sit at the piano for four and a half minutes of nothingness. This was not a performance of complete silence, however, as is the general conception of this composition. Instead, it was supposed to inspire the notion in the audience that music was the random ambient sound around them, and that the piece was made up of every noise they registered during that predetermined time span. Aside from unquestionably challenging and provoking discussion on the very notion of music itself, the roots of latter-day ambient, electronic, and DJ/collage music can be traced back to Cage and his visions.

Cage began working with phonographs in the late 1930s, using them as musical instruments (i.e., playing brief passages as part of a composition, anticipating modern turntablism). He employed this technique in his score *Imaginary Landscape No. 1* (1939). Cage worked most actively with recorded sound in the 1950s when he created several pieces by assembling short fragments of recording tape in the style of *musique concrète*. The best-known of these works was *Williams Mix* (1953), which was created by assembling bits of over 8 reels of tapes consisting of somewhere between 500 and 600 individual sounds, according to Cage. Another, inventive work was *Indeterminacy*, an experiment in which Cage read 90 stories live in the studio while (beyond Cage's hearing) David Tudor played short pieces on the piano as well as short selections from another Cage tape composition, *Fontana Mix* (1958). Each reading and selection was randomly chosen and performed for the same amount of time; Cage had to either read faster or slower (depending on the length of the selection) to meet the time limitations. The result was issued on Folkways Records in 1958, and became a landmark recording for avant-garde musicians (it has been reissued on CD as Smithsonian/Folkways 40804). Also in 1958, a 25-year retrospective concert was held at Town Hall in New York City and subsequently a recording was issued on LP; this helped also spread Cage's music in the early 1960s among younger composers (it has been reissued on Wergo CD no. 6247-2).

Cage turned his attention to live performance from the 1960s forward, although he continued to use various electronic devices—including sound generators of various types—throughout most of his career. Numerous recordings of Cage's music have been issued, although Cage himself did not own a phonograph and did not like the idea of a "fixed" or "permanent" version of his work existing apart from its performance.—Ian Peel/Carl Benson

Campbell, G. A. · *See* LOUDSPEAKER, 9.

Camras, Marvin, January 1, 1916–June 23, 1995 · American electronics engineer, born in Chicago on January 1, 1916. He is noted for research in magnetic recording. He was with the Armour Research Foundation from 1940 through the 1980s. Among his 500 patents are one for AC bias (1941) and U.S. no. 2,351,007 (filed in 1942) for a recording head. He designed a wire recorder that played 30 minutes, at five feet per second, or 60 minutes at 2.5 feet per second, on 0.004 diameter stainless steel wire. General Electric manufactured it for use by the American and British military during World War II. Camras continued his influential research in video recording technology through the 1980s.

Canadian Broadcasting Corp (CBC) [website: www.cbc.ca.] · A Crown Corporation responsible to Parliament but independent of the government, established by Act of Parliament on November 2, 1936; successor to the Canadian Radio Broadcasting Commission (CRBC), a government agency established by Parliament in 1932. The CRBC was intended to broadcast Canadian programs across the country; the agency also made a number of acetate disc recordings of historic interest (speeches, ceremonies, etc.). Unfortunately, there was no practice of preserving the ordinary broadcasts of music and entertainment, so most of popular culture of the 1930s was lost. With the arrival of the new CBC, vast quantities of program material were recorded—although not carefully indexed or cared for. Nevertheless, a substantial record collection did emerge, which was enhanced by wartime documentary material and stimulated by the development of tape recording. In 1959, a Program Archives Department was inaugurated, under the supervision of Robin Woods. Cataloging and preservation developed systematically from that point.

By the year 2000, the archives had grown into a large collection of programs, recordings, books, and even early radio equipment. It holds nearly 250,000 hours of radio programming, stored on CD-ROM, and available to all Canadian radio stations via the intranet. A separate music archive houses 150,000 LPs and 150,000 CDs, including the Clyde Gilmour collection, donated by the broadcaster of the popular "Gilmour's Albums" series that ran from 1956–97 on the CBC. In 1998, The Archives Project was launched to preserve, restore, and catalog the CBC's vast holdings of radio and television programming.

Canby, Edward Tatnall, February 28, 1913–February 21, 1998 · One of the founders of the Audio Engineering Society, Canby, who had a music degree from Harvard, was a choral director, teacher, and writer whose conducting specialty was Renaissance and Baroque music, but whose wide interests led him to work as a writer, folklorist, and as an advocate of electronic music. As a director and singer, he also founded the Canby Singers, in New York, and before teaching at Finch College, in the 1950s, he taught music at Princeton University. In the 1940s, he became fascinated by the relationship between music and audio equipment, and wrote about it in a book, *The Saturday Review Home Book of Recorded Music and Sound Reproduction*, published in 1952. He provided annotations for dozens of recordings on the Nonesuch label, wrote a column for *Audio* magazine for nearly 50 years, reviewed recordings for *Harper's* and *Saturday Review*, and for 20 years hosted a weekly classical-music program on WNYC.—Howard Ferstler

Cans · Another term for headphones.

Cantilever · In a phonograph cartridge, the vertically compliant link between the stylus and armature. It must be sturdy and stiff, as well as well damped to limit resonances. It is usually made of magnesium, boron, or titanium.—Howard Ferstler

Capacitance · The measure, in farads or microfarads, of the energy-storage capability of a capacitor.

Capacitor · An electrical device—often two metal plates separated by an insulator—that can store electrical charge and will block current flow in a DC circuit. In AC circuits, capacitors provide frequency-dependent impedance, useful in filtering and tuning applications. *See also* CAPACITANCE.

Capehart, Homer Earl, June 6, 1897–September 3, 1979 · American industrialist and statesman, born in Algiers, Indiana. He worked on his father's farm until World War I, then enlisted and served until April 1919. After holding various sales posts—one was general sales manager for Holcomb and Hoke, an early maker of coin-op vending machines—he founded the Capehart Co. in 1927. His intention was to manufacture jukeboxes that could play either side of a record; he engaged the inventor of the disc-turning device, a man named Small, to join him in the enterprise. His new device, named the Orchestrope, was successfully placed in roadhouses and bars, but the Depression brought him financial crisis. He then shifted his target market to wealthier homebuyers, and offered a deluxe phonograph that played both sides of discs. This venture was not sufficiently remunerative to save the business, and Capehart endeavored to sell out to RCA and other firms, eventually merging with Farnsworth Television and Radio Corp.

In 1932, Capehart established the Packard Manufacturing Co., another coin-op maker. In 1933, he became associated with Wurlitzer, serving until 1940 as vice president. He was successful in a bid for the U.S. Senate in 1944, and was reelected in 1950 and 1956. Capehart died in Indianapolis.

Capps, Frank L., ca. 1868–June 2, 1943 · American inventor and recording expert. He worked with Emile Berliner, Thomas Edison, and Columbia, and later was production manager for U.S. Pathé. Among his 50 U.S. audio patents were no. 836,089 (granted November 20, 1906) for the Pantograph cylinder duplicating device, and no. 570,378 (granted October 27, 1896) for a spring motor. The motor had three springs; it was used in the 1899 Edison Concert machine. In 1923, Capps produced one of the earliest electrical recordings, of a speech by Woodrow Wilson, pressed by the Compo Co. In the 1940s, he devised a cutting stylus with a burnishing facet. His work for Columbia included making records of Czar Nicholas in Russia, and of many artists in Vienna and Berlin. He retired in 1942. Capps died in New York.

Capstan · The drive spindle of a tape recorder. It consists of a motor-driven cylinder that works with a pinch roller (also known as the puck) to advance the tape at a constant speed. Actual tape speed is determined by the rotational velocity and diameter of the capstan.

Carlos, Wendy, November 14, 1939– · American organist and composer, born in Pawtucket, Rhode Island. She studied music and physics at Brown University and Columbia University. Working with Robert Moog, inventor of the Moog synthesizer, she made an album demonstrating the device. Titled *Switched on Bach* (Columbia MS7194; 1969), it became the first successful record of electronic music, on the charts 31 weeks, and winner of two Grammy awards. She also created the soundtrack for Stanley Kubrick's landmark 1971 film, *A Clockwork Orange*. During the 1980s and 1990s, Carlos turned her attention to creating ambient music. All of her albums have been rereleased under her close supervision in new 20-bit re-masterings by the East Side Digital label.

Cartridge (I) · An enclosure for a roll of magnetic tape, so designed that it will be ready for use when it is inserted into a mated tape recorder or tape player. The advantage of the cartridge over the reel-to-reel tape mechanism is that it is self-contained, and can be inserted without manual threading; it automatically engages the capstan and magnetic heads. The term usually refers to the cassette format introduced by Philips in 1963. With its great size advantage, the cassette made obsolete all the previous configurations, such as the 4-track and 8-track cartridges that had been used in automobiles. This kind of enclosure is also known as the closed-loop cartridge, or continuous-loop cartridge.

Cartridge (II) · A device (also known as a pickup) consisting of a stylus assembly, cantilever, and body. Its function is to convert the groove patterns traced from an analog disc into electric signals. Four basic designs are used: moving iron, moving coil or dynamic, moving magnet, and crystal or ceramic.

In the moving-iron cartridge, a piece of metal (the vane) is attached to the opposite end of the stylus cantilever. As the stylus vibrates in the record groove, it activates a coil of wire that is surrounded by a permanent magnet, producing the audio signal. Designs with "variable reluctance," introduced in the late 1940s, use a minute cantilever of magnetic material to vary the reluctance of a gap between two coils when the stylus is activated by the groove pattern. One example was the British Goldring 500 cartridge, known in the United States as the Recoton. Because of its low-voltage output, the variable reluctance pickup required a preamplifier to boost the output

before regular amplification. With some modifications it was used successfully on LPs, but it never attained widespread use.

More common was the moving-coil cartridge. In that design, the stylus and cantilever moves the coil through a constant magnetic field, setting up electrical variations that comprise the signal. For stereophonic playback, there would be two coils, each responding to stylus movement against one of the groove walls. A cartridge usable for both monophonic and stereophonic discs, such as the Western Electric Model 9A or Westrex Model 10A, could be set so that the stylus moves vertically for mono or laterally for stereo. Problems encountered with this kind of pickup are the need for substantial amplification, and the need with some models to return the entire assembly to the factory for stylus replacement. Denon, Fairchild, Grado, Kiseki, and Ortofon have been associated with this type of pickup. Recent moving-coil cartridges by Denon and Ortofon require no extra amplification stage.

The moving-magnet cartridge is probably the most common design used in high-quality audio systems. The cantilever carries a tiny permanent magnet at the opposite end from the stylus. When caused to move by the action of the stylus in the record groove, it induces voltage in the coil. Among the manufacturers: Audio-Technica, Empire, Fairchild, General Electric, Pickering, Shure, Signet, and Stereotwin. One advantage of the moving-magnet design is its rather high output compared with most moving-coil designs. Another advantage is that the cartridge owner can usually replace the stylus assembly with little effort.

The early crystal cartridges were based on the piezo-electric properties of a material known as Rochelle salt. When a piece of this salt is bent or twisted an electrical output results. The original crystal cartridge had two slices of Rochelle about an inch long, pressed together with a metal foil separating them; each slice had a lead connecting it to an external circuit. At the end opposite the lead, the slices were held in a "torque jaw" clamp. When the stylus, also attached to the torque jaw, vibrated in the record groove, the motion was carried to the Rochelle slices, twisting them enough to generate a voltage. Such a pickup was inexpensive and simple to construct, and did not require equalization as other types do. Certain problems with Rochelle salt—for example, its tendency to absorb moisture and deteriorate—were corrected with the introduction of ceramic piezo materials. Astatic, Electro-Voice, Ronette, and Weathers have made ceramic cartridges.

A less common pickup is the capacitive type, modeled on the principle of the capacitive microphone: Its stylus is attached to a diaphragm biased with a polarizing voltage.

In the 78-rpm era, with steel needles as the styli, the moving-iron pickup was standard. Its efficiency was limited by the mass of the armature, and frequency response was not above 8,000 Hz. The moving-coil cartridge had similar limits based on size of coil. Later designs with smaller moving parts allowed an extension of range to about 16,000 Hz. During the heyday of the LP era, great improvements were made in all aspects of cartridge manufacture. By 1988, quality pickups offered very flat response up to 20,000 Hz.

Other measures applied to cartridges include vertical tracking angle (VTA), which should be between 15 and 20 degrees, channel separation, and tracking ability. Newer products in higher price ranges ($300–$1,300) often perform superbly on discs in good condition, but they do nothing to conceal the defects in worn or dirty grooves. It should be noted that price is no guarantee of quality, and some models, like the Shure V-15, Type V, are reasonably priced and competitive with the best other

brands ever made. *See also* TONE ARM.—Rev. by Howard Ferstler

Cassette · Also known as Audiocassette, or MusiCassette, the analog-audio cassette was introduced by Philips in 1963 as dictating-machine technology. Once introduced into the world of high fidelity, it was supposed to replace the reel-to-reel or open-reel format, and the awkward 8-track tape cartridge. Although it did not displace analog open reel at the professional recording level (digital recorders eventually did, however), it came to dominate the audio-hobby oriented, home-recording field for three decades. The format is itself rapidly being replaced by the MiniDisc, recordable compact disc, and DVD, as well as computer hard-disc technologies. Indeed, few serious audio enthusiasts take the analog cassette system seriously any more, and sales are but a fraction of what they were during the previous two decades.

Early analog cassette tapes did not produce high fidelity output, because of the slow playback speed that made flaws more obvious, and because particle density inhibited high frequency response. Superior tape formulations, better drive systems, and the introduction of noise reduction systems by Dolby and DBX helped to bootstrap the format into the high-fidelity realm.

In the United States, the number of prerecorded cassettes produced each year in the 1970s and early 1980s was about the same as the number of LP albums. Major record companies frequently issued tape versions of their new discs, and both formats were listed in Schwann and other catalogs of new releases. Sales were enhanced by the introduction of the Walkman (a small portable player), by the Sony Corporation, in 1979. The arrival of the compact disc in 1983 changed the market situation, and digital technology was applied to tapes as well. The sale of traditional stereo cassettes remained high, however, particularly among less discriminating enthusiasts, well into the 1990s. *See also* CASSETTE DECK; DAT; HI-FI VIDEO SOUND RECORDING.—Howard Ferstler

Cassette Deck · The transport, recording, and playback device used with cassettes; it is part of an audio system, requiring attachment to an amplifier or receiver, as well as loudspeakers. In principle the analog audio cassette deck is similar to the reel-to-reel tape recorder, but the size and spacing of the drive and rewind components is configured to work with the much smaller and self-contained cassette. Decks available in 2001 included Dolby B and Dolby C noise-reduction systems, with upscale models also including Dolby S. Deluxe versions often have three heads to give a better fidelity and allow instant comparison between the input signal and the recorded output. Many of the more refined decks also have some form of bias or sensitivity adjustment. All the better decks also have two motors, one to turn the capstan, the other to handle fast-forward and rewind operations. The high-end analog cassette deck has been eclipsed by recordable MiniDisc, CD, DVD, and computer hard disk technologies. Recent sales of players and pre-recorded cassettes have plummeted, and the format is not taken anywhere near as seriously by dedicated enthusiasts as in the past.—Howard Ferstler

Cassette Number · The manufacturer's number on a cassette, equivalent to the disc number.

CD · *See* COMPACT DISC.

CD Direct · An input switch on an integrated amplifier that bypasses all circuitry except volume control and perhaps balance control.

CD-Recordable · CD-Recordable (CD-R) is a write-once, read-many (WORM) recording media that is fully compatible with audio compact disc players. The medium was jointly invented by Sony, Philips, and Taiyo Yuden and introduced in 1989 as an alternative to the audiocassette for making private recordings of commercially available music. The recording laser of a CD-R "burns" a spot in a cyanine dye coating on the recordable disc. When played back on a conventional audio CD player, this spot imitates the effect of a pit on a conventional audio compact disc. CD-R uses a sample rate of 44.1 kHz and a sample resolution of 16-bits, the same as pre-recorded audio CDs. CD-R discs are available in two formats, storing up to 74 or 80 minutes of high fidelity sound respectively. CD-R recorders are available as stand-alone audio components that connect to one's stereo system or as computer drives that create audio discs from audio files stored on one's computer.—Thom Holmes

CD-Rewritables · CD-Rewritable (CD-RW) is an audio medium related to CD-Recordables (CD-R). Sony invented CD-RW. Unlike CD-R, CD-RW allows one to erase and reuse discs up to a thousand times. A disadvantage of CD-RW is that the lower reflectivity of the disc itself limits its readability by some commercially available audio compact disc players. A CD-RW drive can record discs in either a CD-R or CD-RW format. CD-RW drives are available as components to be added to one's computer system.—Thom Holmes

CEDAR (Computer Enhanced Digital Audio Restoration) · A reprocessor for 78-rpm records, developed at the National Sound Archive in London. It was made by Cambridge Electronic Design, and first demonstrated at the Audio Engineering Society conference of March 1990. CEDAR is said to outperform other systems that suppress the clicks and noises in 78s. EMI and Columbia have used the system in preparing CD reissues.

Center Channel · In traditional two-channel stereophonic recording, a simulated center-channel image will exist when identical signals from the left and right speakers are produced and the listener sits out in front and equidistant from both systems. In early surround-sound systems, a simulated center could be created from the same input signals by means of electronic circuits in the playback hardware, such as what we have with Dolby Pro Logic, that "steer" identical left-plus-right signals to a discrete center feed. In this arrangement, there is no genuine center, per se, but the steering systems can simulate one quite effectively. More modern systems, such as Dolby Digital, DTS, SDDS, SACD, and DVD-A, actually have a true center channel (as well as discrete surround channels). With proper recording techniques, the addition of a center can greatly enhance soundstaging, imaging, and overall realism, particularly for listeners who are not sitting in the sweet spot that is centered up out in front of the front speakers. *See also* CHANNEL; SURROUND SOUND.— Howard Ferstler

Ceramic Pickup · *See* CARTRIDGE (II).

Channel · The path followed by a signal through a sound system. In a monaural system, there is just one signal and one channel. A basic stereophonic system has two channels, one for the left and right signals, with each helping to create a complete soundstage up front. Modern, consumer-oriented surround-sound systems may have as many as five discrete channels (left, center, right, left surround, and right surround), plus an optional subwoofer channel that handles just the low bass. The latter may also handle explosive low-frequency effects in Dolby Digital, DTS, and SDDS movie soundtracks. The three front channels will deliver the soundstage in most recordings, with the surround channels either re-creating the sense of

hall, church, or studio space or delivering instrumental effects that allow the system to be an artistic form in itself, instead of a way to simulate a live performance. *See also* CENTER CHANNEL; DVD-A (DVD-Audio); SACD (Super Audio Compact Disc).—Howard Ferstler

Channel Balance · The condition of a sound system when all channels (two, three, four, five, or even more) are properly adjusted in terms of levels, so as to properly simulate what the recording or mastering engineers wanted when they created a musical recording. Important with home-theater playback, also. *See also* STEREOPHONIC RECORDING; SURROUND SOUND.—Howard Ferstler

Channel Reversal · An arrangement in which the sound emanations from right and left speakers in a stereophonic system are reversed.

Channel Separation · The extent to which two, three, four, five, or even more channels of a hi-fi playback system are able to keep their signals isolated from each other. Poor separation makes it impossible for the system to properly simulate a live performance or duplicate what the recording engineers wanted when they produced the recording.—Howard Ferstler

Chassis · The frame on which working components of an electronic system are mounted.

Christie, Cary L., August 2, 1944– · Educated in mechanical engineering at UCLA, Christie helped found Infinity Loudspeakers in 1968. He served as vice-president and then president of the company until 1994, and provided much of the creative leadership that helped to establish Infinity as one of the world's premier loudspeaker manufacturers. After leaving Infinity, he went on to found still another company, Christie Designs. He sold his company

Christmas Records

The first Christmas record was "Jingle Bells," played on a banjo by Will Lyle (an Edison cylinder of October 1899). Among the famous early renditions of traditional carols were "O Holy Night" by Enrico Caruso, and by Marcel Journet (Victor 6559), John McCormack's "Adeste Fideles" (Victor 6607), Ernestine Schumann-Heink's "Stille Nacht" (Victor 6723, backed by Engelbert Humperdinck's "Weihnachten"; also on Victrola 88138), and another "Silent Night" by Elisabeth Schumann (Victor 2093, backed by the "Coventry Carol"). In 1908, Victor offered the Irish specialty singer/monologist Steve Porter in "Christmas Morning at Clancy's" (Victor 5604, then 16936), a dramatization of children opening gifts; and in 1918, there was Victor 35679, "Santa Claus Tells About His Toy Shop," a reading by Gilbert Girard. (Texts of the Porter and Girard efforts are in Ault 1987.) Among the novelty records of the acoustic era was "Santa Claus Hides in the Phonograph," on Edison and Brunswick.

Columbia got a late start on Christmas, but had a full list of carols in its catalogs of the 1940s, in addition to Basil Rathbone's version of the Dickens *Christmas Carol* (on six sides, in no. MM-521). *Amahl and the Night Visitors*, by Gian-Carlo Menotti, was a Christmas opera produced for television (NBC, 1951); Victor has the original cast on no. 6485-2.

The best seller among Christmas records is "White Christmas," which has had more than 400 versions on disc; the first and most important is that by Bing Crosby. Crosby also recorded very successful renditions of "Silent Night" and "Adeste Fidelis" (Decca 621) in 1935. Mel Tormé's "Christmas Song"—best known via Nat "King" Cole's Capitol 311 version (1946; no. 3)—and Gene Autry's "Rudolph the Red-Nosed Reindeer" (Columbia 38610; 1949; no. 1) stand out among later examples of the genre. Autry's "Rudolph" may have been the second highest seller of holiday songs; there were about 450 recordings of it by other artists. Another holiday perennial was introduced in 1958 by the Harry Simeone Chorale, "The Little Drummer Boy" (20th Century Fox 121), which returned to the top-ten for the next five years, and is still played during the Christmas season.

The rock era saw a new generation of Christmas songs. Bobby Helms' "Jingle Bell Rock" (Decca 30513, 1957; no. 6), Elvis Presley's "Blue Christmas" (RCA; 1957), and Brenda Lee's "Rockin' Around the Christmas Tree" (Decca 30776, recorded in 1958 and reaching number fourteen in 1960) were among the first. Rock groups often released Christmas albums during the 1960s, most notably The Beach Boys, the Ventures, and the Four Seasons. The Beatles issued an annual record for their fan club with skits and mock carols; these have become highly collectible. Perhaps the most unusual Christmas recording of the rock era was the Bing Crosby-David Bowie duet on "Little Drummer Boy" (RCA BOW 12; 1977).

The first rock benefit record, organized by Bob Geldof to feed starving people in Ethiopia, was "Do They Know It's Christmas" (Columbia 04749), released under the group name Band Aid in 1984. The song inspired other charity recordings, most notably "We Are the World," although it has not become a holiday favorite.

Parodies of Christmas songs are also popular, as are humorous takes on the Christmas spirit. Among these, perhaps the most successful has been "Grandma Got Run Over by A Reindeer" by Elmo & Patsy (Epic; 1984), said to be one of the most-played Christmas recordings of the 1980s and 1990s.

Many of these recordings were reissued on two releases by Rhino (no. 11E-70636/37) titled *Billboard's Greatest Christmas Hits*. Many other Christmas anthology recordings are available by genre, era, and artist.—Rev. by Carl Benson to Recoton Corp. and went on to serve as President of the Acoustic Research brand, which the company had purchased in 1996. During his career, Christie has designed a number of notable loudspeaker systems, including the first high-efficiency electrostatic systems, the EMIM and later-design EMIT mid-range/tweeter drivers, and the classic and monumental Infinity RS and IRS systems. (The EMIT had been initially designed by Daniel R. von Recklinghausen, and both the EMIT and EMIM drivers were configured by Christie to replace the electrostatic and Walsh drivers that Infinity had been using.) He also designed the Black Widow tone arm, and went on to design both the HO series and highly regarded, low-profile Phantom models for AR/Recoton. The audio press has lauded Christie's products, and he has won several design awards. He continues to create innovative speaker designs for the audio industry.—Howard Ferstler

Cinerama · A three-projector motion-picture system designed by Fred Waller that used a wide curved screen and a separate 7-track magnetic soundtrack designed by Hazard E. Reeves for specially equipped Cinerama theaters. Sound was recorded on separate magnetic stock for superior fidelity, in discrete seven-channel stereo. Because of the high cost of equipment and technical complexity, the Cinerama company made only a few feature films in the three-strip process, such as *This is Cinerama*, in 1952; *Seven Wonders Of The World*, in 1956; and *How the West Was Won*, in 1962.—Howard Ferstler

Circuit · A network consisting of one or more closed paths.

Clark, Alfred C., December 19, 1873–June 16, 1950 · American/British inventor and recording industry executive, born in New York. He was educated at City College of New York and Cooper Union, and became an associate of Thomas Edison in 1889. In 1895, he developed, at the Edison Laboratory in New Jersey, the first motion picture films with continuity; he made Edison's only feature film. Joining the Berliner organization in Camden in 1896, he was co-inventor with Eldridge Johnson of a new sound box for the gramophone in 1896; the improved hand drive eliminated much of the old turntable waver. This research led to the Improved Gramophone. In autumn 1896, he moved to Britain, becoming one of the founders and an early executive of the new Gramophone Co. (established in April 1898), and opened the Paris branch in 1899. In 1907, he founded the Musée de la Voix in the Archives of the Paris Opéra. He began using Nipper as a symbol in 1907, several months before the Gramophone Co. From 1909 to 1931, he was managing director of the Gramophone Co., becoming a naturalized British subject in 1928. With the formation of EMI, Ltd., in 1931, he became its first chairman. He was also the managing director of EMI from 1931 to 1939. In April 1946, he was appointed president of EMI; he then retired in September of that year. He was also the first president of the Radio Industry Council. Clark died in London.

Clark, David, April 29, 1941– · Born in Detroit, Michigan, where he served as an apprentice and draftsman under one of the city's most influential architects of the 1950s, and later educated at Lawrence Technological University (where he received a B.S. in engineering in 1977), Clark has worked in the audio industry for over 30 years. He began his adult career as a technician at the University of Michigan, later worked at both management and technical positions in the recording industry for Motown Records, Holland-Dozier-Holland Sound Studio, and the Audio Design and Manufacturing Company, and served as Adjunct Professor of Architecture at the University of Michigan at Ann Arbor.

In 1977, Clark began his own company, DLC Design, initially providing engineering services for concert sound reinforcement, motion-picture theaters, recording studios, and other areas of professional audio. He also co-founded the ABX Company in the early 1980s, with the purpose being to produce a device that would let serious researchers do unbiased, level-matched comparisons of various audio products. The procedure has become an industry standard (being employed by DBX, Dolby, and Lucasfilm, among others), and has become the bane of the lunatic fringe in consumer audio. Now working primarily in automotive audio, Clark also developed DUMAX, a product that enables an entirely new method of predicting loudspeaker drive-unit performance.

An audio consultant for the Detroit Institute of Arts from 1977 through 1987, and a consultant for Delco Electronics, Bosch, Mitsubishi, Chrysler, Harman, and Ford, among others, Clark has also published extensively, both in professional journals and consumer magazines. He has also presented numerous technical papers on subjective testing, room acoustics, loudspeaker design and testing, automotive audio, and psychoacoustics to the Audio Engineering Society, the Acoustical Society of America, and the Society of Automotive Engineers. Clark is a member of each group, helped to found the Detroit section of the AES in 1979, and served six years as Vice President and Governor of the international AES. He became a Fellow of the Society in 1985, for his work in double-blind testing.—Howard Ferstler

Clean Feed · In recording, a version of the program signal that omits one source—for example, the voice part—to allow overdubbing, as in another language.

Clements, Michael, February 18, 1949– · Born in Slough, Buckinghamshire, England, Clements received his early education at Slough Technical High School from 1960 until 1967. After graduation, he was apprenticed as a mechanical engineer at the British Aircraft Corporation and studied engineering at Kingston College of Advanced Technology from 1967 to 1969. Employed by KPM Music Publishing in 1970, he trained and worked as a studio recording engineer until 1975. He has been a freelance recording engineer since 1978, recording diverse material for many companies including Classics for Pleasure, Music for Pleasure, Listen for Pleasure, EMI Records UK, RCA, BMG Classics, Virgin Classics, Collins Classics, Gimell Records, and EMI Classics. During his career, he has won various Gold, Silver, and Platinum discs for U.K. sales achievements, a number of *Gramophone Magazine* Record Awards, including Best Baroque Recording and Best Early Music Recording 1991, Best Engineered Recording in 1991 and 1995, and an NARAS Grammy award for Best Orchestral Recording in 2000.—Howard Ferstler

Clephane, James Ogilvie, February 21, 1842–November 30, 1910 · American inventor and record industry executive, born in Washington, D.C. As secretary of Samuel Seward, U.S. Secretary of State, he became interested in office machines and contributed to the invention of the typewriter, the first of which was built for the use of his staff. Later, he and Ottmar Mergenthaler began the development of the linotype machine, revolutionizing printing technology. Impressed with a demonstration of the Graphophone, he, along with Andrew Devine and John H. White, entered into a marketing agreement with Volta Graphophone Co. on March 28, 1887, in effect establishing the American Graphophone Co.

Clephane was a director of the Mergenthaler Linotype Co., and of the American Graphophone Co. From 1890 to 1893, he was secretary of the Eastern Pennsylvania

Phonograph Co. He died in Englewood, New Jersey.

Click Track · A device used to help conductors and performers to synchronize music with action on a film. The track was at first made up of sprocket holes punched at fixed intervals into a piece of 35-mm film that ran concurrently with the image film; the sprockets clicked in the manner of a metronome, audible through headphones. Later, the click track was electronically constructed, and allowed for tempo variations as needed.

Cliftophone · A line of disc players marketed in Britain by Chappell Piano Co., Ltd., in 1925, offering "new musical joy" and the promise of "Great Artistes … with you, as in life, vivid, real, just as you heard them in living flesh sing or play upon a platform." Console models sold for £7 10s; there was also a portable, 7 × 12 × 14 inches in size.

Clipping · *See* DISTORTION, 3.

Closed Loop Cartridge · *See* CARTRIDGE (I).

CM/S · Centimeters per second; a rate of speed applied to tape velocity in recording or playback.

Coarse Groove · A designation of the 78-rpm disc, in contrast to the microgroove LP. *See also* GROOVE.

Coaxial Cable · An electrical cable in which a center conductor is surrounded by insulation and a braided shield.

Coaxial Loudspeaker · A type of loudspeaker in which a tweeter is mounted concentrically within a woofer, each having its own voice coil. A substantial frequency overlap is desirable between them.

Cobra Pickup · One of the popular cartridges of the high fidelity era, marketed by Zenith ca. 1948. It was a moving iron type, lightweight to give three times as many plays per record without loss of frequency response. A round flat vane was attached to the top of the stylus, with a small coil adjacent to the vane; movements of the vane were transmitted to a connected oscillator.

CODEC (CODER-DECODER) · An electronic program that converts analog signals into digital form and compresses them to conserve bandwidth. Most CODECs employ proprietary coding algorithms for data compression, common examples being Dolby's AC-2 and AC-3, PASC, DTS, ADPCM, MPEG (including MP3), Advanced Audio Coding (AAC), and Meridian Lossless Packing.—Howard Ferstler

Coincident Stereo Recording · A microphone technique (variants being X/Y stereo, M-S stereo, intensity stereo, or a crossed figure eight technique) that involves the use of two dipolar or other directional microphones located and aimed in such a way that sounds reaching them are primarily intensity controlled, instead of controlled by time-of-arrival clues. Often used with small ensemble recording from fairly close-up distances, the result is an often clear and well-focused soundstage and workable monophonic compatibility. *See also* MICROPHONE; SPACED ARRAY MICROPHONE RECORDING; BLUMLEIN STEREO RECORDING.—Howard Ferstler

Coin-Op · The name given to a variety of devices in which playback of one or more recordings is activated by the insertion of a coin into a slot. Also known as coin-slots, or coin-in-the-slots. The final development of the concept was the jukebox.

Louis Glass, manager of the Pacific Phonograph Corp., introduced a coin-op on November 23, 1889, at the Palais Royal Saloon; for five cents, it played a single Edison cylinder audible through any of four listening tubes. These humble gadgets quickly found a national public, and many firms hastened to manufacture and distribute them, principally the Automatic Phonograph Exhibition Co. Before 1900, there were models capable of playing four or five cylinders in sequence, but the customer could not choose among them. The Automatic Reginaphone offered by the Regina Music Box. Co. in 1905 played six cylinders consecutively, requiring a coin for each one; its successor was the Hexaphone of 1908, which offered the customer a choice among six two-minute "indestructible" cylinders—it ran on an electric motor and gave good acoustic results from a wooden horn. Nevertheless, the first machine to give ample choice to the patron was the 1905 Multiphone, which allowed a selection among 24 cylinders. The 1906 Concertophone offered 25 choices; it was sold also in a home model, without the coin slot, becoming the first of its kind. By 1900, there were also disc coin-ops, with the first apparently made for export to Germany by the Universal Talking Machine Co.; it played one seven-inch record. The Gramophone Co. advertised a penny-in-the-slot device in 1902. Soon America had various multi-disc and multi-cylinder devices made by Autophone and the Automatic Machine and Tool Co.—the last-named being the producer of the spectacular John Gabel's Automatic Entertainer in 1906.

The coin-slot idea was also applied to music boxes, player pianos, a combination disc player and music box (*see also* REGINA MUSIC BOX COMPANY), and to machines that showed pictures along with music (*see also* PICTURIZED PHONOGRAPHS). For later developments, *see also* JUKEBOX.

Coloration · In a sound system, the change in frequency response occasioned by resonance peaks; subtle variations of intensity or quality of tone.

Columbia (label) · The story of Columbia Records is a tangle of similar company names. Dating back to the earliest days of recording, the "Columbia" name—in various forms—finally became the basis of one of the "major" labels, recording everything from classical to pop to country and jazz.

The Columbia Phonograph Company of Washington, D.C., was operating as early as 1888. In July of that year, it became a regional representative for the North American Phonograph Co., to sell and service graphophones (dictating machines, cylinder format) and the similar Edison phonograph to government offices. It soon branched out into doing its own recordings. John Yorke AtLee, a whistler, began to make records for the company in 1889, and the label then signed John Philip Sousa and his United States Marine Band to an exclusive contract. In 1890, the firm published its first one-page cylinder catalog, which rapidly grew to 10 pages within a year. By mid-1891, among the items available were marches, polkas, waltzes, miscellaneous hymns and anthems, various solos with piano for clarinet, cornet, and voices "comic," "negro," "Irish" and like material, spoken word records, and 36 of AtLee's specialties accompanied by one "Prof. Gaisberg"—better known later without his (pseudo) academic title as one of the great impresarios of the industry.

The 1893 catalog grew to 32 pages, with such novelties as foreign language instruction and Shakespeare recitations. The first female singer to be identified, Susie Davenport, made her only catalog appearance; and George Diamond, the ever-popular tenor, made his first of many. The company was selling 300 to 500 cylinders a day, mostly by mail. Sales were essentially confined to commercial coin-ops (the early juke boxes), because cylinder machines were still too costly—at $150 or more—for most homebuyers. By November 1891, Columbia was operating 140 coin-ops in the Washington-Baltimore area. The firm continued to grow through the 1990s, expanding to New York and other cities by mid-decade. Sale price dropped to .60¢ per cylinder, for the 575 titles in the 1895 catalog. New artists of 1895 included Sousa's own Grand Concert Band and the famous trombonist Arthur Pryor. In the next year's catalog, "the great and only" Jules Levy appeared with 13 cornet numbers.

By 1897, a boom came to the early recording industry. Economic conditions in the United States were improved, and a lower price line of cylinder machines had become available. Disc sales were rising rapidly. In 1898, a half million cylinder and disc records were produced, a number that tripled the following year and rose to 2.8 million. Columbia was comfortably ahead of its competition, and reduced its cylinder price to .50¢. The firm rapidly expanded, opening offices, between 1896 and 1898, in St. Louis, Philadelphia, Chicago, Buffalo (New York), and San Francisco. In 1897, a Paris office was opened, followed by one in Berlin (1899) and London (1900).

Over the next few years, the industry began to accept the practical superiority of discs over cylinders. In 1901, Columbia began to issue disc records, made by the Globe Record Co. Columbia's major competitor, Victor, bought Globe in early 1902, and used the acquisition as leverage in negotiating a seminal deal with Columbia. In that settlement the two firms agreed to share their patents, effectively closing out other competition in the United States. Cylinders were still made for the Graphophone Grand and other Columbia players—among them the 5-inch Grand that gave a louder playback than the standard size—and were selling at 300 to 550 per day—but attention focused on the new 7-inch and 10-inch records, and in 1903 a 14-inch disc. All were single-sided, with

announcements. The cylinder phonograph began fading from the scene (Columbia discontinued cylinder production in 1908). In 1913, the term "phonograph" was dropped from the company name, which was now the Columbia Graphophone Co. Columbia pioneered in 1904 with the two-sided disc—all their discs were double-sided after September 1908—and in 1907, they marketed an "indestructible" Velvet Tone record that was developed by the inventor Guglielmo Marconi. As a manufacturer of playback machines, in its advertisements Columbia claimed preeminence as the "largest talking machine manufacturers in the world."

Between 1908 and 1910, the company reissued operatic performances made by European labels. None of these initiatives proved to be market sensations, but success was achieved with fine recordings of instrumentalists like Josef Hofmann, Leopold Godowsky, Vladimir de Pachmann, Percy Grainger, Eugen Ysaÿe, and Pablo Casals. Columbia was also very strong on the popular side, with dance music, ragtime, and in 1917 one of the earliest jazz records ever made, by the Original Dixieland Jazz Band: "Darktown Strutters' Ball."

Sales boomed into the 1920s, and then began to fall as the radio appeared on the scene and won the hearts of American consumers. American Columbia—like so many record companies at that time—was headed for bankruptcy. In 1924, the firm's investors reorganized its assets under the name Columbia Phonograph Co. Meanwhile in Britain, Louis Sterling had acquired the firm's London division in 1923, and subsequently purchased the original American company in 1925. A new trademark and label design was introduced by Sterling, who brought in fresh management and equipment, to take advantage of the new technology of "electrical recording," developed by Western Electric and licensed to Columbia.

By the mid-to-late 1920s, economic conditions had improved, encouraging wider purchasing of entertainment products. Acoustic recordings were gradually replaced in the catalogs by electrics. The famous Columbia Masterworks label was introduced, and great energy was poured into the recording of complete symphonies and other large works. American Columbia was also vigorous in the popular field: Bing Crosby's first record was theirs (1926) and Paul Whiteman was stolen from Victor in 1928. In September 1925, the company offered a new low-price label (.50¢ instead of the .75¢ for regular Columbia Recordings: Harmony. These were acoustic recordings, featuring dance and popular material.

Up to the beginning of the Depression, sales were remarkably good in both the United Kingdom and United States. The firm purchased several important smaller labels, including Okeh, which had a large blues and country catalog. The Columbia Broadcasting System (CBS) was incorporated as a subsidiary in 1927, with 16 stations across America. Columbia's answer to the Victor Orthophonic phonograph was its Viva-Tonal, introduced in 1925, heavily promoted from 1927. Intended for playback of the new electrical recordings, it was, however, a windup and fully acoustic in its technology. It did not match Victor's model in the market.

With the Wall Street collapse of 1929, the phonograph industry was nearly destroyed. In April 1931, American Columbia separated from its British owners; the American assets passed to Warner Brothers, the motion-picture giant, who then sold it to the radio manufacturer Grigsby-Grunow. CBS radio was not part of the deal, however; it became an independent company. English Columbia was absorbed into the newly formed EMI. With the collapse of Grigsby-Grunow in 1933, U.S. Columbia was taken over by the American Record Corp. (ARC).

The Columbia label survived these sad days, and discs under that name continued to appear. John Hammond, as recording director from 1933 to 1948, brought many great jazz stars to the label. Finally, in 1938–39, CBS Radio purchased Columbia from ARC to form Columbia Records, Inc.

So the two veteran giants of the industry, Victor and Columbia, faced off once again. Columbia signed up great names in the classical and pop fields, making up for lost time. Columbia's last confrontation with Victor took place from 1949 to 1950, in the "war of the speeds." Both companies had experimented in the early 1930s with discs that rotated 33 1/3 rpm, for cinema, sound effects, and other uses. Both had encountered technical problems. Research and development work was hampered first by the Depression and then by World War II. Even so, in 1948 Columbia Records introduced its long-playing record (LP), revolutionizing the industry. Victor's first response was the 45 in 1949; it was not as useful as the LP for classical music, and served to delay the advent of Victor's 33 1/3-rpm record until 1950. By that time, Columbia and several other LP labels had taken over the classical music area. Columbia stood for the first time as the dominant rival in the half-century struggle with Victor.

Starting in 1951, Columbia made 45s as well as LPs, using the small format for popular singles. Victor used the LP for classical recordings. Columbia rode the crest of an ever-growing wave of disc sales in the United States, joining (if late) in the rock music craze and taking a larger share of that market than any of the major labels. The 1960s were equally strong. *West Side Story* with the original cast was a great multi-million seller; the soundtrack album was even more popular, on the charts for three years. In the mid-1960s Columbia was one of the five giants of the industry, a place that it held through the 1970s.

A curious decision in 1979 led to the dropping of the venerable label name Columbia, in favor of "CBS." The late 1970s marked the peak of the record market in America, followed by a sharp decline in the 1980s. In 1986, Laurence A. Tisch was named chief executive of CBS Inc. He sold the magazine and recording divisions of the firm; CBS Records went to Sony Corp. in January 1988 for $2 billion. As a final coda of the Victor-Columbia rivalry, in 2003, Victor's owner, the German Bertlesmann media conglomerate, merged its assets with Sony's Columbia label to form Sony BMG Music Entertainment.

Comb Filtering, Acoustic · The result of two audio signals interacting in such a way that their combined outputs cause the global frequency response to become more irregular and choppy appearing, like the teeth of a comb. This can happen when the outputs of two speaker systems (or even speaker drivers within the same system that have overlapping responses) reach the listener's ears at slightly different times. The effect is rarely detrimental, unless the alternating peaks and dips are widely spaced. Wall reflections combining with the signals from the speakers also cause comb filtering, and the result is sometimes a pleasant enhancement of spaciousness.

During recording, the comb-filtering effects of spaced microphones can be measurably similar to what is reproduced by speakers, but the result may be subjectively more disturbing. Microphone comb filtering is similar to what is sometimes intentionally applied electrically to a monophonic signal to create a pseudo-stereo effect.—Howard Ferstler

Combination Phonograph · With the 1908 introduction of four-minute cylinders, the Edison Amberols, gearing of new phonographs (by Edison and others) was modified so that either the new records or the older two-minute cylinders could be played. The machines thus designed were the Combination Phonographs. Owners of the older type players were given the opportunity to upgrade their equipment with the purchase of Combination Attachments.

Compact Disc · Commonly known as the CD. A recording made with digital technology instead of the analog recording method that was employed from Edison's time through the LP era. The disc and the machine required to play it were offered first by Philips and Sony in 1983, producing a general sense in the industry that a true revolution had occurred—one that was comparable to the introduction of electrical recording in 1925.

In making a CD, the signal is taped first, just as in analog recording. Then it is sampled electronically: measured 44,100 times a second. The measurements are expressed as strings of digits (zeroes and ones) in binary code. These binary strings are interpreted by a laser beam that cuts millions of corresponding pits into a master disc; from the master, a stamper is made; and from the stamper the final CD is pressed. The playing surface of the disc is of molded plastic—a tough, scratch-resistant polycarbonate that covers an internal aluminum-film coating that caries the pits. Whereas the playing surface is fairly durable, the reverse side of the disc is simply coated with lacquer and labeling paint. This makes that surface of the disc rather fragile, and so a reasonable amount of care has to be taken during handling. Contrary to early ad copy, a CD is not indestructible, or even close to it.

During playback, a laser beam follows the spiral signal path from the inner circumference to the edge, as the disc spins and the pits alternately reflect and scatter the light beam. The CD is a constant linear velocity device, which means that the rotational speed varies as the laser tracks different parts of the surface, thereby keeping the linear speed constant. (*See also* SURFACE

SPEED.) To achieve this linearity, the rotational speed varies from 200 to 500 RPM. Pulses of light reflect off the mirror to an optical sensor, which reads the pits in binary code into a microprocessor. At that stage, the digital signal is changed back to analog by a DAC (digital-to-analog converter), and it can then be perceived as "sound" once again after being amplified in the traditional manner and routed to speaker systems. (*See also* DIGITAL RECORDING.)

A standard CD is 4 3/4 inches (11.9 centimeters) in diameter. "Mini CDs" of three-inch diameter came into production in the late 1980s as 20-minute counterparts to 45s, but did not gain lasting success in the United States. This was in part to the fact that early CD players required a plastic ring-shaped adapter, which snapped on to the outer rim of the disc, to play them.

CD technology offers a number of advantages over its analog predecessors:

1. A standard CD holds a specification-defined maximum of 74 minutes on its single side, but variations can increase the playing time to about 80 minutes. Program loudness levels or bandwidth will not affect that length.
2. A dynamic range of up to 96 dB or more, if noise shaping is employed.
3. An extremely good signal-to-noise ratio, with obnoxious background-noise levels that are very low compared to the LP system or analog cassette; often as much as 30 or 40 dB better.
4. Playback speed that is digitally controlled by an internal clock mechanism, meaning that there is no audible wow or flutter.
5. A subjectively flat frequency response is achieved across the entire audio frequency range, from well below 20 Hz, on out to 20 kHz.
6. Because the surface of the disc is never touched by a stylus or other mechanical part, it does not wear with use.

All decently designed CD players on the market by the early 1990s produced subjectively near-perfect playback, so the only meaningful differences to be noted in the output signal from the whole system came from characteristics of the amplifier and loudspeakers (particularly the latter), and of course from the microphones, mixers, and techniques involved with making the recordings themselves.

During its formative years, a system of codes was used to indicate how a CD was recorded. DDD meant that digital equipment was used in the original tape recording, and in the mixing, editing, and mastering of the music. ADD indicated that the signal was tape-recorded on analog equipment, but mixed and mastered digitally. AAD indicated that only the final master was digitally produced. Since the middle of the 1990s, these terms have been used less and less, as nearly all new digital recordings are produced with the DDD technique.

Despite its huge commercial success and acceptance by the audio-engineering community, some critics and musicians still believe that digital recording is cold, or that it lacks depth and spaciousness. That such doubts still exist among a vocal minority is more a sign of their inability to understand what digital recording and playback does, than their ability to hear advantages with an analog LP record technology that has hundreds, if not thousands, of times the distortion of even the most basic and low-priced compact-disc playback systems.

A lingering doubt about CDs pertains to their longevity. The fact must be faced that there is no long-term research to determine what may happen to the CD signals over time, particularly under adverse conditions of storage. There is little doubt, however, that if repeated and regular playback is contemplated, the CD easily will outlast any LP or tape systems. (*See also* PRESERVATION OF SOUND

RECORDINGS;   PRESERVATION
AND RESTORATION OF HISTORI-
CAL RECORDINGS.)

The LP record has ceased being a mainstream, or even a solidly alternative playback format in the USA. Some small outfits
produce items for those who are still enam-
ored of the format, but very few record
stores sell new LP recordings at all. Many
equipment catalogs do not offer LP turntables, either, and even some hi-fi shops no
longer offer them. CD players are practically standard equipment in many automobiles (*See also* AUTOMOBILE SOUND
SYSTEMS) and there are portable models
for joggers that sell for under $100. Chang-
ers that can handle dozens of CDs are now
available to those who do not care to fool
with single-disc players, and even automobiles offer multi-disc changers as options.

Interactive compact discs (CD-I) were
introduced in 1987, opening yet another
technological door. CD-I is an application
of the CD-ROM format. It allows simultaneous storage of audio, video, graphics, text, and data—displayed on a screen
and played through CD audio systems.
And advance on this technology is the
DVD-ROM.

In terms of state-of-the-art audio performance, the CD itself is now about to be
superseded by the DVD-A or SACD formats, and even Dolby Digital and DTS audio
releases are appearing that surpass the sound
quality of the CD, if only because they offer
more channels. Given the low price and convenience of the CD, however, it is likely that
it will remain the mainstream consumer's
playback format of choice for some time to
come. *See also* MINIDISC (MD).—Rev. by
Howard Ferstler

Companding · A term derived from the
phrase "compressing and expanding,"
indicating an action upon the signal in a
sound system that alternately reduces and
increases its amplitude.

Compatible (I) · In relation to sound
recordings, a term that refers to the stereophonic discs or cassettes that can be played
without damage on monophonic playback
equipment, or to quadraphonic discs playable on stereo equipment.

Compatible (II) · A term applied to elements of a sound system that can be used
efficiently together. For practical purposes,
all parts of a modern analog sound system, regardless of manufacturer, will have
enough compatibility (e.g., in voltage levels
and impedance) to avoid distortion. Problems of non-compatibility may arise in
digital systems, if an element departs from
the original Sony/Philips digital-interface
standard.

Compensation   ·   An adjustment of
responses in a sound system to rectify deficiencies in balance of frequencies. *See also*
EQUALIZATION (EQ); AMPLITUDE.

Compensator · An electronic circuit in a
sound system that modifies the frequency
response in a predetermined manner.

Compliance (I) · The capability of a loudspeaker diaphragm to yield or flex in accord
with the power of the incoming signal.

Compliance (II) · In a cartridge, the capability to respond freely to the groove undulations. High compliance, combined with
low tip mass in the stylus, is the preferred
condition for reducing groove wear; however, excessive compliance can introduce
distortion. The electrical property that
corresponds to compliance is capacitance.
See   also   MECHANICAL-ELECTRI-
CAL ANALOGIES.

Compressed Audio Files · Sound files that
have been reduced in size using any one of a
variety of available digital codec (compres-
sion/decompression algorithm) schemes.
Compression of audio files is widely used
to reduce the time and bandwidth required

to download or play sound files over the Internet. To compress files, a codec converts certain parts of the original audio signal, such as silence, into more compact code. The file is then decompressed upon playback to restore the original signal elements.

The MPEG Layer 3 codec, introduced in 1997 and now known as MP3, reduces an audio signal by as much as 90 percent. This allows the digital storage of hi-fi-quality sound files in one-tenth of the space required by uncompressed audio files. MP3 is currently one of the most widely used audio compression schemes.

The growth of the Internet has led to the widespread development of competing audio compression schemes. In addition to MP3, the most prevalent are RealAudio, QuickTime, and Advanced Audio Coding (AAC) and Windows Media Audio. Unlike MP3, some of these other schemes can also compress video signals. AAC rose to prominence in 2001 as one of the most widely used compression schemes when Apple Computer adopted a secure version of it as the file format for its popular iTunes Music Store and iPod portable music player.

Audio compression and decompression can result in the loss of fidelity of the original signal. Currently, no industry standards govern the quality of compressed audio signals. Results can vary from codec to codec for different kinds of audio content, such as classical music, spoken word, rock music, folk music, and combinations of spoken word and music. *See also* ADVANCED AUDIO CODING; DIGITAL RIGHTS MANAGEMENT (DRM); MP3; WINDOWS MEDIA AUDIO (WMA).—Thom Holmes

Compression · In radio transmissions, the process of making the louder passages a bit quieter and the quiet passages possibly a bit louder, to reduce background noise and make the signals more audible, particularly when listened to in moving automobiles. In analog tape recording, compression is used to mask background noise during the recording process. During playback, the signals would be given expansion back to live-music dynamic range, without the background noise being brought back to previous levels. *See also* DOLBY SURROUND SOUND; DBX CORPORATION; DATA COMPRESSION.—Howard Ferstler

Compression Molding · The process of forming a disc by compressing a quantity of suitable plastic in a cavity. *See also* DISC.

Concentric Groove · The closed circular groove on a disc that follows the lead-out groove; it is also called the finishing groove.

Concert · A term applied to wide (five-inch) diameter cylinders produced by various manufacturers beginning in late 1898, and to the machines used to play them. *See also* CYLINDER.

Condensite · A plastic coating material for discs, developed by Jonas Aylsworth and his associates in the Edison Laboratories around 1910. It was a thermosetting pheno resin, virtually the same as Bakelite, which was being developed by Leo Baekeland at the General Bakelite Co. These inventions marked the beginnings of the modern plastics industry.

Cone · *See* LOUDSPEAKER.

Constant Amplitude · In disc recording, a characteristic of the stylus swing. No change occurs in the amplitude of the swing regardless of frequency changes, and groove displacement is proportional to signal amplitude.

Constant Angular Velocity Discs (CAV) · Audio or video discs that rotate at the same speed throughout their playing time. The most notable version still in use is the 33 1/3-LP recording. Some laservideo discs were also CAV items.—Howard Ferstler

Constant Linear Velocity Discs (CLV) · Audio or video discs that rotate at varying speeds, depending on the location of the tracking mechanism. By controlling speed smoothly in this manner, the linear speed read by the tracking mechanism remains the same, whether the disc is being tracked on its outer or inner circumference. The two most notable examples are the compact disc and the DVD.—Howard Ferstler

Contour Pulse · In magnetic recording, a secondary pulse that occurs when a recorded tape passes over a gap in the read head. This gap results from edges in the core material.

Control Amplifier · *See* PREAMPLIFIER.

Control Unit · The part of an amplifier that contains the controls; it is usually combined with a preamplifier.

Controls · In home audio-playback systems, these devices allow the user to modify or direct the signal. Early sound players were without genuine controls at all. To have a loud or quiet performance with a turn-of-the-century disc, it was necessary to use a pickup stylus designed for one result or the other. Later the problem of volume was approached through size of speaker horn or by opening doors or louvers that affected the output of enclosed horns. The first volume controls appear to have been the so-called tone controls of the 1916 Pathéphone, or the Sonora "tone modifier."

The need for measurement of and control over playing speed of disc recordings was recognized early because there was wide variation in recording speeds and consequently in the pitch of the signal in playback. In 1907, the Phonographic Music Company made available a speed meter for disc-type machines, and phonographs with levers to adjust turntable speed were common into the 1940s. Although there had been an attempt by the U.S. sound industry to stabilize recording speed with the advent of electrical recording, 78s were in fact produced by major recording labels at speeds between 75 rpm and 80 rpm until the end of the 78 era. With the rise of LP and 45-rpm recordings after 1949, most disc players had a control that would allow the turntable rotate at either of those speeds, as well as at 78 rpm. Intermediate speeds were no longer under control, however, until the hi-fi period brought refined concern for pitch and variable speed turntables.

In the late 1950s, with the number of hi-fi enthusiasm growing, an upscale sound system could have any number of controls. Those might include an input-source selector, an output switch (to direct the signal to the tape recorder, or to auxiliary speakers), equalization switches (for the recording curves of various tape and analog-disc formats), treble and rumble filters, an A/B switch, treble and bass controls, a gain compensator, and of course a volume control. Tape recorders and tuners attached to the system would have additional controls of their own. On systems of modest cost, often the only controls were for volume and "tone" knobs, which supplied bass or treble emphasis.

Controls on modern receivers and control amplifiers go well beyond what was available in the old days. For one thing, multi-channel recordings have expanded the playback options immensely. A typical mid-level receiver, in addition to the usual volume, input-selector, tape-monitor, radio tuner, and speaker-output controls, will have controls to adjust the various channel levels and even the degree of ambiance generated by the various surround outputs. More upscale receivers and stand-alone A/V processors might also have controls to carefully fine tune assorted ambiance modes, compensate for the differing distances to each of the speakers, select different crossover points for the subwoofer hookup, and choose the kind of digital decoding desired. Modern digital disc players and recorders will have additional controls of their own, and TV monitors interfaced with those systems will have additional controls, still. *See also* EQUALIZATION (EQ); TONE CONTROL.—Rev. by Howard Ferstler

Cook, Emory, 1915–2002 · Cook was well known for his independent research into improving the phonographic high fidelity medium. In the 1940s, he was a proponent of commercializing the hill-and-dale method of stereo single-groove recording, and to that end, his Cook Labs organization released several early stereo disks before the massive introduction of the monaural compatible, 45/45 system eventually used by all the major labels. Columbia Records pioneered the move toward the development and introduction of stereo "mono compatible" disks in 1958, with everyone else in the industry joining in. This put an end to Cook's hill-and-dale effort.

Mostly overlooked were Cook's refinements of the LP record itself, including the use of thick, virgin-vinyl, low-noise disks, special low-distortion cutting amplifiers, specially designed temperature controlled cutting heads, half-speed mastering, and other innovations, some of which would later become industry standard. From 1952 to 1966, Cook recorded, manufactured, and distributed some of the highest quality audio recordings in the world. Consequently, he paved the way for esoteric labels that came later, such as Mobile Fidelity Sound Labs (half-speed re-mastering), Sheffield (direct-to-disk), Telarc (first digital masters, using the Soundstream system), and others. Awarded an Audio Engineering Society Silver Medal in 1985,

Cook donated all his disks to the Smithsonian in 1990, after he retired.—Howard Ferstler

Cooke, Raymond Edgar, February 14, 1925–March 19, 1995 · Born in Yorkshire, during World War II, Cooke served as a radio operator on a British carrier, and after the war, he obtained a B.S. in electrical engineering from the University of London. After a briefly held job at Philips, he then went to work at the British Broadcasting Corporation's Engineering Designs Department. In 1956, he joined Warfedale Wireless Works, where, among other things, he worked with Gilbert Briggs on a series of books on loudspeaker design, and assisted Briggs with a series of live-versus-recorded concerts at Royal Festival Hall in London. Cooke also joined the Audio Engineering Society in 1956, served for some years on the AES British Section Committee, and was president of the AES Europe Region in 1984. In 1961, he founded KEF Electronics, a highly regarded loudspeaker company that was noted for employing unconventional materials and innovative designs, as well as one of the best engineering staffs in the loudspeaker business. In 1979, Queen Elizabeth II made Cooke an Officer of the Most Excellent Order of the British Empire. In 1980, he won the AES Bronze Medal, and in 1993, he won the Society's Silver Medal.—Howard Ferstler

Cooper, Duane H., 1923–April 4, 1995 · Born in Gibson City, Illinois, during the war Cooper served with the U.S. Army in Italy as a radar specialist, and later on earned both B.S. and Ph.D. degrees, with honors in physics, from the California Institute of Technology. In 1954, he joined the faculty at the University of Illinois, as a professor and research associate, working on statistical detection theory and noise analysis, and also contributed to developments in computer-based instruction.

In the early 1960s, he became interested in problems in audio engineering, and eventually published extensively in that field. He investigated the intricate geometry of the phonograph stylus in relation to the LP record disc surface, and developed a unified treatment of phonograph-stylus tracking and tracing distortion, by utilizing a skew transformation. This resulted in the establishment of the stylus tracking angle that became the industry standard. In 1971, he built the first prototype of an echo-free acoustic delay device, later manufactured as the Cooper Time Cube, which was widely used in recording studios before affordable digital versions appeared. In the later 1960s and early 1970s, he contributed to the theory of surround-sound stereo, inventing the first working version of the surround-sound system that led to Ambisonic surround. Dr. Cooper held over 40 patents, and was a consultant to numerous organizations, including Consumer's Union, Shure Brothers, and Magnavox. He was a Fellow of the Institute of Electrical and Electronics Engineers and the Acoustical Society of America, and was president of the Audio Engineering Society from 1975 to 76. He had become a Fellow of the Society in 1966, won the Emile Berliner Award (now known as the Silver Medal), in 1968, and won the Society's Gold Medal in 1982.—Howard Ferstler

Copy Master (I) · An identical copy of a master tape.

Copy Master (II) · A metal negative disc produced from the positive, for use as a replacement master.

Copycode · A system developed by CBS in 1987 to filter out a narrow band ("notch") of musical frequencies in a master recording. The purpose was to give a cue to a decoder device installed by manufacturers of DAT recorders; the decoder's response to the notch was to shut down the recorder.

Thus, unauthorized copying of a CD onto a DAT blank tape would be prevented. The notch itself was taken from the upper-middle range at 3.838 kHz; it was 112 Hz wide at the 3-dB point and 90-dB deep. Removing this tiny slice of the frequency band did not, according to CBS, affect the quality of the music, but certain specialists claimed to notice differences when the notch was activated. Controversy over the use of Copycode was crystallized in a London conference of the International Federation of Producers of Phonograms and Videograms (IFPI) in May 1987. The producers supported legislation by the European Economic Community and the U.S. Congress to require the Copycode device on all machines imported from Japan; but the Electronic Industry Association of Japan, representing the principal DAT manufacturers, opposed such regulation. Congress asked for an assessment from the National Bureau of Standards (NBS), which reported that "there are some selections for which the subjects detected differences between notched and unnotched material." The NBS conclusion was that the Copycode system "audibly degrades music, and can easily be bypassed." No action was taken by Congress to prohibit import of DAT, or to require Copycode protection.

A pair of anti-copying devices has since been developed by Philips to prevent making more than one DAT copy of a CD; but these pose problems. One system, Solo, has met with disfavor by the record companies because it permits multiple copying of analog material. The other, Solo Plus, is unacceptable to audio users because it permits no copying of analog material at all. Finally, a system was created that appeared to find favor among all parties concerned: Serial Copy Management System (SCMS). The acquisition of Columbia Records by Sony also tended to mute the controversy.

Copyright · Intellectual and creative productions are given legal protection in most countries; this protection insuring that the exclusive rights to distribution, reproduction, display, performance, or any commercial use of a work rests with its author, composer, or artist. Copyright is the equivalent, for intangible property, of the patent.

Problems in the interpretation of copyright issues, particularly when more than one nation is involved, are substantial. The Bern Convention of 1886 has formed a basis for international cooperation; the effectiveness of that agreement was enhanced in 1988 when the United States finally signed into it. The most recent international effort to deal with these matters resulted in the Universal Copyright Convention (UCC) of 1955, signed by all major countries except the Peoples Republic of China. UCC has for a basic principle the acceptance of each country's copyright legalities by all other countries. In most countries, this protection extends 50 years after the death of the author. Types of works protected include literary and musical compositions, all forms of graphic art, motion pictures, sound recordings, and other kinds of audiovisual production.

In the United Kingdom, a record company retains copyright for 50 years; legislation passed in 1925 protects artists against unauthorized reproduction of their performances.

In the United States, the Copyright Act of 1976 (superseding one dating from 1909) became effective January 1, 1976. In 1988, Congress passed the Bern Convention Implementation Act, as an amendment of the 1976 legislation, to account for principles in the Bern agreement. The life-plus-50 years term of protection applies to works created after 1977, but for earlier works, there is a complex system of terms and renewals. Indeed, there are numerous complexities (e.g., in the area of transfers and licenses), which are not appropriate for discussion here. In 1998, the Congress based the Sonny Bono Copyright Act, which extended ownership of copyright material for another 20 years, as big conglomerates like the Disney Company worried that such icons as Mickey Mouse were about to fall out of copyright protection.

One aspect of U.S. law is of special interest to those who are involved with recorded sound: the "fair use" principle. Essentially, fair use means that all or part of a copyrighted work may be copied legally without permission of the copyright holder if the use to be made of the copy is non-commercial and does not interfere with the author's own profits or exploitation of the work. Thus, a teacher may photocopy a periodical article or section of a book for class distribution (not for sale), and anyone may copy a broadcast program for personal use. Libraries have certain privileges in the making of archival copies.

It is also permitted, under the 1976 Act, to copy commercial discs, audiotapes, and videotapes—always for private non-commercial purposes only—and this element of the law has caused great concern among producers of those media. Although one may question the magnitude of financial loss to a record company when someone makes a cassette tape copy of a disc borrowed from the public library—the copy, as often as not, standing in place of non-ownership instead of in place of a personally purchased record—there appears little basis for disputing the claim of great losses to record companies that result from making copies for sale. The making of counterfeit records and tapes, an act usually called "pirating" or "boot-legging," is illegal when the copies are sold, but the practice has been carried on in a brazen manner. Some bootleg records have appeared with distinctive labels, such as Rubber Dubber, and gained legitimacy by being listed among authorized labels in discographies and lists of new releases.

A special problem exists in the case of so-called parallel imports, imported versions of works copyrighted by U.S. firms. When the American firm holding the copyright does not actually release the material on record, or does release it but allows the record to go out of print, imports of the material are still prohibited under section 602(a) of the 1976 Copyright Act. Record dealers, supported by buyer groups, have held that what is not available in the United States should be exempt from import restrictions.

With the advent of digital recording, it became possible for manufacturers to prevent or limit copying by means of protective codes imbedded in the disc or tape. On the other hand, widespread public use of the Internet beginning in the 1990s spurred the rise of music file sharing—both real audio and compressed data formats (e.g., MP3)—via the websites of individual collectors as well as exchange services such as Napster. The universal availability of CD burners has further threatened the economic viability of the record industry, which has responded by pressuring federal legislators to enact stricter protective measures in addition to experimenting with lower pricing policies. *See also* COPYCODE; RECORDING INDUSTRY ASSOCIATION OF AMERICA; SERIAL COPY MANAGEMENT SYSTEM (SCMS).

Corner Horn · A loudspeaker enclosure that utilizes a corner of the room as part of the horn.

Couzens, Ralph, February 9, 1957– · Currently operations director and chief engineer and producer for Chandos Records, Couzens was born in Rochford, Essex, in England. He studied piano and clarinet as a youth, attended Saturday music school, and played in local amateur orchestras and wind bands. He went on to study electronics for 5 years at Colchester Technical College, and attended recording sessions while still in school, in 1972. In 1974, Couzens joined Chandos as an apprentice sound engineer, working mainly as a tape operator on sessions until 1978. He engineered and balanced his first recording for Chandos in 1978, and after that time he engineered numerous high-quality transcriptions, becoming one of the company's in-house producers in 1987. Between 1978 and 1998, he also designed and built various mixing consoles for the company, and currently is involved with the engineering and production of numerous Chandos releases, including those being transcribed for surround-sound release. Over the years, Couzens has won four *Gramophone Magazine* awards for engineering and production, and has been nominated twice for Grammy awards for engineering.—Howard Ferstler

Covering · A term in the popular record industry for the practice of having one performer record another performer's hit material. It was straightforward in the 1940s; for example, Frank Sinatra did a Columbia issue of "Sunday, Monday, or Always"—a Bing Crosby movie hit, originally on Decca—and record buyers had a choice of renditions. There were more than 400 versions of "White Christmas," following Bing Crosby's. Then, in the 1950s—with rhythm and blues and country recordings denied access to mainstream pop radio—A&R staff at the major labels began recruiting middle-of-the-road performers to cover songs from other genres; for example, Tony Bennett offered "Cold, Cold Heart" in a bland style quite removed from the Hank Williams country original. Pat Boone and, to a lesser extent, Elvis Presley, jump-started their careers via this practice. Some rock numbers with racy lyrics were covered in a middle-of-the-road idiom with modified texts. African American doo-wop artists, in particular, and their songs—for example, the Chords' "Sh-Boom" (covered by the Crewcuts), the Jewels' "Hearts Of Stone" (Fontaine Sisters), the Gladiolas' "Little Darlin'" (the Diamonds)—were regularly singled out for covering. Aside from the obvious loss of revenue (even in cases where the original performers were also the composers, songwriting revenues often ended up in the pockets of talent managers and record label executives), helped speed up the synthesis R&B, country, and pop that resulted in the emergence of rockabilly and classic rock and roll. *See also* CROSSOVER.—Rev. by Frank Hoffmann.

Critical Distance · The point at a given distance from a loudspeaker system playing in an enclosed space where the direct signals coming from the system and the boundary-reflected reverberation generated by that same system are perceived at equal levels. The critical distance will be controlled by both the directivity of the speaker and the reflectivity of the room. Because speaker systems usually have multiple drivers of different sizes, it can vary considerably over the operating range of the system. *See also* DIRECT FIELD; REVERBERANT FIELD.—Howard Ferstler

Cros, Charles, 1842–1888 · French poet (his poem "L'archet" was set to music by Claude Debussy in 1883) and amateur scientist. He experimented with sound recording and produced a seminal paper on April 18, 1877, that described a disc machine; sound waves were to be traced on lampblacked glass, then photoengraved into reliefs. Lacking the means to make a model, he did not immediately seek a patent, but merely deposited his paper with the Académie des Sciences. (He did obtain a French patent in May 1878.) A popularizer of science, Abbé Lenoir, described the Cros machine—naming it "phonograph"—in an article of his own, published October 10, 1877. Although the Cros concept was

similar to that of Thomas Edison (and even more similar to that of Emile Berliner), and Edison's working model was not completed before December 6, 1877 (the first sketch dates from November 29, 1877), it is clear that the American knew nothing of Cros. Edison's claim to the invention is firmly based on two points: He was first to demonstrate his idea with a working model and first to patent it.

Crossfade · In the music-broadcasting business, a term most often associated with mixers used by disc jockeys. Devices of that kind usually feature a slide-type potentiometer control that allows the operator create a smooth transition or fade from one program source to another program source.—Howard Ferstler

Crossover · In recording characteristics, the crossover point is that where amplitude adjustment by frequency ceases. It is also known as the crossover frequency, or the turnover. For example, in electrical recording up to about 1935 frequencies above 250 Hz had a pure constant velocity characteristic, with amplitude frequency equaling constant; below 250 Hz—the crossover point—the cut was constant amplitude, with all frequencies being limited to the same amplitude, instead of the amplitude increasing with a decrease in frequency. The rationale for this adjustment was that it allowed a higher recording level at higher frequencies and produced advantageous signal-to-noise ratios. Around 1935, the crossover point was moved up to 500 Hz or 600 Hz in the United States and United Kingdom, to extend the dynamic range. Neither cylinders nor acoustic recordings had this characteristic.

Crossover Network · Also known as a dividing network. In a sound-reproducing system, the circuitry that divides amplifier output into two or more frequency ranges, most commonly the bass, midrange, and treble, and feeds them to separate loudspeaker drivers within a speaker system. The most common crossovers are "passive," and are directly fed with the output of an amplifier. That design will normally be installed within the speaker enclosure itself, with the outputs being directly fed to the drivers. A crossover may also be active, and work with the line-level outputs of a preamplifier, with the outputs then being fed to multiple amplifiers that power the speaker drivers directly. Active crossovers are also commonly used to feed extremely low frequencies to powered, outboard subwoofer systems.

The advantages to using any kind of crossover are a smoother and wider frequency response, less distortion, and higher maximum output levels from the speaker systems. Typical woofer-to-midrange crossover points will be anywhere from 150 to 400 Hz, or sometimes higher. Typical midrange-to-tweeter crossover points will be anywhere from 3 kHz to 5 kHz. In two-way systems, the woofer-to-tweeter transition may take place anywhere from 2 kHz to 4 kHz. Subwoofer crossovers usually work at frequencies between 60 Hz and 100 Hz. *See also* LOUDSPEAKER.—Howard Ferstler

Crosstalk · In both recording and playback, it involves the unwanted propagation of signals from one audio channel to another audio channel. Some recording and playback systems employ crosstalk cancellation between speaker systems to enhance the sound of recordings. *See also* HEAD-RELATED TRANSFER FUNCTION (HRTF); INTERAURAL CROSSTALK.—Howard Ferstler

Cut · Either a band or a groove on a disc. By extension, the song or selection that occupies a band. "To cut" means to record. *See also* LATERAL RECORDING; VERTICAL CUT.

Cutout · A record withdrawn from normal distribution by the manufacturer and removed from the company's catalog. In publishing terms, a cutout is "out-of-print." The number of cutouts in the pop/rock field may be as much as 85 percent of a company's issues. Records that fail to break even, so-called stiffs, are quickly withdrawn and usually sent to a rack jobber for disposal. Like remaindered books, those stiff records are found in bargain sections of the shops, often selling at greatly reduced prices. Retailers have generally denounced this practice as one that undermines their sales of standard material, and requires excessive paperwork. Objections come also from the artists represented on cutout discs, whose royalties are reduced and whose reputations are thought to be injured. Record companies, on the other hand, justify cutouts because they claim that royalty fees are so inflated that only major hit records are profitable.

Cutting Head · Also known as a cutterhead. An electromagnetic device used in disc recording. It includes a moving coil and a cutting stylus; the latter is activated by amplifier signals and transcribes them into the record groove. The "feedback cutting head" was developed at Bell Telephone Laboratories in 1924: It canceled resonances in the cutting head by feeding back a signal from it to the recording amplifier.

Cycle · In a periodic vibration pattern, a cycle is one complete excursion from a given point through two extremes and back to the given point. The unit of frequency is cycles per second (c/s), now generally superseded by Hertz (Hz). The number of Hz in a sound wave determines its pitch.

Cylinder · The earliest practical thinking about the possibility of recording sound was centered on a flat medium as carrier of the signal: the phonautograph invented in 1857 by Léon Scott de Martinville. In 1859, he made a second model, utilizing a cylinder medium. Scott's instrument, which looked quite a bit like Edison's phonograph of two decades later, was designed to trace the fluctuation of sound waves on a sheet of lampblacked paper wrapped around a cylinder on a threaded shaft. Apparently, its inventor failed to consider that his machine, with some elaborations, could have been used for playing back the signal as well as storing it.

There is no evidence that Edison knew of Scott's work as he was developing the first model of the cylinder phonograph in November 1877, but Emile Berliner had seen the phonautograph at the Smithsonian Institution while he was living in Washington, D.C., and devising his approach to sound recording. Berliner took the step that Scott had missed, and made a version of the phonautograph in 1887 that could reproduce the signal. Nevertheless, he soon gave up on the cylinder and developed the disc gramophone, just as Edison had decided to use the cylinder instead of the flat medium that he had also described in his first patent. Through the subsequent competition between cylinder and disc, Edison championed the former while Berliner and his successors held to the latter.

If a definite date is to be ascribed to the birth of the sound recording industry, it should be April 24, 1878, when the Edison Speaking Phonograph Co. was established in New York. In the same year, the London Stereoscope Co., sole British licensee of the phonograph, began to sell—as Edison was doing—machines to record and playback tinfoil records. Sales were good, for the novelty of hearing a voice emerge from a machine had wide appeal. Edison's principal early rivals were Bell and Tainter, who set up the Volta Graphophone Co. in Alexandria, Virginia, in 1886 to sell their variety of cylinder and player; the name of that firm was changed to American Graphophone Co. in 1887. Through the

financial support of Jesse H. Lippincott, the Edison and Volta interests (i.e., the phonograph and the graphophone) were successfully brought together to share a single sales agency under Lippincott's direction: the North American Phonograph Co. (NAPC).

Following the organizational structure of the American Bell Telephone Co., Lippincott leased sales rights for the phonograph to regional and local companies around the United States The individual firms then leased the instruments to customers, and sold them cylinders. Soon there were 33 separate companies in the NAPC. They held a national conference in 1890, dealing with topics like uniform pricing and standardization of equipment. Edison began to supply musical cylinders to NAPC firms in 1891, to be sold at retail. He also offered to make copies of records in high demand. Nevertheless, local companies, and even customers, found they could make their own copies by re-recording, or by pantographic methods, albeit with loss of quality. NAPC member companies began to drop out; in 1894, the organization was liquidated. Meanwhile, American Graphophone was in such poor condition that Columbia, the most successful firm in the industry, was able to absorb it in 1894.

The growth of coin-op markets, improvements in the machines, and some progress in standardization (Columbia cylinders were made to be compatible with Edison phonographs) helped to bring about a national rise in business. In 1896, there were additional firms to compete with Columbia and Edison (who established in that year his National Phonograph Co.). Columbia led the field, however, claiming to sell more records than all other companies combined; its prices were .50¢ per cylinder, or $5 a dozen. The industry's first boom year was 1897, with a half million records produced (including discs). By

1899, sales had reached 2.8 million cylinders and discs per year.

The wax-based cylinders offered poor sound quality and were subject to failure due to heat and other environmental conditions. To meet the need for a more durable cylinder, inventor Thomas Lambert developed a system of making cylinders out of plastic celluloid. Lambert employee William Messer also developed a means of mass reproducing cylinders using a steam press, which enabled them to cheaply and quickly produce large quantities of records. Edison naturally objected, and sued the Lambert Co. over patent infringement based on elements of the cylinder design. Lambert issued about 1200 records through its existence, mostly of popular vocal and band music, although also Yiddish language titles and language instruction and fitness training records for sale by other firms.

After Lambert folded, Messer was associated with the Albany-based Indestructible Phonographic Record Co. The first Indestructible cylinders were advertised in mid-1907, and released that fall. Edison quickly objected to this move, discouraging major dealers from handling a competing cylinder product. At about the same time, Edison competitor Columbia was phasing out its cylinder production, and looking for a source for this material. The two firms got together, and from 1908 to mid-1912, Columbia was exclusive distributor for Indestructible's output, with a joint label (Columbia Indestructible Record) appearing on the product. After the arrangement with Columbia ended, Indestructible cylinders were sold directly by the firm and under a variety of labels through mail order giants Sears, Roebuck (under the "Oxford" name) and Montgomery Ward ("Lakeside"). A factory fire in autumn 1922 ended cylinder production, and the firm formally shut down three years later.

A second process for making "indestructible" celluloid cylinders was developed by Vernon Harris, who licensed his patent to the U-S Phonograph Co. Its cylinders were labeled as the "U-S Everlasting Record," and about 1,100 total titles were issued between mid-1910 and autumn 1913. They were recorded in New York City, with a heavier emphasis on classical music and opera—and larger performing groups—than was featured on its competitors' releases. Like other cylinder makers, the firm was embroiled in lawsuits brought against it by Edison for patent infringement. Although unsuccessful in proving its case, Edison kept U-S tied up in courts—and awash in legal fees—for several years. This undoubtedly contributed to the eventual closing of the firm in 1914.

Columbia continued to make cylinders and discs until 1909. It distributed Indestructibles until 1912, when it abandoned the cylinder field to Edison. The high quality of the Blue Amberol cylinder, introduced in 1912, and the fact that Edison had nurtured a loyal multitude of customers—mainly in rural areas—who kept Edison in business. He had produced more than 10,000 different cylinders by 1912. His price for two-minute standard records was .35¢; for the four-minute Amberols it was .50¢. Grand Opera records sold for .75¢ to $2. Edison phonographs with sapphire reproducers were marketed at all prices from $15 to $200. The fine Amberola phonograph was continually improved from its introduction in 1912 through the late 1920s.

Cylindrography · The study of cylinder records; an equivalent term to discography. It was coined by George Blacker. Apparently, the first serious research in the field was conducted by Duane Deakins, who published an extensive list of early cylinders from 1956 to 1961. In Britain, H. H. Annand was at work at the same time, listing "indestructibles." Sydney H. Carter compiled Edison cylinder lists, as well as lists of Clarion, Ebonoid, and Sterling. Victor Girard and Harold M. Barnes published their important catalog of cylinders, by artist, in London, in 1964. Much of the British research was superseded by the definitive work of Koenigsberg on Edison cylinders. Ron Dethlefson listed the Blue Amberols from 1980 to 1981. Further research by the persons named previously, and by later scholars, has appeared primarily in the collectors' journals, such as *Antique Phonograph Monthly*.

D

D/A · *See* DIGITAL RECORDING

Damping · The action of dissipating part of the oscillating energy in a sound system, usually by the use of non-resonant material. Tone arm or stylus resonance is often intentionally damped to prevent frequency distortion. Unwanted cone movement in a loudspeaker may be damped.

Damping Factor (DF) · In loudspeakers, it is the ratio of the loudspeaker's impedance to the total impedance of the amplifier driving it. Consequently, it is a measure of a power amplifier's ability to control the back-end motion of the loudspeaker cone as the amplifier's output signal varies. Most amplifiers have more than enough damping control, and the impact of damping control has traditionally been overrated.—Howard Ferstler

D'appolito, Joseph, April 13, 1936– · An internationally recognized authority on loudspeaker system design and testing, Dr. D'Appolito earned a B.E.E. degree in 1958 (Rensselaer Polytechnic Institute), S.M.E.E. and E.E. degrees in 1964 (Massachusetts Institute of Technology), and a Ph.D. in electrical engineering in 1969 (University of Massachusetts). He worked in the defense industry for a number of years, but left that field in 1995, and now runs his own consulting firm, Audio and Acoustics, Ltd. He has designed over 60 loudspeaker systems for both private and commercial clients, including the ARIA 5 Point Source for Focal, France that was selected loudspeaker of the year for 1991 by *Hi-Fi Video Magazine* (Paris). One of his more well-known achievements was the MTM (mid/tweeter/mid) vertical loudspeaker geometry, commonly known as the "D'Appolito Configuration." Renowned for its ability to better control vertical system radiation, this driver arrangement has been copied widely by numerous manufacturers throughout the world, and many THX-certified speakers make use of the concept. He is a Contributing Editor to *Speaker Builder Magazine* and has published over 60 articles in both professional and popular hobby journals. His book, *Testing Loudspeakers*, has been published by Audio Amateur Press.—Howard Ferstler

Darrell, Robert Donaldson, December 13, 1903–May 1, 1988 · Editor and discographer, born in Newton, Massachusetts. He attended Harvard College and the New England Conservatory. Darrell edited the *Phonographic Monthly Review* from 1930, and was contributing editor of *High Fidelity* from 1956 to 1984. He wrote the seminal *Gramophone Shop Encyclopedia* in 1936. Darrell was one of the first American critics to focus on recordings, primarily of classical music. He also reviewed discs for *Saturday Review, High Fidelity* (1954–1987), and *Opus*. Darrell died in Kingston, New York.

DAT (Digital Audio Tape) · The first consumer-oriented and pro/semi-pro digital tape recording format to appear in the United States. Actually, it had been around for some time, at least in Japan and Europe, but suffered a delayed introduction in America, because the recording industry was philosophically opposed to consumer-oriented digital recorders from the beginning. They had (and still have) the not altogether unjustified fear that "perfect" recorders of any kind would allow individuals, particularly tape pirates, to expertly steal material. Doing this would deny performers (and of course agents and record producers) their income. The Philips-designed SCMS (Serial Copy Management System) diminished those fears and DAT was released for sale. SCMS allows a user to copy a recording once, but the copy itself cannot be recopied.

DAT has traditionally appealed mainly to professionals and well-heeled, "advanced" amateurs who do live recording. It should also be noted that prerecorded tapes for this format are no longer available, because there was never enough recorders sold to justify tooling up to make them. The limited number of titles that appeared initially were more expensive and less convenient to use than the subjectively equal CD.

Those wanting to go first class, however, particularly if they intend to do live recording in two-channel form, cannot do better than DAT. It takes a back seat to no other type of recording device, unless more than two tracks are needed. It has to be admitted, however, that most people who do recording at the amateur level and want the advantages of digital sound, as well as durability, convenience, and ease of use, would do better to utilize the MiniDisc or the recordable CD.

The measured performance of DAT can exceed that of the CD because a 48-kHz sampling frequency (sampling rate) is available (the CD operates at 44.1 kHz and a DAT deck can use this also, as well as 32 kHz for programs with limited bandwidth needs) giving it the kind of effectiveness

that performance-oriented enthusiasts demand. A DAT tape can hold 1,300 megabytes of information and data is retrieved at a drum-scan speed of 10 feet per second, compared with the 3.9 to 4.9 feet-per-second linear speed of the compact disc. However, Nagra's portable digital recorder—the Nagra V, introduced in February 2002—has been touted as the successor to DAT and various analog tape formats for professional audio personnel.—Howard Ferstler

Data Compression · In digital-audio systems, it can be any of several algorithms designed to reduce the bandwidth requirements for accurate digital audio storage and transmission. The audible consequences of data compression will vary, depending on the degree of compression and the quality of the algorithm used, and the best systems will be subjectively transparent. *See also* COMPRESSED AUDIO FILES; DTS; DOLBY DIGITAL; DATA REDUCTION; COMPRESSION.—Howard Ferstler

Data Reduction · Sometimes called lossy compression. In digital-audio systems, it is designed to reduce the bandwidth requirements for accurate digital audio storage and transmission even further than data compression. Data reduction makes use of psychoacoustic masking to insure that sounds that are eliminated from the mix would not be ordinarily heard. *See also* DTS; DOLBY DIGITAL.—Howard Ferstler

Davis, Arthur C., March 11, 1908–November 7, 1970 · Born in Salt Lake City, Davis spent most of his life in California. In 1938, he founded the Cinema-Engineering company, and after selling it to Aero-Vox sometime later, he went to work for Altec Lansing, heading up their audio-control department. He designed numerous products for the industry, including equalizers, filter sets, loudspeaker systems, audio-console electronics, attenuators, gain sets, and the first mechanical film loudspeaker system. Davis was a member of the Audio Engineering Society, and was named a Fellow in 1955 and won the Society's Potts award in 1962. He was also a fellow of the Society of Motion Picture and Television Engineers, being named a Fellow of that organization in 1967.—Howard Ferstler

Davis, Mark, December 20, 1946– · A noted audio designer and researcher, Davis was responsible for the early dbx Soundfield speaker systems (a groundbreaking design that showed the real-world importance of time-intensity tradeoffs with speaker performance), the MTS audio system for analog stereo TV sound transmission, and most notably the early theater version of the AC-3 coding technology employed with the Dolby Digital audio system that has become the de facto standard for motion-picture sound and surround-sound in home theater. He was part of the team that refined AC-3 for home theater and musical use. Davis has a 1980 Ph.D. from MIT, and has published a number of technical papers on system design.—Howard Ferstler

dB · *See* DECIBEL (dB).

dbx Corporation · Primarily known for a recording noise-reduction system developed in the early 1970s by David E. Blackmer and colleagues, and using more aggressive circuitry than the early Dolby A and B systems. The dbx technology (the company always printed its name in lower-case letters) achieved as much as a 30-dB reduction in tape hiss by means of a wide-range 2:1:2 compressor-expander voltage-controlled amplifier, with pre-emphasis/de-emphasis and true RMS-level detection. In two implementations, it became popular with both pro and consumer recordists, although unlike Dolby it could not be listened to undecoded. In addition, there were potential audible artifacts on some material when record-

ings levels were set too low. At one stage, some outstanding LP recordings also were encoded with the technology, but they never caught on. Eventually, improved Dolby noise-reduction systems (Dolby C and S), not to mention digital recording, put an end to its use.

In its heyday, the company was also a leader in analog signal processing; notably the compressors that make broadcast audio possible, but also in the area of consumer products. dbx was also responsible for the technology behind stereo audio for U.S. television broadcasting. The company did further revolutionary work in digital recording, loudspeaker design, and audio measurement systems. dbx pro exists today as a studio and broadcast signal-processing company, whereas a spin-off, THAT Corporation, provides high-performance audio ICs and technology licensing to the industry.—Howard Ferstler

Dead Studio · In the strict sense, a studio in which there is no reflection of sound waves and no entrance of sound from outside the room; more generally, a studio with relatively little reverberation.

Decca Record Co. · One of the major firms in the record industry of the United States, established as the American branch of Decca Record Co., Ltd. on August 4, 1934, is New York. Decca was begun as a low-priced competitor to the two dominant labels, Victor and Columbia, and was successful in driving prices of 78s down from the average of 75 cents each to the more affordable 35 cents. Decca succeeded partially because of its roster of artists, including the best-selling singer, Bing Crosby. Decca also signed country and blues artists who could be recorded and marketed inexpensively. Victor responded by launching the budget Bluebird label, and Columbia revived the Okeh label. Nonetheless, Decca became the third largest label by the late 1940s.

A major technological improvement was introduced by Decca in 1946: full frequency range recordings (ffrr). It was the outcome of research by Arthur Charles Haddy, who had worked on submarine-detection devices. Used in conjunction with the Decca Piccadilly record player, this shellac 78-rpm disc achieved a range of 50–14,000 Hz, the best in the industry. It was marketed first by American Decca, then by London. The earliest Decca LP appeared in 1949, just in time to be included with 10 other labels in the first *Long-Playing Record Catalog* issued by W. Schwann in October. The firm was among the pioneer stereo labels. An affiliation with Deutsche Grammophon Gesellschaft (DGG) was negotiated in 1956. In 1962, MCA, Inc. acquired the company, continuing the Decca label name into the 1970s. When MCA was absorbed into Universal Music Group in the late 1990s, the Decca name was revived for classical music releases; as of the early 2000s, the Decca Music Group division of Universal includes Decca, Universal, Philips Classics, and Deutsche Grammophon.

Decca Tree · First used in 1954, it is a microphone-placement technique pioneered by engineers working for Decca/London Records (the concept was actually formulated by Roy Wallace), and used to make many of their classical recordings. It involves three omnidirectional microphones set up in a T-shaped array, usually placed 10 to 12 feet above and slightly behind the conductor's podium, with the left and right capsules about 2 meters apart, and with the center unit (feeding both left and right channels equally) placed about 1.5 meters out in front of the axis between them. The microphones were angled 30 degrees downward and clustered tightly together, to exclude reflected sounds from the sides and rear. The resulting geometry, in combination with the microphones chosen (initially Neumann KM-56s, but later M-50s, as finally settled upon by recording engineer Kenneth Wilkinson), imparts a warm and spacious sound to a properly mixed recording. *See also* MICROPHONE; STEREOPHONIC RECORDING.—Howard Ferstler

Decibel (dB) · A logarithmic measure of the relative intensity of sound. It represents a ratio between two acoustical or electrical quantities. One dB expresses a ratio of approximately 1.1:1, between the first and second levels. Human hearing is logarithmic with respect to the perception of loudness: the intensity of a signal must show a certain increase before the human ear perceives change, and the change that is noted is arithmetically smaller than the actual rise in signal intensity. Signal A will be perceived as minimally louder than signal B if it is one dB higher in intensity than B, and it will seem about twice as loud as signal B if their intensities differ by three dB. Signal A will seem four times as loud if there is a six dB increase, and eight times as loud if there is a nine dB increase in the difference between A and B. Twenty dB are 100 times greater than 10 dB, instead of twice as great.

The value of a dB was chosen to match the smallest increment of loudness that the human ear can distinguish in the mid-frequency range. Human hearing has a range from zero dB, the threshold of hearing, to 120 dB, the threshold of pain. (Sustained exposure to sound levels above 120 dB is not only painful, but may lead to temporary or even permanent hearing loss. The noise at rock concerts has been measured as high as 130 dB.) In musical language, the range is from ppp to fff; that 120-dB range actually encompasses a million variations in sound intensity (10^6). A listener 20 feet from a symphony orchestra playing fff would experience about 110 dB. *See also* HEARING.

Deck · In open-reel or cassette tape recording, the name of the unit containing much of the apparatus: it may include the tape transport, amplifier, preamplifier, controls, meters, and a built-in microphone. It may or may not be a recording deck as well as a playback deck. Decks do not have loudspeakers or output amplifiers, so they need to be connected to those components to function. The tape deck is often found as an element in a high-fidelity system or rack system. Recently, many decks have been made with two tape transports, permitting the user to copy a recorded tape onto a blank.

Decoder · A device that assigns each signal in a multi-channel system to its proper channel.

De-Emphasis · A change of frequency response in a reproducing system. *See also* PRE-EMPHASIS.

De Forest, Lee, August 26, 1873–June 30, 1961 · American inventor, born in Council Bluffs, Iowa. His childhood was spent in Talladega, Alabama, where his father was president of Talladega College. As a boy, he was fascinated with machinery, and in time went on to the Sheffield Scientific School at Yale University, where he specialized in electricity and mathematical physics; he took a Ph.D. in 1899. De Forest moved to Chicago, held various jobs, and conducted his own research. His invention of the responder provided an improvement in radio reception, and led him to concentrate in the radio field. In 1907, he formed the De Forest Radio Telephone Co. The triode audion circuit he developed was patented in the United Kingdom (no. 1427; 1908), and his single stage amplifier received U.S. patent no. 841,387 in 1907. These inventions introduced the new age of electronics.

On January 2, 1910, De Forest used his equipment to broadcast from the stage of the Metropolitan Opera House, transmitting the voice of Enrico Caruso. His laboratory produced the first efficient multi-stage amplifier in 1912. He formed a new company, De Forest Radio, Telephone and Telegraph Co.

Acquiring patent rights to several inventions, including the Tellafide photoelectric cell, he was able to work successfully on soundtrack systems. On April 12, 1923, he presented the first commercial talking picture, at the Rivoli Theater in New York. By 1925, he had made a number of "phonofilms"—short subjects with synchronized sound—featuring Al Jolson and other popular performers. He set up another firm, Phonovision Co., to exploit the motion-picture area.

His firm began to have financial setbacks in the early 1920s, and reorganized in 1923. Bankruptcy came in the summer of 1926, and the company was acquired by Powel Crosley, who became president. De Forest remained with his old company as a consulting engineer. He went on to experiment for another 30 years, working in diathermy and color television. He had more than 300 patents, the last issued when he was 83 years old. His nickname, "Father of Radio," was the name he gave to his autobiography (1950).

Degauss · *See* DEMAGNETIZATION.

Delay System · A mechanism that holds back in time all or part of an audio signal passing through all or part of a sound or recording system. With musical recording techniques, the purpose might be to introduce special reverberation effects or even the impression of an increased number of performers. In live radio interviewing, delays may be used to give the controller time to remove potentially offensive material. In home-playback systems, delay circuits, in conjunction with additional channels and ambiance extraction or ambiance synthesis techniques, can often effectively simulate concert-hall, nightclub, theater, or even stadium acoustics from two-channel source material.—Rev. by Howard Ferstler

Dell, Edward T., February 12, 1923– · An important member of the audio-journalism community, Dell was born in Atlanta, Georgia. His father worked as an installer for Western Electric, and the family moved throughout the South until 1935. As a result, Dell attended 17 different public schools before graduating from Ponce de Leon High School, in Coral Gables Florida, in 1941. During World War II, he attended college by day and worked as an electrician in Bethlehem Steel's Hingham Shipyard evenings. Dell holds a B.A. in History and a Th.B. in theology from Eastern Nazarene College, Wollaston, Mass., and an M.Div. From Episcopal Theological School, Cambridge, Mass. He held three Episcopal parish appointments in Massachusetts before moving to a journalism appointment. In 1962, he became a reporter for *The Episcopalian* magazine, a national monthly of the Episcopal Church, and ended his career there as managing editor in 1974. His work involved extensive travel throughout North America, Europe, and in five Pacific Rim countries.

Having written for *Audiocraft* magazine as an avocation in the 1950s and for *Stereophile* in the 1960s, he founded *Audio Amateur*, an audio construction quarterly in 1970, moving the magazine to Peterborough, N.H., in 1975. In 1980, he founded *Speaker Builder* magazine, and then went on to found *Glass Audio* (a tube-electronics-oriented journal) in 1989. In the same year, Dell founded *Voice Coil*, a monthly newsletter. Edited by Vance Dickason, the latter magazine became a business-to-business loudspeaker industry monthly in 1993. Dell's Audio Amateur Press also published all three editions of Dickason's The *Loudspeaker Design Cookbook*, and in addition, the press has published 45 original and reprint titles, as well as software and information CD ROMs. A wholly owned subsidiary, Old Colony Sound Lab, offers a wide variety of audio-related, ancillary products for enthusiasts. In 2001, Dell merged three titles, *Audio Electronics* (formerly *Audio Amateur*), *Speaker Builder*, and *Glass Audio* into a single monthly, *AudioXpress*, which presently has a worldwide monthly circulation of over 15,000.—Howard Ferstler

Demagnetization · A procedure in tape recorder player maintenance, used to counteract the buildup of residual magnetism in the tape heads and in the player's metal parts. The device employed produces an alternate magnetic field that neutralizes polarities on the metal parts, creating a random alignment of the polarities instead of a dominant charge. This procedure, performed after every 40 hours or so of operation, will prevent unintentional signal erasure as tapes are played. Demagnetizer cassettes are available for use with cassette tape equipment.

Demo · A record made for demonstration purposes or as a kind of audition by a performer seeking a label contract.

Denon Electronics [website: www.denon.com] · A Japanese manufacturer of electronics. It was founded in 1910 as Nippon Columbia Co., Ltd. to sell single-sided disc recordings and gramophones. In 1939, Denon introduced the first disc recording equipment made in Japan, and subsequently introduced LPs (1951) and tape recorders (1953) to the Japanese market. In the 1960s, the company moved into manufacturing open reel and cassette audiotape, and in 1971, moved into electronics, primarily components for hi-fi systems. In 1972, Denon developed the first digital recorder for studio use, the PCM system. In 1983, Denon was the first to market commercial CDs, and began producing CD players for the home market. In the 1990s, the company moved into the manufacture and development of DVDs and MiniDiscs. Besides its Japanese main offices, the company has subsidiaries in the United States, Canada, Mexico, Europe, and Asia.

Deutsche Grammophon Gesellschaft (DGG) · A firm established in Hanover, Germany, by Emile and Joseph Berliner on December 6, 1898, to press discs for the European market. The original name of the firm was Deutsche Grammophon GmbH; this was changed to Deutsche Grammophon AG, then reverted to the first form after World War I.

DGG has always been recognized for its implementation of the most advanced recording techniques. Its innovations have included Berliner's twin inventions of the gramophone and accompanying disc, the shift from acid-etched zinc plates to wax recordings in 1901, the introduction of the shellac disc, and the 1922 introduction of the "father-mother-son" process for matrix production.

Masters were originally drawn from Victor and the Gramophone Co. There was quick growth for the firm, which sold both records and players, but the Berliner family did not have the resources to expand. DGG became a joint-stock company on June 27, 1900, owned by three companies, then passed entirely into the hands of the Gramophone Co., and the office was moved to Berlin—headed by Theodore B. Birnbaum—with the factory remaining in Hanover under Joseph Berliner. Within a year the Hanover factory was advertising that it had made more than 5,000 recordings in all languages; a second factory was leased, and purchased in 1908, to handle the demand; it became the "Werk 1" of DGG, located on what is now Podbielskistrasse.

Both 7-inch and 10-inch Grammophon discs were made, sold at 2.5 marks and 5 marks, respectively. With the takeover by the Gramophone Co. of International Zonophone Co. in 1903, discs bearing the Zonophon label were also pressed in Hanover, and sold at 2 marks for 7-inch and 4 marks for 10-inch sizes. Prices were lowered in 1906. The first double-sided discs (12-inch) appeared in 1907, and the 7-inch size was phased out.

The recording division of Siemens merged with the Netherlands-based Philips in 1962 to form the DGG/PPI Group; this company (which maintained its autonomy) was a key component in the establishment of PolyGram in 1971. Siemens sold its assets in the conglomerate in 1987, leaving Philips as the majority shareholder. The Canadian-based Seagram Company Ltd. acquired PolyGram in 1998, forming the Universal Music Group; DGG is now a part of a subsidiary known as the Decca Music Group.

Deutsche Grammophon remains an international leader within the area of classical recordings, due to cutting-edge recording techniques, a prestigious stable of artists, and a comprehensive slate of reissues and collector editions that exploit its illustrious past.—Rev. by Frank Hoffmann

Deutscher Industrie Normenausschus (DIN) · *See* DIN DEUTSCHES INSTITUT FÜR NORMUNG.

DF · *See* DAMPING FACTOR (DF).

DGG · *See* DEUTSCHE GRAMMOPHON GESELLSCHAFT (DGG).

Diaphragm · A membrane, in one of the components of a sound system, that vibrates in response to the incoming signal. In the cylinder phonograph, this membrane was part of the recorder or of the reproducer; in the disc gramophone, it was part of the counterpart sound box. When a record was being made, the vibration of the diaphragm resulted from sound waves produced by the voice or instrument directed at it. When the record was played back, the stylus created the vibration impulses. In early recording the preferred material for a diaphragm was glass, with various thicknesses used for different situations: A thin membrane was suitable for recording a violinist, whereas a thick one was needed for a band. As the vibrating membrane does not produce a sound of great volume, it was soon attached to a recording horn. By 1909, Victor and Columbia were using mica, imported from India, for their membranes; copper and aluminum were other common materials. Instruments often had adjustable gaskets to hold the diaphragm in place, and to vary the quality of output signal. Playback machines might have detachable sound boxes, each with a different diaphragm, such as one of mica for singing and violin music, and one of a larger diameter—made of alloy—for band music. The "Zora diaphragm" advertised by H. Lange's Successors of London (*TMN*, April 1908), was adaptable for playback with either a needle or a sapphire stylus. Modern diaphragms are made of Mylar or other tough plastics.

In addition to the components cited previously, both microphones and headphones utilize these membranes.

Dickson, William Kennedy, 1860–1935 · British inventor. He came to the United States and in 1882 began working for Thomas Edison; he became laboratory chief and assisted in electrical research. During 1888 to 1889, he developed Edison's idea for combining the phonograph with motion pictures. Dickson wrote in his 1895 *History of the Kinetograph* (the first textbook on cinematography) that "the establishment of harmonious relations between Kinetograph [the camera] and Phonograph was a harrowing task, and would have broken the spirit of inventors less inured to hardship and discouragement than Edison's veterans." On October 6, 1889, Dickson showed the first motion pictures with any kind of sound added to them. They ran

about 12 seconds, and included Dickson's voice speaking to Edison.

Although the combination was still in the experimental stage, the camera alone was being demonstrated under the name Kinetoscope. By 1895, Dickson apparently solved the synchronization problem of sound and image, for he wrote in his *History* that "the inconceivable swiftness of the photographic succession, and the exquisite synchronism of the phonographic attachment have removed the last trace of automatic action, and the illusion is complete."

Although Edison did not vigorously pursue the commercialization of the device, he did produce about 50 machines (Kinetoscopes) and made successful short films (*see* KINETOPHONE). Dickson left Edison in 1897 to market his own Mutoscope. *See also* MOTION PICTURE SOUND RECORDING.

Dictating Machines · The original commercial use of the phonograph was to take down office dictation and courtroom proceedings. Edison's early machine used a cylinder four inches long and 2 1/4 inches in diameter for both entertainment and dictation (with space for about 1,000 words of speech). From 1890, the Edison machine used a cylinder six inches long and 2 1/4 inches in diameter for dictation. That became the standard size of records for business machines of all makes until acetate discs replaced cylinders in the 1940s. Graphophone cylinders, however, were six inches long, 1 5/16 inches in diameter.

Differential Amplifier · An electronic device that increases the difference between two input signals.

Diffraction · The characteristic of a sound system that permits longer wavelengths to curve around obstacles.

Diffusor · A diaphragm in the form of a shallow paper cone, used in Pathé phonographs. It resembled Auguste Lumière's pleated paper diaphragm used by the French Gramophone Co. (made by the Gramophone Co., Ltd., for Britain and export). Although the Lumière device was not really a cone, the mechanics of the two diaphragms were similar.

Digital Audio Player · A device for storing, managing, organizing, and playing digital music files. Compact disc and DAT devices are early examples of digital audio players using removable digital media. Today, the term *digital audio player* is most commonly used to describe portable music players that use non-removable erasable digital media instead of removable media as a means for storing and playing digital music recordings. These devices are often called MP3 players even though some brands utilize audio compression schemes and file types other than MP3. The three most prevalent proprietary file formats used by digital audio players at the time of this writing are MP3, Windows Media Audio (WMA) by Microsoft, and Advanced Audio Codec (AAC), adapted by Apple Computer as the file compression scheme for its ubiquitous iTunes and iPod digital music products.

The first commercially available MP3 player in the United States was the Eiger Labs F10, introduced in 1998 with 32MB of file storage. This was followed the same year by the Diamond Multimedia Rio PMP300, the first portable digital music player to gain widespread attention. This led to the rapid development of players by other companies and the incorporation of music players into PDAs and cell phones. Just when it looked as if several digital music players were about to become breakout hits, the public's primary online source of MP3 files—Napster—was shut down because it did not adequately protect the rights of artists whose music files it was distributing.

In 2001, Apple Computer announced the iPod, its first portable music player, and iTunes, a digital music service providing affordable downloads while at the same time protecting artists' rights by incorporating a copy-protection scheme known as Protected Advanced Audio Codec. Although not using MP3 as the file format for its own iTunes service, the iPod remained compatible with MP3 files obtained from other sources. The success of the iPod was astounding. By the first quarter of 2005, Apple was selling more than 5 million units per quarter. Microsoft, Sony, Dell, Samsung, and many other companies now produce digital audio players using a variety of music compression schemes. *See also* ADVANCED AUDIO CODEC, DIGITAL RIGHTS MANAGEMENT (DRM), IPOD, MP3, and WINDOWS MEDIA AUDIO (WMA).— Thom Holmes

Digital Compact Cassette (DCC) · Philips and Matsushita introduced the Digital Compact Cassette (DCC) recorder/player in 1992 as a replacement for the popular analog cassette. DCC was developed as a consumer alternative to DAT, the original digital tape recording medium introduced by Sony in 1987. Selling points for DCC included CD-quality reproduction, durability, and backward-compatibility so that standard analog cassettes could be played (but not recorded) in the same machines. Recording was done using 16-bit linear encoding and any of three different sampling rates: 32, 44.1, and 48 kHz, although all three rates were "dithered" to CD-standard 44.1 kHz before being placed on tape. DCC cassettes were manufactured especially for the format and were available in lengths of 45, 60, 75, 90, and 105 minutes. The medium used a proprietary data compression scheme known as Precision Adaptive Sub-band Coding (PASC) to fit audio tracks onto the tape. Track markers were added during recording to facilitate access to specific tracks during playback, although the linear tape format remained a disadvantage of the medium when compared with the non-linear, instant access of compact discs.

In 1992, the DCC competed head-to-head with the newly introduced Sony MiniDisc, yet another consumer product aimed at supplanting the analog cassette. Neither of these media met with early success and Philips discontinued production of DCC products in 1996, followed shortly by their introduction of CD-R recorders for home audio. The Sony MiniDisc was more resilient and has since become a popular alternative to CD-R for home recording.—Thom Holmes

Digital Counter · A device in a tape deck that displays, usually in three digits, the location on the tape reel that is being recorded or played back. To find a specific spot on a tape, the user engages fast-forward or reverse and stops when the desired point is indicated in the digital counter window. In this context the term "digital" is not drawn from computer digital electronic technology, but from the arithmetic "digit."

Digital Recording · A method of recording, introduced as a consumer product in the late 1970s, in which the signal to be recorded is converted to digital form, allowing the signal to be computer readable. During the production part of the process, a computer/recorder examines the analog input thousands of times per second (the sampling frequency or sampling-rate process) and generates chains of on/off pulses that represent the analog signals. These are transferred to either disc or tape form for storage or duplication. During playback, a computer/player, incorporating a DAC (digital-to-analog converter) restores those pulses back to the instantaneous signal values originally sampled, and special filters form analog curves of them. Thus, the initial audio signal is recreated exactly as originally sampled. This process

preserves all the audio characteristics of the signal, while excluding any extraneous sounds or distortions such as hiss. Current digital recording and playback formats used for musical program material include the compact disc, DAT, DVD, DVD-A, SACD, MiniDisc, and computer hard drives. Before the advent of actual digital discs, some LP recordings were mastered from tapes made with digital recorders. *See also* VIDEO RECORDING.—Rev. by Howard Ferstler

Digital Rights Management (DRM) · Digital Rights Management (DRM) is an umbrella term for various hardware and software initiatives undertaken voluntarily by music product manufacturers to safeguard the sales and use of copyrighted content such as recorded music. The Open Mobile Alliance is an industry organization charged with developing standards for DRM that are operable across different mobile product platforms, such as cell phones, PDAs, and portable MP3 players. One prominent application of DRM is the adoption of Protected AAC by Apple Computer to secure the protection of digital music downloads from its popular iTunes Music Store.—Thom Holmes

Digital-to-Analog Converter · *See* DIGITAL RECORDING.

Din Deutsches Institut Für Normung [website: www.2.din.de] · A German standards organization, founded in Berlin in 1917. It was formerly called Deutscher Industrie Normenausschuss (DIN).

Dipole Loudspeaker · *See* LOUDSPEAKER, 8.

Direct Cut · *See* DIRECT TO DISC.

Direct Disc Recording · *See* DIRECT TO DISC.

Direct Field · The listening position in a room where the direct sound from a speaker, a set of speakers, or a live performance is louder than the sound reflected from nearby room boundaries. Normally, you would have to be very close to the sound source for this to occur at all audible frequencies. *See also* REVERBERANT FIELD; CRITICAL DISTANCE.—Howard Ferstler

Direct Injection · A process of recording an electronic instrument by wiring it directly to the tape recorder. The signal is sent directly to the tape without the use of a microphone.

Direct To Disc · Also known as direct cut, direct-disc recording, or direct recording. This was the original method of disc production, in which the signal was inscribed directly on a master. In this process, the cut disc itself was termed a direct disc if it was the actual record to be played back, instead of a master used to press multiple copies. With the availability of tape recording as an intermediary between signal and master, great advantages were gained over direct to disc: editing became possible, and also enhanced control over groove modulation. Consequently, the commercial recording industry accepted the use of tape as an intermediary for almost all purposes. During the 1970s, however, some direct-to-disc masters were produced by outfits like Sheffield. The supposed advantages included a certain spontaneity in the performance, greater dynamic range, reduced wow and flutter, and the omission of tape hiss and other tape-related distortions. The rise of digital recording and disc-playback systems has rendered direct-to-disc recording superfluous. *See also* INSTANTANEOUS RECORDINGS.—Rev. by Howard Ferstler

Disc · Disc is frequently spelled "disk," most often in the area of digital technology, but sometimes in reference to phonograph records as well. In the present work, "disc" is used for the formats of sound recording.

The earliest term for a flat, circular object employed to receive and retain sound signals was *phonautogram,* from the Phonautograph invented by Léon Scott de Martinville in 1857. Scott's device, which preserved a visual image of the sound waves only, without audio playback capability, actually used a cylinder instead of a disc. Emile Berliner applied the term to his 1887 invention—the gramophone. Berliner's first patent specification refers to the phonautographic recording; later he called the disc a plate. In Thomas Edison's sketches of 1878, a disc was illustrated as a recording format, also named plate. Edison's working format was the cylinder, known also as a phonogram, but usually identified as a record. Both phonogram and record were later used as synonyms for disc.

Emile Berliner is generally credited with "inventing" disc recording, although many others had previously experimented with various types of audio discs, including Edison. Berliner discarded the cylinder in favor of a glass disc 125 millimeters (five inches) in diameter, and from this inspiration, the gramophone was born. Although it took Berliner until 1894 to produce commercial records and playback machines, he was the first to do so. His discs grew to seven inches in diameter, stamped from electrotyped matrices. They gave two minutes of playing time.

In essence, Berliner's system translated an audio signal into an analog groove pattern on a disc surface via a recording horn, a diaphragm, and a needle (later called a stylus). His method was lateral recording, meaning that the groove pattern was lateral (i.e., side-to-side; sometimes called needle-cut). That method contrasted with the vertical-cut method (i.e., up-and-down; also known as phono-cut or hill-and-dale) employed on cylinders.

Although lateral-cut became the industry standard, there was considerable manufacturing of vertical-cut records in the early years. One reason was simply the preference held by certain industry leaders such as Edison, who carried the idea from cylinders to his Diamond Disc of 1912. Another reason was the legal grip on lateral recording achieved by Columbia and Victor in their patent sharing agreement of 1902; this maneuver effectively compelled other producers to follow the hill-and-dale approach. A switch from vertical to lateral occurred after the expiration of Victor/Columbia patents in 1919.

Berliner's earliest discs, for the 1889 toy gramophone, were five inches in diameter; they were recorded on one side only, and turned at about 70 rpm. The first commercial discs, Berliner's of 1894, were seven inches in diameter, and this was the size employed in Europe and America until 1902. A seven-inch disc rotating at 70 rpm would play two minutes; a slow speed cylinder of the time would last three minutes; thus, a larger disc was called for. Over the following years, 8-, 9-, 10-, 12-, and 14-inch discs were produced; by 1908, the industry had settled on 10- and 12-inch as the "standards." Double-sided discs were first introduced in 1902.

That was the situation of the mass market until 1949. Along the way, there were 16-inch, 33 1/3-rpm discs—the first LPs—made by the Vitaphone Co. for use as motion picture sound components (1926). Edison announced his 12-inch LP in the same year, one that played 20 minutes per side; it was not successful because the grooves were too thin for the heavy tone

Disc Jockey

Also DJ or deejay. A person who selects and plays records in a systematic program, either in a discotheque or on the radio, usually adding personal comments on the music. Although the contemporary connotation relates the term to popular music, the earliest radio disc jockeys aired classical music. Christopher Stone was the first disc jockey in regular phonograph concerts on British Broadcasting Corp. programs in 1927; he referred to himself as a "presenter."

In the United States, the first radio programs of recorded music were simply announced like any other fare, and the personality of the announcer was not emphasized. (In fact, early radio announcers were anonymous, and their names were not given to listeners who asked for them.) The first structured presentations of popular music records on American radio were in the *Make Believe Ballroom* programs, hosted by Al Jarvis at KFWB in Los Angeles. Jarvis interjected his personality into the proceedings, and used the clever device of simulating a real ballroom atmosphere—with one band performing all the pieces on each program. The program moved to WNEW in New York, and led to various imitations. Radio announcers who played records, with or without stressing their personalities, were soon recognized as powerful figures in the market. By the 1950s, there was such a concentration of power that a few disc jockeys in major markets could create a hit record or doom another to oblivion.

Performers began early on to pay bonuses to those announcers to have their discs spun. Not far down the road was payola, or outright bribery. The payola scandals of the late 1950s did lead to reforms. One was the development of Top 40 programming in which the best-selling discs of the week were played (WTIX in New Orleans had the first of these). The announcer in that format, known as boss radio, did not have the power to select the material for the show. DJs were relegated to giving continuity and arms of the day. Victor failed with a 1931 LP (not a microgroove) for similar reasons. Then there were numerous specimens of small records issued throughout the acoustic period, with diameters of six inches or less, many for children or as advertising promotions.

The "war of the speeds" between Columbia and Victor in 1949 was also a contest of diameters. Columbia's LP was a 33 1/3-rpm disc available in 10-inch and 12-inch sizes. Victor offered a seven-inch disc at 45 rpm. LPs and 45s were vinyl, and both had the same groove dimension. The war of the speeds ended in February 1950, when Victor marketed its first LP. Nevertheless, it held onto the 45 as well, ingeniously focusing the format on pop music; and the industry followed, using LP for classics and 45 for pop. The last 78 produc-

tion of any significance was in 1957, and the LP and 45 rpm "discs" remained the standards until the coming of the CD era in the early 1980s.

Discman · A trademark name of the Sony Corporation for a portable CD player, an outgrowth of their earlier Walkman.

Disc Number · Also known as the catalog number. The manufacturer's number that appears on the label of a disc recording. *See also* ALBUM NUMBER; MATRIX NUMBER.

Discophone · *See* PICTURIZED PHONOGRAPHS.

Discrete Circuit · *See* INTEGRATED CIRCUIT.

"color" to the total program. Then the announcer regained some lost ground with the introduction of free-form programming, a format that gave the DJ some latitude in choosing material. A wide range of content is typical of this format, including blues, jazz, spoken records, local talent, and folksong as well as material from the charts. Boss remains the dominant mode of popular music broadcasting on AM radio in the United States, while free-form is prominent on FM radio. Larry Miller of Detroit's KMPX-FM is credited with the invention of free-form. There were about 400 free-form stations in the United States during the 1970s; one was Mike Harrison's KPRI-FM in San Diego, where the content was identified as album-oriented rock (AOR).

Beginning in the 1970s club culture, the DJ began to take on a new personality, as a quasi-performer. Assembling long sets of music united by a similar beat, the disco DJ could create 30 minute or longer continuous "sets" to keep dancers moving. Some DJs became as famous (or better known) than the recording artists, and would attract dedicated followers in club culture.

A parallel development beginning in the 1960s in Jamaica and the Caribbean separated the DJ into two related performers: the record spinner and the announcer who goaded the crowd into joining in the party atmosphere. These announcers developed a unique rhymed patter which would become, in hip hop culture, rapping; beginning in the late 1970s-1980s, the DJs developed unique techniques such as scratching, backspinning, and other manipulations of the vinyl LPs that created new musical backgrounds for the rapping. The DJ escaped the confines of the radio studio and became a performer equal to the musicians—in fact, often replacing live musicians. With the introduction of inexpensive electronic samplers and other digital equipment beginning in the mid-1980s, the DJ became a sound engineer creating unique compositions using preexisting recordings and new sounds as the creative elements.

Dispersion · A characteristic of a loud-speaker, referring to its ability to distribute sound widely and evenly throughout the listening area.

Distortion · Any alteration to the input signal as it passes through a sound system. Various types of distortion are listed next. It should be noted that distortions related to analog devices, such as the LP record, are no longer serious problems with the advent of digital-audio recording and playback systems.

1. *Amplitude distortion.* Also known as non-linear distortion. The name given to any change in the ratio of output amplitude to input amplitude for any value of the latter. Both harmonic and intermodulation distortion are outcomes.
2. *Amplitude/frequency distortion.* Also named attenuation distortion. A change in amplification produced by shifts in signal frequency.
3. *Clipping distortion.* A result of overload, usually involving a low-powered amplifier trying to generate higher power levels.
4. *Inner-groove distortion.* In an analog-disc reproducing systems that utilize constant angular velocity, the speed of the disc surface under the stylus is faster at the edge than at the center. On a 12-inch 33 1/3-rpm LP, the speed at the outside edge is 20.9 inches per second. At the center, however, with the radius reduced to about 2.5 inches, the speed is only 8.7 inches per second (*see also* DISC). In practice, this means that the amplitude must be less at the center than at the edge, or amplitude distortion will result, particularly at higher frequencies. Some companies solved the problem by simply putting less music on a side, which made it necessary to flip the recording more often than some people might like. It was this problem that led Thomas Edison to prefer the cylinder, where surface speed is constant. The triumph of digital-discs systems has made this kind of distortion superfluous.
5. *Flutter distortion. See also* FLUTTER.
6. *Harmonic distortion.* A result of amplitude distortion: it refers to overemphasis or underemphasis on certain overtones. The first overtone, or second harmonic (the octave above the fundamental), is not a major problem when it is distorted, but the higher harmonics—third, fifth, seventh, and ninth—can be disturbing if reproduced out of balance. A common reason for this effect is that the volume is turned up to a point where the amplifier is overloaded.
7. *Intermodulation distortion.* A result (like harmonic distortion) of amplitude distortion: it refers to the production of alien frequencies corresponding to the sums and differences of the fundamentals and harmonics of two or more signal frequencies.
8. *Linear distortion.* A type of amplitude distortion in which the input and output signals are not proportionate, but without the introduction of alien frequencies. Modern audio electronics usually have minimal linear distortion, and it most commonly shows up in loudspeaker systems.
9. *Non-linear distortion.* The type of distortion that is most troublesome in an audio system, because it stems from the transmission properties of the system. That is, from the dependency of the system upon the instantaneous magnitude of the transmitted signal. Non-linear distortion produces flutter, intermodulation distortion, and wow.

10. *Phase distortion.* Also called phase-frequency distortion. The type of distortion that results when phase shift is not in direct proportion to the frequency across the entire transmission range. The significance of phase distortion in audio systems is debatable, and probably inconsequential unless the levels are fairly high.

11. *Rumble.* The sound produced by vibrations in the recording or playback turntable of an analog disc system. In digital systems, which do not have problems with mechanical rumble, noise artifacts in the recording studio or concert hall might generate a similar effect. Examples would be traffic noise outside of the building or heater and air-conditioner noises.

12. *Scale distortion.* The result of widely different dimensions between input and output locations. For example, it may occur when a signal originating in a concert hall is reproduced in a small room. To an extent, well-designed surround-sound audio systems and multi-channel recordings can obviate this.

13. *Tracing distortion.* The result of a misfit between the record groove and the playback stylus in an analog record player, usually caused by the swing of the tone arm from the start to the end of the record. The misfit can be diminished by linear tone arm travel, constant groove-to-stylus angle devices, stylus size, and stylus shape.—Rev. by Howard Ferstler [Isom 1972, 1977; Klinger 1991]

Dither · In digital recording systems, it is the addition of random noise at a very low level, before the signal is quantized. Its purpose is to de-correlate the quantization error from the signal, and in doing so, it allows the encoding of signals well below the digital noise floor. The result will be improved resolution of the signals being recorded.—Howard Ferstler

Dolby, Raymond M. (Ray), January 18, 1933– · Dolby was born in Portland, Oregon, and is Founder and Chairman of Dolby Laboratories, Inc. From 1949 to 1952 he worked on various audio and instrumentation projects at Ampex Corporation, where from 1952 to 1957, he was mainly responsible for the development of the electronic aspects of the Ampex video tape recording system. In 1957, he received a B.S. degree from Stanford University, and upon being awarded a Marshall Scholarship and a National Science Foundation graduate fellowship, left Ampex for further study at Cambridge University in England. He received a Ph.D. degree in physics from Cambridge in 1961, and was elected a Fellow of Pembroke College (Honorary Fellow, 1983). During his last year at Cambridge, he was also a consultant to the United Kingdom Atomic Energy Authority.

In 1963, Dolby took up a two-year appointment as a United Nations advisor in India, then returned to England in 1965 to establish Dolby Laboratories in London. Since 1976, he has lived in San Francisco, where his company has established further offices, laboratories, and manufacturing facilities. He holds more than 50 US patents, and has written papers on video tape recording, long wavelength X-ray analysis, and noise reduction.

Dolby is a fellow and past president of the Audio Engineering Society, and a recipient of its Silver and Gold Medal Awards. He is also a fellow of the British Kinematograph, Sound, and Television Society and an Honorary Member of The Society of Motion Picture and Television Engineers, which in the past has also awarded him its Samuel L. Warner Memorial Award, Alexander M. Poniatoff Gold Medal, and Progress Medal. The Academy of Motion Picture Arts and Sciences voted him a Scientific and Engineering Award in 1979 and an Oscar in 1989, when he was also presented an Emmy by the National Academy of Television Arts and Sciences. In 1986, Dolby was made an honorary Officer of the Most Excellent Order of the British Empire (OBE).

In 1997, Dolby received the U.S. National Medal of Technology, the Institute of Electrical and Electronics Engineers' Masaru Ibuka Consumer Electronics Award, and the American Electronic Association's Medal of Achievement. That year he also received an honorary Doctor of Science degree from Cambridge University, and in 1999 was awarded the honorary degree of Doctor by the University of York.

Dolby Digital · A digital, surround-sound audio format that goes well beyond the standard, matrixed Dolby Surround technology pioneered in the 1970s. Making use of data compression and reduction to minimize the number of bits required for storage and transmission, Dolby Digital will typically involve a total of six channels: three up front, two for surround duty, plus a low-frequency effects (LFE) bass channel. It can also involve as few as one channel, however, depending upon the requirements of the source material.

Originally, Dolby Digital was called AC-3 (AC-1 and AC-2 are earlier variants, developed for other applications) and it was originally configured for regular movie theater use. (The first movie to utilize a Dolby Digital soundtrack was *Batman Returns* in 1992.) However, it has evolved into an important home-theater audio technology as well. It is normally called a 5.1-channel system, with the bass-only LFE channel given the point-one designation because of its limited bandwidth. *See also* DOLBY SURROUND SOUND; DTS; DATA REDUCTION; DATA COMPRESSION.—Howard Ferstler

Dolby Noise Reduction System · A device invented by Raymond M. Dolby in 1966 for increasing the signal-to-noise ratio of a tape recording; it removes most recording noise and hiss. Essentially, the Dolby method is to code the audio signal during recording and then decode during playback, thus circumventing hiss production. *See also* DBX CORPORATION; DOLBY DIGITAL; DOLBY PRO LOGIC (DPL); DOLBY SURROUND SOUND; NOISE REDUCTION.

Dolby Pro Logic (DPL) · Strictly speaking, basic Dolby Surround Sound does not offer adequate separation between the left/right channels and the center, or between the left/right channels and the surround channel. Pro Logic, which in many minds has for some time has been synonymous with Dolby Surround, applies automatic gain riding to the decoding, which increases separation markedly. The latest Pro Logic II version, developed by Jim Fosgate and licensed by Dolby, improves upon the steering and also allows the technology to deliver good simulated surround sound from ordinary two-channel music source material. *See also* DOLBY SURROUND SOUND; HOME THEATER; SURROUND SOUND; STEERING SYSTEMS.—Howard Ferstler

Dolby Surround Sound · No longer a dominant format, but at one time used for motion picture soundtracks, some music recordings, and some network video programming, it is a 4:2:4 ambiance-extraction and derived-center surround-sound system that delivers three audio channels up front, plus a single surround channel. The latter is usually reproduced through two or more speakers with home-theater playback and with a considerably larger number used for standard movie-theater playback.

With Dolby Surround, the single-channel surround information is folded into two discrete channels, with the signal sent to one channel being at +90° out of phase and an identical signal routed to the other channel at −90° out of phase. During playback, any signals that are exactly 180° out of phase with each other are extracted by a Dolby decoder and sent to the surround channel. All other signals remain up front.

Center-channel information is handled in just the opposite manner. Identical, in-phase signals in the two discrete channels are electrically routed to a center channel. The result is a stabilized center feed for both theater and home-audio playback. Because of the derived center, Dolby Surround produces a theater soundstage that works better than a stereo phantom center for listeners sitting away from the dead-center sweet spot.

In modern movie theater and home-audio playback systems, basic Dolby Surround, even with Pro Logic decoding, has been mostly superseded by the Dolby Digital and DTS theater and home-theater versions. *See also* DOLBY PRO LOGIC (DPL); AMBIANCE EXTRACTION; SURROUND SOUND.—Howard Ferstler

Domains · The small regions of uniform magnetization (typically magnetized iron oxide particles) that store the sound signals in tape recording. As the domains move past the receptor head, the varying magnetic field induces changing electrical signals that can be converted back to the original sound.

Doppler Effect · In audio speaker systems, the frequency shift caused when a high-frequency signal is being reproduced by the same speaker driver that is also reproducing another signal at a lower frequency. The resulting anomaly may be audible with certain test signals, but is rarely heard with musical program sources.

Dory, Craig D., 1957– · Cofounder, president/CEO, and director of engineering at Dorian Records. While in high school,

Dory was a budding jazz musician. Even so, when he went off to Iowa State University he entered the honors program to study his other interest, mathematics, although he continued to pursue his musical interests. Upon graduating from ISU in 1980, he accepted a job offer from AT&T Bell Laboratories. While working there, he received an M.S. in industrial and operations engineering from the University of Michigan in 1981, and during this time he also began to cultivate his interest in recording music. In 1985, while still a full-time employee at Bell Labs, Dory was named director of engineering for the Musical Heritage Society and Musicmasters labels.

He left Bell in 1986 to pursue his new-found career as an independent recording engineer and producer. Before co-founding Dorian, he produced and engineered recordings for several different labels including, Deutsche Grammophon, Virgin, Musical Heritage Society, Musicmasters, and Orion. He also produced live-concert recordings for New York's 92nd Street Y, WOR-TV in New York, National Public Radio (NPR), Public Broadcasting Service (PBS), and numerous other concert and performing organizations. During this period, he worked with numerous artists, including Dawn Upshaw, whose debut recording he produced and engineered.

As Dorian's chief engineer, Dory has created more than 200 CDs for the label. He is an active member of the Audio Engineering Society (AES) and the National Academy of Recording Arts and Sciences (NARAS). He is also a member of Early Music America (EMA), and sits on the Classical/Jazz Advisory Committee of NARM (National Association of Record Merchandisers).—Howard Ferstler

Double Tracking · A technique in which the same musical material is recorded twice, with one signal superimposed on the other. The effect is to give the listener an impression of multiple performers. Guitarist Les Paul was among the first to use double tracking on a commercial recording, overdubbing several guitar and vocal parts on the hit pop recordings he made in the early 1950s with his wife, singer Mary Ford.

Douglass, Leon F., 1869–1940 · American inventor and recording industry executive. He worked for the Nebraska Phonograph Co., Omaha, then moved to Chicago, establishing the Chicago Talking Machine Co. (sold to Columbia in 1897). A promoter for Eldridge Johnson's Consolidated Talking Machine Co. in 1900, he produced national magazine advertising in the United States, touting the company's new wax disc and offering free samples to gramophone owners. It was once thought that the name of his wife, Victoria, was the inspiration for the name of the Victor Talking Machine Company that succeeded Consolidated.

Douglass was a successful inventor in several fields: he developed the magnetic torpedo used in World War I, demonstrated color motion pictures in 1918, constructed a periscope camera for underwater photography, and at his death was researching the problem of communication between planets. He held 13 U.S. patents in the sound recording area, filed between 1890 and 1909, among them a coin-op (no. 431,883; filed February 14, 1890), a cylinder record duplicating method (no. 475,490; filed March 17, 1892, granted May 24, 1892), and the Polyphone record player (no. 613,670; filed February 14, 1898, granted November 8, 1898). The Polyphone featured two sapphire stylus reproducers, each tracking the same cylinder groove, but 3/8 to 1/2 inch apart, each stylus leading to its own horn. Douglass died in San Francisco on September 7, 1940.

Dowd, Tom, 1925–October 27, 2002 · Dowd was a famed recording engineer long associated with Atlantic Records. He was born in Manhattan; his father worked in the theater as a producer and his mother was trained in opera. Dowd played piano as a youth, but pursued a degree in physics at Columbia; during World War II, he worked there as part of the project to develop the atomic bomb. A job as an engineer with the Voice of America following the war launched his career in recording, and he soon joined the fledgling Atlantic label. Dowd remained there for 25 years as the label's chief engineer, overseeing the label's trademark crisp sound. He also was responsible for the label's early investment in new recording technologies, including stereo recording equipment. Dowd built the label's 8-track console, the first major commercial studio to employ this technology, in the 1960s. Acts that Dowd recorded ranged from contemporary jazz groups, such as the Modern Jazz Quartet and John Coltrane's groups, to pop stars such as Aretha Franklin, Dusty Springfield, and the rock group Cream. In the late 1960s, Dowd went freelance, relocating to Miami and working out of Criterion Sound Studios. In 2002, he was awarded a Grammy lifetime achievement award. He died in Aventura, Florida, outside of Miami.— Carl Benson

Download · A generic name given to anything that is received via computer network. Most often the network in question is the Internet, where downloads might take the form of audio files, video files, and so on. With the rise of the Internet as a major factor in music piracy, downloads became the subject of much debate in the late 1990s as the MP3 became the simplest and easiest way to transfer music across e-mail, the web, or any other facet of the Internet in high sound quality. Other downloads might be executable files which, in the music industry, have been used as promotional tools for longer than MP3s. Executable files are simply computer programs such as screensavers or browser add-ons.— Ian Peel

Drop-In · The insertion of a new signal on a recorded track of magnetic tape by playing the tape to a desired point and switching to the record mode.

Dropout · A very brief reduction in reproduced signal level on a magnetic tape, resulting from dust or some fault in the tape coating. Its magnitude is expressed in terms of decibel loss and length of time. "Dropout count" refers to the number of dropouts on a given length of tape.

DRM · *See* DIGITAL RIGHTS MANAGEMENT (DRM).

Drum Machine · The drum machine or beat box started as a simple studio tool but became an integral part of hip-hop culture in the early 1980s. As Malcolm McLaren noted on the sleeve to his early hip hop hit Buffalo Gals, all a kid needed to create this new style of music was a pair of decks to scratch records and a drum machine to pump out a beat. By the mid-1980s, musicians unions were outraged at the thought of drum machines making traditional, "real" drummers redundant. At the same time, however, musicians such as Peter Gabriel proved instead that this technology could play its own part in music. His anti-apartheid anthem Biko started with a stark, solitary drum machine and finished bolstered by 'live' African percussion. The very sounds that certain drum machines produce have inspired whole cultures and genres of music. Acid house would have been nothing without the bass drum sound of a Roland TR-808 drum machine, as evidenced by the success of the experimental dance outfit known as 808 State who named their group after the device.—Ian Peel

DSP (Digital Signal Processing) · Any recording or playback system that makes use of digital technology to handle program sources in any number of ways. In addition to digital equipment designed for recording and mixing purposes, contemporary technologies that involve DSP include DAT, the compact disc, the DVD, Dolby Digital, DTS, DVD-A, and SACD. DSP is also well known for its use in consumer-oriented, home-playback signal processors, and involves the synthesizing of concert-hall, nightclub, auditorium, etc. environments from two-channel audio sources, or even the enhancement of 5.1-channel source material.—Howard Ferstler

DTS (Digital Theater Systems) · A movie-theater and home-theater audio format that is similar in concept to, but technically different from, Dolby Digital. Like DD, it involves up to 5.1 channels of data-reduced audio coding, but does so at a higher data rate than the Dolby version. Whether this results in superior sound is the subject of debate in the audio community. The first movie to make use of a DTS soundtrack was *Jurassic Park* in 1993. *See also* SURROUND SOUND.—Howard Ferstler

Dual Track · *See* TRACK.

Dubbing (I) · Copying or re-recording; as a noun, the recording thus obtained.

Dubbing (II) · Re-voicing the dialogue of a film track into another language, or by a different artist in the original language.

Dubbing (III) · Recording additional parts on previously taped material (known also as over-dubbing).

Dubbing (IV) · Making a test pressing, known as a dub.

Ducking · In recording, the technique of adding one signal to another without increasing total dynamic level, as when a voiceover is dubbed onto music. *See also* DUBBING (III).

Dummy Head Stereo · Also known by the German name *Kunstkopf*. A process of recording in which microphones are placed in the ears of a model head. The earliest reference to the technique was in a 1927 U.S. patent application by Bartlett Jones of Chicago. *See also* BINAURAL RECORDING.

Dumping · The sales practice of remaindering records at a discount.

Dunlavy, John, January 20, 1929– · Born in Wichita, Kansas, Dunlavy is a highly regarded loudspeaker system designer. He majored in physics at St. Mary's University, and further majored in electrical engineering at the University of Texas at San Antonio. Before professionally entering the field of audio in 1972, he invented several new types of antennas, including the basic log-periodic design, a cavity-backed spiral, the passive-network array, the active-network array, the "time-domain" array, etc., and holds several U.S. patents in the field. He also holds patents in the audio field, the two best known being one that involves the use of acoustical absorbing material to mitigate the effects of cabinet edge-diffraction and one covering the design of high performance audio cables, and has also published several papers on audio and other topics. While living in Australia from 1981 to 1990, he founded Duntech, a high-end-oriented speaker company. He then returned to Colorado, in the United States, and founded Dunlavy Audio Labs in 1992, a high-end loudspeaker company which he currently heads as its CEO and director of R&D.—Howard Ferstler

DVD · Initially, this set of letters was supposed to stand for either Digital Video or Digital Versatile Disc. Ultimately, they ended up not meaning anything but DVD. With home video and audio, it is an advanced technology that involves a digitally coded, data-compressed picture in combination with digitally coded, data-reduced, and compressed audio—usually Dolby Digital. Because of this and also because of the small size of the disc (it is the same size as the compact disc, but because of data reduction and compression it can hold up to 14 times as much data), the technology is ideally suited for home-theater presentations.

As noted, the audio tracks on a pre-recorded DVD movie disc usually involve Dolby Digital technology, but some releases also offer DTS audio. Most discs also feature scads of "bonus" materials, including performer biographies, trailers, multiple language tracks, director commentaries, and featurettes that involve production information. In most cases, the audio is five-channel surround (although fewer channels, at lower data rates, can also be utilized), with a low-frequency effects channel for handling the often very powerful "effects" bass. As noted, DVD programs mostly involve movies, but a large number of music programs are also available. DVD technology, in DVD ROM form, has also been utilized to include computer storage. Current incarnations of DVD technology also allow for video recording.

The DVD has been a runaway sales phenomenon, eclipsing the early success of both the CD and the VCR, and in one form or another it promises to replace both the compact disc and video tape.—Howard Ferstler

DVD-A (DVD-Audio) · A variant of the standard DVD technology, but primarily oriented toward very high-quality sound reproduction in a home-listening environment, the missing or minimal video material on a DVD-A disc allows for a much higher audio data rate and less digital compression than what is possible with Dolby Digital and DTS audio versions. The result is a potentially superior sound reproduction, although the main advantage of the format, compared to the two-channel compact disc, is the addition of the center and surround audio channels. To listen to the DVD-A program material on a disc, a DVD player with a DVD-A, six-channel output must be used; however, most DVD-A discs also have alternate tracks in Dolby Digital or DTS, which allows them to also be played on conventional DVD players. *See also* SACD (Super Audio Compact Disc).— Howard Ferstler

Dynagroove · The RCA trademark for its microgroove record, issued in 1950 as a response to the Columbia long-playing record. [Olson 1964]

Dynamic (I) · Having a moving part; in sound recording the reference is to a moving element related to an electromagnetic field, as in a moving coil or ribbon cartridge; or to a loudspeaker that uses magnetic fields and electric currents to produce sound vibrations. The same principle is found in the dynamic microphone.

Dynamic (II) · The force or intensity of sound (also in plural, dynamics), or volume.

Dynamic Range · In an audio system, the difference (expressed in decibels) between the overload level and the minimum acceptable signal level; that is, the difference between the loudest and softest passages reproduced without distortion.

Dyne · The force that produces an acceleration of one centimeter per second per second on the free mass of one gram. In acoustics, the unit of sound pressure is the dyne per square centimeter. *See also* INTENSITY.

Technology Firsts

Item	Year
The basic principles of the moving-coil electrodynamic loudspeaker, often referred to as the dynamic loudspeaker, were first patented in Germany by Werner von Siemens.	1874
Edison invented the tin foil cylinder phonograph recorder and player.	1877
Edison made the first recording of a human voice.	1877
One of the first wax cylinder recordings was made by Chichester Bell and Charles Sumner Tainter on the graphophone cylinder player.	1881
Emile Berliner invented disc recorder.	1887
The earliest known coin-operated phonograph was invented by Charles Adams Randall.	1888
The first operatic recording was made by Alfred Amrhein, violinist, playing the overture to Fra Diavolo (Edison cylinder recording).	1889
The first working magnetic recorder, the Telegraphone, was made by the Danish engineer Valdemar Poulsen.	1898
The first electronic music synthesizer was built by Thaddeus Cahill.	1900
The first large-scale orchestral recording was made: Odeon's Nutcracker Suite.	1909
Lee De Forest produced the first, practical multi-stage amplifier.	1912
The early condenser microphone was developed by E. C. Wente at Bell Laboratories.	1916
Lionel Guest and Horace O. Merriman (United Kingdom) made the first electrical recording that was commercially sold.	1920
The first condenser microphones were simultaneously developed by Bell Laboratories in the United States, Telefunken in Germany, and AKG in Austria.	1923–24
Brunswick introduced the first all-electric phonograph, the Panatrope.	1925
The first 33 1/3-rpm discs, known as Vitaphone records, were made at Bell Laboratories. They were used for motion-picture soundtracks.	1926
Bristol Co. marketed the first commercially available electrically amplified phono cartridge.	1926

(continued)

Technology Firsts (continued)

Item	Year
The BBC's Christopher Stone was radio's first "disc jockey," playing records on a regularly scheduled series of broadcasts.	1927
The Victor Automatic Orthophonic became the first record changer to reach a mass market.	1927
The single-groove stereophonic recording process was patented by W. Bartlett Jones.	1928
First car radios available.	1930
The Jensen company produced the first permanent-magnet loudspeaker system and the first compression-driven horn tweeter.	1930
First public demonstration of the BASF/AEG (Germany) "Magnetophone," an early magnetic tape recorder.	1935
Experiments by A.C. Keller and I.S. Rafuse of AT&T led to the first U.S. two-channel, single-groove stereo recording system.	1940
Bell Laboratories developed the first solid-state transistor.	1947
The Minnesota Mining and Manufacturing Company (3M), introduced the first successful plastic-based recording tape with a magnetic oxide coating.	1947
Columbia Records introduced the 33 1/3-rpm long-playing record.	1948
RCA Victor introduced the 45-rpm record.	1949
Edgar Villchur built the first acoustic suspension loudspeaker.	1953
Ampex introduced first commercially available multi-track tape recorder.	1954
Harman Kardon company produced the first hi-fi audio receiver.	1954
Ampex introduces the first videotape recorder.	1956
Koss designed the first commercially viable high-fidelity audio headphones.	1958
Philips introduced the audio cassette.	1963
The first commercial Walkman, the FM Walkman, was marketed by Sony.	1976
Sony (Japan) introduced the first digital audio recording systems for professional studios.	1978
The compact disc (CD) was introduced by Philips and Sony.	1983
Dieter Seitzer developed the MP3 digital audio format.	1987
The first commercially available MP3 player in the United States, the F10, was introduced by Eiger Labs.	1998

E

Eadon, Simon, May 14, 1952– · A well-regarded British recording engineer, Eadon did important creative work for the Decca Record Company from 1970 until 1997. He was educated at Sandroyd Preparatory School (1960–1965) and Harrow School (1965–1969). In addition to working for Decca, he began Abbas Records in 1995 (in anticipation of Decca's closure), and continues in that enterprise. The list of artists he has recorded, among many others, includes Dame Joan Sutherland, Vladimir Ashkenazy, Sir Adrian Boult, Sir Georg Solti, Riccardo Chailly, Andrew Litton, Luciano Pavarotti, Cecilia Bartoli, Ian Bostridge, Bryn Terfel, Thomas Trotter, Dame Kiri Te Kanawa, David Zinman, and Gillian Weir. He has also recorded some genuinely notable ensembles, including The Chicago Symphony Orchestra, London Symphony Orchestra, The Choir of King's College Cambridge, The Winchester Cathedral Choir, Waynflete Singers, Bournemouth Symphony Orchestra, and the Holst Singers. He was a 1982 and 1988 Grammy Finalist for Best Engineered Recordings (Classical) and won the 1991 Gramophone Magazine award for Best Engineered CD. In 1996, one of his recordings won the Grammy for Best Choral Recording, and in 1999, a second recoding won the Grammy Award for Best Instrumental Soloist Performance. He is a member of the National Academy of Recording Arts and Sciences and has written articles on recording techniques for *Gramophone Magazine* and *Studio Sound.*—Howard Ferstler

Eargle, John, January 6, 1931– · Graduating with a Bachelor in Music degree from the Eastman School of Music in 1953, Eargle then earned a Masters in Music from the University of Michigan in 1954. Not being satisfied with just learning about the artistic side of the business, he went on to get an engineering degree from the University of Texas in 1962, and a Masters in Engineering from Cooper Union for the Advancement of Science and Art in 1970.

From 1958 to 1960, he worked for Klipsch and Associates and after earning his engineering degree he worked for Jensen Manufacturing (1962–1963), RCA Victor (1963–1969), Mercury Records (1969–1971), Altec (1971–1973), JME Associates (his own company, 1973–1976), JBL (1976–1981), and JME Consulting Corporation (his own company, again, 1981–present), with major clients as diverse as Delos Records, AKG Acoustics, and JBL Professional.

He has engineered over 250 compact discs, has been nominated for Grammy awards in the classical-music category four times, and won once, for classical engineering. He has also published several university-level books on recording and loudspeaker design, including *The Microphone Handbook* (1981), *Stereophonic Techniques* (Editor, 1986), *Handbook of Sound System Design* (1989), *Handbook of Recording Engineering* (1986, 1992, 1996), *Music, Sound, and Technology* (1990, 1995), *Electroacoustical Reference Data* (1994),

The Loudspeaker Handbook (1997), and *The Microphone Book* (2001).

Eargle is a member of the Acoustical Society of America and the Society of Motion Picture and Television Engineers, a senior member of the Institute of Electrical and Electronics Engineers, and a Fellow and Honorary Member of the Audio Engineering Society (AES). He won the latter organization's Bronze Medal in 1984. He is also a member of the National Academy of Recording Arts and Sciences and the Academy of Motion Picture Arts and Sciences, and is also a past president of the AES and a reviewer for the AES Journal.—Howard Ferstler

Early Reflections · In a concert-hall or studio environment, the reflections from nearby wall and ceiling boundaries that may or may not enhance the sound picked up by the recording microphones. With regard to home-listening-room acoustics, they are the reflections that arrive within a few milliseconds of the direct sound coming from the speakers. Depending on the direction from which they are coming, they can either add spaciousness to the sound or muddy the detail. Large-room early reflections can also be simulated by DSP ambiance-synthesis devices. *See also* LATE REFLECTIONS.—Howard Ferstler

Echo · A reflected sound signal, having sufficient magnitude to be audible and reaching the listener long enough after the original signal to be distinguishable from it. *See also* ECHO CHAMBER; FLUTTER ECHO; REVERBERATION.

Echo Chamber · In sound recording, a room used to add an echo effect to a signal. The engineer can control the degree of echo, or reverberation, by combining the program source with the signal as it passes through the microphone and loudspeaker of the echo chamber.

Edison, Charles A., August 3, 1890–July 31, 1969 · American industrialist and statesman, son of Thomas A. Edison, born in Orange, New Jersey. He served as chairman of the board of McGraw-Edison, and as president of Thomas A. Edison, Inc., succeeding his father in August 1926. From 1939 to 1940, he was U.S. Secretary of the Navy, and from 1941 to 1944, he was governor of New Jersey. He died in New York.

Edison, Thomas Alva, February 11, 1847–October 18, 1931 · Eminent American inventor, born in Milan, Ohio. Edison is usually credited with the invention of the cylinder phonograph (*see also* CYLINDER). His earliest patent application for the device was dated December 24, 1877. In July of that year, Edison had through serendipity discovered that paper tape he was using for telegraph relay experiments could retain and play back sound signals. He applied the concept in a sketch for a tinfoil phonograph on November 29, 1877, and conveyed the idea to his assistants Charles Batchelor and John Kruesi. Those men produced a prototype machine and gave it to Edison on December 6, 1877; that phonograph was covered by U.S. patent no. 200,251, granted on February 10, 1878. (The wooden model submitted to the Patent Office went to the Science Museum, London, then to the Henry Ford Museum, in Dearborn, Michigan.)

Although he remained interested in the phonograph, Edison did little work on it for 10 years. During that decade, he concentrated on the electric light and the electric power industry. In 1887, he resumed experimentation with recorded sound, and developed the New Phonograph in which solid wax cylinders replaced the tinfoil of the original invention. He followed this with the Improved Phonograph, and then on June 16, 1888, with the Perfected Phonograph (exhibited at the Crystal Palace, London, in August 1888). A long series of ever-improved models emerged from the Edison work-shops over the next three decades.

With central electric power systems at an unreliable stage, and storage batteries still too bulky to be widely accepted, Edison gave his attention to the spring motor, which he had in fact described in his British patent application (no. 1644) of 1878; and it was the spring motor that operated most of the cylinder machines to come.

The phonograph had been invented in Edison's first laboratory, located in Menlo Park, New Jersey; however, all subsequent phonographic work was performed in the new Edison Phonograph Works, in West Orange, New Jersey. The parent organization in control of the Works and other Edison interests was the Edison Phonograph Co. (1887), but that firm sold its stock to Jesse H. Lippincott in 1888, who formed the North American Phonograph Co. to hold the patents. North American licensed 33 semi-independent subsidiaries, one of which was destined to emerge as a rival to Edison and Victor: the Columbia Phonograph Co. Edison reacquired control of his patents in 1894, but then liquidated North American. He set up another firm, the National Phonograph Co., in January 1896, to manufacture and distribute the spring-motor machines, and within three years had established branches in Europe. There were 12,000 affiliated dealers by 1907.

A final name change occurred in 1910, as the earlier companies were reorganized into Thomas A. Edison, Inc. Edison was president from December 1912 until August 1926, when he became chairman of the board, and his son Charles succeeded him as president. It was this firm that produced the finest Edison sound media, the Blue Amberol cylinder and the Edison Diamond Disc. With much reluctance, Edison conceded that discs were winning the market from cylinders, and he did create an outstanding version in the Diamond Disc. A series of tone tests demonstrated the remarkable fidelity achieved by it, despite the limitations of acoustic recording.

Although the Edison label and the machines made to play them were widely perceived to be of the highest quality, the firm was unable to hold a strong place in the burgeoning sound recording market. Many of the difficulties have been traced to Edison's own strongly held views: for example, his conviction that cylinders were inherently superior to discs because they did not encounter end-of-side distortion (see DISTORTION). His narrow musical taste tended to hold back the repertoire that his company offered, so that he never seriously competed with Victor and Columbia for the classical and operatic market. His preferred audience was rural, and of simple musical requirements. Edison's long-playing record of 1926 failed, for one reason because he did not exploit the repertoire possibilities it presented for uninterrupted renditions of longer compositions. Curiously, the inventor so prominent in the world of electricity was late to enter the field of electrical recording (1927); and he was behind the competition in combining record players and radios (1928). Cylinder production continued until 1929, though market demand had nearly vanished. Edison ceased making discs, cylinders, and machines on November 1, 1929, except for Ediphone dictation records.

Although this article has dealt with the Edison contributions to sound recording, it would be incomplete without mention of his other achievements. His first patented invention was a vote recorder in 1869, forerunner of the modern voting machine. In 1870, he developed a successful stock market printer ("ticker"). His automatic repeating telegraph of 1872 to 1877 allowed the storage and playback of telegraph messages—and led the inventor to the idea of storing and playing back voice signals. The quadraplex telegraph of 1874 expanded the capacity of the national wire system. Although he did not originate the electric light bulb, he labored to produce one that would burn long enough to be useful: the incandescent lamp with a carbonized filament (1879). From that beginning he went on to develop the dynamos, conduits, mains, relay circuits, and so forth that went into a total electric power distribution system; and he did this despite opposition from the reigning gaslight interests. Edison improved Alexander Graham Bell's telephone transmitter in 1877, and advanced the march of electronics in 1883 by discovering the so-called Edison Effect in lamps—a basis for the vacuum tube, radio, and television. He did important pioneer work in motion pictures, beginning in 1889; Menlo Park had the first motion picture studio, and produced the earliest action films (most early movie production took place in and around New York City). The classic *Great Train Robbery* of 1903 was an Edison work, filmed in part at Menlo Park. On October 6, 1889, Edison and William A. Kennedy had synchronized cylinder records with motion picture film to bring sound films into the world. In 1913, he offered a combination of a celluloid cylinder (similar to the Blue Amberol) with film in the Kinetophone. He made 19 talking pictures before 1915, when he abandoned the format.

Thomas Edison's life story is a recitation of the American dream. He was born in a "humble cottage" in a small town in Ohio, lived after age seven with his family in another small town, Port Huron, Michigan. He had little formal schooling, but acquired a wide general and technical education through self study. He would later suffer from deafness, due to a childhood mishap. At age 12, he began to work on the railroad that ran from Port Huron to Detroit, selling newspapers and candy; he soon built this modest post into a fruit and vegetable business. He learned telegraphy from a station agent whose son he had

saved from death, and by the age of 17, he had become a railway telegrapher. Boston was his home for a period, then New York City, where he arrived impecuniously in 1869. Good fortune came at last when his first commercially successful invention— the stock printer—brought in $40,000.

Edison set up a factory and laboratory in Newark in 1870, then the Menlo Park laboratory in 1876. He began to receive patents for electrical developments, and a stream of inventions followed.

During World War I, the genius of Edison (which he described as 2 percent inspiration and 98 percent perspiration) was applied to practical problems. He headed the U.S. Navy research effort that developed submarine detection devices, underwater searchlights, improved torpedoes, and range finders. He was awarded the Congressional Medal of Honor in 1928. At the age of 80, he was still active in experiments, and developed a form of synthetic rubber just before his death in West Orange in 1931.

An early marriage, to 16-year-old Mary Stillwell, ended in 1884 with the lady's untimely death. Edison then met and courted Mina Miller, of Akron, Ohio, and eventually proposed to her—via a Morse code message tapped on her palm, as the story goes—in September 1885. The couple, with Edison's three children, settled in Glenmont, a mansion in West Orange. Another three children were born, including Charles (1890), who was to assist in administering his father's enterprises.

His widow outlived Edison by 16 years, and devoted much energy to preserving her husband's workplaces. This interest culminated in the establishment of the Edison National Historic Site.

Edison lived a simple life, considering his fame and wealth. Despite his consuming interest in science, he was not a cultural blank. His reputed ignorance about music, for instance, must be ascribed to his preferences instead of to lack of familiarity with the masters. (A conversation with John Philip Sousa, printed in the October 1923 issue of *Etude* magazine, revealed an acute musical ear—despite his poor hearing—and his considered views on Mozart, Chopin, and Wagner.) He did not credit himself with genius, yet, in fellow pioneer David Sarnoff's words, "his genius was the spark of history—making advances in the world's social, economic and political life. Imagination, dynamically related to a persistent soul, never discouraged by defeat, comprised the sinew of his fame."

Edison (label) · The name given to the cylinder records sold by Edison's North American Phonograph Co. (1890–1894), the National Phonograph Co. (1896–1910), and Thomas A. Edison, Inc. (1910–1929). *See also* CYLINDER; EDISON DIAMOND DISC.

Edison (Thomas A.), Inc. · A firm incorporated in 1910 in a reorganization of the earlier Edison companies; it was under this name that Thomas Edison carried on his business activities until his death. He himself was president from December 1912, when Frank L. Dyer resigned the post, until August 1926, when Edison turned the job over to his son Charles and became chairman of the board. In 1912, C.H. Wilson, general manager, became vice president as well. The firm included various units for particular products: Phonograph Division, Ediphone Division, and divisions to handle non-audio items like storage batteries. Blue Amberol cylinders were among the first products offered by the company, along with the Amberola player for them, followed by the Edison Diamond Disc. West Orange, New Jersey, was the center of research activity. In fact, the first of the famous tone tests took place there, in 1915, when soprano Anna Case and contralto Christine Miller demonstrated that their

recorded voices on Diamond Discs were indistinguishable from their live ones.

After a remarkable first decade of invention and advanced products, the company fell behind its competitors. Electrical recording of Diamond Discs was put off until 1927. A long-playing record, marketed in 1926, was unsuccessful. Acquisition of Splitdorf Radio Corp. in 1928 marked a belated move into the radio market. Edison was neither able to gather the recording stars of Victor and Columbia, nor handle the sophisticated repertoires of his rivals.

Both discs and cylinders were manufactured by the firm until November 1, 1929, when Edison ordered an end of production except for dictation records. That product was made by the Voicewriter Division, which merged with McGraw Electric Co. in 1956.

Edison Diamond Disc · As early as 1910, there had been experiments in the Edison laboratory directed at the production of a flat disc record. It was put on the market in 1913, as the Diamond Disc, to be played with a diamond stylus in the new Diamond Disc Phonograph. The disc with the earliest recording date was "Dir che ci sono al mondo" from *Zaza*, performed by Carmen Melis. It came from a session of January or February 1910, but was not issued until 1913 (no. 83001). The machine had a heavier reproducer than the one used on cylinders, so a hard surface disc was needed; this was achieved with a plastic named Condensite. The records weighed one pound each, and measured a quarter-inch thick. There were 150 turns (grooves) per inch. At 80 rpm, the 12-inch Diamond Disc played 7 1/2 minutes, and the 10-inch record played five minutes. There was no warping, and no perceptible wearing of the surface, even after hundreds of plays. Outstanding audio fidelity for its time brought the Diamond Disc great acclaim; it was the medium of the remarkable tone tests that Edison used to demonstrate the quality of his product. Considering the longer playing time of the Diamond Discs, their price was competitive with standard discs: $1 for 10-inch records, while standard records were selling for .60¢.

What prevented the Diamond Disc from gaining a greater market share was its excessive surface noise (gradually improved, but a reasonably quiet surface did not emerge until 1924), and the tendency of the earlier discs to separate their layers and to curl or crack. Another difficulty was the need to have an Edison disc player because the Diamond Discs were not compatible with Victors, Columbias, and other machines. Finally, there was the artist and repertoire problem that always dogged Edison; he did not contract the finest artists and have them perform the quality music that was found on competing labels.

Edison did not begin recording electrically until June 1927, two years after the process had been adopted by other firms. He did pioneer in the manufacture of long-playing records, from 1926, but those were not well received. Just before Edison dropped out of the record business, he offered a lateral-cut electrically recorded disc (summer 1929), but it was without outstanding qualities. The final Diamond Disc was cut on September 18, 1929.

Edison Horns · The earliest phonographs and gramophones made use of listening tubes to increase audibility during playback. On the first tinfoil phonographs, the cone-shaped mouth pieces also functioned as volume enhancers. A graphophone of 1886 had a small horn, and so did the Edison New Phonograph of 1887. Around 1895 14-inch brass horns were first marketed with Edison domestic machines and coin-ops.

Horns got larger and larger; by the turn of the century some manufacturers were selling models up to 56 inches in length, collapsible into sections, and held up by cranes or stands. Edison was more restrained, preferring to develop efficient design in place of greater dimension. His products were of curved metal, or later of wood, not more than 19 inches long; they gave superior acoustic results compared with the massive conical shapes of other makers. Music Master was the name given to the wood horns—oak, mahogany, spruce—and to some British versions in hard cardboard or whale skin. *See also* HORN II.

Edison National Historic Site · An entity located at Main St. and Lakeside Ave., West Orange, New Jersey. Thomas Edison opened a new laboratory and manufacturing complex in West Orange on November 24, 1887, 10 years almost to the day after he had invented the phonograph in Menlo Park. His early work in West Orange resulted in the Improved Phonograph, the Perfected Phonograph, and the Kinetophone, as well as a successful storage battery; all his later enhancements in recording were developed there. After the inventor's death, activity at the lab began to phase out, and it closed completely by 1935. Manufacturing of phonographs for business use and of electric storage batteries did continue until 1972. The laboratories were preserved by Edison's widow, Mina. After she died in 1947, the firm opened some of the research areas to the public on guided tours. In 1955, the laboratories were turned over to the National Park Service, which administers the facility as an educational museum. President John F. Kennedy signed legislation giving the site—which combines the labs and the Edison home, Glenmont—its present name.

Edison Phonograph Company · A firm established in 1887 for research and development; Edison's current and future patents (extending to October 1892) were assigned to it. The plant was located in West Orange, New Jersey; its general agent was Ezra T. Gilliland. Actual manufacturing was carried out at the Edison Phonograph Works. On June 28, 1888, the stock was sold to Jesse H. Lippincott for $500,000, and his North Americana Phonograph Co. became sole U.S. proprietor of the Edison patents, though the Edison Phonograph Works retained certain manufacturing rights.

Edison Recorders · The recorder of the acoustic phonograph was the device that carried the audio signal to the record surface. It was basically a diaphragm with a stylus embedded in it, the whole fitted with a speaking tube or recording horn. In the pioneer days, the recorder was set into a spectacle carrier, which also held the reproducer. Such was the form seen in the New Phonograph produced by Edison in 1887. Nomenclature was less than lucid: The recorder was identified in some advertising as a "speaker for recording," whereas the reproducer was also called a speaker. As the emphasis within the sound industry shifted from home or business recording to home listening, attention was concentrated on the reproducer. Edison made many versions of the reproducer, but he produced only minor variations on his basic recorder, which had a mica diaphragm and a sapphire cutting stylus. Nevertheless, he continued to offer the opportunity for phonograph owners to make their own records, even with the Amberola line of four-minute machines, and at reasonable prices (less than $10 would buy a recorder, a recorder fitting, and a special recording horn).

Edison Repeating Attachments · Beginning in 1888, Edison produced devices for his phonographs that allowed repeated playing of the cylinder. This repeating attachment was intended for commercial instead of domestic use. It was a forerunner of the coin-op. Several mechanical principles were tried (cord and windlass, chain drive and pulley, etc.), but they were not successful, and none were offered after 1912; however, the mechanism was important in language instruction.

Edison Reproducers · The diaphragm-and-stylus device used to play back cylinders was first known as a speaker, or sometimes as a repeater. By use of a spectacle carrier, those reproducers were mounted in tandem with recorders; the one employed to play what the other had inscribed on the cylinder. By 1889, Edison had found a way to meld those functions into a single device that he named the Standard Speaker; it had tracking problems and was replaced in 1893 by the Automatic Speaker, also designated as Model A. It must be remembered that the model numbers of the reproducers had no relation to the model numbers of the phonographs. In 1901, there was a special Gem reproducer for the phonograph of that name; this was replaced in a year by the Model B. This complex scenario was simplified in 1902 with the arrival of the Model C reproducer, which was used on most Edison machines until 1913. Glass diaphragms of earlier reproducers were replaced by mica and then copper alloy. Model C was intended for the new hard molded records. The Model D was similar, but adapted for the large concert cylinder. For the four-minute cylinder of 1908, a Model H was introduced. A reproducer to permit playing of Amberol records on five-inch concert machines—the Model J—came out in 1909.

The first reproducer for both two-minute and four-minute records appeared in the 1909 Model K. The required stylus was brought into playing position by turning a swivel. Model L and Model M (1909) were similar devices, intended for Amberola and Opera phonographs. Model N played four-minute Amberol records with a sapphire. Model O (1910) was used on players with large carrier arms. Models R and S (1911) were the final sapphire stylus devices from Edison, offering a large diaphragm usable on a small carrier arm. As for the missing model letters in this summary, Frow states that the Model P "has not been accounted for, but is thought to have been a modification of an earlier model"; "Model I was doubtless omitted as liable to cause confusion"; and "further research is needed to trace what happened to Models E, F, and G."

The advent of the Blue Amberol record called for a new series, the diamond reproducers. They were issued from 1912, and bore no model-letter marks; however, researchers refer to them as Diamond A, B, C, and D. They remained on the market until 1929. Lacquered paper and cork were the diaphragm materials.

Edison Shavers · One of the advantages held by wax cylinders over other recording media was their capability of reuse. From 1887, Edison's home and commercial phonographs had devices for shaving the surface of a used cylinder. Operation was by treadle power at first, then by electric drive. Interest in these gadgets peaked by 1904, when Edison stopped putting shavers on the Home and Standard models. After 1908, he ceased providing them except for the Home Recording Outfit sold in 1912. [Frow and Sefl 1978]

Edmunds, Henry · British engineer who observed Edison's tinfoil phonograph while in the United States in late 1877 or January 1878. On returning to England, he wrote about the phonograph to the *Times*. It was through this notice, which appeared in the newspaper on January 17, 1878, that the British public learned about the invention. Edmunds demonstrated the graphophone in Bath on September 6, 1888, after Colonel George Gouraud had exhibited Edison's Perfected Phonograph there.

Efficiency · The ratio of output power (or energy) to input. In an electronic power amplifier, the ratio of the output power to the power drawn from the mains (alternating current source).

EIA · *See* ELECTRONIC INDUSTRIES ASSOCIATION (EIA).

Eigenton · A German term (Eigentone in English) identifying the resonance set up in a room or enclosure at frequencies determined by the physical dimensions of the space. The lowest frequency will be at a wavelength corresponding to twice the longest length of the space, and others will be at double and three times that frequency, and so on. *See also* ROOM ACOUSTICS.

Eight-Track Tape · *See* TAPE.

Elbow · The part of a disc player that connects the horn to the end of the tone arm.

Elcaset · A modification of the standard cassette introduced by several Japanese firms in the mid-1970s. It used quarter-inch wide tape, instead of the standard 1/8 inch, and ran at a faster speed. Sony was the only company to promote the Elcaset actively. The format failed in the market because the improvements it offered over the standard cassette did not outweigh the considerable cost difference and the fact that it was incompatible with the millions of cassette players already owned by prospective customers. A European version was named Unisette.

Electric Phonograph · A record player driven by an electric motor, with either alternating current or direct current (mains) or direct current (battery) as its power source. Thomas Edison's Perfected Phonograph, which he demonstrated in 1888, had a 2.5 volt battery with a life expectancy of about 15 hours. Certain Edisons had battery power (Class M, certain coin-slots, Domestic, Exhibition, Improved) or mains power (Alva, Class E, certain coin-slots), but the principal Edisons (Amberola, Home, Opera, Standard, Triumph, etc.)

operated with spring motors. The 1915 Columbia Grafonola was available with an electric motor, and in 1921, Victor was advertising two electric console Victrolas, numbers XVI and XVII. A few disc players had, from 1916, electric attachments that wound up spring-operated machines automatically. Brunswick was the first to offer an all-electric record player, the 1925 Panatrope. *See also* TURNTABLE.

Electrical Recording · Also known as electromechanical recording. A number of experiments in several countries during World War I developed the components that were to make up an electrical recording system. The earliest effort that resulted in an actual marketed recording was that of Lionel Guest and Horace O. Merriman in London. They produced a moving-coil recording head (British patent no. 141,790) and set up equipment in a truck outside Westminster Abbey. On November 11, 1920, they recorded part of the service for the burial of the Unknown Warrior, using four carbon telephone microphones placed in the Abbey. The Columbia Graphophone Co. sold the resulting 12-inch double-faced disc for the benefit of the Abbey restoration fund; it contained the "Recessional" by Rudyard Kipling and "Abide with Me." However, the work of Guest and Merriman, as well as that of Adrian Francis Sykes, Frank B. Dyer, W.S Purser, and others, was eclipsed by the accomplishments of engineers at Bell Telephone Laboratories in America.

Research at Bell Laboratories, directed by J. P. Maxfield, had produced experiments in electrical recording as early as 1919. The Bell electrical apparatus consisted of microphones (principally the type 394 capacitor), amplifiers (two-stage), recording heads (balanced armature, moving-iron type), and loudspeakers (also balanced armature, moving-iron type, with response from 300–7,000 Hz). Essentially, what the new system did was to substitute electrical energy for mechanical energy, so that the signal to be recorded no longer had to provide its own (acoustic) power. The microphone replaced the venerable recording horn. There was also an appreciable increase in the amount of the audio frequency range that could be captured; as much as 2 1/2 octaves were added, giving audibility for the first time to higher frequencies (ultimately extended to 9,000 Hz) and to bass notes (down to 200 Hz).

Western Electric Co., the manufacturing division of American Telegraph and Telephone (parent company of Bell Laboratories), became the licensed owner of the process. An offer was made to extend the licensing to Victor, which refused. Columbia Phonograph Co., Inc., which had been reorganized in 1924 by a group of American investors, gained a Western Electric license. When Western Electric sent their master waxes to Pathé's office in New York to be processed, Russell Hunting and Frank Capps—Pathé executives—decided to let Louis Sterling (an old colleague of Hunting) in on the invention. They sent some duplicate pressings to Sterling, managing director of Columbia Graphophone Co., Ltd., in London. Sterling was sufficiently inspired by them to sail at once for New York. There he contrived to acquire the American Columbia firm, making it a part of the British one, thus acquiring the license to the Western Electric process. Victor thereupon consented to a contract also, an agreement inclusive of the Gramophone Co., so that the industry giants had legal control of the electrical recording system. This system remained in use, with modifications, by Victor until after World War II.

Nevertheless, it was an independent company, Chicago's Marsh Laboratories, Inc., that first marketed electrically recorded discs, under the Autograph label, in 1924. Columbia and HMV discs appeared first in the summer of 1925. For Columbia, records no. 3695-140545/140546 were the earliest to come out: They were made by W. C. Polla's Orchestra (under the pseudonym of Denza's Dance Band) and sold in July 1925. A vast choral ensemble was then recorded in the Metropolitan Opera House on March 31, 1925, singing "John Peel" and "Adeste Fidelis" (Columbia no. 9048; September 1925), creating a sensation.

Victor's first electric recording was "A Miniature Concert" by the Eight Famous Victor Artists (no. 35753; June 1925). "Joan of Arkansas," by the Mask and Wig Club, was made later—according to the matrix numbers—but released earlier (no. 19626;

April 1925). HMV's earliest electricals to be marketed were dance numbers by Ramon Newton, Jack Hylton, and the Mayfair Orchestra, recorded during June 24–25, and sold in August 1925. By the end of the first year of electric recording there were eight labels using the system. Brunswick had not licensed with Western Electric, but instead utilized its "Palatrope" or "Light-Ray" process, developed by General Electric. The others—Parlophone, Zonophone, Homochord, Sterno, and Vocalion—worked with alternative systems that did not infringe on the patent rights of the majors. Crystalate and Pathé joined the

Timeline of Early Electrical Recording Techniques

1876—1919	The first microphones were designed for use in telephones, following the first successful design by Alexander Graham Bell with a diaphragm that pressed a small platinum button against a carbon block to create the varying resistances. Improvements included the coil magnet microphone and carbon microphones, but their use was still limited to telephones.
1916	Early condenser microphone developed by E. C. Wente at Bell Laboratories.
1919	J. P. Maxfield of Bell Laboratories (USA) experimented with electrical recording, replacing the mechanical recording "horn" with a capacitor microphone. Western Electric Co., the manufacturing division of American Telegraph and Telephone (parent company of Bell Laboratories), became the licensed owner of the process.
1920	Lionel Guest and Horace O. Merriman (UK) used four carbon telephone microphones to record a public service in Westminster Abbey, resulting in the first electrical recording that was commercially sold.
1924	Marsh Laboratories, Inc. became the first company to sell electrically recorded discs using the Western Electric process.
1925	Electrically recorded discs made using the Western Electric process were issued by Columbia, HMV, and Victor, as well as five other labels. The modern, moving coil, direct radiator, and loudspeaker was developed by Chester W. Rice and Edward W. Kellog at General Electric, and comprised the foundation for modern loudspeaker design.
1925–1926	Rival electrical recording processes were developed by Brunswick (using the "Light Ray" process of General Electric), Parlophone, Zonophone, Homochord, Sterno, and Vocalion.
1926	Vitaphone and AT&T signed agreement to develop sound movies using an improved electrical recording system with a 16-inch acetate-coated shellac disc and a recording speed of 33 1/3 RPM.
1927	Edison made his first electrical records.
1928	Georg Neumann (Germany) introduced a high-quality condenser microphone, marking the beginning of modern electrical microphone design.
1929	Columbia switched from the Western Electric system to a new system developed by Alan Dower Blumlein, whose system reduced background noise and increased frequency response.
1931	RCA introduced a 33 1/3-RPM celluloid transcription disc used to record radio broadcasts.
1935	First public demonstration of the BASF/AEG (Germany) "Magnetophone," an early magnetic tape recorder.

electrics in May 1927. Edison, after holding out because he was concerned about distortions endemic in any electrical system, also began to make electrics in 1927. There was a general reticence by the labels to advertise the nature of their new products, for fear that existing stocks of acoustic records would no longer be salable.

While Victor held to the Western Electric system, Columbia moved from it to a new process developed by Alan Dower Blumlein in 1929. Blumlein sought to overcome some of the technical problems in the Western Electric apparatus, such as high sensitivity to background noise, the tendency for distortion to be more obvious in the extended frequency range, and certain maintenance requirements. Of course, there was also the need to pay royalties to Western Electric. Vocalion's system was developed by an engineer from the Marconi Wireless Telegraph Co.; it was used from 1926 to 1931.

Many refinements were made in electrical recording through the 1930s, primarily in higher quality microphones (including a notable one by Georg Neumann), which began to resemble those of our own time. Other innovations have included disc cutting with the burnishing facet on the stylus (invented by Frank L. Capps), and the "hot stylus" developed in the CBS laboratories while work was going on there to produce the modern long-playing record. Different types of equalization came into use, and modern recording was established. *See also* CARTRIDGE; MICROPHONE; RECORDING PRACTICE; STYLUS.

Electroforming · The technique, originated by Emile Berliner, of producing positive discs from negatives, and vice versa. It permitted the manufacture of positive mothers from negative metal masters, and then the manufacture of negative stampers from the mothers.

Electromechanical Recording · *See* ELECTRICAL RECORDING.

Electronic Crossover · *See* CROSSOVER NETWORK.

Electronic Industries Association (EIA) · A trade organization established in 1924 to represent radio manufacturers. It now encompasses the entire audio and video industry. The EIA has headquarters at 1722 I St., NW, in Washington, D.C. In 1990, Peter F. McCloskey was president; there were 1,200 members. The association absorbed the Magnetic Recording Industry Association in 1965, and the Institute of High Fidelity in 1979.

Electronic Music · Music conceived and created using electronic instruments. Although all recorded music could now be considered "electronic" because of the extensive use of audio processing, instrumentation, and editing techniques, the term *electronic music* has traditionally been used to describe an experimental branch of contemporary classical music. Using this historical perspective, there exists two firmly rooted branches of the electronic music family tree:

Purely electronic music created through the generation of sound-waves by electrical means. This is done without the use of traditional musical instruments or of sounds found in nature. This is the domain of computers, synthesizers, and software-generated sound environments. Purely electronic music can be made through either *analog* or *digital* synthesis. The difference between the two merely lies in the way electricity is controlled. There are no aesthetic differences between the outcomes, and the listener will probably not be able to tell the difference.

Electro-acoustic music uses electronics to modify sounds from the natural world. The entire spectrum of worldly sounds provides the source material for this music. This is the domain of microphones, tape recorders, and digital samplers. The term "electro-acoustic music" can be associated with live or recorded music. During live performance, natural sounds are modified in real time using electronics.

Aesthetic Principles. In practice, of course, the fields of purely electronic music and electro-acoustic music cross over all of the time, making such distinctions about the origin of electronic sounds no more than an academic concern.

What are more pertinent are the material and aesthetic aspects of electronic music that distinguish it from other music. Distinguishing features include:

The sound resources available to electronic music are unlimited and can be constructed from scratch. One of the key differences between electronic music and music composed for traditional instruments is that its sonic vistas are limitless and undefined. The composer not only creates the music, but also composes the very sounds themselves.

Electronic music expands our perception of tonality. The accepted palette of musical sounds is extended in two directions by electronic music. On one hand, the invention of new pitch systems is made easier with electronic music instruments. Microtonal music is more easily engineered by a composer who can subdivide an octave using software and a digital music keyboard than by a traditional instrument builder. On the other hand, electronic music stretches the concept of pitch in the opposite direction, toward less and less tonality and into the realm of noise. All sounds became equal.

Electronic music only exists in a state of actualization. Conventional musical notation is not practical for electronic music. You cannot study it as you would a piece of scored music. Experiencing electronic music is, by its nature, a part of its actualization. A work of electronic music is not real, does not exist, until a performance is realized or played in real-time.

Electronic music has a special relationship with the temporal nature of music. The plastic nature of electronic music allows the composer to record all of the values associated with a sound (e.g., pitch, timbre, envelope) in a form that can be shifted and reorganized in time. The ability to modify the time or duration of a sound is one of the most fundamental characteristics of electronic music.

In electronic music, sound itself becomes a theme of composition. The ability to get inside the physics of a sound and directly manipulate its characteristics provides an entirely new resource for composing music.

Electronic music does not breathe: it is not affected by the limitations of human performance. The arc and structure of electronic music is tolerant of extremes in the duration, pace, and complexity of sounds. The ability to sustain or repeat sounds for long periods of time—much longer than would be practical for live instrumentalists—is a natural resource of electronic music. In addition to its sustainability, electronic music can play rhythms and tonal clusters too complex and rapid for any person to perform. The composer is freed of the physical limitations of human performance and can construct new sounds and performances of an intricacy that can only exist as a product of the machine.

Electronic music springs from the imagination. The essence of electronic music is its disassociation with the natural world.

Having little basis in the object world, electronic music becomes the pulse of an intimate and personal reality for the listener. Its source is mysterious. It is experienced by engaging the imagination.

History. The earliest electronic music instruments were designed for real-time performance of mostly conventional music. Early landmarks in instrument building included the Telharmonium (1900) by Thaddeus Cahill, the Theremin (1920) by Leon Theremin, the Ondes Martenot (1928) by Maurice Martenot, and the Trautonium/Mixturtratonium (1930/1952) by Friedrich Trautwein and Oskar Sala.

With the widespread availability of tape recorders after World War II, numerous government broadcasting, and academic institutions around the world organized tape composition studios for the composition and recording of experimental electronic music. The tape editing, multi-track recording, and special tape effects developed by these studios during the 1950s greatly influenced techniques later applied to the creation of pop, jazz, classical, and motion picture music. Chief among the most influential electronic music studios were the Groupe de Recherches Musicales (GRM, est. 1948 as the studio of French radio, RTF) in Paris, Studio für Elektronische Musik of West German Radio (NWDR, now WDR, est. 1951) in Cologne, the Columbia-Princeton Electronic Music Center (Tape Center est. 1951, the Studio di Fonologia (est. 1953) in Milan, the Electronic Music Studio of NHK (est. 1953) in Tokyo, the Center for Electronic Music (est. 1956) in Eindhoven, the BBC Radiophonic Workshop (est. 1956) in London, Electronic Music Center est. 1959) in New York, the Cooperative Studio for Electronic Music (est. 1958) in Ann Arbor, the University of Toronto Electronic Music Center (est. 1959), and the San Francisco Tape Music Center (est. 1961).

The proliferation of electronic music studios led to the development of several specialized electronic music instruments including the first commercially made synthesizers. Among the early success stories were the Moog Synthesizer and Buchla Synthesizer, both using voltage-controlled analog synthesis and become available by about 1965. The popularity of the Moog-based recording *Switched-On Bach* (released 1968) by Wendy (then "Walter") Carlos nearly single-handedly created such demand for synthesizers that an entire industry was born overnight.

Electronic music is currently produced using a variety of analog and digital means. Tape composition has been replaced by digital composition using personal computers, and live performance has been enhanced by increasingly complex and versatile software controllers, instruments, and sound synthesizers.

After several decades of rapid technological evolution—from vacuum tubes to transistors to integrated circuits to microprocessors to software—we are now firmly grounded on a digital world. The technological obstacles that once limited composers—processing speed, computer memory, and permanent electronic storage—have been overcome. For the most part, memory is cheap, processing power is fast enough, and digital storage (e.g., CDs, mini-discs, DVDs, etc.) is adequate to allow composers and musicians the flexibility they need to create music.

Exciting and highly original electronic music is still being made, and it is more accessible than ever before in its history. Arising from this common technology are the works of a new generation of composers who accept technology as a norm, not as an obstacle to be overcome.—Thom Holmes

Electronic Stereo · *See* REPROCESSED STEREO.

Electrovoice [website: www.electrovoice. com] · A maker of microphones and PA systems founded in 1927 under the name Radio Engineers by Al Kahn and Lou Burroughs. Their original offices were in the basement of a local tire manufacturing company in South Bend, Indiana. In 1930, famed Notre Dame football coach Knute Rockne hired them to develop a PA system so he could coach his players while they worked out on four different fields. He calls his system his "Electric Voice," from which the company took its new name. Four years later, the company introduced its famous "hum-bucking" microphone, designed to operate in close proximity to other electrical devices without exhibiting the annoying interference—or "hum"— that characterized other mikes. In 1940, the firm developed a noise-canceling microphone for military applications. After the war, the company continued to work in the area of amplified sound. In 1957, it invented the stereophonic magnetic phono cartridge, making stereo playback possible of LP recordings. In 1963, it was awarded an Academy Award for its work developing the "shotgun microphone" which became widely adapted in the film industry. During the 1970s and 1980s, the company introduced several new design features to improve the quality and response of their loudspeaker systems. Through the turn of the 21st century, the company continues to work installing sound systems for major theaters, focusing on wireless technology along with improvements in amplification and speaker systems.

Embossed Groove Recording · The use of a blunt stylus in disc recording to push aside the groove material without removing it. Masters can therefore be reused, a factor of value in dictating machines.

Emerick, Geoff, December 5, 1945– · One of the most accomplished recording engineers and producers in the business, Emerick had the fortune and native talent to move from a basic English grammar-school education to a job with EMI Recording Studios, in London (later to be known as Abbey Road Studios). While at EMI, he recorded some of the label's top artists under contract, including Manfred Mann, Adam Faith, Peter Gordon, and, of course, the Beatles. He later left EMI to help build the Beatles' own Apple Studios in London, and when the project was completed he went on to record artists such as Badfinger and Tim Hardin, as well as more of The Beatles. His Beatles recording work included *Revolver* (Capitol 2576; 1966; no. 1), *Sgt. Pepper's Lonely Hearts Club Band* (Capitol 2653; 1967; no. 1), *Magical Mystery Tour* (Capitol 2835; 1967; no. 1), *The White Album* (Apple 101; 1968; no. 1), *Yellow Submarine* (Apple 153; 1969; no. 2) and *Abbey Road* (Apple 383; 1969; no. 1), with his work on the last two winning him engineering Grammy awards, in 1964 and 1969. His work with the Beatles also included the group's *All You Need Is Love* live world television satellite broadcast.

Emerick eventually left Apple and joined George Martin's A.I.R. Studios, also in London, and worked with Martin on most of his projects, including a number of releases by the group America. While there, he also recorded, produced, and remixed material by Elvis Costello and Paul McCartney, including Costello's *Imperial Bedroom* (Columbia 38157; 1982; no. 30) album. His McCartney achievements include *Band on the Run* (Apple 3415; 1973; no. 1), *Venus & Mars* (Capitol 11419; 1975; no. 1), and *London Town* (Capitol 11777; 1978; no. 2), with the former winning him his third Grammy for engineering, in 1974. He has continued to work with McCartney and also other artists, including Art Garfunkel, and in 1991 he won *R.E.P. Magazine's* "Best Acoustic Live Recording" award for McCartney's *Unplugged* Capitol 94613; 1991; no. 14).

Emerick now works out of Los Angeles, where he continues to engineer top-quality recordings.—Howard Ferstler

Emerson, Victor Hugo, 1866–June 22, 1926 · American recording engineer and executive. He was employed by Edison and then by the U.S. Phonograph Co., and was manager of the record department for Columbia from 1897 to 1914. In 1915, he established the Emerson Phonograph Co. A deal with Pathé Frères enabled Emerson to produce six-inch discs from Pathé's recorded repertoire. The company also contracted to have its phonographs made, under the trade names Electrola and Ford. In 1922, Emerson resigned from the presidency of the firm and organized another, the Kodisk Manufacturing Co., but he had to retire because of ill health, and he died in Downey, California. Emerson received 14 U.S. patents.

During its peak years, Emerson produced a number of subsidiary labels: Amco, Clover, Medallion, Symphonola, and Wise.

Enclosure · A housing, usually of wood, for a loudspeaker. *See also* specific types: ACOUSTICAL LABYRINTH; INFINITE BAFFLE.

Enhanced Recordings/Enhanced Stereo · *See* REPROCESSED STEREO.

Equalization (EQ) · Equalization can be applied to sound recordings at either the recording end or at the playback end.

1. *Recording end.* The process by which a master tape or master disc is edited in such a way that it will sound better after the material is transferred to the final product. The term "pre-equalization" is used to describe the alterations made during recording, and with the older, analog technology, such alterations were made in the recording studio to add emphasis or reduce emphasis in certain parts of the audio frequency spectrum (to achieve flat overall characteristics), to minimize distortion, and to limit surface noise. A plot of the relative emphasis given to the various frequencies is known as the recording curve or recording characteristic. The reduction is accomplished by lowering or raising the signal level in the appropriate segment(s) of the spectrum. Discs in the electric era, from 1925, were made with treble emphasis, the bass range being restricted to save groove space. Thus, the compensation intended by the equalization circuits was to restore the original characteristics of the signal, eliminating the artificial boost in the treble and enhancing the low frequencies that had been attenuated.

Standard equalization circuits have existed for some time for analog (LP) discs, and were established by the Recording Industry Association of America (RIAA). They also existed for tapes, as established by the National Association of Broadcasters (NAB). Modern digital systems, which have inherently low electronic noise and no surface noise at all, do not require pre-production equalization, although recording technicians might apply equalization during the editing process to compensate for problems with studio or hall acoustics or poor microphone placement.

2. *Playback end.* The term "post-equalization" is used to describe the compensatory devices in the playback equipment with analog recording and playback systems. With specialized equalization curves applied during the mastering phase, proper re-equalization is required during playback. During the height of the

LP record era, preamplifiers contained special circuits (mainly to work with the standard RIAA curves noted previously) that would restore response to flatness, while reducing background noise inherent with the analog-disc format. Tape recorders utilized similar playback curves for tapes made to the NAB standard. In analog tape production, the treble and bass are both reduced during recording, and playback requires boosting both segments of the range. Standard circuits in the playback recorder usually accomplish this; however, there can be problems when the recording equalization pattern does not correspond to that of the player. The ideal situation is one in which the tape is recorded and played back on the same machine. High quality playback recorders have equalization controls, based on NAB standards, to compensate for differences between the recording curve and the playback curve. Modern digital systems have essentially bypassed the problems noted with analog systems.

Customized sound characteristics may also be attained at the playback end with a variable equalizer, a device that allows the operator to increase or decrease the volume level of selected portions of the spectrum. The bass, treble, and sometimes midrange tone controls found on preamplifiers and audio receivers are simple equalizers. In many cases (particularly in good rooms, with good speakers), those are all the equalization the user should require. More sophisticated equalization can be accomplished with parametric or graphic equalizers. The former allows the user to choose specific frequencies to boost or cut, with the additional option of adjusting the frequency span and slope (the Q) of the boost or cut range. Most parametric equalizers only have a few adjustment points, however. Graphic equalizers usually involve multiple controls that will adjust a large number of fixed frequency points over the range from 20 Hz to 20 kHz. Most one-octave graphic equalizers (ten adjustment points) have limited abilities and are probably not much more useful than good tone controls. However, 1/3-octave equalizers (30 adjustment points) can work to make good systems, in good rooms, become even better sounding. Using any equalizer to smooth the *very* erratic response of poor speakers or even good speakers in poor rooms, is often counterproductive, because the equalizer cannot simultaneously compensate for irregularities in the direct-field and reverberant-field responses. *See also* CONTROLS; DE-EMPHASIS; PRE-EMPHASIS; RECORDING PRACTICE.—Rev. by Howard Ferstler

Erase Head · The device in a tape deck that removes any previous pattern on a recorded tape. When the recorded tape has passed the erase head, the sum of the particles' local magnetic fields is zero at any point, and the tape is said to be neutralized or demagnetized. This neutralization is more difficult with metallic tapes than with ferric-oxide tapes, requiring additional field strength in the erase mechanism.

Exponential Horn · *See* HORN II.

Extended-Play (EP) Discs · *See* LONG-PLAYING RECORD.

External Processor Loop (EPL) · An input/output feature found in some preamplifiers. Similar to a tape-monitor loop, it allows other components, such as equalizers, sound decoders, expanders, and so forth, which possibly work best in fixed-gain situations, to be inserted into a system. Most EPLs are analog in nature, which limits their use when signal inputs are in digital form.—Howard Ferstler

F

Fairchild, Sherman M., 1896–March 28, 1971 · Born in Oneonta, New York, Fairchild was the son of one of the founders of IBM, and himself was founder of the both the Fairchild Camera and Instrument Corporation and the Fairchild Engine and Airplane Corporation. He also became a pioneer in the fields of photography and sound engineering, and he was one of the first to realize the importance of large-scale semiconductor production for a variety of applications. He was keenly interested in music, to the point of being a partner in a music-publishing firm, and in 1931, he established the Fairchild Recording Equipment Corporation to carry out his theories of sound recording. In his lifetime, he was granted 30 patents, and was the recipient of numerous Audio Engineering Society awards. He was strongly involved with that organization during the 1950s, and had a great deal to do with both expanding Society conventions to the point where they were genuinely influential and upgrading the Society's journal to the point where it was able to exercise a genuine influence upon audio and the sound-recording establishment.—Howard Ferstler

Fantasia · An animated motion picture released by Disney studios in 1940. It employed multi-channel recording, called "Fantasound" by Disney, for the soundtrack, and featured the music of J. S. Bach, Tchaikovsky, Dukas, Stravinsky, Beethoven, Ponchielli, Mussorgsky, and Schubert. Deems Taylor narrated the program and the Philadelphia Orchestra, conducted by Leopold Stokowski, performed the music. The performance was recorded at the center of a cluster of polygonal enclosures with rear walls of sound absorbent material. Each enclosure had a separate microphone, so that instrumental groupings were individually recorded. There were also distant microphones to catch the entire orchestra, and the engineers manipulated the separate tracks to create one of the first, large-scale stereo soundtracks. In the theater, the three primary loudspeakers were placed behind the screen, with surround speakers down the side walls for a "surround sound" effect. Although the audio tracks of *Fantasia* were meant to give an accurate reproduction of an orchestra and not to create sound effects or to synchronize character movements on the screen, the discrete-channel system used in this film added a new dimension to motion pictures, and sound reproduction in general. Unfortunately, World War II and the costs of outfitting theaters with proper equipment put surround-sound motion pictures on hold for a number of years. A new version of *Fantasia*, featuring the music of Beethoven, Respighi, Gershwin, Shostakovich, St. Saens, Dukas, Elgar, and Stravinsky, with James Levine conducting the Chicago Symphony Orchestra, was released in the year 2000 (the only scene they share in common is Mickey Mouse's starring turn in Dukas' *The Sorcerer's Apprentice*), and it has been shown in assorted IMAX, 360-degree theaters, as well as theaters in general release. Both the earlier and later versions are also available on DVD, with CD soundtracks also available.—Rev. by Howard Ferstler

Faulkner, Tony, November 16, 1950– · A noted recording engineer, researcher, and consultant, Faulkner has a degree in physics (with additional studies in music) from the University of Surrey. From 1972 to 1976, he was with Angus McKenzie Facilities, Inc., in England, as Chief Engineer. From 1977 to 1980, he was with Enigma Records, and was responsible for running the recording and editing department. From 1980 to date, he was an independent classical-recording engineer with his own company, Green Room Productions. During 1997 to 1998, he also worked for Sony Music Entertainment, U.K.

He has engineered over 2000 classical recordings for dozens of record labels, many of which are award winners and acknowledged to be technical masterpieces. He has recorded hundreds of notable artists, including Claudio Abbado, Charles Mackerras, Peter Maxwell-Davies, Jessye Norman, Seiji, Ozawa, Bryn Terfel, Kiri te Kanawa, Zubin, Mehta, André Previn, and Michael Tilson-Thomas, as well as hundreds of performing ensembles. He was the first U.K. classical engineering specialist to work with digital audio equipment (1980), and has specialized in cutting-edge digital technology for over 20 years.

Faulkner is a member of the Audio Engineering Society Technical Council, was a member of the Board of Directors of EUROLAB, is President of the Federation of British Tape Recordists and Clubs, and is a member of the Music Performance Research Centre, in England. He has taught educational courses in recording techniques in England, Canada, and Japan, and has written articles for a number of audio-related and technical publications.— Howard Ferstler

FCC · *See* FEDERAL COMMUNICATIONS COMMISSION (FCC).

Federal Communications Commission (FCC) · A U.S. federal agency established in 1934, with authority to regulate radio and television, insuring that broadcasts are in the public interest. Although the FCC has no direct control over recordings, it has been able to exert some slight influence on popular song lyrics, endeavoring to expunge more sexual themes and vocabulary.

Federal Cylinder Project · A major program of the Library of Congress, which owns one of the largest collections of field cylinder recordings in the world. In 1979, the Library of Congress inaugurated the project, intending to preserve and duplicate wax cylinder recordings, document and preserve cylinder collections, and disseminate the results to the public. Engineers Robert Carneal and John Howell supervised the delicate task of making tapes from the cylinders. The collection primarily focused on recordings of American Indians made at the turn of the century by ethnographers including Francis Densmore. An inventory of the collection was published in 1984. Further volumes followed through the 1980s on specific regions represented in the total collection.

Feedback · In a sound system, the return of a fraction of the output signal to the input circuit. It may be positive (increasing the output) or negative (decreasing the output). In most cases, feedback is an undesirable distortion, but some rock performers have made deliberate use of it, for example, Jimi Hendrix. *See also* ACOUSTIC FEEDBACK; NEGATIVE FEEDBACK.

Feedforward · The process of mixing a fraction of the input signal in an amplifier with a small amount of the output signal, inverted in phase. This mixing cancels both portions, leaving only the distortions, which can then be amplified and subtracted from the final output. *See also* NEGATIVE FEEDBACK.

Feldman, Leonard, 1928–February 14, 1994 · Well-known as a consulting engineer, writer, lecturer, and technical expert in consumer electronics, Feldman was born in Chicago, and after moving to New York City, enrolled in Brooklyn Technical High School. After a stint in the Navy, as an electronics technician, he went on to City College in New York, where he earned a B.S. degree in electrical engineering in 1950. The next year, he went to work for Fisher Radio in 1951, as a design technician, and stayed with the company until 1956. Feldman then helped to found another company, Madison Fielding, producing a number of components, including the first transistorized preamplifier. Somewhat later, he merged the company with Crosby-Teletronics. In 1970, Feldman, along with John Fixler, present a modified version of Peter Scheiber's quadraphonic-sound matrixing system to Electro-Voice. As a result, the company subsequently developed a quad matrix decoder of its own, which may have been the most compatible of the matrix systems.

After several years of part-time writing while working for the preceding companies, Feldman decided to start writing full time. He became a senior editor of *Audio* magazine, and wrote regularly for *Video Review*, *Popular Electronics*, and *Popular Science*, as well as several business and trade publications covering the consumer electronics industry. As part of his product-testing work, he also operated one of the country's foremost audio-equipment testing laboratories. He was a technical consultant to the Electronics Industry Association, regularly testified before national and state legislative bodies concerning the regulation of consumer electronics, and served for more than ten years as one of the U.S. representatives to the International Electrotechnical Commission. He also published several books, was a member of the Institute of Electrical and Electronics Engineers, and became a Fellow of the Audio Engineering Society in 1991.—Howard Ferstler

Fender, (Clarence) Leo, August 10, 1909–March 23, 1991 · Starting out in the late 1940s as a radio repairman, Fender began tinkering with guitars as a hobby, and eventually became obsessed with producing the best electrical instrument of that kind possible. In 1954, he created the Stratocaster, a design that revolutionized the music business, because it could deal with radically different musical styles, from country-western to blues and heavy metal. Fender sold his Fender Guitar company in 1961. For his work, he was eventually inducted into the Country Music Hall of Fame and the Rock Walk of Fame.—Howard Ferstler

Fender Guitar [website: www.fender.com] · Throughout the 1930s, performers had experimented with using microphone amplification with hollow-body guitars, as a way to make them fill out large areas with sound. It was not until the 1940s, however, that Leo Fender perfected a system whereby hard-body guitars and speaker systems could be properly mated, without the feedback problem. In the 1950s, Fender produced and marketed a number of superior designs that allowed the company to become synonymous with high-quality, electric-guitar sound, and his groundbreaking design was the Stratocaster, produced in 1954. The "Strat" was a near-perfect fusion of electronics, ergonomics, technology, and design aesthetics. Besides its distinctive new look, the design involved a neck that was simply bolted on, thereby simplifying its manufacturer and lowering production costs. One innovation that is practically universal today was an arm that could be pushed to change the pitch of the strings.

Fender sold his company to CBS in 1961, and over the next two decades the product line's quality, and therefore its reputation, began to falter. In 1985, a group of employees, led by William Schultz, purchased Fender from CBS, and they gradually returned the enterprise to its prior glory. In 1987, Fender Guitar acquired the Sunn amplifier company, and in 1995, they purchased Guild Guitar. During this period, and since, the company has expanded to become a worldwide powerhouse in the music-instrument industry, providing everything the pop musician might need, from the guitars, strings, and accessories to the amplifiers and mixing boards.—Howard Ferstler

Fessenden, Reginald Aubrey, October 6, 1866–July 22, 1932 · Born in Canada, with his boyhood years spent in Ontario, Fessenden was a physicist and inventor, and was considered by many to be the Father of Radio Broadcasting. Indeed, his voice was the first-ever to be broadcast by radio waves and heard by another person.

A brilliant student, at age fourteen he was granted a mathematics mastership to Bishop's College in Lennoxville, Quebec. After graduation, he eventually went to work for Thomas Edison, in the inventor's machine shop, where he so impressed his superiors that he was invited to work in the labs. By 1890, he was Edison's chief chemist, but financial difficulties forced Edison to lay him off. After a stint as a professor of electrical engineering at Purdue University, Fessenden came to Pittsburgh in 1893 to serve as the head of the electrical engineering department at Western University (now the University of Pittsburgh). While there, he read of the radio experiments that Guglielmo Marconi was conducting in England and began experimenting himself at a lab at Allegheny Observatory. Marco-

ni's system could only transmit and receive dots and dashes: Morse code.

One of Fessenden's early accomplishments was perfecting a new means of sending Morse code more effectively than Marconi. His work with code transmitting notwithstanding, Fessenden's primary goal was to transmit the human voice and music. To accomplish this he devised the theory of the "continuous wave," a way to superimpose sound onto a radio wave and transmit this signal to a receiver where the radio wave would be removed, leaving the listener with the original sound. This system continues to be used to this very day.

On December 23, 1900, Fessenden made an experimental transmission from an island in the middle of the Potomac River near Washington, and radio broadcasting was born. Six years later, he presented radio's first program from Brant Rock, near Boston. Further experimentation followed, but it was not until after World War I that governments of the United States and Canada would issue broadcasting licenses that would permit development of the new medium. At that time, Fessenden's backers were more interested in radio as a point-to-point medium (a radio telephone), than as a way to transmit sound to large groups of people.

Surprisingly, Marconi's theory of radio transmission still prevailed (time has proven Fessenden correct and Marconi wrong), and because of this, the partnership between Fessenden and his backers began to sour. In the meantime, the phenomenal interest in radio in the 1920s finally allowed him to gain recognition for his pioneering work, and the Institute of Radio Engineers presented him with its Medal of Honor, while the city of Philadelphia awarded him a medal and cash prize for "one whose labors had been of great benefit to mankind."

In 1928, Fessenden returned to Bermuda where he had first met his wife more than

40 years earlier. There, the inventor called by the then head of General Electric Laboratories "the greatest wireless inventor of the age—greater than Marconi," died, largely a forgotten man.—Howard Ferstler

ffrr · *See* FULL FREQUENCY RANGE RECORDING (ffrr).

Filipetti, Frank, November 30, 1948– · Raised in Bristol, Connecticut, with a 1971 degree from the University of Connecticut in psychology, with minors in math and physics, Filipetti came to New York City as a musician and songwriter in that same year. Ten years later, with three production deals, two publishing deals, and three record deals under his belt, he decided that his primary interests lay in the technical side of the business, and from then on he dedicate himself to engineering and production. His natural talent resulted in his first number one single in 1983, with Foreigner's *I Want To Know What Love Is.*

One of the first recording engineers to embrace digital recording and production technology, with its extreme flexibility, Filipetti's additional credits include mixes for Kiss, The Bangles, Carly Simon, Barbra Streisand, Vanessa Williams, George Michael, 10,000 Maniacs, Elton John, Liza Minelli, Luciano Pavarotti, and James Taylor, whose elegant *Hourglass* album Filipetti produced, engineered, and mixed, winning two personal Grammy awards in 1998 for Best Engineered Album and Best Pop Album. He has also worked on projects and with artists as varied as Courtney Love and Hole, Dave Grusin, Celine Dion, Mariah Carey, Paul McCartney, and Bob Dylan.

Filipetti is also an enthusiastic proponent of surround sound. The N2K album, *Dave Grusin—West Side Story*, which he recorded and mixed with producer Phil Ramone in 1997, was one of the first commercially available 5.1 recordings. He has also engineered numerous other 5.1-channel DVD projects, including works for Billy Joel, Meatloaf, Elton John, and James Taylor, whose *Live at the Beacon Theater* DVD video was a landmark example of proper 5-channel sound technology. He has also recorded original cast albums for *A Funny Thing Happened on the Way to the Forum* featuring Nathan Lane, the Grammy-winning *Annie Get Your Gun*, and the Award-winning *Aida*, for which he won a Grammy. He has also recorded and produced live concerts and television broadcasts, including VH-1 *Storytellers*, *A&E Live By Request*, PBS *Sessions at 54th Street*, VH-1 *Live at the Hard Rock*, as well as the last four *Pavarotti and Friends'* concerts, and others for Bravo, HBO and network television.—Howard Ferstler

Film Speed · The rate of film travel in a motion picture, typically 24 frames per second. If the speed is for whatever reason increased, as it is for television in some European countries (to 25 frames per second) the pitch of musical signals is raised significantly, almost a half-tone for each additional frame per second.

Filter · An electronic device that removes unwanted frequencies from a sound signal. Three basic types are used: (1) a low-pass filter screens all but the lower frequencies; (2) a high-pass filter screens all but the higher frequencies; (3) a band-pass filter allows only a certain range of the audio frequency spectrum to pass, screening the lower and higher components. Audio filters are used in equalization and to combat rumble and hum on early discs.

Fine, C. Robert, 1922–1982 · After a stint as a radar specialist in the Marines during World War II, Fine joined Majestic Records in New York City, and from there he moved to Reeves Sound, as chief engineer. During the 1950s, he was an innovator in the new science of multi-channel sound for motion pictures, and he joined with Arthur Loew to head up a special recording operation dedicated to the production of MGM Perspecta Sound films. In the late 1960s, he also developed a process that would allow for the transmission of video pictures over regular telephone lines. He went on to found his own recording studio, Fine Sound, and went on to pioneer in the production of superior sounding stereophonic LP recordings, including those mastered with 35-mm motion picture film stock. Active in the Audio Engineering Society from its beginnings, Fine was chairman of the New York section at the time of his death. He had received a fellowship from the Society in 1973.—Howard Ferstler

Fisher, Avery, March 4, 1906–February 26, 1994 · An audio industry pioneer, musician, and philanthropist, Fisher was born in Brooklyn, graduated from New York University in 1929, and worked professionally for two publishing firms. His main interest was audio, however, and in 1937, in partnership with Herman Scott (who later went on to found his own company), he began Philharmonic Radio, which specialized in tuners, amplifiers, and speakers. In 1945, he sold Philharmonic and started a new company, Fisher Radio, which produced famously high quality high fidelity components. Fisher could produce products of that caliber, because made a point of hiring first-rate technicians away from European companies that could not pay as well as he could.

Fisher is known for producing the first commercially available transistor amplifier, and in 1956, his company produced the first stereo radio and phonograph combination. From 1959 through 1961, the company made important improvements in AM/FM tuner design. As the audio industry became more oriented toward mass-market products, Fisher decided to sell out to Emerson, and later on, Emerson sold the company to Sanyo, in Japan. Fisher continued to be a consultant for both companies.

As a philanthropist, he was very influential, and was a member of the boards of the New York Philharmonic, Chamber Music Society of Lincoln Center, and the Marlboro Festival. Fisher also endowed two award projects, the Avery Fisher Prize, a tax-free, $25,000 award to young American instrumentalists, and the Fisher Career Grant, a $10,000 fund against which recipients can draw for career-related expenses. Lincoln Center's Philharmonic Hall was renamed Avery Fisher Hall after he donated $10.5 million to the refurbishing project. Interestingly, Lincoln Center was built over the site where Fisher's first company was located.—Howard Ferstler

Flanging · In tape recording, a kind of phasing effect achieved by slowing the tape movement.

Flat Response · The ability of an audio system or audio component to produce a constant output level throughout the audio frequency range. A perfect response would exhibit a zero dB level difference from 20 to 20,000 Hz; however, speaker-room combinations, even good ones, often show deviations exceeding +/- 5 dB. An outstanding set up (got that way by means of an excellent room, excellent speakers, proper speaker placement, and perhaps a bit of assistance from a good equalizer) should be able to get that down to +/- 2 dB. Most good audio amplifiers, compact disc and DVD players, and digital recorders have negligible variations over the audible bandwidth.—Howard Ferstler

Fleming, Ambrose, Sir, November 29, 1849–April 18, 1940 · A British engineer, born in Lancaster, who worked as a consultant for Guglielmo Marconi when the Italian inventor succeeded in transatlantic broadcasting. In 1899, he conducted experiments on the "Edison-effect" and in 1904, he patented the Diode (British no. 24,850; 1904, and U.S. no. 803684). Fleming's work was followed by that of Lee De Forest, who transformed the Diode into the Audion. He died in Sidmouth, England.

Fletcher, Harvey, September 11, 1884–July 23, 1981 · Born and raised in Provo, Utah, Fletcher received his early training at Brigham Young University, and graduated in 1907. Continuing study at the University of Chicago, he, along with Robert A. Millikan, measured the charge of an electron. (Millikan won the Nobel Prize for this work.) This fundamental research contributed greatly to the field of electronics, which led to the development of the radio and television industry. Upon completion of his studies at the University of Chicago, Fletcher was awarded a Ph.D. summa cum laude, which was the first ever granted by the Physics Department of that university. After graduation, he returned to Brigham Young University and was appointed Chairman of the Physics Department, in 1911.

In 1916, he went to work at Western Electric Company in New York, where he was assigned to do research in sound. In 1927, he became Director of Acoustical Research at Bell Telephone Laboratories, and in 1933, he was appointed Director of Physical Research, continuing in that position until 1949. During his career, he published 51 papers, 19 patents, and 2 books, *Speech and Hearing* (1929), and *Speech and Hearing in Communication* (1953), which are accepted treatises on the subject. Working with W.A. Munson, Fletcher helped to formulate the well-known Fletcher-Munson equal loudness curves in 1933, and also guided the development of the Western Electric hearing aid (the Model 2A), the first such device to use vacuum tubes. He was also the first to introduce the group audiometer into the school classroom, initiating a program of testing the hearing of school children all over the country.

Fletcher was the first individual to demonstrate stereophonic transmission and stereophonic recording. In 1939, while working with Leopold Stokowski, he presented a concert featuring three-channel stereophonic recording to a capacity crowd in Carnegie Hall in New York. In 1949, He became professor of electrical engineering at Columbia University, and stayed there until 1952. He then moved back to Utah, where he became Chairman of the Department of Engineering Science, in 1953. From 1966 until his death, he was actively involved in the study of musical tones.

Fletcher helped found the Acoustical Society of America and was president from 1929 until 1931. In 1949, he became an honorary fellow of the ASA, and in 1957, he was awarded the Society's gold medal. He was president of the American Society for Hard of Hearing (1929–1930), an honorary member of the Audio Engineering Society (1952, winning the Society's Potts medal in 1958), a member of the National Academy of Sciences and an honorary member of the American Speech and Hearing Society. He was awarded the Louis E. Levy Medal for physical measurements of audition by the Franklin Institute in 1924, was elected vice president of the America Association for the Advancement of Science in 1937, and was president of the American Physical Society in 1945. He was a member of the American Institute of Electrical Engineers (IEEE), Phi Beta Kappa, Sigma Xi, and an honorary member of Sigma Pi Sigma. He received the Gold Medal from the Society of Motion Picture and Television Engineers for development of sound motion pictures.—Howard Ferstler

Fletcher-Munson Effect · A characteristic of human hearing that gives the ear variable sensitivity to frequencies, with the result that low frequencies—and less noticeably high frequencies—are perceived to be less loud than they really are. An audio system may endeavor to compensate for this factor by enhancing the projection of those frequencies that are not received naturally at their correct intensity. This is accomplished through loudness controls in the amplifiers or receivers. The concept is similar to that of equalization, except that it deals with a human imbalance instead of one stemming from the recording/playback process. Fletcher-Munson Curves are graphic representations of frequencies showing which ones are susceptible, and to what degree, to the Fletcher-Munson Effect.

Flutter · A wavering of pitch produced by analog playback equipment. The immediate cause may be fluctuation in turntable speed or tape-transport speed in a tape deck. It may also result from up-and-down movement of the turntable or disc surface. The latter is often called warp wow. Flutter is most evident on notes of long duration, especially at upper frequencies, so it is particularly annoying in piano recordings or bell tones. The National Association of Broadcasters (NAB) has a standard for cassette decks, requiring that flutter shall not exceed 0.2 percent. For open-reel recorders the NAB standard varies, with tape speed, from .05 percent to 0.10 percent. Modern digital recording and playback systems should have no audible flutter at all. *See also* WOW.—Rev. by Howard Ferstler

Flutter Echo · A multiple echo with quick fluctuations.

FM · *See* FREQUENCY MODULATION (FM).

Foldback · A method of cueing performers as they record, by sending signals through their headphones.

45-RPM Discs · Records revolving at 45 rpm were introduced by RCA Victor in the United States in February 1949. They were seven inches in diameter, made first of vinyl and later of polystyrene. Victor intended that the 45 would compete with the Columbia LP in the classical music field; it did have the same groove dimensions and audio quality. Victor made a two-speed turntable (78 rpm and 45 rpm), while Columbia sold a turntable for 78 rpm and 33 1/3 rpm. The Victor player had a 10-disc changing apparatus to make up for the 45's short playing time, which was no more than five minutes 20 seconds. Consumers, forced to choose between the rival turntables and discs, selected the more convenient LP. Victor phased out the 45 and the so-called war of the speeds was won by Columbia. Ironically, each company then began to see the advantages of using the other's new format. Columbia began producing 45-rpm discs of popular songs in late 1950 that carried one song on a side (or two songs, in the extended-play [EP] format), which proved quickly successful with younger buyers. Victor embraced the LP, and used the 45-rpm for popular recordings. By late 1951, both manufacturers were selling three-speed turntables and discs in all the speeds. By 1954, the sales of 45s in the United States reached 200 million, almost entirely in the pop market.

Fosgate, James, December 5, 1937– · Born in Indianapolis, Indiana, Fosgate, whose father owned a radio and TV repair shop, was exposed to electronics at an early age, and was essentially self-trained in audio technology. Later on, he was employed by the Bell System and worked on microwave, video, and carrier systems. In 1970, some years after leaving Bell, he started Fosgate Electronics. The company was later renamed Rockford Fosgate, and the current larger organization concentrates on the production of high-end automotive sound systems. In the early 1980s, he started Fosgate Research (merging in 1986 with Audionics of Oregon, to form Fosgate Audionics, also a branch of Rockford), which continues to specialize in the manufacturing of high-quality surround-sound processors, speakers, and amplifiers.

Fosgate began his career in multichannel audio with the "Tate" surround technology, a quadraphonic circuit, and worked with Peter Scheiber, the inventor of matrix surround decoding. He has made major technical contributions to the advancement of sound reproduction in both home and automobile audio systems. These include pioneering work in the design of sophisticated equalizers, very high-quality amplifiers, surround processors, and surround technologies (including his proprietary Six-Axis system and the Pro Logic II system currently being licensed to the industry by Dolby Labs), as well as a THX surround speaker specifically designed to automatically switch to either a monopole or dipole. He has received several CES Design and Engineering awards, and numerous Audio Video International Awards through the years. He currently has more than 25 worldwide patents in effect, with others still pending.—Howard Ferstler

Foster, Edward J., August 10, 1938– · Born in New York City and raised there and in Bethel, Connecticut, Foster became interested in science as a child and began servicing radios and television sets when he was 12. In 1955, he was among 40 Westinghouse (now funded by Intel) Science Talent Search (STS) winners, with a thesis entitled "Factors Influencing High Fidelity Reproduction in Audio Amplifiers." He went on to work for Electro-Mechanical Research (EMR) and Data Control Systems, going on to earn a B.S. degree in physics from Fordham University in 1959, and graduating with honors and first in class. He went on to work for Shepard Industries in 1960 and 1961 (joining the same people he initially worked with at EMR), doing research in analog and digital tape recorder development and manufacturing. In 1961, he founded S.E.D Memories, and there, he developed the first NASA-approved recording heads for interplanetary use. In 1964, he earned an M.S. degree in solid-state physics from Syracuse University,

and between 1963 and 1973, he worked for CBS Laboratories in various positions, including Branch Manager of Electromechanical Systems Research. As if technological interests were not enough, in 1973, he earned an MBA degree in organizational behavior and finance from Iona College, and between 1973 and 1976, he was Vice President of Technology at By-Word Corporation, where he developed wireless communication systems for museums, historic sites, and for transmission to automobile radios. Since 1976, he has been president of Diversified Science Laboratories, where he specializes in technical and marketing consultation, product development, and product evaluation for major audio-, broadcast-, and recording-industry clients.

Foster has been awarded Woodrow Wilson, National Science Foundation and National Defense Fellowships, is a member of the Institute of Electrical and Electronics Engineers (IEEE), and has been elected to membership in Sigma Xi and Delta Mu Delta national honor societies in science and business. A member of the Audio Engineering Society, he was made a Fellow of the organization in 1980, currently serves on the Board of Editors of the Journal of the AES, and was elected the AES Vice President for the Eastern Region USA/Canada in 1995. He is Deputy Technical Advisor to the U.S. National Committee to the IEC (SC100C), has written two books, has published extensively in technical and mainstream journals (including a current position as Technical Editor of *Pro Audio Review* and a Senior Contributing Editor to *Audio/Video International*), and has presented numerous papers at AES and IEEE conventions. He served as Session Chairman at the AES 46th and 49th Conventions, and was Workshops & Seminars Chair for the AES 95th Convention. Foster has also been Chair of the EIA/CEG Amplifier and Tape Recorder Standards

Committees, is a member of the EIA/CEG R-3 Steering Committee, and is involved with most EIA/CEG standards activity. He has been called as an expert witness before the U.S. Senate in patent cases, and is listed in Marquis *Who's Who in Science and Engineering* and *Who's Who in America.*—Howard Ferstler

Four Channel Stereo · *See* QUADRA-PHONIC RECORDING.

Franssen Effect · Originally formulated by Nico V. Franssen, the Franssen effect is the phenomenon that allows the leading edge of a bass signal to be localized elsewhere from where the body and tail end of the signal is reproduced. The phenomenon is one reason that subwoofer/satellite speaker systems with small satellites and only one subwoofer can simulate an array of larger systems. *See also* PRECEDENCE EFFECT.—Howard Ferstler

Franssen, Nico Valentinus, 1926–December 25, 1979 · After completing grammar school in his native Netherlands, Franssen studied at Delft University of Technology, where he earned a degree in electrical engineering in 1952 and went on to win his doctorate in 1960, with a thesis that involved a study of directional hearing. He had already gone to work for Philips in 1954, in the organization's research laboratories, and remained with the company until his death. Franssen was musically as well as scientifically gifted, and was well versed in the fields of hearing, architectural acoustics, electro-acoustics, and musical instruments, holding patents in some areas, and authoring numerous papers. His most important contribution to audio and recording technology involved his theories on directional hearing, which were based upon "attack" phenomena. He also discovered that by using a multiple-channel surround system, acoustic feedback could be reduced and a higher-level ampli-

fication achieved. *See also* FRANSSEN EFFECT.—Howard Ferstler

Frayne, John George, July 8, 1894–October 31, 1990 · A pioneer in film sound, Frayne was born in Ireland and migrated to the USA as a young man. He earned an A.B. degree from Ripon College, and later on won his doctorate from the University of Minnesota. He first worked for Western Electric, and later on joined the Westrex Corporation, where he did pioneering work in magnetic recording on film. In 1959, he joined Datalab, a division of Consolidated Electrodynamics, in Pasadena, California. While working for those companies, he also developed a noise-reduction system for motion-picture use, as well as methods for the measurement of intermodulation distortion.

Perhaps Frayne's most notable achievement for the history of recorded sound was his development of the Westrex 3-A cutter head, which launched the stereophonic LP record. While at Westrex, he also fostered the use of magnetic recording on motion-picture film, instead of magnetic tape, which allowed for greater dynamic range and reduced print through in the era before Dolby and dbx noise reduction. (The 35-mm technology was used by Everest and Mercury records to produce some of the best-sounding releases of the era.) Another project involved working with Bart Locanthi on horn-loaded loudspeakers for motion-picture-theater use. He also co-authored, with Halley Wolfe, *Elements of Sound Recording* (1949), which was the first handbook on the art and science of recording, and which contains information that is still useful five decades after it was published. Frayne was president of the Society of Motion Picture and Television Engineers from 1955 to 1956, and won several awards from that organization. Among many other awards, Frayne won the Audio Engineering Society Gold Medal in 1978 and an honorary membership in 1985, won the SMPTE Samuel L. Warner memorial Medal Award in 1959, and also won three awards from the Academy of Motion Picture Arts and Sciences, including the 1984 Gordon E. Sawyer Award in 1984, recognizing him as an individual whose technological contributions brought credit to the industry.—Howard Ferstler

Frequency · The rate of vibration of a sound wave; the characteristic that determines the pitch of the signal. *See also* AUDIO FREQUENCY.

Frequency Distortion · *See* DISTORTION, 2.

Frequency Modulation (FM) · The method of radio transmission in which an audio wave is impressed on a so-called carrier wave (of higher frequency). The carrier wave undergoes modification of frequency, but not of amplitude. The modulation process, and the demodulation process of the FM receiver, gives a signal transmission that is much less affected by background noise and static than AM radio.

Frequency Response · The ability of an audio system or component to reproduce the input signals at their original frequencies. In an amplifier, a uniform response is desired, one that does not favor or degrade any segment of the audio spectrum (*see* FLAT RESPONSE). When an amplifier emphasizes particular frequencies, the output signal is distorted (*see* DISTORTION, 1.) In specifications for an audio device, frequency response is often stated in decibels (dB) for a specified segment of the audio spectrum, for example, plus or minus 3 dB from 20 Hz to 20 kHz.

Fried, Irving M. · *See* LOUDSPEAKER, 5.

Full Frequency Range Recordings (ffrr) · A recording system developed by Arthur Charles Haddy, based on submarine detection devices. Decca Record Co. marketed it in the United States in 1946, with great success. A long-coil, moving-coil recording cutting head was used, later modified into a feedback recorder. When discs thus made were played on Decca's new Piccadilly portable, which had a light magnetic cartridge with sapphire stylus, and a three-tube amplifier, the spectrum covered was 50–14,000 Hz, outperforming all competing machines of the time.

Fundamental Frequency · The first harmonic (lowest frequency) of a musical sound; the basic identifying vibration that determines the pitch of the sound. Fundamentals of very low frequency, such as the lowest C on a piano keyboard, are not reproducible in certain recording systems; however, the pitch of a sound may be supplied by the human hearing mechanism even when the fundamental is inaudible. This is done by perception of the second harmonic (i.e., the first overtone), which has twice the frequency of the fundamental and sounds one octave higher. Unless the fundamental or the second harmonic is audible, the pitch cannot be recognized. During the acoustic recording era (before 1924), the lower range fundamentals were often missing. *See also* AUDIO FREQUENCY.

Fuzz · A form of distortion deliberately induced to give a special effect with electronic instruments—for example, guitars, via a device known as a fuzz-box. A harsh timbre can be achieved by means of a frequency multiplier that adds complex harmonics to the fundamental tones.

G

Gain · *See* AMPLIFICATION.

Gaisberg, William, 1878–November 5, 1918 · Recording engineer and executive, brother of Fred Gaisberg, usually called Will. He worked in the Volta Laboratory in Washington, then moved to Philadelphia and opened (with his brother) the first disc recording studio in 1896 or 1897. He went with his brother to London in 1898 to co-manage with him the recording department of the new Berliner firm, the Gramophone Co. While Fred Gaisberg was on his trip to the Far East in 1902, Will brought the temperamental opera star Francesco Tamagno in to record, paying him the first royalties of the record industry. A victim of wartime gassing, which occurred as he was making the first on-site documentary recording (of a gas shell bombardment near Lille), he died in England.

Gap · In tape recording, the space between the record head and the tape. In open-reel recording, the normal gap is between 100 and 500 microinches. In cassettes, the normal gap is 50 microinches. To minimize distortion, especially in higher frequencies, the gap has to be absolutely straight. *See also* GAP ALIGNMENT.

Gap Alignment · The adjustment of the magnetic gap in tape recording. Adjustment in relation to the direction of tape motion is called azimuth alignment; the desired angle is exactly 90°, and even a slight deviation results in loss of high frequency response. Lateral alignment refers to adjustment of the gap parallel to the plane of the tape. Pole face alignment refers to the rotation of the contact surface in a plane, at right angles to the direction of tape motion.

Gaumont, Leon, May 10, 1864–1946 · French inventor, photographer, and motion picture producer, born in Paris. He has a place in the history sound recording as the first person to speak publicly on film, in an address to the Societe Française de la Photographie, November 1902. Gaumont founded a company bearing his name to make and sell photographic equipment in 1885, and then was a backer and collaborator of inventor Georges Demeny. This led to the production of the film apparatus called the Bioscope in 1895. He made feature films in the early 1900s, both in London and Paris, and established branches in Germany and America. The first practical sound system for films, linking a projector and phonograph electrically, was his work; in his demonstration cited above the sound was faint, so he improved it with a compressed air amplifier. His firm used the air-jet principle to make the Elgephone disc record player (operated with a gas jet) in 1906. He also made two-minute wax cylinders.

General Electric Co. · An American firm established in 1892, the result of a merger between the Edison General Electric Co. and the Thomson-Houston Co. Thomas Edison was one of the original directors, but he left the firm in 1894. Various electric products were produced successfully. General Electric (GE) was one of the companies that participated in the establishment of RCA, then sold its RCA holdings in 1930 because of an antitrust ruling. The company was involved in development of the Panatrope, Brunswick's all-electric phonograph of 1926. It also perfected the Photophone sound film method. GE research led to one of the prototype magnetic stereo cartridges in 1958. The British affiliate, General Electric Co., Ltd., was a notable high-fidelity equipment manufacturer in the 1950s.

GE bought RCA in 1986, including the National Broadcasting Co., and including RCA Victor Records (which GE then sold to Bertelsmann). The company continues to manufacture and sell consumer audio products, including radios, televisions, and VCRs.

Gerzon, Michael, 1945–May 6, 1996 · A notable researcher in the fields of acoustics, surround sound, digital reverberation techniques, and signal processing, and father of the ambisonic recording technique that was built upon the pioneering discoveries of Alan Blumlein, Gerzon spent his childhood in Birmingham, England, and graduated from Oxford, with a degree in mathematics, in 1967. After a spell at Oxford's Mathematical Institute, he worked for 20 years as a consultant on digital audio, video, and computer projects.

In addition to his work in surround sound, Gerzon was also responsible for the theory behind the coincident, four-cardioid-capsule cluster Soundfield microphone (with matrixed "B-format" and decoded, steerable 2/4-channel outputs) that was produced by Calrec in 1975. In 1971 and 1976, he published papers on multi-channel versions of the Schroder-Loagan algorithms for unitary networks, a methodology that permits the design of true stereo-in stereo-out reverb algorithms with complex directional patterns of echoes related to the stereo position of individual input sounds.

In the 1980s, Gerzon moved on to digital audio and video, laying the foundation for many contemporary systems. With Peter Craven, he wrote the theory for noise shaping, which lets recording studios squeeze higher fidelity on to compact discs. By 1992, he had published over 100 papers on a variety of topics, ranging from the digitally and mathematically arcane to how to record a typical rock-music group. In designing equipment for the consumer, he was able to bridge the gap between abstract mathematical ideals and the cost constraints of the real world. He had won an Audio Engineering Society Fellowship in 1978 for his work on directional psychoacoustics, won the Society's Gold Medal in 1991, and won the AES Award for Excellence in 1992.—Howard Ferstler

Gilliland, Ezra Torrance, 1848–May 13, 1903 · American inventor and record industry executive, born in Adrian, Michigan. He was a telegraph operator during the Civil War, and then became interested in the telephone. Among his inventions were the telephone switchboard, and the exchange. Gilliland was for many years in charge of the Bell Telephone Company's laboratory in Boston, and he was one of the organizers of the Western Electric Co. He became an associate of Thomas A. Edison and general agent for the Edison Phonograph Co. in 1887. He made the first working model of the new type of Edison phonograph, based on the 1878 British patent, and developed other Edison ideas. As payment for his work, Edison gave Gilliland exclusive sales rights in the United States on Edison products. The Gilliland (Edison) Sales Co. was established to handle those transactions in June 1888. Gilliland patented the Spectacle device, which permitted an easy switch from record to playback mode on the phonograph (U.S. no. 386,974) and made improvements on it; it was used until after 1900 on Edison business machines. A financial imbroglio led to a break with Edison, and to a sale of the Gilliland stock to Jesse H. Lippincott in June 1888 for $250,000. He became associated with the Automatic Phonograph Exhibition Co., and secured a patent on a coin-op for them (no. 443,254) in 1890. Gilliland died in Pelham Manor, New York.

Goldmark, Peter Carl, December 2, 1906– December 8, 1977 · Engineer and inventor, born in Budapest. He was a grandnephew of the composer Carl Goldmark, and son of a chemist and inventor. His interests combined music and science; he played piano and cello, and set up a laboratory at home. He studied in Berlin and took a doctorate in physics in Vienna, beginning the study of television that occupied much of his life. He worked as an engineer in Britain, then in 1933 moved to the United States, becoming associated with CBS in 1936. His greatest achievements with Columbia were the development of color television transmitters and receivers, and the creation of the vinyl long-playing microgroove record. Goldmark and his staff also developed improvements in record turntables, a lightweight tone arm, and a sapphire needle. He was director of engineering research and development at CBS from 1944 to 1950 (interrupted for wartime research on radar), then vice president for engineering research and development (1950–1954) and president of the CBS Laboratories from 1954 until his retirement in 1971. He held about 160 patents of his own, in addition to proprietary developments at CBS. Goldmark was also a university faculty member at Yale and the University of Pennsylvania. He died in Harrison, N.Y.

Goodall, Charles Stanley, May 31, 1934– · One of the industry's more accomplished recording engineers, Goodall went to work for Decca at a very young age, in 1949, becoming involved in a variety of engineering tasks. During the period between 1953 and 1957, he refined his knowledge of disc cutting, starting with 78 rpm acetates, moving on to 45 rpm discs, then to the LP, and beginning in 1957, he began working on experimental stereo cutting. He was one three individuals on the staff who cut all Decca's early stereo releases.

Between 1959 and 1965, he was promoted to senior cutting engineer, and became responsible for the final versions of all Decca stereo releases, including the first of the Vienna Solti *Ring* recordings. In 1966, he moved temporarily to London Records of Canada (in Montreal) to train their resident cutting engineer and help standardize U.K. and Canadian disc-cutting practices. In 1968, he returned to England, worked as a location engineer, and also began working as a balance engineer, arranging studio set-ups, microphone techniques, and mixer operation. In 1970, he was given responsibility of working with The Academy of St. Martins in the Field, beginning a long and successful association with the orchestra, Neville Marriner, and the Argo label. After being promoted to senior balance engineer, in 1975, he recorded numerous works for Decca and Argo, and in 1980, after Decca was taken over by Polygram, he began a three-year association with the Boston Pops Orchestra and John Williams.

Other long-term associations include the Radio Orchestra Berlin and the San Francisco Symphony Orchestra, plus similar long-term arrangements with solo artists such as Vladimer Ashkenazy, Dietrich Fischer-Dieskau, Birgit Fassbinder, and Jorge Bolet. Goodall also has worked with the Chicago Symphony, the Concertgebouw, and the Montreal Symphony. Individual performers include Murray Perahia, Joshua Bell, Joan Sutherland, Marilyn Horne, and Luciano Pavarotti. In 1985, he also co-engineered Decca's first all-digital recording, *Blue Skies* with Kiri

Te Kanawa and Nelson Riddle. Goodall officially retired in 1994, although he freelanced for Decca two more years on ten different projects. During his career, he has won numerous awards for his technical accomplishments, including three Gold Record awards, the Gramophone Magazine Award, and many additional European awards. Recordings he has worked on have received four technical Grammy nominations for his work, and two of them won (1994 and 1996).—Howard Ferstler

Goodman, Paul, February 16, 1927– · One of America's most accomplished recording engineers, Goodman graduated from high school in June of 1945, worked at the Tungsol electric works from the summer of 1945 until enlisting in the Army in September of 1946. He was assigned to the American Forces Network (AFN) in Hoechst, Germany, where he worked as a recording and broadcast technician, and began to learn his trade. After leaving the Army in 1948, he attended Newark College of Engineering for two years, and then went on to work at various radio stations in the New York area, as well as at the United Nations, where he helped to man the communications section during the General Assembly meetings. During this time, he also had a chance to study at the RCA Institute in New York City. While at the Institute, his growing talents were recognized, and he was hired by RCA Records hired him in 1956 as a mastering technician. Within two years, he was moved into the "live area" as an editing, re-recording, and live engineer, and went on to edit many of the opera recordings RCA had recorded in Rome and England. As a staff RCA engineer he also recorded material for many other recording companies, including Columbia/Sony, Bridge, Muse, Atlantic, Musical Heritage Society, New World, Nonesuch, Deutsche Grammophon, and Angel, and did some work for PBS. He retired from RCA in 1992.

Goodman has recorded most of the major ensembles in the USA, including the Boston Symphony, the New York Philharmonic, the Philadelphia Orchestra, the Chicago Symphony Orchestra, the Dallas Symphony Orchestra, and the Saint Louis Symphony Orchestra. He has also recorded numerous Broadway shows, including *42nd Street*, *The King and I*, *Porgy and Bess*, *Into the Woods*, *Jerome Robbins Broadway*, *Fifty Million Frencmen*, *La Cage Aux Folles*, and *Anything Goes*, among many others. The artists and smaller ensembles he has recorded include Artur Rubinstein, Emanuel Ax, Yo-Yo Ma, Sonny Stitt, Vladimir Horowitz, Carla Bley, John Coltrane, André Previn, Roland Kirk, Sonny Rollins, the Canadian Brass, the Cleveland String Quartet, and the Tokyo String Quartet, among many others. He has been nominated for the engineering Grammy award an impressive 22 times and won three of those nominations, for Mahler's *Symphony Number Seven* (RCA, 1982 winner), Prokofiev's *Symphony Number Five* (RCA, 1984 winner), and the highly regarded *Horowitz: The Studio Recordings* (DGG, 1986 winner). Retired now from recording, he has been a member of the National Academy of Recorded Arts and Science (NARAS) both at the local level and as a delegate to the national conventions.—Howard Ferstler

Gouraud, George Edward, Colonel, 1842?–1912 · American military officer, later a recording industry executive. He was the agent sent by Edison to the United Kingdom in 1888, responsible for promoting the "improved phonograph." He brought a model to London in June 1888, quickly got the attention of the press, and then offered a demonstration for journalists at his home on August 15, 1888.

At this and other public demonstrations prominent persons recorded their voices for the ages; among them were Robert Browning, William Gladstone, Henry

Irving, Cardinal Manning, Florence Nightingale, Arthur Sullivan, and Alfred Tennyson. Publicity was highly favorable, but the mechanics of recording still held innumerable hazards, and actual sales of the phonograph were modest. He also sent out traveling agents to the provinces.

Gramophone · The name given by Emil Berliner to his 1887 talking machine, which was the first to use discs as the recording medium. In the 19th century, the term remained exclusive to disc machines, indeed to the laterally cut disc machine; a cylinder player was known as a phonograph. This terminological distinction faded in the United States (Edison referred to his Diamond Disc Phonograph, Columbia to its Disc Graphophone), and the word gramophone was not much used after the early 1900s. In Britain, it has remained in use, although phonograph has become its synonym.

The first patent on a disc gramophone was actually held by Edison, and he made experimental disc records in 1878. In 1879, Ducretet marketed a tinfoil disc player in France. *See also* DISC.

Gramophone Record · A disc recording, in present-day terminology synonymous with phonograph record; but the latter term originally applied only to cylinder recordings. British usage has favored retention of the word gramophone for record players and gramophone records for the discs, while American usage has moved to phonograph in both instances.

Graphic Equalizer · A device that divides the audio spectrum into segments, usually from 12 to 36 parts, and adjusts the amount of energy that passes through each of them. The results are equalization patterns, used to establish the original recording characteristics.

Graphophone · A device for recording and reproducing sounds, patented in the United States on May 4, 1886 (no. 341,214) by Chichester A. Bell and Charles Sumner Tainter, resulting from their research in the Volta Laboratory. It was a wax cylinder machine, and like Edison's phonograph, was primarily intended to accept and replay business dictation. Production was handled by the American Graphophone Co., and marketing by the Columbia Phonograph Co. General.

Greenhill, J. E. · British inventor and "lecturer on scientific matters." He devised the first satisfactory spring motor for the cylinder phonograph, and put it into production in 1893. The machine was made by William Fitch, of Clerkenwell, and sold by J. Lewis Young. Greenhill Mechanical Phonograph Motor Co. was the name of his firm, located in London. The motor is illustrated in Frow and Sefl 1978, p. 164.

Greenleaf, Christopher, August 17, 1949– · An independent recording engineer working in North America, Europe, and East Asia, primarily in the fields of early, organ, and chamber music, Greenleaf earned a B.A. degree from Indiana University in 1972. His recordings for the Gotham Early Music Foundation, in New York City, The Frederick Collection (of 19th-century grand pianos), the Boston Early Music Festival, and prominent international performers have aired over NPR and PRI, as well as on a number of overseas networks. In addition, he has engineered material for Hyperion, Wildboar, EMI, Stradivarius, CRI, Albany, Gothic, Titanic, Centaur, Gasparo, NPR, and Lyrichord, as well as other labels.

As an annotator, repertoire consultant, and recording engineer, Greenleaf has worked with individuals and ensembles to realize album projects noted for their unified esthetic and high standards of production. In addition to his recording work, his translations from German, French, and Flemish-Dutch have appeared in concert programs and albums from Tokyo to Vienna, and encompass writings from the 16th century on. When not engineering recordings, he works as an acoustic consultant in the designing or sonic improvement of halls and churches, as well as for private clients. An important part of Greenleaf's work also involves presenting recording symposia for performers of all ages at conservatories and music schools. Prior to its demise, he also wrote full-time for *Audio* magazine and had been a regular contributor to *Stereo Review*, *High Fidelity*, and *Popular Mechanics*, before becoming a full-time recording engineer, translator, and acoustic consultant.—Howard Ferstler

Greiner, Richard A., 1931– · Now retired as Emeritus Professor from the University of Wisconsin, after a career spanning 36 years, Dr. Greiner earned a reputation as not only one of the more stellar engineering minds in the field of audio, but was equally well regarded as an all-around researcher, engineer, and scientist.

After earning undergraduate and masters degrees in physics (1954 and 1955), with a concentration in molecular spectroscopy, nuclear spectroscopy, and solid state physics, he went on to receive a Ph.D. in Electrical Engineering from the University of Wisconsin in 1957. His doctoral work involved photoconductivity and electrical conductivity in solids, which were directly related to the behavior of semiconductor devices. In 1961, he published a textbook, *Semiconductor Devices and Applications* (McGraw-Hill), which dealt with the physics of discrete transistor operation and applications of a variety of solid-state devices to analog and digital circuits.

From 1979 through 1992, he headed a university research program in acoustics, electro-acoustics, instrumentation, digital signal processing, and adaptive digital control. The core of this research, which resulted in 95 graduate students receiving degrees, was supported by industrial

grants. His lifelong interest in high-fidelity sound reproduction and audio engineering resulted in numerous articles about power amplifiers and loudspeaker system design. These efforts lead to his election as a Fellow of the Audio Engineering Society in 1984.

Since retirement in 1992, Dr. Greiner has continued to consult in acoustics, noise, and vibration control for industrial applications. In addition to his AES membership, he is a member of Eta Kappa Nu, Sigma Xi, Phi Kappa Phi, Tau Beta Pi, Kappa Eta Kappa, and the Institute of Electrical and Electronics Engineers.—Howard Ferstler

Griesinger, David, March 27, 1944– · Born in Cleveland, Ohio, fascinated with music, acoustics, and recording from early childhood, Griesinger attended University School, in Shaker Heights, Ohio, and graduated in 1962. He went on to study at Harvard, getting his B.A. in 1966, earning a Ph.D. in solid-state physics, in 1976, and going on to do additional lecture work in physics at the university in 1977 and 1978. In addition to his scientific studies, he also honed his musical skills by being in the Harvard Glee Club (1963–1966), the Harvard University Choir (1966–1976), and the Boston Camerata (1975–1980). Although his advanced degree was in physics, Griesinger eventually went back to his first love: music, sound recording, and acoustics.

Those interests led him to study the way human neurology decodes the sound field around us into streams that contain information about the direction, distance, and content of sound sources, as well as information about the size, shape, and quality of the playback space. This has lead to a number of papers by him in the field of acoustics and sound perception, to a modest career as a professional sound recording engineer, and to several commercial products, with one of them being the first successful device for generating artificial reverberation with digital techniques: the

Model 224 digital reverberator from Lexicon Corporation. Since that time, he has continued to develop reverberation products for the company.

Griesinger has also produced a number of additional papers on recording techniques, and he has also produced a number of commercially released stereo recordings, as well as a series of highly regarded, consumer-oriented surround products from Lexicon, starting with the CP series of surround processors, and leading to the very highly refined DC and MC series, with the Logic 7 decoding system. His interest in the perception of musical acoustics also led to the development of the LARES reverberation enhancement system, which is capable of substantially improving the musical acoustics of concert halls and opera houses. The system has been installed worldwide, and is currently being used in the Copenhagen Opera, the Amsterdam Opera, the Berlin Staatsoper, and the Adelaide Festival Theater, among many others.—Howard Ferstler

Groove · The wonder of the disc record groove is usually described simplistically. To say that sound waves are cut into analog patterns on a disc surface, or that a groove is the track inscribed by the cutting stylus, is correct; but it suggests an image of compression that is quite misleading. A bundle of sound, like a spoken syllable or an orchestral chord, is not transcribed in a single spot on the record surface, but in a cluster of spots. This cluster is a link in the chain that is the record groove. On a 12-inch, 78-rpm disc, the groove is approximately 244 yards long, or would be in a pristine state. As recording takes place, the spiral path is undulated to account for the pitch, loudness, duration, and timbre of each sound; thus, the final groove length is more like 480 yards. Average speed of the stylus over the groove is about 32 inches per second, if the turntable is revolving at 78 rpm.

The appearance of a groove when a single note is recorded in it is defined by many factors. A sound wave generated by the sounding of a musical note, or tone, is possessed of four basic attributes: pitch, amplitude, timbre, and duration. Pitch is shown in the groove by the periodic repetition of cyclic patterns: the number of cycles (or Hz) determining the place of the tone in the audio frequency range. The patterns themselves, the vibrations, have a size that depends on the intensity of the sound signal; the size, or amplitude, varies with the intensity of the sound, whereas the cyclic frequency is constant as long as the pitch remains the same. Timbre—sometimes referred to as tone quality—results from the characteristics of the instruments or voices that produce tones. In the sound wave, and its analog in the groove shape, the timbre results in distinctive shaping of the cyclic curves. Duration is not exactly a quality of the tone, but it does affect the groove appearance by determining its length. A tone lasting one-fourth of a second takes up eight inches of groove space, and shows a regular pattern of curves diminishing in size as the tone fades. At this point, it should be restated that the groove in a record (disc or cylinder) might be vertical or lateral (see also DISC). Its shape in either case will be the same in terms of movement on and away from its centerline.

Groove shape is complicated by the sounding of complex tones—the kind usually produced by singers and instrumentalists, as opposed to the pure tones produced by tuning forks. Complex tones have perceptible patterns of harmonics, often called overtones or partials. With the presence of harmonics, the wave shape is much elaborated. Yet, up to this point, it is imaginable that the groove shape might be "read" and analyzed to determine by inspection what the sound source could have been. (One can expect certain patterns of harmonics from certain instruments, regardless of the pitches they play.) Nevertheless, groove shape becomes vastly more intricate when it carries the impulses produced by more than one instrument or voice simultaneously. Each source contributes its own frequency, amplitude, and timbre characteristics to the composite shape of the line. The idea of reading or analyzing such a shape to determine exactly what instruments were involved is forbidding, though one always assumes a computer can be taught to do anything. It is even more stunning to realize that the human ear is able to do just this—read and analyze the squiggles on a groove and make correct judgments about the nature of the sound source, and to do this instantly without apparent effort. *See also* HEARING.

Few attempts were made to standardize the shape of the groove in discs until the arrival of electrical recording in the mid-1920s. By 1935, consensus in the industry produced grooves of a V-shape, with an included angle of 80–85° and a bottom radius of 0.002–0.003 inches. At the top of the groove, the width was 0.004–0.006 inches. The actual depth of the groove was about 21 mils in the mid-1930s, as compared with 4 mils in 1908 and 25 mils in the standard British disc of 1962.

Although there is obviously only one groove on a record side, the number of turns or spirals it makes are often named "grooves." The number of turns on a standard 78 varied from 90 to 120 per inch (38–48 per centimeters). The ridge between turns was about 0.004 inch across.

Microgroove discs—usually termed long-playing records, or LPs—are aptly named because the grooves are much smaller than the 78 grooves. LPs have a bottom radius of less than 0.00025 inch (0.0064 millimeters) and a top width of no less than 0.0022 inch; depth is about 0.00125 inch. The included angle is about 90°, with about 200 to 300 turns per inch.

The groove of a stereo disc has to carry two channels of signal information. It does so by inscribing each signal on one side of the groove, one arm of the V, with the axis of operation. *See also* GROOVE SPEED.

Groove Speed · The rate of movement of the disc groove beneath the stylus. It varies with the position of the groove track on the disc surface, even though the turntable maintains a constant rate of revolutions per minute. On a 10-inch disc, for example, groove speed is about twice as fast on the outermost turn of the spiral as it is on the innermost point. *See also* GROOVE; DISC.

Group Delay · In audio systems, the rate of change of phase shift with respect to frequency. The rate of change is a measure of the slope of the phase shift verses linear frequency. If this plot is a straight line, meaning that the delay causes a phase shift that is proportional to frequency, it is said to have a constant phase shift, or a linear-phase characteristic. Therefore, the device exhibiting this characteristic is said to be phase linear. In acoustics, a system that approaches this standard is commonly referred to as a minimum-phase system. Group delay is considered by some to be important with loudspeaker performance, although it is debatable if it is audible in typical listening rooms unless it is pretty extreme.—Howard Ferstler

Grundig, Max, May 7, 1909–December 8, 1990 [website: www.grundig.com] · German electronics industry executive, born in Nuremburg. After training in electronics during World War II, he became successful in radio marketing after World War II with models known as Heinzelmanns or Goblins, introduced in 1946. A self-contained, portable "carrying case" model radio was introduced three years later. By this time, Grundig was the largest manufacturer of radios in Europe. In 1951, the firm introduced the Reporter 300, its first tape recorder. In 1958, the firm introduced the first combined stereo phonograph and tape recorder. Philips acquired a majority of the stock in the firm in 1984, and operated it for the next 16 years. In 2000, Dr. Anton Kathrein, owner of Kathrein Werke AG, acquired controlling interest in the firm. The company continues to manufacture audio, video, and consumer electronic equipment.

Guardband · The space between tracks on a magnetic tape.

Guest, Lionel, 1880–1935 · British engineer, co-inventor (with H. O. Merriman) of the moving coil recording head for electric disc recording, British patent no. 141,790 (1920).

Gun Microphone · A microphone with a long narrow tube along the axis, thus resembling a rifle, leading also to the name "rifle microphone."

H

Haas Effect · *See* PRECEDENCE EFFECT.

Haddy, Arthur Charles, May 16, 1906–December 18, 1989 · British audio engineer, born in Newbury, Berkshire. He was an apprentice for a radio firm, then worked for Western Electric in the late 1920s. He joined Crystalate Gramophone Record Manufacturing Co., Ltd., and remained with the company until 1937, developing improvements in studio equipment. His moving-iron cutting stylus made it possible to raise the upper limit on the recordable spectrum, from 8,000 Hz to 12,000 Hz. Haddy worked with Decca Record Co., Ltd., when the firm acquired Crystalate in 1937, and supervised research on various wartime devices. The most important of these for the history of sound recording was his work on the detection of sonic differences between German and British submarine propellers. Because the differences lay in the upper frequency range, Haddy managed to raise the response of his cutter head to 15,000 Hz. After the war, his innovation was applied to Decca's Full Frequency Range Recording (fffr) system, marking the beginning of high fidelity recording. Later he conducted major research in stereo, and in videodisc technology. In 1970, he received the Audio Engineering Society's Emile Berliner Award "for pioneering development of wide-range recording and playback heads and for his significant part in the international adoption of the 45/45 stereo disc recording."

Hafler Circuit · A simple surround-sound ambiance-simulation technique developed by David Hafler in the 1960s, and made available from his company, Dynaco, in a device called the Quadaptor. It used a left-minus-right extraction process with two-channel source material. Unlike some more complex and effective extraction technologies, such as Dolby Surround, the Hafler circuit did not require additional amplification for the surround, "ambiance" channel. *See also* AMBIANCE EXTRACTION; DOLBY SURROUND SOUND.—Howard Ferstler

Hafler, David, February 7, 1919–May 25, 2003 · Interested in music and music reproduction since childhood, Hafler built his first audio system in 1938, and then went on to earn a degree in mathematics from the University of Pennsylvania in 1940. Although his first post-graduate job involved work as a statistician, the war put him into the U.S. Coast Guard from 1942 until 1945, and during that time, he served as a communications officer, specializing in loran, sonar, and radio equipment. The experience further enhanced his interest in electronics, and after the war, he joined with Herb Keroes to found Acro Products in 1949, specializing in the production of high-quality transformers for use in audio amplifier systems. Hafler also supplied schematic diagrams that allowed an individual to build an amplifier around his transformer. After six successful years of producing transformers, Hafler joined with Edward Laurent in 1955 to co-found the Dynaco Corporation, an enterprise that built completed amplifier units and sold them in kit form at reduced cost. One salient characteristic of his designs was their (for that time) high power output, thereby helping to facilitate the success of the new, low-efficiency, acoustic-suspension speakers beginning to show up in the marketplace. The company went on to build and market preamplifiers and tuners, and imported tone arms and cartridges, as well as a tape deck, all sold under the Dynaco name.

Hafler sold the company to Tyco in 1969, although he stayed on as a consultant for an additional three years. During that time, Dynaco started to import speaker systems built by Scanspeak, selling them under the Dynaco name (the model A-25 being the most notable). Hafler also came up with the Hafler Circuit, a passive, four-speaker ambiance-extraction device that was based upon the research of Peter Scheiber, and sold by Dynaco as the "Quadaptor."

After leaving Dynaco in 1971, Hafler bought a half interest in Ortofon, which itself became part of Harman International in 1977. While at Ortofon, he was awarded a Fellowship in the Audio Engineering Society in 1972. In 1978, he started The David Hafler Company, which replicated what had been done with Dynaco by provided high-quality amplifiers and preamplifiers at reasonable prices, in both kit form and assembled. In 1984, the Hafler's company merged with the Acoustat speaker company and the Hafler Company itself was sold to the Rockford Corporation in 1988, with Hafler himself afterward retiring. An avid chess enthusiast and member of the U.S. Chess Federation, Hafler has one of the world's outstanding collection of chess sets. *See also* HAFLER CIRCUIT; AMBIANCE EXTRACTION.—Howard Ferstler

Half-Speed Mastering · In analog recording systems, a technique of cutting a mas-

ter disc at half the speed of playback time (twice the playback time), thereby reducing distortion levels. The process also offers better dynamic range and improved frequency response. Digital systems gain no benefits from techniques of this kind, and indeed, it is possible to dub digital material at speeds that are faster than standard with no loss in signal quality. *See also* AUDIOPHILE RECORDING.—Rev. by Howard Ferstler

Hall Acoustics · *See* ROOM ACOUSTICS.

Hall, David, August 10, 1951– · Hall earned a degree in mechanical engineering from Case Institute of Technology, in 1974, and is considered by some to be the father of super-quality subwoofers for home-audio use. A versatile and innovative engineer, he has designed a number of machines used in the development of balloon angioplasty, and also patented the design of a hand-held test tachometer. His notable accomplishment in the field of high-fidelity sound reproduction was the design of a subwoofer system that made use of servo-feedback circuitry to keep bass distortion at extraordinarily low levels. This revolution helped to usher in the era of subwoofer/satellite systems, possibly the most significant advance in speaker-system technology because the acoustic-suspension woofer allowed good speaker systems to be built to reasonably small size. In 1983, Hall founded Velodyne Acoustics, which under his leadership continues to specialize in the design, construction, and distribution of both state-of-the-art and affordable subwoofer systems for home-audio use. Hall is a member of the Audio Engineering Society, Acoustical Society of America, and the IEEE, and holds seven patents on product designs.—Howard Ferstler

Hanson, Oscar B. · Hanson ranks among the greatest of the first generation of broadcast engineers. His radio career began in 1912 when he attended the Marconi School in New York, now continuing as the RCA Institute. Completing his course in "wireless," he obtained his operator's license and went to sea. From 1917 to 1920, he worked in the testing department of the Marconi Company, becoming Chief Testing Engineer. When radio broadcasting came into being Hanson became associated with WAAM, a pioneer station in Newark, New Jersey. In 1922, he accepted a position as assistant to the plant engineer at WEAF, then owned and operated by the American Telephone and Telegraph Company. With the formation of the National Broadcasting Company in 1926, he went with the new company and directed technical operations and engineering activities for the rest of his career. No other individual had a greater influence on the look and feel of NBC's broadcast facilities during the network's first decade and a half. Hanson's design masterpiece was the Radio City studio complex in New York, opened in the fall of 1933. He also designed the network's Hollywood facilities. The Audio Engineering Society honored him with its Potts award in 1956.—Howard Ferstler

Harman, Sidney, August 5, 1918– · A major leader in the home-audio equipment business. Harman worked for a public address equipment manufacturer back in the 1940s and decided to bring some equipment home to see if it could be utilized for home-audio use. The results were impressive, both to Harman and his friends, and in 1952, he and engineer Bernard Kardon founded the Harman Kardon company, and were among a handful of individuals who basically started the consumer-oriented hi-fi industry, going so far as to produce the first hi-fi audio receiver in 1954. Harman bought out Kardon in 1956, and in the early 1970s, he began experimenting at his Tennessee factory with a new management technique called the Bolivar Project, which was a precursor to the TQM policies of the 1990s. The Bolivar Project involved cooperative labor-management schedules and goals, and the publicity from the project resulted in Harman being appointed Deputy Secretary of the Department of Commerce between 1977 and 1979, during the Carter administration.

Before Harman came to Washington, he sold his company to Beatrice Foods to avoid a conflict of interest. In 1980, however, after leaving government service he formed Harman International Industries by repurchasing several of the enterprises he had sold to Beatrice, including JBL, Harman Kardon, Infinity, and Epicure. Over time, Harman International acquired additional companies, including UREI, Soundcraft, Allen & Heath, Studer, DOD, Lexicon, AKG, BSS, Orban, dbx, Quested, and Turbosound.

Over the years, Harman, whose thesis was titled "Business and Education—New Experiments, New Hope," earning him a Ph.D. in social psychology, has made a priority of educational support and funding. He is a founder of the Program on Technology, Public Policy and Human Development at the John F. Kennedy School of Government, Harvard University, and is a member of the Advisory Committee of the Science, Technology and Public Policy Program at the same institution. In addition, he is the chairman of the Executive Committee of BENS (Business Executives for National Security); chairman of the Program Committee of the Board of The Aspen Institute for Humanistic Studies; a trustee of the Carter Center; a board member with National Alliance of Business; and a member of the Leadership Institute of the University of Southern California. He also served for three years as president of Friends World College, a worldwide experimental Quaker college. Dr. Harman has been a trustee of the Martin Luther King Center for Social Change, the Los Angeles Philharmonic Association, and the National Symphony Orchestra. He is also a member of the Council on Foreign Relations, the Council on Competitiveness, and is a member of the Board of Advisors at the Carter Center of Emory University. Dr. Harman has written extensively on productivity, quality of working life, and economic policy in *Newsweek* magazine, the *Washington Post*, and *The Christian Science Monitor*. He is the co-author, with Daniel Yankelovich, of *Starting With The People*, published by Houghton Mifflin in 1988.—Howard Ferstler

Harmonic · Any frequency in the audio spectrum that is an integral multiple of a fundamental tone. A pure tone is one that contains nothing but the fundamental (such as the pitch of a tuning fork); it is said to have one harmonic, which is equal to the fundamental. Aside from pure tones, all musical sounds are composite tones, consisting of fundamentals and harmonics of higher frequency that they generate. Harmonics above the fundamental are called overtones; thus, the first overtone is the second harmonic. The physical cause of the overtones is that vibrating bodies, such as strings or pipes of air, vibrate simultaneously as a whole and in sections of 1/2, 1/4, 1/3, etc., of their lengths.

Overtones have much smaller amplitudes than their fundamentals (1/5 to 1/50 of the volume) so they do not confuse the pitch frequency of the fundamental. Their effect is to define the timbre of the musical sound. The extent to which a recording or reproduction system can capture overtones is a measure of its success in achieving realistic depiction of vocal and instrumental quality.

Harmonic Distortion · *See* DISTORTION.

Harris, Gwin, 1897–1985 · Electrical engineer, an associate of Thomas Edison from 1919 to 1931. He supervised disc record production, experimented with electrical recording, and became product engineer in the radio division. Later he worked for Western Electric.

Hartridge, Donald, March 31, 1938– · Educated at Tiffin Boys' School, in Kingston, between 1949 and 1955, Hartridge spent two years in the Royal Air Force, before joining the British Broadcasting Corporation, in 1959. There, he was trained as a sound operator, worked at cutting vinyl disks for immediate broadcast, and edited tapes in over 40 languages. In 1962, he was retrained as a studio manager and transferred to BBC Northern Ireland, where he learned the craft of balance engineering, and worked extensively with the Northern Ireland Light Orchestra. In 1972, he accepted a post as senior sound supervisor with the then BBC Northern Symphony Orchestra (later renamed the BBC Philharmonic), and between 1972 and 1996, he engineered many thousand hours of recorded and live music from across the spectrum, including full orchestra, chamber groups, choirs, quartets, and even incidental music for television. He also designed and built a mobile trolley to allow for swift and reliable recording rigs during extensive touring commitments with the Philharmonic across Europe and America, and in Brazil, Hong Kong, Morocco, Oman, and Prague.

Between 1990 and 1996, Hartridge recorded over 40 compact discs with the BBC Philharmonic, working in close cooperation with Chandos records, and recorded additional CDs for numerous other companies including Nonesuch, Errato, Olympia, Naxos, and Collins. He also recorded cover disks for the BBC Music Magazine, several early Halle recordings, and several operas, including the first recording of Wagner's Rienzi, with Ted Downes.

Hartridge has been associated with several discs that won awards, including two Diapaisons d'Or from the French, as well as a Gramophone Magazine engineering award. Since 1996, he has been working as a freelance engineer, following the downsizing of BBC resources.—Howard Ferstler

HDCD (High Definition Compatible Digital) · Developed by Keith Johnson and Michael Pflaumer, in its purest form HDCD is a specialized noise-shaping, encoding/decoding system that employs dedicated compression during recording and expansion during playback. Supposedly, this allows the 16-bit technology used for the compact disc system to simulate a 20-bit system. Proper playback of certain HDCD encoded compact discs requires an outboard decoder. Without the decoder, the sound may appear somewhat compressed and overly reverberant. The system is mainly used by Reference Recordings, but a number of other companies are also using it, and in 1998 and 1999, more than 10% of all Grammy nominated discs were HDCD mastered.—Howard Ferstler

Head · See ERASE HEAD; PLAYBACK HEAD; RECORDING HEAD.

Head-Related Transfer Function (HRTF) · A characteristic of human hearing mechanism that allows us to localize sound sources in three-dimensional space. Many physical factors are involved: ear spacing, the frequency-response detecting ability of the inner ear, outer-ear shape, and even the shape of the head itself. Indeed, the HRTF is a surprisingly complicated function of four variables: three different space coordinates as well as frequency. In spherical coordinates, for distances greater than about one meter, the source is said to be in the far field, and the HRTF falls off inversely with range. Most HRTF measurements are made in the far field, which essentially reduces the HRTF to a function of azimuth, elevation, and frequency. Because of the different physical variables involved with HRTF, it is likely that no two single people hear the world in exactly the same way.

HRTF plays a big part in the formation of images with stereophonic sound reproduction and also with headphone performance with both standard stereo recordings and binaural sound recordings. Indeed, the HRTF captures all of the physical cues to source localization. Once you know the HRTF for the left and right ears, you can synthesize accurate binaural signals from a monaural source. *See also* CROSSTALK; INTERAURAL CROSS-TALK.—Howard Ferstler

Head Shell · The housing of a phonograph cartridge.

Headphone · An audio device (sometimes called earphone, or simply phone, and often in the plural form) designed to fit over the ears, presenting each with a miniature loudspeaker. The purpose is to allow for individual listening, without disturbance to others nearby, and to focus the listening experience by eliminating much environmental noise. New types of headphone do allow the entrance of external sounds: They are called "open-air," "hear-through," "high velocity," and "dynamic velocity" headphones. Piston speakers are used in less expensive headphones, and electrostatic transducers in more costly types. Low impedance models do not require a separate power amplifier, but the electrostatics and high impedance models do require one. Headphones may transmit monaural signals (both ears receiving the same one) or stereo signals, with the left and right ears receiving the same portions of the signal as full-size loudspeakers do.

Hearing · The remarkable organ that is the human ear is a miniature (about a cubic inch) sound system that includes the equivalents of "an impedance matcher, a wide-range mechanical analyzer, a mobile relay-and-amplification unit, a multi-channel transducer to convert mechanical energy to electrical energy, a system to maintain a delicate hydraulic balance, and an internal two-way communications system" [Stevens 1965, p. 38]. In the act of hearing, sound waves enter the canal of the outer ear and cause the eardrum to vibrate. Those vibrations are taken up by the ossicles of the middle ear, and transferred to the so-called oval window of the inner ear. This much of the process, complex as it is, no longer offers any puzzle to science, but when vibrations act upon the fluid-filled inner ear, certainty gives way to speculation. It is known that sound vibrations produce rippling waves across the basilar membrane of the cochlea, and it is reasonable to picture these waves as having the same contours as those that are drawn by acoustic instruments; indeed their contours are thought to be the same as the tracings of a phonautograph or the cuttings in a record groove. As the waves move along the cochlea, thousands of hair tips are bent, producing minute quantities of hydraulic pressure; this pressure is converted to electrical energy by the organ of corti at the end of the cochlea. And here we cross the border into mystery: The organ of corti transmits its electrical impulses through the nervous system to the brain in such a way that the source signal can be decoded into its original composite of frequencies, amplitudes, and timbres. Although it is comprehensible that a single pure sound wave (e.g., from a tuning fork) may be read and identified by the brain, so that the hearer is able to state what pitch has been struck, it is by no means clear how a signal made up of many pitches, amplitudes, and timbres can at the end of its passage through the ear be again sorted out into its components so that the hearer is able to distinguish it from other simi-

larly complex sounds. Indeed, it is not even clear how the ear and brain are able to distinguish among pitches in a simpler signal. A renowned specialist observes that "we must know how the vibrations produced by a sound are distributed along the length of the basilar membrane before we can understand how pitch is discriminated ... [but] it is hardly possible to observe any vibration in the nearly transparent gelatinous mass in the cochlea of a living organism" [Von Békésy 1960, p. 539]. In the resonance theory of Hermann Helmholtz, each of the transverse fibers of the basilar membrane is "tuned" to a different frequency, and is stimulated only by tones of that frequency. Because there are several thousand of those fibers, it may be further theorized that they are clustered in pitch regions, and that certain ones in a given cluster resonate to different patterns of harmonics; if one accepts that view, it is possible to credit the fibers with ability to discern the sources of tones, that is, different musical instruments. In addition, because each component of a complex sound is carried into the nervous system by distinct fibers, it is also possible to understand how the brain recognizes each bit in the mosaic of an orchestral chord. The trouble with the resonance theory is that the environment of the fibers appears to be hostile to such resonating: They are, after all, buried in a membrane and covered with a fluid.

A variety of theories have been based on the idea of a sound pattern that emerges as sinusoidal movement sets up a series of standing waves along the fibers. Each of these waves is perceived by the nervous system as a single tone, but, as Von Békésy comments, "Because the entire task of analysis is relegated to the nervous system, whose activities are completely unknown, it is not possible to draw any further conclusions on the basis of this theory." Von Békésy himself, after a lifetime of imaginative experimentation, was unable to answer the question of tone recognition and the question of how the ear resolves complex sounds.

Lacking any measurable evidence for the theories suggested previously, it is probably just as reasonable to approach the act of hearing in another way: "We may concede that one day the whole process, including the chemico-electrical actions in the brain, will be bared. The tone, however, will never be found. It is not an object to be found in the outer world; and the organ of corti, the nerves, and the brain are all part of the outer world. One might as well expect to find the soul by dissecting the body" (1965, p. 165).

As we depart from the rigid viewpoint of the physical sciences, we encounter other fascinating questions about "subjective" hearing—recently termed "psychoacoustics." Why, for instance, do we hear music with more pleasure than we hear a screeching noise? Why is a minor chord "sad"? How does our brain allow us to imagine, as we listen to a musical work, what had gone before and what is yet to be heard, and to remember simultaneously other performances of the work? Moreover, how does the brain establish, in response to a stereo recording, the source of the signal as somewhere between the loudspeakers?

Helmholtz, Hermann, August 31, 1821–September 8, 1894 · A groundbreaking German researcher in acoustics, physics, optics, and the physiological effects of sound, Helmholtz was born in Potsdam and initially studied medicine and natural science. From 1849 until 1871, he was professor of physiology at the universities of Königsberg, Bonn, and Heidelberg, and from 1871 until his death, he was professor of physics at the University of Berlin. Helmholtz was one of the great scientists of the nineteenth century, and his contributions to the science of sound were only part of his accomplishments. His analysis of musical signals resulted in the discovery that the tonal quality of a musical sound is created by the overtones or harmonics. In 1862, he published *The Sensations of Tone*, which formed the scientific basis for the study of acoustics. *See also* LOUDSPEAKER.—Howard Ferstler

Hertz (Hz) · The name often given to the unit of frequency formerly identified as one cycle per second. This designation, in use since 1967, was derived from the name of Heinrich R. Hertz, German physicist. One kilohertz (kHz) equals 1,000 cycles per second; one megahertz (MHz) equals 1,000,000 cycles per second.

Hertz, Heinrich Rudolf, February 22, 1857–January 1, 1894 · Modern electronic communication systems, as well as radar, all benefited from the research of Hertz, and his experiments on the reflection, refraction, polarization, interference, and velocity of electric waves triggered the invention of the wireless telegraph, and later on radio. Having received a magna cum laude Ph.D. from the University of Berlin in 1880, where he studied under Helmholtz, Hertz began his studies of the electromagnetic theory of James Clerk Maxwell in 1883. Indeed, he was the first to demonstrate experimentally the production and detection of Maxwell's waves and the validity of Maxwell's theorems.

Between 1885 and 1889, while he was professor of physics at the Karlsruhe Polytechnic, he produced electromagnetic waves in the laboratory and measured both their length and velocity, showing that the nature of their vibration and susceptibility to reflection and refraction were the same as those of light and heat waves. In 1888, in his physics classroom in Berlin, he generated electric waves by the oscillatory discharge of a condenser through a loop provided with a spark gap. With this arrangement, he had demonstrated that the velocity of radio waves was equal to that of light. Hertz was not sure there were any practical benefits possible from his research in this area, but his proofs of Maxwell's theories triggered a flurry of experimentation among other scientists, including Marconi. In 1889, he was appointed professor of physics at the University of Bonn. His writings were translated into English soon after their publication in German and include *Electric Waves* (1883), *Miscellaneous Papers* (1896), and *Principles of Mechanics* (1899). In recognition of his work, the unit of frequency of radio and acoustic waves (one cycle per second, abbreviated Hz) was named after him.—Howard Ferstler

Heyser, Richard, 1931–March 14, 1987 · An audio journalist and inventor who was awarded nine patents in the field of audio and communication techniques, including time-delay spectrometry (TDS), Heyser was by training a scientist at the Jet Propulsion Laboratory of the California Institute of Technology. In addition to his work on TDS, outlined in a 1967 Audio Engineering Society journal article, he published numerous other articles in both technical and popular audio magazines, and was widely known for his patience and ability to clearly present and communicate new and complex technical ideas. Heyser generously aided the AES not only through his technical contributions, but also through his service to its growth and organizational development as an Audio Engineering Society Governor and an AES Silver Medal recipient. He died shortly before he was able to assume office as the President of the Society.—Howard Ferstler

Hidley, Jack, January 29, 1967– · Interested in audio systems since he was 12 years old, Hidley was determined to be a loudspeaker designer by age 20. After five years of electrical engineering at California Polytechnic State University in San Luis Obispo, he went to work for NHT loudspeakers, in Benicia, California in 1992. At NHT, he participated in a wide range of activities, including the electrical, mechanical, and acoustical design of products. When International Jensen moved their Acoustic Research loudspeaker branch to Benicia in 1995, Hidley helped with product development at that company. Early in 1997, he left NHT and began work as an independent loudspeaker consultant, and in early 1998, he joined Vergence Technology (NHTPro) as chief design engineer. In 2001, he returned to NHT, and has been responsible for the design of some of their more notable systems.—Howard Ferstler

HI-FI · *See* HIGH FIDELITY (HI-FI).

HI-FI Video Sound Recording · The two-channel, videotape medium that makes use of specially encoded signals to carry the audio part of a video program. The Beta Hi-Fi version developed by Sony used the video heads on the VCR's rotating tape drum. The VHS Hi-Fi system developed by JVC has separate audio heads, also on the tape drum, in addition to the video heads. Hi-fi video sound, which must make use of Dolby matrixing if it cares to deliver surround sound, is not as capable as current digital systems, particularly the 5.1-channel versions. Nonetheless, it does have impressive performance, and it is more than able to handle the dynamics and clarity requirements of all but the most demanding matrixed-surround motion-picture material.—Howard Ferstler

High Fidelity (HI-FI) · The term given to realistic reproduction of sound, concerned mainly with its frequency-response range and smoothness, as well as distortion levels. The phrase came into use in the mid-1930s in the U.S. record business, although commercial recordings of that time had no deep bass capabilities, and high-range frequency response rarely exceeded 6 kHz. During the 1940s, the 78-rpm disc was able to cover a somewhat wider audio range and even had a fairly decent dynamic range, and because of this, a greater credibility was attached to the term. In the 1950s, there was a popular appetite for achieving maximum fidelity, expressed through the interest in separate components and in the purchase of audio kits to be constructed at home. Two channel "stereo" sound in the 1950s further enhanced playback realism, and got the wider public interested in the concept, particularly after the advent of small, high-quality speaker systems like those pioneered by Acoustic Research and KLH. Modern systems, employing digital technology in the electronic realm and very high-quality speaker designs, have expanded the concept to include bandwidth coverage over the full audible spectrum, dynamic range that can encompass even the most robust symphony orchestra playing, and surround-sound configurations that simulate live-music environments better than ever.—Rev. by Howard Ferstler

High Pass Filter · *See* FILTER.

Higham Amplifier · A sound amplifying device invented by Daniel Higham of Massachusetts, U.S. patent no. 678,566 (granted July 16, 1901). "Amplified vibrations were delivered by means of a variable tension device involving a cord running over an amber wheel, augmenting the pull from the stylus bar by force supplied by the motor turning the amber wheel" (Read). In 1904, the inventor formed the Higham-O-Phone Co., and developed the concept continually (six further patents were granted). The device was shown at the St. Louis Exposition of 1904, and was used in the 1905 Columbia Twentieth-Century Premier Graphophone (Model BC) and in the Home Premier (BM). Thomas Edison obtained the rights for use in the Kinetophone in 1912. [Koenigsberg 1990; Read and Welch 1976]

Hill and Dale · *See* VERTICAL CUT .

Hill and Dale Stereo Recording · An early version of stereophonic recording developed by Emory Cook. The problem with "hill-and-dale" was that it would have made earlier and contemporary lateral groove monaural recordings incompatible, with both channels being 180 degrees out of phase. Hill-and-dale stereo had been used by Bell Telephone Laboratories for the groundbreaking Leopold Stokowski recordings of 1933, and was used in monaural radio program transcription disks through the 1940s. Whatever advantages each had in the monaural format evaporated with the advent of stereo, because the major labels were looking for both compatibility and listener convenience. In 1957, the Recording Industry Association of America ruled that a mono-compatible system would be required, and Cook's system was bypassed.—Howard Ferstler

Hilliard, John Kenneth, October 22, 1901–March 21, 1989 · Born in Wyndmere, North Dakota, Hilliard was one of the most accomplished acoustical engineers of the past century. He received a B.S. in physics at Hamlin University in St. Paul Minnesota in 1925, and a B.S.E.E. at the University of Minnesota. He began work on a M.E.E., but left in 1928 before completing that degree to take a position with United Artists in Hollywood.

This was at the very beginning of the movie sound industry. The first full-length talking picture, *The Jazz Singer*, had been released the year before and there was a mad rush by all studios to develop sound motion pictures. Hilliard was selected from a group of engineers trained in physics, engineering, and acoustics to work at UA Studios, and was placed in charge of the recording, monitoring, and sound-editing operations for studio's first sound picture, *The Coquette*. He was forced by circumstances to develop many recording techniques that later became industry standards.

In 1933, Hilliard transferred to MGM's sound department. His first task was a systematic review and redesign of all recording amplifiers, concentrating on an existing phase-shift problem. The solution was to use transformers with very high self-inductance and relatively large coupling capacities. Transformers with these capabilities had been developed by Lansing Manufacturing Company and this resulted in Hilliard forming a business partnership with James B. Lansing. That connection subsequently led to their most successful collaboration, involving the design of a new, two-way loudspeaker system for theater use. Hilliard was the project manager for this system and was responsible for the overall concept, while Lansing was responsible for the development of the drive units. The end product was a loudspeaker system released in 1944, appropriately named the "Voice of the Theater," that became an industry standard. The work resulted in a technical-accomplishment award from the Academy of Motion Picture Arts and Sciences.

In 1946, Lansing left Altec to found Lansing Sound, Inc., whereupon Hilliard took over Lansing's vacated position as Vice President of Engineering, at Altec, and would hold that position until 1960. During this tenure at the company, Hilliard was responsible for the development of many significant products, including the refined 604B speaker driver, the 603, the "Lipstik" condenser microphone, and numerous amplifier and crossover designs. In 1960, Hilliard became director of the LTV Western Research Center, which was a branch of Altec Lansing's parent company. At LTV, he considerably broadened his field of work to include research on sonic booms, highway noise, hearing conservation, and gun silencing. He left in 1970 to undertake a decade-long career in consulting that focused on noise studies and architectural acoustics.

Hilliard was the author of *Motion Picture Sound Engineering* (1938), published more than 80 technical articles on sound, and received an honorary doctorate from the University of Hollywood, in 1951. He was also an active member of the Institute of Electrical and Electronics Engineers, the Society of Motion Picture and Television Engineers, and the Acoustical Society of America. A long-time member of the Audio Engineering Society, he was awarded the Society's John H. Potts award in 1961, which later became the Society's Gold Medal. *See also* LOUDSPEAKER.—Howard Ferstler

Hirsch, Julian, May 15, 1922– · Arguably the most accomplished and well-known consumer-audio product reviewer of the second half of the twentieth century, Hirsch earned an electrical engineering degree from Cooper Union in 1943, and went on to become an officer in the Army Signal Corps, as part of the forces occupying Japan after the war. After military service, he went to work for General Precision Labs, and later went on to work for Panoramic Instruments, which was later bought by Singer.

Hirsch had long been a ham-radio and sound-quality enthusiast, and his interest in audio eventually had him and three other enthusiasts found the first consumer-interest, audio-testing magazine, *The Audio League Report*. One notable achievement of the journal was the enthusiastic and accurate review it did on a new loudspeaker system being produced by a nearly unknown company at that time—Acoustic Research. The report on the company's revolutionary model AR-1 help to launch AR into the big leagues, and also helped to bring attention to Hirsch's skills as an audio columnist and consumer-product reviewer. The League magazine eventually was bought out, but Hirsch continued to write part time, and produced a number of pieces for *High Fidelity* magazine, while still employed by Singer/Panoramic.

He soon showed himself to be one of the most insightful writers in the business, and he was approached by the Ziff-Davis Company to become a full-time reviewer for *Stereo Review* magazine. He accepted the job and continued in that position until his retirement, in 1998. Hirsch defined the standards for levelheaded and honest audio journalism for over four decades, and during his long career, he was undoubtedly the most accomplished and straightforward product reviewer in the audio-magazine business.— Howard Ferstler

Hiss · Random noise of a sibilant character, a byproduct of tape recording for which no antidote existed until the advent of noise reduction systems. High-speed recording lowers the amount of hiss, but speed of playback has no effect on it.

Hodges, Ralph W., 1944–January 7, 1994 · Born in Hartford, Connecticut, Hodges was educated at several private schools, and went on to graduate from Columbia University in 1965. He joined *Stereo Review* magazine in 1969, and was named its technical editor in 1977. He left to work for Dolby Labs in 1979, but decided to turn to freelance writing and reviewing in 1984. He was contributing insightful monthly columns on the consumer-audio scene to *Stereo Review* right up until his death.— Howard Ferstler

Hoffay, J. · A New York firm, with a branch in London, active in 1915. It produced a disc player advertised as one whose sound does not penetrate walls, "no matter how loud it is inside the flat."

Hofmann, Tony · *See* LOUDSPEAKER, 2; KLH CORPORATION; KLOSS, HENRY.

Holman, Tomlinson, August 6, 1946– · A noted audio researcher and designer, Hol-man has a 1968 B.S. degree in Communications from the University of Illinois at Urbana-Champaign. During his career, he has worked for the Motion Picture Production Center at the University of Illinois, Advent Corporation (chief electrical engineer, assisting Henry Kloss), Apt Corporation (founder and chief engineer), Lucasfilm Ltd. (corporate technical director), and The University of Southern California (Professor in the School of Cinema-Television); during this time, he also started his own company, TMH Corporation. His notable design achievements include the Advent radio and receiver, several television and loudspeaker designs, the highly-regarded Apt/Holman preamplifier and power amplifier, and perhaps most significant of all, the THX Sound System for both theater and home-audio use.

In addition to numerous magazine essays, Holman published *5.1 Surround Sound Up and Running* (1997) and *Sound for Film and Television* (2002). Among other organizations, he is a Fellow of The Audio Engineering Society; a Fellow in the British Kinematograph Sound and Television Society; a Fellow and past Chairman of the Audio Recording and Reproduction Committee; an honorary member of the Society of Motion Picture and Television Engineers; a member of the Institute of Electrical and Electronics Engineers; and a member of the Acoustical Society of America. He has 7 U.S. patents, as well as 23 corresponding foreign patents.—Howard Ferstler

Holt, J. Gordon, April 19, 1939– · One of the most influential journalists in audio, Holt was born in Charlotte, NC, but moved early to Melbourne, Australia, where a music-appreciation course in school and a then "state-of-the-art" record player introduced him to excellent sound. He started collecting records, played them on his family's wind-up acoustical phonograph, and discovered that some phonographs sounded better than others.

Holt returned to the United States, and while earning a journalism degree from Lehigh University, he wrote articles for a magazine called *High Fidelity*, accepting a full-time position with them as an equipment reviewer after graduation. After many tiffs with the publisher about things Holt claimed to hear that the publisher insisted he could not, he left *High Fidelity* to become director of technical services for Paul Weathers, where he started a dealer newsletter that discussed the sound of equipment and recordings. When dealers started ordering extra copies for their customers, he suspected there might be a demand for such a publication, and left Weathers in 1963 to start *Stereophile Magazine*, which featured subjective, as opposed to wholly measurement-oriented, reviewing, thereby pioneering a trend in consumer-audio journalism.

In 1992, Holt sold the ailing magazine to Larry Archibald, who resuscitated it and later hired John Atkinson as editor. Holt stayed on as a contributor and did what he liked best—playing with unaffordable audio equipment and writing about it. Atkinson expanded the magazine's circulation, but took it in directions Holt had no sympathy with. Consequently he left in 1998, to do freelance writing. As of 2002, Gordon Holt was a regular reviewer for *Stereophile's Guide to Home Theater* and *The Absolute Sound*, and was self-publishing booklets of interest to audiophiles and home-theater enthusiasts. His long-time hobby remains recording orchestras.—Howard Ferstler

Home Recording · Making records at home (outside a studio) was always a possibility with cylinder phonographs, and remained one of their selling points in competition with disc machines. The earliest home disc maker was offered by the Neophone Co., Ltd. in Britain, around 1905. The earliest U.S. product was marketed by the Ameri-

can Home Recorder Co. in August 1920. An attachment advertised in 1924 permitted direct home recording from radio programming. Home disc cutting recorders were available from the mid-1920s on, used to make both transcriptions from radio broadcasts as well as personal records.

The introduction of home tape recording equipment after World War II led to a home-recording boom. Open reel tapes were used to record off the radio, TV, and LP records, plus for making personal recordings. Mixers and other equipment enabled hobbyists to create their own home studios. The introduction of the smaller and easier to use audiocassette in the 1960s led to a boom in recordings made for personal use; boom boxes and the later Walkman furthered the popularity of this format. The introduction of digital recording technology to the home market in the 1980s led to further interest in home recording; MiniDisc and other formats became popular for making personal recordings. In the 1990s, the ability to "rip and burn" soundfiles onto CDs using the home computer made piracy an increasing concern for record labels. Into the 21st century, the wide availability of sophisticated sound recording software allows individuals to make home recordings of a quality that could have only been achieved in a professional studio even a few years earlier. *See also* INSTANTANEOUS RECORDINGS.—Rev. by Carl Benson

Home Theater · Film reprints (usually 16 mm) of movies have been available on a limited basis for decades, but the concept never caught on for a variety of reasons. Since the late 1980s, however, video copies of motion pictures have been available for home playback, first as pre-recorded tape with hi-fi video sound (available for sale or rental), later on a smaller scale in laserdisc form, and more recently on a very large scale indeed as the DVD. Home theater has expanded to the point where it is a multimillion-dollar business, eclipsing the home-music business, and its success has resulted in dramatic, market-driven improvements to both audio and video technology. Today, home theater continues to boom, and videocassette and DVD movies (rentals and sales), as well as music videos, are a huge percentage of the total income generated by the entertainment industry. It can also be argued that modern audio-music sound reproduction in the home owes its current state-of-the-art sound quality to the home-theater technology and home-theater economics. *See also* SURROUND SOUND.—Howard Ferstler

Horizontal Tracking Error · The difference between the angle formed by the cutting stylus in disc recording (90°) and the angle formed by the playback cartridge to the disc surface. It results from the pivoting of the tone arm, and the consequent inward slant of the headshell. Distortion in the playback is proportional to the difference between the recording and playback angles. A tangential tone arm eliminates the problem.

Horn (I) · The device used in acoustic recording to capture the sound signal and transmit the vibrations to the cutting stylus.

Horn (II) · The device used in playback of records to amplify the vibrations taken from the disc or cylinder surface by the cartridge. Early recording and playback horns were in simple conical shape, giving poor efficiency and poor tonal quality. As results improved with the length of the horn, manufacturers made them longer and longer; by 1900, a playback horn of 56 inches was marketed, requiring a crane to hold it up.

Experiments led to the exponential horn, in which the cross-sectional area doubles with each increase of x inches in distance along the axis. By 1920, the exponential horn was universally accepted, and in 1925, the orthophonic horn formalized the design and increased the length. Horns were external at first, then (from the Victrola of 1906) were concealed inside the phonograph's cabinet; the concealment was achieved by folding the horn. Internal horns did not improve the sonic quality of the system, and in fact worsened it, but had cosmetic appeal; the term "hornless player" was used in advertising internal horn machines.

The first horns were of spun brass or copper, and brass remained a favored material. Wood horns were introduced in the Regina Hexaphone of 1908, and were in general use by 1911. Later, there were folding cardboard horns on portable machines. With the introduction of electrical recording, the loudspeaker replaced the horn. *See also* ACOUSTIC RECORDING; EDISON HORNS. For the type of horn used on a specific record player, see the player model under the manufacturer's name; for example, *see also* EDISON RECORD PLAYERS.

Hot Air Motor · A drive mechanism used in certain gramophones from about 1909 to 1914, based on the Stirling Cycle Engine patented in 1816 by Robert Stirling and James Stirling. It was an external combustion engine, fired by a methylated spirit burner; the fatal flaw in the design was that a flame was present, one that was difficult to stabilize. This feature, plus the cost— eight times the cost of a spring motor— and overall complexity of its mechanism, prevented the device from gaining wide acceptance. It did have quiet operation and maintained constant turntable speed. The motor was used in the Apollo and Maestrophone gramophones. [Evans, H. 1989]

Howl · Also known as howlaround or howlback. A shrieking animal-like noise that results from excessive buildup of feedback in a sound system. *See also* ACOUS-TIC FEEDBACK.

Hoxie, Charles A., February 26, 1867–October 13, 1941 · American electrical engineer, born in Constable, New York. He made an early career in photography, then in 1895 began to study electrical engineering by correspondence, and two years later was an electrician in Detroit. Hoxie moved to Brockton, Massachusetts, in 1899 to work for the Southern Massachusetts Telephone Co., and in 1901 became wire chief for the New England Telephone Co. He built in his home one of the first wireless transmitting and receiving sets. In 1902, he moved to Schenectady, New York, working first for the Hudson River Telephone Co., then in 1912 as an engineer for General Electric. He worked in the areas of telephony, as well as broader fields of electricity. During World War I, Hoxie was called on to improve radio communications, and developed the pallophotophone, which recorded sound on film for transmission. That invention was followed by the photophone, which converted the photographed film back into sound. The method was to project the exposed film in front of a photoelectric cell (U.S. patent no. 1,598,377); this was basically the Pallatrope system used by Brunswick discs in the later 1920s. It also was used in the synchronization of sound on talking film, with the film carrying both the audio and visual signals, demonstrated by General Electric in the 1922 motion picture *Wings*. This method eventually replaced the disc/film method used in *The Jazz Singer* (1927). Hoxie retired in 1932, and died in Alplaus, New York.

Hsu, Poh Ser, March 30, 1955– · A native of Singapore, with a civil-engineering doctorate from MIT, Hsu is noted for his reasonably priced but still very high-performance subwoofers. He is also an expert in econometrics and statistics, both of which have influenced his "form-is-function" designs. In addition to his role as chief engineer for his California-based company, Hsu Research, he is also a consultant in civil engineering, econometrics, and audio.—Howard Ferstler

Hum · A low droning sound originating in the alternating current power of an electrical device. In the United States, the hum frequency is 60 Hz (approximately B natural), but it may be the first or second overtone of 60 Hz, that is, 120 Hz (also B natural) or (approximately F sharp). In Europe the hum frequency is 50 Hz. Various reasons may be given for a hum in an audio system: multiple grounding, placement of components near a magnetic field, inadequate insulation, or faulty valves.

Hunt, Frederick, 1905–April 21, 1972 · After receiving two bachelor's degrees (one in the arts and one in engineering) from Ohio State University, and later earning a Ph.D. in physics from Harvard, Hunt became widely respected in both academic and government circles for his brilliant work in a variety of fields related to physics, communication engineering, and underwater sound. During the Second World War, he was instrumental in developing technologies that helped to destroy enemy submarines. He eventually won both the post of Rumford Professor of Physics and Gordon McKay Professor of Applied Physics at Harvard University, and was responsible for a number of innovative discoveries, with his most significant work being a brilliant analysis of transducers, with particular emphasis on phono pickups and record players. Among the numerous awards and honors he received during his lifetime were The Presidential Medal of Merit, the Audio Engineering Society's John H. Potts Award (later renamed the Gold Medal) and Emile Berliner Award (later renamed the Silver Medal), and the U.S. Navy's Distinguished Public Service award. Hunt was a member of numerous organizations, including the American Academy of Arts and Sciences and the Acoustical Society of America.—Howard Ferstler

Hunting · The result of a defect in an audio system that causes alternating speeds in the transport mechanism.

I

Image Enhancer · A stereo component that adds the impression of imaging to the sounds reproduced by the system. A potentiometer and two extra speakers are needed. The method is that of adjusting the delay time for signals as they reach the left and right ear of the listener.

Imaging · A characteristic, of advanced audio systems, that duplicates for the listener the placement of the input signals relative to each other. Thus, an orchestral recording will convey a sense of the sound space occupied by each instrument within the larger perceived "stage" of the orchestra itself. Imaging may also be used by the recording engineer to create artificial effects, manipulating the virtual locations of certain signals in departure from their actual placement. *See also* IMAGE ENHANCER.

Impedance · The total opposition (reactance and resistance) to the flow of current in an electric circuit; it is measured in ohms. In an audio system, matching of the impedance value among components will minimize distortion and maximize energy transfer. For loudspeakers wired in series, the total impedance is the sum of their individual impedances. For speakers wired in parallel, however, the total impedance is the sum of the reciprocals of the individual impedances, with the result inverted. For example, two 8-ohm speakers in parallel wiring have a total impedance of four ohms; calculated 1/8 + 1/8 = 1/4, inverted

to 4/1, or 4. *See also* MECHANICAL-ELECTRICAL ANALOGIES.

Inductance · The extent to which an electric circuit or component is able to store magnetic energy when current is flowing. It is measured in "Henrys." *See also* MECHANICAL-ELECTRICAL ANALOGIES.

Infinite Baffle · A loudspeaker enclosure (*see also* BAFFLE) designed to prevent sound waves emanating from the front of the speaker from reaching the back of the speaker. This is accomplished by means of a large open space behind the loudspeaker, causing the rear waves to be completely absorbed.

Infinity Loudspeakers · Founded in 1968, by Arnold Nudell, Cary Christie, and John Ulrich, Infinity quickly became a successful speaker building and marketing enterprise, specializing not only in affordable systems for mainstream consumers, but also producing some of the most monumentally impressive upscale speakers in the industry. The company also produced amplifiers and tone arms. Ulrich left in 1978, after the company was purchased from the original investors by EAD, and Cary, who was VP in charge of operations, product development, and engineering, continued running the operation along with Nudell, who was then President. In 1981, the Infinity was purchased from EAD by Harman International (which still has sole ownership), and under the new corporate banner the company continued to thrive, due mainly to a wise hands-off policy. In 1989, Nudell, who was president, left (he later helped to found Genesis Technologies), leaving Christie as the moving force behind the company. In 1994, Christie left to start still another company.

Some of the more noteworthy Infinity achievements were the first injected-molded polymer driver cones, the first high-efficiency electrostatic driver, the first servo-controlled subwoofer, the first genuinely low mass tone arm, the first class-D amplifier, the first fully integrated sub/sat system (the Servo Static), and the first electromagnetic drivers using high efficiency magnets: the EMIT and EMIM. The company continues to be a dominant force in the speaker business.—Howard Ferstler

Infrasonic Filter · A high-pass filter that is designed to remove audio signals below the audible frequency range. By doing this, components like woofer and subwoofer systems and amplifiers are spared the task of trying to reproduce non-musical signals that are inaudible.—Howard Ferstler

Injection Molding · The method of making a recording disc by injecting the liquefied plastic biscuit into a die cavity of the desired dimensions.

Input Selector · The control on a preamplifier or audio receiver, or even a monitor-type TV set, that allows the user to choose one signal source from multiple inputs hooked up to the system.—Howard Ferstler

Instantaneous Recordings · Records made for nonretail purposes, mostly in the 1930s and 1940s, by a direct to disc process. The material used was typically aluminum, coated with acetate or a nitrate lacquer to make a soft surface. The use of acetate gave the popular name "acetates" to these recordings.

Home recording was a popular use of instantaneous records in the United States from 1920. (In Britain, the Neophone Co., Ltd., had offered a home disc recorder ca. 1905.) Radio stations made transcription discs that way, and researchers made field recordings (some of those on zinc, a more durable material than acetate). Diameters were the same as for commercial discs, except for transcriptions and conference/speech records, which were usually 16 inches in diameter. Most ran at 78 rpm.

The earliest instantaneous records sold for home use in the United States were pre-grooved zinc blanks, six inches in diameter, sold as Echo Disc and Kodisk. They were offered by the American Home Recorder Co. of New York in August 1920. Because the recording method was still acoustic, the recordist had to shout into the horn, and was rewarded with only a faint return. With the arrival of electrical recording in 1925, it was possible to speak at normal volume into the microphone of the player, and to receive an amplified return; the medium was a plain metal disc, the best of them aluminum. The Speak-O-Phone Co. of New York, established in 1926, was a pioneer manufacturer.

Victor introduced a pre-grooved plastic "home record blank" in the early 1930s, to be used on a Victor home disc recorder. As it happened, the audio quality from the pre-grooved record was poorer than that from the ungrooved metal discs, and Victor's apparatus did not gain public acceptance.

An innovation of the early 1930s was the use of lacquer coated discs, first manufactured in France as Pyral records, and marketed in America from 1934 by Presto Recording Corp. of New York. The new surfaces allowed the direct to disc recording of all types of musical ensembles, including orchestras, and gave a clear reproduction. Radio stations embraced the lacquer disc, which could run 33 1/3 rpm on 16-inch blanks, to give uninterrupted programming long enough for broadcast purposes. Lacquer also replaced wax in the major recording studios as the material used for masters in the production of commercial recordings. The lacquer was applied to an aluminum or glass base, or later to inexpensive fiber or paper bases. Presto solved the problem of freshly cut thread clogging the grooves by means of a blower system introduced in 1940, but a more practical and less expensive solution was provided by Audio Devices, Inc.: a wiper blade that brushed the fresh threads toward the center of the disc. Eventually, a vacuum suction device was developed to draw off the threads.

Early lacquer-coated discs usually had three drive-pin holes, equally spaced around the center hole; the purpose was to secure the disc (onto drive pins on the turntable) and prevent slipping during the process. By 1940, there was a flourishing market for domestic disc recorders and their discs. The advent of the LP in 1948 had, in a few years, its application in the instantaneous field. Recordists of the 1950s could select from the 33 1/3, 45, or 78 rpm. Wire recording did not affect the home disc market, but tape recording ultimately obliterated it.

Manufacturers of the home recorders included Recordio (manufactured by Wilcox-Gay), Howard, Federal, Packard-Bell, Phono-Cord, Rek-O-Kut, Universal, and Motorola. Montgomery Ward sold their house brand Airline, and Sears, Roebuck sold Silvertone machines. The most popular models had a built-in radio, allowing direct recording from the air (a feature first available in 1924).

Preservation has been a serious problem with instantaneous discs because the surfaces permitted only a few playbacks without noticeable wear, and the unstable chemical structure leads to oxidation and brittleness of the entire record. A further problem arose from the breakdown of the bonding between the recording medium and its backing, so that the coating would peel or flake away. Finally, a greasy film often formed on the surfaces, from the castor oil used as an additive, rendering the disc unplayable. Archives seek to re-record an instantaneous disc immediately.—John Case

Institute of Electrical and Electronics Engineers [website: www.ieee.org] · An American organization established in 1963. It was formed in a merger of the American Institute of Electrical Engineers (established 1884) and the Institute of Radio Engineers (established 1912). The Institute sets standards in areas of impact on audio manufacture, among many other activities. More than 377,000 members are in 150 countries, consisting of scientists in all fields related to electrical and electronic engineering. The national organization is broken down into 10 regions, 37 societies, 4 councils, approximately 1,200 individual and joint society chapters, and 300 sections. A total of 1,000 student branches are located at colleges and universities worldwide. Among the 37 societies are several devoted to the study of sound and its reproduction, including the Broadcast Technology Society, Consumer Electronics Society. Support for the Engineering Societies Library in New York is an important activity. The IEEE established the IEEE History Center in 1980, in anticipation of its Centennial celebration in 1984. In 1990, the Center moved to the campus of Rutgers University, which became a cosponsor.

Insulator · A substance that presents a strong resistance to the flow of electric current, or—in an audio system—to the passage of sound waves. *See also* BAFFLE.

Integrated Amplifier · A device that unifies the functions of a power amplifier and a preamplifier. When the integrated amplifier is combined with a tuner, the result is called a receiver. *See also* AMPLIFIER.

Integrated Circuit · A group of electronic components joined into a single package. It is distinguished from a discrete circuit, which consists of individually packaged elements.

Intensity · In an audio system, the strength of a sound signal. It is measured in dynes or newtons, or in watts per square meter. The intensity of a sound depends first of all on the amplitude of its vibrations. This value is affected by various factors and components, especially the amplifier. For high fidelity reproduction, peak levels reach 20 dynes per square centimeter (100 dBs) above the threshold of hearing. What the listener finally perceives to be the relative intensity of the reproduced signal is referred to as loudness. Loudness is a physiological impression of the level of the sound; it has no quantitative measurement.

Intensity Stereo · *See* BLUMLEIN STEREO RECORDING.

Interaural Crosstalk · An effect created when the signals from a pair of stereo speakers are heard as individual events, instead of a coherent blend. The effect can muddy stereo imaging and soundstaging realism, particularly when not listening from the sweet spot. Several recording techniques, such as Q Sound, Spatializer, and Roland RSS, are designed to take advantage of the effect. *See also* CROSSTALK; HEAD-RELATED TRANSFER FUNCTION (HRTF).—Howard Ferstler

Intermodulation Distortion · *See* DISTORTION.

Internet Music · The music industry has provided content on the Internet since it was invented. When the USENET discussion groups system started in the 1980s, several were set aside for the discussion of genres and artists; now there are thousands. In the late 1980s, well before the dawn of the World Wide Web (WWW), "talkers," Internet Relay Chat (IRC), mail exploders (e-mail forums), and Multi-User Dungeons (MUDs) all had thriving music communities. In 1990, when Tim Berners-Lee of the European Particle Physics Laboratory unveiled his new system for moving intuitively between data and computers (aka the WWW), it is unlikely that he foresaw the revolutionary ripples this would send across the music industry. Record companies and artists (both signed and unsigned) used the web to promote their work. Magazines set up online versions and, like the labels and artists, reached a global audience for the first time. The WWW also revolutionized fanzine culture. Idiosyncratic publications with small print runs by fans of particular artists were transformed into multimedia centers accessible worldwide. Many of the earliest and best examples were adopted by the artists and given an official seal of approval. With the arrival of the MP3 format for saving and transferring music digitally, the Internet became a hotbed to hear both new, unsigned music from around the world, and for sharing and bootlegging pirate recordings. The latter reached a head with the Napster file sharing system court case in 2000.—Ian Peel

Ionophone Speaker · A type of tweeter that uses a corona discharge to produce a direct acoustic effect through electrical vibration. It operates by application of a high voltage radio frequency oscillation between a Kanthal electrode housed in a small quartz tube and a counter electrode; the result is a glow discharge of the Kanthal. Air pressures in the Kanthal tube vary with the audio modulation. If the open end of the tube is connected to an exponential horn, the horn will be without resonance or amplitude distortion.

iPod · A brand of portable, MP3 music player made by Apple Computer. Introduced in October 2001 and backed by an eye-catching media campaign, the iPod's sleek design and easy-to-use interface made it a favorite of the music consuming public. By early 2006, Apple had already sold more than 40 million iPods since their introduction in 2001, 30 million of these units were sold in 2005 alone. Apple commands about 70% of the U.S. digital music player market. Anthony Fadell, an independent audio engineer who was trying to find a market for his idea, conceived the concept and design of the iPod. Apple hired Fadell in 2001 to develop its audio products, where Fadell is currently Senior Director of iPod, iSight & Special Projects Group. The iPod is compatible with a variety of digital audio formats including MP3 (8 to 320 Kbps), MP3 VBR, AAC/M4A (8 to 320 Kbps), Protected AAC (from Apple iTunes music store, M4A, M4B, M4P), AIFF, and WAV. The iPod is not compatible with Microsoft Windows Media Player or Windows Media Audio formats, but can be used with a Windows machine in conjunction with Apple's popular iTunes music store. In addition to playing music, iPod models feature PDA functions, color digital photo storage, and games. By 2005, the fourth generation iPod lineup included the following models: iPod (20GB storage, in white); iPod Photo (30 GB, 60 GB storage, in white); iPod Special U2 Edition (20 GB storage, in red); iPod Mini (4 GB and 6 GB models in silver, blue, pink, or blue); the iPod Shuffle (512 MB, 1 GB storage); iPod Nano (1 and 2 GB models); and ability to play video files. A lithium polymer battery provides power. The original iPod could play 10 hours of continuous music and by 2005, this had been improved to about 15 hours for the iPod Photo model. Playback controls, such as the ability to shuffle music selections by song, album, or artist and to set equalization settings by type of music, make the iPod the standard by which other future MP3 players will be measured. *See also* WINDOWS MEDIA AUDIO (WMA). —Thom Holmes

J

Jaffe, Christopher, October 4, 1927– · A noted leader in the field of architectural acoustics, Jaffe graduated from the School of Engineering at Rensselaer Polytechnic Institute in 1949 and then went on to complete his graduate studies at Columbia University. He has been the consultant for more than 250 concert halls, opera houses, theaters, and music pavilions in the United States, Mexico, and the Far East. His company, Jaffe Holden Acoustics, designed the Sala Nezahualcóyotl in Mexico City and the Boettcher Concert Hall in Denver, the first surround concert halls built in North America. Among his other completed works are the Bass Performance Hall in Fort Worth, the renovation of the Kennedy Center Concert Hall and Severance Hall, home of the Cleveland Orchestra, and the four performance spaces at the Tokyo International Forum. No other acoustical consultant has worked with as many professional symphony orchestras, opera companies, dance groups, and theater companies. Dr. Jaffe has presented over 100 papers to professional societies and has received nine patents. He is a Fellow of the Acoustical Society of America, the Audio Engineering Society and the Institute of Acoustics, United Kingdom, and has held professorships at the Juilliard School, Rensselaer, and the City University of New York. Most recently, Jaffe received the Year 2000 Honor for Collaborative Achievement Award from the American Institute of Architects.—Howard Ferstler

Janszen, Arthur A., 1908–October 16, 1992 · A leading proponent and designer of electrostatic loudspeaker systems, Janszen was a native of Yoakum, Texas, and graduated from the University of Texas in 1943. A short time later, he joined the staff of the Underwater Sound Laboratory at Harvard, working to conceptualize sonar-guided torpedoes for the war effort. His war-work experience and his interest in audio allowed him to develop an interest in electrostatic loudspeaker technology, which had been developed in the 1920s, but which had also been dismissed as impractical. Using thin-film plastics technology, however, he introduced an electrostatic tweeter in 1952 (patented in 1953) that not only worked, but also was considered by many to be the best tweeter of that era. In 1954, he started his own company, Janszen Laboratory, Inc., and produced electrostatic tweeters for use with existing full-range systems having limited treble abilities. In 1959, he sold his company to KLH, in Cambridge Massachusetts, became a vice president of that company, and produced the legendary KLH Model 9 system. In 1960, he left KLH, joined Acoustech (also in Cambridge), and produced the legendary Acoustech 10 speaker system. From the early 1970s, until his death, he was a freelance consultant to various speaker manufacturers. *See also* LOUDSPEAKER.—Howard Ferstler

Japanese Victor Company (JVC) · A firm established in 1927 as a subsidiary of the Victor Talking Machine Co.; it manufactured records and record players. From

1929, when Mitsubishi and Sumitomo acquired substantial shares of the company, it was operated as an American-Japanese venture. Products were labeled Victor in Japan and JVC elsewhere until 1989, when the single label Victor/JVC was adopted for worldwide use. Matsushita now owns a majority of the stock shares in the firm.

Research at JVC resulted in the "45–45" stereo phonograph (1957); a color video tape recorder (1958), the VHS ("video home system," 1976), and various other audio devices. A recent product is the K2 Interface, a component designed to eliminate distortions in compact disc recording before the analog processing step. Another is the CD+G/M player, which adds still-picture graphics to the basic CD format.

In 1986, JVC America was established as a subsidiary, and in 1989 Nippon Victor (Europe) GmbH, was organized in Germany.

Jensen, Peter Laurits, 1886–1961 · Born in Denmark, and sometimes called the Danish Edison, Jensen began working in the laboratory of Valdemar Poulsen soon after Poulsen's public demonstration of the telegraphone at the 1900 Paris Exhibition. Jensen helped Poulsen develop a continuous wave arc transmitter that made voice transmissions from a radio station at Lyngby near Copenhagen in 1905. Jensen came to America in 1909, to help develop products for the Poulsen Wireless Telephone and Telegraph Company, then financed by Palo Alto investor Cyril Elwell. The idea was to compete with General Electric's system, which was based on Reginald Fessenden's patent. While building a radio station in Sacramento, he met Edwin Pridham who had an electrical engineering degree from Stanford and was working for the Elwell company.

Pridham helped Jensen learn English and American history. When Elwell was reorganized into Poulsen Wireless and Federal Telegraph, Pridham and Jensen left and joined the new Commercial Wireless and Development Company. In 1911, Jensen and Pridham moved to Napa, California, and began a small research laboratory. They experimented with Poulsen's arc radio transmitter, adding thicker wires connected to a diaphragm, and putting a coil of copper wire between magnets. In 1915, they made a working model of what they called the "electro-dynamic principle" for voice reproduction. The incorporated a gooseneck horn from an Edison phonograph on their device and sold the device, called a "Magnavox," as a public address system.

In 1917, Jensen and Pridham merged with the Sonora Phonograph Corp. and formed the Magnavox Company in San Francisco. In 1919, they provided loudspeakers for a speech by Woodrow Wilson in San Diego, and Magnavox gained national attention. Its speakers were used in the 1920 political conventions, by the campaigns of James Cox and Warren Harding, and at the March 4, 1921, Harding inauguration. AT&T dominated public address system technology, however, especially after the 1921 Armistice Day demonstration, and Magnavox shifted its focus to radio and phonographs.

Jensen left the company in 1925 and founded the Jensen Radio Manufacturing Co. in 1927, moved it to Chicago, and made improved loudspeakers with the help of engineer Hugh Knowles. In 1930, his company produced the first permanent-magnet loudspeaker system and also the first compression-driven horn tweeter. In 1936, it produced the first bass-reflex speaker enclosure and in 1942, it introduced the first commercial coaxial two-way loudspeaker. Jensen resigned from the company in 1943, because of disputes with his backers, and later founded Jensen Industries. (Magnavox continued to operate, eventually becoming part of Philips Electronics in the late 1980s, which continues to market home electronic items under this name.) In 1956, the King of Denmark knighted Jensen, and he was made an Honorary Member of the Audio Engineering Society in that same year. In 2001, he was inducted into the Consumer Electronics Hall of Fame.—Howard Ferstler

Johns, Glyn, February 15, 1942– · Born in Epsom, England, Johns is a noted recording engineer and producer who worked with several major rock acts of the 1970s and 1980s. He began his career as a would-be rock star in the early 1960s, but after failing to achieve much success, apprenticed with pop producer Shel Talmy. He began working with the Rolling Stones in 1965, with engineering credits on the group's *Their Satanic Majesties Request* (1968) and *Beggars Banquet* (1969). In 1968, he began working with the Steve Miller Band, producing, engineering, and performing as a backup musician on their landmark *Brave New World* album a year later. Johns did his most famous work in the early 1970s, producing and engineering all of The Who's albums from the 1970s and 1982's *It's Hard*; engineering for the Rolling Stones (*Sticky Fingers*, 1971; *Exile on Main Street*, 1972); producing The Faces (*A Nod Is as Good as a Wink to a Blind Horse*); and producing and engineering the Eagles' first two albums (their self-titled debut and the hit album *Desperado*). Later in the decade, he worked with Eric Clapton, notably on his *Slowhand* album in 1977. Johns has continued to produce through the 1980s and 1990s, working with lesser-known artists including Nanci Griffith, Belly, and John Hiatt, among many others.—Carl Benson

Johnson, Eldridge Reeves, February 6, 1867–November 14, 1945 · American recording engineer and industry executive, born in Wilmington, Delaware. He worked as a machinist in Philadelphia, then managed a small machine shop owned by Andrew Scull in Camden, New Jersey.

Johnson became Scull's partner in 1891, and bought the business from him in 1894. He built the spring motor for the Berliner gramophone, and in 1896 got the contract to supply them. In 1897 he and Alfred C. Clark developed the "improved gramophone" with a better motor and sound box; this is the machine immortalized in the Nipper painting (U.S. patent no. 601,198; filed August 19, 1897; granted March 22, 1898). He also devised the method of recording on wax blanks, which were then covered with gold leaf; this led to a master that produced stampers and finally a pressing of a new, smooth, relatively quiet surface. The records were the seven-inch "Improved Gram-O-Phone Records" that set the industry standard. The first 10-inch disc is also credited to Johnson, who reasoned that with a larger turntable and stronger motor the enhanced record size would be feasible. It sold as the Victor Monarch, following a favorable court decision in litigation brought by Frank Seaman. Johnson sold British rights to the wax process and the paper label to the Gramophone Co., which became the Victor partner in Europe. (In 1907 an agreement between the firms divided the world market between them.)

Johnson went on to receive 53 other patents, most of them in his own name alone. He developed the famous and frequently litigated tapering tone arm design "which would dominate the industry through the acoustical period" (Koenigsberg) and gained U.S. patent no. 814,786 (filed February 12, 1903; granted March 13, 1906). On August 8, 1900, he filed to patent a disc with a slightly recessed center area to allow placement of a paper label (U.S. no. 739,318; granted September 22, 1903). He developed a cabinet for a table model record player with all movable parts enclosed, for enhanced appearance, although the horn was still exposed during operation (U.S. patent no. 774,435; filed November 19, 1902;

granted November 8, 1904). It was a step toward the Victrola—the fully enclosed record player, also patented by Johnson (U.S. no. 856,704; filed December 8, 1904; granted June 11, 1907).

Johnson established the Consolidated Talking Machine Co. in 1900, and made both discs and players with the Nipper trademark; this firm merged with Berliner to become the Victor Talking Machine Co. (incorporated on October 3, 1901), with Johnson as president. Victor acquired the Berliner patents and took the lead in the development of the phonograph industry.

The success of Victor was in large part due to the unprecedented promotional campaign directed by Eldridge Johnson and Leon Douglass, Victor vice president. The firm advertised in newspapers and periodicals, presenting the public with an image of quality and sophistication that no rival was able to match. In 1903, Johnson initiated the Red Seal series (based on the Red Label celebrity records of Gramophone & Typewriter in the United Kingdom) in a special recording studio in Carnegie Hall. The Red Seals presented Metropolitan Opera stars and other great artists, some on 10-inch discs, and others on the new 12-inch discs.

Among Johnson's other contributions to the industry was the exclusive artist contract, which captured Enrico Caruso in 1904 and many other international artists. He continued to experiment with improvements in equipment, and made an experimental model of a record changer in 1920; this was developed into a marketable Victor machine in 1927.

In December 1926, Johnson sold 245,000 shares of Victor stock for $28,175,000 and retired. Control of the firm passed to a pair of New York bankers, Speyer & Co. and J.W. Seligman & Co., and then to the Radio Corporation of America in 1929. Eldridge Johnson died in Moorestown, New Jersey.

Johnson, Keith O., March 29, 1938– · A noted recording engineer, Johnson graduated from Stanford University in 1960, with a B.S. degree in electrical engineering, and with minors in music and physics. He then went on to do graduate work in mathematics and circuit theory. From 1955 to 1963, he worked for Ampex Corporation, first as a technician and later on as an engineer working in the company's advanced technology group. From 1963 to 1964, he worked for Winston Research Corporation as a designer of instrumentation recorders. Between 1965 and 1973, he worked for Gauss Electrophysics, MCA, and Cetec Corporation, helping to pioneer several recording technologies, including endless-loop duplicating, RF bias, real-time log-sweep alignment techniques, and high-speed servo transports.

From 1974 to today, he has been self-employed and has helped to design or consulted with the design of loudspeakers, music synthesizers, laser projectors, servo motors for recorders, and multi-channel optical reproducing systems, among other things. He has also been, and continues to be, the technical director and recording engineer for Reference Recordings, where his classical-music recording techniques have become industry standards. He holds several design patents, and has published numerous articles in the *Audio Engineering Society Journal*, *Radio-Electronics*, and *Journal of the Society of Motion Picture and Television Engineers.*—Howard Ferstler

Johnston, C. R. · British recording expert, known as Johnnie Johnston. He worked with Colonel Gouraud's Edison Phonograph Co. in London, then with Edison Bell, Clarion, Pathé, and Marathon records. He recorded various notable persons for Gouraud, including Alfred, Lord Tennyson, Florence Nightingale, and the explorer Henry M. Stanley. He was with the Orchestrelle Co., Ltd., in London in 1917. During 1918 he was in New York, working in the recording laboratory of the Aeolian Co. Johnston was the recording expert for Chicago's Rodeheaver Record Co. in 1921, and in 1922 he was director of recording and then vice president of Bell Recording Laboratories.

Johnston, James, 1953– · Born in Northeastern Ohio, Johnson received his B.S.E.E. and M.S.E.E. from Carnegie-Mellon University in 1975 and 1976. He is employed by AT&T Bell Laboratories, and has worked in the company's Acoustics Research Department, Signal Processing Research Department, and in the newly formed AT&T Labs—Research. During this time, he has worked on speech, image, and audio coding for transmission and storage, and also co-invented the field of perceptual audio coding. He is a Fellow of the Audio Engineering Society and Senior Member of the Institute of Electrical and Electronics Engineers. In 1998, he received an AT&T Technology Medal and AT&T Standards Award, and in February 2001, he received a New Jersey Inventor of the Year award for his contributions to MP3 and audio coding in general. Recently, Mr. Johnston has been working on Perceptual Soundfield Reconstruction (PSR) for accurate reproduction of live music on high-fidelity sound systems, as well as on issues related to audio coding and image and auditory perception.—Howard Ferstler

Jones, Joseph W., ca. 1876–? · American inventor. As a youthful employee of Emile Berliner, he worked a summer at age 17 in the Washington, D.C., laboratory and closely observed the recording process (which employed acid-etched zinc matrices). Jones devised a method of cutting a wax disc with a lateral groove, similar to the method of Eldridge Johnson, and applied for a patent on the process in November 1897, receiving it on December 10, 1901 (U.S. no. 688,739). His success was in part due to the clever adjustments in the appli-

cation (at first rejected) by Philip Mauro of American Graphophone Co. That firm then bought the patent for $25,000 and hired Jones as a research engineer, gaining an entry into the disc business in 1901. Upheld at first, the Jones patent was finally invalidated after litigation brought by the Victor Company against American Graphophone (1911). Jones had already gone to Europe by then, to make Vitaphone records. In addition, Columbia had taken over American Graphophone and made an agreement with Victor in 1903 for cross licensing, so the final court decision had no effect on anyone. Jones received 10 other patents in the sound recording field.

Jones, W. Bartlett · *See* STEREOPHONIC RECORDING.

Joyce, Thomas F., August 8, 1904–September 8, 1996 · American record and television industry executive. A vice president at Victor in the late 1930s, he established the Victor Record Society in 1937. Society members were entitled to buy an inexpensive ($14.95) record player, developed by Joyce, which would play through a radio. It was said that 150,000 of these machines were sold within a year. After World War II Joyce became recognized for his enthusiastic promotion of television, and in 1952 he left RCA to become president of the Raymond Rosen & Co., a leading distributor of television sets and other appliances. He died in Philadelphia.

Jukebox · A coin-operated record player, originating with the coin-op of 1889. The name "juke" is probably related to an old southern U.S. word of African origins, "jook," meaning to dance. When coin-ops went out of favor around 1910, as a result of the thriving home phonograph industry and the competition in public places of the player piano and nickelodeon, the concept was dormant for many years. With the development of electric amplification after

1925, there was a revival of interest in the record machines. In 1927, a model made by the Automatic Musical Instrument Co. of Grand Rapids, Michigan, was able to play either side of 10 discs; about 12,000 of them were on location by 1930. Other manufacturers taking part in the juke box golden age of the 1930s and 1940s included the J. P. Seeburg Co., Capehart Co., Rock-Ola, AMI, and, most prominently, the Wurlitzer Co. It is estimated that there were 25,000 jukeboxes in operation in America by 1934; 225,000 by 1938; 300,000 by 1939 (making use of 30 million 78-rpm discs per year). Indeed, the jukebox sales were significant in keeping the record industry afloat during the Depression.

An important contribution of the jukebox to American musical culture was the exposure it gave, from around 1935, to country and western music. It should be noted that all juke boxes were devoted to pop music, suitable to the preferences of patrons in the places where they were installed: saloons, pool halls, drug stores, ice cream parlors, inexpensive restaurants, and roadhouses. The jukebox era came to a close in the late 1970s, following the passage of a new copyright law in the United States that required licensing and compensation to the record labels. There had also been a decline in the production of single 45-rpm records as opposed to LP albums. In addition, of course, television had become the source of background noise in drinking places, whereas Muzak or radio music seemed to serve the needs of restaurants.

By the turn of the 21st century, antique jukeboxes, particularly fancy Wurlitzer models, had become high-priced collectibles. Many bars and clubs seeking to enliven their decors installed reproductions or originals of elaborate jukeboxes. Meanwhile, the jukebox format was imitated in multiple-disc CD changers as well as in electronic "virtual" jukeboxes, designed to hold large numbers of recordings that could be easily accessed. [Hoover 1971 provides good illustrations, pp. 107–113; Kirvine 1977]

Jump · *See* BUMP.

JVC · *See* JAPANESE VICTOR COMPANY (JVC).

K

Kantor, Ken, September 7, 1956– · One of America's preeminent speaker designers, Kantor earned an S.B.E.E. degree from MIT in 1979, with a thesis titled "A Psychoacoustically Optimized Loudspeaker," and in 1982, he earned an M.S. from the same university, with a thesis titled "Radio Frequency Performance."

After completing post-graduate work at MIT, he worked for Teledyne Acoustic Research from 1983 to 1986, as director, R&D, and was with NHT Loudspeakers from 1986 to 1990, as co-founder, chairman, and head of research and development. In 1990, NHT was purchased by International Jensen and from 1990 to 1997 Kantor remained with the company as VP technology, and chairman of the Corporate Technology Department. From 1997 to 2000, he was with Vergence Technology, as co-founder, managing director, and chief technical officer. He has also had technology consulting and product development relationships with Boston Acoustics, NAD, Faroudja Laboratories, MultiVision Products, Denon, and Hewlett-Packard, among others. Current projects include research in acoustics toward the goal of improved loudspeaker performance.

His design accomplishments include a number of very highly regarded speakers from AR, NHT, and Vergence. He has had numerous articles published in consumer and trade journals, was elected to the Administrative Committee of the Institute of Electrical and Electronics Engineers Consumer Electronics Society for four years, and was also elected to the Administrative Committee of the Northern California chapter of the Audio Engineering Society. He has been awarded numerous patents, awards, and honors relating to audio technology and product design, and as of 2002, he was CTO and co-owner of Intelligent Audio Systems, and working on proprietary loudspeaker/electronics technology.—Howard Ferstler

Katz, Bob, March 12, 1949– · A noted recording engineer and producer, and former technical director of Chesky Records, Katz earned a B.A. degree in Communications and Theatre from the University of Hartford in 1972, and went on do private studies with Ray Rayburn and Al Grundy. From 1972 through 1977, he was Audio Supervisor of Connecticut Public Television, and later on was an independent recording engineer and producer, with recordings and mastering work done for numerous labels, including BMG, Chesky, Sony, EMI, Virgin, and Sierra. He also has done extensive recording for radio and film, built several recording studios, and consults throughout the world on audio and computer topics. Among his many accomplishments in the recording business, Katz built the first working model of the Bob Adams 128× oversampling analog-to-digital converter, and recorded the world's first compact disc using 20-bit, 128× oversampling technology.

He has also recorded over 100 audiophile-quality albums of popular and classical music, using minimalist miking techniques and custom-built equipment, and recorded the music used on the world's first 96-kHz/24-bit DVD release. Katz co-owns Digital Domain, a CD mastering house that masters music from audiophile classical to pop, rock, and rap, and manufactures selected products used in the professional- and consumer-audio industry. He has published hundreds of articles since 1972 on recording and computer technology, in numerous magazines including *Byte, RE/P, dB, Pro Audio Review, Audio Media*, the *Journal of the Audio Engineering Society*, and is in the process of completing a textbook on digital and analog mastering.

Katz has recorded or mastered three Grammy winners, and has had his recordings named disc of the month more than 10 times in *Stereophile* magazine and numerous times in *Stereo Review*. He is a member of the Audio Engineering Society, being Chairman of the New York Section Committee, Facilities Chair of the AES Convention, Workshops Chair of the AES Convention, and has been chairman of several mastering and recording workshops at various AES Conventions.—Howard Ferstler

Keele, D. B. (Don) Jr., November 2, 1940– · Born in Los Angeles, Keele has worked for a number of audio-related companies in the area of loudspeaker R&D and measurement technology including ElectroVoice, Klipsch, JBL, and Crown International. He holds three patents on "constant-directivity" loudspeaker horns and is a fellow of the Audio Engineering Society (AES). For 11 years, he wrote for Audio Magazine as a Senior Editor performing loudspeaker reviews. He recently joined Harman-Becker Automotive Systems as a Principal engineer in the advanced development engineering group. He is currently doing loudspeaker reviews for *The Audio Critic* and *The Audiophile Voice* magazines.

Keele holds two B.S. degrees in electrical engineering and physics from a state college in California and an M.S.E.E. degree from Brigham Young University. He has presented and published a number of AES technical papers on loudspeaker design and measurement techniques, and has written many magazine articles. He is perhaps best known for his AES paper describing how loudspeaker low-frequency responses can be measured using near-field measurement techniques. Mr. Keele is a frequent speaker at AES section meetings and workshops, has chaired several AES technical paper sessions, and is a member of the AES review board. He is also a past member of the AES Board of Governors and is past Vice President, Central Region USA/Canada of the AES. Mr. Keele recently received the 2001 TEF Richard C. Heyser Award.—Howard Ferstler

Keller, Arthur Charles, August 18, 1901– August 25, 1983 · A major pioneer in high-fidelity and stereophonic sound recording and reproduction, Keller spent his entire career with the Bell System, beginning with his first job in 1918 as a laboratory assistant for the Western Electric Company. While employed at Bell, he completed his education, graduating from Cooper Union in 1923. He then went on to do graduate work at Yale and later Columbia, earning a master's degree.

Keller's early work at Bell Laboratories was in sound recording and reproduction, under the direction of Henry Harrison. Keller was particularly interested in stereophonic recording, and in December of 1931, working with Harvey Fletcher and Leopold Stokowski, Keller used improved electrical recording equipment installed at the Academy of Music in Philadelphia to record and transmit stereophonic sound.

Keller held 40 patents related to his work in sound recording and other areas, including one in the late 1930s, which covered the basic principles of stereophonic recording, and his work with sound engineer Irad

Rafuse led to the first single-groove stereophonic recordings. Their proposal for recording two sound channels onto a master disc eventually became the standard stereophonic recording technique. Interestingly, in one patent application, Keller described the 45/45 method that utilized the single groove. The application was not filed until 1936, however, because Bell did not see an immediate commercial use for the method. Keller was unaware of the stereo work of Blumlein, at least until the 1950s, when Westrex independently re-invented Keller's 45/45 system.

During World War II, Keller was involved in the development of four major sonar systems for the U.S. Navy, and for his services he received two Navy citations. After the war, he continued his work with Bell Laboratories, which included the development of the wire spring relay and solderless wire wrapping. Keller retired from Bell in 1966, after a long and productive career. During that time, he authored 35 technical papers, and for his achievements, he received the Audio Engineering Society Emile Berliner Award (now known as the Silver Medal) in 1962 and the Society's Gold Medal in 1981. He died in Bronxville, N.Y.—Howard Ferstler

Kellog, Edward W., 1882–1960 · Some sources give his name as "Kellogg." Kellog was a pioneering researcher, who, along with Chester Rice, came up with the basic design of the modern, direct-radiator loudspeaker, which had a small coil-driven, mass-controlled diaphragm in a baffle with a broad mid-frequency range and relatively uniform response. (Edward Wente at Bell Labs had independently discovered this same principle, and filed a patent for it in 1925, with the patent granted in 1931.) Kellog and Rice worked for GE, and together they published their "hornless loudspeaker" design in 1925, after five years of work. The Rice-Kellog paper also published an amplifier design that was important in boosting the power transmitted to loudspeakers. In 1926, RCA used this design in the Radiola line of AC-powered radios. Kellog also went on to independently design the first electrostatic loudspeaker system in 1929, with a patent being granted on the design in 1934. *See also* LOUDSPEAKER.—Howard Ferstler

Kinetophone

In 1889, Thomas Edison and William Kennedy Dickson developed the first device that added sound to motion pictures. It came to be called the Kinetophone. In a 1912 version the audio playback was provided using a Higham amplifier and large Blue Amberol cylinders measuring 4-3/8 inches in diameter and 7 1/4 inches long. The cylinder played up to six minutes, running 120 rpm, with groove pitch of 100 lines per inch. Kinetophone films (projected with the Kinetoscope) were single-reel shorts of six minutes or less in duration; they included "Sextette from Lucia," "Jack's Joke," "Scene from Julius Caesar," "Charge of the Light Brigade," and "Revenge of the Indian Girl." Synchronization of the cylinder with the film was the main problem. It required the record operator to observe certain cueing on the cylinder, then to start the machine at the right moment. Adjustments were possible once the film had started, but they needed to be made with great precision. Because Edison required users of the cylinders to be authorized purchasers of the entire audio-visual apparatus, his records were not widely sold. Theater managers were already showing films with costly projection equipment and were not inclined to duplicate it to acquire Edison cylinders. *See also* MOTION PICTURE SOUND RECORDING.

Klein, Larry, July 9, 1928– · A highly regarded and influential editor for *Stereo Review* magazine during the 1960s, 1970s, and 1980s, Klein grew up in New York City and became interested in audio and electronics at an early age. When he joined the Army in 1945, he had already learned enough while working for radio-repair shops in the city to earn a position at the White Sands Proving Grounds, where he worked with scientists in setting up instrumentation for early rocket experiments. After his discharge from the Army, he attended Brooklyn College, NYU, and Hunter, studying social sciences and philosophy, instead of electronics. He also worked for various electronics companies as a consultant and paid troubleshooter during the early 1950s. This eventually led to a job for *Popular Electronics* magazine as technical editor. Two years after that, he moved on to a similar post at *Electronics Illustrated*, and in 1963, he became technical editor (later technical director) at *Stereo Review* magazine, a post he held for 20 years.

While at *Stereo Review*, Klein, along with Julian Hirsch, established a rational approach to audio system performance, and his influence in this area has been far-reaching and long lasting. Part of Klein's job as technical editor was to deal with industry experts and designers and convert their often-complex ideas about audio system performance and recording technologies into language understandable to typical audio enthusiasts. (He earlier had demonstrated this ability in a book titled *It's Easy to Understand Electronic Test Equipment*.) As a result, a small multitude of audio enthusiasts became adept at understanding the hobby at a time when it was expanding and becoming a powerful segment of the consumer electronics industry.

Klein left *Stereo Review* in 1983 and went on to be a contributing editor to *Audio Times*, *Sound & Vision* (Canada), *Car Audio*, *Electronics Now*, and *High Fidelity*. He also wrote manuals and advertising copy. A life member of the Audio Engineering Society, he is currently retired from writing and listens to music without being overly concerned about how it is reproduced.—Howard Ferstler

Klepper, David, January 25, 1932– · Born in New York and the son of a father who was an ear, nose, and throat specialist and mother who was a pharmacist, Klepper graduated from grammar school in 1949, and then went on to enroll at MIT with the intention of becoming a railway electrification engineer; however, academic studies under acoustician Leo Beranek got him interested in architectural acoustics as well as sound systems. He went on to earn an S.B.E.E. degree in 1953, and earned his S.M.E.E. degree in 1957, with a thesis titled "A Binaural Recording System for Concert Hall Evaluation."

He then worked for the acoustic consulting firm of Bolt, Beranek, and Newman between 1957 and 1971, and moved on to be a partner at Klepper, Marshall, and King, between 1971 and 1996. During his career, Klepper has been responsible for several innovations in sound system design, including seat-back loudspeakers in reverberant spaces and coaxial loudspeakers for ceiling distributed systems. Design projects he is responsible for include the Danny and Mitzi Kaye Theatre, the Bruno Walter Auditorium, and the St. Thomas Episcopal Church renovation in New York; the Tanner Building at Brigham Young University in Provo, Utah; Boston's Holy Cross Cathedral sound system and Harvard's Memorial Church renovation, in Massachusetts; and The Congregation Young Israel of Southfield, Michigan.

Klepper is a Charter Member of the Institute of Noise Control Engineers, a Fellow of both the Acoustical Society of America and Audio Engineering Society, and active member of several music, railway, and historical societies. In 1987, he won the AES Silver Medal for his work in acoustics. After retiring in 1996, he moved to Israel, where he is has been working on several books in both Hebrew and English, studying toward a Rabbi's or Cantor's career, and studying Arabic.—Howard Ferstler

KLH Corporation [website: www. klhaudio.com] · A high-fidelity equipment company started by Henry Kloss, Malcolm Lowe, and Tony Hofmann, in 1957, hence the letters K, L, and H. From the beginning, the company produced a variety of consumer-oriented products, most of which were loudspeaker systems with acoustic suspension woofer designs licensed by Acoustic Research Corporation, which all three KLH principles had helped to start before moving on to found KLH. (The three sold their AR shares to Edgar Villchur, the primary founder of AR, before moving on to begin their new company.) In addition, the company marketed the six-foot-tall, Model 9 electrostatic speaker system (designed by Arthur Janszen), and produced a top-quality (and expensive for its time, at $160) table radio, as well as the first high-quality portable stereo hi-fi system, both designed by Kloss. In 1968, the company also produced the first consumer-grade tape recorder utilizing Dolby noise reduction, the reel-to-reel Model 40. *See also* LOUDSPEAKER.— Howard Ferstler

Klipsch, Paul, March 9, 1904–May 5, 2002 · A noted audio pioneer and speaker designer, Klipsch received a Bachelor of Science in electrical engineering from New Mexico State University in 1926, worked in Chile maintaining locomotives from 1928 to 1931, and obtained a Masters of Science in electrical engineering from Stanford University in 1934. After receiving his Masters Degree, Mr. Klipsch worked as a

geophysicist for a Texas oil company, and later served in the U.S. Army during World War II, earning the rank of Lt. Colonel. In 1981, he earned a Doctor of Laws from New Mexico State University (NMSU). The NMSU engineering department was renamed the Klipsch School of Electrical and Computer Engineering in 1995, in his honor. In 1978, Klipsch was awarded the Audio Engineering Society's Silver Medal, for his contributions to speaker design and distortion measurement. In 1984, he was inducted into the Audio Hall of Fame, and in 1997 he was inducted into the Engineering and Science Hall of Fame, an honor shared by Thomas Edison, George Washington Carver, and the Wright brothers. One of his most notable design achievements is the well-known Klipschorn, which was designed to be located in a room corner, so as to be able to utilize the two wall surfaces as the mouth of the horn. The system was designed and patented in 1945, with further upgrades in 1948, and models using the design principles are still in production. *See also* LOUDSPEAKER, 7.—Howard Ferstler

Kloss, Henry, February 21, 1929–January 31, 2002 · Born in Altoona, Pennsylvania, Audio Hall of Fame member and Emmy award winner Henry Kloss founded or helped to found five different and successful electronics companies, and is justifiably considered to be a legendary figure in consumer-audio (and video) history.

In 1954, Kloss and Edgar Villchur co-founded Acoustic Research, Inc. (Kloss had been one of Villchur's students at NYU, and had previously been building Baurch-Lang loudspeakers for mail-order sale). The company's first product, the model AR-1 loudspeaker, incorporated the first acoustic-suspension woofer. Villchur invented and patented the acoustic-suspension woofer system; however, Kloss quickly realized the value of Villchur's invention, and was responsible for most of the mechanical and production design work on the AR-1 loudspeaker. By 1957, Kloss left AR to help found KLH Research and Development Corporation. While at KLH, Kloss (with Malcolm Low and Tony Hofmann) produced acoustic-suspension speaker systems under license to Acoustic Research and designed the first high-quality, portable stereo system and the first high-fidelity table radio, the Model Eight.

Kloss sold his share in KLH in 1967, and went on to form Advent Corporation, where he worked with both Tomlinson Holman and Andy Kotsatos, who quickly became fine designers in their own rights. Kloss's primary interest in starting the new company involved the development of a high-quality, front-projection video system. To fund his research, however, he also designed and marketed the low-cost but very high-quality (and also very popular) Advent line of loudspeakers, many of which became borderline audio-cult items for some hi-fi enthusiasts. In addition, the company produced the first high-fidelity audio cassette deck, the Model 200, which worked as well as it did, because it employed Dolby noise reduction circuitry. In 1977, Kloss became founder and president of Kloss Video Corporation, which marketed a refined version of the projection TV system he had worked on and sold while at Advent.

In 1988, Kloss and Tom DeVesto joined forces to form Cambridge Soundworks, which continues to specialize in an assortment of consumer electronics products (including conventional and powered speaker systems that were designed by Kloss) sold by mail order. Kloss left Cambridge Soundworks after selling it in 1997 to Creative Labs, and in 2000, he unveiled an elegant tabletop radio, the Model One, from yet another company, Tivoli Audio. Kloss was a giant in the audio industry (and even won an Emmy for his video designs), and it could be said that he was one of the origina-tors of modern, affordable, and high-quality consumer audio products. *See also* LOUD-SPEAKER.—Howard Ferstler

Koss, John C., 1930– · Koss designed the first commercially viable high-fidelity audio headphones in 1958. They were successful because up until that time audio-playback hardware had been heavy and anything but portable. The advent of the transistorized, portable players made headphone listening more attractive, however, and the Koss product line benefited from the requirements of the new small-player technology. Today, the Koss family still has a 60% share in the company (now run by the founder's son, Michael J. Koss) and the products include studio and home-audio stereo headphones, portable headphones, cordless headphones, noise-reduction headphones, and microphones and headsets with microphones.—Howard Ferstler

Kotsatos, Andrew, February 14, 1940– · Born in Baltimore, Kotsatos initially worked for KLH Corporation, where Henry Kloss mentored him. In 1969, he joined Advent Corporation where he worked on specific design aspects of all speakers. Indeed, working closely again with company president Kloss, Kotsatos helped to create one of the great success stories of its era—the original Advent Loudspeaker. He then went on to design the highly successful Advent/2, Advent/3, and New Advent loudspeakers. Kotsatos left Advent in 1978, and in 1979, he joined with Frank Reed, who had worked with him at KLH and Advent, to establish Boston Acoustics.—Frank Hoffmann

Kruesi, John, May 15, 1843–February 22, 1899 · Swiss/American machinist, born in Speicher. He learned the machinist's trade in Zurich, and from 1867 to 1870 he worked in the Netherlands, Belgium, and France. In 1870, he crossed to America, taking a job with Singer Sewing Machine Co., then going to the Edison plant in Newark, New Jersey, in 1871. He became foreman of the machine shop, responsible for the mechanical execution of many Edison ideas. He assisted with the installation of the electric light system in New York; he patented the Kruesi Tube, an insulated underground cable. Kruesi and Charles Batchelor were responsible for the building of Edison's great plant in Schenectady, New York, which became the Edison General Electric Co.; in 1889, he became its assistant general manager. In 1895, he was appointed chief engineer of the new General Electric Co. He died in Schenectady.

Kruesi is best known in the history of recorded sound as the man who made the first working model of the phonograph, following a sketch given to him (and Charles Batchelor) by Thomas Edison on November 29, 1877. Kruesi and Batchelor had the model ready on December 6. An unfortunate error in dating the sketch has only recently been corrected (by Allen Koenigsberg in 1969); the mistake resulted from Edison's much later (ca. 1917) inscription on a copy of the drawing "Kreuzi make this Edison Aug 12/77." The inventor evidently forgot the date of his original instruction to Kruesi, and also the spelling of his machinist's name. Kruesi also made the patent model of the phonograph.

The spelling of Kruesi has had a varied history in the literature. It appears as Kreusi, Kreuzi, Krusci, and Kruesci in various respected sources.

Kudelski, Stefan · In 1951, a Polish immigrant named Kudelski was a physics student at what is now the Swiss Federal Institute of Technology at Lausanne. That year, he built the first portable and self-contained audio recorder (using a windup motor), thereby freeing on-sight recording engineers from dependence upon power-line electrical sources or electrical generators. He named the recorder the Nagra, which

in Polish means "will record," started a business, and began producing the device, but only in limited quantities. In the early 1960s, however, Jerry Lewis, after visiting Kudelsky at his factory, brought the first Nagra to Hollywood, showed it to some film executives, and the device went on to revolutionize movie making.

In 1968, Kudelski's private company became Kudelski SA, and moved into a new factory at Cheseaux-sur-Lausanne. Under his leadership and that of his son, Andre, after 1991, the Kudelski Group's product line, including the Nagra audio recorders and advanced digital recording systems, continued to be an important part of audio and video production industry. The Academy of Motion Picture Arts and Sciences awarded Kudelsky its Gordon E. Sawyer award in 1990, which recognizes an individual in the motion picture business whose technological contributions have brought credit to the industry. Kudelsky is also a three-time Oscar winner for technical achievements, in 1966, 1978, and 1979. In addition, he won the Audio Engineering Society's Gold medal in 1984, is an honorary member of the Society of Motion Picture and Television Engineers, and is also an honorary fellow of the Association of Motion Picture Sound, in the United Kingdom.—Howard Ferstler

Kunstkopf Stereo · *See* DUMMY HEAD STEREO.

Kurlander, John, May 25, 1951– · Born in London, Kurlander has been in the recording industry since 1967, with the first 28 years spent at EMI's Abbey Road facility. He began his career working as an assistant to Geoff Emerick on The Beatles album, *Abbey Road*, with Emerick winning the engineering Grammy for that album. Expanding his horizons, Kurlander did some singles with Paul McCartney, and in the early 1980s he engineered the popular *Hooked on Classics* series. Later, he recorded Toto and Elton John, layering 80-piece orchestra tracks on top of the rock-music tracks. This led to doing some serious classical recordings around 1980, which included projects with the Berlin Philharmonic and the Philadelphia Orchestra. In 1985, Kurlander became Abbey Road's chief balance engineer and also chief classical engineer for EMI. Today, he is a highly sought, Hollywood-based independent engineer specializing in major motion-picture film scoring and soundtrack albums.—Howard Ferstler

L

Label · A paper attachment to a disc or cylinder, giving identification data on the music and or the performers. Before 1900, discs had no paper labels, but carried identification scratched into their surfaces. Eldridge Johnson began using paper labels on discs in 1900, and the practice soon became widespread.

Labyrinth · *See* LOUDSPEAKER, 5.

Lacquer Disc · Another name for the acetate disc; one usually made of metal, glass, or fiber, and coated one or both sides with a lacquer compound. Lacquers were used in home recording and in making instantaneous recordings between the introduction of electrical recording and the advent of the 1948 LP. Around 1950, the industry generally began to abandon wax in favor of lacquer surfaces.

Lambert, Thomas Bennett, 1862–January 9, 1928 · American inventor and recording company executive, born in Chicago. In 1900, he received British patent no. 13,344 for an "indestructible" cylinder record, and U.S. patent no. 645,920 (where the term used was "infrangible"). His process involved coating the usual wax master with a form of carbon, then depositing copper on it by electrolysis to make a shell. When the wax master was cooled and removed, a copper negative matrix remained; it was used to form duplicate cylinders in celluloid ("cellulose" was Lambert's term). The Lambert Co. was established in Chicago to produce and market the records. With the bankruptcy of that firm in 1906, Lambert turned to telephone research, and then was vice president of the Marsh Laboratories in Chicago, producers of the earliest commercial electrical discs.

Land · A term for the surface of a record between adjacent grooves.

Lansing, James B., January 14, 1902–September 24, 1949 · An early pioneer in high-fidelity loudspeaker design. Lansing was born James Martini and for unknown reasons changed his name to James Bullough Lansing just before starting the Los Angeles located Lansing Manufacturing Company in 1927. The company later made notable contributions to the design and building of large horn systems for motion-picture sound reproduction. In 1941, Lansing sold the company to Altec Service Corporation (Altec stood for "all technical," and the original company had been formed in 1938 by M. Conroe and George Carrington), and the new combination was called Altec Lansing. After the merger, Lansing stayed on and helped to design several notable monitor and theater-horn systems, including the 604 coaxial and the A-4, mainly designed by John Hilliard. In 1946, Lansing left Altec and formed a new company, Lansing Sound, with several other partners. Later on, the company came to be called James B. Lansing Sound, Incorporated (JBL). Between the time he helped to start the new company and his death, in 1949, he was responsible for several notable speaker designs and manufacturing methods. The company continued to prosper after his death, and since 1969, JBL has been owned by Harman International. *See also* LOUDSPEAKER.—Howard Ferstler

Lansing Manufacturing · *See* LANSING, JAMES B.

Laserdisc · A laser-read, video-recording format supported in the 1980s by a number of manufacturers, the most notable of which was Pioneer. Most laserdiscs were 12-inches in diameter and early versions had both the picture and sound in analog form. Although the picture was always a frequency-modulated analog signal, later configurations had the sound in potentially very high quality two-channel, PCM digital form, with the very last versions having Dolby Digital or DTS audio tracks. Discs were available in two forms, standard (constant angular velocity) and extended play (constant linear velocity), with the former having as much as 30 minutes of sound on a side and the latter doubling that to 60 minutes. Repertoire offered by various labels until the demise of the format near the end of the 1990s included operas, ballets, concerts, and motion pictures, with the latter being the most common use. The laserdisc was eclipsed by the rapid success of the DVD in the late 1990s, and both laserdiscs and players eventually went out of production.—Rev. by Howard Ferstler

Laser Turntable · A turntable designed to reproduce sound from analog vinyl recordings using a laser beam instead of a phono cartridge. Introduced to great fanfare in 1986 by Finial Technology of Sunnyvale, California, the company was unable to find adequate distribution for the product and sought outside investors to acquire the technology. In 1988, ELP Corporation of Japan, a consumer audio company formerly known as BSR Japan, acquired the patents for the laser turntable and began produc-

tion. After several years of producing the turntable for institutional use, ELP introduced its first commercial models in 1995 and targeted them at the high-end audiophile. By 2001, the company was making a profit.

The primary advantage of the laser turntable is the reproduction of analog records without subjecting them to the wear associated with phono cartridges. Each turntable is constructed by hand and includes laser reading optics that can be adjusted to the speed of groove depth of all commercially produced vinyl recordings. The speed of the turntable is fully adjustable in 1-RPM steps within the range of 30 to 50 RPM, and in 2-RPM steps within the range of 60 to 90 RPM. Vinyl discs measuring 7, 8, 9, 10, 11, and 12 inches can be played, as can RPM speeds that are the equivalent of traditional vinyl playback speeds of 45, 33 1/3, and 78 RPM. The laser turntable has notably low distortion and can faithfully reproduce the sound of records that may even have scratches or warps. The height of the scanning laser can be adjusted within the groove of a record to fine-tune its reproduction.

The high price of the laser turntable—ranging from about $13,500 to $23,500, depending on features—has proven to be a worthwhile investment for institutions and collectors concerned about preserving their vinyl heritage.—Thom Holmes

Late Reflections · In concert halls, churches, and recording studios, they are the sounds reflected from more distant room boundaries. These reflections allow for a recording made in those spaces to partially simulate a large-space environment. In home listening room situations, they are the sounds that arrive at the listening position after being reflected from multiple room surfaces that are considerably closer to the listener than what we have in studios, concert halls, and churches. As a result, those small-room reflections are not delayed enough to do a proper simulation, and they therefore tell the listener that they are listening to a music ensemble recorded in a large room being played back in a smaller one.

To counter this artifact with two-channel recordings, DSP ambiance-synthesizing devices that incorporate surround channels and extra channels can be employed to simulate a larger space. One purpose of well-done, dedicated surround-sound recordings, like what we have with DVD-A, SACD, Dolby Digital, and DTS, is that they are able to reproduce those late reflections from the surround channels.—Howard Ferstler

Lateral Alignment · *See* GAP ALIGNMENT.

Lateral Recording · The process—also known as lateral cut or needle cut—of cutting disc records in which the vibrations are represented by sidewise deflections in a groove of uniform depth. It was developed commercially by Emile Berliner and was accepted widely in the United States and Europe by 1900. The other system, vertical cut or "hill-and-dale," was preferred by a few labels, such as Pathé and Edison, into the 1920s, but the industry had standardized on lateral recording by the beginning of the 1930s. Both lateral-cut and vertical-cut recordings were made in the Volta Laboratories in the early 1880s, as shown by the notes of Charles Sumner Tainter; however, the lateral method is not mentioned specifically in the key U.S. patent of Tainter and Chichester Bell, no. 341,214 (1886). Berliner's method was not strictly a cutting, as it was the old method of acid etching. Berliner could not use a true cutting process because of the wax-cutting Bell and Tainter patent.

Layering · The recording of a musical part with several, similar sounding inputs playing simultaneously. The technique is an outgrowth of the multi-track tape recorder.—Howard Ferstler

Leader · A short length of uncoated tape attached to the beginning of an open-reel magnetic tape or cassette tape of facilitate winding the recording tape on the take-up reel.

Lead-In Groove · The plain unrecorded groove that is found at the edge of an analog-disc record; it has the function of guiding the stylus to the beginning of the recorded part of the groove.—Rev. by Howard Ferstler

Lead-Out Groove · The plain groove that follows the recorded groove on an analog-disc record; it has the function of keeping the stylus silently in place on the revolving disc until the machine's operation is either automatically terminated or terminated by the user.—Rev. by Howard Ferstler

Lebel, Clarence Joseph, December 16, 1905–April 14, 1965 · One of the founders of the Audio Engineering Society, in 1948, LeBel was also the Society's first president. He earned a degree from MIT in 1926, and went on to obtain his masters from the same institution in 1927. His first job was as a research physicist at Raytheon, from 1927 until 1929, where he worked on lamps and rectifiers. After Raytheon, he worked at Sylvania from 1929 through 1932, where he worked on lamps and ozone tubes. In 1937, his growing interest in audio systems helped him to found Audio Devices, where he was chief engineer and was active in the development of lacquers used for the machine production of recording discs. During this period, he also worked on the development of high-grade recording tapes. In 1940, he became vice president of the company, a position he held (with a five-year sabbatical hiatus to work for the Maico Company, doing hearing-aid research) until his death. From 1945 through 1946, he also worked as a project engineer at Cambridge Instrument, and went on to found still another company, Audio Instrument, in 1947. LeBel was also a member of the Acoustical Society of America and the Society of Motion Picture Television Engineers. He had a profound impact on the audio technologies of the era and his influence has been honored at MIT with a teaching position called the C. J. LeBel Professor of Engineering.—Howard Ferstler

Lede (Live End/Dead End) · Formulated by Don Davis in the 1980s, and relating to recording control rooms or even home playback rooms, it involves acoustically treating the front area of the room with absorbing materials, to minimize reflections that would muddy the direct sound coming from the speakers. In contrast, the back of the room remains reflective, often with special surfaces designed to scatter reflections and delay their reception by the ears as long as possible, to enhance the sense of space and envelopment.—Howard Ferstler

Leek, Bruce · Freelance recording engineer and occasional consultant for Telarc Records. Leek holds degrees from Los Angeles State and Long Beach State Universities. He has recorded the Philadelphia Orchestra, the Los Angeles Chamber Orchestra, the Luxembourg Symphony, the Utah Symphony Orchestra, the Mormon Tabernacle Choir, and the United States Air Force Band, as well as ensembles from the University of Cincinnati, the University of North Texas, and Indiana University of Pennsylvania. He has mastered albums for The Rolling Stones, The Beatles, Jefferson Airplane, The Beach Boys, Crosby, Stills, Nash & Young, Judy Collins, Fleetwood Mac, and The Fifth Dimension.—Howard Ferstler

Level · The intensity of output from an audio system, referring either to the signal or to noise; it is technically measured in decibels against a standard reference level (zero level) that is equivalent to a power of one milliwatt in a resistance of 600 ohms.

Lexicon Corporation · One of the most important and influential producers of recording hardware and super-grade consumer-audio processors in the world, Lexicon was the initial brainchild of MIT Professor Dr. Francis Lee, who had developed a digital delay unit for heartbeat monitoring. With engineer Chuck Bagnashi, he went on to found American Data Sciences in 1969, with offices over the Lexington Savings Bank in Lexington, Massachusetts. The company changed its name to Lexicon in 1971, when it appeared that there would be a future in digital technology for language instruction. Barry Blesser, then a teaching assistant to Dr. Lee at MIT, and later another luminary at Lexicon, suggested putting audio through the system. The result was a 100-millisecond audio delay line—not so impressive today, but at the time, it was more than state of the art.

The new technology interested the late Steve Temmer at Gotham Audio in New York, who commissioned 50 units from the Lexicon team, to be used to overcome propagation delays in live sound installations and as a pre-delay for echo-plates. Thus, in 1971 the Delta T-101 (the world's first commercially available professional digital audio product) was born, followed by the T-102, which offered even better performance. The two components helped convince many in the industry that digital audio was the way to go.

The year 1972 saw the introduction of a Lexicon product for the language instruction market—the Varispeech, the first digital time-compression system. Its successor, the broadcast-quality Model 1200, went on to win an Emmy in 1984. Ron Noonan joined the company in 1973 as CEO (a position he held until 1996), and realized that Lexicon needed to also target the professional audio market. The breakthrough was the development of the 224, one of the first commercially viable digital reverb systems, which was shown at the AES Convention in 1978 and shipped the following year. Designed by David Griesinger, a Ph.D. physicist from Harvard who is still with the company, the 224 remained an industry standard until the introduction, in 1986, of its successor, the 480L, which was itself superseded by the 960L, with its 24-bit/96kHz capability and true multichannel surround reverb processing.

Lexicon went public in the United Kingdom (which had always been a strong market for the company) in 1985, and raised the funds needed for the development of the groundbreaking Opus digital audio workstation, which was released in 1988. In the same year, the company introduced the first all-digital surround-sound processor for the home-theater market, the CP-1, and as a result Lexicon has been justifiably dominant in the high-end home theater ever since. That unit was followed by the CP-2 and CP-3, and later on by the even more advanced DC and MC series, which make use of Lexicon's proprietary Logic 7 circuitry, a technology that is capable of creating a simulated 7.1-channel output from any two-channel source. Presently, the "Lexicon sound" is heard on more than 80% of the world's most successful music albums and theatrical soundtracks. In the early 1990s, the company became a part of Harman International.—Howard Ferstler

Limiter · A circuit used in tuners and amplifiers to control the volume during signal peaks; it prevents overloading that would be caused by unwanted overmodulation.

Lindenberg, Theodore, 1911–December 12, 1995 · A founding member of the Audio Engineering Society, Lindenberg was born in Columbus, Ohio, and went on to study engineering at Ohio State University. In the mid 1930s, he had a recording studio in Columbus, and soon after became interested in phonograph cartridge design. In 1941, he joined Sherman Fairchild at his company, with Fairchild soon after marketing a cartridge designed by Lindenberg. In 1950, Lindenberg was elected president of the AES, and from that year until 1959, he was chief engineer at Pickering & Company, working for Walter Stanton. He was responsible for refining the design of the molded pickup cartridges featuring the replaceable stylus assemblies that Stanton had designed. He also designed an integrated arm/cartridge combination, electrostatic loudspeakers, and a turntable. He left Pickering in 1960, and until 1967, he was director of engineering at the Astatic Corporation. After leaving Astatic, he worked for Martin Marieta until his retirement, researching optics, electronics, piezoelectric devices, and laser components.—Howard Ferstler

Line Source Loudspeaker · *See* LOUDSPEAKER.

Linear Predictor · A device that allows modification of one characteristic of speech sounds (e.g., pitch change) without altering other characteristics (e.g., duration). In terms of a recording, it permits playback at various speeds without changing pitch, or a shift in pitch without change of turntable or tape velocity.

Linkwitz, Siegfried, November 23, 1935– · Born in Germany, Linkwitz studied electrical and electronic engineering at Darmstadt Technical University, Germany, from 1955 to 1961, and received a "Diplom Ingenieur fuer Nachrichtentechnik" degree in 1961. He went on to attend M.S.E.E. classes at Stanford University between 1962 and 1964, as part of Hewlett-Packard's Honors Cooperative program. He worked for Hewlett-Packard Co. (now Agilent) from

1961 to 1998, in R&D of radio frequency and microwave electronic test equipment, and joined Audio Artistry Inc. as partner between 1993 and 1999.

While at HP, he worked on and was responsible for a number of test instruments, most notably the 8566A Spectrum Analyzer, which was the first fully automated and programmable test instrument with a frequency range from 20 Hz to 20 GHz. He also developed a well-known loudspeaker crossover together with R. Riley, known as Linkwitz-Riley crossover, and developed a novel biquad circuit topology, known as the Linkwitz Transform, which is often used for woofer equalization. Linkwitz is a member of Institute of Electrical and Electronic Engineers and the Audio Engineering Society. *See also* LOUDSPEAKER, 9.—Howard Ferstler

Lioret, Henri Jules, June 26, 1848–May 19, 1938 · French clockmaker and manufacturer, born in Moretsur-Loing. His clocks won the bronze medal at the 1878 Paris Exposition, where Thomas Edison had his exhibit; it is possible that Lioret became interested at that time in sound recording. He gained several important patents in the field. He made a talking doll in 1893 for the Emile Jumeau doll manufacturer of Paris, sold successfully at 38 francs under the name of Bébé Jumeau. Having seen the Edison doll, Lioret improved on its weak points: The Edison cylinder could not be changed and it was too fragile. The Lioret doll operated with a spring mechanism and had unbreakable, interchangeable celluloid cylinders. In 1898, he used the mechanism in a talking clock. A talking mechanical doorman greeted visitors to Lioret's workshop at 18 rue Thibaud. There was also a talking kiosk, developed by Lioret for advertising Chocolat Menier. His Lioretgraph No. 3 was a large weight-driven phonograph with oversized horn; he actually leased the Trocadéro auditorium in 1897 and brought in a substantial audience (to judge from a contemporary drawing) to admire it.

A complicated electroplating molding method duplicated Lioret cylinders. By 1900, he was able to produce a four-minute unbreakable record about 3 1/4 inches long and playable at 100 rpm on a phonograph. Lioret also made these—some weight-driven—with the trade name Lioretograph. He also made non-molded brown wax cylinders, and vertical-cut discs. The Lambert Co. of Chicago purchased a Lioret patent and used it in defense against litigation brought by Edison over the molding process. Lioret was in business until 1911. He also collaborated with Léon Gaumont and others in motion picture work, and then turned to landscape painting. He died in Paris.

Lipshitz, Stanley, November 25, 1943– · Decidedly, one of the more important academics involved with the concepts that make modern audio systems behave as they do, Lipshitz was educated in primary and secondary schools in Durban, South Africa, and went on to graduate with a B.Sc. (with honors) in applied mathematics from the University of Natal, Durban, in 1964. He then earned an M.Sc. in applied mathematics from the University of South Africa, Pretoria, in 1966, and then earned a Ph.D. in mathematics from University of the Witwatersrand, Johannesburg, in 1970. Shortly after graduation, he moved to Canada, taking a position as Professor of Applied Mathematics and Physics at the University of Waterloo.

Lipshitz is one of the founding members of the Audio Research Group at the University of Waterloo, which conducts research in many areas of audio and electroacoustics. His current interests include the mathematical theory of dithered quantizers and noise shapers (and their relation to stochastic resonance and chaos), physical acoustics, and active noise control. He has presented numerous technical papers, on a wide range of topics, at conferences both in North America and overseas, and has published numerous important papers on audio in the Journal of the Audio Engineering Society, the Institute of Electrical and Electronics Engineers *Transactions on Signal Processing*, the *Physical Review E*, and *Computing in Science & Engineering*. Lipshitz won an AES Fellowship in 1982, and went on to win the Society's Silver Medal in 1993, and won the Society's Publication Award in 1994. He was president of the AES from 1988 to 1989, and is a member of the IEEE, the Acoustical Society of America, and the Canadian Acoustical Association. *See also* LOUDSPEAKER, 8.—Howard Ferstler

Liquid Audio · Digital file format and online music distributor. Launched in May of 1996, the Liquid Audio venture recruited computer-music veterans from Stanford University, audio manufacturer Ampex, and the Grateful Dead. Based on the idea that the imminent digital-music revolution would be nothing without legally licensed content and corresponding delivery technology that protected against online bootlegging, Liquid Audio provided record labels and artists a means of distributing music electronically without rampant loss of revenue. Perhaps surprisingly, the company's insistence on copy protection did not successfully attract the participation of major labels, which are involved in proprietary online distribution methods. Music retailers sometimes have been more threatened by Liquid Audio's distribution model than the labels, and Capitol Records withdrew its plan to pre-release a Duran Duran single in "Liquid" format after a threatened retailer boycott of the CD. Liquid Audio failed to become a standard for such distribution, and in 2002, the service went bankrupt. In early 2003, Anderson Merchandisers, a wholesaler of major-label recordings that services Wal-Mart and other retailers, purchased Liquid Audio's

assets, with the support of the Universal Music Group. They hope to revive the format as a means of delivering audio files to consumers and to retailers.—Brad Hill

Live Recording · A recording made at an actual public performance instead of in the studio. In August 1888, recordings of an organ at Westminster Abbey, and at the Crystal Palace in London, were undertaken by Colonel Gouraud for the Edison Phonograph Co. to demonstrate the utility of the phonograph; parts of *Israel in Egypt* were inscribed (*see also* OLDEST RECORDS). The Mapleson cylinders of 1901 were the earliest series of live recordings, and the first live recordings made in the United States.

Live Studio · *See* REVERBERATION.

Live to 2-Track · During recording, this usually involves using a direct feed from the recording microphones and amplifiers to a two-channel master, bypassing any mixing stages. It can also involve multiple microphones that are mixed to a 2-track master during the recording process. This has the potential to deliver a cleaner, less-manipulated sound. If not done correctly, however, it can result in a recording that is possibly worse than what one would get by employing multiple microphone feeds, mixers, and equalizers, and doing methodical post-production editing to get the balances perfect. In the 1970s, Sheffield Records produced some demo-grade-sound LP recordings from disc masters that were cut directly during a live, 2-track feed.—Howard Ferstler

Locanthi, Bartholomew Nicholas (Bart), 1919–January 9, 1994 · Born in White Plains, New York, Locanthi earned a B.S. degree in physics from California Institute of Technology, in 1947, after his war service had split his educational experience into two parts. In the early 1950s, while working for the analog computer development group at Cal Tech, he published a paper on modeling loudspeaker performance, via electrical equivalent circuits. Reprinted later in the Audio Engineering Society's journal, it became the foundation of most of the loudspeaker driver and enclosure programs available today.

From 1953 until 1960, he was a partner in Computer Engineering Associates, a company specializing in large-scale computer services, and in 1960, he joined James B. Lansing Corporation, where he served as vice president of engineering until 1970. During that time, he engineered the designs of numerous JBL loudspeaker systems. In addition, he developed the "T-Circuit," an output configuration for solid-state amplifiers that became a standard for the industry. After an association with Cetec Gauss, a manufacturer of professional sound components, he joined Pioneer North America in 1975, and continued with the company until 1986. During that time, he was responsible for the design of a number of loudspeaker drivers, as well as some of the company's digital technologies. After 1986, he formed his own consulting company, with Pioneer remaining his principle client. Locanthi was a member of the Acoustical Society of America, the Institute of Electrical and Electronics Engineers, the Society of Motion Picture and Television Engineers, and the Audio Engineering Society, which awarded him a Fellowship in 1972, a Silver Medal in 1990, and a posthumous Gold Medal in 1996. *See also* LOUDSPEAKER.—Howard Ferstler

Long-Playing (LP) Record · The early commercial cylinders had a two-minute playing time, a span insufficient for rendition of a typical song or instrumental work. Efforts began to extend playing time, both through the production of larger cylinders (e.g., five-inch "concert records") and through finer grooving. Various solutions were tried, but it took a combination of several new technologies to make the true LP possible.

Both Victor and Edison had tried to develop 12-inch "long-playing" discs, but were hampered by the current playback technology. The heavy tone arms then in use could not play the tighter grooves necessary to contain the additional audio information. Columbia is generally credited with coming up with the first workable solution, albeit it for use in motion pictures. In 1932, the firm introduced 12-inch records to provide intermission music in motion picture theaters. The discs played from the center outward. A 12-inch record could play, like the later commercial LP, for 20 minutes. The 33 1/3-rpm speed was found to be suitable also in adding sound when a motion picture film was projected because a 20-inch diameter disc at that speed would cover the time used by one film reel, and gave respectable quality.

Eventually that speed was employed by Columbia as it introduced the modern LP record, developed by Peter Goldmark and William S. Bachman, in 1948. It had between 250–400 grooves per inch, in contrast to the 96–125 grooves per inch of the standard 78-rpm record. Stylus diameter was .001 inch (1 millimeter), and the stylus exerted only 6 grams of pressure, with a tip radius of less than 0.025 millimeters. This format became the new industry model, and remained so until the arrival of the compact disc.

Looping · A mixing technique used by disc jockeys to extend the playing time of a song by blending two records of it into a continuous play.

Lord-Alge, Tom, 1963– · A noted mixing engineer and two-time Grammy winner for engineering, Lord-Alge has worked on more than 150 albums since 1983. His credits include producing albums for Steven Winwood, REO Speedwagon, and Starship. He was engineer on albums for artists including Jeff Beck, TKA, REO Speedwagon, Sun City Artists, and Steve Winwood. He mixed albums by Earth, Wind, and Fire, Billy Joel, Fuel, Dave Matthews, Verve Pipe, the Rolling Stones, Dog's Eye View, Shawn Mullins, Bare Naked Ladies, Limp Bizkit, Marilyn Manson, Hole, Hanson, and Collective Soul, among many others.—Howard Ferstler

Loudspeaker · Often referred to simply as speaker. This article consists of nine sections, much of which relates to system bass reproduction.

1. *Introduction.* The year 1925 heralded the most significant advance in the history of recorded sound, the commercial introduction of electrical recording and reproduction. Two technological developments made electrical recording feasible: the transducer and the vacuum-tube amplifier. The transducer made it possible to convert mechanical energy into electric current and vice versa. Electrical recording required two transducers: a microphone to convert sound vibrations into electricity, and an electrical disc cutting head to convert the electricity into a mechanical vibration that would cause a cutting stylus to cut a physical replica of the original sound wave into the record groove. On the reproduction end, a phonograph cartridge (pickup, as it was originally called), traced the mechanical picture contained in the record groove and converted the resulting vibration into electricity. Finally, the loudspeaker converted the electricity, after it was amplified, back into sound vibrations.

A microphone cannot provide sufficient voltage and current to feed a disc cutting head directly; the small signal from the microphone requires considerable amplification to drive the cutting apparatus. Similarly, the phonograph pickup is incapable of driving a loudspeaker. In both cases, the vacuum tube amplifier of the era provided the means of increasing the voltage and current of the electrical signal provided by the first transducer to a level sufficient to drive the second transducer. Today, solid-state amplifiers have generally replaced their tube counterparts.

Werner von Siemens first patented the basic principles of the moving-coil electrodynamic loudspeaker, often referred to as the dynamic loudspeaker, in Germany in 1874. In Britain, John William Rayleigh described radiation theory for a circular diaphragm mounted in a baffle in his Theory of Sound (1877). In 1898, British physicist Oliver Lodge received a patent for a sound reproducer consisting of a moving coil attached to a wooden board. The modern dynamic loudspeaker is generally credited to C. W. Rice and E. W. Kellogg, who produced a working model in 1925. The essential elements of a modern moving coil loudspeaker, which has changed very little in its basic operation since Rice and Kellogg, are a coil of wire (the voice coil) surrounded by a magnetic field and attached to a vibrating diaphragm or cone. The voice coil and the cone are suspended by the "spider" at the rear of the cone and the flexible rim suspension (the surround) at the front. As electricity flows through the voice coil, the coil generates its own magnetic field that interacts with the field of the permanent magnet, causing the cone to move back and forth. During the early days of radio and electrical phonographs, single full-range loudspeakers, which attempted to reproduce the entire range of frequencies available on recordings, were commonplace. Since the 1950s, however, nearly all loudspeaker systems claiming to have high fidelity performance have used more than one speaker element to cover the entire audible frequency spectrum from 20 Hz to 20,000 Hz. The speaker enclosures described below are most commonly used with low frequency loudspeakers, normally called woofers. Separate speakers called midranges and tweeters are normally used for the middle and high frequency portions of the spectrum, and these individual loudspeaker components are often called drivers.

A moving-coil loudspeaker normally radiates sound from front and rear because the loudspeaker frame (basket) is open in the back. When the loudspeaker cone moves forward, a compression of air is produced in front of it, and a rarefaction is produced behind it. Conversely, when the loudspeaker cone moves backward, a rarefaction is produced in front of the loudspeaker, along with a compression at the rear. Thus, the radiation of sound waves from the front and the back of the speaker cone are out of phase with each other. At low frequencies, the wavelengths reproduced are quite long with respect to the size of the cone, and when the front and rear radiations meet, at the outer edge of the loudspeaker, cancellation occurs. This results in little low frequency output from the loudspeaker, despite large cone movement in this region.

Consequently, since the first use of dynamic loudspeakers, it has been important to somehow isolate the front radiation of the cone from the back radiation. The simplest method is to mount the loudspeaker on a large, flat baffle. The distance from the front of the speaker, around the baffle to the rear of the driver, determines the low frequency cut-off point for the system. When the distance is less than 1/4 wavelength of the frequency being reproduced, the output from the system is greatly reduced. Many early radio receivers and phonographs used flat-baffled loudspeakers, as well as the variant open back enclosure. Early radios and electric phonographs were often housed in five-sided wooden boxes that contained both the electronics and the loudspeaker. Open-back cabinets provided a reasonable distance between the front and rear of the driver, but with a much smaller front profile. Unfortunately, the baffle size required to handle really low frequencies satisfactorily would have been too large to be practical. Fully enclosed boxes were necessary to achieve accurate bass with a front baffle of manageable size, and a choice had to be made regarding what kind of enclosure would be used.

Two basic options are available: The rear radiation can be completely absorbed inside the enclosure or a portion of the rear radiation can emerge, through a port or vent (or opening that is mass controlled by a dummy-radiator diaphragm), to reinforce the front radiation at low frequencies. The major types of loudspeaker enclosures are noted below, beginning with those that completely absorb the rear radiation of the driver.

2. *Completely closed box woofer systems.* The infinite-baffle enclosure was popular through the mid-1950s. A true infinite baffle would isolate the front radiation of the driver from the rear radiation at the lowest

operating frequencies. Because it has never been possible to build a baffle of infinite size, such an enclosure was always approximated using a box of manageable proportions. One common approach to building an infinite baffle was to mount the driver on the wall of a room, in which case the room at the rear of the loudspeaker became the enclosure and the room at the front of the driver became the listening room. Very large, stand-alone enclosures, which approximated infinite baffles, were built by a number of manufacturers during this era. Bozak was a leading proponent of such enclosures, exemplified by its B-310 loudspeaker system. The B-310 contained four 12-inch woofers housed in an enclosure with an internal volume of nearly 18 cubic feet. Electro-Voice manufactured a loudspeaker system known as the Patrician, the second version of which contained a single 30-inch woofer in an enclosure of comparable size.

In 1949, Harry F. Olson and J. Preston received a patent on what they called the air-suspension loudspeaker. This configuration involved mounting a woofer in a small, sealed enclosure in which the air became part of the cone's suspension. The RCA LC-1 loudspeaker system was the first commercial product based on the Olson and Preston patent. It is important to note that the woofers used by Olson were not substantially different than those used in large infinite baffles or open-back enclosures; they had relatively stiff suspensions, with fairly high free-air resonant frequencies. When such drivers were placed in a small enclosure, the system resonance will be even higher than that of the driver in free air, resulting in relatively weak low bass,

unless extremely large woofers are used.

One of the most significant developments in the history of the high fidelity loudspeaker occurred in 1953 when American designer Edgar Villchur built his first acoustic suspension loudspeaker. What distinguished Villchur's loudspeaker from Olson's air-suspension design was the use of an extremely high compliance woofer. By itself, the high compliance woofer had a very low free-air resonance frequency of less than 15 Hz. When it was placed in a sealed box of less than two cubic feet, however, an initial low-frequency roll-off point of 38 to 40 Hz was achieved. The trapped air inside the small, airtight enclosure provided most of the support for the woofer cone, and served as a restoring force for the cone at frequencies near system resonance. In Olson's air-suspension designs, the compliance of the air inside the enclosure was greater than that of the driver's suspension. In an acoustic suspension loudspeaker the situation would be reversed, with the compliance of the air being less than that of the driver suspension. Before the development of the acoustic suspension loudspeaker, a low frequency cutoff of 38 Hz was unheard of in such a small enclosure. One problem with acoustic suspension loudspeakers is their relative electrical insensitivity, or lack of what is commonly called efficiency. That is, more amplifier power is required for a given playback level than with most larger woofer systems. As a result, a trend toward higher-powered amplification began in the late 1950s.

These small-box systems were commonly called "bookshelf" loudspeakers and their introduction played a major role in public acceptance of stereophonic recording. When high fidelity enthusiasts contemplated converting their monaural systems to stereo, adding a second enormous enclosure to their living rooms was, in most cases, an unwelcome prospect. The compact size of the acoustic suspension loudspeakers made installing a pair of them considerably more practical. Tony Hofmann developed the original formulas for acoustic suspension loudspeaker design . In 1972, the mathematics of closed box loudspeaker design was analyzed and described by Richard Small in a series of landmark articles that formed the basis for most of the later designs.

3. *Bass reflex (vented) woofer systems.* The bass reflex loudspeaker uses a fully enclosed box, except for a port or vent that may be located on the back, side, or even the bottom with certain subwoofer designs, with the port area with the latter configuration kept above the floor by small feet on the enclosure bottom. Some of the back radiation from the woofer cone emerges from the port in phase with the front radiation, reinforcing the low frequencies. A. L. Thuras of Bell Laboratories performed the first experiments with ported loudspeaker enclosures in 1930. His model was based on the Helmholz resonator. The Thuras patent application (1932) described the interaction of the driver and the port. Voight in England and Olson in the United States did similar work in the early 1930s; then in 1937, Jensen introduced the first modern bass reflex loudspeaker system.

Early bass reflex woofer systems had inaccurate low-frequency performance by today's standards, and their excessive output at resonance often made them sound boomy. Nevertheless, they were extremely popular during the days of low power amplifiers due to their relatively high electrical efficiency. During the 1950s, L. L. Beranek, Bart Locanthi, R. H. Lyon, and J. F. Novak developed more precise mathematical models; however, Australian A. N. Thiele first portrayed the modern vented loudspeaker in 1961. Thiele described vented loudspeakers in terms of their electrical equivalent circuits, and showed that it was possible to achieve a smooth low frequency response that was equivalent to an ideal electrical high pass filter.

Thiele's work did not receive wide attention until 1971 when his paper was reprinted in the United States. Richard Small did much to enhance the work of Thiele, showing that the vented loudspeaker was a fourth order high pass filter, and that the filter could be adjusted for a wide variety of mathematically predictable response characteristics. He also showed the effect of enclosure losses on the performance of the loudspeaker system, and presented the mathematics for matching an enclosure design to a specific driver, using the driver's electrical and mechanical specifications. These driver specifications are now universally known as Thiele/Small parameters. Modern terminology refers to the bass reflex as the design type that preceded Thiele and Small, and to the vented loudspeaker as the type that followed their work. Vented designs characteristically roll off their outputs much faster below the lower resonance point than acoustic suspension designs, and their woofers are also more prone have problems with extremely low frequency, sub-resonance inputs than sealed-box systems. It is possible, however, to configure vented systems to go very deep into the low-bass range, and subwoofers built by Hsu and SVS have proven that point.

4. *Passive radiator woofer systems.* This category of loudspeakers is related to vented designs. A passive radiator configuration actually contains two woofers, one with the usual, powered voice coil and magnet structure, and the other without. The passive driver is acoustically coupled to the active loudspeaker at low frequencies, and the passive driver contributes as much to the output at low frequencies as the vent does in a vented design. One advantage of passive radiator systems is the absence of wind noise and pipe resonances sometimes found in vented systems. Harry F. Olson received the first patent on these systems in 1935, and followed his original work with research published in 1954. He referred to the passive drivers as "drone cones." An early commercial proponent of passive radiator systems was Polk Audio, an American firm based in Baltimore. The Sunfire Corporation has also produced some high-output, small subwoofers using the design. Some of their systems employed multiple 6 1/2-inch active drivers with much larger passive units.

5. *Transmission line woofer systems.* The transmission line loudspeaker is a refined descendant of the Stromberg-Carlson acoustic labyrinth, which was invented by Benjamin Olney in 1936. The acoustic labyrinth is a long pipe into which the back radiation of the woofer is loaded. The length of the pipe is normally a quarter wavelength of the woofer's free air resonant frequency, which produces a pressure node at resonance, controlling the cone motion of the woofer. Because the labyrinth is a completely open pipe, except for a lining of fiberglass, a substantial amount of sound emerges from the end of the tube.

A. R. Bailey first described the modern transmission line loudspeaker in 1965 (Bailey 1965; Galo 1982). Although superficially resembling the acoustic labyrinth, the transmission line operates quite differently. A classic transmission line is completely filled with absorbent material, either long fiber wool or Dacron polyester. That damping material acts as an acoustic low pass filter, effectively increasing the length of the line as the frequency drops. At the lowest operating frequencies, the woofer is mass-loaded by the air in most of the length of the line. This results in excellent woofer control at low frequencies. The transmission line is a theoretically non-resonant enclosure, and the internal pressures found in closed box designs are nearly absent in a well-designed system. In a classic transmission line, all of the back radiation from the driver is absorbed in the line, but some variations on this concept have made use of a portion of the back radiation. A negative side effect, as with reflex systems, is the relatively poor control of the woofer cone below the system cutoff frequency. The transmission line is probably the least scientific of all present day loudspeaker enclosures, and there are no hard and fast formulas for determining line length and stuffing density. Recent research by Robert Bullock and Peter Hillman (Bullock 1986; Hillman 1989) has led to a more precise understanding of the transmission line, but designs are not as mathematically predictable as they are for closed and vented boxes. Since 1965, only a handful of commercial designs have employed transmission lines because their relatively large size and complex internal construction making them somewhat expensive and impractical. Among home loudspeaker builders, they have attained a kind of cult status. Irving M. Fried is the best-known commercial proponent of the transmission line, having marketed many such systems under the brand names of IMF and Fried Products.

6. *Aperiodic woofer systems.* The aperiodic loudspeaker is a closed box system that contains a vent stuffed with damping material. The stuffing, usually foam or fiberglass, provides a pressure release for the system at low frequencies. The term aperiodic literally means an absence of resonances at any specific frequency or multiples thereof. Aperiodic damping is defined as "damping of such a high degree that the damped system, after disturbance, comes to rest without oscillation or hunting" (Turner 1988). In a standard acoustic suspension system the trapped air in the box is quite reactive, or springy, at very low frequencies. The reactive nature of the air will cause excessive cone excursion at system resonance. Adding an aperiodic vent to the system releases internal pressure at resonance, resulting in better control of the cone motion at very low frequencies. The aperiodic loudspeaker offers some of the performance advantages of the transmission line in terms of excellent woofer control and a reduction in internal pressure at frequencies near system resonance, but with enclosures much more manageable in size. It is important to note that no sound emerges from an aperiodic vent, so this design does not resemble a vented loudspeaker in any way.

The first patent on such a loudspeaker enclosure was issued in 1936 to Marvel W. Scheldorf, an engineer for RCA; he described his invention as an acoustic resistance device. Scandinavian firms have shown the greatest interest in this concept. In 1969, Dynaco Corporation introduced the model A-25, the first in a series aperiodic loudspeakers made for them in Denmark by Seas. Another Danish firm, Dynaudio, has also been an advocate of aperiodic loading. For many years it manufactured a device called a Variovent, which contained tightly packed fiberglass stuffing held in place by a plastic grill and frame. A third Danish firm, ScanSpeak, has manufactured a similar device. Audio Concepts, an American loudspeaker manufacturer based in LaCrosse, Wisconsin, has also produced loudspeakers with aperiodic loading.

7. *Horn-loaded loudspeakers.* Since the first acoustic phonographs appeared, horns have been used as acoustic amplifiers or impedance-matching device. A horn does this by coupling the relatively small surface area of the radiator to the large volume of air in the room, with the size of the mouth opening determining the low frequency cutoff for the horn. Horn shapes on acoustic phonographs made before 1925 were determined largely by trial and error. No mathematical procedures had been developed for determining the size and rate of expansion between the throat and the mouth, and the horns usually had very uneven frequency response. In 1919, the American physicist Arthur G. Webster received a patent for the first exponential horn. As the name implies, the cross-sectional

area of the horn increases exponentially with distance from the throat, resulting in a more uniform frequency response. Webster's work failed to have an impact on the phonograph industry until 1925, when acoustical recording was abandoned in favor of the electrical process. The Orthophonic Victrola was the first commercial phonograph to incorporate an exponential horn. It was also the first to use a folded horn design. An exponential horn with low frequency response adequate for the reproduction of electrical recordings required a large mouth opening, and consequently had to be quite long. The folded horn reduced the size to manageable proportions.

In 1925, Rice and Kellogg conducted the first experiments with horns coupled to dynamic loudspeakers. Because of the very high efficiency of horn-loaded loudspeakers, they were highly effective where large rooms had to be filled with a high volume of sound. This made them especially suitable for use in talking motion picture theaters because the vacuum tube amplifiers available at that time had limited power output capability. Although horn systems were used extensively in theaters during the 1930s, their large dimensions made them impractical for home use because woofer horns had to be quite large. That situation changed in the middle 1940s when the American engineer Paul W. Klipsch invented the corner-horn woofer system, a complex folded design in which the walls of the room form the mouth of the horn. The Klipschorn loudspeaker in production today is still based on the original model, and it uses a horn midrange and tweeter to fill out the remainder of the audible spectrum.

(Klipsch was not the first engineer to advocate corner placement of loudspeakers. In 1925, M. Weil made the first corner loudspeaker patent, and his patent was issued in 1931.) Today, Klipsch is the only major manufacturer of home high fidelity loudspeakers that continues to advocate horn and corner-horn designs over all other types. Due to their exceptionally high efficiency, however, horn systems continue to be the preferred loudspeakers for sound reinforcement and motion picture applications.

8. *Electrostatic loudspeakers.* Unlike the dynamic speaker, an electrostatic loudspeaker does not make use of electromagnetism. Instead, it uses a thin plastic sheet, stretched over a rectangular frame, as the vibrating diaphragm. The plastic sheet is coated with a conductive material, connected to a high voltage power supply that charges the diaphragm to a potential of several thousand volts negative DC. Suspended on either side of the plastic diaphragm is a pair of metal screens, called stators, to which the audio signal is applied. The output from the amplifier is connected, through a transformer, to the two screens, allowing it to interact electrostatically with the polarities of the signals on the screens. When the audio signal on the front screen is positive, the signal on the rear screen will be negative. The negatively charged diaphragm will be attracted toward the positively charged screen, and repelled by the negative screen. When the audio signal reverses polarity, the opposite will occur, with the diaphragm moving back toward the rear (positive) screen and away from the front (negative) screen.

As with the moving-coil systems previously discussed, the output from the two sides of the diaphragm will be out of phase with respect to each other, and because of efficiency requirements panels slated for bass-response duty are usually not installed in an enclosure. Consequently, there can be low-bass cancellation problems. How significant this can be will depend upon the size of the panel area, and how low in bass the designer wants the system to operate. As a result, electrostatic panels that are slated for use as bass reproducers are usually very large, floor-standing arrangements. Smaller electrostatic elements, configured for midrange and high-frequency reproduction are often used in conjunction with the large, bass panels, or even with dynamic woofer systems.

Indeed, the earliest electrostatic loudspeakers were small units used only for high frequency reproduction. They were normally used in conjunction with a conventional dynamic woofer forming a two-way package. During the 1920s, there was a considerable amount of experimentation with electrostatic loudspeakers, particularly in Britain and Germany, but there were few commercial products. Among the first was the Kyle condenser loudspeaker, which was used by Peerless in a radio receiver introduced around 1930. The Automatic Musical Instrument Co. used one of the first electrostatic loudspeakers in a jukebox, also introduced in 1930. These early electrostatic speakers employed a single screen, in front of the diaphragm, and were enclosed at the rear. Thus, they were not dipoles. The first modern dipole electrostatic loudspeaker was the Quad, introduced in 1958 by Acoustical Manufacturing Co., Ltd. The following year, KLH introduced the Model 9

electrostatic loudspeaker, with two tall dipole speakers, held at a fixed angle by a pair of brackets. A stereo installation, therefore, required the use of four panels.

Because of the extremely low mass of the plastic diaphragm, electrostatic loudspeakers are capable of exceptional clarity and inner detail in the midrange and high frequencies. As has been noted, however, because electrostatic speakers often suffer from a lack of extreme low bass, many designs use a conventional dynamic woofer system, coupled to electrostatic elements for the midrange and high frequencies. Martin Logan is noted for building such systems.

A related category is the planar loudspeaker. It is nearly identical in radiation concept to an electrostatic loudspeaker, having a large, thin, vertically oriented plastic diaphragm as the vibrating element. Planar speakers use conventional magnetic principles, however, and are, therefore, dynamic loudspeakers. Thin wires are embedded into the plastic diaphragm, forming the equivalent of a voice coil stretched out lengthwise. Magnetic strips are placed in the front and back of the diaphragm, where the stators would be in an electrostatic loudspeaker. Magnetic instead of electrostatic interaction causes the diaphragm to vibrate. Magnepan, a Minnesota firm, is the best-known manufacturer of planar-magnetic loudspeakers. Its first such speaker, designed by company founder Jim Winey, was the Magneplanar Tympani I of 1971. It contained three tall panels that operated as dipoles.

Most electrostatic and planar-type loudspeaker systems have their driver elements arranged vertically or in vertical arrays, allowing the system to behave as a tall "line source." In some larger systems, the tall, narrow driver or array of drivers may reach nearly from floor to ceiling. In a 1986 paper presented at the 81st Audio Engineering Society convention, mathematician Stanley Lipshitz showed that the acoustic radiation of line-source speaker systems of finite length could exhibit significant direct listening field anomalies at midrange and treble frequencies because the total surface area of the tall line could not be the same distance from a point receptor like the ear. Therefore, because large-panel systems are nearly always going to put the listener predominantly in the direct listening field, instead of in the reverberant listening field, where the signals will blend to an average, comb-filtering artifacts will exist. Nevertheless, many audio enthusiasts still strongly prefer the sound of such systems.

9. *Multi-way loudspeakers.* As early as 1925, Rice and Kellogg realized that the very large loudspeakers suitable for low frequency reproduction were far from optimum for reproducing the midrange and high frequencies. Their first multi-way system, developed that year, consisted of three horn-loaded drivers, each dedicated to a limited portion of the frequency spectrum. There was little practical use for such a system until the sound motion picture industry was formed because most early electric phonographs and radios used single drivers to cover the entire available range. In 1934, Shearer and Hilliard built the first modern two-way horn loudspeaker system for the MGM studios in Culver City, California. James B. Lansing also built such systems.

Until the late 1950s, multi-way systems for home use employed either small direct radiator cone drivers for the midrange and treble (a direct radiator is a loudspeaker that radiates directly into the room, without any horn loading to improve efficiency), or cone drivers with horns attached. Then in 1958, Edgar Villchur introduced the first commercially viable dome tweeter, bringing several advantages over the cone drivers previously used, not the least of which was increased efficiency and power handling for the size of the radiator. In addition, because of its physical shape, the dome was more rigid than the cone, resulting in less distortion at high frequencies. In addition, the small size of the dome (typically one inch or less in today's systems) results in much wider dispersion at high frequencies, giving a uniform frequency response in a large number of listening positions. By the mid-1960s, dome drivers had also become common for midrange reproduction, although cone designs continue to be popular into the 1990s and beyond with many designers. In the early 1970s, Roy Allison designed a variant on the dome tweeter that exhibited even wider dispersion characteristics.

Today's high-performance, multi-way dynamic loudspeaker systems usually employ small dome drivers as tweeters, and either dome or cone drivers for the midrange. Dome drivers are typically manufactured as sealed, self-contained units, and do not require the construction of any enclosure. Cone midrange drivers, typically four to five inches in diameter, but sometimes larger, are not sealed at the rear and will normally require some kind of sub-enclosure that can be incorporated into the complete system. Sub-enclosures for midrange drivers can be either closed, aperiodic, or vented boxes, depending on the driver used and the preference of the system designer. Transmission line loading, though less popular, has also been used effectively with midrange loudspeakers.

Multi-way loudspeaker systems require the use of a combination of filters that, together, form the crossover network. In a two-way system, a low-pass filter feeds the low frequencies to the woofer and a high-pass filter sends the high frequencies to the tweeter. A three-way system contains both of these filters, plus a band-pass filter to feed the middle portion of the frequency spectrum to a dedicated midrange driver. The earliest multi-way crossover networks were based on the theories of Bell Telephone Laboratory engineers G. A. Campbell and O. J. Zobel. Their crossovers were known as constant-K and M-derived designs, in which each filter section was designed individually, matching electrical impedance to the other sections. The constant-K and M-derived filters were replaced by Butterworth filters in the 1950s. Butterworth filters, using calculus-based network theory, were designed as a whole, allowing simpler and more precise matching of the filter sections.

A crossover that uses filters rolling off at the rate of six decibels per octave outside of the passband (first order, 6 dB/octave) yields minimum phase response across the entire spectrum, but this rate of attenuation is not sufficient to insure low distortion with many drivers. In 1971, Richard Small indicated that a 12-dB/octave roll-off was the minimum necessary to reduce driver distortion. Because

the 12-dB/octave (second-order) crossover has both amplitude and phase problems, at least in the direct listening field, many engineers in agreement with Small's premise have sought higher rates of attenuation. Siegfried Linkwitz introduced the 24-dB/octave (fourth-order) all-pass crossovers in 1976. Known as Linkwitz-Riley crossovers, they have received wide acceptance, particularly with subwoofer systems, due to their symmetrical vertical radiation pattern.

In 1956, C. P. Boegli analyzed the effects of improper time alignment between crossover-controlled speaker elements. Time alignment of the drivers in a multi-way system has become a concern of some speaker-system manufacturers during the past two decades, particularly high-end designers like John Dunlavy. There is no consensus today, however, among loudspeaker engineers as to the relative importance of flat amplitude response versus time alignment of drivers and minimum-phase response across the audible spectrum. Nor is there consensus on which type of crossover roll-off characteristic is best, with excellent sounding systems making use of a variety of different crossover designs. Every loudspeaker system is the result of compromises, and each engineer has a preference regarding which compromises to make.

The personal computer has revolutionized loudspeaker design during the past decade, and is now considered an essential tool for loudspeaker engineers and manufacturers. A large quantity of software has been written for both crossover and enclosure design, bringing sophisticated loudspeaker design within the reach of the non-mathematician, while enabling those who are mathematically inclined to work in a fraction of the time that would otherwise be required. With an appropriate interface card and software, the computer can also function as a test and measurement system. The Maximum-Length Sequence System Analyzer (MLSSA), developed and marketed by DRA Laboratories, is an example, and has become a de facto standard for loudspeaker measurements.

The authors wish to express their gratitude to C. Victor Campos for providing a large quantity of unpublished historical information on the acoustic suspension loudspeaker.—Rev. by Howard Ferstler

Loudspeaker Imaging · In studios and home-listening rooms, particularly as it relates to traditional two-speaker stereo, it is the ability of those speakers to form a realistic sound stage up front, with precise instrumental or vocal localization. In fact, imaging is often more dependent upon recording techniques than speaker system design or listening-room acoustics, and it remains important even with multi-channel, surround-sound audio technologies. *See also* HEAD-RELATED TRANSFER FUNCTION (HRTF); SWEET SPOT; STEREOPHONIC RECORDING.— Howard Ferstler

LP Record · *See* LONG-PLAYING RECORD.

Lowe, Malcolm · *See* KLH CORPORATION; KLOSS, HENRY; STOCKHAM, THOMAS.

Ludwig, Robert, 1944– . One of the most important mastering engineers in the recording business, Ludwig graduated from the Eastman School of Music, in Rochester, NY, in 1966, earning a Bach-

elor of Music degree, and he holds a Master of Music degree from Eastman in Performance (trumpet) and music literature. While at Eastman, he also announced at a commercial classical radio station, worked in the school's recording department, and did lots of independent recording. Later, he played principal trumpet with the Utica Symphony Orchestra. His big recording-business break occurred when Phil Ramone, who directed Eastman's first recording workshop, hired Ludwig to work at his studio, A&R Recording, in New York. While working there, he learned the art of mastering, with Ramone as his mentor. Later, he moved to Sterling Sound shortly after its incorporation and became vice president. After seven years at Sterling, Ludwig moved to Masterdisk Corporation where he was vice president and chief engineer. In January 1993, he opened his own business, Gateway Mastering Studios, in Portland, Maine.

Ludwig has mastered 13 RIAA "Diamond" award albums and countless Gold and Platinum records, won numerous Pro Sound News mastering awards, and won *Mix Magazine's* TEC Award for "Creative Achievement Mastering Engineer" ten times. In addition, he has personally won the TEC Award ten times, and his company, Gateway Mastering & DVD has won the TEC award for Mastering Studio work five times. He was also the first person to be honored with the Les Paul Award for "... individuals who have set the highest standards of excellence in recording and sound production over a period of many years." In 1997, Ludwig's mastering studio was the first in the world to offer DVD authoring, and they were the first to be able to create DVD-Audio 0.9 spec discs. Gateway is a complete authoring facility doing DVD Video, Audio, Graphic design and state-of-the-art video compression.

Ludwig is a member of SPARS and NARAS, was active in the New York

Section of the Audio Engineering Society, and was a past Chairman of the New York section. He has been the keynote speaker at the SPARS BizTech convention in Chicago, and has been a panelist or guest speaker at SPARS (New York, Chicago, and Montreal), and at Consumer Electronic Shows, NARAS, Society of Broadcast Engineers, MPGA, Audio Engineering Society, the RIAA, and many other conferences. He has been a guest lecturer at State University of New York campuses in Purchase and Fredonia, as well as at the University of Connecticut, the Institute of Audio Research in New York City, the University of Miami, the University of Massachusetts at Lowell, the University of Southern Maine, Full Sail School for Recording Arts, and many times at Berklee College of Music in Boston. He has also been a guest instructor at McGill University, the Banff Centre for Performing Arts, and the University of Iowa. He has written numerous professional-magazine technical articles and has often been interviewed in consumer audio magazines. Feature articles on Ludwig and his studio have appeared in the *Portland Press Herald, USA Today, The New York Times*, and *the Associated Press* wire for 1,500 newspapers nationwide. Ludwig is listed in *Who's Who In Finance and Industry, Who's Who in the East*, and *Who's Who in Entertainment.*—Howard Ferstler

M

Macdonald, Thomas Hood, 1859–December 3, 1911 · American inventor, born in Marysville, California. He was a research scientist at the Bridgeport, Connecticut, plant of the American Graphophone Co., and developed many key devices in the cylinder and disc fields. Macdonald was granted 54 individual patents, and two as joint inventor with Frank L. Capps. An invention of special interest was the 1902 invention, the Multiple Graphophone, marketed as the Multiplex Grand. This was the first attempt at stereo recording, using three separately recorded tracks on the same cylinder. As all the records have been lost, it cannot be ascertained how well the process worked, but it was shown at the Paris Exposition of 1900. Macdonald went to England to organize Columbia's British factory at Earlsfield, Surrey, in 1905; cylinder and disc records were produced there.

Mackie, Gregory Clark, September 22, 1949– · Professional audio designer. Mackie was a frustrated rock musician who took to making his own amps and PA systems because he was unhappy with the quality of what was commercially available. Mackie formed his first company in 1969 as cofounder of Technical Audio Products (TAPCO) with partner Martin Schneider, operating out of a house in the Pacific Northwest. The company introduced the first six-channel mixer designed to handle the heavy demands of rock bands. The mixers became very popular because of their heavy-duty construction. In 1977, Mackie left the firm to form another company, AudioControl, to manufacture home stereo equipment, particularly equalizers and analyzers. In 1989, he returned to the mixer business, recognizing the needs of contemporary bands that utilized banks of synthesizers as well as conventional instruments. Today, the company produces highly regarded recording mixers, digital recording products, studio consoles, studio loudspeaker monitors, and professional amplifiers. In 1993, the company produced the first reasonably priced, eight-bus analog console.—Carl Benson and Howard Ferstler

Magnavox Corporation · Electronics manufacturing firm founded in 1917 by Peter Jensen and Edwin Pridham when they merged their own Commercial Wireless and Development Company with the Sonora Phonograph Corp. The company began by manufacturing loudspeaker systems, but could not compete with the bigger AT&T. So, they moved into making radios and phonographs. Jensen left the firm in 1925. After World War II, Magnavox became a prominent manufacturer of television sets, and then in the 1970s video recorders. In the late 1970s, Magnavox developed the video game Odyssey, which became a classic of its type. In the 1980s and 1990s, the company has made TVs, video recorders and players, DVD players, and portable camcorders, among other products. Philips NV owns the Magnavox name. *See also* JENSEN, PETER LAURITS.

Magnepan Loudspeakers · Pioneered in 1969, by Jim Winey, the flat-panel magnetic-driven loudspeaker design has been intriguing audiophiles for more than 30 years. Winey had previously owned flat-panel electrostatic systems and admired their dipolar-radiation signature; however, he wanted to create something that worked similarly in terms of acoustic output and radiation pattern, but would also not require an external power source and present a friendlier load to amplifiers. The result was the thin-film magnetic equivalent to the electrostatic design, and the company he created to produce and market the systems was called Magnepan.

Corporate and manufacturing facilities are located in White Bear Lake, Minnesota, a small community north of St. Paul, and Minneapolis. Having outgrown its original facilities, Magnepan's current plant is over 50,000 square feet, in addition to corporate and engineering offices, with over 40 people involved. Magnepan manufactures two different kinds of proprietary drivers for its systems: true ribbon tweeters with response beyond 20 kHz and planar-magnetic/quasi-ribbon midrange and bass drivers. This latter driver is the one upon which Winey built his company, and it operates without an electrostatic driver's transformer, essentially behaving like a very large, very light dynamic driver, although the design is more like a series of dynamic drivers that fire along a vertical axis. Each model is still designed by Winey, and to this date, over 200,000 pairs of his Magneplanar speakers have found their way into the homes of panel-speaker enthusiasts. *See also* LOUDSPEAKER.—Howard Ferstler

Magnetic Recording · Varying magnetic patterns, which correspond to sound waves, can be imposed on a moving magnetizable surface. Such patterns can be played back; the magnetic patterns can be read and transduced to sound waves. This principle, which underlies all modern tape recording systems, was discovered independently by several 19th-century inventors. Thomas Edison, while working on the cylinder phonograph in the late 1870s, observed that it would be possible to magnetize indented tracks on a tinfoil cylinder, then to record in the tracks, and read the deformations in the foil with an electromagnet. He did not develop that idea, but Charles Sumner Tainter did some experiments in the Volta Laboratory. Tainter's approach was to propose a fountain pen attached to the recording diaphragm, the pen to carry ink that contained bits of iron; the pen would then write on a paper-covered cylinder in response to the sound signal. He decided to concentrate on mechanical cylinder recording instead of pursuing the electromagnetic trail, however.

An article by Oberlin Smith, "Some Possible Form of Phonograph," appeared in *Electrical World* on September 8, 1888; in it, Smith proposed that particles of steel, carried by cotton or silk thread, could serve as the magnetized medium for recording telephone speech. Those particles could be scanned by an electromagnet, but Smith did not develop the notion into a patent.

The first working magnetic recorder was the Telegraphone of the Danish engineer Valdemar Poulsen, dating from 1898. That device looked something like a cylinder phonograph, with its cylinder grooved to hold a carbon steel wire. An electric motor rotated the cylinder at 84 inches per second, running the wire past the poles of an electromagnet. Signals were indeed inscribed on that wire; one message remains playable to this day, but there was a lack of amplification and a major obstacle of short playing time—limited to no more than a minute per length of wire. One of Poulsen's patents suggested variant media, such as a band (steel tape) machine, and a paper strip coated with magnetizable metal dust. Later he and Oscar Pedersen did construct a usable wire machine for dictation, with 20 minutes playing time. Both the British Post Office and War Office—and the U.S. Navy—bought these devices before and during World War I.

Lee De Forest suggested in 1924 the possible application of his amplifier to the wire recording process, thus allowing music reproduction, but he did not follow up on the concept. A year later Henry C. Bullis got a U.S. patent for the application of magnetic recording in motion pictures; this concept was not immediately developed either. A strong deterrent to all magnetic systems designers was the success of the talking machine in both its cylinder and disc formats. In the years before World War I, improvements in recording machines and media poured from hundreds of thriving manufacturers, and the public in America and Europe was apparently insatiable for the products.

Nevertheless research continued. W. L. Carlson and G. W. Carpenter patented their substitution of high-frequency bias in place of direct-current bias applied to the recording head in 1921. In addition, in Germany, Kurt Stille made diverse ameliorations and innovations. He developed a finer wire, capable of longer duration; and a steel-tape recording machine with sprocket holes in the tape, the purpose being synchronization with motion picture film. His wire machine had a cartridge containing supply and take-up reels similar to today's cassette. It was patented in U.K. in 1928. He described it in a 1930 article, under the name of Dailygraph, and saw it receive some commercial production: Rights were acquired by the International Telephone and Telegraph Co. in 1932, who redesigned it and produced it in Germany as the Textophone (1933).

Stille's steel tape machine was noisy and erratic, and ran too fast (six feet per second) to be practical. A demonstration in London in 1929, by film producer Ludwig Blattner,

was not successful in blending film and speech. Blattner—who had acquired the rights from Stille by license—persisted with this sound carrier, and sold some devices to the British Broadcasting Corp. in 1930. New models were devised with playing time up to 30 minutes per spool, and a British Blattnerphone Co. was chartered. Later the rights passed to Guglielmo Marconi's Wireless Telegraph Co., where further improvements were forthcoming, sufficient to make the machines usable at the BBC into the 1950s. A comparable machine was developed by the C. Lorenz AG in Germany and adopted by the German radio system.

Military research in World War II led to American wire recorder models with 0.1-millimeter stainless steel wire moving at 30 inches/second; one spool could run 60 minutes. The Brush Development Co. and Western Electric Co made commercially available recorders, both with steel tapes. Marvin Camras, of Armour Research Foundation (Chicago), received many patents in the early 1940s, and saw production of steel wire machines by General Electric Co. Wire recording reached high quality in the late 1940s, notably with an Armour Research model and the Magnecorder in the United States, and a Boosey & Hawkes device in Britain. The rapid improvements in plastic tape recording soon eclipsed the wire machines, however.

Fritz Pfleumer, of Dresden, brought to a practical stage the idea of a paper or plastic base for a recording tape. He began experiments in 1927, using soft iron powder as the magnetic coat, attaching it to the base with sugar or other organic binders. Various improvements in the tape were made in Germany through the 1930s. By 1934, the Badische Anilin und Soda Fabrik was producing cellulose acetate tapes coated with ferric oxide. The Allgemeine Elektrizitäts Gesellschaft (AEG) was able to record a symphonic concert on their Magnetophon in 1936, albeit not very satisfactorily. It took another two years of research by AEG before a machine suitable for broadcasting was available, and music could at last be presented in decent rendition, with a frequency response of 50 to 6,000 Hz.

In the post-war period, tape recording spread throughout the world. The introduction of Mylar as a thinner, durable base accompanied numerous technical refinements. The Ampex Corp. was the first to market high quality tape equipment in the United States (1948). Sales of pre-recorded reel-to-reel tape began around 1954, but the medium was not commercially successful because of the clumsy manual process required to thread a tape onto the take-up reel. Quality did reach high levels, and tapes were soon utilized by record companies as the original recording media, with the signal later transferred to disc.

Philips took a monumental stride in 1963 with the introduction of the audiocassette (see also CASSETTE) and its compact portable recorder. Improvements in fidelity followed. Then in 1986 Sony brought out the DAT (Digital Audio Tape), transforming the field. See also TAPE; TAPE RECORDER.

Magnetophon · The magnetic tape recorder first made by Allgemeine Elektrizitäts Gesellschaft (AEG) in 1935. It was demonstrated at the Berlin Radio Fair, showing the new cellulose acetate base tapes coated with ferric oxide. Although intended for business dictation, the machine was used also for musical recording. When Thomas Beecham and the London Philharmonic Orchestra performed in Germany in 1936, the Magnetophon recorded the concert. In 1938, AEG produced an improved version, type K4. It had a frequency response of 50–6,000 Hz, adequate for radio use. In 1942 another improved version, type HTS, was put into service; it carried the frequency range of 50–9,000 Hz, while reducing distortion characteristics and signal-to-noise

ratio. During World War II, the machine was used for broadcasting taped concerts, with a fidelity that puzzled listeners outside Germany; when the Allies captured Radio Luxembourg on September 11, 1944, they found the Magnetophon, in the last version, type K7. It ran the tape at 30.31 inches/second (77 centimeters/second), and gave up to 10,000 Hz in response. It had facilities for editing, a time clock, and a means of running two or more machines in synchronization for continuous play. One tape reel ran 22 minutes.

Manufacture of high quality machines based on the Magnetophon began outside Germany in 1947—one of the first was the EMI's BTR1. In America, Jack Mullin and Ampex Corp modified the design.

Main Amplifier · See POWER AMPLIFIER.

Manual Sequence. Also known as standard sequence. The recording sequence of 78 rpm or LP discs in an album in which the material flows from disc one, side one, to disc one, side two; then to disc two, side one, etc. With the advent of automatic record changers, manufacturers provided alternative sequencing that would keep the material in order when the discs dropped one after the other onto the turntable; in that "automatic sequence" the material flowed from disc one, side one, to disc two, side one, etc. Album numbers showed the distinction: For example, for Columbia Masterworks, M or X prefixes denoted manual sequence, and MM or MX denoted automatic sequence.

Marantz, Saul, 1902–January 16, 1997 · Marantz became fascinated by electronic devices when a boy in Brooklyn. In the early 1950s, in New York, he and Sidney Smith started the Marantz company, with the idea being to make and market very high-quality audio equipment (mainly record players, amplifiers, and speakers) for the nascent hi-fi sound business. After several years of design research, his first commercial product, the Model 1 Audio Consolette Preamplifier, was released in 1953. Working with such audio engineers as Smith and Richard Sequerra, Marantz continued to produce vacuum-tube components that became synonymous with upscale audio. In the early 1960s, he and his people developed the first all-transistor hi-fi audio receiver (combination tuner, pre-amplifier, and amplifier) for consumer use. After building up the company to the point at which the Marantz name was almost synonymous with the high-end high fidelity, Marantz realized that he needed more capital with which to expand his research and development, particularly after putting so much capital into the Model 10B tuner. This led to purchase of Marantz by the Japanese company Superscope in 1964. Marantz continued to work with the new operation until 1968, after which he retired—but only for a short time. In 1972, along with John Dahlquist, he founded the Dahlquist speaker company, and Marantz served as president until 1978. He also helped to form two other audio businesses: the New Lineage Corporation and Eye Q Loudspeakers. (In 1991, Superscope sold the Marantz company to Philips Electronics in The Netherlands.)—Howard Ferstler

Marconi, Guglielmo, April 25, 1874–July 20, 1937 · Born in Bologna, Italy, of an Italian mother and an Irish father, Marconi was educated first in Bologna and later in Florence. Then he went to the technical school in Leghorn, where he studied physics. In 1895, he built the equipment and transmitted electrical signals through the air from one end of his house to the other, and then from the house to the garden. A bit later, he transmitted the Morse Code letter "S" for three miles, with the receiver located behind a hill, for good measure. These experiments were, in effect, the dawn of practical wireless telegraphy or radio. A couple of years later, he built a transmitter 100 times more powerful than any previous station at Poldhu, on the southwest tip of England, and in November 1901, he installed a receiving station at St. John's Newfoundland. On December 12, 1901, using those facilities, he received signals from across the ocean. News of this achievement spread around the world, and outstanding scientists, including Edison, acclaimed him for his accomplishment. Marconi received many honors in his lifetime, including the Nobel Prize for Physics in 1909.—Howard Ferstler

Margin Control · A disc recording technique developed in the early 1950s, which controlled groove spacing one revolution ahead of the signal being recorded; it utilized an extra head on the tape reproducer.

Marsh Laboratories, Inc. · A Chicago firm established ca. 1921 by Orlando Marsh (1881–1938); successor to Cullen, Marsh & Co. T. B. Lambert. The principal claim to fame of the laboratories was the creation and production of the first electrical recordings, issued on the Autograph label in 1924. Marsh apparently sold his interest to the New York Recording Laboratories around 1927. In 1931, the firm was engaged in "electrical transcription service," providing material for radio stations. Although no terminal date is available for the firm, Marsh himself was known to be active in the recording business until at least 1936.

Masking · An audio phenomenon that involves the ability of louder or more complex sounds to obscure the sound of simultaneous sounds—usually at lower sound levels. Masking is very important with data-reduction recording and playback techniques, because it allows inaudible data to be ignored during the encoding process, thereby increasing the storage capacity of the medium.—Howard Ferstler

Massenburg, George Y., August 18, 1947–
· Born in Baltimore, Maryland and raised between there and Macon, Georgia, Massenburg was interested in music, electronics, and sound recording at an early age. Indeed, he was working part-time both in the recording studio and in an electronics laboratory at 15 years old, and worked on an engineering degree at Johns Hopkins University. In 1972, he presented a paper at the Audio Engineering Society convention on parametric equalization, and he is credited with being the first person to come up with a viable design for studio use. He was chief engineer of Europa Sonar Studios in Paris, France, in 1973 and 1974, and did freelance engineering and equipment design in Europe during those years. In 1982, he began GML, Inc., to produce specialized equipment for recording applications, including parametric equalizers, dynamic gain controllers, mixing consoles, and microphone preamplifiers. GML also consults and provides independent design for several major audio electronics manufacturers. He has designed, built, and managed several recording studios, notably "ITI" Studios in Huntsville, Maryland, and "The Complex" in Los Angeles, and has contributed acoustical and architectural designs to many others, including Skywalker Sound and "The Site" in Marin County.

Individually or collaboratively, Massenburg has also participated in the production of over two hundred record albums during the past 30 years. His engineering and producing credits include working with Billy Joel, Kenny Loggins, Journey, Madeleine Peyroux, James Taylor, Randy Newman, Lyle Lovett, Aaron Neville, Little Feat, Michael Ruff, Toto, and Linda Ronstadt. He has been nominated many times for the non-classical engineering Grammy, for Record of the Year in several years, and has won a number of Grammys for his work as a producer. In 1998 he received the Grammy for Technical Achievement, one of only four such awards presented in the history of NARAS. He also won the Academy of Country Music award for Record of the Year in 1988. In 1989, he received the Mix Magazine TEC Award for Producer and Engineer of the Year, as well as Engineer of the Year Award in 1991, and 1992. Massenburg is currently Adjunct Professor of Recording Arts and Sciences at McGill University in Montreal, Quebec, Canada, and visiting lecturer at UCLA and USC in Los Angeles, California, and MTSU in Murfreesboro, Tennessee.—Howard Ferstler

Master · The copper or nickel shell made from an original disc or tape recording, from which copies are made, leading to the final pressing. It is also known as a "metal master." It may also be a lacquer disc (in instantaneous recording). In the early days of recording, the master was usually of wax for cylinders and discs. *See* DISC; RECORDING PRACTICE.

Master Tape · The tape that is used to produce the final product after the recording and editing process. In some cases, it might be created live from two tracks during the recording session. Usually, it is put together from multiple recorder tracks later on, during mixing and post-production work. A master tape may have two or more channels, depending on the playback medium required.—Howard Ferstler

Masters, Ian, April 25, 1944– · Born in Toronto, and earning a B.A. degree from the University of Toronto, in 1968, Masters took a stab at the accounting business, and decided that the work did not suit him. Consequently, he started writing about audio and video equipment, and has continued to do so since 1972. He spent more than a decade as editor of *AudioScene Canada*, and for another three years, he was editor of *Inside Audio Video*. In 1984, he became a contributing editor for the Toronto-based magazine *Sound & Vision*, that country's leading consumer electronics magazine (not affiliated with the U.S. magazine of the same name). In May 1996, he was appointed editor of the magazine, although the publication ceased production some months later.

During the same period, Masters had been a regular contributor to the U.S. magazine *Stereo Review*, and since the magazine merged with *Video* magazine in 1999 to form *Sound & Vision*, he has been a contributing technical editor and regular columnist. He also writes a weekly audio and video column for Canada's largest newspaper, the *Toronto Star*, and has contributed articles on audio and video topics to *Home Computing & Entertainment* magazine. Over the years, Masters has also been a regular contributor to such diverse publications as *Car Stereo Review*, *Audio*, Ottawa's *Canadian Consumer* magazine, Sydney's *Australian Hi-Fi*, and *Home Goods Retailing*, a national trade publication, as well as a number of other publications, plus the *Journal of the Society of American Archivists.*—Howard Ferstler

Matrix (I) · An alternative term for master.

Matrix (II) · A circuit in an electrical system that mixes or separates signals.

Matrix Number · A serial number engraved or embossed on each side of a disc record by the manufacturer, usually near the center; or on the circumference of a cylinder record. This number is a guide to the date of the record; it may indicate which take or performance is on the record; and it may provide other data as well. The matrix number is sometimes useful in the case of reissues because it suggests whether the reissue does in fact offer the identical take as the earlier record.

Mauro, Philip · Legal counsel for the American Graphophone Co. in the 1890s and early 1900s. The graphophone patent no. 569,290, granted to Thomas A. Macdonald on October 13, 1896, was acquired in part because of the arguments of Mauro and his fellow attorney Pollok; the patent examiner had at first cited a German and an American patent as prior conceptions. Mauro became known for aggressive patent litigation, and won injunctions against Hawthorne & Sheble, Frank Seaman, and Emile Berliner. American Graphophone Co. was enabled to produce disc records in 1901–1906 on the strength of Mauro's case for the validity of the Joseph Jones patent; he had to rewrite the claims several times to demonstrate their novelty to a skeptical patent examiner. On January 31, 1899, he gave a "brilliant paper" (Read) before the Washington Academy of Sciences, "Development of the Art of Recording and Reproducing of Sound," and repeated it for the Franklin Institute in Philadelphia; he credited Macdonald and American Graphophone scientists for the invention and improvement of the talking machine.

Maxfield, Joseph P., December 28, 1887–1977 · Born in San Francisco, Maxfield had a Ph.D. in architecture, but his chosen field of interest was audio and acoustics. After World War I, while at Bell Laboratories, he and Henry Harrison devised the first recording and reproducing system using electricity. Using microphones and amplifiers, they extended the reproducible sound range by more than an octave and appreciably improved fidelity, resulting in the Orthophonic phonographic player of 1925. That same year, he also led the project that produced E. C. Wente's moving coil speaker, and pioneered the Vitaphone talking motion picture system in 1926. Maxfield also developed the 33 1/3-rpm rotational speed for electrical recordings. The chosen speed was based upon the need for disc systems to properly synchronize with motion-picture reel length during the early era of talking pictures, and a patent was granted for his work in 1927. Although it was more than twenty years before consumer versions of this design showed up for home-audio use, the 33 1/3-speed was chosen for precise mechanical and mathematical reasons that Maxfield had worked out. For his pioneering work, the Audio Engineering Society awarded him its Potts Award in 1954. *See also* SURFACE SPEED; DISC; TURNTABLE.—Howard Ferstler

Maxicut Process · A technique developed by EMI, Ltd., using an electronic logic circuit in the preview computer, to recognize frequencies and levels otherwise difficult for average record players to reproduce.

McIntosh, Frank, July 12, 1906–January 1990 · A notable manufacturer of consumer-audio amplifiers, preamplifiers, and tuners, McIntosh was born in Omaha, Nebraska. As a young man, he was an accomplished cellist, but he was more interested in engineering, and eventually became chief engineer at radio station WOAW. He also taught math and radio at a YMCA school, wrote columns on radio for various newspapers, and was radio editor for *Popular Mechanics* magazine. In 1929, he went to work for Bell Telephone Laboratories. During his eight years there, he either installed or worked on the equipment for 235 radio stations. He joined the Radio and Radar Division of the War production Board in early 1942. In 1945, he started his own consulting business.

While working for Frank Stanton, who was then president of CBS, he learned of the need for better quality audio amplifiers. He decided to build his own, employing a unity-coupling circuit, and he patented this in 1949 and set up is own manufacturing company, McIntosh Laboratories, in Silver Spring, Maryland. McIntosh. His company specialized in extremely high-quality amplifier, preamplifier, and tuner components, beginning in an era when high-end audio was almost unheard of. McIntosh retired in 1977, and sold his stock shares to top management and a few dedicated McIntosh investors, although he was retained with a salary on a consulting basis. He moved from his home in Endicott, New York, to Scottsdale, Arizona where he lived until he passed away.— Howard Ferstler [Information obtained from Roger Russell.]

McProud, C. G., 1904–April 16, 1986 · A graduate mechanical engineer, McProud joined Paramount pictures during the early talking-picture era and stayed with the company for over a decade. During World War II, he helped produce sonar manuals for the Navy, which triggered an interest in technical writing. Following the war, he got into freelance work, and ended up as managing editor of *Audio Engineering*, which eventually became *Audio* magazine. In 1949, he became the magazine's editor, and served in that capacity until 1971. He is credited with conceiving the audio show as a major element in popularizing high-fidelity music systems. A life member of the Institute of Electrical and Electronics Engineers, in 1953 the Audio Engineering Society presented him with an award for helping to advance the Society, and in 1954 he won a Fellowship from the organization for his work in the recording and reproduction of sound, and for his work in transducer design, development, and production. In 1959, he also won a citation from the Society for his magazine's work in educating the audio community.—Howard Ferstler

Mechanical-Electrical Analogies · The properties that determine the passage of an electric current are analogous to properties concerning mechanical motion. The analogies are: (1) inductance = mass; (2) capacitance = compliance; (3) resistance = friction or viscosity. Thus, for every mechanical situation, there is an equivalent electric circuit situation, and the solution of a problem in one medium is equivalent to the solution in the other. This fortunate fact of nature makes possible, among other things, electrical recording of sound.

Mechanical Recording · *See* ACOUSTIC RECORDING.

Merriman, Horace Owen, November 21, 1888–1972 · Canadian audio engineer, born in Hamilton, Ontario. He received a B.A. in Science from the University of Toronto. During World War I, he and Lionel Guest were engaged in efforts to enhance air to ground communication via electric loud-speakers; with the Armistice they turned to other applications and decided to develop a method of making phonograph records electrically. After considerable experimentation, in later stages at the studio of Columbia Graphophone Co., Ltd., in London, they produced the moving coil recording head for electric disc recording (British patent no. 141,790; 1920). He and Guest recorded a part of the Ceremony of Burial of the Unknown Warrior, in Westminster Abbey (London), on November 11, 1920. Microphones and signal buttons were placed at three points in the Abbey, wired to a sound recording van located near the south transept entrance. Although an attempt to record the entire ceremony was made, only two hymns were well enough transcribed to be issued commercially (by Columbia Graphophone Co., Ltd.: Kipling's "Recessional" and "Abide with Me." These recordings were the first to be sold using any type of electrical process. Merriman later served as engineer in charge of the Interference Section, Radio Branch, Dept. of Transport, until his retirement in 1954. (*TMR* 40 [June 1976] carries Merriman's own account of the Westminster Abbey project.) *See also* ELECTRICAL RECORDING.

Microcassette · A small version of the audiocassette, using tape 1/8-inch wide and moving at a speed of 15/16 inches per second. Its case is 5.5 × 3.3 × 0.7 centimeters (2 3/16 × 1 5/16 × 9/32 inches). It is used in telephone answering machines and for other business functions, and to a limited extent for musical programming.

Microgroove Record · *See* LONG-PLAYING RECORD.

Microphone ·

1. *Types of microphone.* A microphone converts sound energy into electrical energy, and the earliest microphones were of the pressure type. Over the years, there have been several basic microphone designs put to use. Carbon microphones use pellets, rods, or granules of carbon sandwiched between two electrodes. A DC current passes through the carbon, while a diaphragm vibrates, compressing the carbon, which causes a change in the electrical resistance of the carbon, creating an AC voltage component across the electrodes.

Piezoelectric microphones rely on the properties of certain materials that create a voltage when they are mechanically distorted. A diaphragm vibrates, bending the piezoelectric material, creating an AC voltage. Crystal microphones use Rochelle salts, a naturally occurring piezoelectric substance.

Ceramic microphones use a synthetic material that is more rugged. More recently, certain plastics, such as Kynar or PVDF, have been used. Piezoelectrics are inexpensive but somewhat fragile.

Dynamic microphones work much like an electrical generator, and essentially function as a dynamic loud-speaker in reverse. The diaphragm is attached to a coil of wire suspended between the poles of a magnet. As the diaphragm vibrates, the coil cuts the magnetic field, generating an AC voltage. Ribbon microphones work like dynamics, but use a pleated metal ribbon suspended between a horseshoe magnet's poles, essentially functioning as a ribbon-type loudspeaker in reverse. Ribbons are frailer than dynamics and have lower output voltages. Ribbon microphones are also called velocity microphones.

Condenser microphones consist of a capacitor having one fixed electrode and one movable electrode serving as the diaphragm. A DC bias voltage is applied to both electrodes. As the diaphragm electrode vibrates, the change in capacitance caused by its movement creates an AC voltage. Modern electret microphones are permanently charged, but still require a supply of electricity, usually a penlight battery, to power a circuit used to convert their very high impedance to a lower impedance to minimize noise and loss of high frequencies. "Condenser" is an older name for a capacitor; most new designs use the term capacitor microphone.

Some microphones, called "omni" models, are sensitive to sound equally in all directions, whereas others exhibit directionality, especially at higher frequencies. Cardioid microphones are more sensitive to sound arriving from the front, less so from the sides, and lesser still from the rear. Cardioid means "heart shaped," and the term refers to the shape of a two-dimensional graph of its directional sensitivity. Supercardioid microphones are more directional cardioids. Bidirectional (sometimes called figure-8) microphones are sensitive mainly from the front and rear, and

much less so from the sides. Ribbons are the most common bidirectional types, and Harry Olson did cardioid microphone experiments by "shading" one side of a ribbon. Single-tube line microphones (sometimes called rifle or shotgun microphones) use an interference tube in combination with a hypercardioid element for a highly directional pickup pattern. More directional still are parabolic microphones, which use a curved dish to focus sound energy onto the microphone diaphragm. Contact microphones use rubber discs or solid rods to sense vibrations in solid materials, such as walls or rock. Hydrophones are underwater microphones.

2. *The First Microphones: 1870s to 1920s.* The very first microphones were designed for use in telephones. As such, they were called transmitters, not microphones. Alexander Graham Bell's design of April 1876 used a carbon rod suspended vertically in a pool of diluted sulfuric acid to cause a change in resistance to a DC voltage, creating what he called "undulating current." A diaphragm of sheepskin mounted horizontally at the bottom of a funnel vibrated the carbon rod. This "liquid" microphone was a meager success, and was quickly superseded because of the hazards involved with the open cup of acid. Later that year, Bell's improved design used a diaphragm that pressed a small platinum button against a carbon block to create the varying resistances. All the principal manufacturers of transmitters followed this pattern, including Ader, Berliner, and Edison. Batteries supplied the DC voltages.

Another design used in many early Bell telephones was the "magnetic" transmitter. This design was the same as a telephone receiver: a coil of wire was wound around the end of a magnet. A steel diaphragm was placed at the end of the magnet by the coil. As it vibrated, it induced a weak AC voltage in the coil. Although this simplified telephone design allowed the same device to send and receive, it limited the telephone's range and usefulness, and battery-driven carbon microphones quickly superseded the design. Carbon microphones developed higher voltages in the era before electronic amplifiers existed.

By 1880, carbon rods began to substitute for carbon blocks, improving reliability and sensitivity. It was with a rod-type carbon microphone that Bell demonstrated binaural sound, with a pair of transmitters placed on either side of a mannequin's head. In a separate room, "auditors" experienced "binaural audition" by listening to a pair of receivers, much like modern headphones. In 1881, Clement Ader placed pairs of his transmitters in the footlights of the Paris Opera. Visitors to the Electrical Exhibition Hall ten miles away could hear the opera through pairs of receivers, connected by telephone circuits to the transmitters there. The year 1885 brought the Blake transmitter, which for the first time used carbon granules instead of rods or blocks. The White transmitter of 1890 placed the carbon microphone in its familiar, modern form. Called the "solid-back" transmitter, it allowed vertical mounting for the first time, and greatly reduced the "packing" of the carbon granules that plagued earlier designs. Various improvements in materials, manufacturing, and power supply occurred up to the 1920s, but no major improvements in sound quality derived, because the

sole application of microphones was in telephone systems.

3. *The Radio Age.* The advent of radio, talking movies, and electronic amplifiers in the 1920s gave impetus for better designs to meet the quality demands of these applications. Whereas telephones were concerned with speaking voice only, radio and the movies often included music. Although the very first radio microphones were still carbon types, new designs quickly arrived. Bell Laboratories in the United States, Telefunken in Germany, and AKG in Austria simultaneously developed the first condenser microphones, during 1923 and 1924. Bell Laboratories' Model 103 was used in their early experiments into "wide-range electrical recording," and the 1932 landmark stereophonic recording experiments in Philadelphia with Leopold Stokowski. The Radio Corporation of America (RCA) seven-inch square box condenser, and the Western Electric cathedral shaped model became standards of film and broadcasting.

The 1930s were an era of rapid improvements in microphone design and use. Bell Laboratories upgraded its condenser models, largely because of recording experiments begun in the late 1920s. In England, Alan Dower Blumlein used omni microphones and derived first-order directional patterns (at low frequencies) through a technique called "shuffling," ultimately leading to his pioneering successful stereo recordings. Other ribbon microphones gained rapid acceptance too, most visibly by the distinctive angular RCA Model 44, and models by Shure Brothers, Electro-Voice, and others. Huge cylindrical Telefunken microphones festooned the podium during rousing speeches by Adolf Hitler. Crystal microphones, such as those made by Astatic, Amperite, and Brush, adorned the podiums of less grandiose public address systems.

Western Electric marketed the first cardioid microphone, their model 639 "birdcage," which used a ribbon and omnidirectional dynamic inside the same housing. A switch could select only the ribbon element for bidirectional pickup, only the dynamic element for omnidirectional pickup, or both to create a cardioid pickup. Their models 630 "8-ball" and 633 "saltshaker" also became mainstays.

Dynamic microphones arrived with the discovery of better magnetic materials. Besides RCA, Shure, Electro-Voice, AKG, and Calrec, companies such as Turner, Universal Microphone Company, and American Microphone Company marketed less costly models. Ben Bauer developed the classic Shure Unidyne in 1939. During the Second World War, microphone development continued. The huge Telefunken U-27 became a world standard following the War. RCA's innovative model 77 ribbon became almost universal in film and radio, and later in television. Adjustable vanes inside the "time capsule"-shaped, perforated metal housing allowed it to be bidirectional, cardioid, or nearly omnidirectional. RCA 77s are still sought after today.

4. *The Post-War Boom.* The arrival in America and Europe of German tape recording technology in the late 1940s brought fresh demand for even higher quality microphones. Electro-Voice created a cardioid dynamic that vented the rear of the diaphragm, creating partial cancellation of the sound resulting in a cardioid pickup pattern. This technique became quickly copied, and is the method still most used cardioid microphones.

Radio, stereophonic movies, television, and home tape recording led to a proliferation of microphone designs. In 1956, court actions forced the divestiture of Western Electric's microphone division to speaker giant Altec. Telefunken introduced their classic U-47 (which was actually a relabeled Neumann U-47), a condenser in which a pair of elements was electronically switched to create different pickup patterns. (Some years later, Gotham Audio picked up the line directly.) Other models came into being: the Electro-Voice 635, 644, and 664; Shure 515, 545, and the 55, associated with the birth of rock-and-roll; and AKG C-12 brought back as "The Tube." The C-12 had also been marketed by Telefunken, relabeled as the ELAM 251, until AKG made other foreign distribution arrangements. Many of these microphones are still made today.

5. *The Rock Era: 1960s.* Improved materials, lower manufacturing costs, and a proliferation of models characterized the 1960s. Neumann, Schoeps, AKG, Shure, Electro-Voice, Altec, Peavey, and Calrec marketed a wide range of successful models, primarily dynamic and condenser types. Carbon microphones remained in telephones, and crystal types became used only in the cheapest home models. Neumann updated the Telefunken U-47. B&K (Bruel & Kjaer) introduced what many claim is the best microphone ever created. Sennheiser and Electro-Voice marketed their very rugged designs. Nearly all quality microphones were dynamics or condensers. Pressure

from the demands of television and movie sound brought the lavaliere microphone, inconspicuously worn around the speaker's neck.

6. *The "Golden Era": 1970s.* New technologies arrived in the 1970s. Electro-Voice marketed the Mike Mouse, an innovative product based on research into boundary layer effects. An omnidirectional microphone was placed inside a specially shaped foam windscreen and laid on the floor. This eliminated the comb filter effect that occurs when sound from a nearby floor or wall arrives at the microphone, blends with direct sounds, and causes partial cancellations. Crown took this idea a step further with their Pressure Zone Microphone, or PZM. A PZM mounted a tiny condenser upside down a very short distance from a metal boundary plate. The unique configuration duplicated the Mike Mouse but gave greater freedom of placement.

The electret microphone was introduced, in which the "bias" DC voltage was replaced by a permanent static charge. Nearly every recorder manufacturer could then offer quality condenser models. Studio and broadcast microphones dropped in cost. Electrets were built into portable cassette recorders. Lavaliere microphones using electrets became so small as to be nearly invisible. Electrets replaced crystals in low cost models, and were used in telephones. Piezoelectric models using conductive plastics, such as Kynar or PVDF, were introduced in operator's headsets, music instrument pickups, hydrophones, ultrasound microphones, and contact microphones.

The direct-to-disc audiophile record craze brought a generation of transformerless condensers. Originally modifications of existing units, they improved transient response by eliminating losses caused by transformer core saturation. AKG C-414, C-451, and C-461 condensers became popular and the cosmetically distinctive D-190 dynamic became one of the most visible European models. AKG two-way dynamic models D-200 and D-202, with separate high/low frequency dynamic elements, gave condenser-like quality. Neumann updated the U-67, which became the U-87. (This was some time after the U-47 had been discontinued.) Shure SM-57 and SM-58 cardioids became arguably the two most visible public address microphones.

7. *Modern Microphones.* In the 1980s, rare-earth magnets led to a new generation of dynamic microphones. Electro-Voice marketed the N-Dym line, and Shure the Beta line. Their neodymium magnets created such high magnetic flux that they exhibited a clarity normally associated with condensers, along with higher output. Digital microphones built the quantization circuits into condenser microphones to attain remarkable results. Great improvements in wireless microphone technology occurred.

8. In the 1990s, innovations were appearing quickly. One was B & K's "Ball" accessory for the 4000 series omnidirectional condensers. The 7-cm diameter solid plastic ball made the omnidirectional microphone into a somewhat cardioid pattern. —Kermit V. Gray; updated by Howard Ferstler, with thanks to John Eargle for some detail corrections. *See also* ELECTRICAL RECORDING; ORCHESTRA RECORDINGS.

Microsoft Windows Media Audio · *See.* WINDOWS MEDIA AUDIO.

MIDI (Musical Instrument Digital Interface) · The industry standard bus and protocol (digital signal system, or system of number signals) used to communicate performance information to and from musical instruments making music. First utilized in 1983, it has been expanded to include both signal processing as well as lighting control.—Howard Ferstler

Mil · One-thousandth of an inch. A measure used to describe the thickness of the base in a magnetic tape, stylus dimensions, groove dimensions, etc.

Miller, Walter, 1870–1941 · American recording engineer and inventor, an associate of Thomas Edison from ca. 1888 to 1929. He had various duties, including direction of research, supervision of entertainment cylinder production, and general supervision of recording. Miller had 18 U.S. patents in the area of sound recording between 1898 and 1904, five of them in his name alone, and the others with Jonas W. Aylsworth or Alexander N. Pierman. His principal invention was the molding technology that made mass production of cylinders possible.

MiniDisc (MD) · A small-disc (slightly larger than half the diameter of the compact disc), recording and playback format pioneered by Sony. By using 5-to-1 data reduction and data compression, a program that would just fit on a 5.25-inch compact disc can be installed upon the MD surface with only minimal fidelity loss. The technology allows for both pre-recorded programs and recording to blank discs, and allows for portable players of very small size. The format has never caught on in the USA, although it remains popular in Japan.—Howard Ferstler

Minimalist Recording Techniques · *See* LIVE TO 2-TRACK.

Minnesota Mining and Manufacturing Company (3M) [website: www.3m.com] · A diversified American firm, established in 1902, located in St. Paul. 3M is of interest in the sound recording field for its development of magnetic tape players and (1947) "Scotch" recording tapes. Research under direction of Wilfred W. Wetzel led to an improved magnetic tape with an iron oxide coating; this was the Scotch tape. It reached a high frequency of 15,000 Hz, moving at 7 1/2 inches per second. When this tape went into production in 1947 it almost immediately replaced discs in professional work, such as making of radio transcriptions. The firm has also manufactured videotapes and CD media, and many other non-audio products.

Mitchell, Peter, 1942–December 30, 1995 · Born in Quincy, Massachusetts, Mitchell graduated from Vermont Academy in 1960, and received a B.A. in physics and astronomy from Boston University in 1966. For a while, he worked for Avco Corporation, studying ablative nose-cone materials, in preparation for future Apollo landings. Throughout the 1970s, he and co-host Richard Goldwater had a weekly, audio-oriented talk show on WBUR-FM in Boston, called *Shop Talk*. Mitchell was also one of the founders of the Boston Audio Society. Mitchell was a gifted writer, and during the last 25 years of his life, he published several hundred articles on audio, many very influential, in *The Boston Phoenix*, *Stereo Review*, *High Fidelity*, *Stereophile*, *Atlantic Monthly*, and *db* magazine, among others. He also wrote a number of audio instruction manuals for Apt, NAD, and other companies. As a long time member of the Audio Engineering Society, he presented papers, chaired workshops, and served on a working group of the Digital Standards Committee.—Howard Ferstler

Mixdown · A reduction in the number of channels from the original recording, as signals are transferred from a multi-track reproducer to a 2-track master record, or to a monaural master, etc. *See also* MIXER.

Mixer · A device that blends two or more recorded signals. In recording, the mixer permits a manipulation of outputs from several channels, so that they may be faded, selected, or combined in any combination and in any arrangement of volumes. *See also* MIXDOWN.

Mobley, Edwin H. · American inventor, holder of nine early patents in sound recording: diaphragms, sound boxes, a turntable for discs, and a phonograph-reproducer (patent no. 690,069; filed July 3, 1901; granted December 31, 1901) that improved stylus tracking and volume of the Edison Automatic Reproducer. Edison sued him successfully because Mobley had no right to alter Edison's patented device.

Modulation · The technique of varying a characteristic (i.e., amplitude) of a wave (the carrier) as a function of the instantaneous value of another wave (the modulator). Amplitude modulation (AM) and frequency modulation (FM) are basic to radio broadcasting. Modulation is also a factor in acoustic and electrical recording, telephony, etc.

Monaural · Single-channel sound transmission or recording, another term for monophonic; it is often shortened to "mono."

Mono; Monophonic · *See* MONAURAL.

Moog, Robert, May 23, 1934–August 21, 2005 · Born in Flushing, New York, Moog was interested in electronic musical instrument design even as a youngster, and following instructions in an electronics magazine, built a theremin when he was only 14 years old, and published an article about building theremins when he was only 19. His academic degrees include a B.S. in Physics from Queens College, a B.S. in Electrical Engineering from Columbia University, and a 1965 Ph.D. in Engineering Physics from Cornell University. In 1954, while still in school, Moog founded the R.A. Moog Company as a part-time business to design and build electronic musical instruments, and between 1961 and 1963, he sold over 100 theremin kits, while working out of his three-room apartment. The company became a full-time business in 1964 (the year before he earned the Ph.D.), and that year it introduced a line of electronic music synthesis equipment. Significantly, Moog's was the first synthesizer to use attack-decay-sustain-release (ADSR) envelopes, set with four different knobs, which control the qualities of a sound's onset, intensity, and fade.

Moog's synthesizers were designed in collaboration with the composers Herbert A. Deutsch, and Walter (later Wendy) Carlos, and after the success of Carlos's album *Switched on Bach*, entirely recorded using Moog synthesizers, Moog's instruments made the leap from the electronic avant-garde, into commercially successful popular music. In 1971, after being sold to a private investor, the name of the company was changed to Moog Music, Inc., and in 1973, the company became a division of Norlin Music, Inc. Moog served as president of the Moog branch, mainly designing guitar effects and guitar amplifiers, until 1977.

In 1978, he moved himself and his family moved to Asheville, North Carolina, and there he founded Big Briar, Inc., for the purpose of designing and building novel electronic music equipment, especially new types of performance control devices. At the International Computer Music Conference in 1982, he introduced the multiple-touch-sensitive keyboard, developed with John Eaton of Indiana University. From 1984 to 1988, Moog was also a full-time consultant and vice president of new product research for Kurzweil Music Systems. Moog's awards included honorary doctorates from Polytechnic University and Lycoming College, as well as the Silver Medal of The Audio Engineering Society, the Trustee's Award of the National Academy of Recording Arts and Sciences, the *Bilboard Magazine* Trendsetter's Award, and the SEAMUS award from the Society of Electroacoustic Music in the United States. He wrote and spoke widely on topics related to music technology, and contributed major articles to the *Encyclopedia Britannica* and the *Encyclopedia of Applied Physics*. In 2002, Moog won the Grammy award for technical achievement, the same year he regained the use of Moog name on his instruments. He died of brain cancer in 2005.—Howard Ferstler

Moorer, James A., November 25, 1925– · Moorer earned an S.B. degree in applied mathematics from MIT in 1968, and had already picked up an S.B. degree in electrical engineering from the same university in 1967. He went on to earn a Ph.D. in computer science from Stanford University in 1975, and is a founder and director of advanced development at Sonic Solutions. He is an internationally known figure in digital audio and computer music, with over 40 technical publications and 2 patents to his credit. He personally designed and wrote much of the SonicSystem and developed the advanced DSP algorithms for the NoNOISE process that is used to restore vintage recordings for CD re-mastering. To date, NoNOISE has been used in the production of over 50,000 CD's.

While vice-president of research and development at Lucasfilm DroidWorks between 1980 and 1987, he designed the Audio Signal Processor (ASP), which was used in the production of sound tracks for *Return of the Jedi*, *Indiana Jones and the Temple of Doom*, and other high-impact films. Between 1977 and 1979, he was a

researcher and the Scientific Advisor to IRCAM in Paris. In the mid-1970s, he was co-director and co-founder of the Stanford Center for Computer Research in Music and Acoustics. In 1990, he received the Audio Engineering Society (AES) Silver Award for Lifetime Achievement and in 1999 he received the Academy of Motion Picture Arts and Sciences Scientific and Engineering Award for his pioneering work in the design of digital signal processing and its application to audio editing for film. Moorer is currently working at Adobe Systems, Inc. as senior computer scientist in the DVD Team.—Howard Ferstler

Motion Picture Music · There were various systems in early days of the film that provided mood music related to action on the screen. The photoplayer arrived around 1912. It was an orchestrion with various special effects under operator control. These were made by the North Tonawanda Musical Instrument Co., Rudolph Wurlitzer Co., Justus Seeburg, American Photoplayer Co., The Operators Piano Co., Chicago, Lyon & Healy, and the Automatic Music Co. (later the Link Piano Co.) The photoplayer thrived until around 1923. Only a few of the thousands made have survived.

Motion Picture Sound Recording · The first motion pictures with any kind of sound added to them were shown in Thomas Edison's laboratory, in West Orange, New Jersey, on October 6, 1889. The system, developed by William Kennedy Dickson, used a cylinder synchronization device. Running about 12 seconds, at 46 frames per second, the resulting films included Dickson's own voice giving a greeting to Edison. That was the forerunner of Edison's Kinetophone, developed in a 1912 version to the point of making short subjects and selling the system to theaters. In 1897, George W. Brown claimed invention of a device to synchronize the projector with the phonograph; in 1900, Léon Gaumont made the first practical synchronizer, linking the projector and phonograph electrically. He presented a filmed speech to the Société Française de la Photographie in November 1902, with a type of Auxetophone amplifier. (His product was sold in America by the Gaumont Co., under the trade name Chronophone, in 1904.) Oskar Messter in Germany had similar success in 1903-1904. Other systems of synchronizers were Viviphone (1907), Cameraphone (1908), Synchronoscope (1908), and Cinephone (Britain, 1909).

All these early systems faced the same problems:

1. Getting the synchronization exactly right and keeping it so throughout the showing
2. Coping with the short playing time of early records
3. Finding ways to enhance the phonographic volume to fill a theater

While these difficulties were being researched, the main use of the phonograph in the early theaters was to bring customers in as it played through large horns that projected through the wall into the street.

In 1903, Eugen Lauste demonstrated a method of getting sound from film through photographed sound waves, with the light passing through the film onto a selenium cell. He gained British patents and gave successful demonstrations, but did not do well commercially. Theodore W. Case patented the soundtrack idea, with the sound inscribed on the film with the pictures, in 1919. Lee De Forest joined in the research, acquiring the Case patent and improving the quality of voice and music reproduction. He made a stock of short films by comedians and musicians, under the name of Phonofilms, by 1925, including one by Al Jolson, *Sonny Boy*. The first Mickey Mouse cartoon with sound, *Steamboat*

Willie (1928), used this method. William Fox used the system in Movietone News short subjects, shown first in 1927 in New York and London. The British Talking Picture Corporation used the De Forest system in early Pathé newsreels. The concept of the soundtrack (a strip on the film, 0.1 inch wide) replaced the idea of the synchronized disc by 1928. Ortofon, a Danish company was also working on a system for putting sound into motion-picture presentations. By 1923, they were able to demonstrate a sound film, using the "variable area" method that required two films run simultaneously—one carrying the audio, the other the video. The method was licensed in Europe and America.

Edison's sound film research had been detoured by a fire in the plant in 1914, plus there were difficulties with the unions and Edison's own multitude of other activities. Indeed, he had lost interest in the Kinetophone project by 1915. Meanwhile, Bell Telephone Laboratories made some improvements. One was the reduction of record speed from 78 rpm to 33 1/3 rpm to give more playing time in the synchronized system. They also developed amplifiers and large horns to extend the sound range. Bell's process was called Vitaphone, an inadvertent use of an old company name. Vitaphone discs were lateral cut, center-start items, 12 to 16 inches in diameter, and running 33 1/3 rpm. The Vitaphone Corporation, under contract with Warner Brothers, made a series of short subjects (four to ten minutes each) between 1926 and 1932 they included work by Giovanni Martinelli, Mischa Elman, Harold Bauer, and Efrem Zimbalist. Vitaphones were shown in New York in February 1926, and on October 6, 1927, the famous Al Jolson film, *The Jazz Singer*, was premiered. This feature-length motion picture, the first with speech, ushered in the era of talking pictures. When it was released, about 100 theaters in the United States were equipped to show sound films, out of about 7,500 Warner Brothers houses. By the end of 1929, some 4,000 theaters had undergone sound installation.

During the 1930s, there were many areas of progress. Reliable film-drive systems were developed, noise reduction was achieved, post-synchronizing in the studio instead of on location, and various improvements in theater installations and in sound reproducing apparatus. In 1940, Disney even released a sound film, *Fantasia*, in multi-channel form. After World War II, magnetic recording became operational for motion picture use. When wide-screen films were made in the early 1950s, soundtracks were made on a separate 3-track magnetic coated film. Those soundtracks were then dubbed onto the film print itself. Cinemascope carried three tracks that were 63 mils wide and one track that was 29 mils wide. The Todd-A-O system used six magnetic tracks on 70-mm film. With most of these systems, three to five separate channels were up front, with one surround channel feeding a multitude of speakers along the side walls of the theater; however, many theater owners could not afford to install systems elaborate enough to deal with such source material.

In the late 1970s, Dolby introduced Dolby Surround Sound to the movie industry, which allowed theaters with more modest budgets to deliver exemplary full-theater sound. The most famous film to make use of this new technology was *Star Wars*, released in 1977, but *A Star Is Born*, released in 1976, was the actually the first widely released movie to make use of the technology. The sonic impressiveness of *Star Wars* did allow the technology to grab people's attention, however, and after that, action movies were not really action movies without surround sound. The Dolby system was carried over into videotapes and laserdiscs for home-theater use,

which further enhanced the public's interest in surround sound.

Somewhat later, Lucasfilm Corporation attempted to standardize theater-sound parameters by introducing the THX program. By allowing theaters to achieve THX "certification" after an appropriate upgrading of playback hardware and an inspection by THX officials (these were to be done at intervals, to insure continuous adherence to the THX theater-sound standards), a theater was allowed to advertise its superior sound system, further whetting the public's appetite for superior theater sound. The THX program was later expanded to include home-theater hardware and software.

Modern theater sound has for the most part become digital, with six-channel software technologies (five satellite channels, plus a subwoofer channel for low-frequency effects) available from several companies, including Dolby, Digital Theater Systems, Sony, and for a while, even Eastman Kodak. The Sony and DTS systems even allowed for as many as seven or even eight satellite channels. With these systems, there would continue to be three-to-five channels up front, with the surround feed split into two or even three separate channels, allowing for often-stupendous theater surround effects. In the late 1990s, these digital systems also became available to the home-theater industry as part of the DVD system.—Rev. by Howard Ferstler

MP3 · MP3 is an abbreviation for MPEG-1 Audio Layer III, the audio component of a digital media compression protocol that is widely used for reducing the size of digital music files without loss of sound quality. Development of the audio file format that would become MP3 began in Germany in 1987 under the direction of Dieter Seitzer at the University of Erlangen in Nuremberg. The Fraunhofer Institut Integrierte Schaltungen holds key patents for the technology. As an industry wide standard, MP3 was the first such audio file format of significant importance to be adopted by the Industry Standards Organization (ISO).

Music from a compact disc transferred to a computer in pure digital form is known as a wave (or in PC-speak a .wav) file where one minute of music occupies approximately 10 megabytes of data and drive space. The advent of MP3 allowed such files to be compressed to 10 percent of their original size. Not only did this make them easier to play back on a computer (smaller files being quicker and easier to manage) but it also made them easier to transfer. Attaching an MP3 file to an email for example made it possible to send an entire CD-quality music tracks around the world in seconds. The music industry was transformed because of this new file format. Underground consumer cultures of "ripping" (the process of extracting audio to a computer's hard drive) and "burning" (recording received files onto normal audio CDs) took firm hold. New systems, such as peer-to-peer networking (a famous example being Napster), also sprang up as illegal MP3 "sharing" (i.e., bootlegging) portals. With the seemingly impossible task of clamping down on MP3 music piracy, the music industry has been working frantically to develop its own fee-based, file-sharing services. Some switched-on record companies have embraced the concept by putting time and energy into promoting and talent scouting artists via MP3 files on public websites. As of this writing, the dominance of the MP3 file format has been challenged by improvements both to MPEG file compression (e.g., MP4 for audio and visual content) and rival compression schemes. The most noteworthy competing audio scheme is Advanced Audio Coding (AAC), which stole the spotlight from MP3 with its adoption by Apple Computer as the compression scheme of choice for its best-selling iTunes and iPod products. The coexistence of this and established formats,

such as CD, remains to be seen. See iPod.
—Ian Peel; Rev. by Thom Holmes

MP3 Players · *See* DIGITAL AUDIO PLAYER.

MS (Mid/Side) Stereo Recording Technique · *See* COINCIDENT STEREO RECORDING.

Mullin, John, T. (Jack), October 5, 1913–June 24, 1999 · Born in San Francisco and growing up in Larkspur in Marin County, Mullin graduated from Santa Clara University in what is today Silicon Valley, with a major in electrical engineering. He was a member of the U.S. Army Signal Corps during World War II, and during the post-war occupation in Germany he visited a studio near Frankfurt that was occupied by the Allies and was shown a small storehouse of magnetic quarter-inch tape and machines. He had already suspected that the Germans had some kind of superior recording device from his monitoring experiences when he was stationed in England. The device he discovered that was most important was the high-fidelity version of the German AEG Magnetophon K-4 audio tape recorder, a machine with extremely low distortion and a frequency response almost matching the human hearing range. Getting official permission to send home samples of what he felt was important, he shipped 50 reels of tape, head assemblies, and two of the tape transports back to America (in pieces in multiple mailbags), and later worked to improve the technology.

In October of 1946, at a meeting of studio executives, Mullin used his modified Magnetophone recorders to demonstrate how the new recording technology worked. Soon Bing Crosby, who hated the pressure of live broadcasting, started using the then revolutionary technology to pre-tape his radio show for ABC. The show included laugh tracks, which Mullin also invented. Before Mullin, prerecorded programs (usually done on 16-inch transcription discs) presented terrible sound quality. His new technology (which not only allowed for production during convenient time periods, but also allowed for scissors-and-tape editing that removed bloopers) revolutionized the industry and set a precedent in broadcast production that remains the norm to this day.

Mullin's prototype machines proved the feasibility of the new tape technology to Ampex Corporation, a small northern California company that then decided to become the first American manufacturer of the Mullin-enhanced German technology. The result was the Model 200A, and later the Model 300, tape recorders, which went on to revolutionize the entertainment and information industries. Mullin went on to work for Minicom, a division of 3M,

and helped to formulate many recording industry standards, including the NAB equalization curve that is still in use for analog recording. He remained Minicom's chief engineer until his retirement in 1975.

At that time, he began a second career of voluntary teaching, writing, and lecturing, in addition to helping to work out recording technology for the blind and dyslexic. He created over 2000 hours of books on tape that now reside at the university library at Princeton, and which are still nationally distributed to the reading impaired. He also created one of the finest collections of historic entertainment technology available, including radios, recorders, microphones, tapes, and discs. The Mullin Museum is now a part of the Pavek Museum of Broadcasting in St. Louis Park, Minnesota, near 3M in St. Paul. For his work in recording technology, the Audio Engineering Soci-

Multi-Track Recording

The use of two or more multiple tracks of recorded sound to create a composite audio recording from separately recorded parts. Before the introduction of multi-track recording, music performances were usually recorded as complete performances in real time. The introduction of 2-track stereo recording in the early 1940s permitted two tracks to be recorded separately and then mixed to create a composite recording. This was the generally accepted practice by the late 1960s.

Multi-track recording originated with the use of multiple track tape recorders and is currently emulated by digital studio recorders using magnetic, optical, and other computer media.

Experiments in multiple track recording began soon after the magnetic tape recorder became available in the United States following World War II. Some notable achievements in the early history of multi-track recording included:

1931, England. Alan Blumlein of Columbia Graphophone Co. applied for a patent for a binaural or two-channel sound system, an early conception of stereophonic sound recording.

1936, United States. Unaware of Blumhein's earlier work in England, Arthur Keller of Bell Labs applied for a patent for single-groove stereo. Westrex used a similar approach in the 1950s when single-groove two-channel stereo recording and reproduction became widespread.

1940, United States. Earlier experiments by A. C. Keller and I. S. Rafuse of AT&T led to the first U.S. two-channel, single-groove stereo recording system. The first commercial use of stereo sound was in movie theaters when the Walt Disney Studios released the movie *Fantasia.*

ety presented him with numerous awards, including the organization's Silver Medal, in 1994.—Howard Ferstler

Multiplexer · A switching circuit in an audio system that makes possible the serial transfer of signals from various sources in a defined sequence intended for a single output.

Musicassette · The enclosed cassette launched by Philips in a compact cassette portable recorder in 1963.

Musique Concrète · Pre-empting sampling and DJ culture by almost 50 years, *musique concrète* was first theorized in the 1940s by French composer Pierre Schaeffer. Schaeffer was convinced that music of the future would be created from recycled recordings of the past. He was a mainstay of Club D'Essai, the experimental studio at Radio France, recording tracks that were "concrete" (i.e., of the future) as opposed to "symbolic" (i.e., of the past). Other collaborators and regulars at the Club D'essai included Boulez and Henry, both key figures in France's input into early, experimental musical thinking. In the post-hip-hop era of dance music, where the majority of records are created from fragments of others, extending *musique concrète* into the mainstream, Schaeffer is considered an early visionary. John Cage's "William's Mix" was perhaps the most ambitious tape composition ever conceived, randomly assembled from thousands of pieces of tape over a period of 9 months, to create a 4.25-minute work; the "score" for the work runs 192 pages. *See also* ELECTRONIC MUSIC; SCHAEFFER, PIERRE, TAPE COMPOSITION.—Ian Peel

1953, United States. Raymond Scott built two multi-track tape recorders. His patented machines could record 7 and 14 parallel tracks on a single reel of tape.

1953, Germany. In the newly opened electronic music studio of West German Radio (WDR) in Cologne, founders Meyer-Eppler, Beyer, and Eimert equipped the studio with a 4-track tape recorder.

1954, United States. Guitar player and instrument designer Les Paul built a prototype 8-track multi-track tape recorder.

1955, Canada. Hugh Le Caine invented the Special Purpose Tape Recorder that mixed six separate but synchronized tapes down to one track. Models of the recording device were later improved and installed in the electronic music studios of the University of Toronto and McGill University in Montreal. Although inventors such as Scott and Le Caine had created sophisticated multi-track tape recorders during the 1950s, it was not until the mid-1960s that 4-track machines were generally available. The Beatles' album *Sergeant Pepper's Lonely Hearts Club Band* (1967) was recorded using the painstaking process of connecting two 4-track tape recorders to get eight tracks.

1956, United States. The Recording Industry Association of America (RIAA) formally adopted the Westrex system of single-groove stereo recording and reproduction as the industry standard. This made stereo records incompatible with monophonic record players, although mono records could still be played on stereophonic systems.

The advent of multi-track recording spawned the related industry of noise reduction systems, most notably those made by Dolby. Dolby introduced its Type A noise reduction system in 1965. Noise reduction systems are used to reduce tape hiss associated with magnetic tape recording, a problem that is magnified by the use of multiple tape tracks.

Multi-track recording using digital mixing panels can often use as many as 128 separately recorded tracks of sound.—Thom Holmes

Mute · To silence, to reduce, to soften the output of an audio instrument. *See also* MUTING CIRCUIT.

Muting Circuit · In an audio system, the circuit that silences audible sound during the change cycle of a record player, or in a tape deck when the tape is rewinding or fast forwarding, or in a radio receiver when it is tuned across the band.

N

Nagata, Minoru, April 26, 1925–· An internationally known expert on architectural acoustics, Nagata was born in Fukuoka, Japan, and graduated from Tokyo University in 1949. Between 1949 and 1971, he was employed by NHK (Japan Broadcasting Corporation), in the company's technical research laboratories. In 1962, while still working for NHK, he received his doctorate from Tohoku University, and during 1963 and 1964, he engaged in further studies at Goettinngen University, Germany. In June of 1971, he left NHK to establish his own company, Minoru Nagata Acoustic Engineer & Associates Co., Ltd. (later renamed Nagata Acoustics Inc.). During his career, he has acoustically engineered a large number of fine concert halls, including Suntory Hall, Casals Hall, and Tokyo Metropolitan Art Space Concert Hall in Tokyo, as well as Kyoto Concert Hall and Sapporo Concert Hall in other parts of Japan, and Walt Disney Concert Hall in Los Angeles. Nagata is a member of the Acoustical Society of America, the Audio Engineering Society, the Acoustical Society of Japan, and the Japan Organ Society. He has won the Sato prize from the Acoustical Society of Japan, a Best Technical Paper prize from the Acoustical Society of America, and won the prestigious Prize of the Architectural Institute of Japan.— Howard Ferstler

NAGRA [website: www.nagraaudio.com] · Since Swiss Federal Institute of Technology physics student Stefan Kudelski built the NAGRA I portable audio recorder, the firm's equipment has been widely utilized by audio professionals due to its sound quality and mechanical reliability in the fields of scientific research, radio broadcasting, the cinema, journalism, and the record industry. With the introduction of the NAGRA III, a transistorized tape recorder with electronic speed control, for the first time a unit weighing only five kilograms could be relied to produce recordings the equal of those achieved by the best non-portable studio recorders. Models such as the NAGRA 4.2 and NAGRA IV-S Time Code were pivotal developments within the film industry. The company's products have garnered three Oscars and an Emmy (for development of digital Pay-TV in the United States) as well as many electronics-related awards.

In 1997, the firm entered the high-end audiophile market with the PL-P preamplifier and the C-PP (a recorder/editor/CODEC, a companion of the Academy Award-winning ARES-C). The VPA (Vacuum Tube Power Amplifier) appeared the following year. February 2002 saw the introduction of the NAGRA V—a 2-channel, 24-four-bit portable digital audio recorder offering all features required contemporary sound recording engineers—which has signaled the demise of analog and DAT recorders then in use within the film, television, and music industries.

Nagra products fall within the Kudelski Group, a combine encompassing digital television and broadband network applications, Pay-TV systems, professional and prestige hi-fi hardware, physical access and ticketing solutions, health sector applications, and the e-voting and cyber-administration sector. *See also* KUDELSKI, STEFAN.—Howard Ferstler

Nakajima, Heitaro, 1921–· Interested from childhood in math and physics, Nakajima was one of the first individuals responsible for actually recording digitally processed sound, and is considered by many to be the father of the compact disc, along with Johannes (Joop) Sinjou, of Philips, and Toshitada Doi, of Sony. Nakajima earned a degree in electrical engineering from the Tokyo Institute of Technology in 1944, with a concentration in telecommunications, because the school had no degree program in math and physics at that time. Shortly later, he earned a master's degree at Kyushu University, and in 1947, he went to work for NHK Industries, doing research in acoustics and microphone design. In 1958, he earned his doctorate from Kyushu, continued to advance in the NHK hierarchy, and from 1965 through 1968, he was the general manager of the Acoustic Research Division, later on being promoted to the head of the Science Research Laboratory. During this time, he began to experiment with prototype digital recording systems. In 1971, he left NHK and joined Sony, working at first on analog recording systems but eventually working on the digital technology that resulted in DAT and later, in consort with engineers at Philips, the compact disc. He is past president of the Japan Audio Society, and for his pioneering work in digital recording systems, he was awarded the Audio Engineering Society Gold Medal in 1989.—Howard Ferstler

Nakamichi [website: www.nakamichi. com]· Founded by Etsuro Nakamichi in 1948, the Tokyo-based Nakamichi Corporation is known worldwide for the manufacture of high performance audio-visual and multimedia electronic hardware. The firm originally designed and developed portable radios, speakers, phonograph tone arms, and communications equipment. By 1951, the company was manufacturing open reel tape decks for the "Magic Tone" line.

Nakamichi created proprietary magnetic tape heads in 1957; with the appearance of the cassette configuration, the firm assumed a leadership role in the development of a tape head capable of reproducing sound ranging from 20 Hz to 20 kHz. In 1967, the company began supplying cassette and open-reel decks on an OEM basis to many of the top hi-fi brands. By 1972, the first products bearing the Nakamichi name—geared to the audiophile—entered the marketplace; the premium item was the first ever three-head cassette deck, thereby enabling the audiocassette to became a high quality music medium.

Shifting its Research and Development emphasis to the digital domain, Nakamichi introduced its widely acclaimed Music-Bank CD changer mechanism in 1990. The device would also provide the impetus for the company's entrance in to the computer peripheral market. By the 21st century, Nakamichi had emerged as the foremost manufacturer within the "design-driven" category of audio and home theater systems. Seven SoundSpace systems—the 1, 2, 3, 5, 8, 9, and 21—received the Consumer Electronics Association Innovations Award (overseen by the Industrial Designers Association of America) in 2000, 2001, and 2002. A 24-bit CD player/tuner for mobile applications, was introduced in 2000, claiming to have the best sound quality of any in-automobile system available.

The E. Nakamichi Foundation was established in 1982. The nonprofit, philanthropic organization advances the musical arts through the subsidizing of competitions, public concerts, and public radio programming.—Howard Ferstler

Napster, Inc. [website: www.napster. com] · In August 1999, Napster, Inc. was launched as an Internet file swapping service. It helped Internet users locate files, particularly music files in MP3 format, available for uploading from other users. The Napster software sorted files by type, artist, title, and speed of user connection. Users selected the file they wanted and the Napster software would tell the two computers to connect to each other and begin the transfer of the designated file. Within months transfers of music files using Napster reached into the millions per day. In December of 1999, record labels and artists sued to shut Napster down for copyright infringement

The record labels were largely victorious in their suit, *A & M Records, Inc. v. Napster, Inc.* A federal court of appeals ruled that it was likely that:

1. Napster users were copyright infringers, engaging in unauthorized copying and distribution of recordings and songs.
2. Napster, Inc. was liable for this infringement either as a vicarious or contributory infringer.
3. Napster, Inc. was not sheltered by the Digital Millennium Copyright Act because it was not a "service provider" as defined in the statute.
4. Napster must take positive steps to screen out infringing files and transfers.

By July 2001, BMG Music had bought a share of Napster to turn the service into a licensed digital music distribution company. In January 2002, Napster launched a subscription version in competition with other pay services, MusicNet, PressPlay, and Rhapsody; in May 2002, Bertelsmann purchased Napster completely, hoping to realize this goal. It closed the operation in September 2002, however, and subsequently Napster's assets were purchased by Roxio, Inc., a maker of CD-burning software. Napster has since been revived as a pay service. *See also* MP3.—G. P. Hull

National Academy of Recording Arts And Sciences (NARAS) [website: www. grammy.com] · An organization established in 1957 to promote creative and technical progress in the sound recording field. The first chapter office was opened in Los Angeles in 1957, followed by 11 more offices, including New York (1958), Chicago (1961), Nashville (1964), Atlanta (1969), Memphis (1972), San Francisco (1974), Austin (1998), Philadelphia (1999), Florida (2000), and Washington, D.C. (2000). The membership consists of performers, producers, engineers, and others engaged in the industry; as of 2002, there were over 20,000 members. A Producers and Engineers Wing was also established in early 2000 as a means of representing members in special areas of the recording profession; other wings are planned. From 1958, NARAS has presented the annual Grammy awards for outstanding recordings. The NARAS Hall of Fame was established to honor records issued before the Grammys began. NARAS has also established several charitable and advocacy organizations, including MusiCares Foundation, established in 1989 to provide health and other services to musicians; the Grammy Foundation, supporting education in music; and the National Coalition for Music Education. In 1997, NARAS founded the Latin Academy of Recording Arts & Sciences with offices in Miami and Santa Monica, California, as its first international membership organization, representing Spanish-speaking artists. The First Latin Grammy awards were held in September 2000.—Rev. by Carl Benson

National Association of Broadcasters (NAB) [website: www.nab.org] · Formed in 1922, initially to work for rational rules related to spectrum allocation related to

U.S. radio broadcasting, the NAB was crucial in bringing about the Radio Act of 1927. This created legislation for station licensing and frequency allotment, while avoiding government control of station's business operations and programming. A second major concern of the organization's founders focused on demands made by the American Society of Composers Authors and Publishers (ASCAP) that broadcasters license and pay for all music played over the air. In working out relations with ASCAP, and later with other licensing organizations, the NAB became the chief business representative as well as the governmental lobby representing the broadcasting industry. With headquarters in Washington, D.C., the NAB is one of the most active lobbies in the United States. It represents more than 900 television stations and almost 5,000 radio stations, as well as 7,500 members from the radio and television industry. It monitors FCC activities and legislation, as well as economic, legal, social, and technical trends that might affect the industry, and holds yearly conferences and conventions that deal with the radio and television business and technology, including aspects related to recording.

Needle Chatter · Vibration of the pickup in a disc player, caused by insufficient vertical compliance of its moving parts.

Needle Cut · *See* LATERAL RECORDING.

Needles · Replaceable needles were a hallmark of the 78-rpm period. They were made of various materials: steel, chrome, fibers, thorn, cactus, sapphire, and diamond. Some needles were designed for a single play only (e.g., the Beltona), others played as many as 10 records (e.g., the Petmecky), and some went on to 20 or more performances (e.g., the Euphonic). With the popularity of the jukebox in the 1930s, there was improved needle design: Alloy-tipped shockproof needles, capable of many plays, came into use. The diamond needle was theoretically non-wearable. Some sapphires, such as the one marketed by Neophone in 1905, were also "permanent"—advertised to play from 500 to 800 times.

As early as 1906, there were nine types of needle available: three to play quietly, three to play at medium volume, and three types for loud playback. (These were sold by Universal Talking Machine Co. of New York.) Loud needles had rounded tips, and softer-sound needles had sharper tips. The problem with all metal and jewel needles was that they chewed up the record grooves. Fiber, thorn, and cactus needles were popular with collectors in the 1930s and 1940s because they produced minimal record wear, but of course, the needles themselves wore out instead. They could be shaved for replay, and shaving devices something like pencil sharpeners were sold for the purpose. Victor sold a fiber "needle cutter" in 1909 that used a plunger action, "enabling you to use each fiber needle at least ten times." Major manufacturers offered a choice of materials; for example in 1924 HMV was advertising steel, fiber, and "tungstyle"— said to be semi-permanent—varieties.

The Petmecky Co. had the favorite brand name needles of the acoustic period, made by the W. H. Bagshaw Co., of Lowell, Massachusetts. In the electric era, the Recoton brand was among the most popular in America.

With the arrival of LP records, the lightweight stylus took the place of the needle.

Negative Feedback · The inversion and return of a portion of an amplifier's output to its input. It is used intentionally to reduce distortion and to provide more predictable amplification and response. Because negative feedback also reduces gain, the amplifier must have a greater open-loop gain to compensate for this factor. Nevertheless, the considerable improvement in many other characteristics often outweighs the reduction in gain. *See also* ACOUSTIC FEEDBACK.

Neumann, Georg, October, 1898–August 30, 1976 · Born in Chorin, near Berlin, during most of the 1920s, Neumann worked for Eugen Reisz, who was credited with developing the first decent-quality carbon microphone. Neumann went on to design a still better version, which was called the Reisz microphone, after the firm's owner. During this period, Neumann was also responsible for numerous phono pickup, capacitive loudspeaker, and electro-mechanical cutter head designs. In 1928, in Berlin, Neumann, along with Erich Rickmann, started the company that still bears his name, and went on to design and build condenser microphones, which became famous throughout the recording and radio industry for their quality. The company also produced some fine test equipment, the most notable of which was the linear motion, logarithmic pen recorder. After the Second World War, Neumann temporarily moved to Paris, where he worked to develop a new storage-battery design. The result was the gas-tight NiCad battery, which revolutionized the portable power industry. In 1947, the company was reorganized, and the result was Neumann's U-47 microphone, a device that changed what was possible to hear with recordings. After a long career of building innovative products for the audio and recording industries, Neumann won the Audio Engineering Society's Gold Medal in 1976. Years after his death, in 1999, the company that bears his name won a Grammy for technical achievement, and many of those achievements were a direct result of the genius of Georg Neumann. *See also* MICROPHONE.—Howard Ferstler

Neve, Rupert, 1926– · One of the most famous audio-recording console designers of all time, Neve was born in Newton Abbot, Devonshire, England. From the beginning he been interested in electronics, and at age 13, he designed and built audio amplifiers and radio receivers. He was educated at Belgrano Day School and St. Alban's College, Lomas de Zamora, Buenos Aires. When World War II erupted, he returned to England to serve in His Majesty's Royal Signals. Peacetime found him running a public address and disc recording business in England, and later he worked for several other companies, specializing in transformer design. During this time, he also designed one of the first ever, bookshelf-oriented loudspeakers, and was invited to lecture on it at the Royal Society of Arts in London in 1958. For four additional years, he designed and manufactured hi-fi equipment.

In 1961, he started Rupert Neve & Company, located near Cambridge, specializing in custom equipment for the recording, television, film, and broadcasting industries. The enterprise, and his reputation as a designer, grew rapidly, and in 1969, the company moved to a new factory at Melbourne. In 1975, he sold control of the company, and by 1978, he had ceased to design equipment for them. With the later sale of the Neve companies to Siemens in 1985, the company was reorganized, although it ceased operations in 1992. Neve continued as an independent designer, and 1985, Beatles producer George Martin commissioned Neve to build a no-compromise microphone-preamp and EQ circuit that he could add to the Neve console in his A.I.R. Montserrat studio. Neve is now a long-term design consultant to Amek (a Harman International company), whose expertise in the audio sound control and manufacturing fields is supported by Neve's innovative approach to the sound path. Recent designs include new analog rack-mount microphone preamps, equalizers, dynamic-control units, and consoles for live sound, film, and music recording.

Neve won a Grammy for technical achievement in 1997.—Howard Ferstler

Nichols, Roger, September 22, 1944- ·
One of America's most notable recording engineers and producers, Nichols was born in Oakland, California, and was interested in astronomy as a child. Indeed, when he was in the seventh grade he constructed a hand-ground telescope lens, built a reflecting telescope, and used it to discover a comet in 1957. After graduating from high school, he won an appointment to the Air Force Academy, but declined and went to Oregon State University instead, and later completed a nuclear engineering course through Capitol Radio Engineering Institute, in Washington, D.C. After earning his degree, he initially worked as a nuclear engineer at the San Onofre Nuclear Generating Station in Southern California. While at San Onofre, he and two other sound-recording enthusiasts built a studio in Torrance, and worked there on weekends. Plans were canceled for other nuclear plants, and Nichols, who was becoming more interested in expert recording technologies than nuclear reactions, left for full-time recording in late 1969.

Nichols has recorded and produced recordings in a number of musical styles. Those he has collaborated with read like a veritable performing who's who, including John Denver (producer for 17 years), Steely Dan (engineering for 30 years, winning four engineering Grammys in the process), Donald Fagan (independently from Steely Dan), Frank Sinatra, Motorhead, Rosanne Cash, Reba McIntyre, Natalie Cole, Jim Messina, Gloria Estefan, The Beach Boys, Placido Domingo, Bela Fleck, Yo Yo Ma, Walter Becker, Michael Franks, Rickie Lee Jones, Lee Greenwood, John Klemmer, Crosby, Stills & Nash, Diana Ross, Flora Purim, Rodney Crowell, Sly Stone, Michael Bloomfield, Mark Knopfler, Frank Zappa, Patti Austin, John Lee Hooker, and numerous others. In addition, he has mixed soundtracks for a number of TV shows and films. The material he has produced or recorded has been nominated for 11 Grammys, with 7 winners, and he has had several TEK award nominations and wins.

Nichols has been deeply involved in digital recording technology since 1977. As part of his engineering work, he designed and built WENDELjr, a high-fidelity digital audio percussion replacement device used by many major artists, including Pink Floyd, Heart, Donald Fagan, and Paul Simon, as well as sound companies such as Clair Brothers in the production of their albums and live shows. He has worked on a technique involving tape restoration process, as well as a completely new kind of microphone, with patents for three of his designs pending. He serves on the Board of Governors for the Miami Chapter of the National Academy of Recording Arts & Sciences (NARAS), gives master class lectures at the Berklee School of Music, the Musicians Institute, the Recording Workshop, Full Sail, and University of Miami. A sought after guest speaker, he has also given seminars on digital audio and recording techniques in Hong Kong, Buenos Aires, Singapore, and Sweden, and at various AES and NARAS functions in the USA. He also serves as a consultant on digital audio technology for the Culpepper Archiving Facility at the Library of Congress. Starting in 1984, he archived and restored digital/analog tapes for *The Big Chill* soundtrack (Motown), all the Steely Dan original master tapes, the entire Roy Orbison catalog, early Blue Thumb catalog tapes for re-release, the JVC Jazz catalog, and many more. He also designed the recording curriculum for the Musicians Institute in Hollywood, and is a regular columnist and equipment reviewer for *EQ* magazine.—Howard Ferstler

Nipper, 1884–1895 · A white fox terrier with black markings—the dog in the painting

"His Master's Voice" by Francis Barraud, famous as the Victor/Gramophone Company trademark. Born in Bristol, United Kingdom, Nipper was owned first by the painter's brother, Mark Henry Barraud. When Mark Henry died in 1887, Nipper moved in with Francis, in Liverpool, and the painting followed at some uncertain date. He was seen in advertising by Emile Berliner, who registered the trademark with the U.S. Patent Office in July 1900; and by Eldridge Johnson's Consolidated Talking Machine Co., in 1900. The dog was next seen on Victor Monarch record labels from January 1902, and on Gramophone Co. labels from February 1909. He appeared in other countries as well, wherever Gramophone affiliates were found, with the text translated appropriately into "*Die Stimme seines Herrn*," "*La Voce del Padrone*," etc. In Germany, the dog trademark was used by the affiliate until 1949, whereas the Gramophone Co. branch, Electrola (established 1926) used it only on products sold outside Germany until 1949, when EMI gained control of the trademark and used it on early LPs in Germany.

In 1949, a plaque was placed (according to undocumented reports) over Nipper's supposed grave, near a mulberry tree on Eden St., Kingston-on-Thames. That was the place of employment of Mark Barraud, nephew of the painter and son of Nipper's first owner; he took the dog to work with him each day. Later developments in that location, however, resulted in a parking lot, under which Nipper apparently lies. The property, now addressed as 83 Clarence St., belongs to Lloyds Bank. A marker was laid in the parking area on August 15, 1984, by David Johnson, Chairman of HMV Shops, Ltd., and a memorial plaque was placed in the foyer of the bank. Nipper's birth and death dates, as given previously, are taken from the memorial plaque and marker.

In late 1990, RCA began to use two "Nippers"—a grown dog and a puppy—in advertising its new line of television models and camcorders. RCA was acquired from General Electric by Thomson Consumer Electronics, a French company, in 1987. Thomson has the right to use the Nipper symbol and so does General Electric. The latter firm owns the four green stained glass windows—circular, 14 1/2 feet in diameter—now in the nine-story tower in Camden, New Jersey, which was for years the centerpiece of Victor's vast establishment there. Eldridge Johnson commissioned Nicola D'Ascenzo Studios of Philadelphia to make the windows in 1915. They remained in place until the late 1960s, when RCA changed its logo and donated three of the windows to the Smithsonian Institution, Widener College, and Pennsylvania State University. The fourth window was stored by RCA until 1988, when it was given to Camden County Historical Society. A revival of interest in Nipper resulted in a fresh commission by RCA to D'Ascenzo in 1979, and four new windows, copies of the originals, were installed. *See also* DEUTSCHE GRAMMOPHON GESELLSCHAFT (DGG); VICTOR TALKING MACHINE COMPANY.

Noise (I) · Any undesired signal in a recording or transmission system; an interfering disturbance. *See also* DISTORTION.

Noise (II) · In acoustics, noise is a sound with a large number of frequencies outside the harmonic series of the fundamental.

Noise (III) · White noise is a random signal, having the same energy level at all frequencies, sometime used as a mask to conceal disagreeable sounds.

Noise (IV) · Pink noise is a band-limited random signal with the same amount of energy in each octave.

Noise (V) · Ambient noise is the total of the undesired signals in the listening environment. It renders inaudible the desired portion of a received signal that falls below a certain decibel level; in an average home situation, it is estimated that signals of volume below 30 dB are not actually heard because of ambient noise.

Noise (VI) · Surface noise is the result of friction between a record surface and the playback stylus, friction that is enhanced and more audible when the surface is scratched or damaged or when the stylus is worn. Even with all elements in perfect condition, however, there was an audible hissing noise in playback of 78-rpm records. LP records in fine condition, played with proper lightweight styli, were for practical purposes free of surface noise. Some cylinder records had extremely quiet surfaces when new. *See also* NOISE REDUCTION SYSTEMS; SIGNAL-TO-NOISE RATIO (S/N RATIO).

Noise Filter · *See* SCRATCH FILTER.

Noise Reduction · In recording technology, any number of electronic processes that are designed to reduce background noise and increase dynamic-range potential.

Surface noise was a nuisance from the beginning of the sound recording industry. Early discs were so noisy from the contact of hard needles with gritty grooves that the desired performance signals could nearly disappear into the background. Improvements in materials lessened the seriousness of this problem, which in any case appeared to have been solved in the advertising of the manufacturers—who promoted "silent surfaces" long before such things were practical. Indeed, the audience for 78s did learn to listen through the surface noises to a certain extent, ignoring them somewhat like white noise (*see also* NOISE (III)). The best Edison Diamond Discs possessed nearly silent surfaces, and other good discs could be rendered almost free of noise when played with fiber, thorn,

or cactus needles. Tape recording brought its own noise, tape hiss.

Real work on noise reduction through technical means began in the 1950s. D.T. N. Williamson gave a lecture in Britain in 1953 on "Suppression of Surface Noise," using a capacitor/inductor delay line and valve equipment. His ideas were employed by the Garrard MRM/101 of 1978, intended to cancel clicks on stereo LPs. Essentially the system analyzed waveforms as they occurred, delayed those with frequencies that matched click frequencies, shunted them out of the signal, and returned the entire cleaned signal to its place in the audio stream. This approach to noise reduction, the "dynamic noise filter," has been used in most of the popular modern systems: Burwen, SAE, SEA, Dolby, MicMix, dbx, and Packburn. Another approach, the "static filter," was adapted by Owl, Orban, UREI, and Pultec.

Digital processing has opened a new pathway to noise reduction. A computer with appropriate instructions can translate a sound signal into digital (numerical) form, sample it for specific patterns named in its program, eliminate those patterns that have been designated as unwanted, and replace them with the average of neighboring number patterns. CEDAR is a functioning digital system that operates along the line just described. It is also able to compare several records of similar content, to find the points where there is least noise, and to produce a new combined recording with the best characteristics of all of them and the fewest intrusive sounds. Klinger 1991; Tuddenham and Copeland 1988. — *See also* CEDAR (Computer Enhanced Digital Audio Restoration); DBX CORPORATION; DOLBY NOISE REDUCTION SYSTEM; PACKBURN AUDIO NOISE SUPPRESSOR.

Noise Shaping · In digital recording systems a technique that reduces subjectively important, in-band noise levels by moving the more audible parts of the background-noise spectrum to areas where the ear is less sensitive. *See also* HDCD (High Definition Compatible Digital).—Howard Ferstler

Non-Magnetic Tape Recording · The idea of cutting a groove into a ribbon of some kind, by acoustical means, is an old one. Thomas Edison's first reproduction of sound in fact took place on a paper ribbon, and he alluded to this kind of medium, as well as other sound carrier formats, in his British patent no. 1644. U.S. patent no. 944,608 was granted to Franklin C. Goodale on December 28, 1909; it was for a talking machine based on a celluloid tape instead of a cylinder. Frank E. Holman had a U.S. patent granted on November 9, 1909, for a talking machine with a belt for a carrier; it was claimed to play for 50 minutes.

Optical (photographic) sound recording on film was another non-magnetic approach; it was developed by Frenchmen Eugene Lauste and Eugene Boyer before 1913. These early systems failed to replace the short-playing noisy discs because they lacked amplification devices, and their unamplified playback was very weak. With the development of electron tubes by Lee de Forest, optical systems became significant, especially in motion picture sound. In the United Kingdom, British Ozaphane, Ltd. used sound films without pictures, offering an eight-millimeter film soundtrack with playing time up to 90 minutes. The Dutch Gramofilm of 1934 was similar in concept; and there were comparable devices in other countries.

The many promising features of the non-magnetic systems were eclipsed by the arrival of magnetic recording, first on wire, then in its several tape manifestations.

NOS Recording Technique (*Nederlandsche Omroep Stichting*) · A microphone-positioning technique that involves two directional cardioid microphones placed 30 cm (11.8 inches) apart, with them angled outward at approximately 90 degrees to each other. The spacing is somewhat further apart than what is used with the ORTF system, and the result is coincident microphone behavior at lower frequencies, combined with some pronounced time-delay-related clues at higher frequencies that add a degree of spaciousness to the sound.—Howard Ferstler

Notch Filter · A way to electronically null out certain, potentially obnoxious frequency-related anomalies in a recording during the mixing/editing phase of the production process. The better filters can simultaneously adjust frequency, bandwidth, and depth, whereas cheaper versions have fixed bandwidth and depth settings, with only the frequency being adjustable.—Howard Ferstler

Nousaine, Thomas A. (Tom), October 15, 1944– · A major audio writer and journalist, Nousaine was born in Brainerd, Minnesota, and went on to receive an M.B.A. from Michigan State University in 1971. He retired in 1996 from Ameritech, where he had managed a staff of graduate analysts investigating economic and technology obsolescence, and has since been a regular contributor to *Audio* magazine (until it folded), *Car Stereo Review*, *Stereo Review*, *The Sensible Sound*, *Sound & Vision*, *Mobile Entertainment*, and *The Audio Critic*. He was co-founder and president of The Society of Depreciation Professionals, has been Central Region U.S. Vice President of The Audio Engineering Society, and was the founder of the Prairie State Audio Construction Society. In addition to his regular journalistic and product-reviewing work, Nousaine has designed, conducted, analyzed, and published the results of an extensive series of controlled listening tests, as well as in-room low frequency and surround-speaker placement experiments.—Howard Ferstler

Nyquist Frequency · The digital sampling rate required to obtain an undistorted signal at half that frequency and all lower frequencies. To obtain accurate waveform reproduction out to 20 kHz (the upper hearing limit for those with excellent hearing), the Nyquist theorem determines that it is necessary to have a sampling rate of 40 kHz. In practice, a guard band is necessary between the upper program frequency and the Nyquist frequency, and so a sampling rate of 44.1 kHz is utilized for the compact disc. Modern digital recording systems often have sampling rates substantially higher than this. Although this allows for more flexibility with digital recording procedures, it is not necessary for adequate sound reproduction in final-product, digital playback systems. *See also* OVERSAMPLING.—Howard Ferstler

O

Offset (I) · The slight inward slant of the mounting of the headshell on a phonograph pivoted tone arm. Its purpose is to minimize the angle of the stylus in the groove.

Offset (II) · In a CD system, the difference between access time and start time.

Olive, Sean, September 10, 1959– · Born in Brockville, Ontario, Canada, Olive received a bachelor's degree in Music from the University of Toronto in 1982 and a master's degree in Sound Recording from McGill University in 1986. From 1986 to 1993, he was a research scientist in the Acoustics & Signal Processing Group at the National Research Council in Ottawa, Canada. During that time, he was a member of the research team of the ATHENA project, which developed one the first room-adaptive loudspeakers.

Since 1993, he has been the Manager of Subjective Evaluation for the R&D Group of Harman International Industries, Northridge, California. He is a Fellow of the Audio Engineering Society, past-Governor, and past-chair of the Los Angeles AES Section, and has authored and co-authored over 25 papers and preprints in the *AES Journal*, for which he received AES publications awards in 1990 and 1995. Olive is a member of two AES Technical Councils and the AES Working Group for Listening tests. For nine weeks a year, he teaches a critical listening course to recording engineering students at UCLA. He recently co-authored a chapter on "Subjective Evaluation" with Dr. Floyd Toole in John Borwick's third edition of the *Loudspeaker and Headphone Handbook*, published in 1988.—Howard Ferstler

Olney, Benjamin · *See* LOUDSPEAKER.

Olson, Harry, 1901–April 1, 1982 · Born in Mt. Pleasant, Iowa, Olson was a pioneer in musical sound reproduction and one of the most important researchers and designers in the history of audio. He received his B.E. degree from the University of Iowa in 1924, continued his graduate studies at the same institution, and was awarded a master's in solid mechanical wave filters in 1925 and went on to obtain a Ph.D. in atomic physics in 1928. He joined RCA in 1928 and stayed with the company for 40 years.

Some of the primary things Olson tackled at RCA included the development of the RCA magnetic tape recorder for television, as well as the music synthesizer. Another problem involved the problem of poor quality sound in the new talking pictures that had recently been introduced. Part of the solution Olson came up with involved the development of the velocity microphone, and he was instrumental in work done on RCA's second-order gradient microphone. In 1932, he patented the first cardioid ribbon microphone using a field coil instead of a permanent magnet. In 1934, he was placed in charge of acoustical research for the RCA Manufacturing Company, at the company's Camden acoustic laboratory, where he went on to develop the electronic synthesizer with

Herbert Millar. Subsequently, he became director of the acoustical and Electromechanical laboratory at RCA Laboratories, in Princeton, New Jersey.

In 1938, under his supervision, Leslie J. Anderson came up with the design for the RCA 44B ribbon bi-directional microphone and the 77B ribbon unidirectional, and in 1942, Olson patented a single-ribbon cardioid microphone and a phased-array directional microphone. Apart from microphone design, he worked to develop high-directivity horn speaker systems for theater and sound-reinforcement use, and also designed a loudspeaker woofer system that was a precursor to the acoustic suspension design further developed by Edgar Villchur some years later. Between 1958 and 1963, Olson, drawing on profits from Elvis Presley's record sales for RCA, developed what became known as the "Dynagroove" record. This was actually a system of recording and reproducing music that retained the phase relationships while compressing the 70- to 90-dB dynamic range of live classical music to the 60-dB limit of LP phonograph records. In the 1960s, Olson also experimented with surround sound, and 1966, he was appointed staff vice president of acoustical and electromechanical research for the entire company.

During his long career, Dr. Olson was granted more than 100 patents, published more than 130 technical articles, and wrote a number of important books, including *Applied Acoustics*; *Acoustical Engineering*; *Modern Sound Reproduction*; *Music, Physics, and Engineering*; and *Musical Engineering*.

Elected to the National Academy of Science in 1959, and later becoming a fellow of the American Physical Society and Society of Motion Picture and Television Engineers, Olson received numerous additional awards in the field of audio engineering. Among these awards were

Oldest Records

The oldest known record in existence today is one made in 1878 by Augustus Stroh (inventor of the Stroh violin). Still on the mandrel of his machine, and never played, it was reported in *Sound Box*, November 1990, and *ARSC Journal*, vol. 22, no. 1 (Spring 1991). Among extant records that have been played, the oldest may be an engraved metal cylinder made by Frank Lambert in 1878 or 1879. It was intended to be the sound track in a talking clock, and offers the hours: "One o'clock, two o'clock, three o'clock . . ." through twelve o'clock, with ten o'clock for some reason omitted. A very interesting account of the discovery and explication of this unusual artifact appears in Cramer 1992. Another venerable record is the white wax cylinder made by composer Arthur Sullivan, praising Thomas Edison for inventing the phonograph, but saying he shudders to think how much horrible music it will cause to be recorded. Jim Walsh (*Hobbies*, April 1965) gives the date of that record as October 5, 1888.

Another group of cylinders from 1888 was reported to be at the Edison National Historic Site, West Orange, New Jersey, in 1988 (*NAG*, vol. 65, July 1988). It consists of 22 records, 21 in white wax, made by Colonel Gouraud in London, during August 1888. They include a whistling number by "Mrs. Shaw," a "letter from Col. Gouraud to Mr. Edison," three live recordings of a Handel Festival at the Crystal Palace, and an "organ solo played on the grand organ at Westminster Abbey by Prof. Bridge." There was no announced plan by officials at the Historic Site to play or reissue the cylinders, and it was not stated when (if ever) the records had been played in the past [Cramer 1992].

the Audio Engineering Society's John H. Potts Award, in 1949 (later to become the Gold Medal), an Honorary Membership, in 1957, and the AES Award, in 1965. A past president of the organization, he was editor of the Society's journal from 1966 until 1969, and was editor emeritus for 13 years. He also received three awards from the Institute of Electrical and Electronics Engineers, including a fellowship, and was awarded the first Silver Medal in Engineering Acoustics ever offered by the Acoustical Society of America, in 1974, and the Society's first Gold Medal, in 1981. *See also* LOUDSPEAKER, 2, 3, 4; MICROPHONE, 1.—Howard Ferstler

Open Loop Gain · The added gain before feedback, required of an amplifier to compensate for negative feedback amplification loss.

Open Reel Tape · *See* REEL-TO-REEL TAPE.

Optical Recording (I) · A system of recording sound on film through a photographic process. The sound signal activates a light valve, causing variations in the light that falls upon and exposes the film as it moves past the valve. The changes in density that result are analogs to the frequency and amplitude of the original signal. Playback is achieved by drawing the film between a photoelectric cell and a light source, producing a fluctuation that is converted back into sound. Because the fidelity of this kind of recording is inferior to that of other processes, magnetic recording is used on film sound tracks for improved reproduction. The idea of recording with light beams is an old one, traceable to the Photophone of 1879. *Talking Machine World* described such a process in May 1912. *See also* MOTION PICTURE SOUND RECORDING.

Optical Recording (II) · In CD systems, optical recording has a wide application, meaning any kind of medium using laser light to convey data to or from the disc.

Optical Sound Track · On a motion picture film, the narrow band that carries a photographic record of sound. *See also* OPTICAL RECORDING (I).

ORTF Recording Technique (*Office de Radiodiffusion-Television Francaise*) · A microphone-positioning technique developed by the French broadcasting system, but now used world wide, that spaces two, directional cardioid microphones 17 cm (6.7 inches) apart (roughly the same distance as between human ears) and angles them outward at approximately 110° to each other. The angle may be varied, depending upon the needs of the recording engineer. The result is coincident microphone behavior at lower frequencies, combined with some time-delay-related clues at higher frequencies that add a degree of spaciousness to the sound. *See also* NOS RECORDING TECHNIQUE (*Nederlandsche Omroep Stichting*).—Howard Ferstler

Orthophonic · The Victor gramophone introduced in 1925 to play the new electric records. *See also* VICTROLA.

Ortofon · A Danish firm established in 1918 in Copenhagen, by Axel Petersen and Arnold Poulsen, to develop sound motion pictures. By 1923, they were able to demonstrate a sound film, using what they called a "variable area" method that required two separate film strips to run simultaneously, with one carrying the audio and the other the video. The method was accepted and licensed in Europe and America (*see also* MOTION PICTURE SOUND RECORDING). Later the firm developed new disc cutter heads and amplifying systems, with records issued by Tono. Improvements were made also in tape recording and in recording long-playing microgroove discs. Ortofon moving-coil and moving-magnet pickup cartridges became universally praised, and during the heyday of the LP record the company was one of the world's leading manufacturers. The firm's stereo cutterhead was also widely used. The company is also known for rugged, disco-oriented pickups that are admired by disc jockeys. High quality audio equipment is still being produced, and is marketed around the world.—Rev. by Howard Ferstler

Otala, Matti · *See* AMPLIFIER.

Out of Phase · The term given to the situation when the moving elements of two loudspeaker systems, in response to simultaneous identical signals, move in opposite directions. The sonic effect, if the listener is seated an equal distance from each speaker, will be for normally centered images to take on a vague and directionless characteristic. Bass response will also be reduced in strength. It is therefore important to have all speaker systems in an audio installation, including those in multi-speaker surround set ups, wired as much in phase as possible. If the speaker models are different from each other (the center and surrounds are typically different from the left and right mains), this can be tricky to pull off effectively.—Rev. by Howard Ferstler

Output · In an audio system, any signal leaving any component.

Out-Take · Material that is recorded (or filmed) but not retained in the final master.

Overdubbing · *See* MULTI-TRACK RECORDING.

Overload · *See* DISTORTION, 3, 6.

Oversampling · A better term might be "re-sampling." In a digital playback system, it is one of several ways to enhance the performance. It involves sampling at a rate higher than the sampling Nyquist theorem. The Nyquist theorem states that a band-limited, continuous waveform may be represented by a series of discrete samples if the sampling frequency is at least twice the highest frequency contained in the waveform, meaning that each sample from the data converter at the playback end is sampled more than once (i.e., oversampled). This multiplication of samples permits digital filtering of the signal, thereby reducing the need for sharp analog filters to control aliasing (unwanted frequencies created when sampling a signal of a frequency higher than half the sampling rate). The result is a more effective way to eliminate problems at frequencies above the audible range. *See also* COMPACT DISC; NYQUIST FREQUENCY; SAMPLING FREQUENCY.—Rev. by Howard Ferstler

P

P Channel · On a compact disc, a sub-code (inaudible) channel used for carrying information on lead-in, lead-out, and playing areas.

Packaged System · A complete audio playback system, also known as a rack system, including all components with necessary connections. During the early hi-fi period of the 1950s, enthusiasts preferred to have separate components. Nevertheless, modern packaged systems demonstrate quality equivalent to that of assembled sets of components, and they may be harmoniously clustered as well as less costly.

Packburn Audio Noise Suppressor · A device designed to suppress transient noises (ticks, pops, clicks, crackle, scratch, etc.) In phonograph records, mono or stereo, wherever or however made, as well as the audible hiss characteristic of all audio media before the development of successful encode/decode noise suppression systems, and more recently, digital audio. This article describes Model 323A, which has three principal components: a switcher, a blanker, and a continuous noise suppressor.

The switcher is designed specifically for the reduction of transient noises in monophonic disc and cylinder records. The switcher does this by taking advantage of the circumstance that, whereas the same signal is engraved on each side of the groove wall, the noises caused by dirt, mildew, scratches, cracks, particulate matter in the record material, etc., are not the same on each side of the groove wall.

Before the development of the Packburn switcher, a monophonic disc or cylinder was best reproduced for stereo by summing (in the appropriate polarity) the signals from the left and right channels. The switcher also does this, in the rest position. At any moment when the reproduction from the left or right channel is more noise-free than the sum signal (by a user-adjustable threshold amount), however, the switcher can reproduce from the quieter groove wall only. At frequencies lower than 300 Hz, where switching would not accomplish anything, the two channels are mixed to minimize rumble. The switching process is applicable to vertical-cut recordings as well as to lateral-cut records, as a correct playback stylus rides on the side walls of the groove; it is, however, more effective with lateral records.

The switching process is the least compromising mode of noise reduction, as it has no effect on the fidelity of reproduction and does not introduce distortion or have any other undesirable side effect. In fact, its audible effect is one of decreased distortion in the reproduction of records that have any substantial amount of transient noises. The output of the process is a monophonic signal in which the noise content consists of the residual noise that has survived the switcher's three-way choice.

Stereo records, monophonic tape recordings, and broadcasts cannot be processed with the switcher. For these the blanker is used. The blanker is designed to cope with transient noises from any source: the output of the switcher, a stereo disc, a tape, compact disc, or broadcasts. It will usually be most effective in dealing with an original record, as copying and broadcasting processes, which typically employ filtering, compression and limiting, tend to dull the leading edge of a noise transient, and thus lower its detectability by the blanker circuitry. Transient noise suppression is achieved by clipping the amplitude of each individual positive-going and negative-going pulsation of a noise transient whenever the amplitude of the transient exceeds a threshold value determined by the peak program level in the vicinity of the transient; and by the setting of the "blanker rate" control. The blanker does not attempt to eliminate the totality of the transient, which would require momentarily reducing the signal level to zero. Therefore, a slight ghost of lower frequency components of certain noise transients will sometimes remain. Cracks, pits, gouges, dents, or bumps may still be audibly detectable but as low frequency thumps which normally will not be painful to listen to.

Once the switcher and blanker have completed their tasks—to cope with transient noise—there remains the need to reduce audible hiss. The continuous noise suppressor accomplishes this. In the case of recordings containing no transient noises, such as master tapes or copies thereof, the continuous noise suppressor will be the only processor needed.

The Packburn continuous noise suppressor is classified as a dynamic noise suppressor. In such devices, the cutoff frequency of a variable low-pass filter varies with the dynamics of the program material in such a way that audible noise is minimized with a zero or minimal degradation of the perceived fidelity of reproduction and without introducing extraneous noises because of the dynamics of the filter operation.

The success of such a device is crucially dependent on the design of its sensing and control circuits and on the user-operated controls that are provided. The operation of the filter in the Packburn continuous noise suppressor is controlled as follows:

1. The signal amplitude in the frequency range of 1.7 kHz to 3.4 kHz is employed as an index of the high frequency content of the signal in the audible range;

2. The time rate of change of the total signal-plus-noise is employed as an index of the audible surface noise;

3. A voltage derived from the ratio of measurements a) and b) is employed to control the width of the pass band;

4. Separate user-adjustable controls are provided to select the minimum cutoff frequency in quiet passages and the maximum cutoff frequency in loud passages;

5. User-adjustable means are provided for a rapid increase of the pass band width at the onset of signal transients.

Because the continuous noise suppressor functions best if it "hears" the program material with the same treble equalization that one chooses for listening, the Packburn unit provides a treble equalization switch that allows one to select the RIAA curve or one of five other equalization curves that match those historically used in cutting records before the standardization of the RIAA curve by the record industry in 1953.

Other controls are provided in the Packburn 323A to assist in obtaining optimum results. Meters assure proper adjustment of the input level, and a frequency meter reads out the fluctuating value of the cutoff frequency as the continuous noise suppressor operates. The user can audition the separate groove walls of a record, which can be of assistance in selecting the optimum size stylus for record playing; and can audition the vertical component of lateral-cut records as well as the lateral component of vertical-cut records.

The channel balance control, which is important in adjusting the switching process, also serves as a canting control for vertical-cut records.

To accommodate stereo recordings, Model 323A is provided with two blankers, two treble equalization networks, and two continuous noise processors. It is designed to interface with contemporary stereo playback systems. It can be inserted in a tape loop of a preamplifier, amplifier, or receiver, or it can be interposed after the preamplifier.

In professional installations, the Packburn Audio Noise Suppressor is used immediately after the stereo preamplifier and before such devices as equalizers, filters, volume expanders, reverberation synthesizers, etc., save that, in record restoration work, one may prefer to utilize the continuous noise suppressor in the final stage of processing. (Packburn is registered with U.S. Patent and Trademark Office.) *See also* NOISE REDUCTION.—Richard C. Burns

Padgham, Hugh, February 15, 1955– · One of the industry's top recording engineers, producers, and mixers, Padgham's youth involved being educated at St. Edwards School, in Oxford, England. After graduation, he started out working for Advision Studios, in 1974, where he began learning his future trade. He moved on to Lansdowne Studios between 1975 and 1978, and then got a house-engineer job with the studios of Virgin Records (the Townhouse & The Manor Studios), which lasted from 1978 until 1981. Since 1981, he has been self employed, and has gone on to record a number of music-industry notables, with one of his credits being the "inventor" of Phil Collins' big-drum sound and another being his work with helping to develop the early SSL mixing computer systems.

A member of NARAS, Padgham has won numerous awards and acknowledgments for his producing, engineering, and mixing work, including: BPI Best Producer nominations, in both 1985 and 1986; a Grammy Award for Producer of the Year and also a Grammy for Album of the Year, in 1985 (Phil Collins' *No Jacket Required*); a Music Week Award for Best British Producer, in 1985, plus Top Album Producer, in 1990; a British Award for Best Single, in 1989, as well as the Grammy for Record of the Year, in 1990 (both for Phil Collins' "Another Day in Paradise"); an acknowledgment as one of the Top Ten Most Influential Producers of the Mix Magazine Era, in 1992; the TEC Award for Outstanding Creative Achievement by a Recording Engineer, in 1993; a Grammy Award for engineering in 1994 (Sting's *Ten Summoner's Tales*); and a tribute for achievement from Billboard magazine, in 1997. During the 1980s, the multi-faceted Padgham was also co-owner of a private sports car racing team that took second place at the Le Mans 24-hour race in 1985.—Howard Ferstler

Panasonic [website: www.panasonic. com] · One of the world's largest electronic companies, Panasonic was founded in 1918 by Konosuke Matsushita as a vehicle to exploit his invention of a two-socket light fixture. Originally known as the Matsushita Electric Industrial Co., Ltd., the firm established a major share of the U.S. videocassette hardware market in the 1980s with its VHS line, ranging from basic playback machines to high-end recorders.

Panasonic presently manufactures dozen of consumer electronics products (e.g., CD and DVD players, televisions) as well as electronic components such as semiconductors, DVD-ROM drives for PCs, and flat screen plasma TV displays. The company received a technical Emmy Award for its development of many of the technologies relating to the DVD format. A leading producer of DVD entertainment

Paris Exposition, 1889

The world's fair named Exposition Universelle ran only six months, from May 6 to November 6, 1889, but attracted some 25 million visitors. Thomas Edison had a major 9,000 square foot exhibit there, displaying 45 phonographs. Sarah Bernhardt and other celebrities were featured making records. The public could hear recordings through ear tubes. Edison presented a phonograph to Gustave Eiffel, who installed it in his apartment on the third level of the Tower. There was also an exhibit of the graphophone by Charles Tainter, but it was a less elaborate display. Henri Lioret had an exhibit of his clocks at the fair, and became interested in the talking machine; it is believed that the stimulus of meeting Thomas Edison and hearing the phonograph inspired his own work in the field. Valdemar Poulsen's telegraphone was also exhibited.

software, it was the first to introduce the recordable DVD for the PC and led the way in developing recordable DVD players for the video marketplace at the outset of the twenty-first century.

With the establishment of the Panasonic Foundation in 1984, the firm began its long-term commitment to public education in North America. Since then, it has implemented programs such as Kid Witness News—providing video resources to more than 200 schools as a means of stimulating student cognitive, communication, and organizational skills—and the Creative Design Challenge, which introduces high schoolers to real-world engineering problems.—Howard Ferstler

Panoramic Potentiometer · A device used in multi-channel recording to locate the signal from each channel into the stereo field. It is also called a pan pot.

Pan Potting (or Panning) · The pan pot itself is an electrical device that distributes one audio signal to two or more channels or speakers. As used on recording mixers, pan potting involves moving or panning the apparent position of a single channel between two outputs—usually left and right for stereo outputs, but also with a center feed for three-channel soundstaging. At one extreme of travel, the sound source is heard from only one output. At the other

extreme, it is heard from the other output. In the middle, the sound is heard equally from each output, but is reduced in level by 3 db relative to its original value. With multi-track inputs, pan potting allows the mixing technician to properly lay out a soundstage with only two or three front channels.—Howard Ferstler

Parabolic Reflector · A curved sound reflector that is intended to direct signals to a microphone.

Parametric Equalizer · A type of equalizer that allows a boost or cutout of any frequency or any bandwidth.

Parsons, Charles Algernon, Sir, June 13, 1854–February 11, 1931 · British engineer and inventor born in London. He studied at Cambridge University, then apprenticed in Newcastle-upon-Tyne. He set up a turbine generator business, and worked with marine equipment. As a diversion, he experimented with sound amplification, and developed the Auxetophone. He demonstrated the device for the Royal Society in May 1904, and sold the gramophone rights to G & T sometime before March 21, 1905. He died at sea in 1931.

Patch · To patch is to connect items of equipment, as in an audio system, with cords and plugs. Such connections are usually controlled by break-jacks. The cord used for patching is the patch cord.

Patch Bay · A rack-mounted, recording-studio component containing at least two rows of connectors used to "patch in" or insert into the signal path a piece of external equipment, usually console sections and tape machines. The two rows consist of send and receive jacks, with the better designs configured for balanced interconnection, instead of unbalanced. The two rows are tied together by shorting contacts, meaning that during normal operation the send and receive points will be connected, maintaining the signal path until something is plugged in. Patch Bays are popular in recording studios where it is common to change the units in the signal path for each new session or client.—Howard Ferstler

Patents · Millions of patents of all kinds have been issued since the birth of the U.S. patent system in 1790 (over 5 million since the Patent Office began its current consecutive system of numbering). Originally, working models of each invention were required by the examiners, but this condition was cancelled by Congressional Statute on July 8, 1870, and by Office Rule on March 1, 1889, saving the potential inventors some precious funds, and lessening massive storage problems for the Patent Office and the National Archives. Many of the wood and metal models were destroyed by neglect and fire, especially in 1836 and 1877. Others were sold off and dispersed from 1925 to 1926, but a number still exist today in private collections and institutions.

After six days of intensive labor, John Kruesi completed the first working cylinder phonograph—invented by Thomas Edison—on December 6, 1877; on the seventh day, he constructed the still-required model for submission to the Patent Office. It was returned to Edison on June 22, 1926, and is preserved today at the Henry Ford

restoration of Menlo Park in Greenfield Village, Dearborn, Michigan. The model had been sent to Washington with the formal application less than three months after the devastating Patent Office fire of September 24, 1877, in which over 76,000 models were destroyed (about one-third of the total then existing).

Between 1877 and 1912 (when the external horn machines lost their popularity), the U.S. Patent Office granted over 2,000 Utility (invention) Patents to about 1,000 inventors in the sound recording field, and more than 70 Design Patents. A patent remained in force for 17 years from the date of the grant and could not be extended, except under extraordinary circumstances. In the patent titles, the word "phonograph" outnumbered "graphophone" five to one, although the subclass headings themselves used the latter term more often. "Talking machine" was a distant third. Although the "paper average" was about two phonograph patents per inventor, the reality was quite different. Thirty-two inventors received—either singly or jointly—10 or more patents apiece. Although numbering only about 3% of the inventors surveyed, they received more than 33% of the patents. In that sense, relatively few inventors, financed by the larger companies, dominated the field. Yet, others who received only one or two patents—for example, Charles Batchelor, John B. Browning, Heinrich Klenk, Henri Lioret, William F. Messer, Stanislaus Moss, and Werner Suess—still managed to make a substantial impact.

Although millions of dollars were invested on the strength of a handful of major patents, other entrepreneurs gambled smaller sums—but frequently everything they had—on a single clever idea. For example, Louis Glass built and applied for a patent on the first U.S. coin-operated phonograph in 1889. Edward Amet constructed the first spring-wound motor for

These were the most prolific U.S. phonograph invention/design patentees, from 1877 to 1912, with the number of patents they received:

Thomas A. Edison, 134	Victor H. Emerson, 14
Thomas H. Macdonald, 56	Isidor Kitsee, 14
Eldridge R. Johnson, 54	Horace Sheble, 14
Jonas W. Aylsworth, 38	Leon F. Douglass, 13
Louis Valiquet, 33	Emile Berliner, 12
John C. English, 31	Edward D. Gleason, 12
Peter Weber, 27	Edward H. Amet, 11
Charles S. Tainter, 25	Robert L. Gibson, 11
Ademor N., 23	Joseph W. Jones, 11
Alexander N. Pierman, 22	Wilburn N. Dennison, 10
Edward L. Aiken, 18	Alexander Fischer, 10
Walter H. Miller, 18	George W. Gomber, 10
Thomas Kraemer, 15	Luther T. Haile, 10
Gianni Bettini, 14	Frederick Myers, 10
Frank L. Capps, 14	John F. Ott, 10
George K. Cheney, 14	William W. Young, 10

Edison's personal involvement with the field was the longest of any inventor, spanning 1877 to 1930. Ironically, his first U.S. phonograph patent, which established the industry, had little importance in the subsequent commercial development because of an unfortunate choice of words. Although Edison was aware that his first recorder would engrave paraffined paper in 1877, he had difficulties with wax clogging the stylus, and his lawyer failed to mention this detail in the original U.S. application, specifying "indentation" instead of "engraving." This lack of foresight would cost Edison dearly in the later struggles with Columbia.

phonographs by 1891 (probably brought to market in mid-1894), and Thomas Lambert developed the first standard-size, unbreakable (celluloid) cylinder record by mid-1900.

A number of patentees were known in other, though allied, fields. Recording artist Steve Porter (Stephen C. Porter) had already been a founder of the American Phonograph Record Co. in 1901, when he later received a phonograph patent (no. 1,012,910). The only other singer with a patent was Berliner artist James K. Reynard (no. 666,819 and no. 776,941), but Hulbert A. Yerkes, Columbia's later jazz band director and vice-president, received a design patent on a Grafonola (no. 41,902)

and two other invention patents after 1912. Byron G. Harlan was the one-fifth assignee of Rudolph Klein's double-volute disc (no. 814,053), and the famed Victor recording engineer (and Berliner alumnus) William Sinkler Darby also managed to obtain one: no. 786,347. The keeper of Edison's musical accounts book from 1889 to 1892, and the world's first recording director, Adelbert Theo Wangemann, later received two patents (no. 872,592 and no. 913,930)—but both posthumously.

Patents and the suits fought over them often changed the form of competing products. The early Echophones of Edward Amet had deeply indented mandrels, thus to avoid Edison's patent on the continuously tapered interior of a cylinder record. Thomas Lambert had to remove the little angular guide blocks from the title end of his first (hollow) white and pink celluloid cylinders. Columbia's Type AZ Graphophone with its fixed frame and Lyre Reproducer was only permitted on the market in late 1904 when Edison's patent no. 430,278 was held invalid. U-S Phonograph's unusual coiled-tube tone arm cylinder phonographs, developed by Harry McNulty and Thomas Towell with a double feedscrew, successfully avoided Victor's patent on the solid tapering tone arm and Edison's two-minute to four-minute gear-shifting devices.

Some inventions and ideas that later became important in the industry were buried in earlier applications. For example, although Ademor Petit received a patent for a two-sided disc record in 1904 (no. 749,092), this very feature was mentioned as early as 1891 in the United States by Joseph Wassenich (no. 505,910) and indicated by Edison in his British Patent no. 1644 of 1878, not to mention the 1878 abandoned patent application of William Hollingshead, which fortuitously survived. Even the concept of a cabinet-styled phonograph with concealed horn slowly emerged in 1899 with a music box mechanism (J. Philips. no. 632,925). Eventually, after years of litigation (and assistance from Keen-O-Phone and Brunswick), John Bailey Browning, in 1927, finally received credit for his prior conception of the Victrola. Other ideas, such as tapered tone arms, radial tracking, anti-skating devices, magnetic recording, tone-modifiers, disc-changing mechanisms, and the ideal horn, weave their way through the work of many inventors.

Extended litigation over patents marked the early years of the industry; much of it was brought on by brazen, unauthorized imitations. After the Victor Talking Machine Co. had spent $1 million buying and defending Emile Berliner's pivotal patents (especially for the groove-driven reproducer), Eldridge Johnson (in the May 1909 issue of *Talking Machine World*) reacted to his own Supreme Court victory on this issue over Leeds & Catlin on April 19 by commenting on patent infringers: "Injunctions, fines, and even danger of imprisonment do not stop them. People infected with this curious spell seem more like the followers of some strenuous religious belief than simple business men who are working for a livelihood."

Research into the formative decades of the phonograph is greatly facilitated by use of Patent Office documents. Copies of the original applications are still available on request from the U.S. Patent and Trademark Office, Washington, D.C., 20231, at a cost of $1.50 each.

Patents issued by European countries followed various principles, bringing about a number of challenges for American inventors and firms. Foreign patents had varying terms, and many were subject to renewal. The U.S. statutes limited the American patent to the term of the inventor's shortest-running foreign counterpart (a practice not ended until the implementation of the Treaty of Brussels). The situation became so complex that some patents filed before 1898 expired before they were granted! American practice demanded that a U.S. citizen apply for a patent simultaneously in the United States and in any foreign country chosen. Edison's failure to file a U.S. application in 1878 (or promptly convert his March caveat) at the same time as his second English phonograph patent (Series 1878, April 24 and October 22, 1878, no. 1644) led to denial of the American patent application filed December 15, 1878, on the grounds of prior publication. Edison tried to repair the damage by reapplying, to no avail. Partly as a result, American Graphophone Co. Was able to negotiate a royalty of $10 for every Edison machine sold until 1894.

Some of the pivotal names in European recorded sound had their own patent histories. Léon Scott's important phonautographic patent was registered in France on March 25, 1857 (no. 17.897/31.470), with illustrations showing a flat recording surface; the July 29, 1859, amendment displayed the familiar traveling drum inspired by Young, Duhamel, and Wertheim. Charles Cros did not register a formal patent on his sealed Paleophone description of April 16, 1877 (opened December 3), until April 28/May 1 and August 2–3, 1878 (French patent no. 124.313), and as far as is known never "reduced the idea to practice," built a model, nor even made a drawing. His explicator, Abbé Lenoir, did use the word "phonograph" in the October 10, 1877, issue of *La semaine du clergé*. The word had been previously used by Edison in August, however, and long before—in the 1840s—by Isaac and Benn Pitman to describe their newly invented system of shorthand transcription.—Allen Koenigsberg (The preceding text is a modified version of introductory material in Koenigsberg's *Patent History of the Phonograph 1877–1912*, 1990, used with permission. Copyright 1989 by Allen Koenigsberg. All rights reserved.)

A number of significant patents were granted after 1912. Electrical recording systems were made possible by the prior invention of the Audion—British patent no. 1427, issued in 1908—and the single-stage amplifier—U.S. no. 841,387; 1907—by Lee De Forest. Among the great innovations of the 1920s was the pioneer moving coil recording head for disc recording, patented by Horace Owen Merriman and Lionel Guest (British patent no. 141,790; 1920).

Alan Dower Blumlein and H. E. Holman developed the moving coil microphone in the 1930s, gaining a patent from Britain, no. 350,998. They also patented a single turn moving coil cutting head (British patents no. 350,954 and no. 350,998).

At Bell Telephone Laboratories in the United States, the research of Joseph P. Maxfield and Henry C. Harrison led to several related patents in 1923: U.S. no. 1,562,165; no. 1,663,884; no. 1,663,885; no. 1,678,116; and no. 1,709,571; plus British patent no. 262,839. Microphone research at Bell led to the patents for several instruments (U.S. no. 1,333,744; no. 1,456,538; no. 1,603,300; no. 1,611, 870; no. 1,675,853; British no. 134,872). The so-called rubber-line electrical recorder, designed to give a flat, extended range frequency response, also came from Bell Laboratories, in 1923 (U.S. no. 1,562,165; no. 1,663,884; no. 1,663,885; no. 1,678,116; no. 1,709,571; British no. 262,839). Advances in microphone design came from RCA in 1931, with the ribbon microphone (U.S. no. 1,885,001; British no. 386,478); there were numerous further developments of microphone design.

Full frequency range records (ffrr), introduced by Decca Record Co., Ltd., around 1945, was the result of Arthur Haddy's research; it ushered in the age of high fidelity. *See also* FULL FREQUENCY RANGE RECORDING (ffrr).

In magnetic recording, based on the early work of Valdemar Poulsen (first British patent no. 8,961; 1899), progress was slow. Among the key patents of the 1920s were one for applying bias by W. L. Carlson and G. W. Carpenter in 1921 (U.S. no. 1,640,881), and Curt Stille's steel tape recorder (British no. 331,859; 1928). The Blattnerphone of the late 1920s was improved and patented by Guglielmo Marconi (British no. 458,255 and no. 467,105). Wire recording developments in the 1940s were largely credited to Marvin Camras of the Armour Research Foundation in Chicago. Among his patents were U.S. no. 2,351,003 and no. 2,351,007, filed in 1942. The use of coated tape as the magnetic medium was first patented in Germany in 1928 (no. 500,900 and no. 544,302; then British no. 333,154) by Fritz Pfleumer.

Stereophonic recording began with the work of W. Bartlett Jones, who patented in 1928 his idea of putting two channels into a single groove (U.S. no. 1,855,150), but he did not develop the concept into production. Alan Blumlein was researching the subject also, and put many basic ideas into his patent applications of December 1931 (British no. 394,325; U.S. no. 2,095,540). He laid the foundations of the modern stereo disc. Blumlein thought of spacing pressure microphones to provide the listener with localizing ability (British no. 394,325; 429,022).

Peter Maxfield's successful long-playing record, issued by Columbia in 1948, was based on a combination of ideas and processes previously patented, as well as some new ones. For example, W. S. Bachman's U.S. patent no. 2,738,385, for a variable-pitch system of recording, allowed the extension of recording time to 30 minutes per side of the 12-inch LP.

Pathé Frères Compagnie · A firm established by Charles Pathé and Emile Pathé in Paris, in 1896. It succeeded their earlier company, Les Phonographes Pathé (1894).

The Pathé brothers had seen an Edison phonograph demonstration and had begun to put on exhibitions themselves. They went on to wholesale Edison machines, and to market their own cylinders for it. They also became interested in motion pictures. In 1898, the Pathé brothers issued a catalog of their cylinders, offering nearly 800 recordings. "Celeste Aida" was number one in the catalog; like most of the records, it bore no artist's name; however, announcements on the records did reveal the identity of the performers. The cylinders were made of perishable light-brown wax compounds, and only a few have survived.

Deluxe cylinders with prominent artists were offered from late 1901 or 1902; however, the composition of the cylinder was unchanged. The "Céleste" five-minute cylinder was issued during 1903 to 1905, but because it required a new playback machine, the innovation was not a market success. In about 1903, Pathé abandoned its brown wax formula for the more durable black wax. In November 1906, the firm introduced its disc records, vertical cut, with shallow, wide grooves. They started at the center and played outward, using a sapphire stylus. Because the wide grooves reduced playing time, the disc diameter was larger than the conventional discs of other firms: up to 14 inches at first, then to 20 inches by 1909. Pathé gave up its cylinders in Britain in 1906 (carrying on with them a few more years in France) to concentrate on disc production.

Pathé was also active in the sale of record players, cylinder at first, then (from 1906) both disc players (Pathéphones) and cylinder players. It sold Edison machines, and Columbia Graphophones, at one time re-labeling the Graphophone Eagle as their own Le Coq. The firm also produced its own brand of players, and in time discontinued the import of American machines. A line of office dictating machines, named Ronéophone, was available as well. The Pathé cylinder machines were of high quality, but the disc players were prevented from attaining the standard of Victor machines because of the Victor patent on the tapered tone arm.

The company was highly successful throughout Europe, and had branch offices in many countries before 1910. Pathé Frères (London) Ltd. was established in 1902; it issued a catalog of cylinders in 1904 and a catalog of record players on sale in 1906. Hurteau and Co. of Montreal were the agents for Pathé goods in Quebec. There were other factories elsewhere in Canada. There were also U.S. offices in New York. *See also* PATHÉ FRÈRES PHONOGRAPH COMPANY, INC.

Rights for France and the colonies (not the United States) were acquired by

Columbia Graphophone Co., Ltd., in October 1928. Discs with the Pathé label were still made in France until 1932, although the company had been absorbed by the Société Pathé Marconi, which brought together the French interests of the Gramophone Co., Columbia, and Pathé. All became part of EMI, Ltd., in 1931. (The company's history in the cylinder period is chronicled in Girard and Barnes 1964. *TMR* no. 58 (June 1979) reproduced a 1904 cylinder catalog.)

Pathé Frères Phonograph Company, Inc. · A New York firm established in late 1911 or January 1912, incorporated in Delaware. The arrangement with the French firm, Pathé Frères Compagnie, allowed the American company to buy and market Pathé goods. Emil Pathé was consulting engineer for the American firm. In March 1913, Pathé products were demonstrated in New York, including Pathéphones, Pathégraphs, twin-turntable Duplex Pathéphones, and a Pathé Reflex machine, along with Pathé discs. In May 1914, it was reported that the firm had leased the entire second floor of a newly erected building. Russell Hunting was named director of recording at a new pressing plant to be constructed.

In subsequent months, as shipments continued to arrive from Europe despite the war, dealers were named in several American cities. An extensive factory was occupied in Belleville, New Jersey, responding to great demand for Pathé discs. In July 1915, the American firm claimed to command the largest record catalog in the world, with over 96,000 selections. Frank L. Capps became production manager in October 1915, in charge of all experimental, mechanical, and development work. The Pathé Pathéphone Shop opened opposite the New York Public Library on Fifth Ave. at 42nd St.

Standard outside-start records replaced the center-start records in February 1916. Record labels bore the characteristic rooster trademark. The Pathé Frères Pathéphone Co., Ltd., of Canada was established, with a factory in Toronto.

An agreement was made with Brunswick-Balke-Collender in 1916; Brunswick to make record players for Pathé, and Pathé to supply discs to be sold through Brunswick dealers. Pathé's output in 1917 was reported to have increased 500% over the previous year.

A revolutionary new record player, the Actuelle, was demonstrated. It had a cone-shaped parchment diaphragm fitted into a gold-plated aluminum frame and attached to the needle holder by a wire. It could play either vertical-cut or lateral discs with a twist of the needle. Two doors on one side of the cabinet and a device with a wire (a remote) were used to control the volume.

In November 1918, the Pathé Military Band marched on Fifth Ave. as part of Peace Day celebrations, joined by the office staff and administration. One of the Pathé artists, Kathleen Howard, sang the national anthem on the Public Library steps. Pathé News, a house organ, was published from June 1919.

Financial difficulties arose in 1921, due to the popularity of radio. Receivers in equity were appointed to take charge of the firm and deal with the claims of its creditors. A reorganization emerged, and a name change took place in August 1922, to Pathé Sound Wave Corp. In November 1922, the name was changed to Pathé Frères Phonograph and Radio Corp. Actuelle discs were still selling well, at .55¢ each. A new subsidiary was set up, called Perfect Record Co. Perfect lateral discs were issued around September 1922, at .50¢ each. Vertical-cut discs were no longer advertised. Throughout 1924, the company advertised Pathéphones, Pathé radios, and lateral-cut discs.

In September 1925, the firm announced a new process of recording, based on extensive research in electrical and photoelectrical sound wave reproducing methods—a system differing from any other. It was not an electric process, but by 1927, a new Pathéphonic electrical method was in use. In 1928, Pathé and Cameo Record Corp. merged. Many records were then issued on both labels simultaneously.

The record industry was in economic crisis in 1929. Pathé was among the companies that were merged into the new American Record Corp. (ARC) in August. Actuelle records were no longer produced, but Perfect continued, pressed from Cameo masters. Until 1938, Pathé and Perfect masters were used in Britain to produce some of the Pathé discs there, and for Actuelles and Pathé Perfect; and for subcontracted work to Homochord, Grafton High Grade Record, Scala Record (7000 series), and Scala Ideal Record. Through further subcontracting, it was also used for Gamage and Vox Humana records.

PCM (Pulse Code Modulation) · A conversion method used in recording, in which digital words in a bit stream (actually, amplitude pulses encoded on to magnetic tape or disc) represent samples of analog information. Invented by Alec Reeves in 1937, it remains the basis of most digital audio recording and playback systems. *See also* DIGITAL RECORDING; COMPACT DISC; DAT (Digital Audio Tape).—Howard Ferstler

Peak · The maximum numerical value for any given event; in audio systems usually applied to the maximum instantaneous output (peak output) of a given component. Usually, the peak is occasioned by a musical fortissimo.

Pellowe, John, September 21, 1955– · With an educational background mainly involving telecommunications, Pellowe joined Decca Records in 1974, and trained for a recording engineer career under the direction of the one of the great engineering masters, Kenneth Wilkinson. He started recording and mixing session tapes in 1978, and went on to develop a successful partnership with James Lock, who had succeeded Wilkinson as chief engineer at Decca. In addition to working with opera and classical music, Pellowe also has mixed a number of pop-music albums, and has become adept at mixing multi-channel surround sound.

In addition to his recording and mixing work, Pellowe started engineering for live-sound production with Luciano Pavarotti's concerts in 1986, and as a live-concert engineer, he has mixed the "front of house" sound for over 200 concerts in some of the world's largest and most prestigious venues. He now has over 180 albums to his credit, including recording, live broadcast, and post-production work done on the 1990, 1994, and 1998 Three Tenors World Cup albums from Rome, Los Angeles, and Paris. Pellowe has recorded a substantial number of Grammy-nominated albums, with many of them winning, including his 1992 recording of Richard Strauss' Die Frau Ohne Schatten effort, which gained him a Grammy for engineering.—Howard Ferstler

Personics · The practice of making customized tapes for clients.

Perspecta Sound · The system premiered with the movie *White Christmas*, in 1954, as part of Paramount's VistaVision, horizontal 35-mm wide-screen format. Perspecta Sound employed a single, conventional monophonic sound track, onto which were encoded sub-audible control signals. Tones of 30, 35, and 40 Hz were detected by an integrator unit connected to the projector's sound head and used to turn up the gain on left-, center-, and right-hand speaker channels. Although this did not provide true stereo, it did create directional effects, with the additional advantage that mixing for Perspecta was considerably quicker than mixing for a cinemascope magnetic sound track, because it only required that the sound to be panned between the three channels to follow the action on screen.—Howard Ferstler

Phantom Center Image · With traditional two-channel, stereophonic sound reproduction, this involves the ability of a pair of speakers to simulate a real performer in the middle of the array. A proper phantom image requires that the listener be located out in front of the speakers, and equidistant from both, and a good recording should be able to create additional phantom images all the way across the soundstage. Aside from the need for a sweet spot listening position, a major problem with a phantom image with two-channel stereo is that the center image is formed by four arrival clues: one for each ear from each of the two speakers. Moreover, two of those clues are delayed in time, because the ears are not equidistant from each speaker. A true center channel, such as what exists not only with DSP steering systems, but also with Dolby Digital, DTS, SACD, and DVD-A (at least potentially because not all engineers take full advantage of the technologies), overcomes this problem. It can do so because it simulates a genuine performer at center stage, with the image being formed by only two arrival clues: one from the centered source for each ear. *See also* PRECEDENCE EFFECT; CENTER CHANNEL; HEAD-RELATED TRANSFER FUNCTION (HRTF).—Howard Ferstler

Phase Inverter · A circuit in an amplifier that derives the opposing voltage polarity required to drive the push-pull output stage.

Phase Shift · A distortion in an audio system produced when signals originally simultaneous are heard with a small delay between them. This delay, often occasioned by ultrasonic filters in modern systems, may be as tiny as a thousandth of a second, but it will result in a mismatch of the signal peaks. If the signal peaks are at exact opposite stages of their cycles, they are 180° out of phase, and cancel each other out. Out-of-phase program material is a particular problem in stereo playback because it may cause loudspeakers to vibrate out of step with each other. Some out-of-phase programming is fundamental to the stereo effect, however: When signals are separately reproduced through different loudspeakers, it is phase shift (at very low frequencies) that suggests to the listener that the sound is coming from somewhere between the two speakers. *See also* PHASING; PHASING SWITCH.

Phasing (I) · The correlation between cone movement in one loudspeaker with respect to that in another loudspeaker. *See also* PHASE SHIFT; PHASING SWITCH.

Phasing (II) · A special effect obtained in the sound studio by dividing a signal between two tape machines or networks, and subjecting one to a minuscule time delay. *See also* FLANGING.

Phasing Switch · A control on an amplifier, also known as the phase reversal switch, which reverses the leads to one loudspeaker, thereby changing its relative phase. *See also* PHASE SHIFT.

Phonautograph · The device invented by Léon Scott in 1857 to record (but not reproduce) sound signals on a lampblack-covered cylinder. Emile Berliner adapted the principle in his gramophone.

Phonet · In Thomas Edison's early terminology, the stylus/diaphragm assembly of the phonograph.

Phono-Cut · Another name for vertical cut, the process of inscribing sound signals on record surfaces through an up and down movement of the cutting stylus.

Phonogram · The original name given by Thomas Edison to his cylinder records, suggesting their intended use for business purposes. Later, musical cylinders were called "records."

Phonograph · In current terminology, any disc or cylinder record player. Originally, it meant only the cylinder player, whereas the disc player was a gramophone, but that distinction faded early in the United States. In Britain, the specific terminology was retained through the 78 rpm era, and lingers today in some contexts (e.g., the name of the principal sound recording journal, *Gramophone*). For history and technical

Timeline of Phonographs, Gramophones, and Digital Music Players	
1857	Phonautograph invented by Léon Scott de Martinville.
1877	Thomas Edison made the first recording of a human voice using a tinfoil cylinder phonograph.
1878	The Edison Speaking Phonograph Co. was established to produce tinfoil cylinder recording and playback machines. Cylinders were largely viewed as dictation machines to be used for business.
1887	Emile Berliner coined the word "gramophone" for his disc player.
1890	Cylinders were composed of wax on an inner core of cardboard or other materials.
1891	Edison began to produce musical cylinders for entertainment.
1893	Henri Jules Lioret of Paris pioneered the production of celluloid cylinders, which improved the mass production of cylinders.
1894	Berliner Gramophone Co. founded in Philadelphia.
1896	Levi H. Montross invented a spring motor record player that was used by Eldridge Johnson in his Improved Gramophone. The hand-cranked motorized gramophone made disc players more marketable.
1900	Lambert Co. began producing cylinders made of celluloid, their "Indestructible" line. Eldridge R. Johnson and Leon F. Douglass formed the Consolidated Talking Machine Co. to market disc records and players. The name was changed to the Victor Talking Machine Company in 1901.
1901	The Columbia Phonograph Co. introduced its first disc machine.
1902	Separately, Edison and Columbia began producing their first molded cylinders. Edison established a standard speed of 160 rpm that was maintained by most other manufacturers from this point on.
1905	Following Victor's lead, most American record labels were recording discs at 78 RPM (actually 78–80 RPM) by this time.
1909	Columbia ceased producing cylinders.
1910	Discs and disc players begin to outsell cylinders and cylinder players. Victor and the Gramophone Co. were market leaders in disc sales.
1912	Edison acquired the rights to Lambert's process for producing celluloid cylinders, resulting in the Blue Amberol line. Edison also introduced its first disc player, the Diamond Disc phonograph.
1920	In Great Britain, Horace Owen Merriman and Lionel Guest patented the pioneering moving coil recording head for disc recording.
1923–1925	Electrical recording and amplification systems introduced by Bell Laboratories, General Electric, and others.
1928	In Germany, Fritz Pfleumer patented the use of coated tape as a magnetic recording medium.
1929	The last commercial cylinder recordings were released (Edison Blue Amberols).
1931	Alan Blumlein patented several key ideas leading to the development of the modern stereo disc.
1937	The Brush Development Company introduced the Soundmirror, one of the first commercially available magnetic recorders in the United States.

Timeline of Phonographs, Gramophones, and Digital Music Players

1945	Decca Record Co. introduced full frequency response records, ushering in the era of high fidelity recording.
1947	The Minnesota Mining and Manufacturing Company (3M), introduced the first successful plastic-based recording tape with a magnetic oxide coating.
1948	Columbia issued the long-playing disc, which operated at 33 1/3 RPM. Ampex Corporation manufactured its first professional tape recorder, the model 200.
1949	RCA Victor introduced the 45-RPM disc.
1951	Most record makers and record player manufacturers were offering three-speed disc players by this time, accommodating discs recorded at 33 1/3, 45, and 78 RPM.
1963	Philips (Netherlands) introduced the audiocassette tape format.
1978	Sony (Japan) introduced the first digital audio recording systems for professional studios.
1979	Sony introduced the TPS-L2 Walkman portable audio cassette player.
1980	The Philips/Sony audio compact disc technology was introduced.
1982	Music distributed using the Philips/Sony audio compact disc becomes commercially available.
1986	Digital Audio Tape (DAT) introduced.
1987	Development of the MP3 digital music file format began in Germany in 1987 under the direction of Dieter Seitzer at the University of Erlangen.
1988	Sony introduced the Discman, a Walkman that played a compact disc instead of a cassette. In addition, CD sales first exceeded the sales of vinyl long playing records.
1991	Pro Tools introduced, a software program allowing the digital editing and mixing of audio. It marked a significant shift from analog to digital music production. Sony introduced the DAT Walkman, using DAT tape.
1992	Sony introduced the MiniDisc portable music player using its MiniDisc format.
1998	The first commercially available MP3 players in the United States were introduced, including the Eiger Labs F10 and the Diamond Multimedia Rio PMP300.
1999	Napster was launched, becoming the primary consumer source for MP3 music files until it was shut down by law for infringing on the copyrights of music companies and artists.
2001	Apple introduced the iPod and its music download service, iTunes.
2002	Napster was re-launched as a paid music service à la iTunes.

aspects of the cylinder phonograph, *see also* CYLINDER and EDISON, (THOMAS A) INC. *See also* GRAPHOPHONE.

Phonograph Parlors · Establishments that provided coin-op phonographs for public listening, popular in the United States after 1889, and then worldwide. Notable parlors were the Pathé Salon de Phonographes in Paris and a similar establishment in London; and the lobby of the Vitascope Hall motion picture theatre in Buffalo, New York (the first deluxe movie house in the United States), where 28 Edison phonographs were deployed. In Italy, the parlor was known as the Bar Automatico. Parlors declined in popularity with the introduction of automatic pianos and music boxes, but they persisted for years, often grouped with other coin machines in penny arcades.

Phonograph-Graphophone · The commercial designation first given to the instrument of Chichester Bell and Charles Tainter when it was leased by the North American Phonograph Co. Later, it was simply the Graphophone, the name they had given to their original experimental models, and later still, it was the Columbia Graphophone.

Photophone · A light-ray system of sound recording, invented by Charles A. Hoxie, based on experiments of Alexander Graham Bell in 1879. The Bell concept was not practical at the time, because electronic amplification was not yet available. General Electric later adapted the principle for the Brunswick Pallatrope system of 1925.

Pickup · *See* CARTRIDGE (II).

Picture Discs · Records with illustrations on their labels or playing surfaces, issued by many companies from 1905 as postcard records, then by Talk-O-Photo in 1920, and as Emerson children's records in 1922 (six inches in diameter, with color pictures on one side). From 1932 to 1933, there were 30 items by Victor, including sides with photos of Enrico Caruso and Jimmie Rodgers. Picture discs—along with colored vinyl—enjoyed a revival in popularity during the early 1980s because of record company efforts to boost sagging retail sales. A recent price guide listed about 6,000 picture discs, worldwide. The most famous label in the picture field was Vogue from 1946 to 1947.

Picturized Phonographs · Devices that showed illustrations as accompaniment to records played in coin-op phonographs during the early years of the 20th century. Some of the brand names were Illustraphone (Hawthorne & Sheble), Cailophone, and Scopephone (both by Caille Brothers), and the Illustrated Song Machine (Rosenfield Co., New York). The Discophone was the first in use with disc players in the United States; it was made by the Valiquet Novelty Co. in Newark, New Jersey.

Pierce, Richard (Dick), 1952– · Involved in audio and technical software development professionally for over a quarter of a century, Pierce's activities have ranged from high-fidelity audio to radio astronomy to software development management. He has been the technical director of company designing and manufacturing high-quality loudspeaker drivers for OEM customers, senior development engineer for sophisticated CAD/CAM, data acquisition and process control, professional digital audio products and more.

Since 1990, Pierce has been working as an independent consultant in the audio fields. For much of that period, he was the principal software engineer for the AKG DSE-7000 and Orban AUDICY digital audio editing workstations. As an offshoot of this work, he has proposed and developed (what will soon be) an AES standard for exchanging metadata along with audio between diverse professional audio applications. In addition to this, he has consulted with a wide range of loudspeaker manufacturers, providing technical assistance and advice in design, measurement, quality control, and manufacturing, and has acquired an extensive acoustics measurement and analysis facility that has allowed him to develop a comprehensive suite of loudspeaker-simulation and modeling tools. He has served on a number of technical review committees for organizations such as the Audio Engineering Society, and continues to write and present

---

Phonolamp

A device invented by George E. Emerson, marketed in the United States in 1916 by the Electric Phonograph Corp. of New York. It was an electric lamp with an electric motor phonograph in the lamp base. Doors in the base opened to give access to the turntable and reproducer, from which "the tone is carried upwards through the stem of the lamp, which acts as a concealed horn, and at the top is reflected downward by means of a globe and thereby producing a tone of unusual clarity"—this according to a *Talking Machine World* advertisement of June 15, 1916. The apparatus appeared in at least five models, selling from $75 to $200. A record with the same label name was produced by the Grey Gull organization, and given to purchasers of the lamp.

tutorials on subjects such as digital audio and loudspeaker operating principles.

Apart from his professional interests, Pierce has an active interest in fine-art photography, having had a number of photographs accepted in juried art shows, and will be teaching several upcoming course on the subject. Additionally, he has had a long-term involvement in Baroque keyboard instruments and music, having built a dozen instruments including harpsichords, clavichords, and small pipe organs.—Howard Ferstler

Pinch Effect · In disc recording, the situation caused by the fact that the cutting stylus does not twist to face the groove direction, although the reproducing stylus does; thus, points of contact between the one stylus and the groove are not identical to the points of contact of the other stylus and the groove. The result is tracing distortion. *See also* DISTORTION.

Ping Pong Effect · A stereophonic separation of signals in which the sound output appears to come from one or the other of the loudspeakers, instead of from the space between or around them; the term coming from the alternating sounds of table tennis rackets striking the ball.

Pink Noise · Broad-band noise whose energy content is inversely proportional to frequency. The rate of change as the frequency climbs is minus 3 db per octave, which results in equal energy in each octave. Pink noise is often used as a sound source for testing audio components. *See also* WHITE NOISE.—Howard Ferstler

Pioneer Electronics (USA), Inc. [website: www.pioneerelectronics.com] · A division of the Tokyo Pioneer Corporation, which was founded in 1938 as a radio and speaker-repair company. The U.S. branch opened in 1972, and as of 2002 employs over 300 people at its Long Beach, California, headquarters.

The firm is best known for its home and mobile (in-car) audio equipment, marketed under the Pioneer and Premier names. Pioneer introduced several new technologies, including the unsuccessful laserdisc player, an early home-video format; however, it did serve as a model for the more successful DVD format, also introduced by Pioneer. In car audio, Pioneer introduced the first in-dash CD player, and the first detachable face-plate car stereo.

Pitch (I) · The property of musical tone that is determined by the frequency of the sound wave that produces it. In order for musicians to play in ensemble, an agreement is necessary among them regarding the pitch to be sounded for each note of the score. Various standards for pitch have been in use, though none have found universal adoption. These agreements have gradually resulted in a raising of the pitch standard; it is believed now that musicians of the 18th century played any given note about a semitone lower than the same note would be played today. In the early 19th century, pitch in European opera houses was 425.5 cycles per second for the note A in the treble staff. A Paris agreement of 1859 established that the note A would be played at 435 cycles per second (435 Hz). In 1939, an international agreement set the pitch of A at 440 Hz, and this remains the most accepted norm.

Pitch in recording is affected by the speed at which the cylinder or disc rotates, the factor being applicable both in making the record and in playing it back. A 6% deviation in playing speed results in a change in pitch by a semitone: 6% faster meaning the pitch rises a semitone, and 6% slower that it falls a semitone. A 6% deviation is achieved on a 78-rpm disc by 4 1/2 revolutions per minute on either side of the correct rotation rate, and by only two rpm for an LP record. Early discs made to be played at speeds above 78 rpm (e.g., at 80 or 82 rpm) will result in a noticeably lower (flattened) pitch when the playback turntable is set for 78 rpm. These problems have been a prime concern to those who reissue acoustic discs in LP or CD format. As examples of artists whose records need careful speed monitoring. *See also* STROBOSCOPIC DISC; TUNING BAND.

Pitch (II) · The distance between tracks on a recording medium. For example, on a compact disc, it is 1.6 microns.

Pitch (III) · The number of grooves (i.e., turns, or threads) per inch on a cylinder or disc record, expressed as a decimal; "0.1 inch pitch" refers to a configuration of 10 grooves per inch. Most cylinder records of the early 1890s had 1.0 pitch, or 100 grooves per inch. Standard 78-rpm discs have a pitch of 0.9 to 1.2. Microgroove LPs have a pitch of 2. to 3. *See also* CYLINDER, 4; DISC.

Pits · The bumps on a compact disc, carriers of the signal. They are read by the laser pickup by diffracting the light they receive and decreasing the light returned to the pickup according to the characteristics of the signals they represent.

Pitts, Eugene, August 3, 1940– · Awarded B.A. in English literature from Northwestern University in 1962, Pitts was editor in chief of *Audio* magazine from 1973 to 1995. During that time, he played a key roll in determining the magazine's style and the way it balanced the need for hard, engineering-style data and the also important need to satisfy the reading requirements of a broad subscription base. Since he left *Audio* (which folded a few years after he left), Pitts has been manager/owner/publisher of *The Audiophile Voice* (formerly the magazine of the Weschster Audiophile Society), an audio journal that stresses the analysis of recordings and performance aesthetics as much as equipment quality.—Howard Ferstler

Plate · The name given to the early hard rubber disc recordings made by Emile Berliner, issued by the U.S. Gramophone Company. In 1894, Berliner continued referring to his discs as plates until 1896.

Platter · A disc record.

Plaut, Fred, 1907–1985 · Noted recording engineer for Columbia Records from the mid-1940s through the 1970s, Plaut specialized in classical music and Broadway shows, and won two Grammy awards for engineering. During the years he worked as an engineer, he recorded notables such as Miles Davis, Virgil Thomson, Ned Rorem, Aaron Copland, Leonard Bernstein, John Williams (the guitarist), Robert Casadesus, Glenn Gould, Eugene Ormandy, Rudolf Serkin, and Igor Stravinsky. Plaut was also an avid photographer, and his photos of numerous musical personalities are housed in the Archives at Yale University. Yale also has a recording facility named after him.—Howard Ferstler

Playback Curve · The reciprocal of the recording curve in an audio system; the degree of frequency compensation or equalization required in playback.

Playback Head · The element of a tape deck that generates electric currents from the recorded pattern on the tape passing by it; it may be the same head as the recording head.

Playback Loss · The difference between recorded and reproduced levels at a given point on a disc record. It results from the variance in formation between the two walls of the modulated groove (one side being concave, the other convex).

Playboy · A jukebox introduced by Seeburg in 1939; it was the first to have a wall box with selections in it, separated from the speaker apparatus.

Playing Speeds · *See* PITCH; SPEEDS.

Pohlmann, Ken C. · Pohlmann is a tenured full professor and director of the Music Engineering Technology program in the School of Music at the University of Miami in Coral Gables. He holds B.S. and M.S. degrees in electrical engineering from the University of Illinois in Urbana-Champaign, and is the author of *Principles of Digital Audio* (4th edition, 2000, McGraw-Hill) and *The Compact Disc Handbook* (2nd edition, 1992, A-R Editions), co-author of *Writing for New Media* (1st edition, 1997, Wiley), and editor and co-author of *Advanced Digital Audio* (1st edition, 1991, Macmillan Computer Publishing). He has written over 1,500 articles for audio magazines. He contributes to *Sound & Vision* and *Mobile Entertainment* magazines.

Pohlmann chaired the Audio Engineering Society's Conference on Digital Audio in 1989 and co-chaired the Society's Conference on Internet Audio in 1997. He was presented two AES Board of Governor's Awards (1989 and 1998) and an AES Fellowship Award (1990) by the Audio Engineering Society for his work in the field of audio engineering. He is a non-board member of the National Public Radio Distribution/Interconnection Committee, and a member of the Board of Directors of the New World Symphony.

He serves as a consultant in the design of digital audio systems, for the development of mobile audio systems for automobile manufacturers, and as an expert witness in technology patent litigation. Some of his consulting clients include: Alpine, Baker & McKenzie, Bertlesmann, Blockbuster, DaimlerChrysler, Darby & Darby, Fish & Neave, Ford, Fujitsu Ten, Harman/Becker, Hyundai, IBM, Kia, Lexus, Microsoft, Motorola, Nippon Columbia, Onkyo, RealNetworks, Sony, TDK, Time Warner, Toyota, and United Technologies.—Howard Ferstler

Polar Response: Loudspeakers · A graphic display of the speaker's dispersion at specific frequencies. Polar response will usually be quite wide if the driver diameter is small in relation to the frequencies being reproduced. Typical loudspeakers will therefore have variable polar response as the frequency varies, with it narrowing considerably in the top octave. *See also* LOUDSPEAKER.—Howard Ferstler

Polar Response: Microphones · A graphic display of the audio output levels of the microphone at different frequencies, caused by sound waves arriving at the diaphragm from different directions. Microphone polar response will vary from omnidirectional to very narrow, with dispersion patterns also varying considerably as the signal frequencies change. *See also* MICROPHONE.—Howard Ferstler

Pole Face Alignment · *See* GAP ALIGNMENT.

Polyphone. A phonograph with two sapphire-stylus reproducers, each tracking the same groove but 3/8 to 1/2 inch apart. Leon Douglass was the inventor.

Poniatoff, Alexander Mathew, March 25, 1892–October 24, 1980 · Russian-American electrical engineer responsible for the development of the professional tape recorder and the first commercially successful video tape recorder (VTR).

Poniatoff was born in Kazan District, Russia, and educated in Moscow and Karlsruhe, gaining degrees in mechanical and electrical engineering. In 1927, he immigrated to the United States and became a citizen. He was employed by the General Electric Company and later by Dalmo Victor.

In 1944, taking his initials to form the title, Poniatoff founded the AMPEX Corporation. By 1946, AMPEX had turned from the manufacture of airborne radar to the production of audio tape recorders developed from the German wartime Telefunken Magnetophon machine (the first tape recorder in the truest sense). In this, Poniatoff was supported by the entertainer Bing Crosby, who needed high-quality replay facilities for broadcasting purposes. By 1947, Poniatoff was able to offer a professional-quality product and the business prospered.

With the rapid post-war boom in television broadcasting in the USA, a need soon arose for a video recorder to provide "time-shifting" of live TV programs between the different U.S. time zones. Many companies therefore endeavored to produce a video tape recorder (VTR) using the same single-track, fixed-head, longitudinal-scan system used for audio, but the very much higher bandwidth required involved an unacceptably high tape-speed. AMPEX offered a machine with twelve parallel tracks, but it proved unsatisfactory. Next his development team, which included Charles Ginsburg and Ray Dolby, devised a four-head transverse-scan system in which a quadruplex head rotating at 14,400 rpm was made to scan across the width of a 2-inch tape with a tape-to-head speed of 160 ft/sec (about 110 mph) but with a longitudinal tape speed of only 15 in/sec. In this way, acceptable picture quality was obtained with a reasonable rate of tape consumption.

By April 1956, commercial production of studio-quality machines began to revolutionize the production and distribution of TV programs, and the perfecting of time-base correctors, which could stabilize the signal timing to a few nanoseconds, made color VTRs a practical proposition. In the face of emerging competition from helical scan machines, where the tracks are laid diagonally on the tape, AMPEX developed its own helical machine in 1957. They also developed the Videofile system, in which 250,000 pages of facsimile could be recorded on a single tape, offering a new means of archiving information. Poniatoff was President and then Chairman of AMPEX Corporation until 1970; he died a decade later. Although quadruplex VTRs were obsolete by 1986, Poniatoff's role in making television was decisive.—George Brock-Nannestad

Port · A vent or auxiliary opening in a bass reflex baffle. It must be precisely located and of correct dimension to allow passage of rear sound waves through the enclosure while keeping them in phase with the front waves.

Portable Record Players · The ability to carry music with you—today embodied in many ultra-miniature playback devices—is almost as old as the phonograph itself. The Decca portable gramophone, introduced in 1912 and made popular at the front in World War I, was the first famous portable, but the Pigmy model of the Gramophone Co., introduced in 1909, was the earliest of the genre.

During the 1920s, portables became popular that were modeled after inexpensive box cameras; like these cameras, they would fold into a small, easy-to-carry box. These often featured folding leather-covered horns, and took names like "Cameraphone" (from Britain) and "Brownie" (from America) in imitation of the popular folding cameras of the day. The Peter Pan Gramophone, made in England, is among the earliest in this style, introduced in August 1923; they even built a version that incorporated a clock, with the phonograph serving as the alarm (an early form of clock-radio!). During the mid-1920s, various models were made in Britain, Germany, and Switzerland, many using mechanical movements made by Thorens.

More conventional, suitcase-sized models were widely marketed by Victor during the later 1920s and into the 1930s. These all-in-one units lacked the novelty and extreme compactness of the box-camera

---

Postcard Records

Max Ettlinger & Co., of Long Acre, England, marketed Discal postcards in March 1905. In June of the same year, Zonophone GMBH advertised singing postcards, and a few days later, there was advertising from M. Taubert & Co. of Berlin for postcard records. Ettlinger was still selling the cards in May 1908. Such cards could be played on a standard turntable, but needed a clamp to keep them from slipping. Postcard records became common throughout the industry, and were issued in both 331/3- and 45-rpm speeds.

---

models, but offered better sound without being too bulky to carry. Sewing machine manufacturers, such as Singer, also made these spring-driven model. They were ideal for door-to-door salesmen and even traveling preachers, particularly the Jehovah's Witnesses, whose leader, Joseph Franklin Rutherford, provided his troops with portable phonographs and recordings of Bible talks to carry with them during the 1930s. These phonographs became quite popular in rural areas of the United States and even Mexico, where electric floor models would have been impractical.

The introduction of the 45-rpm record after World War II launched a new era of portable phonographs, mostly aimed at young children and teenagers. "Singles" became the favorite method of selling pop songs to teens, and they could listen to them in their own rooms thanks to the introduction of small, self-contained, portable players. Spindles were developed so 45s could be stacked and played in sequence automatically. From the 1960s forward, firms such as Fischer-Price made portable toy phonographs for use by younger children. The phonographs were often decorated with cartoon characters like Mickey Mouse.

Once cassettes and other media were introduced, an entire new generation of portable players not relying on discs was made possible. Of modern portable audio players, the most important has been the Sony Walkman, a cassette machine small enough to fit in the palm, used for headphone listening. Similar players have been introduced for the CD and MiniDisc formats. The introduction of the MP3 format in 1997 allowed music to be stored digitally in compressed files, leading to the development of several portable digital players, most notably Apple's iPod player, introduced in 2001.—Rev. by Carl Benson

Post Sync · New audio material added in synchronization to a previously filmed motion picture.

Pot · *See* POTENTIOMETER.

Potentiometer · In an amplifier, the variable attenuator, or potential divider, used to control volume; it is often referred to as a pot.

Poulsen, Valdemar, 1869–1942 · Danish inventor and engineer, credited with the development of magnetic wire recording around 1898. His machine was named the telegraphone, first patented in Britain (no. 8961) in 1899. He also invented a process for magnetic recording on iron discs and metal tape, but did not exploit it. Poulsen set up a corporation to hold his patents: A/S Telegraphonen Patent Poulsen; and a manufacturing firm: Dansk Telegraphone Fabrik A/S (1903). He showed his recorder at the Paris Exposition of 1900, and registered the voice of Emperor Franz Joseph. Later he recorded King Edward VII, and presented the wire to Queen Alexandra (its whereabouts are not known). In 1905, he sold those interests to the Telegraphone Corp. (U.S.) and the American

Telegraphone Company became the manufacturer. Among Poulsen's eight American patents, no. 661,619 (filed July 8, 1899, granted November 13, 1900) was most important, as the bearer of his basic ideas for wire recording.

Power Amplifier · The main amplifier, or basic amplifier; the device that boosts the voltage supplied by the pre-amplifier to the level required to drive a loudspeaker. *See also* AMPLIFIER.

Preamplifier · A device, commonly known as a preamp, added to an amplifier to accommodate the very low voltage output from pickups and tape recorders and to raise that voltage to a point that will drive the amplifier. For example, the output level of a cartridge may be 1–5 millivolts; the preamplifier could raise it to 1–1.5 volts. The preamp may also provide frequency-response equalization, and may have other functions as well. It may be built into the turntable or the amplifier, or may appear as a separate component. *See also* AMPLIFIER; CONTROLS.

Precedence Effect · The phenomenon of correctly identifying the direction of a sound source heard in both ears but arriving at different times. Due to the spacing of the ears, the direct sound from any source first enters the ear closest to the source, with the more distant ear getting

---

Euphonious Euphemisms

The coming of the phonograph, gramophone, and other music-related consumer products ushered in an unprecedented effort on the part of manufacturers to invent catchy, high-minded names for their new products. On one hand, product makers were trying to impress an impressionable public. On the other hand, they often sought to confuse the buyer by inventing names that were much like those of their better-known competitors. Here is a sampling from the first 70 years of music technology taken from the pages of this guide:

Adler	Echophone	Multiplex Grand
Amberola	Grafonola	Orchestrope
American Indian	Graphophone	Panatrope
Ampliphone	Graphophone Grand	Peerless
Angelica	Hexaphone	Perfected Graphophone
Automatic Entertainer	Home Grand	Phonogram
Autophone	Home Queen	Phonograph
Baby	Illustraphone	Picturized Phonographs
Baby Grand	Invincible	Polyphone
Bardini	Jewel	Polyphone Concert Grand
Bijou	Languagephone	Premier
Cailophone	Leader	Scopephone
Columbia Grand	Luxus	Sovereign
Concert	Lyric	Standard
Crown	Lyrophone	Symphonola
Dance Master	Magnetophone	Twentieth-Century Grand
Deuxphone	Mignon	Twentieth-Century Premier
Double Eagle	Monarch	Ultona
Eagle	Multinola	Universal
Ebonoid	Multiphone	

a delayed signal. Research on this mechanism has shown that humans localize a sound source based upon the first-arrival sound, even if the subsequent arrivals are within 25–35 milliseconds. The phenomenon also describes how a stereophonic soundstage is possible from only two up-front loudspeakers.

A practical example of the precedence effect working against realistic stereophonic sound reproduction can be observed when identical sounds come from two different speaker systems. When this occurs, the identical sounds form a phantom center image if the listener is seated in the sweet spot out in front of but equidistant from the two speakers, and then moves to the side, therefore becoming closer to one of the two speakers. The result is a tendency for the signal from the more distant speaker (for example, the phantom-center image) to collapse toward the nearer speaker. *See also* FRANSSEN EFFECT.—Howard Ferstler

Pre-Emphasis · A high-frequency boost used during the recording process. During playback, reciprocal de-emphasis would be applied, and the result will be an improved signal-to-noise ratio.—Howard Ferstler

Premier Cylinders · The "Columbia Gold Moulded" cylinder records, six inches long, announced in April 1905. (There had been prior demonstrations.) Because of the enhanced volume produced—by the Higham mechanical amplifier built into the reproducer mechanism—the player marketed for these records was called the Loud Speaking Graphophone; it cost $100 minus horn; later the name Twentieth Century Graphophone was given to the machine, and to the records. The cylinders were issued to April 1909, despite poor sales.

Presence (I) · The impression given to the listener of an audio system that the original program source is actually present.

Presence (II) · A boost given to frequencies in the region of 2,000 to 8,000 Hz, intended to enhance the forwardness of a recorded signal on playback, thus to give a greater impression of presence.

Preservation and Restoration of Historical Recordings · This article has 10 sections:

1. Introduction, Definition of Sound Preservation
2. Formats, especially Obsolete Formats
3. Deterioration of Formats
4. Cleaning and Repairing Formats
5. Playback Equipment
6. Current Standard Preservation Formats (Analog and Digital)
7. Recording Equipment
8. Equalization
9. The Re-recording or Transfer Process
10. Definition of Sound Restoration

Introduction. Sound preservation is the process of saving and protecting any auditory material, which has significant historical and cultural value from a deteriorating recording medium before the medium becomes unplayable. Sound preservation is also protecting any articulation made by vocal apparatus (oral histories including radio broadcasts, speeches, interviews, and literature) or any recorded rhythm, melody, or harmony composed to create music (jazz, folk, blues, classical and rock 'n' roll) from injury or destruction. Sound preservation is the professional cleaning and transfer of the original recording to the highest quality technology using the best recording medium available at the time the work has to be done for the sake of saving it for years to come. The resulting sound preservation master should be the fairest representation of the original recording.

Before Sound preservation, archivists should consider a conservation program.

Conservation includes assessing a sound collection to establish a condition baseline or triggering immediate preservation reformatting if the conditions or the technology indicate such action. Conservation consists of re-housing sound materials into new containers and placing these materials in a monitored temperature (between 65°–75°F) and humidity-controlled (between 40 to 60% relative humidity [RH]) environment until either a deterioration issue occurs in the collection or before the playback equipment for the sound format becomes obsolete.

Sound preservation is done by sound preservation engineers in specialized commercial sound preservation laboratories or by in-house sound archivists at universities or institutions. The purpose of sound preservation is to preserve the sound of original source material that may be deteriorating. This article focuses on the craft of sound preservation. The definition of sound restoration can be at the end of the article.

Formats · The recordings to be preserved can range from wax cylinders, to broadcast transcription discs or acetate disc recordings, to wire, open reel tape that are acetate or polyester base, audio cassettes, belt or band recordings or vinyl recording discs, audio on film or VHS tapes, digital audio tapes (DATs) and MiniDiscs, among other formats. These recordings are made of a variety of materials. There have even been recordings made on unusual materials, such as X-ray film, that needed to be preserved. *See also* DISC for wax cylinders, and acetate and vinyl records, TAPE for various tape formats, and see the following list for a few obsolete belt formats and an obsolete cellulose acetate disc format.

1. *Dictabelt.* As stated in a Dictaphone brochure, "Ahead of your time with the Dictaphone Time-Master" was their invitation to prospective buyers and in language that dates the machine: "Thousands of business executives, doctors, lawyers, government men and others whose thoughts are important rely on Time-Masters and Dictabelts as their thoughts thruway." Dictabelt was the medium, or software, as we would call it today, for the famous Dictaphone machine, which was introduced in 1947 by the Dictaphone Corporation. At one time, tens of thousands of them were in the offices of American insurance companies alone. Ten years later, Dictaphone introduced its first magnetic recorder, the Dictet, but the Dictabelt had another decade of life in it, and a few Dictabelts were in service even as late as the 1980s. By 1979, however, when Pitney Bowes acquired Dictaphone, they had virtually disappeared. Today, it is difficult to find even one.

   Dictabelts are composed of a soft cellulose acetate material and contain visible grooves on them. They come in a variety of colors including red, purple, and blue.

2. *Magnabelt.* In dictation machines, the switch from stylus-and-groove to magnetic belts occurred mainly in the mid 1960s, and IBM was manufacturing magnetic belt dictation machines as late as the mid-1980s. The new machines were similar in appearance to the older machines, but boasted greater fidelity and the ability to erase and re-use belts. Dictaphone was, of course, a major player in this new technology, which it continued to call the Dictabelt, but Dictaphone had a serious competitor, IBM, with machines that were not compatible with Dictaphone's. There was also a third player, Gray Manufacturing, with machines that were compatible with IBM but not with Dictaphone's. The Gray's were known for their exceptional rugged-

ness. Lanier Worldwide eventually bought Gray Manufacturing's technologies. Those technologies were sold to companies in Germany.

Magnabelts are quite similar in appearance and operation to the Dictabelt visible belt machines but obviously do not contain grooves. The magnetic belt is made with either acetate or Mylar backing.

3. *Dictalog Magnabelt.* The Dictaphone Corporation manufactured the Dictalog Magnabelt in the 1950s. Only 1,000 of the DL-3A model were made. The U.S. Government used these machines in the DEW line radar defense system and by corporations and law firms, who used them for dictating letters because they held twice as much information than the traditional magnetic belts. A well-known sound engineer in the Midwest with extensive experience on this equipment recounted that often a lawyer on a business trip would phone in letters after hours for his secretary to type in the morning. As technology created smaller units that recorded more information, these machines became obsolete; however, the belts were sold into the late 1960s.

Dictalog Magnabelts are similar in appearance to Magnabelts but are longer in length than the Magnabelts.

4. *Memovox Disc.* The essential technology of a Memovox is stylus-and-groove. An amplified signal was used to drive a stylus that cut analogous grooves into a 16-inch cellulose acetate disc ; however, Memovox incorporated a lead screw that kept the disc rotating at a constant linear velocity across the stylus. This feature greatly increased the capacity of the medium. The disc is often clear or milky white and the recording plays from inside out.

Deterioration Issues of Formats. Identifying deterioration issues in the formats is an essential step in sound preservation before cleaning so that the engineer does not cause further distress to the format. All formats will collect dirt and debris depending on how they have been stored. Some formats will have developed mold or fungus and others will display other deterioration issues depending on their composition and how they have been stored. The problems can range from tape with sticky shed syndrome or vinegar syndrome, to broken discs, to discs that have lacquer peeling off. Certain discs in the collection could have issues such as palmitic acid and powder residue. Some sound collections can even suffer from biological infestation. Identifying the deterioration issue is key in deciding how the format should be cleaned. Here are some common deterioration issues:

1. *Peeling Lacquer.* Moving to first generation or instantaneous discs, these so-called acetates were manufactured with an aluminum, glass, or cardboard base. The base was then coated with nitrocellulose lacquer plasticized with castor oil. This was an unstable mixture making these acetates not suitable for long-term storage. Symptoms or problems include continuous shrinking of the lacquer top coating, embrittlement, and irreversible loss of recorded sound because of the loss of the castor oil plasticizer. Because the core does not shrink and the lacquer coating does (or expands under changes in temperature), cracking and peeling of the lacquer coating results.

2. *Palmitic Acid.* The production of palmitic acid is caused by the hydrolysis of the castor oil from heat and

humidity, which then oozes through the lacquer on a disc. The specks or small mounds on the groove look similar to powder residue but have a more crystallized appearance. Palmitic acid is stubborn to remove and requires extensive hand cleaning.

3. *Powder Residue.* Powder residue may appear on lacquer discs as dried white specks or pasty mounds on the grooves. The main symptom is caused by glue from the paper label, which has spread over time onto the recording surface of the disc. Sometimes powder residue is mistaken for mold or palmitic acid.

4. *Vinegar Syndrome.* Cellulose acetate reel-to-reel tapes and acetate discs are subject to a slow form of chemical deterioration known as vinegar syndrome. The main symptoms of this problem are a vinegar-like odor and buckling, shrinking, and embrittlement of the tape or cellulose disc. Low-temperature storage conditions can aid in slowing down this process. More on Vinegar Syndrome can be found in an article, "Vinegar Syndrome: An Experience with the Silent but Stinky Acetate Tape Killer" published at www.cuttingarchives.com. There is a product by the Image Permanence Institute for measuring the level of acidity. The color on the strip, blue, will change to mustard yellow as it detects high acidity.

5. *Sticky Shed Syndrome.* Polyester magnetic tape stock, which came into wide use in the 1960s, can develop a condition known as sticky shed syndrome. This problem occurs when oxidation of the tape sticks to the guides and magnetic heads of the playback machine. All polyester based tapes are susceptible to hydrolysis—the absorption of water molecules into the tapes' binder. Over time, particularly for tape stored in moist environments, this accumulation of water molecules causes the binder to become gummy and sticky. Upon playback, this tape will stick to the heads and guides of the playback machine and will shed flakes of iron oxide. This causes distortion to the sound of the recording that is called separation or shed loss and can sometimes bring the tape playing on the machine to a grinding halt. It results in very low-level volume, fuzzy sound, or inaudible audio.

Tape manufacturers changed the chemistry of their binders in the mid-1970s (approximately 1975) and tapes produced between that time and the mid-1980s are particularly at risk for signs of this sticky shed syndrome.

6. *Mold Growth.* Mold is caused by the growth of fungus in elevated temperature or humidity conditions. It can cause serious distortion and physical breakdown in most audio formats, both grooved and magnetic formats alike. The other major agent involved in fungal action is the presence of organic material on the recording medium due to unclean storage areas.

7. *Biological Infestation.* On occasion, due to the environment of where the audio materials are stored, the materials will be affected by unusual conditions such as biological infestation. For example, in hot and humid conditions and flood conditions, termites have been known to make their home in open reel tapes. They ate through the reel cardboard boxes and took residence on the tape under the plastic reels.

Cleaning and Repairing Formats. To clean and repair the various sound formats, it is important to know the composition of the format and understand the deterioration or problem condition. As a rule of thumb, the formats should be cleaned with the most non-invasive methods as possible. There are times, though, when to save the audio from the format, heroic measures might be taken with the approval of the sound collection owner.

Most disc recordings are cleaned with record cleaning solutions, which are usually composed of a degree of dish detergent to many parts distilled water. For more stubborn or complex conditions, for example, acetate reel-to-reel tapes suffering from vinegar syndrome need to be isolated and transferred from all other sound collections especially acetate based recordings and transferred on dedicated playback machines. Polyester-based reel-to-reels suffering from sticky shed syndrome either can be baked in a convection oven or undergo treatment in a food dehydrator. In certain cases, commercially manufactured solutions followed by a distilled water washing can be employed.

Playback Equipment. The sound preservation lab should be equipped with a wide assortment of playback machines. For example, the lab should have a variety of tape playback machines that accommodate various speeds, tracks, and tape sizes. The lab should be equipped with turntables that can accommodate various sized discs and variable disc speeds. It is also important to be equipped with a large array of styli and cartridges. It is important to have a variety of sizes and shape styli. Having the proper phono pre-amp is also an essential part of the playback equipment. A variable EQ preamplifier can allow the engineer to transfer disc recordings at a pre-Recording Industries Association of America (RIAA) curve setting or a RIAA curve setting depending on when the disc was originally made.

Often, playback equipment is not readily available especially for obsolete audio formats. In those cases, sound labs usually rebuild machines or reverse engineer trans-fer machines cannibalizing parts from old machines. Experienced technical engineers should routinely maintain all playback machines.

Current Standard Preservation Formats (Analog and Digital). Today, some institutions still prefer to preserve their sound collections on 1/4-inch open reel analog tape, while others choose to digitize their sound collections. Some archivists prefer to have both analog and digital preservation masters and user reference copies on CD-R. The following are typically the standards for both:

- *1/4-Inch Open Reel Tape Preservation Master.* One each to be a 7.5 ips, full track, 1/4-inch analog recording made on 1.5-mil polyester audiotape stock. A 1-khz, 250-nwb/m test tone will be placed at the head of each new preservation recording for reference purposes. This will be the preservation master able to replace the original recording media. This open reel copy shall be made with minimum signal processing so that it will be a fair representation of the original recording.

- *Digitized Files.* These are master files in 96-khz, 24-bit WAV file stored on CD-R, DVD-R, or removable hard-drives depending on size and archivist's needs. Service files or reference copies are made at 44.1-khz, 16-bit WAV or MP3 (monaural at a data rate of 128 kbps or stereo at a data rate of 256 kbps). Some archivists request service files in streaming audio format. Reference copies are often made available on CD-R format. The master and service files are usually recorded onto hard disc and can be FTP'd (file transfer protocol) directly to the archivist's secured server. The CD-R stock is normally an archive grade CD made with a phthalocyanine-based dye.

Recording Equipment. Quality assurance starts with the condition of the recording equipment. Analog tape decks should be checked by technical engineers for the following: distortion, frequency response, signal to noise ratio, crosstalk, gain difference, and phase difference. The machine specifications should be teched out with appropriate calibration tapes. Burned CD-Rs are analyzed by compact disc quality analyzers for any errors. The engineer also A/Bs the original recording to the preservation recording that is being made to assure the fairest representation of the original recording.

Equalization for Sound Preservation. The archivist tends to seek a clear and fair representation copy or "forensic" copy not a "restore" copy of their original recordings. The sound preservation engineers use selective filtering only in cases where quality or intelligibility of original recording should be improved. The engineers do not apply specific technical applications if it is beyond appropriate filtering and moderate noise reduction without consulting the archivist first.

The Rerecording or Transfer Process
- Inspect the sound format.
- Identify any deterioration issues.
- Clean or repair the format before transferring.
- Reference signals are recorded.
- Format is transferred.
- During transfer, the engineer will A/B to compare preservation recording with new recording to ensure the fairest representation.
- Reference or service copies are made.
- Original recording is re-housed.

Definition of Sound Restoration. Sound restoration is the process of restoring, renewing, reviving, re-purposing, or re-establishing auditory material as well as the restitution of music or vocals that have been lost. Where sound preservation is a fair representation of the original recording, sound restoration is a recovery of the original recording and even an enhancement to authenticate the original recording. Today with the aid of advanced digital audio software, sound engineers can enhance and work to restore lost audio by removing clicks, pops, tape hiss, and surface noise to improve the sound beyond the preservation master.—Ranjita (Anji) Kalita Cornette

Pressing (I) · The final form of the disc, made from the stamper; it is the form sold to the end user. *See also* DISC.

Pressing (II) · As a verb, the process of molding the biscuit as it is kneaded and squeezed flat between warmed bed plates. *See also* DISC.

Preston, J. · *See* LOUDSPEAKER, 2.

Print-Through · The transferal of signal information from one portion of a magnetic tape to another portion, with the effect of simultaneous playback of the transferred signal and the signal already present. This is a major problem of the format, arising from the tight winding of tape on its reel, tape coercivity, or temperature aberrations. Thickness of the base is an important factor also.

Print-through is most likely to occur immediately after recording, and becomes less likely with the passage of time. It may be helpful to rewind a freshly recorded tape a few times before playback. Annual winding of little used tapes—fast-forward and slow reverse—is recommended by some authorities as a means of reducing the tendency of tape layers to adhere to each other; however, "winding retightens the tape-pack and this freshly accumulated tension restarts the tape stretching cycle anew. Thus, ritual rewinding may cause more ills than it cures" (Smolian 1987). No device or method will remove print-through once it has occurred (Smolian 1987). *See also* PRESERVATION AND RESTORATION OF HISTORICAL RECORDINGS.

Production Master · *See* MASTER.

Pro Tools · A computer-based multi-track recording hardware and software system, Pro Tools was first released in 1991. Over the next decade, it became the top selling digital audio workstation. Some versions used only a computer's own CPU, whereas others required adding DSP cards to increase the number of available channels and effects. This created a platform that third party companies could develop for, with hooks that allowed other pieces of software (plug-ins) to affect the audio stream. A number of control surfaces became available, providing buttons and sliders to ease access to and tactile feedback.

Pro Tools was developed by Digidesign, an innovative company begun in 1984 by Peter Gotcher and Evan Brooks, who started by producing sound replacement chips for drum machines. They went on to make the program Sound Designer, and then used its editing tools to create hard disk recording systems, capitalizing on the convergence of new technologies: programmable DSP chips, affordable 16-bit converters, computers with expansion slots, and the very rapid increase in hard drive storage capacity and chip processing power.

Computer-based systems revolutionized the recording industry by greatly lowering the cost of high quality systems. They began a trend away from tape-based facilities with expensive consoles and out-board gear toward integrated systems that can handle recording, mixing, processing, editing, and playback.—Robert Willey

Psychoacoustics · The scientific study of the perception of sound, particularly important when we think of recorded musical or motion-picture-sound listening in home- or studio-listening environments. A knowledge of psychoacoustics will help the recording engineer produce recordings that have maximum realism and impact in home-playback situations. Those who design home-audio hardware, particularly speakers and surround processors, can use the same knowledge to produce superior products.—Howard Ferstler

Puck · *See* CAPSTAN.

Pulse Code Modulation · *See* PCM (Pulse Code Modulation).

Push-Up Player · The type of 1890s piano roll player that was mechanically independent of the piano, and had to be pushed up to it to function. Aeolian Company's Pianola was the most popular, and gave its name to the genre.

Putnam, Milton T. (Bill), 1920–April 13, 1989 · A pioneer in recording studio acoustics, Putnam was born in Danville, Illinois. As a young man, he was influenced by his father, a businessman who also put on radio programs, including a number- one country music show. By age 15, Putnam had passed the ham radio operator's exam and was constructing his own equipment. In high school, he worked repairing radios and renting out PA systems, while also singing on weekends with dance bands, developing his interest in the music business. Technical studies at the Illinois Institute of Technology were followed by work at radio stations, such as WDAN in Chicago, and WDWS in Champaign; during

World War II, Putnam did radio engineering work for the Army.

In 1946, he started his own recording studio, in Evanston Illinois. His goals at the time, besides having a successful business, were the development of new recording techniques and the production of specialized equipment for recording studios. Putnam is acknowledged as the first person to use artificial reverberation for commercial recordings, and the whole modern control-room concept in common use was his invention. He also developed the first multi-band equalizers, a specialized limiter, the first low-noise tube microphone preamplifier, and a half-speed mastering technique. His company, Universal Recording, was responsible for the development of classic equipment like the United Recording Electronics Industries (UREI) Time Align monitors, and he was involved in the early development of stereophonic recording, at a time when other studios were afraid to fool with it. Putnam also published a number of articles on high-fidelity sound reproduction, and even conducted seminars and classes. During that time, he mentored upcoming engineers like Alan Sides and Bruce Swedien.

As success followed success, he founded additional facilities in Chicago, Hollywood, and San Francisco. A number of recording-industry firsts occurred at Universal: the first use of tape repeat, the first vocal booth, the first multiple voice recording, and the first 8-track recording trials and experiments with half-speed disc mastering. Universal was becoming famous, doing recordings for the Chicago-based labels Veejay, Mercury, and Chess. The studio was a hub for rhythm and blues recordings, including cuts for Muddy Waters, Willie Dixon, Bo Diddley, Little Walter, and Chuck Berry. Jazz and more mainstream artists recorded by Putnam included Stan Kenton, Patti Page, Vic Damone, Dinah Washington, Tommy Dorsey, Count Basie, Dizzy Gillespie, Ella Fitzgerald, Sarah Vaughan, Nat King Cole, and the master, Duke Ellington, who considered Putnam his favorite recording engineer. During the 1960s and 1970s, the studios were sometimes busy 24 hours a day, 7 days a week with artists such as Frank Sinatra (for many years, Putnam was the only engineer that Sinatra would allow into the recording booth), Bing Crosby, Dean Martin, Sammy Davis, Johnny Mercer, and Ray Charles. Putnam was also producing records for Decca, as well as writing songs and lyrics. Putnam was a member of the Audio Engineering Society, became a Fellow of the Society in 1959, and became an honorary member in 1983. In 2000, he won a posthumous Grammy for his technical accomplishments.—Howard Ferstler

Q

Q Channel · An inaudible sub-code channel on a compact disc that carries information on tracks, index numbers, product codes, and the like.

Quad · *See* QUADRAPHONIC RECORDING.

Quad Loudspeaker Company · Founded in 1936 by Peter Walker. One of the oldest audio-product enterprises still in operation, Quad was founded by Peter Walker in 1936, under the name Acoustical Manufacturing Company. Although it originally specialized in producing public address systems and amplifiers, Walker was also interested in loudspeaker design, and in 1949, he introduced the Corner Ribbon Loudspeaker, a system that was notable for its ability to reproduce very clean high frequencies. In the same year, the company name was changed to QUAD, which cryptically stood for "Quality Unit Amplified Domestic." During this same period, Walker and Gilbert Briggs, founder of Warfedale, arranged a series of audio-system demonstrations at Royal Festival Hall in London and Carnegie Hall in New York. Briggs was trying to prove that recorded music could compete with live music. At one session, a capacity audience of 3000 at Royal Festival Hall heard a demonstration of the clarity and quality of a well-designed hi-fi system. This technique presaged the live versus recorded demonstrations done by Acoustic Research in the 1960s.

In the late 1950s, Walker and David Williamson developed the world's first full-range electrostatic loudspeaker, which later came to be called the Quad ESL-57. (The technology was based in part on designs pioneered decades earlier by E. W. Kellog and Hans Vogt.). The ESL-57, for all of its maximum-output and low-bass limitations, was admired by a whole generation of direct-field listening audio enthusiasts, due to its very clean midrange performance

In the early 1980s, Quad introduced the ESL-63, a more advanced electrostatic design that was unique, in that it used a concentric ring of sound-radiating electrodes fed through a calibrated delay line. The bulls-eye-styled radiating surface worked to create a simulated point source, even though the system was still at its best when precisely aimed at the listener. The ESL-63 was an immense success in high-end circles, with an entire year's production selling out within two months. Later iterations of this system, the ESL-88 and larger ESL-89, offered even more advanced performance. The current company produces both electrostatic and dynamic loudspeakers, in addition to electronic components. *See also* LOUDSPEAKER, 8.

Quadraphonic Recording · Also known as Quadraphonic, Quadrasonic, or Quad. A four-channel sound reproduction system, promoted heavily in the 1970s, that was intended to reproduce or simulate concert hall, nightclub, studio, etc. ambiance. Four microphones were used in recording, and four loudspeakers—one in each corner—had to be set up in the listening room.

Acoustic Research, Inc. made a number of experimental quad recordings in the late 1960s, but they never resulted in marketable products. Outfits, such as Sound Concepts, Advent, and Audio Pulse, also made some ambiance simulators that delivered a quadraphonic effect.

There were marketing difficulties almost from the beginning. The cost of a four-channel amplifier and two additional speakers was sufficient to keep many audiophiles at bay, as was the problem of loudspeaker placement (even with small, bookshelf systems) in many home-listening environments. Then there was the nuisance of incompatible rival systems being offered by major firms. For example, EMI used the CBS matrix system, while Pye and others took the Sansui QS system, and RCA used still another. Record companies waited to see which system would prevail before investing in large-scale record production, although small quantities were produced in the various formats to test the market. The public also waited, and meanwhile sales were too small to form the basis for commercial viability; however, the biggest drawback was that the analog technology of the era simply could not deliver four discrete channels with any genuine fidelity, at least at a reasonable cost.

Nevertheless, the concept was at least educational. For experimentation on a practical level proved that a pair of speakers mounted up front cannot simulate the three-dimensional effect of a genuine performance environment in a typically small home-playback room; however, four-channel sound, at least if reasonably well executed, can be impressively realistic. In the late 1980s, there was a rebirth of interest in quad, but with the addition of a center channel, and a discussion of that can be found under SURROUND SOUND. *See also* DOLBY SURROUND SOUND; DOLBY DIGITAL; DTS (Digital Theater Systems); DVD-A (DVD-Audio); SACD (Super Audio Compact Disc).—Rev. by Howard Ferstler

Quarter Track · *See* TAPE.

R

Radio Phonographs · The rise of radio in America from 1921 severely damaged the phonograph industry. The idea of combining the competing formats into one cabinet, a radio phonograph, was articulated first in advertising of August 1922, by Jewett Radio and Phonograph Co. of Detroit. The only other firm to advertise a combination in 1922 was George A. Long Cabinet Co., Hanover, Pennsylvania. Emerson announced its new Phono Radio in January 1924. In all these early combinations, it was necessary to remove the phonograph reproducer and attach a radio receiver to hear radio stations through the phonograph horn, but a Talking Machine World advertisement of February 1924 offered a model with a switch, by the Oro-Tone Co., of Chicago. Sonora then marketed its Sonoradio, also with a switch controlling the two functions.

It was the RCA 1924 product, Radiola, that dominated the combination market in the 1920s, and the model name became a convenient generic term for all radio phonographs. Brunswick announced a similar machine in July 1924. The Gramophone Co. marketed its table model Lumiere around that time, containing a crystal radio set and a folding external horn. Phonograph attachments for radio sets were a later approach; these were called Radiograms, a name also given to radio phonograph combinations.

Radiogram/Radiola · *See* RADIO PHONOGRAPHS.

RCA (Radio Corporation of America) · An American firm established on October 17, 1919, in New York. It had an early association with Victor Talking Machine Co. in 1925, through an arrangement for RCA radios to be included in certain Victrola record player models. Then, on January 4, 1929, RCA bought Victor. The Victor label name was retained, with RCA added, and the record remained in the forefront of the industry. On April 15, 1986, RCA became part of the Bertelsmann conglomerate. For the history of RCA, *see also* VICTOR TALKING MACHINE COMPANY.

RealAudio [website: Real.com] · Unlike traditional, stand-alone downloads, RealAudio is a system of listening to music "live" via the Internet. Launched in 1995 by Progressive Networks, the system spread like wildfire thanks in part to the fact that users need not install detailed software to start enjoying music "streamed" from websites. Seven years later, an inordinate number of online radio stations are using RealAudio to broadcast with sound quality improving all the while. The only drawbacks are those that were there at the beginning. RealAudio users still suffer from Internet congestion and restrictions placed on playback due to their connection speed, both of which stagger and break up the audio that is heard. The company also sells downloadable music files through its Rhapsody subscription service.—Ian Peel

Real-Time Spectrum Analyzer · An instrument that displays signal strength in the frequency domain, usually at specific one-, one-third-, one-sixth-, or one-twelfth-octave intervals, plotting level versus frequency on an easy-to-read panel. One-octave versions have only limited use, but with a proper microphone, properly used, more refined one-third-octave and better versions can be especially useful for making accurate measurements of loudspeaker room response in home-listening environments. They can also help with calculating large room and hall acoustics, calibrating theater equalization, and determining background noise levels. Useful versions have been produced by Rane, AudioControl, Behringer, TerraSonde, Ivie, and dbx, and programs have been developed that allow personal computers to perform as RTAs.—Howard Ferstler

Receiver · A unit in an audio or audio-video system that traditionally incorporates a tuner, a preamplifier control section, and the required number of amplifiers. Modern versions also include a Dolby Digital and often a DTS surround processor and video switching, and many current models include fairly powerful multi-channel amplifier sections and DSP ambiance extraction or ambiance synthesis circuitry. The receiver has become the dominant control center and power source in modern audio and home-theater systems, and upscale versions can compete in terms of quality with many high-end separates.—Howard Ferstler

Recklinghausen, Daniel R. VON, January 25, 1925– · Born in New York City, von Recklinghausen graduating from M.I.T. with an engineering degree in 1951. He was employed for a while at Rohde & Schwartz, in Munich, Germany, but later joined Herman Scott at the H.H. Scott company in the USA as a project engineer. His tenure at Scott spanned more than 22 years and influenced nearly all the products the company produced, including amplifiers, tun-

ers, turntables, loudspeakers, consoles, sound analyzers, and acoustic testing instruments, and he is also known for his pioneering efforts with FM Stereo (Multiplex) broadcasting. After leaving Scott, he served as an in-house consultant for Electro Audio Dynamics, then parent of Eastern Air Devices, KLH, and Infinity. Recklinghausen is the designer of the first EMIT planar ribbon tweeter, and patented a system of dynamic equalization, the father of all processor-controlled loudspeaker systems. Since 1991, he has served as Editor of the Journal of the Audio Engineering Society. He is a Fellow of the Institute of Electrical and Electronics Engineers and AES, was president of the AES in 1967, and won the AES Gold Medal in 1978. He holds 24 US patents and has authored dozens of technical papers, and has actively supported and chaired many industry standards committees.—Howard Ferstler

Record · Term usually associated with analog audio recordings distributed on cylinders or discs. The term "record" acknowledges the early use of audio recordings to make a "record" of events by preserving them for repeated playback.

Record Changer · Traditionally, this involved a turntable and tone arm assembly that stacked records and played them in succession. It was also known as an automatic turntable. A disc changer was described in Scientific American in 1921, but none reached the market until 1927, sold by Victor. A model of the Victor Orthophonic Victrola played 12 discs, on one side only, holding the stack at a 60° angle; it shut off after the last disc was played. The first British disc changer was made by Garrard; the same firm produced the first changer that could play both sides of each record in the stack, in 1938. Garrard machines (and their counterparts by the Capehart Co. in America) actually turned each record over; another approach was illustrated by the Sharp player of 1981, which held the disc vertically and played each side with its own tone arm assembly.

In most record changers of the 78-rpm and LP eras, the stack of discs to be played was directly above the turntable and parallel to it. The records were held in a level position by a record leveler arm (or record support arm, or record balance arm). The same arm activated the shutoff mechanism after the final disc had been played. Breakage of the 78s was avoided on the drop from the stack because there was a cushion of air that developed and provided a reasonably soft landing. Other formats existed: For example, some machines pushed each record off the turntable after playing it, into a hopper of some kind (the records awaiting play were stacked on the turntable).

Some record changers were able to handle only six records, but most could play 10 or more. It seemed that 12 was the maximum because as the fallen discs piled up on the turntable, the tone arm had to reach up to play the top one, creating an awkward playing (tracking) angle. Records also tended to slide around on each other, especially if any were warped. Finally, there should be mention of the RCA novelty of 1949, the 45-rpm disc and its compact record changer. It was a high-speed operator, and reasonably quiet about it, but only in the wildest fancy could anyone have expected it to equal the speed of an LP moving from one band to the next. Outfits such as Dual, PE, Garrard, Sony, and Pioneer Produced good record changers.

Good though some of them might be, record changers were not popular with many serious audio enthusiasts because it was felt (with complete justification) that stacked records could not be properly cleaned just before being played, greatly increasing the chance of dust-related damage. Consequently, many changers were configured so that their changing mechanisms could

be removed and replaced with a single spindle that allowed them to perform more like "audiophile" players. The advent and subsequent runaway success of the compact disc not only reduced the LP record to being a niche product, but also practically put an end to the LP record changer. Only serious analog-sound enthusiasts remained loyal to the LP, and those individuals were not likely to be interested in playing their prized jewels on a changer.

Interestingly, the CD changer (and later on the DVD/CD changer) that first showed up as a somewhat novel item in the late 1980s has become the dominant CD playback device of the new century. Some early versions used a stacked cartridge system, but the most popular type now involves the use of a rotating carousel mechanism that makes it easy to play singles or up to five or even six discs at a session. [Hoover 1971, pp. 82–83, illustrates the Automatic Orthophonic; Kogen 1977. Updated by Ferstler.]

Record Condition · A topic primarily of interest to those who collect cylinders, 78-rpm, 45-rpm, and 33 1/3-rpm analog recordings. The term mint (M) or near mint (NM) describes records never played, in mint condition. A mint rating (M) is never a certainty because the usual sign of an unplayed record is its factory packaging, but a record may have been removed from its package and resealed into it. Very good condition (VG) is the state of a record free from marks and scratches, although showing evidence of some playing; it is practically as good as new, but not NM. A good record (G) has been played but is not badly worn or damaged. A record in fair (F) condition has had heavy play but is usable. One in poor (P) condition is close to unplayable, and would be kept for historical reasons only.

Such designations have not been applied to open-reel or cassette tapes, or to compact discs, where noticeable wear or damage is not a factor of concern. Tapes do develop problems such as print-through or simple breakage. These are not gradual forms of decay, however; either they exist or they do not. Older tapes may exhibit oxide shedding, however, and when that happens the tape is usually no longer usable. For a while in the 1980s, certain laserdiscs exhibited deterioration of the aluminum substrata. The problem was traced to impurities in the plastic coating, and later discs showed no sign of such chemical deterioration.

The compact disc, laserdisc, and the DVD have not evidenced operational wearability, due to the lack of physical contact between the player and the laser pickup, and properly made versions should be very durable as long as they are not damaged by scratches or chemical blemishes. Although there have been fears that the aluminum substrata might deteriorate over time, it is likely that most discs will outlive their owners. Some deluxe CD releases produced by upscale smaller labels made use of gold, instead of aluminum, thereby insuring a very long life, indeed. Minor scratches on the plastic-coated playing side should not bother some laser-pickup assemblies, although scratches on the label side of a CD or DVD could cause problems if they penetrate deep enough to make contact with the aluminum. The label side is actually the weak point with such discs, and some CD releases did have problems with silk-screen printing damaging the lacquer coating, and ultimately the aluminum; however, such incidents are now nearly unheard of.

Another documented problem has involved the use of foam dividers in multiple-CD jewel box sets. Although a number of major labels—most notably, the PolyGram empire (including subsidiaries such as Deutsche Grammophone, Archiv, London, and Polydor)—have downplayed the negative effects of this 1980s practice, the plastic surface coming into contact with the dividers over long time periods

would erode to the point where playback was impossible.

Some time back, when demand was outstripping supply, a Philips facility in England used a wet-process silver coating instead of vacuum-evaporated aluminum to form the layer that holds the digital data. Although aluminum is fairly stable and protects itself with a self-generated coating when attacked by most airborne pollutants, silver does not self-protect and can tarnish. This is unlikely to happen if the plastic and lacquer coatings are properly applied. However, if they were not, particularly if the disc was stored in proximity to paper or cardboard materials containing sulfur by-products, the silver might gradually turn black, starting at the disc's outer edge and working inward. Fortunately, the wet process has been abandoned, but a number of discs produced by Hyperion, ASV, Unicorn, and a few other British labels that had "Made in the UK by PDO" printed around the center hole might still be exhibiting the problem.—Rev. and updated by Howard Ferstler

Record Out Switch · A control in a recording system that permits the recording of one signal while listening to another signal.

Record Player · A device consisting of components necessary to play and listen to a sound recording. For a cylinder record, it consists essentially of a mandrel to support and rotate the cylinder, a reproducer to track the grooves and produce vibrations, a motor or hand crank, and a horn to amplify the vibrations so they can be heard. For a disc record, an acoustic record player consists of a turntable to spin the record, a sound box and needle to track the grooves and produce vibrations, and a tone arm to hold the sound box and carry the vibrations to the horn. An electric record player translates the vibrations to electrical impulses in a cartridge (pickup), enhances their volume in an amplifier, and then translates them back to audible sound vibrations in the loudspeaker(s).

In a CD record player a spindle drive rotates the disc, a laser beam pickup reads the pits on the record, and one or two D/A converters translate the digital signals to stereo analog signals that can be enhanced in the same kind of amplifier and loudspeaker that is used in an LP player.

Recording Characteristic · *See* RECORDING CURVE.

Recording Curve · Also known as recording characteristic. With analog recording systems, a plot of the relative emphasis given to the various frequencies in the audio spectrum to ensure low levels of distortion, reduced background noise, and reasonably long playing time. With analog disc systems, lower frequencies must recorded at lower volume levels than higher frequencies to prevent cutting into adjacent grooves. Standards for the curve have been established by the RIAA. Such frequency balancing is not required with digital systems. *See also* AUDIO FREQUENCY; PLAYBACK CURVE.—Rev. by Howard Ferstler

Recording Head · In a tape recorder, the electromagnetic device that impresses the signal, by means of a varying magnetic field, on the tape surface. It may be the same head as the playback head.

Recording Industries Association of America (RIAA) [website: www.riaa.com] · A trade organization established in 1952. Its membership is open to "Legitimate record companies with main offices in the United States that are engaged in the production and sale, under their own brand label, of recordings of performances for home use." Its purpose is to promote the interests of the industry and to "foster good relations among all concerned" with it. Among its active concerns are record piracy, technical standards, freedom of speech, copyright, music and the web, licensing and royalties, audio technologies, and rewards for achievement.

On March 14, 1958, the RIAA awarded the first Gold Record award for sales of over a million dollars to Perry Como's single "Catch A Falling Star," and four months later the cast album of *Oklahoma!* became the first gold album. In 1976, due to rising sales of albums, the Platinum award was launched for sales of over 1 million records; Johnny Taylor's "Disco Lady" was the first Platinum single, and the Eagles' *Greatest Hits* the first platinum album. Multiplatinum was soon introduced to cover sales of 2 million, 3 million, and so on. In 1999, a new award, the Diamond Award, was created for sales of over 10 million copies. A year later, to address the growing Latin/Spanish language market, the "Los Premios de Oro y Platino" awards were introduced, with Disco De Oro representing 100,000 copies sold; Disco de Platino, 200,000 copies; and Multi-Platino, 400,000 copies. The RIAA awards are based on total number of records shipped in the United States, less returns, to all accounts.

Recording Practice · The genesis of any commercial recording project is the careful selection of artist and repertoire. Once these artistic considerations have been determined, it is the task of the producer to make all the necessary musical, technical, physical, and monetary arrangements for the recording.

When searching for the proper venue to make the recording, the first decision the producer must make is where—in a studio or on location—the session should be held. This prompts a fundamental question: "Where will the music be performed to its best advantage?" If the answer is that a recital or concert hall, a nightclub or cocktail lounge, or any other "real" environment is where the performers and their music are most comfortable, this is where the producer should consider scheduling

Recording Industry Charts

The charting of sound recordings was inevitable in American society, where competition is a birthright and trivia—such as that included in countless best-selling "book of lists" publications—has become a national obsession. Charting appears to have begun shortly after Thomas Edison filed for a patent to his phonograph on December 24, 1877.

Its prime purposes then—as now—were to promote the recording industry (as associated business interests) by focusing interest on new releases, and to provide retailers a gauge of relative demand. The charts accomplish these ends by tracking the performance of a given entertainment unit through a number of distinguishing features:

Numbered position

Time frame (generally expressed in weeks or the interval in which the chart is issued)

Special features: most notably, bullets, which designate fast upward movement, and outstanding performance within a specialized sector such as sales or radio plays

Supplementary charts, which delineate activity (in greater detail) within these specialized sectors

For industry insiders and outsiders alike, the analysis and interpretation of charts can be problematical at best. The process of translating prior unit sales, airplay, online downloading, etc., into a present-day breakdown by positions represents a highly subjective process. Various elements must be weighted according to perceived consumer behavior and industry needs. The stakes for record companies are high enough to render chart tampering—whether consciously or subconsciously—an everyday fact of life. A major type of bribe consists of a record company buying expensive—often self-congratulatory—ads in the publication that reward its releases with favorable chart positions. For researchers and chartographers, any attempt to compare the chart performance of recordings from different eras is fraught with pitfalls. For example, the tabulation for any given chart edition does not measure intensity (i.e., specific unit sales, number of radio plays, etc.). Therefore, it is possible that a compact disc barely reaching the Top Ten in one period might actually outperform the top-rated title from another time frame by all quantitative measures employed by the chart compiler.

Phonogram, an early record industry periodical established in 1891, anticipated charting by including ongoing mention of top popular recordings. *The Phonoscope* featured monthly listings (though not in precise rank order) during the 1896 to 1899 period. Data on sheet music sales, and lists of popular song releases from ASCAP and the leading record labels served as early chart prototypes.

Billboard, the bible of the recording industry throughout most of the 20th century, instituted weekly lists of sheet music in 1913, and published lists of the most popular songs in Vaudeville from 1913 to 1918. During 1914 to 1921, the major record companies provided *Talking Machine World* with monthly lists of their best-selling records. *Variety* advanced the practice to a considerable degree with ore systematic listings from late 1929.

By 1934, both *Billboard* and *Variety* were regularly charting the top songs in radio airplay and sheet music sales. From November 1934 through early 1938, *Billboard* carried the best-selling charts of the individual record labels, and in late 1938 instituted weekly surveys of the most popular records in jukeboxes. As a result, two separate weekly charts emerged within the industry at this time: best-selling records and radio airplay-sheet music sales. As far as the public was concerned, however, the long-running radio show, *Your Hit Parade*, provided the principal format for top hits; it continued to be influential on television during the 1950s. A similar top ten countdown was employed by Dick Clark on *American Bandstand*.

During the early 1940s, the pace-setting *Billboard* evolved the triad of charts that dominated the industry until the late 1950s: "Best Sellers in Stores" (July 20, 1940–October 4, 1958), the first comprehensive listing combining data from all labels; "Most Played by Disc Jockeys" (1945–July 19, 1958); and the previously instituted "Most Played in Juke Boxes" (which ran until June 12, 1958). After World War II, *Billboard* began running supplementary charts to focus further the industry picture; for example, "Up & Coming Hits" (1947–1948), "Regional and Up & Coming Hits" (1952–1954), and the "Honor Roll of Hits" (which ran through November 16, 1963—a compilation of tunes instead of individual records).

With *Billboard*'s publication of the weekly "Hot 100" (of 45s) beginning on August 18, 1958, the industry could look to one chart for a combined factual account of a single's popularity. Similar listings soon appeared for other genres (country, rhythm & blues, classical, etc.) and formats (long-playing albums).

In the meantime, many radio stations and retail outlets began producing their own charts as a marketing tool (for example, to encourage listening to their local countdown programs). These proved particularly useful in spotting local talent and regional breakout hits. While initially available only by mail or pickup at the local outlets, the industry trade publications began running selected charts of key markets in the 1960s based on such listings.

The late 1970s and 1980s saw the widespread proliferation of charts to include the important new genres and formats appearing at the time. These included disco/dance/12-inch singles, rap music, college/alternative rock, new age, easy listening, album-oriented radio, videotapes, videodiscs, video clips, computer software, video games, and compact discs (until subsumed by the mainstream pop album charts). One particular marketing stratagem, midline catalog albums (i.e., older classic releases still popular with buyers), proved sufficiently successful in the early 1980s to have its own chart for a time within the trade.

Industry trade journals, long the chief means of disseminating chart data, have included *Billboard*, *Cash Box* (which ceased publication in the mid-1990s), *Variety*, and *Record World* (ceased publication in 1981). By the late 1980s, a number of fanzines and serious music journals (e.g., *Rolling Stone*) have begun including their own listings as well. A decade later, the Internet had become a major player, both in terms of sound recording transactions and dissemination of the charts themselves. Notable web publications charting on-line music distribution include the EvO:R Street Journal (www.evor.com) and Radio & Records (www.radioandrecords.com). Literally thousands of other net-based chart sites now exist, including many devoted to reprinting past editions of radio and trade listings.

(continued)

Recording Industry Charts (continued)

Billboard's utilization of SoundScan (beginning with the "Hot 100" singles and "Top 200" albums in its May 25, 1991 issue) represented a concerted effort to counteract criticisms that industry charts were either falsified to reflect the interests of the highest bidder, or grossly inaccurate in reflecting actual performance (particularly sales). At the outset, SoundScan compiled computerized barcode information form store registers. The sudden rise of country recordings, and corresponding fall of alternative music titles, led many industry insiders to deride the system because it tended to be concentrated in large retail chains that catered more to middle-of-the-road/rural customers, instead of independent and specialty record stores. Adjustments in its sampling approach—combined with efforts to gather data from an increasingly broader range of sources, all geared to assessing the relative popularity of various information and entertainment media—has assured the institutionalization of the SoundScan formula; it remains a key factor in the compilation of industry charts up to the present day.

The following charts were included in the January 31, 2004, issue of *Billboard*:

TOP ALBUMS—The Billboard 200, Bluegrass, Blues, Christian, Country, Electronic, Gospel, Heatseekers, Independent, Internet, Pop Catalog, Latin, R&B/Hip-Hop, Reggae, Soundtrack, World Music;

TOP SINGLES—Hot 100, Adult Top 40, Adult Contemporary, Country, Dance/Club Play, Dance/Radio Airplay, Dance/Singles Sales, Hot Digital Tracks, Hot Latin Tracks, Mainstream Top 40, Modern Rock, Hot R&B/Hip-Hop, Rap Tracks, Rhythmic Top 40;

VIDEOS—VHS Sales, DVD Sales, Health & Fitness, Kid Video, Music Video Sales, Recreational Sports, Video Rentals, Video Game Rentals;

UNPUBLISHED—Classical, Classical Crossover, Jazz, Jazz/Contemporary, Kid Audio, New Age.—Frank Hoffmann

the recording session—keeping in mind, however, that there are technical considerations which also influence the decision. For example, a noisy room, acceptable for a live performance with an audience, may not prove satisfactory for a recording because the other aural and visual stimuli of the live experience will not be present to "mask" the record listeners' awareness of the intruding noise. Recording studios, on the other hand, generally offer a very controlled acoustical environment—in most modern studios, this is usually means rather dry acoustics, so that any sense of "liveness" will need to be added artificially during recording.

Technical and other cost factors must be considered as well; on-location sessions often cost more than in-studio sessions because all of the equipment needs to be brought to the site, set up, calibrated, and tested before recording, and then it all must be removed at the end. In addition, risers, chairs, stands, and instruments (and sometimes even acoustical treatment) also need to be brought to the site. All these technical factors aside, sometimes the music will "just sound better" when recorded on location. These, and numerous other tradeoffs between cost and result will be evaluated when making the decision.

Today, digital recording formats are readily available in both direct-to-stereo and multi-track processes and the costs are no longer so widely different as they were in earlier days of digital recording. Because both formats can be used to produce analog or digital products (e.g., LPs, cassettes, CDs, DVDs, etc.), the primary factors involved in choosing the recording format will be based on the "sound" of the recording and the preferences of the producer.

For stereo release projects, the next decision the producer will need to make is whether to record direct-to-stereo (2-track) or to use a multi-track process. (Surround-sound recordings, by definition, require a multi-track process.) Both methods have their advantages as well as disadvantages. The decision between the two approaches will be determined primarily by the type of music being recorded and the capabilities of the performers and the recording facility. Traditionally, music intended to be played "live" (classical, folk, small jazz ensembles, and the like) has been be recorded direct-to-stereo, and with the growth in popularity of home-theater systems, these styles now are being recorded in surround-sound formats as well.

Direct-to-stereo has been a time-proven method for recording music that can be performed in "real time," as in a live performance. The recording techniques are, generally, less complex than multi-track, and when properly implemented, will result in a realistic, lifelike sound. Similar "minimalist" microphone and recording techniques are employed even for surround-sound recordings. Contemporary recording practices generally tend toward multi-microphone, multi-track methods to avoid problems with musical balance. Thus, even if a direct-to-stereo mix is recorded, a multi-track "protection" tape will be made simultaneously.

Complex musical performances (Broadway musicals, opera, etc.), "popular" genres (rock, rap, etc.), electronic music, or other musical formats requiring "layering" or "over-dubs" will almost always be recorded via a multi-track process. Multi-track recording is employed whenever the artistic intent is to create a "new reality" that does not exist (either conveniently or at all) in real time or space. Multi-tracking becomes a necessity when overdubbing or layering parts, or where performance difficulties or the instrumentation dictate that a proper musical blend cannot easily be achieved in actual performance.

Multi-tracking also affords the opportunity for electronic manipulation of existing sounds to create new sounds, or for the replacement of one voice or line with another. It gives the producer and performers, therefore, the ability to "bend reality" to suit their art. This is the primary benefit of, and reason for, multi-track recording: the ability to mix or re-mix the individual voices (tracks) after the initial recording session, to achieve the exact balance desired.

Cost factors always are of significant importance to the commercial success of any recording project, and because producers are always concerned with money will also be considered when making the decision where and how to produce the recording. Direct-to-stereo recording sessions take much less time, and when they are finished, the basic recording is complete. Multi-track sessions not only take much more time during the initial recording (and usually at much higher hourly rates), but the result is not yet a finished recording. The producer must then spend additional time to mixdown the multi-track tape to produce the final stereo master tape. As a general rule, the total time required to complete a multi-track recording will be at least six to eight times that of a direct-to-stereo session. Surround-sound projects, as mentioned previously, always require multi-track production.

During the recording sessions, (except, of course, for "live concert" recordings) the performances are accomplished in a number of individual takes. Each take is a segment of the entire musical piece. With some forms of music—particularly classical music or short songs—a take of a complete movement or song will be made to provide an overall sense of continuity. Then, if needed, short segments ("pickups" or "inserts") will be recorded to replace spots that did not go well during the full recording.

In modern recording practice, it has become commonplace for individual instruments, groups of instruments, or vocalists to be recorded separately sometimes at widely different times, or even in entirely different locations, depending on the availability of the performers or instruments. This process is called tracking because each part is recorded to a separate track on the tape. A related process, called overdubbing, comes into play when one performer is required to record more than one part or line of the musical composition. In both processes, the original track is played back to the performer, via headphones, and the new part is performed and recorded onto another track in synchronization with the original. During the mixing process, the two or more parts are mixed together to provide the complex texture so vital to modern musical performances.

Once the session master tape has been recorded, the next step in the process is post production. During editing, the first stage, the individual takes are selected and combined (spliced together) to produce a finished performance of each song or piece; these pieces are then sequenced to produce the complete recording as it will be released. Numerous artistic and technical processes are involved in this stage, and are dictated by the musical genre, stylistic considerations, including the relationship of each piece to all of the others in the album, and technical matters, such as the final release format for the recording.

As mentioned earlier, multi-track recordings must be mixed-down to a stereo (and as appropriate also a surround-sound) master. This usually occurs after the editing, although some producers prefer to mix first, and then edit. In popular music, special signal processing (compression, equalization, reverberation, phasing, etc.) effects are frequently employed during the mixing process to augment or enhance the texture.

The days of the vinyl LP having passed, projects are now usually released as CDs, sometimes also with cassettes as a secondary format. The cost of CD production has fallen at the same time as the widespread adoption of CD players has grown, so that the CD is now more viable than the cassette for most recording projects today.

Editing and mixing a recording can be done in either the analog or the digital domain, and the decision as to how to proceed will usually follow the format of the original recording. With the growth and proliferation of digital "workstation" technology, however, most editing now is done digitally, even if the original recordings were analog. Once completed, this recording will then be the final edited master.

The total time available on the various release formats requires that different "duplication masters" be created for each. Cassette sides generally have a maximum running time of 45 minutes; two sides afford a total program length of 90 minutes. Compact discs provide a playing time of around 72 minutes (although up to 79 minutes can fit safely onto a CD). Thus, the different program lengths will determine how the tapes are edited.

"Mastering" is the final stage in the creative process. Here, the edited masters will be reworked one more time to create the "duplication masters" for each release format required. Dynamic range of the release format will also play an important role in the mastering process; because cassettes have a more limited dynamic range than compact discs, the technical limitations of the different release formats will also be taken into consideration when producing these duplication masters. For cassettes, this master will be an equalized, often compressed, stereo master and may be either an analog or digital tape or CD-ROM. For compact discs and DVDs, the duplicating-master will be a digital tape, CD-ROM, or, as is becoming more common, a file on a computer drive, containing the musical program material or files, time code, and all the special data and codes necessary to indicate track numbers, timings, table of contents, surround-sound track formats and coding, etc.

During the preparation of these final duplicating masters, the producer has a last chance to change the sound or order of the recording. Once the duplicating masters have been made, the remainder of the process is just mechanical replication.—Ron Streicher

Reduction · The combining of tracks from a multi-track recording (often involving more than a dozen feeds) into a lesser number of tracks, such as for a two-channel stereophonic or five-channel surround-sound recording. *See also* DATA REDUCTION.—Rev. by Howard Ferstler

Reel-to-Reel Tape · A magnetic tape format, also known as open reel tape, popular in the 1950s and 1960s, in which the recorded tape is played back by attaching its end to an empty take-up reel and running it past the playback head. After play, the tape is rewound to its original feed reel. A reel seven inches in diameter contains about 1,200 feet of tape, and plays at 7 1/2 inches per second, for a total playing time of about 30 minutes. Although the running time of such a tape exceeded that of an LP record side, sales for pre-recorded open reel tapes were poor. The use made of them was in home recording and in making copies of disc material. Open reels were also used in professional studio work, to make the original recording from which the disc masters, stampers, etc. were prepared. With the introduction of cassettes in 1963, inter-

est in reel-to-reel taping virtually vanished in the United States. *See also* MAGNETIC RECORDING; TAPE.

Regina Music Box Co. · A firm established in 1892 in Rahway, New Jersey, with offices later in New York and Chicago. A German named Brachausen formed the company. He was one of the founders of the Polyphonmusikwerke in Germany a few years earlier, and had been employed by the German company that made the Symphonion brand of music boxes. Regina music boxes were essentially Polyphon music boxes at first. In 1898, Regina was marketing coin-op music boxes. The Regina Disc Changer of ca. 1900 played a dozen two-minute steel tune discs. The Reginaphone could play either gramophone records or steel tune discs, and the Automatic Reginaphone of 1905 was able to play six cylinder records consecutively, one for each coin inserted. A selective coin-op, the Hexaphone, was offered in 1906. The Reginapiano (an inner player) was another product, vacuum cleaners still another.

In 1909, the firm name was shortened to the Regina Co. A contract with Columbia Phonograph Co. allowed the two firms to distribute each other's products, so Regina began to sell Columbia records. Regina was bankrupt in 1922. [Hoover 1971 has illustrations of the Hexaphone (pp. 36–37) and Reginaphone (pp. 40–41).]

Remote Control · A small device that allows the user to turn on or off, adjust the volume, or perform other functions of an electronic device from a distance. The earliest example of a remote control for an audio system was a 1931 HMV device that had a 12-foot cord. Sophisticated remote control without a cord had to wait for the 1950s, when such features became available for television. Infrared LED remotes for television sets were introduced in the mid-1970s, and remotes for the videocassette player and the record player followed.

Remotes in the early 2000s offered a full command of all audio and video functions, making it virtually unnecessary for the user ever to approach the sound source directly.

Renner, Jack, April 13, 1935– · A major American recording engineer, Renner has a 1960 B.S. in Music Education from The Ohio State University School of Music, plus all the course work for Masters in Music Education from the same university. In 1998, he was awarded an honorary Doctorate from The Cleveland Institute of Music, and is on that institution's faculty as Adjunct Professor of Recording Engineering. In October, 1978, Renner engineered the first digitally recorded and commercially released recording of a major orchestra and conductor: the Cleveland Orchestra, conducted by Lorin Maazel, performing Mussorgsky's *Pictures at an Exhibition*. In 1977, along with Robert Woods, he began Telarc Records, and both men continue to run the company. Renner's technical acumen is legendary, and to date he has won a total of seven engineering Grammy awards. *See also* STOCKHAM, THOMAS G.—Howard Ferstler

Reprocessed Stereo · Simulated stereophonic recordings made from monophonic masters; also known as electronically reprocessed stereo, electronic stereo, re-channeled stereo, simulated stereo, enhanced recordings, and enhanced stereo. Various different techniques were used, mostly involving a slight delay between the left and right channels of the original recording, resulting in a distant, "echoey" sound quality that was less-than-satisfactory to many listeners. Nonetheless, from the mid-1960s through the early 1970s, many mono recordings were issued in this new format to appeal to owners of stereo playback equipment.

Reproducer · The name given during the acoustic period to the pickup and its assembly; also known as the sound box. Weight varied, always with the intent of achieving the lightest pickup that would track the grooves properly; in the Victor Orthophonic, the reproducer weighed 142 grams (about 5 ounces).

Resonance (I) · A vibration in a sound system that results from a relatively small periodic stimulus having the same or similar period as the natural vibration period of the system.

Resonance (II) · The intensification of a musical signal by supplementary vibration of the same frequency.

Reverberant Field · In home, studio, and live-music listening environments, it defines the sound field that exists when the reflected sound predominates over the direct sound coming directly from a source, be that source loudspeaker systems or live performers. Obviously, the strength of the reverberant field will depend upon the listening distance and the room's layout and reflectivity. *See also* DIRECT FIELD; SURROUND SOUND.—Howard Ferstler

Reverberation · Multiple reflections of sound waves within a closed space, resulting in echo effects that may be heard along with the original signals. The time taken up between the introduction of a sound wave to the closed space and the return of the reverberation to the point of introduction is the reverberation time. A room, or recording studio, is said to be "live" if it has a comparatively long reverberation time; "dead" if the reverberation time is comparatively slow. Reverberation can be created artificially with electromechanical devices or electronic circuits. *See also* RESONANCE; ROOM ACOUSTICS.

Reverberation Time · The interval required for the sound that remains after a primary signal stops to decay to a specific loudness level. It is normally quantified by measuring how long it takes the sound pressure level to decay to one-millionth of its original value. Because one-millionth equals a 60 dB reduction, reverberation time is usually abbreviated RT60.—Howard Ferstler

Reverse Equalization · *See* EQUALIZATION (EQ).

Re-Voicing · *See* DUBBING.

Revox · *See* STUDER/REVOX.

Rhapsody · *See* REALAUDIO.

Rice, Chester, W. · Rice was a pioneering researcher who, along with Edward W. Kellog, came up with the basic design of the modern, direct-radiator loudspeaker, which had a small coil-driven, mass-controlled diaphragm in a baffle with a broad mid-frequency range and relatively uniform response. (Edward Wente at Bell Labs had independently discovered this same principle, and filed a patent for it in 1925, with the patent granted in 1931.) Kellog and Rice worked for GE, and together they published their "hornless loudspeaker" design in 1925, after five years of work. The Rice-Kellog paper also published an amplifier design that was important in boosting the power transmitted to loudspeakers. In 1926, RCA used this design in the Radiola line of AC-powered radios. *See also* LOUDSPEAKER.—Howard Ferstler

Rich, David, January 7, 1958– · A design engineer, Rich has B.S., M.S., and Ph.D. degrees in electrical engineering, with the latter earned from The Polytechnic University of New York in 1991. Between 1981 and 1992, he worked for General Instruments and TLSI, moving on to Bell Labs from 1992 until 2001. In 1987, he co-founded Precision Audio, where he helped design an analog circuit to solve problems caused by slow-settling time in the current-to-voltage converter of early CD players. In 1995, he co-discovered tonal behavior in commercial delta-sigma analog-to-digital and digital-to-analog converters, and demonstrated that the problem could be eliminated with proper architectural choices and appropriate levels of dither. As technical editor for *The Audio Critic* (1989–), he analyzed a number of amplifiers, preamps, tuners, and CD players, and developed a circuit analysis review method capable of demonstrating that topological differences in amplifiers do not correlate with sound quality. In addition to his AES presentations and preprints, Rich has published numerous papers in Institute of Electrical and Electronic Engineering proceedings and journals. He is a member of the AES and IEEE, serving as a reviewer for the latter organization, and also for National Science Foundation proposals. He currently is associate professor of Electrical and Computer Engineering at Lafayette College in Easton, Pennsylvania.—Howard Ferstler

Riggs, Michael, 1951– · Michael Riggs was born in Frankfort, Kentucky, and is a graduate of Washington University in St. Louis, where he studied physics and philosophy. He began writing professionally about audio and video in the mid-1970s, at a time when he was editing the Boston Audio Society's monthly newsletter. In 1980, he left *Mini-Micro Systems* (a Boston-based computer magazine) to join the staff of *High Fidelity* magazine in New York as a technical editor, and he served as that journal's chief editor from 1986 until its demise in 1989. Later that year, he joined *Stereo Review* (now *Sound & Vision*), where he became executive editor. In 1995, he was appointed editor of the foundering *Audio* magazine, which ceased publication at the beginning of 1999. Currently a technology writer and consultant to the consumer electronics industry, Riggs is a member of the Audio Engineering Society and author of *Understanding Audio and Video* (Pioneer, 1989).—Howard Ferstler

Ripper · Name given to a software program that converts audio files from a compact disc and transfers them directly to a computer's hard disc storage device. The software bypasses the audio sound card of the host computer, preserving the original digital integrity of the sound file. To "rip" a file is to move an audio file from a compact disc to a computer's hard drive. Rippers convert compact disc files to a variety of common file formats, including WAV, MP3, Windows Media Audio, and AIFF. —Thom Holmes

Robe, The · Released in 1953, *The Robe* had 4-track stereo sound and was the first CinemaScope film. It was also the first of 33 stereo films to appear in 1953. Stereo technology, however, due to the complexities involved, failed to transform motion picture soundtracks and would not reappear until 1975 with Dolby Surround sound. *The Robe* used directional sound, including footsteps of Roman legions marching from right to left, and panning thunder, wind, and rain in the crucifixion scene. For the first time, off-screen voices were actually heard off-screen. With later stereo releases, only Fox and Todd-AO would record dialogue with directional sound. All other studios provided some music in stereo for magnetic soundtracks, but recorded voices and sound effects in mono.—Howard Ferstler

Rockola, David C., 1897–January 26, 1993 · Canadian business executive, born in Verden, Manitoba. Before the age of 20 he was in the food processing business, manufacturing coolers. In 1924, he began distributing vending machines and scales, and patented a new scale mechanism. In 1932, he established the Rockola Manufacturing Corp. in Chicago. (The company

address in 1945 was 800 N. Kedzie.) His firm acquired the patents of John Gabel, and began leasing the Entertainer instruments in 1934. A dial device for selection of tunes was added later, permitting a choice among 12 discs. Rockola was one of the four successful jukebox companies in the 1930s.

Rockola was one of those visionaries who believed that people would pay to telephone a central record center and request music to be played; he designed a "mystic music" service to accomplish this, but it failed to attract customers. He tried another remote system during World War II, which was also unsuccessful. After the war, he developed the very popular Magic-Glo jukebox. He had a 200-selection box in operation in 1958.

Roland Corporation [website: www.rolandus.com] · In business since the early 1970s and located in Los Angeles, Roland is a leading manufacturer and distributor of electronic musical instruments including keyboards and synthesizers, guitar products, digital pianos, electronic percussion kits, digital recording equipment, amplifiers, and audio processing devices, such as digital mixers. The company also manufactures urban, dance and techno-music production equipment, used by disc jockeys, rappers, and dance music producers worldwide. Roland's BOSS division produces a line of guitar and bass effects pedals, rhythm machines, personal digital studios, and other easy-to-use instruments for all musicians.—Howard Ferstler

Room Acoustics · Room size, shape, furnishings, physical integrity, speaker locations, and listening position can all have a considerable impact upon the sound quality of an audio system. A large room requires greater acoustic output from the loudspeakers, particularly in the bass range. A room with lots of curtains, overstuffed couches, and dense carpeting tends to be "dead" (non-reverberating), and requires more acoustic output, particularly at mid-range and higher frequencies, than a "live" room.

Room shape and size are both factors in the creation of standing waves, which are the result of the enhancement or weakening of signals at certain wavelengths that are sub-multiples of the distance between room surfaces. Obviously, then, an irregularly shaped room can do a lot to mitigate standing-wave problems (although it cannot remove them, and can sometimes make them worse), and it can be seen that the least desirable room for audio listening would be a small one in the shape of a perfect cube. Rooms with dimensions that are multiples of each other will also cause problems. The larger the room, the less impact there is from these resonances because the more problematic ones will be at lower frequencies. The stiffness of the room walls can have an impact on the strength of standing waves, and of course, weak walls may also generate spurious sounds of their own. In some cases the effect of standing waves can be somewhat mitigated by shifting the location of the loudspeakers or by making use of a separate subwoofer speaker, preferably located in a corner to excite all room modes uniformly.

Reflective surfaces close to woofer systems will have an impact on speaker performance by reinforcing low frequency output, although they can also generate mid-bass suckout effects that are independent from standing waves. Where these nulls and reinforcements occur on the frequency spectrum will depend upon the woofer-to-boundary distances, and Roy Allison first analyzed their behavior. Reflective surfaces can also have an impact on midrange and treble imaging and strength, and this can work against proper soundstaging if one speaker in a stereo pair is not the same distance from an adjacent wall as the other, or one boundary is damped with a drape and the other is hard surfaced.

Good quality equalization can sometimes correct for bass and mid-bass suckout artifacts, and even for standing waves to an extent, but equalization may only slightly correct problems involving image-degrading midrange and high-frequency reflections. Speakers often sound better if located some distance from room walls, and smaller ones probably work better if they are placed up on stands. Placement of this kind will usually have a negative impact on mid-bass smoothness, however, meaning that designs that are built to work close to room boundaries may have an inherent advantage. Whatever is done about these matters, there will always remain good and bad places to sit while listening, and with two-channel stereo systems, listeners should try to position themselves equidistant from both speakers, forming one tip of an equilateral triangle with them. With modern surround-sound systems that also employ a center channel, the listener position may be less critical, and other room-related artifacts may be better controlled.—Howard Ferstler

Rotating Head Recorder · A tape recorder that uses pickup and recording heads attached to a fast-spinning drum to increase the tape-read speed. This can be done because the slow-moving tape passes over the heads at an angle, and the fast rotation of the head allows it to put a succession of electronically controlled, short, angular scans down the length of the tape. This greatly increases the linear tape speed above what would be possible by simply having the tape itself speeded up and passed over stationary heads. The most common use is with standard, hi-fi video tape recorders, but the technology is also used with DAT recorders.—Howard Ferstler

Rotational Speed · *See* SURFACE SPEED.

Rumble · A low-frequency noise, usually between 20 and 35 Hz, brought about in a phonograph by motor or transport vibrations. In some cases, rumble originates in the recording mechanism, and is thus a part of the recorded signal. Aside from motor rumble, there is the possibility of rumble caused by resonance in the springs, which keep the idler wheel in contact with the turntable rim. Rumble also occurs in cylinder playback. A rumble filter is a control on an amplifier that may reduce audible rumble that originates in the turntable or record changer. *See also* DISTORTION, 11.

Russell, Roger, September 13, 1935– · Earning a B.E.E. degree from Rensselaer Polytechnic Institute in 1959, Russell went on to work for Sonotone Corporation, a maker of hearing aids, phonograph cartridges, ceramic microphones, nickel cadmium batteries, tubes, and tape heads, from 1959 to 1967, ending up as Senior Engineer. In 1967, he went to work for McIntosh Laboratory, as Director of Acoustic Research, and stayed there until his retirement in 1992. While at McIntosh, he designed the highly regarded C26 preamplifier, and went on to set up the company's then new loudspeaker division. Over the years, he created 21 different speaker designs for the company, including column-type and equalized systems, and won patents for several of them. Russell has published audio-related articles in numerous consumer magazines and is a member of the Audio Engineering Society and the International Society for General Semantics.—Howard Ferstler

S

Sabine, Wallace C., June 13, 1868–January 10, 1919 · An American physicist and Harvard University professor credited with founding the systematic study of acoustics around 1895, Sabine is particularly regarded by many as the father of the science of architectural acoustics. One of the first notable things he accomplished as a 27-year old assistant professor of physics at Harvard was to correct the acoustics in Harvard's Fogg Lecture Hall. During World War I, he became a staff member of the Bureau of Research for the Air Service of the American Expeditionary Forces and provided services for the British Munitions Inventions Bureau in England, for the French fleet at Toulon in the Mediterranean, and for Italy on the Italian front. After the war, in 1922, he came up with a formula for calculating the reverberation time of a room, although he may have been using it as early as 1911. He also helped to design Symphony Hall, in Boston, considered by many to be one of the finest concert halls in the world. The "sabin," a non-metric unit of sound absorption used in acoustical engineering, was named in his honor.—Howard Ferstler

SACD (Super Audio Compact Disc) · An extremely high-quality disc-playback system designed by Philips and Sony to surpass what was possible with the compact disc. The original technical proposal was for the disc to have a multi-channel SACD program on a semi-transparent middle layer, with a standard density, two-channel CD layer underneath. This would allow the disc to be played on conventional CD players as well as SACD players. The SACD tracks could also be done in high-quality two-channel form, for two-channel purists. For some reason, early SACD releases were done only in two channels, but surround versions followed somewhat later. *See also* DVD-A (DVD-Audio).—Howard Ferstler

Sampling · In the mid 1980s, the concepts first theorized by John Cage 40 years before, of constructing music from details and samples of other recordings, became a physical possibility with the launch of the Fairlight CMI combined computer/keyboard. The Fairlight took fragments of sound—recordings of anything from people talking to sections of records—and then replicated and transposed them across a full piano keyboard. Vastly expensive at the time, one of the first musicians able to afford a Fairlight was Trevor Horn who used it to create his wall of sound production style on records for *Frankie Goes to Hollywood*. Heading up the Art of Noise, he pushed the Fairlight further to create a completely new style of music based almost solely on "found" sounds.

Scratching and hip-hop culture took sampling to the streets and some of the earliest rap records are set to a backing track of music sampled from other singles from the time and cut-ups of 1950s rock and roll. By the late 1980s, sampling was a creative force pushing dance and pop music into a new dimension. It was also threatening the very nature of the music industry as record

Salon Du Phonographe

A phonograph parlor located on Boulevard des Italiens, Paris, around the turn of the century. It followed the practice of a century later in inviting customers to order selections through a speaking tube, upon which the record would be played in another room and heard by the customer through ear tubes. It was said that 1,500 cylinders were in the Salon collection. In a sense, it was the earliest record library.

labels scrambled to recoup royalties on the snatches of their recordings used in others. Sampling continues to this day—in a more visible way than ever—although now the rights of the "samplee" as well as the sampler are observed. Bringing the story almost full circle was *Firestarter* by Prodigy. The worldwide dance hit from the late 1990s featured a single word sampled from the Art of Noise's first hit *Close to the Edit* (1984). This garnered all five members of the Art of Noise a co-writing credit for *Firestarter*, alongside the Prodigy's single member Liam Howlett.—Ian Peel

Sampling Frequency · Also called the sampling rate. The frequency or rate at which an analog signal is sampled or converted into digital data for storage or eventual playback, with the reading expressed in Hertz (Hz). For example, the compact disc's sampling rate is 44,100 Hz (44.1 kHz). Because the earliest commercial digital audio recorders used a standard helical-scan video recorder for storage, it was necessary to have a fixed relationship between the sampling frequency and the horizontal video frequency. This allowed those frequencies to be derived from the same master clock by frequency division. For the NTSC 525-line TV system used in the United States, a sampling frequency of 44,055.94 Hz was selected, whereas for

the European PAL 625-line system, a frequency of 44,100 Hz was chosen. The 0.1% difference shows up as an imperceptible shift in pitch. It is important to remember that there are other rates than those used by the compact disc, with common examples being 32 kHz, 48 kHz, and even 50 kHz. Those are mostly used by digital recording devices. *See also* DAT (Digital Audio Tape); DIGITAL RECORDING.—Howard Ferstler

Sarnoff, David, February 27, 1891–December 12, 1971 · Inventor, programmer, network founder, futurist. Although not technically the inventor of broadcast technology, David Sarnoff's visionary and hard-working influence on the double innovations of radio and television gave him the enduring reputation as the father of both media. Straddling the lines between profit-pouncing executive, patent-pursuing futurist, and artist-shmoozing programmer, Sarnoff was first to realize the consumer benefit of bringing both radio and TV into the home. His vision of home radio began in 1915, and was scorned by the technology industry of the time. Not until after World War I, when Marconi (Sarnoff's employer) was absorbed by recently created General Electric subsidiary RCA, did the home-radio idea gain traction. Sarnoff swung into the role of programmer, arranging to broadcast a prizefight in 1921. Within a few years, RCA's new product (the Radiola) was a success despite its hefty price of 75 pre-Depression dollars. With a media mogul's unerring sense of leverage, Sarnoff imagined the benefits of networking hundreds of local broadcast stations, and formed the National Broadcasting Company in 1926.

Television was next; Sarnoff saw its potential and began the first NBC television station in 1928. He demonstrated the technology at the 1939 World's Fair, but further progress was delayed by World War II, after which TV was released upon the American public. Sarnoff fought for controlling patents to develop the technology. NBC produced the first videotape telecast and the first made-for-TV movie. Sarnoff became president of RCA in 1930, chairman of the board in 1947, and retired in 1970.—Brad Hill

Schaeffer, Pierre, August 14, 1910–August 19, 1995 · French audio engineer and composer, inventor of the style of electronic music known as *musique concrète*, a form of music composed primarily by manipulating tape recordings of natural ambient sounds and instrumental sounds. Schaeffer graduated from L'École Polytechnique in Paris in 1931 and continued his studies in the field of electricity and telecommunications. He later accepted an apprenticeship as an engineer at the Paris facilities of French National Radio and Television—Radiodiffusion-Television Francaises (RTF), which led to a fulltime job as both a technician and broadcaster. In 1947, Schaeffer met the audio engineer Jacques Poullin, who became his close collaborator on the design of specialized audio equipment for the radio studio. By January 1948, Schaeffer was ready to stretch the limitations of turntable technology for a series of five compositions collectively known as the *Études de bruits*. He worked on them all year and premiered them on the radio on October 5, 1948. These were the first completed works of *musique concrète*, a term that Schaeffer coined to denote the use of sound objects from nature, "concrete" sounds of the real world. These were opposed to the "musical objects" of tonal music, whose source was the abstract value system of the mind. His first "concert of noises" included montages of sounds made by locomotives, toys, musical instruments, saucepan lids, voices, and other everyday sources. His first works were composed using only turntable technology, but by 1951, he and colleague Pierre Henry (b. 1927) had begun to work with tape recorders to compose electronic

music. Many of the recording techniques and tricks still employed by recording studios were first pioneered by Schaeffer and Henri, including reversal of sounds, variable speed manipulation, quick cuts and transpositions of sound, reverberation, and echo. After jump-starting the RTF studio, Schaeffer pulled back from composition and was content to observe the development of the medium at arm's length while he served as a kind of guiding influence. One of his achievements was bringing several other composers to the studio, including Luc Ferrari (b. 1929), Iannis Xenakis (1922–2001), and Edgard Varèse. These composers created some of the most influential tape compositions of all time there. *See also* ELECTRONIC MUSIC; MUSIQUE CONCRÈTE; TAPE COMPOSITION.

Scheiber, Peter · *See* AMBIANCE EXTRACTION; BAUER, BEN; FELDMAN, LEONARD; FOSGATE, JAMES.

Scheiner, Elliot, March 18, 1947– · One of America's premier recording engineers, Scheiner started out as a musician playing percussion in various bands, including Jimmy Buffett's Coral Reefers, and began his recording career under the tutelage of Phil Ramone, in 1967. By 1973, he had begun to freelance as an engineer and producer, becoming the first person ever to work as a freelance engineer for other artists. Since then, he has produced, recorded, or mixed for performers as diverse as Steely Dan, Toto, Boz Scaggs, Fleetwood Mac, Glenn Frey, Sting, Ricky Martin, Aretha Franklin, Natalie Cole, Barbra Streisand, Luciano Pavarotti, The Eagles, Van Morrison, Queen, The Doobie Brothers, Roy Orbison, and James Brown. He also recorded the soundtrack for *The Godfather*, parts I and II. His talents have been recognized with 16 Grammy nominations, five of which he has won, plus two Emmy nominations and three TEC award nominations.—Howard Ferstler

Schmitt, Al, April 17, 1938– · One of America's top recording engineers, Schmitt gained his first recording studio experience at the early age of seven, while working for his uncle, Harry Smith, who was the owner of New York's first independent recording studio. Smith was a well-known engineer who had worked with the likes of Caruso, the Andrews Sisters, Art Tatum, Bing Crosby, and Orson Welles. Between the ages of 17 and 19, Schmitt served in the U.S. Navy and, when he came out, his uncle found him an apprenticeship at Apex Recording Studio in New York, where Schmitt was to meet and be strongly influenced by engineer Tom Dowd. He moved to Los Angeles in 1958, where he went to work at a studio called Radio Recorders. Soon after he was hired by RCA to become an engineer at RCA Studios in Los Angeles, and in 1963, he became staff producer. In 1967, he left RCA to become an independent producer, and in 1970, he returned to engineering work, realized that he thoroughly enjoyed that part of the trade, and went on to record many outstanding releases.

During his career, Schmitt has been involved in over 150 gold or platinum records. He has been honored with 25 Grammy Award nominations and won eleven of them—more than any other recording engineer. In addition, he was a 1997 inductee into the Technical Excellence and Creativity Awards Hall of Fame. The list of people he has recorded reads like a who's who in contemporary music: Frank Sinatra, Barbra Streisand, Madonna, Steely Dan, Toto, Ray Charles, Dave Grusin, Joe Sample, Luther Vandross, Sam Cooke, Henry Mancini, Jefferson Airplane, Brandy, David Benoit, Toni Braxton, Dr. John, Quincy Jones, Les Brown, Natalie Cole, Horace Silver, Robbie Robertson, Vanessa Williams, Greg Adams, Ruben Blades, Duke Ellington, Jackson Brown, George Benson, and Diana Krall, among others.—Howard Ferstler

Schnee, William, July 4, 1947– · A major American recording engineer, Bill Schnee was born in Phoenix, Arizona, took keyboard lessons at age 8, started studying the trumpet when he was 9, and switched to the saxophone when he was 11. At age 13, he moved with his family to San Francisco; when he was 16, the family moved again, this time to Los Angeles, where he spent his last year in high school. In Los Angeles, Schnee put his keyboard talents to good use and formed a band with the help of several of his friends. While he honed the band's sound and engineered their demos, the group's producer noticed his talents and encouraged Schnee to pursue the professional recording techniques that would later build his craft. Throughout college studies at California Polytechnic Institute (1965–1968) and Loyola Law School (1969–1970), Schnee continued to write songs and play music, but his natural gifts in sound engineering convinced him that recording work was what he wanted to do.

His natural engineering talents paid off, and one technical triumph followed another. In 1975, Schnee engineered the groundbreaking album from Thelma Houston on the Sheffield Labs label, *I've Got the Music in Me*, a live direct-to-disc recording that set new standards in sound engineering and still ranks as a favorite of audiophiles everywhere. In 1981, he opened his own recording facility, Schnee Studio. State of the art in every way, it is equipped with a custom made console, custom tube-microphone pre-amps, and an extensive collection of old tube microphones, and is regarded as one of the finest tracking rooms in Los Angeles. Since its opening, the studio has generated even more gold and platinum triumphs by hosting artists like Don Henley, Anita Baker, Aaron Neville, Cher, Natalie Cole, Bette Midler, Teddy Pendergrass, and Dionne Warwick.

Today, Schnee's musical background continues to help in communicating with artists and musicians in the studio as producer, engineer, and mix master. In a career that spans four decades, he has engineered gold or platinum releases with such artists as Three Dog Night, Barbra Streisand, Neil Diamond, Carly Simon, The Pointer Sisters, Whitney Houston, Michael Bolton, Amy Grant, and Chicago. Schnee has also mixed four projects for Mark Knopfler and engineered the last Dire Strait's album, *On Every Street*, one of the better engineered rock recordings created by anybody, anywhere. Switching to his producer role, Schnee also has worked on multiple projects with Huey Lewis & the News, Boz Scaggs, and Pablo Cruise.

Schnee has been Grammy-nominated 10 times for Best Engineered Recording and has won twice for *Aja* and *Gaucho*, both from Steely Dan. Those two multi-platinum releases add to a list of hits that include over 60 gold records, 35 platinum projects, and 50 top-20 singles. In 1992, he took an Emmy Award for Best Sound Mixing for a Variety Special, Natalie Cole's live concert for PBS, and in 1996, he won a Dove Award for *Raise The Standard*, a praise album for the Promise Keepers.—Howard Ferstler

Schoeps [website: www.schoeps.de] · A microphone manufacturing company, founded in 1948 by Karl Schoeps, known as Schalltechnik Dr.-Ing. Schoeps. At the beginning, the company dealt with sound recording and reinforcement systems, and engineered systems for use in motion-picture theaters, even manufacturing a tape recorder model for a short time. When it was started, the Schoeps "factory" was housed in private apartments. Before long, however, it moved to a rented house in Durlach, the oldest district of Karlsruhe. The company's current residence is one of the oldest houses preserved in Durlach, with its cellar and foundation walls dating back to 1662. The firm expanded into an adjacent building in 1965, doubling the available floor space, and in 1990, it expanded again into a former ballroom on the premises.

In the first twenty years of its history, Schoeps had practically no distribution network of its own. Nevertheless, its circle of customers steadily increased, thanks to the friendship between Dr. Schoeps and a French businessman, who had very good contacts at radio stations. Consequently, Schoeps gained a strong market position in the French recording industry during the 1950s, which it has managed to preserve to the present day. In the years that followed, Schoeps also developed contacts in German radio and television stations, making the name Schoeps well known in Germany. Throughout the years the company was known for its innovative small-capsule designs, and in 1973, the Colette series was launched, possibly the most extensive and versatile microphone system ever conceived. This series was used by a number of important American recording companies, including Telarc.

In 1980, the son of Dr. Schoeps, Ulrich Schoeps, joined the company, becoming second director in 1986, with his father remaining first director. At the end of 1993, Dr. Schoeps died, whereupon his son became head of the firm. In this position, the younger Schoeps has continued the tradition begun by his father. No doubt, part of the company's success is because, in a space of only 1,500 square meters, only 35 employees develop, manufacture, and distribute the whole range of Schoeps products. Today, Schoeps is one of the most innovative microphone manufacturers in the world, leading the way in many developments. Central to its design philosophy over the years is the company's insistence on absolute sound neutrality of the microphones, making them ideal for recording classical ensembles.—Howard Ferstler

Schroeder, Manfred, July 12, 1926– · A major researcher in the fields of concert-hall acoustics, the monaural phase sensitivity of human hearing, and computer graphics, among many other disciplines, Schroeder studied at the University of Göttingen in Germany, where he earned a B.S. in mathematics (1949), an M.S. in physics (1951), and a Ph.D., also in physics (1954), and spent time investigating the distribution of resonances in concert halls using microwave cavities as models. The chaotic distribution he discovered is now recognized as characteristic of complex dynamical systems. In 1954, Schroeder joined the Research Department of Bell Laboratories in Murray Hill, New Jersey. In the late 1950s, he helped to formulate the U.S. standards for stereophonic broadcasting, which is now used worldwide. From 1958 to 1969, he directed research at Bell on speech compression, synthesis, and recognition.

Since 1969, he has served as professor of physics at the University of Göttingen, commuting between the university and Bell, and in 1991, he became a professor emeritus at the university. He is also a founding member of the Institut de Recherche et Coordination Acoustique/Musique of the Centre Pompidou in Paris. He is the author of over 150 papers and book chapters, as well as several complete books including: *Number Theory in Science and Communication*; *Fractals Chaos, Power Laws: Minutes from an Infinite Paradise*; and *Computer Speech: Recognition, Compression, Synthesis*. Schroeder also holds 45 U.S. patents in speech and signal processing and other fields, and has been awarded Gold Medals from the Audio Engineering Society (1972) and the Acoustical Society of America (1991), the Lord Raleigh Medal of the British Institute of Acoustics, as well as the Helmholtz Medal of the German Acoustical Society. He is a fellow of the American Academy of Arts and Sciences and the New York Academy of Sciences, and is also a member of the National Academy of Engineering in Washington, and the Göttingen Academy of Sciences.— Howard Ferstler

Scott, Hermon Hosmer, March 28, 1909– April 13, 1975 · Scott was born in Somerville, Massachusetts. A straight-A student at Massachusetts Institute of Technology, where he earned a master's degree, Scott went on to earn his doctorate at Lowell Technological Institute. In 1947, he founded the H. H. Scott Company in Maynard, Massachusetts, with the idea being to provide high-quality products at reasonably affordable prices. In that respect, he was in direct competition with Avery Fisher's company. Indeed, for years the two equipment manufacturers practically defined the state of the moderately high-end audio market. Scott held more than 100 patents for innovations in the electronics field, including the first commercial noise-level meter, the RC oscillator (used in electronics laboratories all over the world), and the dynamic noise suppresser, which greatly reduced the sound of electronic and mechanical background noise in radio broadcast situations. The device worked so well that it allowed Paul Whiteman to pre-record his radio program for later broadcast. With the help of Daniel R. von Recklinghausen, the H. H. Scott company went on to earn an enviable reputation as one of the technically best in the business. Scott's reputation was such that he won the Audio Engineering Society's Potts Memorial award in 1951, and became a Fellow of the organization in 1952. Unfortunately, Scott's unwillingness to master marketing issues, and his inability to match the cost-cutting techniques of his competitors, particularly Japanese companies that were able to use advanced design and construction skills, forced H. H. Scott into bankruptcy in 1972. Emerson Radio purchased the brand name in 1985, but the company has never regained the ironclad reputation it enjoyed in the 1950s and 1960s. He died in Newton, Massachusetts.—Howard Ferstler

Scott, Leon, 1817–April 26, 1879 · French inventor, printer, and librarian; born Edouard-Léon Scott de Martinville. His work in the printing trade gave him the opportunity to read scientific treatises, leading to an interest in invention. He developed the phonautograph in 1857, a device that recorded sound but did not play it back. Although he patented the invention (no. 17.897/31.470; March 25, 1857), he was unable to market it. He became a librarian, and wrote several books unrelated to recorded sound. When Edison's phonograph was announced in 1877, Scott claimed recognition for his prior work, but unsuccessfully; he was by then reduced to selling prints in a stall behind 9 Rue Vivienne, Paris. He died, poor and forgotten.

Scott De Martinville, Edouard-Léon, April 25, 1817–April 29, 1879 · Scott de Martinville was a French amateur phonetician who developed a recorder for sound waves. Born in Paris, he became interested in making a permanent record of sounds in air. He constructed a phonautograph in collaboration with the leading scientific instrument maker in Paris at the time, Rudolph Koenig. The instrument was a success, and Koenig contracted Scott and published a collection of traces in 1864.

Although the membrane was parallel to the rotating surface, a primitive lever system generated lateral movements of a bristle that scratched curves in a thin layer of lampblack on the rotating surface. The curves were not necessarily representative of the vibrations in the air. Scott did not imagine the need for reproducing a recorded sound; instead, his intention was to obtain a trace that would lend itself to mathematical analysis and visual recognition of sounds. The contract with Koenig

left Scott without influence over his instrument, and eventually he became convinced that everyone else, including Edison in the United States, had stolen his invention. He died in Paris.—George Brock-Nannestad

Scott, Raymond, September 10, 1908–February 8, 1994 · An American bandleader and inventor of electronic music instruments. Scott was best known as a bandleader during the 1930s, 1940s, and 1950s. Many of his catchy melodies (e.g., *Powerhouse, Twilight in Turkey, Dinner Music for a Pack of Hungry Cannibals*) were adapted for use in cartoons by legendary Warner Brothers music director Carl Stalling. The other side of this man was little known to the public. He was at heart an inventor and a self-trained electronics wizard. He spent many of his early years soldering, tinkering, and inventing musically oriented contraptions. By the late-1940s, he had accumulated enough wealth from his work as a bandleader and composer to purchase a mansion in North Hills, Long Island.

Scott was a sought-after composer of commercial jingles and invented electronic music instruments and recording devices to facilitate his work as a one-man production house. Scott formed Manhattan Research Inc. in 1946 as an outlet for his commercial electronic music production. By about 1960, he was manufacturing a grab bag of gadgets for various musical applications, including four models of electronic door bells, an electronic music box, and three models of an instrument he called The Electronium. By the mid-1960s, his advertising slogan billed the company as "Designers and Manufacturers of Electronic Music and Musique Concrète Devices and Systems." His most original inventions included a variety of keyboard instruments, multi-track recording machines, and automatic composing instruments.—Thom Holmes

Scratch Filter · A control on an audio pre-amplifier that serves to reduce the noise on an analog disc containing scratches or other surface defects. Scratch filters are rarely found on modern, consumer-grade equipment, because digital-audio software does not react to scratches the way analog systems do; however, computer systems that can nearly eliminate scratch sounds from analog recordings are now available, allowing rare and valuable performances on such discs to be fairly cleanly transferred to digital storage for archiving or reproducing.—Howard Ferstler

Scroll · An inaudible segment of the groove on a recorded disc, used to separate and link the recorded bands. It would only be needed when a side carried more than one song or instrumental piece, so it was not much used in the acoustic era. The earliest example noted in the literature was Victor 16863 (1911), which has two songs by Henry Allan on side A, and five "Mother Goose Songs" by Elizabeth Wheeler on the flip side. Another Wheeler disc of Mother Goose songs, with separation scrolls, was no. 35225 (1912).

A French language set issued by HMV in 1927 (no. C-1353+) had such dividers for lessons. The HMV *Instruments of the Orchestra* had scrolls that were "locked," so that the needle would not pass to the next band without human intervention; evidently, the purpose was to give a teacher time to talk about the instruments as they were illustrated (HMV C-1311+, 1927). In 1932 and 1933, the British labels Durium and Broadcast Four-Tune used scroll separators. Scrolls became standard on LP records.

SDDS (Sony Dynamic Digital Sound) · Sony's competing format for the digital soundtrack system for motion picture playback. Unlike like DTS and Dolby Digital, this format has never been used for home audio. For theater use, the signal is optically printed outside the film sprocket holes, along both sides of the print. The first movies to make use of the SDDS system in theaters were *In the Line of Fire* and *Last Action Hero*, in 1994.—Howard Ferstler

Seas · *See* LOUDSPEAKER, 6.

Seeburg, Justus P., 1871–October 21, 1958 · Swedish/American industrialist, born in Gothenburg. After technical training there, he transferred to the United States in 1886. He worked in a piano factory in Chicago, and became superintendent of Cable Piano; then he was co-founder of Kurz-Seeburg Co., Rockford, Illinois, which made piano actions. He sold his interest in 1902, and established the Seeburg Piano Co. in Chicago, 1907. That firm made coin-op pianos with electrically driven bellows and perforated paper rolls. A line of Orchestrions appeared in 1910, used in silent film theaters.

In 1927, Seeburg began to manufacture automatic electric coin-op phonographs. He discontinued the Orchestrion with the arrival of sound films. Two interesting products followed: the Audiophone, with 8 turntables for selective play (1928), and the Melophone, allowing 12 selections (1930). In 1935, the Selectophone and the Symphonola were introduced. A wall-mounted jukebox, the Playboy, was introduced in 1939. The firm was in receivership during the 1930s, and diversified to other products. Finally, the family sold out in 1956 to Fort Pitt Industries. Seeburg died in Stockholm, Sweden.

Selectophone · A Seeburg jukebox, 1935, developed by Wilcox. It had many turntables on a single revolving shaft.

Sennheiser [website: www.seinheiser.com] · Founded in 1945, by Dr. Fritz Sennheiser, near Hannover, Germany. The company has built its professional reputation on high-quality studio microphones and wireless microphone systems, and it produces headphones that are used by both professionals and hi-fi enthusiasts, worldwide. One of its more notable consumer-product breakthroughs was the "open-air" headphone design. An American branch of the company, SEC, was started in 1963, and it has since become Sennheiser's largest distributor.—Howard Ferstler

Sensitivity · In an audio system, the response-signal ratio of a microphone or other transducer, taken under specified conditions.

Sensurround · A motion-picture, surround-sound recording/playback process developed by W. O. Watson and Richard Stumpf at Universal Pictures, which debuted with the movie *Earthquake* in 1974. Four large low-frequency horns were located behind the screen, two in each corner. The "Model W" horn in each corner was eight feet long, four feet wide, and four feet high. The "Model C" horn in each corner was a modular unit a foot wide and five feet high. Two additional horns were located on a platform in the rear of the theater. Each horn was driven by a 1,000-watt amplifier controlled by inaudible tones on a special optical control track along with the normal 4-track magnetic soundtrack of the 35-mm Panavision filmstrip. The tones turned the horns on and off at preset volumes, creating low-frequency vibrations 5–40 cycles at sound pressures of 110–120 dB, causing the audience, chairs, floor to feel the vibrations of the earthquake and dam-destruction scenes.—Howard Ferstler

Separation (I) · The ability of a microphone to accept signals from certain sources and not from other sources.

Separation (II) · In elements of a stereo system, the degree to which individual channels are kept distinct.

Separation Recording · A method of recording that assigns microphones to each performer or group of performers in an ensemble, inscribing their contributions independently of the other participants. The separate signals are mixed in the control room, not necessarily in a manner to duplicate the original event. Elements may also be recorded at different sessions, and combined later in a mixdown.

Serial Copy Management System (SCMS) · *See* DAT (Digital Audio Tape).

Session. The event of actual recording, in a studio or on location. Sessions comprise a variable number of takes. The date of a session, which occupies no more than one day, is important in discography to establish precedence and the identification of personnel.

Session Tape · The tape of all the material performed during a recording session, including both the accepted material that appears on the master, and the rejected (outtake) material.

78-RPM Discs · Records revolving at 78 rpm, also known as standard or coarse groove discs, were the international industry norm from the 1920s until the introduction of the Columbia long-playing record (LP) in 1948. Earlier discs had displayed a variety of speeds, from 70 rpm to more than 90 rpm (*see also* SPEEDS), although 78-80 was most common after 1900. By 1957, mass commercial manufacture of 78s had ceased. There were a few later releases: 15 are listed in Biel 1982/1 and 3 others in Biel 1982/2. Not mentioned in those two lists was the 1962 Pickwick release in Britain of 36 children's records on 7-inch 78s. Sound effects records for professional use also continued to appear in 78-rpm format.

The 78s have been the prime focus of record collectors. Although no complete inventory of 78s exists, many useful lists have been published (*see also* DISCOG-RAPHY). Much attention has been given by audio experts to the best means of replaying 78s on modern equipment, to eliminating hiss and scratch noises (*see also* NOISE REDUCTION), and to improving the sound on them (*see also* REPRO-CESSED STEREO). *See also* DISC.

Shavers · Cylinder record blanks had to be turned smooth for both initial use and for re-use, this task being accomplished by a shaver. Thomas Edison's British patent no. 17175 (1887) included such a device, attached to the carrier arm of the new phonograph. Later the shaver (or planer, or parer) had a separate existence, which might have been powered by a treadle (1890s to ca. 1905) or by electricity (from ca. 1897). An electric drive could spin a cylinder under the planer at 1,500 rpm to 2,800 rpm. In March 1908, Edison marketed his Universal Shaving Machine, usable on both regular size and six-inch business cylinders. A simple hand-cranked machine was available in 1912, employing a steel blade that could smooth a cylinder with just a few turns.

Sheble, Horace · Philadelphia recording industry executive and inventor, a partner in Hawthorne & Sheble with Ellsworth A. Hawthorne. He held 14 patents in the audio field, notably a 1907 patent for a tone arm. The tone arm was Sheble's answer to the patented tapered tone arm of Eldridge Johnson; it was a "sound-conveying tube consisting of a plurality of sections of progressively increasing cross-sectional area." This configuration was used on the Hawthorne & Sheble Star Talking Machine. Sheble went to work for Columbia Phonograph Co. in 1911.

Shellac · The name given to the compound that was used to make most disc records from about 1896 to about 1948. Shellac is also the name of the principal ingredient in the compound. Shellac is a resinous compound secreted by the lac, a tree insect native to India, Burma, and Thailand. The secretion is utilized to form a protective shell for the insect and for its unhatched eggs, such shells being about the size of a grain of wheat. This shellac is scraped from twigs and branches, and shipped in dry powder form. For the disc record application in its developed state, shellac itself formed 13.6% of the shellac compound. Other ingredients were vinsol (8.7%), Congo gum (.92%), white filler (37.4%), red filler (37.4%), carbon black (1.3%), and zinc stearate (.49%). In 1896, Fred Gaisberg discovered the utility of the shellac compound for discs; he found it being used for button making by the Duranoid Co., of Newark, New Jersey.

Problems in the use of shellac for records included the uncertain quality of the shellac itself, which was often loaded with impurities; the variable inclusion of scrap (including, in times of shortage, old records returned for recycling) in the compound by different manufacturers; and the basic difficulty of getting enough of the material from India. During the Second World War, the supply was virtually cut off. Even under the best conditions, however, shellac was subject to gross surface noise produced by the abrasive filler—most of it limestone. Another great problem was the brittleness of the record, requiring great care and cost in handling, packaging, and shipping.

Lamination of the final shellac disc, initiated and produced briefly by Columbia in 1906, reduced surface noise. Columbia returned to the laminated record in 1922 and presented a technically superior product that worked well later with jukeboxes. The laminated record also sustained the label through the shellac shortage of the war (because lamination reduced the need for so much shellac).

Shellac was finally replaced as a disc ingredient by vinyl, introduced in the 1930s, and rendered ubiquitous by the LP record.

Shoemaker, Kathryn (Trina), June 14, 1965– · Born in Illinois, and graduating from Joliet Central High School in 1983, Shoemaker has worked as an independent recording engineer for dozens of labels, and has had numerous articles published about her, her talent, and her work in professional journals, such as *EQ*, *SPIN*, and *MIX*. In 1998, she won an engineering Grammy award for the best non-classical album, being the first woman ever to win that award.—Howard Ferstler

Shure, Stanley N., March 27, 1902–October 17, 1996 · An Audio Engineering Society member, Shure was born in Chicago and earned a degree in geography from the University of Chicago. Known professionally as S. N. Shure, he started the Shure Radio Company in 1925, which was a distributor of parts for home radio set builders. Eventually he was joined by his brother in the business, and the company was renamed Shure Brothers. Shure was interested in technology as much as business enterprise, and it was not long until he became interested in microphone design. In 1938, he helped Ben Bauer invent the world's first single-element directional microphone, called the Unidyne, which was marketed in 1939 and later became the design foundation for the later, world-renowned SM57 and SM58 models.

Somewhat before that time, in 1935, Shure had begun to design and produce phonographic cartridges, and this diversification helped the company to expand into the growing and lucrative home-audio market. In 1954, he began doing research on stereophonic phonograph cartridges, and within a few years, at the dawn of the stereophonic era, he introduced the M3D stereophonic cartridge. Because of this and other design innovations, the company expanded into being one of the world's major phonograph cartridge enterprises.

Shure was also an avid photographer, an internationally recognized philatelist, and an expert on linguistics and languages. A portion of his extensive stamp collection has been donated to the Smithsonian Institution.—Howard Ferstler

Shure Brothers · American audio firm located in Evanston, Illinois. Established in 1925 by Stanley N. Shure as Shure Radio Co., which specialized in selling radio parts kits. In 1926, the founder's brother, S. J. Shure, joined the company and the name was changed to Shure Brothers. The company branched out into the production of microphones in 1932, and one major product was a two-button carbon microphone. The first single-diaphragm unidirectional microphone, the Unidyne (invented by Ben Bauer), was introduced in 1939. Later designs, such as the SM57 and SM58 models, introduced in 1965, were very popular and are still used internationally for recording rock and pop concerts. In the world of live sound, the Beta series of microphones (1989) took the proven design philosophy of the SM58 and applied it to the special needs of the modern concert stage. Similarly, Shure's UHF wireless system (1996) has become an industry standard. Other sound recording and reinforcement products include a line of in-ear wireless stage monitoring systems that give performers control of how they hear themselves while aiding in hearing conservation. Recent product innovations for professional installations include digital feedback reducers and automatic mixers.

Among audiophiles, the company was probably best known for its innovative and often reasonably priced phonograph cartridges than for its microphones. Shure's important V15 series of cartridges were continually upgraded reference standards for years, and the latest version is still being produced.

Sides, Alan, September, 1951– · After attending Pepperdine University, Sides, later to become one of the most respected producers and recording engineers in the industry, inched his way into the recording business, and got his first job working for United Western Recording, in Hollywood, in 1968. He later started a small studio, named Ocean Way, in Santa Monica, and after several years of honing his skills and building up the business, he went back and purchased United Western, in 1977, and changed its name to Ocean Way Studios. After still more recording successes, he went on to also found Record One Studios, in Los Angeles, as well as a second Ocean Way facility in Nashville.

With over 400 albums to his credit, Sides' engineering and mixing work includes releases by Eric Clapton, Alanis Morissette, the Goo Goo Dolls, David Benoit, Neil Diamond, John Lee Hooker, Barry Manilow, Olivia Newton-John, Oscar Peterson, Benny Carter, Andre Previn, Diane Schuur, Frank Sinatra, Mel Tormé, Aerosmith, Patti Austin, Count Basie, Dolly Parton, Zoot Sims, Vanessa Williams, and Nancy Wilson, among many others. His engineering work also includes the film scores to *Primary Colors*, *Dead Man Walking*, *Phenomenon*, *Runaway Bride*, *City of Angels*, and *Last Man Standing*, among quite a few others. Other credits include Beck, Ry Cooder, Emmylou Harris, The Brian Setzer Big Band, Deana Carter, the GRP All Star Big Band, and *The Songs of West Side Story*, featuring Phil Collins, Natalie Cole, All For One, Trisha Yearwood, Wynonna Judd, Tevin Campbell, Kenny Loggins, Michael McDonald, Little Richard, and Aretha Franklin.

Signal · In audio terminology, the complex of sound waves that is introduced to the recording system to be captured and reproduced.

Signal-to-Noise Ratio (S/N Ratio) · Often arbitrarily assigned, in an audio system, it is the ratio between the desired signal level and the extraneous audible material, such as hum, surface scratches, vibrations from components, etc. It is usually expressed in decibels (dB). For instance, an S/N ratio of 50 dB means that the signal is 50 dB louder than the extraneous noise. Obviously the higher the ratio, the better the result, because an overlay of equipment-generated background noise is undesirable in audio recording and playback systems. The noise should be measured using a true RMS type voltmeter over a specified bandwidth, and sometimes weighting filters should be used to account for audibility differences at various frequencies. All these things must be stated for a S/N spec to have meaning, and simply saying a playback device or recorder has a S/N ratio of 70, 80, or 90 dB means nothing, without giving the reference level, measurement bandwidth, and any weighting filers. Note also that a system's maximum S/N should equal its dynamic range.

Early equipment and record materials yielded very low ratios. For example, it was said about Emilé Berliner's hard rubber discs that "in terms of signal-to-noise ratio, the best probably did not exceed 6 dB and the average was very near unity." The shellac record that came later was better, but "the best signal-to-noise ratio never exceeded 32 dB and 28 dB was a high average performance." With the vinyl record, 55 dB to 60 dB ratios were reached. A good CD player with 16-bit resolution has a S/N ratio of 96 dB (6 dB per bit, with the range expanded if noise shaping is employed), which is more than adequate for all but the most robust symphonic music. Ideally, there should be no noise at all in a CD output, but the optimal situation is not achieved in practice because of noise in the analog circuitry. [Isom 1977, source of the quotations; Pohlmann 1989; further updates by Howard Ferstler.]

Simulated Stereo · *See* REPROCESSED STEREO.

Siney, Philip, April 3, 1966– · The only recording engineer still actually working for Decca Records, at company headquarters in Chiswick London, Siney initially pursued an education in electronics engineering, and received musical training as counter tenor and organist. In 1989, he joined Decca as a location engineer, and went on to receive training as a balance engineer under the tutelage of James Lock, Stan Goodall, and John Dunkerley.

Today, Siney continues to record for Decca, using the classic Decca Tree, three-microphone technique pioneered by Roy Wallace and later refined by Kenneth Wilkinson. At Decca, he regularly works with musical artists such as Flemming, Pavarotti, Scholl, Dutoit, Ashkenazy, Thibaudet, and Chailly, using 24 bit, 96-kHz technology for both stereo and surround mixes. He has worked with recordings that received Grammy awards for best opera (1992 and 2000), and won the 2002 French Diapason Award for a piano album of Fauré's works, performed by Kung Wo Paik.—Howard Ferstler

162/3-RPM Discs · In the 1950s, several manufacturers produced discs that rotated at half the speed of the long-playing record, to double the amount of content material. Turntables were marketed with the 16 2/3 speed as well as 33 1/3 and 45 rpm. Sound quality did not prove acceptable for music, but the speed was used for talking books and other literary recordings until the cassette became available.

Skating Force · The tendency of a spinning disc on an analog record player to draw the cartridge, stylus, and playing end of the pivoting tone arm toward its center. The result will be slightly higher stylus tracking pressure on one side of the groove than the other. Anti-skating mechanisms are often used to combat this tendency. A tangential tone arm, which tracks the record by mounting the arm on a sliding mount that does not pivot at all, eliminates skating force. Skating force is a non-issue with digital recordings.—Rev. by Howard Ferstler

Skywalker Sound · Possibly the best facility of its kind in the world, Skywalker was the brainchild of film maker George Lucas in the mid 1970s, and is located in the midst of a 2,600-acre tract in Marin County, about 40 miles north of San Francisco. It is a special effects, image-manipulation, and movie sound editing and production facility, as well as a top-quality recording environment for music-only productions of nearly any kind. It offers everything from on-site recording to final soundtrack work, in any format from standard 2-channel productions, through Dolby Surround and 5.1-channel Dolby Digital and DTS, on up to 8-channel SDDS. The operation markets its services to first-time directors and independent producers, as well as to established organizations, and it also offers music-production engineers, producers, and performers a recording facility that is second to none. Indeed, the scoring stage has a recording area that measures 60 feet wide × 80 long, with 30-foot ceilings, and the area is capable of easily accommodating a 125-piece orchestra. In addition to being responsible for many high-tech motion-picture productions, numerous top-quality sound recordings have been produced in the facility.—Howard Ferstler

Sleeve · The jacket or envelope used for protecting, storing, or marketing a disc recording; also known as a slipcase or record cover. Usually the material is paper or cardboard. Often there is a second envelope inside the sleeve, made of paper or Mylar, intended to give the surface additional protection. Sleeves may do more harm than good to their records, however; this point is discussed in PRESERVATION OF SOUND RECORDINGS.

Small, Richard, March 29, 1935– · A major researcher in audio system theory and design, Small received a bachelor of science degree from the California Institute of Technology in 1956, and went on to obtain an M.S. degree in electrical engineering from the Massachusetts Institute of Technology in 1958. He was employed in electronic circuit design for high-performance analytical instruments at the Bell & Howell Research Center in California from 1958 to 1964, except for a one-year visiting fellowship to the Norwegian Technical University from 1961 to 1962.

After a working visit to Japan in 1964, Small moved to Australia, and in 1972, following the completion of a program of research into direct-radiator electrodynamic loudspeaker systems, he was awarded the degree of doctor of philosophy by the University of Sydney. He then joined the teaching staff of the School of Electrical Engineering of that university. In 1986, he resigned his position as Senior Lecturer to return to industry, as Head of Research at KEF Electronics Limited in Maidstone, Kent, England. In 1993, he returned to the United States, and he currently holds the position of Senior Principal Engineer with Harman/Becker Automotive Systems in Martinsville, Indiana.

Dr. Small has published dozens of articles and conference papers in AES, Institute of Electrical and Electronics Engineers, and IREE publications, and is well known for mathematically formulating the performance parameters, the Thiele-Small parameters, of all modern loudspeaker systems. He is a senior member of the Institute of Electrical and Electronics Engineers and a member of the Institution of Engineers Australia. He is a fellow of the Audio Engineering Society and a recipient of the Society's Publication Award (1976), Silver Medal (1982), and Gold Medal (1996). He has served the AES as a member of the Editorial Review Board since 1973, a governor from 1989 to 1991, vice-chairman of the Technical Committee on Transducers from 1992 to 1994, and chairman of the Publications Policy Committee since 1992. *See also* BASS REFLEX SYSTEM; LOUDSPEAKER.—Howard Ferstler

Smithsonian Institution · The American national museum, founded in 1846, now consisting of several component museums, most of them in Washington, D.C. The National Museum of American History (NMAH) has a collection of recordings and artifacts pertaining to recorded sound. Included are a phonautograph; an 1877 Edison tinfoil phonograph; a cylinder ostensibly recorded by Alexander Graham Bell in the Volta Laboratory, 1881; a Berliner photoengraved record dated July 26, 1887, and a Berliner gramophone of

---

Small Records (in the 78 era)

Disc records of lesser diameter than the typical 10-inch size of the 78-rpm era appeared from time to time in the United States, more commonly in Britain and Germany. The smallest playable record known was made for Queen Mary's dollhouse, 1924; it measured one and 5/16 inches. Among the diminutive British and German labels were Baby Odeon, Beka, Broadcast Jr., Crown, Crystalate, Favorite, G & T, Globe, Homo Baby, Homophon, Kiddyphone, Little Marvel, Little Wonder, Marspen, Mimosa, Nicole, Neophone, Odeon, Oliver, Pathé, Phonadisc, and The Bell (some of those labels produced standard size records as well). In America, the Harper Bubble Books appeared during 1920 and 1921, and were marketed in Britain as Hodder-Columbia Books That Sing. Little Tots' Nursery Tunes were published in New York by Plaza Music Co. during 1923 and 1924.

1888. The Department of Social and Cultural History of NMAH holds important collections of jazz, popular, blues, and country records dating from 1903; there are more than 1,000 artists represented. Armed Forces Radio and Television Service transcription discs are there, plus the series *Hit of the Week Records*.

The Department of History of Science in NMAH has Columbia's experimental microgroove recordings of 1943 to 1946. It also has numerous records of geophysical phenomena, such as radio noise from Jupiter, and tapes representing engineering standards. Examples showing the development of audio components are found, including complete phonographs, headphones, tone arms, loudspeakers, receivers, magnetic recording devices, and microphones. Early recordings and early record players are abundant.

In the NMAH Department of National History, there is a collection of radio transcription discs from the World War II period. There is also a collection of recordings from political campaigns of 1896.

The Smithsonian has issued many recordings, including the *Smithsonian Collection of Classic Jazz* (1973), consisting of six 12-inch LPs. This was enlarged and re-mastered on five CDs in 1989. Individual albums have been released on country, jazz, and swing artists, and for American musicals. *Voices of the Civil Rights Movement: Black American Freedom Songs, 1960–1966* is an important contribution. A recreation of the Paul Whiteman 1924 concert in Aeolian Hall (which featured the premiere of *Rhapsody in Blue*) was issued on two LPs. Another CD album of special interest is *American Popular Song*, a collection of 110 selections by 62 artists, covering six decades on five compact discs (1988). *Big Band Jazz* won a Grammy in 1984 as the best historical album.

In 1986, the Smithsonian purchased the assets of Folkways Records, establishing Smithsonian Folkways Recordings. The Folkways archives were made part of the Center for Folklife and Cultural Heritage. Subsequently, several other small labels were also incorporated into the archives, including Dyer Bennett, Cook, Fast Folk, Monitor, and Paredon.

Snow, William B., May 16, 1903–October 5, 1969 · A pioneer in audio and acoustics, Snow was born in San Francisco and earned B.S. and E.E. degrees from Stanford University. During the golden years of sound research between 1923 and 1941, he worked at Bell Laboratories, playing a major role in the advancement of acoustic science. During the war years, he was assistant director of the U.S. Navy's underwater sound laboratory, at New London, Connecticut. In 1946, he took employment with the Vitro Corporation of America, and became director of physical research and development at the company in 1950. From 1952 to 1960, he ran a consulting practice in Santa Monica, California, and in 1961, he went to work for Bissett-Berman Corporation as head of electro-acoustics. Snow's contributions to audio and the science of recorded sound are manifest, and in 1968, the Audio Engineering Society awarded him its John H. Potts award.—Howard Ferstler

Society of Motion Picture and Television Engineers (SMPTE) · A professional engineering society that establishes standards for movie production and distribution, including a time-code standard used for audio synchronization.—Howard Ferstler

Society of Professional Audio Recording Services (SPARS) · Founded in 1979, a professional trade organization that unites professional customers with the manufacturers of audio recording equipment and providers of services.—Howard Ferstler

Solid State · A term applied to various semiconductor devices (e.g., the transistor)

to distinguish them from their electron tube counterparts.

Sony Corporation [website: www.sony. com] · A Japanese firm established in 1946 as Tokyo Telecommunications Engineering (current name taken in 1958) in the bombed-out shell of a department store. It made audio components, and experimented constantly to find new products and applications. Sony marketed the first Japanese tape recorder in 1950, and the world's first transistor radio in 1955, and went on to miniaturize other components; their pocket radio came out in 1957, gaining great popularity in world markets. Sony transistor television was introduced in 1959, and the solid-state video recorder in 1961. Other successful innovations included the desktop electronic calculator (1964), the Trinitron color television tube (1968), and the Walkman (1979). From 300 employees in the early 1950s, the firm went to 4,400 employees in 1961, 22,000 by 1975, and 26,000 by 1980. As of 2002, Sony employed 168,000 people worldwide.

In the audio field, Sony joined with Philips in developing compact disc technology, and has become the market leader in CD players. The firm has invested heavily in DAT and high definition television. Sony acquired CBS Records from CBS in 1988, for $2 billion, and Columbia Pictures from Coca Cola in 1989 for $4.9 billion. As of 2002, Sony's principal U.S. businesses include Sony Electronics Inc., Sony Pictures Entertainment, Sony Music Entertainment Inc., and Sony Computer Entertainment America Inc.

Soria, Dario, May 21, 1912–March 28, 1980 · Italian/American recording industry executive, born in Rome. He took an economics degree from the University of Rome in 1934. His family fled Italy in 1939 and came to America. Soria worked for the U.S. Office of War Information during World War II, becoming a citizen in 1945.

He was head of overseas news broadcasting for CBS (1943–1948). In that period, he organized the Cetra-Soria label, drawing on the Cetra matrices, which offered a major catalog of operatic material.

Artists on the Cetra-Soria label included Maria Callas, Cesare Siepi, Ferruccio Tagliavini, and Italo Tajo. Sixteen complete Verdi operas were issued over a seven-year period. In 1953, Soria sold the label to Capitol, and assumed leadership of a new EMI American subsidiary, which revived the Angel label. He was responsible for elegant packaging as well as high quality material on Angel until 1961, when he moved to RCA Victor as vice-president of the international division. From 1970, he was managing director of the Metropolitan Opera Guild. When he died in New York, Soria was at work on a planned release of a Metropolitan Opera historic broadcast of *Ballo in maschera*.

Sound File · A digital sound file contains one or more sequences of data points that directly or indirectly describe sound in such a way that a suitable program can reconstruct it. Consequently, not only would a computer hard drive downloading MP3 data from an Internet site be considered a sound file, but commercially produced CD and DVD recordings are sound files, too.—Howard Ferstler

Sound Recording · The process of registering and reproducing sonic signals. Various means and devices have been applied to this task, beginning with the Phonautograph of 1857, proceeding through cylinder phonographs and disc gramophones, wire and tape recordings, cassettes, compact discs and DAT. A description of the way each of those recordings is made is given in the appropriate article. *See* CYLINDER; DISC; RECORDING PRACTICE.

Soundbox · A common designation for the reproducer of an acoustic phonograph; it is usually applied to disc machines. Its parts are the diaphragm, needle arm and screw, spring, cushions, casing, and gasket. It was supplanted in the electric era by the cartridge, or pickup.

Soundstaging · *See* STEREOPHONIC RECORDING; SWEET SPOT.

Soundstream · A system of sonic enhancement for acoustic records, invented by Thomas Stockham. Using digital technology, soundstream adds harmonics that were not produced in the original recording by means of a parallel modern recording of the same work. It reduces surface noise, and brings the singer's voice forward; but also increases the presence of low pitched rumble. The most notable soundstream recordings are those of Enrico Caruso, issued by RCA.

Soundstream, Inc. · *See* STOCKHAM, THOMAS G.

Spaced-Array Microphone Recording · Sometimes called A-B stereo or difference stereo, uses two spaced-apart microphones to record stereo audio signals. Depending upon the distances between the microphones, the spacing introduces time and phase differences between the signals that results in a realistic, but still somewhat ersatz sense of spaciousness that often works very well in typical home-listening environments. Focus and imaging may be vague, however, unless additional spot microphones are used. The technique is often used to record large orchestral ensembles. *See also* MICROPHONE; COINCIDENT STEREO RECORDING; BLUMLEIN STEREO RECORDING.—Howard Ferstler

Spatializer · Developed by Desper Products and utilized in some VCRs, TV sets, and playback devices to improve the sound of two-channel program sources, it is a spatial enhancement technique that adds matrixing, crosstalk cancellation, and frequency-response manipulations. It is also employed by some motion picture and music recording systems, with the required enhancements applied during the mixing and editing process. The result in either case simulates a large-stage image up front and phantom-surround effects, doing so without the need of extra channels. *See also* CROSSTALK.—Howard Ferstler

SPDIF (Sony/Philips Digital Interface) · A consumer version of the AES3 (old AES/EBU) digital audio interconnection standard based on coaxial cable and RCA connectors.—Howard Ferstler

Spectacle · A combination recorder and reproducer assembly invented by Thomas Edison (U.S. patent no. 386, 974; filled November 26, 1887; granted July 31, 1888) with improvements by Ezra Gilliland (U.S. patent no. 393, 640; filed June 7, 1888; granted November 27, 1888). The device enabled the user to make a record and then play it back quickly on the same machine, simply by pivoting the spectacle, which held—in a form similar to a pair of eyeglasses—the recorder diaphragm and stylus along with the counterparts of the reproducer. The spectacle was first marketed in Edison's Perfected Phonograph of 1888.

Speeds · A major challenge to all forms of sound recording has been to establish the optimal and agreed-upon speed of the medium as it spins on a turntable, turns on a mandrel, or passes a given point. Too slow of a speed will result in unacceptable distortion products and one that is too quick will use up the recording surface in a short time. Another problem with analog systems is to make sure that the playback speed is exactly the same as the recording speed. If it is not, there will be a change in musical pitch.

The experiments and conclusions of recording manufacturers are outlined in the articles CYLINDER, 5, and DISC, 4. Analog discs are supposed to rotate at a constant number of revolutions per minute (rpm). In other words, they operate as constant angular velocity (CAV) systems. There was a fair range of differing standards among principal manufacturers of discs during the acoustic period. For example, following Victor's lead, most American labels were recording at 78–80 rpm shortly after the turn of the century; however, 75 rpm was the norm for Columbia acoustics made in France, Italy, and Spain, and for Odeon acoustics in all countries. Parlophone used 75 rpm for 1 series, and 80 rpm for another. Victor itself announced in its May 1917 catalog that "all records should be played at a speed of 76"; however, the November 1917 catalog gives the correct speed as 78, suggesting the possibility of a misprint in the May edition.

Other labels showed similar variations from the "standard" 78 rpm. Even the first electric-produced recordings may sometimes be odd. Ault reports on his study of Columbia set X 198 (1927) of Les Préludes by Felix Weingartner and the London Symphony: "The four sides were recorded at four different speeds, the first side at about 74 rpm, with each side a little faster until the last side was at about 77 rpm." Ault also points out the slow recording speed for the first Bing Crosby record (70 rpm) and the fast speed (83 rpm) of Columbia 50-D, of the Original Memphis Five (1924). Variations in speed were even found from one session to another in the same studio.

In modern discographies of old records, the compiler often endeavors to indicate the correct recording (and playback) speed of each disc. John Bolig's Recordings of Enrico Caruso, for example, notes all the correct speeds, which range from 75 to 80 rpm. The Phonometer was a 1907 device intended to monitor turntable speed. Eventually, standardization took hold and the 33 1/3-rpm LP microgroove discs and 45-rpm

discs that were the mainstay of recorded sound in the home accurately maintained the advertised speeds.

The compact disc operates on a completely different level. The CD requires constant linear velocity (CLV) for its tracking mechanism to maintain a constant tracking speed, meaning a variable angular velocity. Because the CD playback mechanism is digitally controlled, the required speeds can be very accurately maintained. Compact discs rotate from 200 to 500 rpm, as do DVD recordings. Laserdiscs come in two forms, with some having constant linear velocity at from 600 to 1,800 rpm, or constant angular velocity at a steady 1,800 rpm. *See also* SURFACE SPEED; TUNING BAND.—Ault 1987; Brooks; updated by Howard Ferstler

Spindle (I) · The vertical post at the center of a gramophone turntable. It keeps the disc in position during play, and in certain types of record changer it holds the stack of records to be played, or which have been played. The standard size in the 78 era was 0.25 inches in diameter; this was the size used by Berliner in his original instruments. Other sizes were used, among smaller manufacturers in the early 1900s, notably those based in Chicago: 1/2 inch and even 3 inches. The RCA 45-rpm record player of 1948 had a 1 3/8-inch spindle to accommodate the little vinyl discs; spindles of that diameter were later available as attachments to LP record players.

Spindle (II) · On a compact disc player, the spindle is the part of the drive that spins the disc.

Spindle Hole · The hole in the middle of a disc recording through which a record is mounted onto a turntable spindle for playback.

Splicing Tape · An adhesive tape used in editing recorded tapes; it is not magnetized.

Sizes for open-reel tapes and cassettes are available. In studio work, a splicing machine applies the tape.

Spring Motor Record Players · Because early sources of electrical power were expensive and unreliable, most of the pioneer phonograph and gramophone makers used spring motors to rotate their mandrels and turntables. The first such motor was developed by Edward H. Amet in 1891 and used on the Edison Class M phonograph of 1894. Frank L. Capps invented a motor with three springs (1896) that was used with the Edison Concert machine of 1899. The motor of J. E. Greenhill was perhaps the first to be used in a phonograph (1893). Henri Lioret made a talking doll in 1893 with his own spring mechanism. Columbia's first spring motor phonograph was the Type F Graphophone of 1894.

The earliest spring motor for a disc machine was patented by Levi H. Montross (1898). He sold these in Camden. Eldridge Johnson used the Montross motor in the 200 gramophones he manufactured for the U.S. Gramophone Co. (Berliner's firm) in 1896. He then took an order for another 3,500 machines. An improved governor, invented by Johnson, was used in the Berliner "trademark" model, the Improved Gramophone.

Even after the use of electric power became convenient, spring motors were used to drive portable 78 rpm disc players and cylinder or disc machines used in field recordings.

SRS (Sound Retrieval System) · Developed by Arnold Klayman and employed in some TV sets, desktop personal computers, and stand-alone processors, it adds matrixing and frequency-response manipulations to two-channel, stereophonic program sources (shaping extracted ambiance signals so that they mimic the side- and rear-surround response contouring provided by the pinna of the outer ear), thereby simulating a large-stage effect up front and phantom surround channels, and does so without the need of extra channels.

Stamper · The mold part in the disc record making process that is used to create the final pressing. *See also* DISC .

Standard Play · A designation for the 78-rpm disc, in contrast to the 33 1/3-rpm LP microgroove disc.

Standard Sequence · *See* MANUAL SEQUENCE.

Standing Waves · Irregularities, often quite audible and unwanted in the bass range, that result when sounds reflected back and forth between the walls of a room interact with each other and with the direct sounds from the speaker systems (or even musical instruments) that produced them to form alternate reinforcements (peaks) and nulls. The effect is dependent upon the size and shape of the room, and to some extent upon the location of the source. The structural integrity of the walls can also have an effect on the strength of the artifacts. Standing waves can be detrimental to sound reproduction at lower frequencies in small or badly proportioned rooms, where their effects are often extreme. In addition to the obvious axial modes that involve opposing walls, the phenomenon also involves tangential and oblique effects that are more difficult to calculate and are thought by some experts to be as negative in impact as the axial modes. *See also* ROOM ACOUSTICS.—Rev. by Howard Ferstler

Stanton, Walter O., 1915–April 16, 2001 · Born in Canton, Ohio, Stanton graduated in 1939 from Wayne State University, with a degree in electrical engineering. In the late 1940s, he invented the easy-to-replace, slide-in phonograph-cartridge stylus, which made it possible for users to replace their own stylus assemblies, thereby helping to revolutionize and expand the nascent hi-fi industry. In 1950, he purchased Pickering and Company, which had been selling his patented stylus, and in 1960, he founded Stanton Magnetics, one of the first American companies that produced truly high-fidelity phonograph cartridges. In later years, he started still another company, branching out into producing headphones and loudspeaker systems. He ran both companies until his retirement, in 1998. A former president of the Audio Engineering Society, Stanton was made a Fellow in 1959, received a Citation from the Society in 1961, and was also instrumental in founding the Institute of High Fidelity.—Howard Ferstler

Steering Systems · Most visibly employed by Dolby Pro Logic, but also used in some digital and analog music-ambiance systems, steering involves the electronic spatial manipulation of recorded two-channel audio signals. Doing this allows matrixed center-channel or surround-channel signals that would ordinarily only be vaguely imaged to be positively routed to a center channel or surround channel (or channels). Steering thereby strives to simulate multiple independent channels from two-channel sources, and with DSP ambiance systems it may also strive to simulate a sense of hall space around the listener. *See also* CENTER CHANNEL; DOLBY PRO LOGIC; DOLBY SURROUND SOUND; DSP (Digital Signal Processing); PHANTOM CENTER IMAGE; STEREOPHONIC RECORDING.—Howard Ferstler

Stereophonic Recording · Usually referred to as stereo, the modern term comes from a Greek word that translates as "solid." It involves the process of recording a sound source so that the result will deliver the impression of a fully developed, three-dimensional soundstage between just two loudspeaker systems. Stereophonic record-

ing is somewhat different from "binaural" recording, which involves headphone reproduction of sounds picked up by a microphone array that simulates the human head. True binaural sound reproduction can deliver a genuine full-dimensional effect, whereas stereophonic sound can only simulate the breadth and depth of the soundstage, and not the acoustics of the original performance space. Both techniques are in contrast to surround-sound recording that involves additional reproduction channels both in front of and adjacent to the listener and extends the three dimensionality clear out into the listening room, and expands the size of the listening area accordingly.

Stereo sound reproduction is based on a theory first propounded by Alan D. Blumlein: a pair of left-right microphones and just two playback speakers could imitate the human hearing mechanism. The stereo effect creates far greater realism than monaural recording, producing an illusion of depth that may be compared to the effect of stereoscopic photography. Stereo works because the brain compares the intensities of incoming sounds and contrasts the input received by each ear. It notes the arrival time from right and left sources, the reverberations, and the intensities. Thus, it is able to determine source direction as well as distance instantaneously (and unconsciously). Although the phantom images between the speakers cannot exactly simulate direct sources, the overall effect can be very realistic, at least if the listener occupies a location out in front of and equidistant from each of the speakers. *See also* HEARING.

Early experiments with binaural sound transmission preceded the phonograph; there were such efforts in Britain in 1876, by Lord Rayleigh. Silvanus Thompson of Bristol University carried on in 1877 and 1878. The use of two listening tubes, spaced like human ears, was found to produce a certain localizing ability of the source signals on the part of the listener. Alexander Graham Bell in America was also interested in "stereophonic phenomena," and apparently, he was the first to use the term. In Paris, 1881, Clément Ader demonstrated two-channel telephone transmission for a large enthusiastic audience in the Opéra auditorium. Listeners wore pairs of headphones. Thomas Edison's second British phonographic patent (1878) referred to multiple sound boxes on a single cylinder or disc, probably an effort to secure greater volume in reproduction, instead of a stereo effect. The Columbia Multiplex Grand Graphophone of 1898 utilized the concept.

Real efforts to record stereophonically began with the work of W. Bartlett Jones in the United States. He patented the idea of putting the left and right sound signals in adjacent grooves of the disc or on opposite sides of the record. Both methods required two replay styli, and difficulties of synchronizing these were a serious flaw in the design. (A curiosity in this genre was the perhaps unintentional stereo recording made by Duke Ellington in 1929.) Jones then patented a single groove, single stylus system. Simultaneous vertical and lateral modulation of the groove was involved. This idea was not developed commercially at the time.

EMI made experimental 78 rpm stereo discs at the Abbey Road studios in 1933. Pressings of these test discs (one of them Thomas Beecham conducting the Mozart Jupiter Symphony) exist, and sound effective. Arthur Charles Haddy and colleagues of the Decca Record Co., Ltd., in London, performed other important research. Haddy's work, and that carried on in Germany by Teldec, led to an increased frequency spectrum in stereo playback, and to solving the problems of groove spacing so that space on the disc was not wasted by the dual signals. In the United States, an experimental stereo recording was made in

March 1922 at the Philadelphia Academy of Music, as Arthur Charles Keller and a Bell Telephone Laboratories team made records of the Philadelphia Orchestra with two microphones. The output was on two parallel vertically cut tracks in 78-rpm discs. They were demonstrated at the Century of Progress Exposition in Chicago, 1933.

In later analog-disc recording, the twin signals were cut into the same record groove, at an axis of operation of 45/45 degrees. This was also one of the methods Alan Blumlein worked on, and the Blumlein patent applications of 1931 helped to establish all later practice. Westrex and Bell Telephone Laboratories received a U.S. patent for the their elaboration of the 45/45 disc technique in 1957. With each sidewall of the disc groove impressed with one program channel, the stereo cartridge distinguishes between them as it picks them up and sends one to each loudspeaker.

RCA initiated commercial recording in stereo in Boston's Symphony Hall from February 21–22, 1954, inscribing the *Damnation of Faust*. They followed that with a recording of the Chicago Symphony Orchestra under Fritz Reiner. These transcriptions did not actually show up in stereo form on discs until a few years later. EMI unveiled its "stereosonic" records in April 1955. Decca's first commercial recording in stereo-using the three-microphone "Decca Tree" assembly took place in Geneva, with the Orchestre de la Suisse Romande, in May 1954. Decca also began to use extra microphones, "outriggers," to capture flanking sounds from the boundaries of the orchestra. Eventually the company recorded the famous Georg Solti Rheingold in 1958 "where a KM-56 Tree captured the main orchestral sound" with a "six-channel unit augmented by a three-input outboard mixer and a single-channel pan-potted amp, a total of just 10 mikes to record what is universally recognized as a landmark achievement in stereo production" (Gray).

In May 1958, the first 45/45 stereo discs were marketed in the United States by three independent labels: Audio-Fidelity, Urania, and Counterpoint. That summer RCA and Columbia came out with their discs. The Recording Industry Association of America (RIAA) had finally determined which of the several available systems to endorse, and worldwide mass production followed. Pye issued the first commercial stereo discs in the United Kingdom in June 1958.

Multi-channel optical motion picture recording was first used commercially by Walt Disney studios in Fantasia (1940). It had a 4-track sound film, derived from eight recording channels. It could best be described in today's terms as surround sound, instead of stereo because it did not observe the natural sound perspectives of stereo. Cinemascope, developed by Bell Telephone Laboratories and demonstrated in January 1953, was an attempt to created true stereophonic sound on film.

Two-channel tape recording was also produced in the Bell Laboratories. At the New York World's Fair, 1939, demonstration tapes of Vicalloy were successfully displayed. Further important work in stereo tape was performed by Marvin Camras, with a three-channel wire recorder. Domestic stereo tapes were introduced commercially by EMI in October 1955—a 2-track system, also labeled "stereosonic," with a two-tape set of Nozze di Figaro performed at the Glyndebourne Festival. RCA's 4-track system appeared in 1958. For several years, the companies produced their releases in both monaural and stereo versions, to accommodate users who did not have the new stereo playback equipment. Then compatible systems were developed, with which a stereo disc could be played as if it were only monaural (i.e., without the twin loudspeakers and stereo amplifier).

Thus, the user without the means or desire to acquire a stereo system could buy stereo records, and the need for manufacturing monaural records evaporated. By the end of the 1960s, virtually all commercial recording on disc and tape was stereophonic.

The digital era continued the stereophonic revolution, and because digital systems offer considerably better channel separation than the 45/45 system used to produce the LP record, it was possible for recording engineers to do an even better job of simulating a phantom soundstage between the speakers. Unfortunately, the enhanced separation also required that some tried and true practices be modified or even shelved, and so many early CD releases seemed to lack the air and spaciousness of their LP counterparts. Eventually, recording engineers became aware of the requirements of the CD, and many contemporary releases offer up the best stereophonic sound ever produced. *See also* RECORDING PRACTICE.

Stockham, Thomas G., 1933–· Considered by many to be the father of digital recording, Stockham earned an Sc.D. degree from MIT in 1959 and was appointed Assistant Professor of Electrical Engineering at the same school. In 1962, he began experimenting with digital audio tape recordings using a large TX-0 computer and a A/D-D/A converter. (During this time, he also helped fellow MIT professor, Amar Bose, work on loudspeaker design.) In 1968, he left MIT for the University of Utah, and in 1975, he founded Soundstream, Inc., along with Malcolm Lowe, who had previously helped to found KLH. At this new position, he developed a 16-bit digital audio recorder using a high-speed instrument magnetic tape recorder. Soundstream, located in Salt Lake City, was the first commercial digital recording company in the United States. Other companies had been experimenting with digital recording since 1971, but Stockham was the first to make a commercial digital recording, using his own Soundstream recorder in 1976 at the Santa Fe Opera.

Using Soundstream technology, the first commercial digitally mastered LP recording to be released for sale was recorded by Jack Renner, of Telarc in 1978 (Frederick Fennell and the Cleveland Symphonic Winds), and the company released the first compact disc version of this material in the United States in 1982. From 1975 to 1980, Stockham with the help of scientists, such as Jules Bloomenthal, made over 500 digital masters with a completely computerized editing system and pioneered tapeless hard disk editing. The company sold about 16 of its editing systems at $160,000 each that were used by companies such as Bertelsmann. These machines used a Honeywell 16-track transport and sampled at 50 kHz. Stockham also played a key role in the digital restoration of Enrico Caruso recordings. Soundstream merged with Digital Recording Corporation in 1980 and became DRC/Soundstream.

In 1980, after leaving Soundstream, Stockman became chairman of Electrical and Computer Engineering at the University of Utah. He was named a Fellow of the Institute of Electrical and Electronics Engineers, served as president of the Audio Engineering Society (AES) in 1982 and 1983, and has received numerous awards for his contributions to audio technology, including the Poniatoff Gold Medal from the Society of Motion Picture and Television Engineers (SMPTE), the Gold Medal from the AES, and an Emmy in 1988 for the development of tapeless audio recording and editing technology used in television studios. The National Academy of Recording Arts and Sciences (NARAS) awarded him a Grammy in 1994 for his role in pioneering and advancing the era of digital recording. In 1999, the Academy of Motion Picture Arts and Sciences awarded Stockham and Robert B. Ingebretsen a

1998 Scientific and Engineering Award for their work in the areas of waveform editing, cross-fades, and cut-and-paste techniques for digital audio editing.—Howard Ferstler

Stokes, Jonathan, April 10, 1964– · After graduating from the University of East Anglia, with a master's degree in music, Stokes joined Decca in 1987 as an audio editor. Within three years, he had learned enough about recording and recording technology to move on to the location department, where he eventually was promoted to senior engineer, a position that involved responsibility for projects ranging from recording solo recitals to recording grand opera productions, live events, and video productions. In addition to his engineering tasks, Stokes also occasionally worked as a producer, and during his time with Decca, he worked with some of the finest artists in the world, including Bernard Haitink, Cecilia Bartoli, George Solti, Luciano Pavarotti, Placido Domingo, Bryn Terfel, Kiri Te Kanawa, and Al Jarreau, as well as with ensembles such as the Berlin Philharmonic, Vienna Philharmonic, Chicago Symphony Orchestra, Cleveland Orchestra, and the Montreal Symphony, among others.

During his career, Stokes has won a Deutsche Schallplaten award for best opera recording (1994), has won Grammys for best engineered recording twice (in 1992 and 1995), and has had recordings win performance Grammys four times (two in 1995, for best choral and best solo instrument, plus one in 1996 and one in 2001). He has also has won numerous best-recording awards from *Gramophone* magazine. In November 1997, he left Decca, and with Neil Hutchinson, formed a new recording and mastering facility in London, Classic Sound, built from the ground up to deal with both traditional and the new 5.1-channel formats.—Howard Ferstler

Stollwerk Chocolate Record

A vertical-cut disc issued by Gebrüder Stollwerk AG, a firm that had acquired Edison patents for Germany ca. 1898. Remarkably, the records were made of chocolate, with a foil covering. Stollwerk also made other records, in wax or on a coated, compressed card base. In 1903, the firm produced spring motor disc players.

Storage of Recordings · *See* PRESERVATION AND RESTORATION OF HISTORICAL RECORDINGS.

Stroboscopic Disc · A special record or printed disc used to check the speed of a turntable. Radial lines on the disc appear to be stationary if the turntable is rotating at true speed. Some commercial discs carrying normal programming have also served as stroboscopics, via an edge marking to assist in turntable speed adjustment; W. D. Sternberg used this device on records issued by British Homophone Co. in 1930 (4-in-1, Plaza, and Sterno labels). The British label Great Scott had strobe marks on the edges of 1934 releases. Decca had a similar marking on certain 1938 discs, and DGG had an edge pattern used, even on LPs, into the mid-1960s.

Stroh, John Matthias Augustus, 1828–1914 · German inventor, born in Frankfurt-am-Main. A British Post Office employee, he made a cylinder phonograph for the chief engineer of the General Post Office and demonstrated it to the Royal Institution on February 1, 1878. He then designed various improvements to steady the cylinder movement with counter-weights and a clockwork train. His most renowned invention was the Stroh violin. His son Charles was an industry executive, a director with the Russell Hunting Record Co., Ltd., and a manufacturer of the Stroh violin.

Stroh Violin · The instrument invented by John Matthias Augustus Stroh for use in acoustic recording, and used widely by the industry for about 10 years from 1904. His son Charles was the first manufacturer. It had the strings of a violin, but instead of a sound box, it had a diaphragm and metal trumpet; these changes presented an amplified, if rather artificial, sound to the recording horn. The first commercial record on which a Stroh violin is heard was Victor 2828, Charles d'Almaine performing "Military Serenade" (April 23, 1904) the instrument was identified as a "viol-horn." In *Talking Machine World* for 1909, there were various advertisements by George Evans, 4 Albany St., Regents Park, London, claiming to be the sole maker of the Stroh violin, as successors to Charles Stroh.

Studer, Willi, December 17, 1912–March 1, 1996 · Born in Switzerland and a child prodigy and natural entrepreneur, the 19-year-old Studer founded his first company in 1931, building and marketing radio receivers. Although the designs were very good, the cost/profit ratio involved put him out of business before the company could become firmly established. After passing an important radio engineering exam, Studer began still another technical-business career in 1948, in Zurich, by building still another electronics equipment factory. The first products were specialized oscilloscopes, but he eventually decided to specialize in audio technology, specifically tape recorders. The experience gained from the adaptation of U.S. tape recorders for the European market helped him to design and build such equipment himself, with extremely high reliability and overall performance quality being the goals. In 1960, he began a cooperating enterprise with EMT Wilhelm Franz GmbH, which led to a worldwide expansion of Studer/Revox products. Sticking to the concept of quality over quantity, over the years, Studer built his company, now named Revox, into an organization known for superior tape-recording equipment, including the A36 (1956) and A77 (1967) models. In 1978, Studer was awarded an honorary doctorate in Technical Sciences by the Swiss Federal Institute of Technology in Zurich, and in 1982, the Audio Engineering Society awarded him its highest award, the Gold Metal.—Howard Ferstler

Studer/Revox · Founded by Wili Studer in 1948, in Zurich, Switzerland, the following year the Studer company produced its first professional-level tape recorder, named the Dynavox. By the early 1950s, Studer had settled on a new brand name for his amateur and professional recording products: Revox. By 1986, the company had 2,000 employees in production centers and subsidiaries in 10 countries, with annual sales reaching 220 million Swiss Francs. In 1990, Studer sold his company to the Swiss Motor Columbus Group, and eventually Studer/Revox joined the Harman International group of businesses. Over the years, the organization has earned a well-deserved reputation as a producer of very high quality tape-recording equipment, mixers, and recording consoles, as well as some consumer-oriented recording and electronic hardware. *See also* TAPE DECK.—Howard Ferstler

Stylus · The jewel or metallic element or needle in a cartridge that tracks the record groove; it is attached by a stylus shank to the magnet in the cartridge. The term needle was applied to this element through the 78 era, when steel needles were the norm. There were sapphire needles and diamond needles, as well as fibers and alloys; they were spherical or conical. The microgroove LP record (1948) required a lightweight tracking device, leading to the various kinds of cartridge and their stylus tips. To avoid surface noise from the groove bottom, styli were often truncated.

Stylus types in use at the end of the LP era (late 1980s) were spherical (conical), suitable to early LP records; elliptical, used with later lighter tone arms; hyper-elliptical, with a wider and thinner contact area to improve high-frequency response; and micro-ridge, with the smallest contact area. Diamond styli (1,000 + hours of playing time) were common, with tips almost invisible to the naked eye. Sapphire tips (about 40 hours of playing time) were a second choice; other materials included tungsten carbide, osmium, and various alloys.

The standard dimensions of styli used on LPs were 0.001 inches (0.6 millimeters) radius and 40—50 degrees included angle. With a 90° groove angle, such a tip had an effective radius at the point of contact of 0.0007 inches. Despite close similarity in dimensions, actual standardization of LP styli never occurred. Every manufacturer had slight modifications that made replacement of worn styli a matter of finding specific type numbers in a cross-reference list bearing hundreds of types. [Blacker 1978.]

Subcode · Data encoded on a compact disc with miscellaneous inaudible information (e.g., track numbers, copyright, copy inhibit codes).

Subwoofer · A loudspeaker system, sometimes of rather large size (although there also some rather small models that can work surprisingly well), that is dedicated to reproducing only low-bass signals. A subwoofer can be integrated with an array of smaller satellite speakers, and the result will be large-speaker sound from a small package of speakers that are not visually intrusive. Some subwoofers are able to go deeper and cleaner into the low bass than all but the largest and most expensive full-range systems. *See also* WOOFER; LOUDSPEAKER, 3, 4, 9; ROOM ACOUSTICS; INFINITY LOUDSPEAKERS .—Howard Ferstler

Surface Noise · The unwanted sound heard in playback of 78-rpm discs, and to a lesser extent in playback of LPs, is sometimes caused by mistakes in cutting, mastering, and plating, but especially by abrasives in the shellac compound and by wear in the grooves and playback needle or stylus. Some surface noise can be suppressed as original records are transferred, by means of equalizer and dynamic static filters. *See also* PACKBURN AUDIO NOISE SUPPRESSOR.

Surface Speed · In contrast to turntable rotational speed, this is a measure of the linear velocity of the record surface as it moves beneath the pickup stylus with an LP recording or laser beam with a digital-disc recording. With the LP record, although the angular, rotational velocity remains constant, the linear velocity will obviously decrease as the groove diameter becomes smaller toward the center of the record. This reduction in linear speed can seriously compromise sound quality in the inner-groove area, even if the record/playback system is designed to compensate for the change in linear speed. This factor influenced Thomas Edison to hold to the cylinder record, where surface speed would be constant. Charles Tainter applied for a patent on a device that maintained uniform surface speed on discs in 1887, but he did not follow it with commercial production. Discs issued in the United Kingdom from 1922 to 1924, by the World Record Co., did play at constant linear speed. A record controller device, one that was made available for standard gramophones by Noel Pemberton Billing, achieved this. Modern digital-disc playback systems of all kinds utilize a variable rotational speed to keep the linear speed constant. (British patents no. 195,673 and 204,728). *See also* DISC; SPEEDS; TURNTABLE; CONSTANT ANGULAR VELOCITY DISCS; CONSTANT LINEAR VELOCITY DISCS (CLV).—Rev. by Howard Ferstler

Surround Sound · This concept goes back to well before the quadraphonic recording era, and also before the period when outfits like Sound Concepts, Audio Pulse, Advent, Acoustic Research, Lexicon, and Yamaha were experimenting with or marketing four-channel surround processors of one sort of another for home-audio use. Indeed, on a commercial level it goes back at least as far as Disney's work on the movie *Fantasia*, released in 1940.

Modern (and successful) surround sound in home-listening situations is mainly the result of the home-theater boom that began in the late 1980s and continued through the 1990s and into the new century. Mainstream movies had been produced in matrix-surround form since the advent of Dolby Surround (which offered left, center, and right channels, plus one surround channel, embedded into the left and right channels of a stereo mix), and that technology was easily transferred to videotape copies of movies that were sold or rented to consumers. To take advantage of the technology, more enthusiasts demanded surround decoders and amplifiers for home use, and manufacturers accommodated them by building hardware that would do the job. Dolby Labs also made its Pro Logic technology available to manufacturers, and this greatly enhanced the separation between channels, particularly the center, left, and right, which was one way that modern surround sound is superior to the old four-channel quadraphonic arrangement. The center channel was not only important for dialog reproduction in movies, but with music reproduction it was found that a genuine center channel improved sound-stage realism, particularly when listening from anywhere but the sweet spot.

As the digital audio/video age dawned and home theater became even more popular, outfits like Yamaha, Lexicon, Carver, Pioneer, Sony, Onkyo, Denon, Technics, and quite a few others began to produce very high quality hardware at often very reasonable prices, and that hardware usually included assorted ambiance modes that allowed two-channel compact disc recordings to decently simulate the surround ambiance of genuine concert halls, nightclubs, etc. Thus, it could be said that home theater helped to usher in the era of surround-sound music playback in the home. Home theater also pretty much forced people who normally would not be concerned with proper speaker positioning for musical playback to rethink the placement of their speakers for a proper soundstage effect. In other words, the location of the TV monitor made proper speaker soundstaging more important than ever.

Modern systems have better DSP ambiance simulations than in the past, and the technology that has given us discrete-channel DVD movie surround sound is now giving us multi-channel music sound that eclipses the two-channel stereo sound that has existed in commercial form since the 1950s. Indeed, surround sound, at least if we are talking about state-of-the-art, or even reasonably upscale audio, is the future of home-music sound recording and reproduction. *See also* DOLBY DIGITAL, DTS (Digital Theater Systems), DVD-A (DVD-Audio), SACD (Super Audio Compact Disc), AMBIANCE EXTRACTION, AMBIANCE SYNTHESIS.—Howard Ferstler

SWARF · In the recording process, the material cut or scraped from the surface of a record by the cutting stylus.

Sweet Spot · The listening position out in front of a stereo pair of speakers that puts each of them the same distance from the listener. The result is an enhanced sense of soundstage realism and imaging from two-channel source material. Sweet-spot listening can even be important for multi-channel, surround-sound systems, but it will not be as critical as it

is for two-channel setups. *See also* STEREOPHONIC RECORDING; DOLBY SURROUND SOUND; INTERAURAL CROSSTALK; PHANTOM CENTER IMAGE; PRECEDENCE EFFECT.—Howard Ferstler

Symphonola · A coin-op produced by Seeburg in the mid 1930s. It operated with a single turntable, which moved to play up to 20 different records.

Szymczyk, Bill, February 13, 1943– · Born in Muskegon, Michigan, Szymczyk became a major producer of rock and pop acts during the 1970s. After serving in the Navy in the early 1960s, Szymczyk got a job as an engineer at a small New York studio, where many of the Brill building songwriters cut their demos. He worked as an engineer at New York's Regent Sound from 1965 to 1967, doing his first production work for rock bassist Harvey Brooks in 1967. A year later, he was hired by ABC/Paramount as a house producer. He first produced B. B. King there, and then signed a new Detroit-based rock group, the James Gang (with lead guitarist Joe Walsh). Szymczyk moved to Los Angeles in 1970, and then a year later relocated to Denver, where he went independent. He had success in the early 1970s with the J. Geil Bands and R.E.O. Speedwagon; but he was best known for his production work with the Eagles (being brought to the band by Joe Walsh, who had been hired to toughen up their sound), overseeing most of their 1970s-era hits. In the mid-1970s, he took a job with Criterion Sound in Miami, and then in 1976 built his own studio. He continued to produce through the mid-1980s, overseeing albums by Jefferson Starship, the Who, Santana, and Elvin Bishop, but then took some time off. He returned to production work in the 1990s, although with less visibility and success then he had previously enjoyed.—Carl Benson

T

Tainter, Charles Sumner, August 25, 1854–April 20, 1940 · British instrument maker and inventor. In 1879, he began working with Alexander Graham Bell in a research facility in Washington, D.C., and in 1881, he was invited by Bell to join him and with Chichester Bell in the formation of the Volta Laboratory Association. The purpose of Volta was to carry out acoustical and electrical research. Tainter was probably responsible for the emphasis on developing a talking machine that would improve on Edison's tinfoil phonograph. He applied the principle of engraving into wax as early as 1881, and created a demonstration cylinder that was sealed in the Smithsonian Institution; the record—presenting the voice of Alexander Graham Bell—was apparently played for the first time in public, at the Smithsonian, in 1937; documentation of the event is not positive. Tainter eventually filed on June 27, 1885, a patent application for his method of "recording and reproducing speech and other sounds." His application specified that the recording surface was solid beeswax and paraffin, and that the signal vibrations were inscribed vertically (hill-and-dale); but the word cylinder did not appear. Another patent application, for a machine with a removable wax-coated cardboard cylinder, was filed on December 4, 1885. The instrument he developed came to be called the graphophone, giving its name to the new organization established in 1886 by him and the Bells: Volta Graphophone Co.

Tainter's notebooks show diverse experimentation. He worked on a variable-speed turntable to derive constant surface speed in disc recording on lateral-cut records, and on a wax paper strip medium. On July 7, 1887, he filed for a U.S. patent on a foot-treadle graphophone that turned the cylinder at 200 rpm; it used a wax-coated cardboard cylinder, 6 × 1 5/16 inches. Although the treadle feature (an adaptation of the Howe sewing machine) did not succeed commercially with the graphophone, it was used later in shavers. A coin-op graphophone was developed and patented in time for exhibition at the World's Columbian Exposition, Chicago, 1893; it became the Columbia Graphophone Type AS (1897). Tainter received 25 U.S. patents in the phonograph field.

Take · The name given to the smallest identifiable unit of a recording session. In the early period of recording, before the use of magnetic tape to receive the original impression of the signal, a take necessarily included an entire presentation: a song, instrumental composition or discrete movement of a large composition, literary reading, etc. With modern technology, a take may include a minute portion of a presentation, and many takes of the same portion may be made. The best takes are then edited into a satisfactory whole version of the signal presentation, and used to make the negative master. (*See also* DISC.) Takes that are not used to make masters are called outtakes.

Talking Dolls

This medium was the earliest format for entertainment records. Thomas Edison's U.S. patent no. 423,039 (filed July 2, 1889; granted March 11, 1890) was for a doll with a cylinder record. The Edison talking doll was shown at the Paris Universal Exposition of 1889, and first sold to the public in April 1890, in New York. The doll was not a commercial success, with only about 500 eventually sold, at $10 to $25, and many returned by unsatisfied buyers. Twelve pre-recorded records were available.

Emile Berliner's 1889 doll used a disc record; it was also unsuccessful. Maison Jumeau, established 1842, was the most famous doll maker. The firm produced dolls for a world market, with the most exotic creations emanating from the 1860s through the 1890s, a "golden age" of French doll making. The dolls were called Poupées (lady-types) and Bébés (child-types). A successful line of the Bébés (at 38 francs), offered in 1896, was fitted with a talking mechanism made by Henri Lioret. [Koenigsberg 1990; Marty 1979 shows three Bébés on p. 74.]

Record manufacturers sometimes give identification numbers to takes, possibly as parts of matrix numbers. Outtakes are sometimes preserved, and may be used later to make pressings when it is desired to have complete documentation of a performer's work. *See also* RECORDING PRACTICE.

Talking Book · The name given to the recorded version of a book. Originally, talking books were discs made for blind persons. They appeared in Britain in 1934, made by Decca and EMI for the National Institute for the Blind, using slows speeds, such as 24 rpm. Talking books are circulated in the United States by the Library of Congress through a network of local libraries. Cassette tapes replaced the discs in the 1960s, and a wider audience was identified as cassette players became common in automobiles. By the 1980s, a large repertoire of fiction and nonfiction works was available on cassette. In most cases, long books are abridged on record, but some firms specialize in complete texts. Readings are done by actors who sometimes dramatize fiction material by using different voices for the characters, and many talking books have sound effects or background music, simulating radio dramas. "Bookcassettes" marketed by the Brilliance Corp., do not

have sound effects or music; they use digital speech compression to achieve a quick reading speed, and use four tracks of a stereo cassette to increase the capacity of their monophonic recordings. The firm Books on Tape advertises itself as having the "world's largest selection of audio books."

Talking Machine · The generic term for the phonograph, and later for the gramophone, as used in the trade literature and in company names from the early days of the industry into the 1920s. This designation was sometimes abbreviated to "talker."

Tangential Tone Arm · Also called a linear tracking arm. A type of tone arm that moves straight across a disc record along the disc's radius, instead of in an arc. It is designed to eliminate skating and horizontal tracking error.

Tape · In common audio terminology, a strip of thin plastic, coated with iron oxide or similar substance that may be magnetized to record sounds. (*See also* NON-MAGNETIC TAPE RECORDING.) Through the 1950s, tapes had an acetate base, and tended to become brittle with age and to break easily. More recent tapes have a polyester base, such as Mylar; they do not grow brittle, though their elasticity may be a problem (better tapes are pretensilized to overcome this).

Dupont improved upon the widely used iron oxide coating in the late 1960s with the development of chromium dioxide coatings. Better response at high recording levels was achieved in 1978 as 3M introduced pure metal particle (non-oxide iron) tape. For nomenclature of current tape types, *see also* CASSETTE.

Tape thickness is 1.5 or 1.0 mils (38 or 25.4 micrometers) for the open-reel variety and 0.47 or 0.31 mils for cassette type. *See also* MAGNETIC RECORDING; PRESERVATION.

Tape Composition · In electronic music, the composing of music using sounds recorded on segments of magnetic tape. Until the availability of the magnetic tape recorder following World War II, electronic music had only been a live performance medium. The influence of the tape recorder on the very nature and definition of "music" was profound. On one hand, it led to the creation of a new kind of music that existed *only* as a recording. On the other, it led to an obsessive quest for new and different electronic music technology and the development of the modern music synthesizer.

The tape recorder transformed the field of electronic music overnight by making it a composer's medium. They sought other sounds, other structures, and other tonalities and worked directly with the raw materials of sound to find them. In the heyday of classic electronic music, nearly every piece of music and every audio effect were somehow dependent on the skills needed to record and edit magnetic tape. *Musique concrète*—the name given to the music created by the first electronic music studio in Paris—was a recording medium, first using acetate discs and then magnetic tape.

The following is a compendium of the classic sound-editing techniques produced using tape recorders and tape editing. Most of these ideas are still relevant even when transcribed to the digital-editing medium.

Tape Splicing: The cutting and splicing of magnetic tape is, in effect, no different from moving sound around in time and space. A given sound that occurred at one time can be moved to another. Every sound has a given length. The mechanics of magnetic tape splicing are simple. Tape is provided on open reels, mounted on a tape recorder, and manually moved across the playback head to locate a precise sound on the tape. The composer's only other tools are a ruler to "measure" time in inches or centimeters of tape, a razor blade, and a splicing block. Tape is then cut into segments and spliced to other pieces of tape to form a composition. Splicing could be used in a limited way to change the attack and decay patterns of recorded sounds.

Degeneration of a Recorded Signal: A sound will decay over time when it is played back, re-recorded, and played back again.

Tape Echo, Delay, and Looping: The tape recorder makes possible several basic techniques for repeating sounds that have been popular since the earliest experiments

---

Talk-o-Photo (Label)

A single-sided six-inch record issued by the Talking Photo Corp. of New York from 1919 to 1920. The discs featured photographs of the recording artists (in the known issues, all were movie stars) on one side and performances by them on the other. Emerson cut the masters. Items listed by Blacker appear to be spoken material (e.g., "How to Become a Star" by David Powell; "My Real Self," by Mae Murray; and "Happiness" by Gloria Swanson). There were 91 records in the series, but only 16 have been identified and just 3 have been seen and discussed in the literature.

with tape composition. The idea of taking a piece of magnetic audio tape, splicing it end-to-end to form a loop, and then playing it back on a tape recorder so it constantly repeated itself is as old as the field of recorded electronic music and continues to be popular with digital sampling techniques. Unlike echo, during which each repetition of the trigger sound becomes weaker until it diminishes entirely, the sound repeated by a tape loop does not weaken with each repeat.

Echo: The repetition of a single sound that gradually decays in amplitude and clarity with each successive repeat. This was first achieved using tape recorders equipped with three "heads"—the erase, recording, and playback elements across which the reel of tape passed to record, play, and delete sounds. To create echo with a tape recorder, the playback output signal of the machine is fed back into the input, or record head, of the same machine. When this connection is made and the tape recorder is simultaneously recording and playing back, the sound being played is immediately re-recorded by the record head. The distance that the tape must travel from the record head to the playback head and the tape speed determine the length of the delay. Continuing in this manner without interruption creates the echo effect. The signal degrades slightly with each successive playback. The strength or persistence of the echo—how many repeats you hear—is determined by the amplitude of the playback signal being fed back into the recorder.

Echo and reverberation should not be confused. Echo is the periodic repetition of the same sound signal whereas reverberation is the modulation of single sound signal to produce weaker ghost frequencies, or depth. Reverberation is used, for example, to replicate the ambience of a large room or space.

Tape delay: Combines the recording and re-recording of a sound using a tape loop or combination of tape recorders. The most interesting approach used two or more widely spaced tape recorders through which a single length of magnetic tape was threaded. A sound was recorded on the first machine and played back on the second, creating a long delay between repeats to form a kind of extended echo effect. If the sounds being repeated were also fed back to the recording head of the first machine, a diminishing effect was created that accumulated on the tape as layers of repeating sounds of various amplitudes.

Tape Reversal—Playing Sounds Backward: The idea of playing recorded sounds in reverse had crude beginnings with the turntablism of primordial *musique concrète*. With tape composition, the effect came into its own as an essential ingredient of the electronic music repertoire. Tape reverse is created by literally snipping out a length of recorded tape and splicing it back into the reel backward or, on a tape recorder that only recorded on one side of the tape, by turning the tape over and running it backward past the playback head.—Thom Holmes

Tape Deck · The mechanical element of a tape recorder, nearly always the open-reel design, instead of a cassette version, including its motors, reels, linkages, recording head, erase head, and playback head, but not including the electronic components and electric circuits. It is also known as a tape transport. A deck must be connected to an amplifier to drive loudspeakers. The use of separate tape decks arose in the early high fidelity period (1950s), when users began to demand distinct components in the audio system.

A conventional grading of tape decks assigns them to one of three categories: professional, semi-professional/audiophile, and consumer. Libraries often use good consumer-grade decks, whereas sound archives should use only professional or semiprofessional grade. Recording engineers should always opt for professional versions. There is no significant difference in performance between the two better grades, but the professional grade tends to be more rugged and reliable, and probably also offers more flexibility. Among the makers of professional-grade tape decks marketed in America are Ampex, 3M, Scully, Crown, Nagra, and Studer. Widely used semiprofessional decks come from Revox, Tandberg, Sony, and TEAC. Sony and TEAC are also major producers of consumer-grade decks.

Over the years, various firms offered refinements in the basic mechanism. Ampex developed an automatic threader for open-reel tapes. Bell and Howell marketed a "tape inhaler" that pulled the tape to the take-up reel with a vacuum. Sony marketed at one time a tape changer for four open-reel tapes, with a total playing time of 60 hours.

Tape Guides · In a tape deck, the rollers or posts that keep the tape in proper position as it moves across the heads.

Tape Leader · The section of a tape that precedes the part with the program material. It may be magnetic, carrying technical signals and production information. Alternatively, it may be a plain paper or plastic attachment to the magnetized tape, intended merely to aid in the affixing of the tape end to the take-up reel, and to protect the recorded portion in storage.

Tape Pack · The name given to the fully wound tape on its reel, or to the portion of tape that is wound on the reel.

Tape Recorder · An audio recording device using magnetic tape as the record-

---

Outline of the Historical Development of the Tape Recorder

1857, France—Irish-born E. Léon Scott invented the "phonautograph," a device capable of inscribing a visual record of sound being directed into a diaphragm. The device used a stylus to record sound on a disc of smoked paper. The phonautograph had one serious problem: although it could indeed inscribe representations of sound onto paper, it could not reproduce the sound in any way. Twenty years later, in 1877, French physicist Charles Cros conceived of a way to reverse Scott's process so that one might playback the recorded sound. Cros called this device the paleophone but never succeeded in building a working model.

1876, United States—Edison successfully reproduced recorded sound for the first time. In 1877, he patented his first "talking machine." With this device, a recording of sound was made on a piece of tinfoil wrapped around a rotating brass drum. The recorder consisted of a membrane of parchment stretched over the end of a short brass cylinder. The membrane had attached to it a spring-mounted chisel needle that would vibrate as incoming sound caused the membrane to vibrate. The action of the needle on the piece of revolving tinfoil inscribed a mark that corresponded to the sound. The recording could be reproduced by rotating the cylinder again but with the needle resting in the existing cut groove. Edison called this device the "phonograph." Edison also tried wax cylinders as a recording medium. He envisioned the phonograph being used for such practical applications as dictation.

1878, United States—Oberlin Smith, an American engineer, filed a patent caveat, but not a formal patent, for a steel wire recorder. He conceived of it as a way to record telephone conversations. Ten years later, after having never pursued the idea further, he published his theory about magnetic recording in the magazine *Electrical World*.

1887, United States—Emile Berliner introduced disc recording, solving some of the recording and reproducing problems associated with the cylinder recorder of Edison. His first discs consisted of glass that was coated with a thick fluid of ink or paint. When a turntable rotated the disc, a stylus cut into it a spiral groove that corresponded to the sound being picked up by a diaphragm. Berliner called his first machine the "gramophone" and imagined that it could be used to supply voices for dolls or to reproduce music.

(continued)

Outline of the Historical Development of the Tape Recorder (continued)

1896, United States—Windup mechanical turntables were introduced to play disc recordings. The disc gramophone soon gained acceptance. Berliner began to use recording discs from which copies, or imprints, of master recordings could be printed. Gramophone records made available at this time were usually made of thick, brittle shellac, operated at 78 rpm, and had recording on only one side.

1898, Denmark—Valdemar Poulsen of Copenhagen built the first magnetic recorder. It was called the telegraphone and recorded crosswise (vertically) on a steel piano wire as it was rotated between the poles of an electromagnet. Unlike modern tape recorders, which use iron-oxide-coated tape as a medium, the recording medium was an uncoated metal wire. Calling his device an "apparatus for electromagnetically receiving, recording, reproducing, and distributing articulate speech," Poulsen took the 1900 Paris Exposition by storm and won the Grand Prix for scientific invention. He envisioned the device as an office dictation machine. Poulsen had two versions of the telegraphone. The most widely known was the one that used wire as the recording medium. Because the twisting of the wire caused distortion in the sound, he next tried to use steel tape as a medium. The American Telegraphone Company was formed around 1900 to produce and sell Poulsen's wire model, which had two spools to transport the wire, a 100-volt motor and manual rewind. It could record for 30 minutes on a wire moving at 7 feet per second. The recorded sound was listened to using earphones because no practical electrical means (e.g., the vacuum tube) had yet been developed for amplifying sound. The machine was a marketing failure, largely because of the inferior quality of its sound when compared with the gramophone. ATC ceased operation in 1909. A Dutch firm also licensed to sell the device folded in 1916. Other wire recorders, primarily those made by Air King in Brooklyn, New York, appeared during the 1940s, but were soon superseded by magnetic tape recorders.

1905, United States—By this time, various forms of sound boxes—loudspeakers—had been developed for use with the gramophone. These ranged from simple diaphragms connected to large horns, to delicately balanced "tone arms" with spring-mounted styli, mica diaphragms, and horns that could be either internally or externally mounted.

1906, United States—Lee De Forest invented the vacuum tube. Sometimes called the thermionic valve, audion, or triode tube, the vacuum tube was capable of controlling electrical current with precision. A vacuum tube could be used for the generation, modulation, amplification, and detection of current and was thus useful for everything from amplifying the sound of gramophones to detecting radio waves and generating audio signals in tube oscillators.

1912, United States—In an experiment that went largely unnoticed, Lee De Forest succeeded in amplifying the magnetically recorded sound of a Poulsen Telegraphone by using his triode vacuum tube.

1916, United States—E. C. Wente of Western Electric invented the condenser microphone. It was capable of making high-quality, distortionless sound recordings in the frequency ranges associated with speech and orchestral instruments, becoming the industry standard for radio broadcasting and the production of gramophone records.

1917, United States—G. A. Campbell built an early frequency filter.

1919, United States—A. G. Webster published his paper "Acoustical Impedance and Theory of Horns and Phonograph," which alluded to the possibilities of applying electrical theory to the design of microphones and audio reproducing systems.

Early 1920s, Germany—Kurt Stille, in yet another effort to salvage the telegraphone, organized the Telegraphie-Patent Syndikat Company to sell licenses to produce magnetic recorders in Europe. Several firms took part, a number of them using the improved version of the telegraphone that used steel tape instead of wire. The device was considered for use in the production of sound for movies, and some experimental films using synchronized sound were actually produced in England.

1924, United States—J. P. Maxfield and H. C. Harrison of AT&T successfully built an electrically operated recording and reproducing system using recently developed microphones and vacuum-tube amplifiers. Their system extended the frequency range of prior gramophone recording systems by more than an octave and with much improved fidelity.

1925, United States—The Maxfield-Harrison recording system was adopted by the recording industry under such brand names as "Orthophonic" (Victor).

Outline of the Historical Development of the Tape Recorder (continued)

Mid-1920s, United States—The AC bias technique for recording sounds was first tried by W. L. Carlson and G. W. Carpenter of the U.S. Navy. They used it to send recorded telegraph messages. Until that time, all attempts at recording had used DC methods. The AC technique eliminated the background noise found in earlier DC recordings and is still the principal method used today.

1929, United States—Special oversized disc recordings were introduced for broadcast use. Called "transcriptions," these ran at 33 1/3 rpm and could carry a fifteen-minute program on one side of a 16-inch platter. These were the first long-playing records but required special playback equipment and were not available to the public.

1930–1931, United States—Bell Telephone Laboratories undertook a research project in magnetic recording under the guidance of engineer Clarence N. Hickman. He immediately suggested that they use steel tape instead of wire as the recording medium because the greater surface area for recording the magnetic signal did not require high speeds to maintain fidelity. This meant that they could slow the speed of the recorder down from the rate of seven feet per second required for a wire recorder to about nine inches per second. Hickman conceived several applications including a telephone answering machine, a dictation device, and a portable reel-to-reel tape recorder, but none were manufactured.

1932–1935, Germany—Due to Kurt Stille's licensing activity, many varieties of wire and steel-band recorders were being sold in Germany. The Echophone Company produced a cartridge-loaded unit that simplified operation of the machine. ITT eventually acquired this company, but resold it to the German firm of C. Lorenz Company, which redesigned the recorder and introduced it as the Textophone in 1933. The Nazi party and secret police began to acquire large numbers of such magnetic recording devices.

AEG introduced the Magnetophone in 1935 at the German Annual Radio Exposition in Berlin. This unit employed a coated paper tape instead of steel bands or wire. The supplies themselves cost a mere 15 cents per minute of recording time in comparison to the more than $1 cost of using steel tape. This fact, no doubt, contributed to the success of the device at the exposition.

1935, United States—Bell Laboratories, one of the few American firms interested in magnetic recorders, designed the mirrorphone. This recorder employed steel tape and was used to broadcast weather reports over the phone lines.

1937, United States—The Brush Development Company introduced the soundmirror, one of the first commercially available magnetic recorders in the United States. This steel tape unit could record only one minute of sound. Brush supplied the armed forces with many of these during World War II.

1938, Germany— German engineer Fritz Pfleumer began experimenting with a number of new recording mediums in an attempt to improve on the basic design of magnetic recorders. He tried paper and plastic tapes coated with iron oxide particles as an alternative to wires and steel tapes. The Allgemeine Elektrizitäts Gesellschaft (AEG) became interested in Pfleumer's work and bought all the rights to it. Such early recording tapes used large iron particles as coatings and had the feel of sandpaper. When run through a recorder, the earliest versions immediately clouded the air with residue and dust.

1940–1945, The World War II Years—While American firms including General Electric (GE) continued to improve the design of wire recorders for military use, the Germans shifted their attention to tape units. The AEG magnetophone was further developed, and when the victorious Allies moved into Germany in 1945, they were stunned to find the German tape units to be far superior to wire recorders. By 1945, the magnetophone had adapted AC bias recordings and coated paper tape, and possessed a surprising frequency response of 10,000 cycles, which was much higher than earlier wire and steel tape units. These German recorders were capable of accurately recording midrange frequencies. The Americans quickly adapted the tape medium. Following the war, the U.S. alien-property custodian held all patents on the AEG magnetophone and licensed any American company that desired to build it. The only three small companies to earnestly take on the magnetic tape project were Magnecord, Rangertone, and the Ampex Electric Company. The first technical problem that needed to be solved was to replace the low-grade coated paper tape used by the Germans with something more durable and of higher quality.

1947, United States—The Minnesota Mining and Manufacturing Company (3M), introduces the first successful plastic-based recording tape with a magnetic oxide coating. It quickly became an industry standard.

(continued)

Outline of the Historical Development of the Tape Recorder (continued)

1948, United States— Ampex Corporation manufactured its first professional tape recorder, the model 200.

1949–1950, United States—Magnecord demonstrated the first prototype two-channel stereo tape recorders.

1950, United States—A. H. Frisch patented a method for recording sound directly onto magnetic tape without the use of a tape recorder. Using a process called magnetic stenciling, hand-made metal stencils made from paperclips and wire were placed directly on top of the magnetic tape itself. A magnet was passed over this assemblage to imprint a signal pattern onto the tape. The result was played using a tape recorder. Frisch fully developed magnetic stencils, creating electronic music directly onto tape, controlling pitch, and modifying amplitude and envelope characteristics using several direct techniques.

1951, France—By this year, Pierre Schaeffer and Jacques Poullin of the *Groupe de Recherches Musicales* (GRM) had completed three special-purpose tape machine designs to assist them in composing electronic music for magnetic tape. These included the morphophone, a tape machine with 10 heads for the playback of loops and the creation of echo effects; the Tolana Phonogène, a keyboard-operated version of the Morphophone with 24 preset speeds that could be triggered by the keyboard; and the Sareg Phonogène, a variable speed version of the Tolana Phonogène tape loop machine.

1963, Netherlands—Philips introduced the compact cassette tape format.

1965, United States—Ford and Mercury introduced the 8-track tape cartridge as a stereo music system option in its luxury cars. It quickly becomes the most widely used commercial tape format. The increasing popularity of the Philips cassette eventually drew interest away from the 8-track format, which was discontinued in 1980.

1978, Japan—Sony introduced the first digital audio recording systems for professional studios.

1980, Japan—The Philips/Sony audio compact disc format was introduced.

1986, Japan—Philips/Sony introduced the first digital audio tape (DAT) recorder.

1992, Japan—Philips and Matsushita introduced the digital compact cassette (DCC) recorder/player.— Thom Holmes

ing medium. The tape recorder was an outgrowth of earlier sound recording efforts using the technologies of cylinder and disc recording, developed by Thomas Edison and Emile Berliner. The first magnetic sound recorder was actually invented in 1898 by the Danish inventor Valdemar Poulsen, but further technical development of a device that was practical for commercial distribution did not occur until the late 1940s.

Tape Speed · The rate of tape motion, usually stated in inches per second (IPS), of a magnetic tape as it passes the recording or playback head of a tape recorder or tape deck. In the United States, professional tape speeds have been 30 inches per second (IPS) and 15 IPS. Consumer recording has been at 7 1/2 IPS or 3 3/4 IPS, although 1 7/8 IPS and the higher speeds are sometimes available. In the Philips audiocassette, the tape travels at 1 7/8 IPS. Microcassette recorders use a speed of 15/16 IPS.

Tape Transport · *See* TAPE DECK.

Tate, Alfred O., 1863–April 6, 1945 · An associate of Thomas Edison, born in Petersborough, Ontario, Tate was Edison's personal representative at the convention of the National Phonograph Association in 1893. Tate served as secretary of the Edison Phonograph Works and the Edison Manufacturing Co. In 1887, he became Edison's private secretary. He emerged as a dissident within the Edison circle, and provided his employer with crucial misinformation in the 1888 controversy involving Ezra Gilliland; as a result, he came between Edison and his trusted colleague Charles Batchelor. Tate died in Brooklyn, New York. [Welch 1972.]

Tefifon · A phonographic device that recorded sound on an endless band of 35-millimeter film—up to 100 feet long— inscribing lateral grooves on the film with a stylus. The film was housed in a cartridge, and played back at 7 1/2 inches per second with a sapphire needle and a crystal pickup. Tefifon was marketed in Germany from about 1950, though the development of it is traced to the 1920s; the main work was carried out by Karl Daniel (1905–1979) of Cologne, who organized a company to handle it: Tefi-Apparatebau. Because of its long playing time—an hour for a small cartridge, up to four hours for larger cartridges—the device appeared to have a promising future, even in competition with the new LP disc. A catalog was issued in 1954 with 264 prerecorded tapes listed, mostly light music. Inability of the firm to secure the services of major artists, who were under contract to the record labels, prevented the Tefifon from achieving long prosperity, and it passed from the scene around 1960.

Telegraphone · The magnetic wire recorder developed by Valdemar Poulsen around 1898. It used steel piano wire of 0.01-inch diameter, moving past the recording head at 84 inches (213 centimeters) per second. Poulsen's concept included the possibility of magnetic recording on coated paper strips and even discs. The telegraphone was patented in the United States (1900) and in a dozen other countries. It was demonstrated at the Paris Exposition of 1900, and used to record the voice of Emperor Franz Joseph I in Vienna (the recording still exists in the Danish Technical Museum, Hellerup). King Edward VII recorded words of appreciation for the invention, and the wire was given to Queen Alexandra, but its whereabouts are unknown.

Despite its early fame, the telegraphone proved unable to compete with the cylinder phonograph because its playback sound was very faint (there were then no adequate means of amplification), its playing time per spool of wire was very brief because of the high speeds required, and the wire tended to tangle in transport to its take-up reel. Later Poulsen and Oscar Pedersen worked out a longer playing wire machine that would run 20 minutes, and some of them were used by the British Post Office and the War Office during World War I, and by the U.S. Navy. Nevertheless, the telegraphone was a commercial failure, and little was heard about it after 1910. *See also* MAGNETIC RECORDING.

Theremin · Patented in 1928 by Leo Theremin, and commercially licensed by RCA that same year, the theremin uses an electronic oscillator as a stable reference tone of a very high frequency. It has another electronic oscillator, initially in tune with the reference, which has a variable frequency controlled by the proximity of the hand to a capacitive sensing element, usually an antenna of some sort. The difference between the two frequencies is a pitch in the audible range that is detected and amplified. Move your hand near and away from the sensing element and get musical pitches. The theremin is perhaps the first electronic musical instrument, and is unique in that it is the first musical instrument of any kind that can be played without being touched. It has been used for decades in movie and television soundtracks and rock bands, and has also been played as a serious solo instrument.—Howard Ferstler

Thiele, Albert Neville, December 4, 1920– · One of the most important modern researchers in audio and video system theory and design, including the mathematical profiling of all modern loudspeaker parameters, Thiele was born in Brisbane, Queensland, Australia. He was educated at Milton State School, Brisbane Grammar School, and the Universities of Queensland and Sydney. Interested in the reproduction and transmission of sound as a young man, he decided to study the topic formally and graduated with a bachelor's degree in mechanical and electrical engineering in 1952.

That same year, he joined EMI (Australia) Ltd., and was employed as a design engineer on special projects, including telemetry. After spending several months studying video systems in England, Scandinavia, and the United States, he returned to Australia and led the design team that developed EMI's earliest Australian television receivers. In 1962, he joined the Australian Broadcasting Commission as a senior engineer, designing and assessing equipment and systems for sound and television broadcasting. In 1978, he was appointed assistant director Engineering NSW (TV), responsible for engineering of the ABC's Gore Hill television studios in Sydney. In 1980, he was appointed director, engineering development and new systems applications, where he was responsible for the ABC's engineering research and development and served in this position until his retirement from Gore Hill at the end of 1985.

In 1991, Thiele was appointed Honorary Visiting Fellow in the University of New South Wales, and since 1994 has been Honorary Professional Associate at the University of Sydney, where he teaches loudspeaker design in its graduate audio program. He continues to be a consulting engineer in the fields of audio, radio, television, and electronic filter design.

Thiele has published more than seventy papers on electroacoustics, network theory, testing methods, and sound and vision broadcasting in *Electronic Engineering* (U.K.), *Proc IREE* (Australia), the *Journal of the Audio Engineering Society* (U.S.), and other journals. Some of his papers, notably on loudspeaker design, television testing, and coaxial-cable equalization, have become accepted internationally as references on these topics, including origination of the Thiele-Small parameters for measuring and designing loudspeakers, and the total difference-frequency distor-

tion measurement of audio transmission and recording.

Thiele has lectured extensively throughout the United States, both at the university level, at Audio Engineering Society, IEE, and Institute of Electrical and Electronics Engineers conventions, and at numerous AES meetings, and in 1994, he was awarded the AES Silver Medal for pioneering work in loudspeaker simulation. In addition to being a Fellow of the AES, and vice president of the International Region from 1991 until 1993, and again in 2001, he is a Member of the Society of Motion Picture and Television Engineers and a Fellow of the Institution of Engineers Australia. He was President of the Institution of Radio and Electronics Engineers Australia from 1986 to 1988, and has been involved internationally in committees of the International Electrotechnical Commission (IEC) and of the Audio Engineering Society, concerned with loudspeaker design and digital audio. *See also* BASS REFLEX SYSTEM; LOUDSPEAKER.—Howard Ferstler

Thiele/Small Parameters · *See* LOUDSPEAKER; THIELE, ALBERT NEVILLE; SMALL, RICHARD.

331/3-RPM Discs · *See* LONG-PLAYING (LP) RECORD.

Thuras, Albert L. · *See* LOUDSPEAKER.

3M · *See* MINNESOTA MINING AND MANUFACTURING COMPANY (3M).

THX · A Lucasfilm Corporation performance certification program for A/V hardware and software. Although the program began with movie theaters (the first film shown in a THX-certified theater was *Return of the Jedi*), it later spread to home-theater equipment and even discs and tapes. THX certification involves quality-control and compatibility standards for hardware and software, but it also involves special emendations to those standards for supposedly enhanced performance, particularly if every component in a home A/V system (players, speakers, processors, amplifiers, and even wires) is so certified. *See also* MOTION PICTURE SOUND RECORDING; DOLBY SURROUND SOUND; SURROUND SOUND.— Howard Ferstler

TIM · *See* TRANSIENT INTERMODULATION DISTORTION.

Timbre · The tone color or tone quality of a musical sound. Timbre varies with different patterns of harmonics generated as a tone is produced; it is the principal basis for the audible differences among musical instruments when they play the same pitches. Because many of the harmonics that give specific instruments their identifiable tone color are in the upper range of the audio spectrum, early acoustic recordings (unable to capture that portion of the range) failed to give recognizable representations of numerous instruments, the piano among them. Although today's studio recording apparatus is capable of dealing with all timbre problems, some playback equipment may be so poor (e.g., cheap portable cassette players) as to recall the performance limitations of the acoustic era.

Tinfoil Phonograph · The first cylinder phonograph of Thomas A. Edison, constructed according to his design by John Kruesi and Charles Batchelor between December 4–6, 1877. Edison's basic sketch was completed on November 29, 1877. "Mary Had a Little Lamb" was the first phrase successfully repeated by the tinfoil phonograph. Edison filed a patent application for the device on December 24, 1877, and received U.S. patent no. 200,521 on February 19, 1878. *See also* CYLINDER.

Tone Arm · Often written as one word: tonearm. The usually pivoted device in an analog-disc record player that holds the cartridge and playback stylus. The stylus tip is propelled across the record surface by the groove wall, and the tone arm moves to accommodate the traverse. In early acoustic systems, the hollow tone arm carried the needle/diaphragm vibrations to the horn. In electrical systems, the tone arm includes wires that conduct transmits the electrical signals generated by the stylus/cartridge combination to the preamplifier and after "preamplification," to the amplifier. In upscale systems, with upscale cartridge/stylus combinations the normally the downward stylus tracking force is usually between one and two grams, allowing proper tracking without bringing damaging pressures to bear on the grooves.

The position of the tone arm should ensure that it locates the stylus on a tangent to the record groove. The stylus assembly should always be at a right angle to the groove being tracked. This kind of perfection over the full disc surface is not possible with pivoted arms because the arm ascribes an arc as the stylus traverses the disc surface. The technical compromise has been to use a bent tone arm: one that keeps the stylus reasonably close to tangent all the way across the disc. Longer arms also help to minimize the problem, but the downside is increased arm mass, which can affect dynamic tracking pressure with even moderately warped recordings. Radial- or linear-tracking arms, which move straight across the disc on a low-friction carriage, have no problems with tangent error. The vertical tracking angle of the stylus has traditionally been about 15°, and good tone arms allow one to adjust the cartridge body for this kind of angle.

A tone arm may be an integral part of the turntable or sold as a separate item that is custom installed on a blank turntable. Separate tone arms can give superior performance but are expensive and may be relatively difficult to install. If not installed properly, the arm may perform worse than integral arms that have been factory installed. The arm must also be free of audible resonances that lead to sympathetic vibrations, and there must be synergy between the arm mass, cartridge mass, and stylus behavior for such vibrations to not be a problem.

The earliest phonograph with a distinct tone arm, as opposed to a stylus/diaphragm attached directly to the horn, was the Echophone invented in 1895. Eldridge Johnson made a key improvement by inventing the tapered tone arm (U.S. patent no. 814,786; filed February 12, 1903; granted March 13, 1906), allowing "the sound waves to advance with a regular, steady, and natural increase in their wave fronts in a manner somewhat similar to ordinary musical instruments." The tapered-arm patent was held by Victor, which used it in constant litigation against imitators. The arm was first used on the Victor IV of April 1903. February 1905 advertising from Zonophone announced its "Gibson Patent Tapering Sound Arm."

Major advances in tone arm design followed the research of Percy Wilson in the early 1920s; he attacked the problem of tracking error through mathematical analysis, devising an "overlap and offset" method for achieving the correct tracking angle and overhang. E. G. Lîfgren, H. G. Baerwald, B. B. Bauer, J. D. Seagrave, and J. K. Stevenson wrote significant papers on the same problem of tracking distortion in the 1938–1966 period. Frederick Hunt, although writing primarily on record wear, contributed important findings on tracking force in a 1962 paper. Skating force was effectively addressed by having enough vertical pressure to insure that the stylus sat firmly anchored in the groove, although other solutions followed once it was seen that low tracking pressures greatly reduced record wear.

Garrard introduced articulated tone arms in record changers, to give near-zero lateral tracking angle error, although the downside of this design was increased lateral friction and arm mass. The previously noted radial tone arm, which rides on a straight rail instead of pivoting in an arc from its base at the corner of the turntable, was made commercially viable in the early 1980s, although it had appeared some time before then. It combined low arm mass, straight-line tracking, zero tracking error, and zero skating force. In practice, however, it was not judged audibly superior to the finest pivoting arms. In addition, it was complex and expensive, and the typical short arm length magnified problems with warp wow.

Other features in the latest-generation tone arms included cueing mechanisms, height adjustments, vertical tracking angle adjustments, anti-skating compensation, and damping mechanisms. The overall trend in later designs involved toward lower mass, which allowed for still lower tracking pressures. A problem not fully dealt with at the end of the LP era was the electrostatic attraction of the tone arm by the records in the stack of a record changer, and the fact that the vertical tracking angle would change as the stack piled up. *See also* CARTRIDGE (II).

Tone Control · A knob on an audio or audio/video receiver or preamplifier that adjusts the relative balance of treble, midrange, or bass. Most preamp control sections have separate bass and treble tone controls, and some include a midrange control. In many cases, each channel will have its own set, and some preamplifier units will have switches that allow one to configure different roll-off slopes for each of the tone controls. Some also include a spectral-tilt control that slightly rotates the entire audible spectrum around a specific frequency in the midrange. A tone control can be used to adjust for minor frequency imbalances in a recording (not unusual with older releases), correct for room-acoustics problems, or compensate for loudspeaker deficiencies. *See also* EQUALIZATION (EQ); CONTROLS.

Tone Tests · A puzzling phenomenon of recording history, consisting of recitals sponsored by the Thomas A. Edison Co. to illustrate the quality of Edison Diamond Discs. In those recitals, which were held from 1915 to 1925, singers or instrumentalists would perform a program in partnership with Diamond Disc recordings and would from time to time cease their live performance, allowing the disc to continue the music. A darkened stage permitted the performer to slip away, and the audience would not have been aware of that departure until the lights went back on. The point was to demonstrate that the audience would be unable to distinguish between the live performance and the recorded version. Difficult as it is for those of a later generation to believe that such suspension of disbelief might have occurred on the wide scale that it apparently did, all contemporary reports testify that the illusion was remarkable.

Although special pressings were made of the Diamond Discs used in the tone tests, to minimize the surface noise that plagued regular issues until about 1924, there was no way to improve upon the limited audio frequency range of the acoustic process: about 1,000 to 2,000 or 3,000 Hz.

The earliest test to be reported in the press was held in February 1915 in New York. Participants were Christine Miller, Elizabeth Spencer, Donald Chalmers, and John Young. It was organized by a man named Hallowell, who was succeeded by Verdi E. B. Fuller, a superintendent for Thomas A. Edison, Inc. A test was held for a dealers' group in August 1915, followed by a series of national tests. Alice Verlet sang a tone test recital in Orchestra Hall, Chicago; as reported in *Talking Machine World* of December 15, 1915, there was no claim that the audience was unable to distinguish between voice and machine. Nevertheless, an advertisement in *Talking Machine World* on January 15, 1916, stated that observers found it "almost impossible" to tell the difference. By May 15, 1916, the Edison advertisements were saying that audiences found it "impossible" to make the distinction.

Newspaper critics offered glowing praise, in statements that were quoted in Edison promotional material. Among the quotations given in a 1919 publication were: "Impossible to distinguish between the singer's living voice and its re-creation by the musical instrument . . ." (Boston *Herald*); "No one in the audience . . . could tell which was the real and which the reproduced" (Brooklyn *Daily Eagle*); "A convincing demonstration of the power of a man to produce tone from an instrument so perfectly as to defy detection when compared side by side with the tone of the original producing artists" (*Musical America*).

Artists who engaged in tone tests included Anna Case, Thomas Chalmers, Arthur Collins, Byron G. Harlan, Frieda Hempel, Mario Laurenti, Margarete Matzenauer, Arthur Middleton, Marie Rappold, Elizabeth Spencer, Maggie Teyte, Jacques Urlus, Alice Verlet, and Giovanni Zenatello. It was during a tone test that Arthur Collins fell into a trap door on the darkened stage, sustaining injuries that affected his career.

Albany, New York, was the site of the largest tone test audience, as 6,000 teachers heard Laurenti sing in the State Armory; they were reportedly unable to detect any difference between the disc and the person. More than 4,000 tests were held by the end of 1920. Overseas tests were reported from Liverpool (England) in 1923, and Melbourne (Australia) in 1924. Mexico City was a site in 1923. The final notice of one of these events appeared in the *Talking Machine World* of August 15, 1925.

One of the tone test singers may have offered a partial solution to the puzzle of the illusion created by the tone tests, in saying that the performers endeavored to imitate the records. This possibility was explicitly denied in Edison promotional material. Surely there was at least an imitation of volume. A remarkable comment by Albert Spalding is more directed toward the persuasiveness of the actual recordings: He observed that nobody could have distinguished between the live artist and the record, but that on modern records (he was speaking in 1953) anybody could. Frow suggests that the illusion was accomplished because it "the world was a simpler place, people were simpler too."

On occasion, Brunswick and other labels conducted demonstrations of their products in live/recorded recitals, but it is not reported that they carried out the dramatic lights-out routine of the Edison tests.

Toole, Floyd, June 19, 1938–. A major researcher in audio systems and design, Toole was born in Moncton, New Brunswick, Canada, and studied electrical engineering at the University of New Brunswick, receiving a B.Sc. in 1961. He then attended the Imperial College of Science and Technology, University of London, where he received a Ph.D., also in electrical engineering, in 1965. Upon graduation, he joined the National Research Council, in Ottawa, Canada, in the Acoustics and Signal Processing Group. There, he expanded his interests into the complicated interactions of room acoustics and loudspeakers, particularly as they related to the psychoacoustic relationship between what listeners hear and the technical measurements that are used in the design and evaluation of audio products.

The research resulted in improved methods for subjective evaluations and technical measurements. For a paper on this subject, he received the Audio Engineering Society (AES) Publications Award in 1988. Later work focused on one of the fundamental problems in audio, the perception and measurement of resonances, for which (with Sean Olive) he received the 1990 AES Publications Award.

In 1991, he joined Harman International Industries, Inc. in Northridge, California, where he is Corporate Vice President of Acoustical Engineering. In 1998, he was appointed to the additional position of Senior Vice President of Acoustical Engineering for the Harman Consumer Group.

Dr. Toole has published several papers in the *Journal of the AES* and the *Journal of the Acoustical Society of America* (ASA), numerous AES preprints, chapters in two audio engineering handbooks, the entry on Sound-Reproducing Systems for the ninth edition of the *McGraw-Hill Encyclopedia of Science and Technology*, and dozens of articles in consumer audio publications. He is a Fellow of the AES, a member of the ASA, a Past President of the AES, and in 1997, he was awarded the AES Silver Medal Award, presented in recognition of outstanding developments in the subjective and objective evaluation of audio devices.—Howard Ferstler

Toy Records · Small discs (usually five to seven inches in diameter) intended for children, often sold with small record players. Thomas Edison held a patent for toy and doll cylinder phonographs (U.S. no. 423,039; filed July 2, 1889; granted March 11, 1890), but exploited only the doll. Emile Berliner marketed toy gramophones in 1889 in Germany, with five-inch "plates" (*see* BERLINER (LABEL)). In view of the repertoire on those plates, it may be that the product was miniature in size but not necessarily for children. In December 1900, the Consolidated Talking Machine Co., immediate predecessor of Victor, advertised a Toy Gram-O-Phone for $3, with 6 records and 100 needles included.

After World War I, there were several sets of toy records in the U.S. Emerson Phonograph Co. distributed Mother Goose Records in 1920. Harper Brothers issued Bubble Books in 1919. Both the Emerson and the Harper releases were combinations of children's books with small discs.

In Britain, there were numerous examples in the 1920s. The Bob-o-Link Talking Book was offered from 1922. Other labels in the field included Little Marvel, Kiddyphone, Mimosa, Victory, Broadcast Junior, HMV (Nursery Series), Homo Baby, Savana, Pigmy Gramophone, and The Bell. J. E. Hough offered The Bell, whose matrices were used to press under other labels as well, namely Marspen, Savana, Boots the Chemists, The Little Briton, John Bull Record, The Dinky, and The Fairy.

The smallest discs (diameter 1 5/16 inches) were the HMV records made for the Queen Mary's Doll House gramophone, shown at the Wembley Empire Exhibition in 1924.

Little Tots' Nursery Tunes records appeared in 1923, with releases in Britain and the U.S. HMV presented a series of seven-inch records of children's material in 1924, featuring Auntie and Uncle characters. Another seven-inch children's issue in the United Kingdom was on the Goodson label 1930. In the same year, Crystalate offered a Nursery Rhymes series. Other nursery rhymes were issued on the Durium label in 1932. Kid-Kord was another seven-inch label of 1932.

LP toy records appeared from Oriole Records, Ltd., in about 1951. Others came from the Children's Record Co., London (the Cricket label), Selcol Products, Ltd. (Gala Nursery Records), Lumar, Ltd., of Swansea, Wales (Kiddietunes—Extra Long Play), and Pickwick International, Inc. (G.B.), Ltd. (Happy Time Records).

Track · The path on a magnetic tape that is used for recording and playback. Full track means that the entire width of the tape is used; dual track means that half the width of the tape is used for each continuous signal. An 8-track tape employs eight side-by-side tracks, representing four separate stereo programs of two channels each, or two programs of four channels each. *See also* MULTI-TRACK RECORDING.

Tracking · The movement of the needle or stylus as it follows the undulations of a record groove. Failure of the stylus to follow the groove variations closely results in the distortion known as tracking error. *See also* TRACKING FORCE.

Tracking Error · In disc playback, a failure in tracking. Ideally, the stylus movement should trace a perfect radius from its axis at each point on the disc groove to the center hole. However, the radius is closest to perfect only as the stylus approaches the inner rim, farthest from its starting point at the outside of the record. Thus, the stylus is not always equally able to follow the groove undulations perfectly, with tracking error as the distortion that results. To overcome this problem, the pickup may be designed with an angle of twist, such as 14.5°.

Tracking Force · In a disc player, the pressure exerted by the pickup or cartridge on the stylus. A low tracking force is advantageous in terms of disc wear, but too little tracking force will allow the stylus to bounce in the groove—that leads to disc wear too, and to distortion. Modern LP cartridges track at 2 grams or less. The Shure V-15 tracks at about 1 gram (optimum value).

Transcription Discs · Large diameter (between 16 and 20 inches) acetate, later vinyl, discs used in film recording and in radio, in the 1930s. A vertical-cut disc came from Bell Telephone Laboratories, playing at 33 1/3 rpm, with 200 grooves to the inch;

it had a thin wax cover on an aluminum backing, with gold sputtering. Playback discs were translucent acetate, later vinyl. *See also* DISC; INSTANTANEOUS RECORDINGS.

Transducer · Any device that converts one form of energy to another. In an electrical audio recording system, such conversions occur as input signals (mechanical energy) are changed to electrical energy by the microphone, then back to mechanical energy by the cutting head as it creates the groove pattern. The sequence is reversed in playback. *See also* DISC; MECHANICAL-ELECTRICAL ANALOGIES; MICROPHONE.

Transient Intermodulation Distortion (TIM) · The type of distortion in playback of an audio system that follows sudden overloads of the amplifier, too quick for the compensating negative feedback to counteract it. A loud sforzando in a musical work, like those in Haydn's "Surprise Symphony," is a typical cause. The result is a ringing effect or, in piano recording, a ping sound. *See also* TRANSIENT RESPONSE.

Transient Response · In audio playback, the reaction of the system to a sudden change in amplitude of the signal or of its frequency. Poor transient response, often caused by loudspeaker inadequacy, brings a boom in the bass or an edgy sound at the top of the spectrum. *See also* TRANSIENT INTERMODULATION DISTORTION (TIM).

Transistor · A semiconductor device that can amplify or (with power gain) switch electrical signals. Transistors generally replaced vacuum tubes in audio systems during the 1960s.

Transport · The element in a CD player that spins the disc while isolating it from vibration.

Tuner · In a radio receiver, the device that selectively converts radio signals to audio signals. It is often a separate component in an audio system, used with an audio amplifier.

Tuning Band · On certain early discs, a band that followed the program material; it reproduced a fixed pitch, for the purpose of setting the correct turntable speed. A 1904 G & T record, no. 053048 (a song by Giordano sung by a soprano named Frascani) and a 1909 Gramophone Concert Record, no. GC-37851 ("Ave Maria" for cello and piano) had such bands, termed "key-notes" by G & T. Fonotipia copied the device, but gave it up following protests from the Gramophone Co. (Italy), Ltd.

Turntable · The platter or platform on which analog-record discs are rotated in recording or playback. By extension, the term is applied to the complete assembly: platter, spindle, driving components, and motor. An ideal turntable has a constant and accurate speed of rotation, without rumble, and without effects from outside vibrations or feedback. These desired conditions were hardly to be found in the early turntables of Emile Berliner, operated by hand cranking, or later models with treadle power. Spring motor phonographs ran more dependably, and finally electric mains power made constant speed possible.

Three types of operation are found: belt drive, in which a resilient belt connects the motor to the turntable platter; idler-wheel drive, where the motor drives the inner rim of the platter via a rubber-covered outrigger wheel; and direct drive, in which a slow-speed motor is directly coupled to the platter's center shaft. Either of these three can give satisfactory results, although direct drive has been preferred in professional work for its simplicity and durability. (Interestingly, although there was no motor but the human engine involved, Berliner record players can be classed as both belt driven and direct; some had a belt to carry the cranking energy to the platter, some had the crank attached to the platter.)

Heavy turntables (about eight pounds) offer greater stability and are used in studio work, but they require a stronger motor than consumer turntables (weighing about four pounds, or less). Some consumer designs, such as the classic model produced by Acoustic Research in the 1960s and 1970s, used a fairly lightweight platter, driven by a moderately powerful motor. Felt covering was used on turntable platters in the 1890s. The first advertising for velvet-covered turntables appeared in 1921. Mats produced for turntables in the modern era emphasized anti-static qualities and non-conductivity.

In the best LP turntables, beginning in the 1960s with the previously noted Acoustic Research player, and exemplified later on by the Linn product line and Yamaha PF-800, there was a suspended sub-chassis isolation system, to prevent any unwanted feedthrough from the mounting shelf or floor. Many turntables also feature a fine-tuning speed control, a built-in strobe light, and strobe markings on the edge of the platter. *See also* FLUTTER; PITCH; TONE ARM; CARTRIDGE (II); RECORD CHANGER; WOW.—Long 1988; updated by Howard Ferstler

Tweaking · A method of suppressing resonances and vibrations in audio playback by the placement of dampers under components. The dampers, made of various kinds of absorbent materials, are sometimes called isolation feet. Good results have been reported with such feet positioned beneath a turntable. [Whyte 1989]

Tweeter · A high-frequency (treble) loudspeaker.

U

U.S. Everlasting Record · *See* U-S EVER-LASTING RECORD.

U.S. Phonograph Co. · Edison's phono-graph export agency during the 1890s, located in Newark, New Jersey. (This was a brown-wax era firm, with no connection to the later U-S Phonograph Co. of Cleve-land.) U.S. Phonograph Co. began in the spring of 1893 as a successor to the New Jersey Phonograph Co., one of the North American Phonograph Co. local compa-nies, and was reorganized in January 1894. Victor H. Emerson served as general man-ager from the beginning, and as president from January 1894. George Tewksbury, formerly of the Kansas Phonograph Co., was another executive of the firm. Frank L. Capps invented the early U.S. spring motor in 1895. These men were to become influential personalities in the recording industry.

U.S. Phonograph produced a variety of musical and spoken-word selections on cylinders by mechanical duplication in their laboratory at 87-91 Orange Street, Newark, NJ. Popular artists included Rus-sell Hunting, Dan W. Quinn, Len Spencer, John Yorke AtLee, and Issler's Orchestra.

When Edison organized his National Phonograph Co. in January 1896, he was not in a position to meet the demand for entertainment records. U.S. Phonograph Co. supplied master cylinders to Edison until U.S. Phonograph was bought out by National Phonograph in late 1897.—Bill Klinger

U.S. Phonograph Co. (Cleveland) · *See* U-S PHONOGRAPH CO.

Ultona · The reproducer marketed by the Brunswick-Balke-Collender Co. in 1916. It could play vertical-cut or lateral-cut discs.

United States Gramophone Co. · The sec-ond American firm established by Emile Berliner, succeeding his American Gramo-phone Co. in April 1893. Located at 1410 Pennsylvania Ave., Washington, D.C., the firm marketed gramophones as well as one-sided seven-inch discs with the Berliner label. The machines produced included hand-driven models and battery-operated models; about 1,000 were sold in 1894. In fall 1894 a factory and salesroom opened in Baltimore. The Berliner Gramophone Co. took over both manufacturing and sales of all products (except for the District of Columbia region). United States Gramo-phone Co. continued to hold the Berliner patents. [Wile 1979/2.]

United States Phonograph Co. · *See* U-S PHONOGRAPH CO.

United States Record Manufacturing Co. · A firm established in 1920 in Long Island City, New York, where its factory was located, with offices in New York. Victor H. Emerson was president. It was announced in March 1921 that the com-pany was prepared to press 10-inch discs in substantial quantities and to supply stock matrices for the presses of others. Thomas H. McClain, an engineer formerly with

Thomas Edison, supervised the factory. A label named H.I.T.S. was advertised by the firm in September 1921. [Andrews.]

United States Talking Machine Co. (I) · A Chicago firm active in 1897. It sold a finger-wound disc player at a cost of $3, and records for it (disguised Berliner discs). Joseph N. Brown was the inventor of the machine (U.S. patent #653,654, filed April 22, 1897; granted July 17, 1900), which had a wooden tone arm, steel needle, and *gutta percha* listening tubes. Despite its low selling price, and a manufacturing cost of only 12½ cents per unit, the device was a market failure and remainders were sold off at .98¢ each. [Koenigsberg 1990.]

United States Talking Machine Co. (II) · A Newark, New Jersey, firm established in 1916. It advertised in that year a line of Ideal disc players, in eight models, selling from $12 to $85.

United Talking Machine Co. · A Chicago firm, established in 1911 as a division of the Great Northern Manufacturing Co. Record players were sold under the Symphony name, and discs with the United label. The players had 1½-inch spindles to accommodate the extra large spindle holes that were cut into the discs (which were Columbia overstock records, relabelled by United). The firm seems to have been absorbed by the Consolidated Talking Machine Co. sometime before March 1918. [Fabrizio 1980.]

U-S Everlasting Record · A brand and type of cylinder record manufactured by the U-S Phonograph Co. of Cleveland, Ohio. The cylinder was formed from thin sheet celluloid, rolled into a tube and butt-joined. After pressing under steam heat and pressure in a metal matrix, the still-warm molded record was slipped over a core of wax-impregnated wood pulp. This "unbreakable" construction proved less vulnerable to the effects of atmospheric moisture and temperature changes than most other forms of celluloid cylinders.

The end rims of standard-production U-S Everlasting records are all impressed with a patent grant date of December 11, 1906, identifying the record construction developed by Varian M. Harris.

Some 1,100 U-S Everlasting and Lakeside titles were issued between 1910 and 1913. It is likely that all were recorded in New York City. The catalog included separately-numbered series for Grand Opera and Foreign Language items. A generous proportion of "cultural" titles were offered in the U-S catalogs, compared to the typical range of popular material then being recorded by the major cylinder record companies.—Bill Klinger

U-S Phonograph Co. · The last firm to challenge Edison's market dominance in the cylinder field, originally formed in August 1908 as the Cleveland Phonograph Record Co. The corporate name was changed to United States Phonograph Co. on July 14, 1909, and to U.S. Phonograph Co. on September 4, 1912. Advertisements often styled the company name and products as "U-S," a practice that helps to distinguish it from the earlier (unrelated) brown-wax-era firm, U.S. Phonograph Co. of Newark, New Jersey.

The Cleveland management (under president E. C. Beach) attracted the services of Chicago chemist Varian M. Harris, who had developed the processes that would be used in manufacturing U-S Everlasting Records. Harris felt that thinner celluloid would take a more faithful impression in the molding operation, but such thin material was not yet available in tubular form. Working in his home laboratory in Chicago in 1904, Harris rolled very thin sheet celluloid into tubes and bonded the edges together with a solvent. Granted U.S. patent #837927 for this technique on December 11, 1906, Harris assigned it (and at least one other) to the Cleveland Phonograph Record Co. on August 20, 1908.

In October 1909, Harris came to Cleveland to direct the setting up of the U-S record pressing plant. After pressing the very first lot of records on October 29, 1909, he rejected, as unacceptable, 55 of the first 90 matrices that had been made from masters recorded in New York City by Isaac Norcross. Charles L. Hibbard (an engineer who left Edison to join U-S Phonograph) took over the New York recording operation and improved the quality of the masters.

Around November 1909, musician Albert W. Benzler became music director for U-S Phonograph. He had been in charge of the music room at the Edison Laboratory, but disagreed with Edison's methods for choosing the selections to be released. (Edison reportedly employed a "Jackass Committee" of factory employees to audition candidate recordings; Benzler thought this practice too vulgar. There may have also been a rivalry with Victor Herbert for the Edison post of music director.) It seems likely that all U-S masters were made in the New York City area; no recording facilities are known to have existed in Cleveland.

Meanwhile F. L. Fritchey, in the U-S machine shop at 1013 Oregon Ave., Cleveland, Ohio, was preparing to build the first U-S phonograph. Cleveland inventor Harry B. McNulty had designed a unique dual-feedscrew machine with a pair of reproducers for playing either two- or four-minute cylinders by turning a single knob. Eventually, at least nine different models of U-S cylinder phonographs were offered, ranging in price from $24 to $200. U-S treasurer and general manager Thomas H. Towell took samples of the first U-S records to New York in November 1909 to show to R.D. Cortina; the Cortina Academy of Languages had already placed an order for 5,000 language records in August 1908.

U-S products were announced to the trade in May 1910. Two-minute and four-minute records and three models of machines were then available to dealers. By June 1910, U-S was in full production with a capacity of some 5,000 records per day. New U-S Everlasting records were released monthly through April 1913, with a few titles issued as late as October 1913. Among the total of 1,100 selections were many well-recorded popular items, tunes from Broadway shows, foreign-language pieces, and operatic arias.

In addition to the U-S Everlasting brand of record, the firm manufactured Lakeside cylinders, a parallel series numbered identically with the Everlasting releases, for distribution by the Chicago mail-order house, Montgomery Ward and Co.; celluloid Cortina foreign-language instruction series; and the more obscure Medicophone series, for dissemination of medical information by the Medicophone Post-Graduate Co., also of New York City. All these label variants are identical in materials and construction.

Attacked in litigation by Edison's legal department, U-S Phonograph incurred heavy legal fees for several years, but Edison's attorneys never established any patent infringement or other offenses.

U-S Phonograph received continued support through an association with the Bishop-Babcock-Becker Co., under Kirk D. Bishop, who was USP president from 1910. But by spring of 1914, U-S Phonograph succumbed to market realities and ceased production.

Interestingly, some very late U-S recordings have been discovered on cylinders made by the Indestructible Phonographic Record Co. of Albany, New York. The Indestructible records numbered in the range from 3280 through 3316 were almost all made from U-S masters or matrices. The exact circumstances of this transfer remain to be understood.

While Edison's National Phonograph Co. was still producing only "wax" records, the U-S Phonograph Co. of Cleveland introduced the first truly high-quality unbreakable cylinders. The U-S Everlasting records delivered better sound quality with lower surface noise than the earlier Lambert Co. or Albany Indestructibles. Some collectors consider the U-S cylinders to have remained unsurpassed throughout the acoustic recording era.—Bill Klinger

Universal Phonograph Co. · A New York firm. The January 1899 issue of *Phonoscope* advertised its records guaranteed to be original, and invited clients to "come and take the records off the rack as they are being made." Material included "catchy music" as well as selections from "works of Wagner, Meyerbeer, etc." George Rosey and his orchestra and Albert Campbell were artists identified in the promotion copy. Joseph W. Stern & Co. was proprietor and Mitchell Marks was manager.

Universal Talking Machine Co. · A firm which Frank Seaman took part in establishing on February 10, 1898, with Orville La Dow as president. The purpose of Universal was to make machines for Seaman's National Gramophone Co. Seaman was sole sales agent for Berliner gramophones and discs, and the Berliner Gramophone Co. objected to Seaman's attempts to handle alternative cheaper machines. As a consequence, Seaman took part in organizing the National Gramophone Corp. on March 10, 1899, as sales outlet for the Universal Talking Machine Co. machines (called Zonophones) as soon as they would be in production. The first products were in fact unauthorized disguised Berliner items, a situation that led to a break between Berliner and Seaman. After litigation brought by the graphophone interests over alleged infringements by Seaman of the Bell-Tainter patent for incising in wax, there was a consent agreement allowing Columbia to use the Zonophone line of players. Universal held a sheriff's sale of patents and equipment on October 28, 1901. Then the Zonophone business was reorganized under control of a new company founded for the purpose on December 19, 1901, the Universal Talking Machine Manufacturing Co. (The continuing Universal Talking Machine Co. acted as sales representative for some time.) Failure of the National Gramophone Corp. followed, but Seaman maintained his rights as sole sales agent for the Berliner Gramophone Co. The original Universal Talking Machine Co. kept its corporate existence to June 6, 1903, when its share stock was acquired by G&T, along with the share stock of Universal Talking Machine Manufacturing Co. and that of the American and German International Zonophone Co. In September 1903, G&T sold the Universal assets to Victor.

As a Victor subsidiary the Universal firm continued to produce the Zonophone line of discs and players. In 1908, it offered five discs by Luisa Tetrazzini, in 9-inch size for .75¢, and in 11-inch size for $1.25. The address of the UTMMC was given in a July 1911 advertisement as 4th and Race Streets, Philadelphia. Columbia successfully litigated UTMMC out of business in 1912, on grounds of patent infringement, as it had never been licensed by Columbia. All masters and factory stock of American-made Zonophone records had to be destroyed by court order.

The American company was not related to the British Universal Talking Machine Co., Ltd. [Andrews.]

Universal Talking Machine Co., Ltd. · A British firm, not related to the American company of like name, registered on November 9, 1907, in London. It was a successor to the gramophone branch of Aldridge, Salmon and Co., Ltd. British gramophones were sold. The firm wound up operations on May 5, 1908, then reorganized and continued in business under the same name. E. J. Sabine and Thomas F. Bragg were among the directors, while controlling interest was held by Aldridge, Salmon and Co., Ltd. A record with the Elephone label was issued from November 1908. Liquidation came on June 6, 1909. The Universal name was used for a time in 1910 by William Andrew Barraud, before he gave his company his own name. [Andrews 1990/6.]

Universal Talking Machine Manufacturing Co. · *See* UNIVERSAL TALKING MACHINE CO.

V

Valiquet, Louis P., 18??–1925 · Inventor of several important audio components, holder of 33 U.S. patents filed from 1897 to 1909. His research formed the basis for products of the Universal Talking Machine Co. (for which he was factory superintendent) and the National Gramophone Corp. His patents included designs for playback machines, a horn-support device (needed in the days of large, heavy horns; 1902), and the disc turntable with a spring-loaded pin for securing the record (1905); it was used in 1900 models of the Zonophone even before the patent application had been filed. Other Valiquet patents were for a coin-op, a case, sound boxes, and a motor.

Van Gelder, Rudy, November 2, 1924– · Noted jazz recording engineer, Van Gelder was a professional optometrist who, in the early 1950s, became interested in recording jazz music. In the late 1940s, he built a studio in the living room of his parents' home in Hackensack, New Jersey, and in 1953 began to record for the Blue Note label. By the mid-1950s, he was also overseeing most jazz sessions for Prestige. (Thelonious Monk named one of his pieces "Hackensack," after the location of Van Gelder's studios.) In 1959, Van Gelder moved to a professional studio in Englewood Cliffs, New Jersey, and continued to record for Prestige and Blue Note along with a variety of small jazz labels, notably Impulse and CTI, through the early 1970s. Van Geller was known for his crisp, unadorned recording style and for creating a relaxed atmosphere where musicians could be creative. Beginning in 1999, Blue Note began a "RVG Editions" reissue series, inviting Van Gelder to re-master his original recordings in 24-bit format for CD.—Carl Benson

Varigroove Recording · The method of making a disc record that allows the lateral movement of the cutting stylus to determine the spacing between adjacent grooves. Thus, the louder signals will have wider spaced grooves than the quieter signals. This practice permits a longer playing time for a given disc diameter.

V-Discs · Records produced during and after World War II by the U.S. War Department for distribution to military personnel. The earliest issues appeared in October 1943, the final ones in May 1949. V-Discs were made of unbreakable vinyl, in 12-inch size; Victor and CBS did the pressing. By means of tight grooving (136/inch) a playing time of up to 6 1/2 minutes was achieved, allowing more than one piece to appear on each side. Leading popular and classical artists donated their time for original recordings, and others were heard from contributed matrices. Often the performer would introduce a disc with some spoken lines, in the manner of the old announcements on acoustic discs and cylinders. It is interesting that many of the V-Discs were made during the recording ban ordered by the American Federation of Musicians, the only instrumental commercial records officially created during that period. More than 8 million V-Discs were distributed, and all the matrices were publicly destroyed when the project terminated.

Vertical Cut · The name given to a recording process (also known as hill and dale) that utilizes a vertical modulation or pattern made in the spiraling groove on a cylinder or disc. Vibrations are cut into the medium perpendicularly to the surface. This was the method of the Thomas Edison phonographs. Both lateral-cut and vertical-cut recordings were made in the Volta Laboratories in the early 1880s. First used on commercial discs by Neophone Co., Ltd., in 1904, it was popularized by Pathé from 1906. Vertical cut was never as popular as the lateral-cut method, although Edison preferred it, making vertical-cut cylinders and Diamond Discs until 1929, at which time he also made some lateral records. *See also* LATERAL RECORDING.

Victor Talking Machine Company · Eldridge R. Johnson was a machinist providing gramophones for Emile Berliner, the first producer of commercial disc records. Johnson began to make records himself in January 1900. He released his first commercial records a few months later, with gold print on black paper labels (Berliner discs had no labels) that were seven inches in diameter. Those discs bore the label name Improved Gram-O-Phone Record, and sold for .50¢. The first recording, listed as number A-1 in Johnson's matrix log, was a recitation by George Broderick of Eugene Field's poem "Departure."

In summer 1900, Johnson and Leon F. Douglass formed the Consolidated Talking Machine Co. to market Johnson's machines and records, and to utilize his improved recording process. There were daily recording sessions, and a few discs were pressed from material recorded in Europe by Fred Gaisberg and Belford Royal for the Gramophone Co., Ltd. The company name was changed to "Eldridge Johnson, Manufacturing Machinist,"

to avoid a name conflict with Berliner's holding company, Consolidated Talking Machine Co. of America.

In January 1901, the first 10-inch discs were made. Johnson issued them at first with the label name Victor Ten Inch Record, then as Victor Monarch Record. The cost was $1. Yet, another label name was introduced on March 12, 1901, when Johnson registered the trademark Victor Record for the seven-inch discs. A report of September 1901 indicated that the previous 12 months had been successful for the Johnson firm, with a profit of $180,000.

Berliner and Johnson agreed to pool their patent, trademark, and manufacturing interests, and incorporated the Victor Talking Machine Company on October 3, 1901. A large manufacturing complex was soon developed around Johnson's machine shop in Camden, New Jersey, across the Delaware River from Philadelphia. Nipper—the "His Master's Voice" dog logo—appeared for the first time on Victor record labels in January 1902. By the end of that year, Victor had produced about 2 million records. Some 2,000 discs per day were coming from Camden.

In Europe, the Gramophone Co. and others were releasing recordings of classical music by operatic artists such as Feodor Chaliapin and the new sensation, Enrico Caruso. The records had special red labels and sold at higher prices than non-classical records. In the United States, most of the early recorded material consisted of popular songs, comic songs and recitations, and band music. Victor did have a little classical material in 1900, by George Broderick (opera arias in English), Rosalia Chalia, and Emilio de Gogorza, but the great advance came with first Red Seal records, announced in March 1903. That was the 5000 series, 25 imports (including Enrico Caruso's Milan recordings) from the Gramophone Co., selling for $2.50 each.

Victor made its own first Red Seal recording on April 30, 1903, in room 826 at Carnegie Hall with Australian mezzo-soprano Ada Crossley singing "Caro Mio Ben" on a 10-inch Monarch (no. 81001). In early 1904, Victor signed Enrico Caruso to an exclusive contract. The first Red Seal duet was extremely popular: "Solenne in quest' ora" from *Forza del destino*, sung by Caruso and Antonio Scotti (no. 89001; March 1906), and the first recording of the *Rigoletto* Quartet was a great hit, selling for $4. It presented Caruso, Bessie Abott, Louise Homer, and Scotti (no. 96000; February 1907).

Eldridge Johnson continued to improve the instrument line. The tapered tone arm and gooseneck were introduced in 1903. A trade publication, *The Voice of the Victor*, was introduced for dealers in April 1906 to keep them informed about new records, sales methods, and artist tours. The Victor dealers formed the National Association of Talking Machine Jobbers. In 1906, Victor introduced a new phonograph with the horn enclosed within its cabinet. It was named the Victrola, and was priced at $200. It was a success in many console and table models, setting the industry standard.

At the end of its first decade, Victor was in an excellent position. More than 35 million records had been sold, and the phonographs (606,596 sold through 1910) had gained acceptance as the finest made.

Over the decade of the teens, the Camden complex continued to grow in response to the volume of sales. In 1911, 124,000 phonographs were sold. In April 1911, an educational department was established, under the direction of Frances E. Clark, to develop an interest in music among school children. Additions to Victor's artist roster from 1910 to 1913 included George M. Cohan, Al Jolson, John McCormack, Mischa Elman, Fritz Kreisler, Alma Gluck, Victor Herbert, Jan Paderewski, Jan Kubelik, Giovanni Martinelli, and the Flon-

zaley Quartet. Amelita Galli-Curci began recording for Victor in October 1916. About 600 titles were in the Red Seal catalog in 1912. In 1916, Calvin Child became head of Victor's artist department and Josef Pasternack became musical director. In February 1917, the Original Dixieland Jazz Band made their first records, the first jazz ensemble to be recorded.

The *Victor Book of the Opera*, edited by Samuel H. Rous, appeared in the first of many editions in 1912, offering opera plots along with photos and promotions of Victor artists, for .75¢. No fewer than six Lucia Mad Scenes were noted in the book.

Victor's instrument production was severely curtailed by the company's effort to supply material for World War I, as skilled workers of the cabinet factory made aircraft assemblies, rifle stock, and detonator cases. Recording artists appeared at war bond rallies, and their recordings helped boost morale. A new label design, the so-called Wing label, was introduced in 1914.

After Pasternack and the 51 musicians of the Victor Symphony Orchestra made satisfactory recordings, the Boston Symphony, under Karl Muck, and the Philadelphia Orchestra, under Leopold Stokowski, were brought to Camden to make their initial recordings. Jascha Heifetz began recording for Victor in November 1917. Normal production in Camden after the war was reached in October 1919 and instrument sales reached 560,000 in 1920. More than 205 million Victor records had been sold by the end of 1919. Sergei Rachmaninoff and Paul Whiteman became Victor artists in 1920. Caruso made his last recordings in Camden on September 16, 1920. His death in August 1921 ended the career of the single artist who contributed most to the success of Victor and the early phonograph industry.

Hard times were coming to the record industry, however, with phonograph sales being greatly eroded by the increasing popularity of radio as a form of home entertainment. Victor's phonograph sales were also hurt when competitors, such as Brunswick and Sonora, began selling flattop cabinets, which were preferred by the customers. In addition, the phonograph industry had been doing little to improve its product. Early in 1924, Victor had rejected an offer made by Bell Telephone Laboratories to witness a demonstration of a new electrical recording process and improved acoustical playback equipment. Nevertheless, by December of that year, Victor arranged to have a demonstration for its technical staff in Camden. Victor and Columbia obtained rights to use the new recording and reproduction systems.

Victor introduced its new electrical recordings under the name of "Orthophonic Records." In a short time 10,000 Credenza Orthophonic Victrolas were built, hand-wound acoustic taking machines with re-entrant horns. The new products were introduced to the public on November 2, 1925, and by the end of 1926, Victrola introduced 43 new models. Included in the new line were models with a radio chassis and electrical playback apparatus made by RCA. An "Electrola" line had electric amplification. The electrically recorded discs had a new scroll design on their labels. Public acceptance of the new records and instruments was satisfying, and by the end of 1926, the working loss of $6.5 million incurred in 1925 had been recovered. Great hit records emerged from the electrical process, including the J. S. Bach "Toccata and Fugue in D-Minor" in a brilliant transcription for the Philadelphia Orchestra.

Eldridge Johnson sold his interest in Victor in December 1926 to bankers Speyer and Co. and J. & W. Seligman of New York, for an estimated $30 million. Johnson's inventiveness and business sense had developed the wheezy instrument and noisy discs of the 1890s into a product line

that through 1929 resulted in the manufacture of nearly 8 million instruments and more than one-half billion records. Many new dance bands and popular groups were Victor artists during the late 1920s, including the Coon-Sanders Orchestra, Jan Garber, Ray Noble, Fred Waring, and Ted Weems. Jazz artists included Duke Ellington, Jean Goldkette, Jelly Roll Morton, Bennie Moten, Ben Pollack, and Fats Waller.

Nathaniel Shilkret was the principal conductor of the Victor Orchestra and accompanist of popular vocalists. Field recordings were made with portable electrical recording equipment during the summers of 1927 and 1928 in Virginia, Tennessee, North Carolina, and Georgia. Jimmie Rodgers and the Carter Family were among the artists discovered in these sessions. New Red Seal performers of the 1920s included Marian Anderson, Pablo Casals, Richard Crooks, Vladimir Horowitz, Wanda Landowska, Lauritz Melchior, Yehudi Menuhin, Ezio Pinza, Rosa Ponselle, Sergei Rachmaninoff, Elisabeth Rethberg, Paul Robeson, Tito Schipa, and Lawrence Tibbett. Toscanini made records with the New York Philharmonic Symphony Orchestra, and Serge Koussevitzky recorded with the Boston Symphony Orchestra. Another instrument advance came in March 1927, with the first record changer. The early version played either 10-inch or 12-inch records, whereas a later model could mix the two sizes.

In 1929, RCA (Radio Corporation of America) acquired Victor Talking Machine Co. Victor, in its 28-year existence, had made a major impact on home entertainment. It was an industry pioneer in the use of the advertising media. It provided jobs for 10,000 workers, and at least 30 investors in the company received investment returns of more than $1 million each. By the end of 1929, record sales had reached around 600 million. Some $700 million in total sales had been posted. About 8,130,000 instruments had been made.

The acquisition of Victor cost RCA $150 million, but the value received was enormous. A prize item gained was the "His Master's Voice" (Nipper) trademark, with its heritage of customer loyalty and confidence. Another valuable item in the package was the extensive Victor phonographic and record business, which had earned more than 25% in average annual dividends for 20 years. More than 1,000 artists were in the Victor catalog, and the sales and distribution network was unequaled in the industry. A third significant item was the Camden manufacturing complex, one of the largest in the nation, with 16 buildings and more than 10,000 employees. Camden was immediately pressed into radio manufacture, to meet the ever-increasing demand, while continuing to produce records.

The U.S. national economy was at its lowest point in 1931 and 1932, giving RCA its only deficit years. The radio business remained profitable, leading to demands within the firm that the phonographic products be eliminated. Yet radio stations and broadcast networks were dependent on records for program material. The technology developed for Vitaphone discs in the 1920s was applied to the transcription of continuing radio shows and commercials. These were "transcribed" on 16-inch plastic lacquers in studios in Chicago and New York. The lacquer was immediately heavily plated to produce a copper master that was used for pressing a few (never more than 50) approval copies. When approval was given, the lacquer was given normal matrix processing in the plant and pressings were made. These 33 1/3-rpm, narrow-groove (2.5 mil) "Thesaurus" records on 16-inch plastic (Vitrolac) discs served the radio broadcast industry for more than 30 years.

Between radio applications and jukebox sales, the record industry had enough business to survive the early years of the Depression. The 50,000 jukeboxes in operation in 1930 accounted for about half of the 6 million records sold in that year. At the same time, Victor's recording facilities and manufacturing plant were held in readiness, and had some opportunities to bring some profits. In 1934, the Duo Jr. record player was sold for plug-in use with a radio; a second version had a lighter weight crystal pick-up, a smaller turntable, and a lower price. That was the machine used in 1937 to promote membership in the Victor Record Society.

During the 1930s, popular records outsold Red Seals by a ratio of three to one. An advance for the Red Seals was made with the formation of the NBC Symphony Orchestra for Arturo Toscanini in 1937. Toscanini's weekly broadcasts created an audience for classical music and an increase in classical record sales. During the period 1932 to 1938, industry-wide record production increased by 661%; Victor's production increased 440%.

Artists who made their first Victor records in the 1930s included E. Power Biggs, Jussi Björling, the Boston Pops Orchestra, Budapest Quartet, Nelson Eddy, Kirsten Flagstad, José Iturbi, Helen Jepson, Lotte Lehmann, Lily Pons, Artur Rubinstein, Artur Schnabel, Rudolf Serkin, and John Charles Thomas.

During 1939 to 1945, RCA Victor was engaged in a variety of activities related to the war effort. At the same time, research continued in phonographic products, among them the vinyl disc (introduced in 1945), and record sales climbed in both popular and classical categories. A large percentage of the internationally acclaimed classical soloists and orchestras were under contract. Alexander Kipnis, Andrés Segovia, and Helen Traubel made their first appearances on Victor. Red Seals were sold for $1, black label discs for .75¢ and .50¢, and Bluebird (a pop label introduced in 1933) records for .35¢. Bluebird carried important material by Shep Fields, Earl Hines, Vincent Lopez, Freddy Martin, Glenn Miller, Artie Shaw, Fats Waller, and many others. Big Bands heard on regular Victor black label discs included Sammy Kaye, Wayne King, and Tommy Dorsey. Benny Goodman's Victor releases defined the swing era. Duke Ellington's Victors from 1940 to 1942 display his band at its creative peak.

The seven-inch vinyl record, with a narrow groove for a lightweight crystal high-fidelity pickup, was introduced in 1949 with a speedy record changer. Critical analysis had established that a record speed of 45 rpm was required for good performance of a seven-inch record. The next objective was to have the 33 1/3-rpm long-play RCA Victor record with a three-speed record changer available within one year. In the light of Columbia's acclaimed 33 1/3 microgroove LP disc (1948), the technical wisdom and the commercial expediency of the 45 was widely doubted, but by February of 1951 the small disc had found universal acceptance for popular music, and billions were sold in the next 30 years.

With the introduction of its 33 1/3-rpm LP in 1950, RCA Victor was able to compete effectively with other LP labels in the classical field. The next technical advance in the industry was stereophonic recording. In 1954, John F. Pfeiffer of RCA Victor's New York recording studio worked with Fritz Reiner and the Chicago Symphony Orchestra (in Orchestra Hall, Chicago) to capture Strauss' *Also Sprach Zarathustra* and *Ein Heldenleben* in stereo. By today's standards, the setup in Orchestra Hall was primitive: a 30 ips 2-track tape and two Neumann M-50 omni microphones positioned 12 feet high and 24 feet apart with the orchestra between them. Nevertheless, the recordings are superb.

Stereo tape recordings spurred activity to develop stereo disc records. H.

E. Roys, chief engineer of RCA Victor and chairman of the Electronic Industries Association (EIA) committee on the phonograph, was heavily involved in the establishment of worldwide industry standards for full stereo records before major producers placed them on sale in 1958. It took more than statesmanship to accomplish this. The "more" ingredient was the analytical skill that had established 45 rpm as the correct speed of a seven-inch record with five 1/2-minute playing times and less than 10% tracing distortion. In 1957, Roys asked Murlan S. Corrington of the Advanced Development Section of Home Instruments to make a comparative analysis of the 45/45 degree and the vertical-lateral proposals for stereo discs. Corrington reported on January 27, 1958 to the EIA committee on recording. His conclusions served as the basis for the choice of the 45-45 degree system and its standardization by the record industry.

In 1961, an electronic processor was sold that reproduced monaural records in stereo. The RCA New Orthacoustic Response Curve was adopted by the record and broadcast industries in June 1953. From 1953 to 1956, the Indianapolis plant installed 12 seven-inch automatic presses, adding an annual production potential of 32 million to the 18 million of the 46 seven-inch manual presses.

By 1977, the record plant in Indianapolis had reached a production capacity of 165 million discs a year, of which 90 million were 45s. There were three other U.S. plants, with additional capacity of 32 million discs. International plants in Argentina, Australia, Brazil, Canada, Chile, Great Britain, Greece, Italy, Mexico, and Spain had about 200 presses and a 45-million production capacity. Thus, the total RCA Victor capacity was 224 million records per annum. A fully automatic plant completely dedicated to tape duplication and cassette loading was opened in 1984 in Weaverville, North Carolina.

Abraham M. Max, manager of the chemical and physical laboratory, RCA Victor Records Engineering (1944–1972), and research director of the American Electroplating Society, applied and adapted state-of-the-art processes to change the plating time of a record stamper, which had been as long as 60 hours, to 1 hour, and to increase the life of a Red Seal stamper from 100 to 2,500 records. For other pressings from unfilled compounds, 10,000 records per stamper was not uncommon.

RCA Victor sealed records in shrink-wrap beginning in 1964 and thereby participated in a bold change in product marketing. Other innovations did not fare so well (e.g., four-channel sound). Near success was achieved even though the technology applied proved to be overextended; however, there was no great demand in the marketplace for something beyond stereo. The 1973 Dynaflex record was designed to have laminar flow of the compound in the press and to have a positive profile to achieve performance goals through the conformity of flexibility instead of the precision of rigidity. Record plant production facilities and personnel were not yet ready for this approach.

The Victor name, its trademark, its artists, its catalog, its studios, its RCA Music Services, its manufacturing business, and its heritage became a part of Bertelsmann AG on April 15, 1986. In 2003, Betelsmann's holdings were merged with Sony Columbia, to form Sony BMG Music Entertainment. Thus, the holdings of the two oldest and largest U.S. labels—Columbia and Victor—were brought together.

Victrola · A trade name registered by the Victor Talking Machine Co., filed December 1, 1905, for a disc record player; it became the most popular and famous disc phonograph in the industry. Distinctive features of the instrument were the enclosure of all mechanical parts and the horn within a cabinet, a door on the front of the cabinet that could be opened or closed to control the volume, and storage space for records inside the cabinet. Eldridge Johnson held the patent covering these features, although in 1927 John Bailey Browning received credit for prior conception of the Victrola.

The Victrola (derivation of the name is uncertain) was announced to the trade on August 7, 1906. Advertising in 1906 identified the machine as a "Victor-Victrola," but the name was simplified to Victrola in 1907; it was also known as "Victrola the Sixteenth" or Model XVI. Table models were available from 1911, with sales rivaling those of the floor models. Either a spring motor or (from August 1913) AC (mains) electric power was offered.

By 1910, some 40,000 Victrola consoles had been sold. The table model quickly reached 50,000 sales in its first year, 1911. Thereafter, the annual sales for each model were in six figures. In 1920, the console Victrola had its peak sales—333,889. In addition, 212,363 table Victrolas were sold that year; however, the arrival of the radio brought about a slump from 1922. Production was halted in 1924, but resumed in the next year with the introduction of the Orthophonic Victrola.

Electrical recording created the need for an appropriate record player because the new electric discs reproduced with excessive volume and stridency on the regular Victrolas. In June 1925, Victor announced its plan for a solution, a completely new machine (and set up a half-price sales campaign to move the older stock). On "Victor Day," November 2, 1925, there were nationwide demonstrations by dealers of the new Credenza model ($275.00–$405.00) of the Orthophonic Victrola—sales were strong from the outset: 42,446 before the end of 1925 and 260,436 in 1927.

Technically, the novelties in the Ortho-phonic were its pleated aluminum dia-phragm (in place of the mica disc of the standard Victrola), a stylus assembly in ball bearings, and a folded exponential horn. Response was from about 100 Hz in the bass to about 5,000 Hz in the treble.

Varieties of the Orthophonic were numerous. The most expensive was the electric Borgia II model, at $1,000. It was housed in a double cabinet, with a radio in one of them (the Radiola 28); and the records could be played through the radio amplifier for complete volume control. There were also spring motor machines, and table mod-els as well as elaborate consoles. Victor's all-electric instrument was known as the Electrola-Victrola; it competed with the Brunswick Panatrope, made from the same RCA components. Victor's first record changer was introduced in 1927, the Auto-matic Orthophonic; it was the first changer to reach a mass market. With the creation of these combination radio-phonographs, run by electric power, and complete with disc changers, Victor established the format of the record player that was to remain the norm until the high-fidelity era of the 1950s and the move toward separate components.

Video Recording · The storage and repro-duction of visual images, perfected by the Ampex Corp. in the United States in 1956, and offered commercially for professional studio use in 1957. The Ampex system was in tape format, using two-inch-wide tapes running at 15 ips. Telefunken and Decca first accomplished videodisc recording in 1966, using a microgroove record with 25 grooves in the space of a typical LP record groove. Signals were vertically inscribed and frequency modulated. The pickup sensed changes in pressure. In a demon-stration at the AEG Telefunken building in Berlin, June 24, 1970, the discs were of thin flexible plastic foil, with a playing time of five minutes. They revolved at television picture frame rates: 1,500 rpm (in Europe;

the American speed was 1,800 rpm). This was basically a mechanical system.

An optical videodisc system was launched by Philips in 1978 and named the "Laser Disc." In this process, a laser beam traces a spiraling track of depressions or pits in a highly reflective aluminum layer on a vinyl disc. The spot of reflected light activates a photo-diode to produce the electric signal that is then processed to reproduce a color picture and audio signal in a conventional television set. From this technology, the compact (audio) disc (CD) emerged. The format was not initially suc-cessful, because it was more expensive and less flexible than the popular video-tape formats (VHS and Beta), which also allowed home recording. In the late 1990s, the DVD, a CD-sized video disc, took its place, and has since become equally popu-lar as videotape for home rentals, thanks to the low cost of DVD players and new recording technologies that allow for home recording on some machines.—Howard Ferstler

Villchur, Edgar M., May 28, 1917– · After earning an M.S.Ed. degree from the City College of New York in 1939, Villchur served as a Captain in the Army Air Corps during World War II, specializing in elec-tronics. After some postwar courses and self-study, he became a teacher of acous-tics and sound reproduction at New York University. During this time he was also writing articles on sound reproduction for *Saturday Review, Audio Magazine, the Journal of the Audio Engineering Society,* and other periodicals. In 1957, he published *The Handbook of Sound Reproduction,* and in 1965, he published *The Reproduc-tion of Sound.*

In 1953, Villchur developed and built a prototype acoustic-suspension woofer sys-tem. To supply the restoring force to the woofer cone, the acoustic-suspension design substitutes the elastic body of air in a sealed speaker cabinet for the usual mechanical suspension. Because the elastic cushion of air is essentially linear for these small pressure changes, harmonic distortion for this type system is much less than for a system with an all-mechanical restoring force. He applied for and received a patent for acoustic-suspension loudspeaker.

In 1954, Villchur and former student Henry Kloss founded Acoustic Research, Inc., (AR) with Villchur as president. (Kloss left AR in 1957 to form his own company, KLH, which manufactured acoustic-suspension loudspeakers under license from Acoustic Research.) Villchur went on to develop the dome tweeter (first used in the 1958 AR-3 speaker system) and an award-winning turntable.

Although the primary purpose of the acoustic-suspension system was to reduce bass distortion, the necessary reduction in cabinet size was at least as important in creating public acceptance, and by 1966, AR had approximately 32% of the domestic speaker market. The AR-3, with an acoustic-suspension woofer, dome tweeter, and dome midrange, is part of the Smithsonian Institution's Museum of American History exhibit on the history of sound reproduction.

In 1967, Villchur sold AR to Teledyne, Inc., and left to establish the Foundation for Hearing Aid Research, a nonprofit laboratory. Since that time, he has worked as a Visiting Scientist at the Massachusetts Institute of Technology and the Albert Einstein School of Medicine. He has pioneered the use of multi-channel compression in hearing aids. His latest book, *Acoustics for Audiologists*, was published in 2000. *See also* LOUDSPEAKER.—Howard Ferstler

Vinyl · The compound used in making disc records, replacing shellac gradually in the 1940s and then totally with the advent of the LP record. Union Carbide developed a vinyl resin in the 1930s ("Vinylite") that was compatible with production equipment of the time, so that factories set up

to make shellac records could make vinyl records as well, or change over completely. Western Electric used vinyl for radio transcriptions, and Muzak used it for its music services. RCA made vinyl ("Victrolac") radio transcriptions, and then the unbreakable V-Discs during the Second World War. In 1944, RCA issued a few Red Seal records on transparent cherry-red vinyl. Cosmo Records made the first major seller on vinyl, a children's item named "Tubby the Tuba." Red vinyl was also used for the RCA 45 rpm record, and for the Columbia microgroove LP of 1948.

The basic vinyl material is polyvinyl chloride (PVC). It is produced by cracking the hydrocarbons in petroleum products to derive vinyl monomer, which is the PVC raw material. Coal and agricultural products are alternative sources for the monomer. LP discs were compression molded of vinyl chloride vinyl acetate copolymer. Injection molding of seven-inch 45-rpm discs used modified polystyrenes.

Important factors in the vinyl disc manufacturing process include careful selection of the resins and stabilizers in the compound, use of carbon black with ideal particle size and distribution, selection of fillers, and blending of special additives.

Vitaphone Corp. · A New York firm, established April 20, 1926, as a joint venture of Warner Brothers and Western Electric. The purpose was to make disc records that would provide sound for motion pictures. This was one of the two active approaches to the making of talking pictures, the other being the optical soundtrack. Although the optical soundtrack became the norm eventually, in the late 1920s, both systems were competing for attention in the film industry, which was of course dealing only with silent films at the time. For a year, the Vitaphone work was carried on in the Manhattan Opera House, then from 1927 in Hollywood.

Vitaphone is of special interest in the history of sound recording not only for its technology, which soon took second place and was forgotten in a few years, but for the content of its productions, many of which were made by outstanding musical artists. The most famous of the 400+ Vitaphone films was *The Jazz Singer* of 1927, with Al Jolson, the first commercial talking picture to achieve national success.

Discs used in the Vitaphone system were shellac, but with less of the usual abrasive filler, so that the surfaces were smoother and quieter. The disadvantage was rapid wear of the discs, which had to be replaced frequently in the projection room. Records played from inside to outside, probably to give the projectionist a better chance of seeing the needle come to the end of its playing surface, thus allowing a timely transfer to the next disc. The diameter was 16 inches, and the speed was 33 1/3 rpm (the same as the later commercial LP record). Synchronization between film and records was accomplished through manual placement of the needle at the starting point in the center of the disc when a cue flashed on the screen. Although this seems a risky method, synchronization did not prove to be a problem in practice. Projection of the sound was from behind and below the theater screen, using four long horns (12–14 feet).

Despite the success of the Vitaphone short subjects, Warner discontinued making them in 1930, as the advantages of soundtracks became more apparent.

Vivatonal · The Columbia counterpart of the Victor Orthophonic record player, introduced in 1925. Major advertising took place in 1927, which claimed a frequency range exceeding that of any "ordinary" player, but the instrument did not succeed in its competition with Victor.

Voecks, Kevin, September 19, 1956– · Currently Director of Research and Tech-

nology at the Revel division of Madrigal Audio Laboratories, a Harman International company, Voecks has a background that includes a mixture of engineering, manufacturing, and retailing high-end audio equipment that dates back to his time in high school, when he imported and sold high-end audio from his parent's home. In 1975, while attending Worcester Polytechnic Institute, one of the few schools to offer specialization in audio engineering at the time, Voecks founded "Natural Sound," a high-end audio store in Framingham, Massachusetts. He sold the operation somewhat later, and then began Symdex, a small high-end company specializing in the production of upscale loudspeaker systems.

In 1979, Voecks moved on to join Mirage Loudspeakers as chief engineer, with the job of designing all of their models, and in 1985, he went to work for to Snell Acoustics, also as chief engineer, shortly after Peter Snell's untimely death. While at Snell, he designed the entire Snell speaker line for many years, making good use of the Canadian National Research Council's famed loudspeaker research facilities, headed at that time by Floyd Toole. In January 1996, Dr. Sidney Harman announced the formation of Revel Loudspeakers within the Harman International group, with Voecks signing on as chief engineer. In that position, he continues to have responsibility for all technical details with the company's very high-end line of loudspeaker systems.—Howard Ferstler

Voigt, Paul Gustavus Adolphus Helmuth, December 9, 1901–February 9, 1981 · Voigt was an English/Canadian electronics engineer who developed electromechanical recording and reproductions systems, amplifiers, and loudspeakers. Born in Forest Hill, London, Voigt had an early interest in the application of valve amplifiers. After graduating with a B.Sc. from University College, London, he was employed by J. E. Hough, Edison Bell Works. He became interested in the mechanical (and later electrical) side of recording and developed principles and equipment, in particular capacitor microphones for in-house and commercial purposes. When the Edison Bell Company closed in 1933, Voigt founded his own company, Voigt Patents Ltd., concentrating on loudspeakers for cinemas and developing horn loudspeakers for domestic use and gramophone pickups. In 1950, he immigrated to Toronto, Canada, and taught electronics; from 1960 to 1969, he was employed by the Radio Regulations Laboratory in Ottawa. After retirement, he worked with theoretical cosmology and fundamental interactions. He died in Brighton, Ontario, Canada.—George Brock-Nannestad

Volta Laboratory Association · A group organized in Washington, D.C., on October 8, 1881, by Alexander Graham Bell, Chichester Bell, and Charles Sumner Tainter. The purpose of the association was to carry on electrical and acoustic research. An early emphasis on the telephone was shifted to phonographic research, probably because of the interests of Tainter. Having developed and filed for a patent on the wax surface principle of the graphophone, the association endeavored in vain to bring Thomas Edison into the enterprise (Tainter spent two months in New York trying to stimulate the interest of Edison and Edward H. Johnson), and then went ahead with the project independently. The Volta Graphophone Co. was established on February 2, 1886, to carry on with development.

Volume · The intensity of an audio signal, the function of the amplitude of the sound wave. It is expressed in decibels relative to a standard reference volume. *See also* AMPLITUDE; LEVEL.

Volume Control · Early playback systems had no means of adjusting the intensity of the output signal, other than to change needles; there were needles that gave degrees of louder to softer output. In 1916, Pathé advertised an "exclusive on Pathéphone": a "tone control" knob on the side of the cabinet to adjust volume. Sonora had a comparable "tone modifier," and the Aeolian Graduola, marketed in 1920, had the same function, although advertising copy clouded its purpose.

VU Meter (Volume Unit Meter) · The standard unit of measurement in a recording system is the Volume Unit. Jointly developed by Bell Labs, CBS, and NBC, and put into use in May 1939. A VU Meter, whose response is supposed to be closely related to the perceived loudness and dynamics of the audio signal, will register zero level on its scale when the potential corresponding to one milliwatt in 600 ohms (0.775 volts) is applied. The dynamic characteristics of a proper VU meter are such that it reaches 99% of its 0-dB maximum in 0.3 second if a steady sine wave of 0 dBm is applied to it. Obviously, the traditional VU meter has an inherent weakness: It will not respond quickly enough to measure certain transient program material. Due to the requirements of digital recording systems, it has been replaced or augmented in some instances by peak program indicators that allow the recording engineer to be guaranteed of no signal clipping. The use of peak indicators increases the chance of background noise becoming audible, however, and in many cases, the standard VU Meter still has operational advantages.—Howard Ferstler

W

Walkman · Small, portable cassette player, developed by Sony Electronics, and first marketed in 1979 under the name the "Soundabout." By the end of the 20th century, Sony alone had sold over 100 million Walkman-type players, and countless other manufacturers had copied the original machine. The Walkman revolutionized portable music listening in much the same way that the earlier Boombox had done, but now, thanks to small headphones that offered excellent fidelity, the listener could enjoy music without disturbing his or her surroundings. Later Walkman-style machines were developed to play Mini-Discs, CDs, MP3s, and other audio file formats.—Carl Benson

Walsh, Lincoln, November 3, 1903– November 17, 1971 · Educated at Stevens Institute of Technology, and earning an M.E. degree from there in 1926, Walsh also studied at Columbia University and Brooklyn College. Before the Second World War, he founded the Brook Amplifier Company, and during the war itself, he worked with Rudy Bozak at the Dinion Coil Company in Caldonia, New York, developing power supplies for radar use. After the war, he worked with Bozak to develop some of the first Bozak speaker systems and later on, he came up with a single-driver speaker design, the Walsh Driver, which has been utilized in some Ohm Corporation loudspeakers for many years. Walsh was an early member of the Audio Engineering Society, and was also a member of the IRE and AIEE (these later merged to become the Institute of Electrical and Electronics Engineers).—Howard Ferstler

Watt · The unit of electrical power measurement. In an audio system wattage is a consideration with regard to an amplifier (indicating the amount of work it can perform, primarily in the driving of loudspeakers) and to loudspeakers (referring to a speaker's efficiency in converting electrical power into acoustic power).

Wax · One of the earliest and most used materials for records, both cylinder and disc. Initially, waxes were carnauba (brittle yellow), from Brazilian palm leaves, or a mineral derived from brown coal. *See also* CYLINDER, 2; DISC.

Webster, Arthur G. · *See* LOUDSPEAKER, 7.

Western Electric Co. · A firm established in 1869 by Enos Barton and Elisha Gray, manufacturer of the equipment used by the Bell Telephone Co., and controlled by Bell after 1882. It has remained in the Bell family, currently as a subsidiary of American Telephone and Telegraph Co. (AT&T). In the 1920s at Western Electric, J. P. Maxfield and H. C. Harrison made important experiments in electrical recording, and developed the major system used by Victor and Columbia. Western Electric developed a steel-tape magnetic recorder in 1940.

White Noise · Broadband noise having constant energy per unit of frequency, as opposed to pink noise, which has constant energy per octave. White noise can sometimes be used for testing audio equipment and can be used for rapidly setting up levels in a surround system by ear or meter.—Howard Ferstler

Winamp · Winamp is one of the most popular software devices for playing back MP3 files on an Apple Mac or PC. It was one of the first to appear, which gave it an instant foothold. It has retained this by being very small—both in terms of the size of the installation software and the space it occupies on screen. At the same time, Winamp has incorporated extra functionality and hi-fi-like components such as graphic equalizers. Produced by Nullsoft in Arizona, it is one of many success stories from comparatively tiny companies that has driven the multimedia development of worldwide operating systems such as Microsoft Windows and driven acceptance of the MP3 music file format. Founded in 1995 by Justin Frankel, Nullsoft and Winamp were sold to AOL Time Warner in 1999. Winamp now co-exists with the company's other, complimentary creation Shoutcase, a system for receiving streaming, radio-style Internet transmissions.—Ian Peel

Windows Media Audio (WMA) · Windows Media Audio (WMA) is a proprietary audio compressed audio format developed by Microsoft, Inc. Originally created as an improvement over MP3, the adoption by Apple Computer of the Advanced Audio Coding (ACC) system for its iPod and iTunes music products shifted Microsoft's competitive aim at Apple. Like ACC, WMA improves upon MP3 audio playback and access while also providing digital rights management of copyrighted content. A WMA file is usually encapsulated in an Advanced Systems Format (ASF) file, a proprietary Microsoft for multimedia files. A WMA song file may have the filename suffix "wma" or "asf," but a file containing more than just audio content must have the suffix "asf." *See also* ADVANCED AUDIO CODING.—Thom Holmes

Winey, James · *See* LOUDSPEAKER, 8; MAGNEPAN LOUDSPEAKERS.

Woofer · The loudspeaker driver in a speaker system that handles the bass-frequency range. In a three- or four-way system, the woofer will probably cover the range between a lower cutoff point of 20 to 60 Hz on up to anywhere between 130 to 600 Hz, before the midrange driver begins to cut in. In a two-way system, the woofer may also handle a substantial percentage of the midrange, all the way up to 2, 3, or even 4 kHz, before the tweeter gradually cuts in. *See also* SUBWOOFER.—Howard Ferstler

Wow · A fluctuation in pitch (frequency) that results when a phonograph turntable does not rotate at constant speed, or when the disc is not fully stabilized on the turntable. In a tape player there is wow when the tape slips somewhere in the transport system, usually at the capstan.

Wurlitzer (Rudolph) Co. · A music instrument manufacturing firm, established in 1861 in Cincinnati, Ohio, by Rudolph Wurlitzer. At first, it made drums and bugles for use in the Civil War, then other band instruments. It was soon the largest retailer of its kind. In 1890, the firm incorporated as the Rudolph Wurlitzer Co., Inc.

Wurlitzer made pianos, electric pianos, coin-op instruments, automatic piano roll changers, and other automatic musical devices. By September 1904, the firm had become an official jobber for Edison products. Before 1913, the firm was located at 122 E. Fourth St., Cincinnati, and after 1913 at 982 Fourth St. It was active in furnishing theatre instruments. An advertisement in *Billboard*, September 1913, claimed that "thirty-three motion picture theatres in twenty-five cities installed Wurlitzer music during August alone." The reference was to the "One-Man Orchestra," a photoplayer (*see also* MOTION PICTURE MUSIC). The company had 20 branches, including one at 115-119 W. 40th St., New York.

In the late 1920s, there were also Wurlitzer coin-op phonographs, and then the fully developed jukebox of the 1930s. About 750,000 jukeboxes were made up to 1974, when production ceased. [Hoover 1971, cover, shows jukebox model no. 1015, 1946.]

Wyoming Phonograph Co. · A firm affiliated with the North American Phonograph Co., established in 1890 in Cheyenne, in business at least to 1893. E. L. Lindsay was manager in 1890.

X-Y-Z

X-Y Stereo Recording · See COINCIDENT STEREO RECORDING.

Yale Collection of Historical Sound Recordings [website: www.library.yale. edu/musiclib/collections.htm#hsr.] · One of the principal archives of its kind, established as a department of the Yale University Libraries in 1961 with an initial deposit of about 20,000 recordings by Mrs. and Mrs. Laurence C. Witten II. Many other individuals and organizations have since contributed records and documentation to the collection, which numbered over 160,000 recordings in various formats as of 2002. Composer recordings are a major concentration; another focus is on early singers. Jazz collecting has been emphasized in recent years. Important holdings also include musical theater, poetry, and drama.

Yamaha Corporation [website: www. yamaha.com] · Founded by Torakusu Yamaha as Nippon Gakki, Ltd., in 1887, Yamaha has grown from a company that specialized in the making of excellent pianos and organs to the world's larger producer of musical instruments. The company is also a leading producer of recording and playback hardware, and of products as diverse as semiconductors, specialty metals, machine tools, motorcycles, golf clubs, industrial robots, furniture, and even bathtubs. The company now owns 44 subsidiaries and representative offices in overseas markets, in addition to numerous related companies in Japan. Yamaha Music Corporation, founded in 1966, has generated a wide range of music activity throughout global society, including Yamaha music schools and the Junior Original Concert.

In 1986, the audio-products division introduced the first DSP ambiance synthesizer to home audio. Since then, the company and its subsidiaries, including the Yamaha Corporation of America established in 1960, have been a dominant force in the world consumer-audio marketplace, producing both affordable and state-of-the-art surround-sound receivers, CD players, cassette and hard-drive CD recorders, and even video projectors, as well as highly regarded professional recording equipment available from the company's professional product group.—Howard Ferstler

Bibliography

Abell, G. O., L. E. Abell, and James F. E. Dennis. "Richard Tauber." *Record Collector* 18 (8, 12) (Oct.–Dec. 1969): 171–272; 19 (3, 4) (June 1970): 81–86.

Adamson, P. G. "Berliner Labels." *Talking Machine Review International* 24 (Oct. 1973): 247–254.

———. "Berliner and 7-inch G & T Records." *Talking Machine Review International* 65, 66 (1983): 1793–1794. A commentary on Rust 1981.

Adrian, Karlo, and Arthur Badrock. *Edison Bell Winner Records.* Rev. ed. Bournemouth, England: *Talking Machine Review International*, 1989. Includes 9 parts in 1 vol.; unpaged. (1st ed. 1974)

Aeppli , Felix. *Heart of Stone: The Definitive Rolling Stones Discography, 1962–1983.* Ann Arbor, Mich.: Pierian Press, 1985. 575 p.

Aldridge, Benjamin L. *The Victor Talking Machine Company.* Camden, N.J.: RCA Sales Corp., 1964. 120 p. Reprinted in Fagan 1983.

Allen, Walter C. *King Joe Oliver.* Stanhope, N.J.: Author, 1955; London: Sidgwick & Jackson, 1959. 224 p.

———. *Hendersonia: The Music of Fletcher Henderson and His Musicians: A Bio-discography.* Highland Park, N.J.: Author, 1973. 651 p.

———, ed. *Studies in Jazz Discography. I. Proceedings of the First and Second Annual Conferences on Discographical Research, 1968–1969, and of the Conference on the Preservation and Extension of the Jazz Heritage, 1969.* New Brunswick, N.J.: Rutgers University, Institute of Jazz Studies, 1971. 112 p.

Albert, George and Frank Hoffmann. *The Cash Box Black Contemporary Charts, 1960-1984.* Metuchen, N.J.: Scarecrow Press, 1986.

Altamirano, Antonio. "Ellen Beach Yaw." *Record Collector* 10 (7) (Dec. 1955): 149–161.

American Music Recordings: A Discography of 20th-Century U.S. Composers. Edited by Carol J. Oja. Brooklyn: Institute for the Study of American Music, 1982. 368 p.

Andrews, Frank. "The 'Jumbo' Story as I See It." *Hillandale News* 61 (June 1971): 21–22. [Andrews 1971/1]

———. "Toward the Complete Documentation of All So-Called 78 RPM Records." *Talking Machine Review International* 12 (Oct. 1971): 108–110. [Andrews 1971/2]

———. "Record Research No. 5." *Talking Machine Review International* 16 (June 1972): 108–210.

———. "Lambert in Britain." *Talking Machine Review International* 27 (Apr. 1974): 70–91; 29 (Aug. 1974): 152. [Andrews 1974/4]

———. "Guiniphones." *Hillandale News* 80 (Oct. 1974): 233–235. [Andrews 1974/5]

———. "The International Indestructible Cylinder Records." *Talking Machine Review International* 30 (Oct. 1974): 190–196. [Andrews 1974/10]

———. "The North American Phonograph Company." *Talking Machine Review International* 38 (Feb. 1976): 571–582. [Andrews 1976/2]

———. "A Fonotipia Fragmentia." *Talking Machine Review International* 40–42, 44, 45, 48, 49b (1976–1977). Serialized in seven parts. [Andrews 1976/5]

———. "Some Errors in the Society's Cylinder Catalogues." *Hillandale News* 90 (June 1976): 508–509. [Andrews 1976/6]

———. "The Columbia Bubble Books." *Hillandale News* 92 (Oct. 1976): 46–49. [Andrews 1976/10]

———. "Minstrels, Minstrel Shows, and Early Recordings." *Talking Machine Review International* 47 (1977): 1,063–1,066, 1,071–1,076. [Andrews 1977/1]

———. "The Recordings of 1907 in Britain." *Hillandale News* 98 (Oct. 1977): 239–241. [Andrews 1977/10]

———. "Neophone." *Talking Machine Review International* 51 (Apr. 1978): 1,304–1,313; 52, 53 (June–Aug. 1978): 1,333–1,339; 54, 55 (Oct.–Dec. 1978): 1,397–1,400. [Andrews 1978/3]

———. "EdisoniaEdison Bell." *Talking Machine Review International* 51 (Apr. 1978): 1,301–1,302. [Andrews 1978/4]

———. "Star Records." *Talking Machine Review International* 60, 61 (Oct.–Dec. 1979): 1,617–1,622; 68 (June 1984): 1,873–1,874. [Andrews 1979/10]

———. "A Further Look at the International Zonophone Company, May 1901 to June 1903." *Talking Machine Review International* 62 (1980): 1,691–1,696; 63, 64 (1981): 1,717–1,725; 65, 66 (Feb. 1983): 1,811–1,818. [Andrews 1980/2]

———. "From Orchestrelle to Vocalion: An Account of the Aeolian Companies and Their Involvement with Talking Machines." *Hillandale News* 116 (Oct. 1980): 99–106; 117 (Nov. 1980): 120–155. [Andrews 1980/10]

———. "British Brunswick: The History of Brunswick Cliftophone, Brunswick Cliftophone Ltd., and Brunswick in the 1920s." *Hillandale News* 122 (Oct. 1981): 265–273. [Andrews 1981/1]

———. "Broadcast: The Story of a Record." *Hillandale News* 129 (Dec. 1982): 126–131; 130 (Feb. 1983): 148–149. [Andrews 1982/12]

———. "The History of the Crystalate Companies in the Recording Industry, 1901–1937." *Hillandale News* 134 (Oct. 1983): 259–290; 135 (Dec. 1983): 291–297; 136 (Feb. 1984): 317–324. [Andrews 1983/10]

———. "Duo-Trac." *Hillandale News* 137 (Apr. 1984): 16–23. [Andrews 1984/4]

———. "Genuine Edison Bell Records." *Hillandale News* 141 (Dec. 1984): 125–130; 142 (Mar. 1985): 159–164; 143 (Apr. 1985): 179–184; 145 (Aug. 1985): 233–242. [Andrews 1978/12]

———. "Imperial Records." *Talking Machine Review International* 69 (Dec. 1984): 1,908–1,912. [Andrews 1984/12]

———. *Columbia Ten-Inch Records Issued 1904 to 1930.* London: City of London Phonograph and Gramophone Society, 1985. Unpaged. Lists U.K. issues of the various Columbia labels. [Andrews 1985/1]

———. "The Birth of Electrical Recording." *Hillandale News* 144 (1985): 199–202. [Andrews 1985/6]

———. "Homophone in Britain." *Hillandale News* 147 (Dec. 1985): 284–290; 148 (Dec. 1986): 312–317; 149 (Apr. 1986): 5–8; 150 (June 1986): 32–35. [Andrews 1985/12; 1986/4]

———. *The Edison Phonograph: The British Connection.* Rugby, England: City of London Phonograph and Gramophone Society, 1986. 140 p.

———. "The Coming and Demise of the Marathon Records and Machines." *Talking Machine Review International* 72 (Apr. 1987): 2,081–2,105. [Andrews 1987/4]

———. "The His Master's Voice Record Catalogues." *Hillandale News* 158 (Oct. 1987): 255–261; 159 (Dec. 1987): 284–291; 160 (Feb. 1988): 320–329. [Andrews 1987/10]

———. "John Bull Records and Ercophone Gramophones." *Talking Machine Review International* 73 (Feb. 1988): 2,139–2,150. [Andrews 1988/2]

———. "The Under-Twenty-Fives: A History of British Disc Records of Less than 25 cm (10 Inch) Diameter." *Hillandale News* 161 (Apr. 1988): 6–11; 162 (June 1988): 40–46. [Andrews 1988/4]

———. "Joseph Leonard Blum and His Gramophone Records." *Talking Machine Review International* 75 (Autumn 1988): 2,182–2,196. [Andrews 1988/10]

———. "The Zonophone Record and Its Associated Labels in Britain" *Hillandale News* 166 (Feb. 1989): 150–156; 167; 168 (June 1989): 206–211. Corrections by Andrews in *Hillandale News* 170 (Oct. 1989): 276.

———. "Nipper's Uncle: William Barraud and His Disc Records." *Hillandale News* 174 (June 1990): 37–42; 175 (Aug. 1990): 67–72; 176 (Oct. 1990): 112–116; 177 (Dec. 1990): 134–138.

———. "Records in Store." *Hillandale News* 181 (Aug. 1991): 268–276.

Andrews, Frank, and Ernie Bayly. *Billy Williams Records: A Study in Discography.* Bournemouth, England: Talking Machine Review, 1982. 72 p.

Annand, H. H. *The Complete Catalogue of the United States Everlasting Indestructible Cylinders, 1905–1913.* London: City of London Phonograph and Gramophone Society, 1966. 38 p.

———. *Block Catalogue of the Cylinder Records Issued by the U.S. Phonograph Company, 1890–1896.* Hillingdon, Middlesex, England, 1970.

———. *The Catalogue of the United States Everlasting Indestructible Cylinders, 1980–1913.* 2nd ed. Bournemouth, England: *Talking Machine Review International,* 1973. 36 p.

Aranza, Jacob. *Backward Masking Unmasked.* Shreveport, La.: Huntington House, 1984. 115 p.

Arfanis, Stathis A., and Nick Nickson. 1990. *The Complete Discography of Dimitri Mitropoulos.* Athens: IRINNA, 1990. 111 p.

Association for Recorded Sound Collections. *Preliminary Directory of Sound Recordings Collections in the United States and Canada.* New York: New York Public Library, 1967. 157 p.

———. *Audio Preservation: A Planning Study: Final Performance Report.* Elwood A. McKee. Rockville, Md.: Association for Recorded Sound Collections, Associated Audio Archives Committee, 1988. 2 vols., looseleaf.

Atchison, Glenn. "The Musical Theatre in Canadaon Stage and on Record." In Hummel 1984, pp. xxxiv–xl.

Audio Cyclopedia. Edited by Howard M. Tremaine. 3rd ed. Indianapolis: Sams Publishing, 1977. 1,757 p. (1st ed. 1959)

Audio Key: The Canadian Record & Tape Guide. Winnipeg: Audio Key, 1985 (annual).

Ault, Bob. "CBS and the Columbia Phonograph Company." *Antiques and Collecting Hobbies* (Nov. 1986): 53–56.

———. "A Few Observations on the Art of Playing Old Records." *Antiques and Collecting Hobbies* (Feb. 1987): 48–50.

The Australian Music Industry: An Economic Evaluation. Music Board of the Australian Council. Sidney: The Board, 1987. 298 p.

Bachman, W. S., B. B. Bauer, and P. C. Goldmark. "Disk Recording and Reproduction." W.S. Bachman. *IRE Proceedings* 50 (May 1962): 738–744. Reprinted in Roys 1978.

Backensto, Woody. "Red Nichols Memorial Issue." *Record Research* 96, 97 (Apr. 1969): 2–18.

Backus, John. *The Acoustical Foundations of Music.* New York: Norton, 1969. 312 p.

Badmaieff, Alexis, and Don Davis. *How to Build Speaker Enclosures.* Indianapolis: Sams, 1966. 144 p.

Badrock, Arthur. *Dominion Records: A Catalogue and History.* Bournemouth, England: Talking Machine Review, 1976. 31 p.

———. "Unravelling Ariel." *Talking Machine Review International* 75 (Autumn 1988): 2, 197–2,199.

———. *The Complete Regal Catalogue.* Arthur Badrock and Frank Andrews. Malvern, England: City of London Phonograph and Gramophone Society, 1991. 358 p.

Badrock, Arthur, and Derek Spruce. "Aco." *R.S.V.P.* 2 (June 1965) to 15 (Aug. 1966); 17 (Oct. 1966) to 25 (June 1967); 27 (Aug. 1967) to 31 (Dec. 1967); 34 (Mar. 1968); 35 (Apr. 1968), 40 (Sept. 1968) to 42 (Nov. 1968). Additions and corrections in 43 (Dec. 1968), 47 (Apr. 1969), 52 (Jan.–Feb. 1970).

Bahr, Edward. *Trombone Euphonium Discography.* Stevens Point, Wis.: Index House, 1988. 502 p.

Bailey, A. R. "A Non-Resonant Loudspeaker Enclosure." *Wireless World* (Oct. 1965): 483–486.

Baker, Darrell, and Larry F. Kiner. *The Sir Harry Lauder Discography.* Metuchen, N.J.: Scarecrow Press, 1990. 198 p.

Barnes, Harold. "Ninon Vallin." *Record Collector* 8 (3) (Mar. 1953): 52–65.

Barnes, Harold, and Victor Girard. "Conchita Supervia." *Record Collector* 6 (3) (Mar. 1951): 51, 54–71; 8 (2) (Feb. 1953): 41–44.

Barnes, Ken. "Record Cleaning." *Antique Phonograph Monthly* 2 (10) (Dec. 1974): 3, 8; 3 (1) (Jan. 1975): 5–7.

———. "The Bristophone: An 'L' of a Reproducer." *Antique Phonograph Monthly* 3 (3) (Mar. 1975): 3–5.

Barr, Stephen C. "Gull(s) of My Dreams." *New Amberola Graphic* 39 (Winter 1982): 3–12.

———. "Ring Out Wild Bells! A Study of Bell Records." *New Amberola Graphic* 46 (Autumn 1983): 3–7.

Basart, Ann P. *The Sound of the Fortepiano: A Discography of Recordings on Early Pianos.* Berkeley, Calif.: Fallen Leaf Press, 1985. 472 p.

Batten, Joseph. *Joe Batten's Book: The Story of Sound Recording.* Foreword by Compton Mackenzie. London: Rockliff, 1956. 201 p.

Bauer, Benjamin B. "Tracking Angle in Phonograph Pickups." *Electronics* 18 (Mar. 1945): 110–115. Reprinted in Roys 1978.

———. "Vertical Tracking Improvements in Stereo Recording." *Audio* (Feb. 1963): 19–22. Reprinted in Roys 1978.

Bauer, Benjamin B., Daniel W. Gravereaux, and Arthur J. Gust. "A Compatible Stereo-Quadraphonic (SQ) Record System." *Journal of the Audio Engineering Society* 19 (8) (1971): 638–646. Reprinted in Roys 1978.

Bauer, Robert. *The New Catalogue of Historical Records, 1898–1908-09.* 2nd ed. London: Sidgwick and Jackson, 1947. 494 p. Foreword signed by Roberto Bauer. (1st ed. 1937) Reprinted by Sidgwick and Jackson 1970.

Baumbach, Robert W. *Look for the Dog: An Illustrated Guide to Victor Talking Machines, 1901–1929.* Woodland Hills, Calif.: Stationery X-Press, 1981. 326 p.

Bayly, Ernie. "The Decca Portable." *Talking Machine Review International* 26 (Feb. 1974): 596–597. [Bayly 1974/2]

———. "Small Records." *Talking Machine Review International* 28 (June 1974): 116–119. [Bayly 1974/6]

———. "Double Sided Records." *Talking Machine Review International* 38 (Feb. 1976): 596–597.

———. "Zonophone Pseudonyms." *Talking Machine Review International* 43 (Dec. 1976): 857–858. [Bayly 1976/12]

———. "DeWolf Hopper." *Talking Machine Review International* 70 (Dec. 1985): 1,966, 1,979.

———. "5-Inch Berliner." *Hillandale News* 163 (Aug. 1988): 71.

Bebb, Richard. "The Actor Then and Now." *Recorded Sound* 47 (July 1972): 85–93; 48 (Oct. 1972): 115–124.

Bennett, Bill. "Capitol, 1942 to 1949 and Beyond." *Record Research* 183, 184 (July 1981): 11; 185, 186 (Oct. 1981): 12; 187, 188 (Dec. 1981): 12; 189, 190 (Mar.–Apr. 1982): 11; 191, 192 (July 1982): 12, 14; 193, 194 (Oct. 1982): 10; 197, 198 (Mar.–Apr. 1983): 11; 199, 200 (June 1983): 13.

———. "Capitol 15000 Series 78 RPM, Oct. 1947 to Mar. 1949." *Record Research* 227, 228 (Mar. 1987): 1–2; 229, 230 (June 1987): 10; 231, 232 (Oct. 1987): 10; 233 234 (Feb. 1988): 9; 239 240 (Apr. 1989): 8; 241, 242 (Sept.–Oct. 1989): 24; 243, 244 (May–June 1990): 23; 245, 246 (Jan. 1991): 23.

Bennett, John. "Fonotipia Catalogue." *Hobbies* (Feb. 1954): 25–27.

———. *Melodiya: A Soviet Russian L.P. Discography.* Westport, Conn.: Greenwood Press, 1981. 832 p.

Benson, Joe. *Uncle Joe's Record Guide: The Rolling Stones.* Glendale, Calif.: J. Benson Unlimited, 1987. 124 p.

Berger, Karol. "The Yale Collection of Historical Sound Recordings." *Association for Recorded Sound Collections Journal* 6 (1) (1974): 13–25.

Berger, Monroe, Edward Berger, and James Patrick. *Benny Carter: A Life in American Music.* Metuchen, N.J.: Scarecrow Press, 1982. 877 p.

Bergman, Billy. *Hot Sauces: Latin and Caribbean Pop.* New York: Quill, 1985.

Berliner, Oliver. "Wags and Tales that Started a Revolution." *Audio* (Dec. 1977): 36–40.

Betrock, Alan. *Girl Groups: The Story of a Sound.* New York: Delilah Books, 1982. 175 p.

Bettini Catalog for June 1898; *Bettini Catalog for April 1900*; *Bettini Catalog for June 1901.* Stanford, Calif.: Stanford University Archive of Recorded Sound, 1965. (Reprint Series, 1)

Betz, Peter. "Uncle Josh before Cal Stewart." *Talking Machine Review International* 41 (Aug. 1976): 726–728.

———. "John Kreusi [sic] The Man Who 'Made This'." *Hillandale News* 177 (Dec. 1990): 131–133.

Bianco, David. *Heat Wave: The Motown Fact Book.* Ann Arbor, Mich.: Pierian Press, 1988. 524 p.

Biel, Michael. "For the Record." *Association for Recorded Sound Collections Journal* 14 (1) (1982): 97–113. [1982/1]

———. "For the Record." *Association for Recorded Sound Collections Journal* 14 (3) (1982): 101–111. [1982/2]

Blacker, George. "Disco-ing" columns. *Record Research*, 1955–1990. Cited by date only.

———. "How to Play Old Records on New Equipment." *High Fidelity* (Apr. 1973): 48–57.

———. "The Pennsylvania Vertical Group Preliminary Report." *Record Research* 131 (Jan. 1975): 1, 6; 132 (Apr. 1975): 5–6; 133 (June 1975): 5–6. Considers relationships among vertical-cut labels including Domestic, Keen-O-Phone, McKinley, Phono-Cut, Rex, and Rishell.

———. "Playing Oldies the New Way." *Antique Phonograph Monthly* 3 (7) (Aug.–Sept. 1975): 3–6. [Blacker 1975/8]

———. "The Data Sheet Again!" *Record Research* 139, 140 (May–June 1976): 12. [Blacker 1976/5]

———. "Some Pointed Remarks about Styli." *Record Research* 159, 160 (Dec. 1978): 2.

———. "Parade of Champions, 1925 to 1930, 1500 to 16133." *Record Research* 169, 170 (Jan. 1980): 2–16; 171, 172 (Mar. 1980): 6–6; 173, 174 (June 1980): 8, 24; 175, 176 (Sept. 1980): 12; 179, 190 (Feb. 1981): 11. [Blacker 1980/1]

———. "Further Remarks on Electronic Cylinder Playback." *Record Research* 175, 176 (Sept. 1980): 2. [Blacker 1980/9]

———. "Some Comments on the Edison Kinetophone Cylinders of 1912." *Antique Phonograph Monthly* 6, 10 (1981): 3–7.

———. "Cylindrography or Cylindrographically Yours." *Record Research* 179, 180 (Feb. 1981): 2, 23. [Blacker 1981/2]

———. "Little Wonder Records." *Record Research* 197, 198 (Mar.–Apr. 1983): 1–2; 199, 200 (June 1983): 8; 201, 202 (Sept. 1983): 12; 203, 204 (Dec. 1983): 7; 205, 206 (Mar. 1984): 10–11; 207, 208 (June 1984): 10; 209, 210 (Oct. 1984): 11; 211, 212 (Feb. 1985): 10; 213, 214 (May 1985): 12; 215, 216 (July 1985):10; 217, 218 (Oct. 1985): 11; 219, 220 (Jan. 1986): 14; 221, 222 (Apr. 1986): 12.

———. "The English Singers and Roycroft Revisited." *Record Research* 209, 210 (Oct. 1984): 3–4; 211, 212 (Feb. 1985): 4–5, 11.

———. "Beginning of the Emerson Dynasty." *Record Research* 239, 240 (Apr. 1989): 1–2; 241, 242 (Oct.–Nov. 1989): 2; 243, 244 (May–June 1990): 5; 245, 246 (Jan. 1991): 6; 247, 248 (Sept. 1991): 6.

———. "Talk-O-Photo." *Record Research* 243, 244 (May–June 1990): 4; 247, 248 (Sept. 1991): 5.

Blackmer, David E. "A Wide Dynamic Range Noise Reduction System." *dBMagazine* (Aug.–Sept. 1972): 54–56.

Blair, Linda W. "The Yale Collection of Historical Sound Recordings" *Association for Recorded Sound Collections Journal* 20 (2) (Feb. 1989): 167–176.

Bloesch, David. "Artur Schnabel: A Discography." *Association for Recorded Sound Collections Journal* 18 (1, 3) (1986): 33–143.

Blyth, Alan. *Opera on Record.* London: Hutchinson, 1979, 1984. 2 vols.

———. *Song on Record.* New York: Cambridge University Press, 1986, 1988. 2 vols.

Bolig, John. *The Recordings of Enrico Caruso.* Dover, Del.: Delaware State Museum, 1973. 88 p.

Bond, Johnny. *The Recordings of Jimmie Rodgers: An Annotated Discography.* Los Angeles: John Edwards Memorial Foundation (JEMF), University of California, 1978. 76 p. (JEMF Special Series, 11)

Bondesen, Poul. *North American Bird Songs: A World of Music.* Klampenborg, Denmark: Scandinavian Science Press, 1977. 254 p.

Boots, Robert C. *Military Music Holdings at the United States Army Military History Institute.* Carlisle Barracks, Penn.: U.S. Army Military History Institute, Audio Visual Archives, 1981. 391 p.

Bordman, Gerald. *American Musical Theatre.* New York: Oxford University Press, 1978. 749 p.

Borwick, John. "The Diamond Stylus Company." *Gramophone* (July 1975): 258.

———. "Dual Gebrüder Steidinger." *Gramophone* (Apr. 1976): 1,693.

———. *The Gramophone Guide to Hi-Fi.* London: David & Charles, 1982. 256 p.

———. *Sound Recording Practice.* 3rd ed. New York: Oxford University Press, 1987. 557 p. (1st ed. 1976) [Borwick 1987/1]

———. "A Music-Lover's Guide to CD and Hi-Fi." *Gramophone* (Mar.–Aug. 1987). A series of six articles. [Borwick 1987/3]

———. *Loudspeaker and Headphone Handbook.* London: Butterworths, 1988. 573 p.

———. "The British Library National Sound Archive." *Gramophone* (July 1989): 251–252. [Borwick 1989/7]

———. "JVC, Japan." *Gramophone* (Oct. 1989): 787–788. [Borwick 1989/10]

———. "Microphone Balance." *Gramophone* (May 1990): 2,094.

Bott, Michael F. "Riccardo Martin." *Record Collector* 26 (1, 2) (May 1980): 5–42.

Bridges, Glenn. *Pioneers in Brass.* Detroit: Sherwood, 1968. 129 p.

Brooks, Edward. *The Bessie Smith Companion: A Critical and Detailed Appreciation of the Recordings.* New York: Da Capo Press, 1982. 229 p.

Brooks, Tim. "Columbia Acoustic Matrix Series: Preliminary Research." *Record Research* 133 (June 1975): 1–8; 134 (Aug. 1975): 3–4; 135, 136 (Nov.–Dec. 1975): 8–12.

———. "Vogue, the Picture Record." *Record Research* 148 (July 1977): 1–8; 151, 152 (Jan. 1978): 4–10; 153, 154 (Apr. 1978): 10; 159, 160 (Dec. 1978): 10; 161, 162 (Feb.–Mar. 1979): 3.

———. "Columbia Records in the 1890s: Founding the Record Industry." *Association for Recorded Sound Collections Journal* 10 (1) (1978): 5–36.

———. "A Directory to Columbia Recording Artists of the 1890s." *Association for Recorded Sound Collections Journal* 11 (2, 3) (1979): 102–138.

———. "Current Bibliography." *Association for Recorded Sound Collections Journal* 10 (2, 3) (1979). Continuing series. [Brooks 1979/1]

———. "The Artifacts of Recording History: Creators, Users, Losers, Keepers." *Association for Recorded Sound Collections Journal* 11 (1) (1979): 18–28. [Brooks 1979/2]

———. "ARSC: Association for Recorded Sound Collections—An Unusual Organization." *Goldmine* (Feb. 1983): 22–23.

———. "A Survey of Record Collectors' Societies." *Association for Recorded Sound Collections Journal* 16 (3) (1984): 17–36.

———. "One-Hit Wonders of the Acoustic Era (... And a Few Beyond)." *Antique Phonograph Monthly* 9 (2) (1990): 8–11.

Brown, Alan. "The Kinetophonograph." *Talking Machine Review International* 40 (June 1976): 716–719.

Brown, Denis. *Sarah Vaughan: A Discography.* Westport, Conn.: Greenwood Press, 1991. 192 p.

Brown, Jake. *Suge Knight: The Rise, and Fall, and Rise of Death Row Records.* New York: Amber Books, 2001. 206 p.

Brown, Scott, and Robert Hilbert. *The Life and Music of James P. Johnson.* Metuchen, N.J.: Scarecrow Press, 1986. 503 p.

Brownstein, Mark. "One Disc at a Time: Moldy Discs." *CD-ROM Enduser* (Feb. 1990): 29.

Bruun, C. L., and J. Gray. "A Bibliography of Discographies." *Recorded Sound* 1 (7) (1962): 206–213.

Bruyninckx, Walter. *60 Years of Recorded Jazz.* Mechelen, Belgium: Author, 1980. 36 vols.

Bryan, Martin F. "Columbia BC Half-Foot-Long Records." *New Amberola Graphic* 41 (Summer 1982): 3–9.

———. "Orlando R. Marsh, Forgotten Pioneer." *New Amberola Graphic* 71 (Jan. 1990): 3–14. Supplemented in *New Amberola Graphic* 72 (Spring 1990): 3–5.

Bryan, Martin F., and William R. Bryant. *Oxford and Silvertone Records, 1911–1918.* St. Johnsbury, Vt.: New Amberola Phonograph Co., 1975. 56 p.

Bryant, E. T. *Collecting Gramophone Records.* New York: Focal Press, 1962. Reprint Westport, Conn.: Greenwood Press, 1978. 153 p.

Bryant, E. T., and Guy Marco. *Music Librarianship: A Practical Guide.* 2nd ed. Metuchen, N.J.: Scarecrow Press, 1985. 449 p. (1st ed. 1959)

Bullard, Thomas R., and William R. Moran. "Lawrence Tibbett." *Record Collector* 23 (11, 12) (Aug. 1977): 242–287; 24 (1, 2)(Jan. 1978): 36–46.

Bullock, Robert M., III, and Peter E. Hillman. "A Transmission Line Woofer Model." Paper read at the 81st Conference of the Audio Engineering Society, Nov. 1986.

Bunnett, Rexton S. "The British Musical." In Hummel 1984, xix–xxvi.

Burlingame, Roger. "Emile Berliner." *Dictionary of American Biography.* Supplement 1, 1944, pp. 75–76.

Burros, Harold. "Frida Leider." *Record Collector* 1 (5) (Sept. 1946): 50–53. Burros also wrote the discography in *Playing My Part,* by Frida Leider (New York: Da Capo Press, 1978).

Burt, Leah. "Chemical Technology in the Edison Recording Industry." *Journal of the Audio Engineering Society* 25 (10, 11) (Sept.–Oct. 1977): 717–717.

Buth, Olga. "Scores and Recordings." *Library Trends* 23 (Jan. 1975): 427–450.

Capes, S.J. "Early Pianoforte Records." *British Institute of Recorded Sound.* Bulletin 3 (Winter 1956): 13–19.

Carolan, Nicholas. *A Short Discography of Irish Folk Music.* Dublin: Folk Music Society of Ireland, 1987. 40 p.

Carreck, J.N. "Early Organ Recordings." *Hillandale News* 1 (Oct. 1960): 4, 8.

———. "Obituary: Dr. Ludwig Koch, Sound Recording Pioneer, 1881–1974." *Hillandale News* 79 (Aug. 1974): 223–224.

Carter, Sydney H. *Edison Two-Minute Cylinder Records: The Complete Catalogue of the Edison Gold Moulded Two-Minute Cylinder Records, 1901–12.* Abbots Close, Worthing, England: Author, 1965? 156 p.

———. *Edison Amberol Cylinder Records ... Foreign Issues, 1908–12.* Abbots Close, Worthing, England: Author, 1965? 39 p.

———. *A Catalogue of Clarion and Ebonoid Records.* Bournemouth, England: Talking Machine Review, 1977. 70, 27 p.

———. "Air-Pressure Operated Amplifying Gramophone." *Hillandale News* 94 (Dec. 1977): 98–101. [Carter 1977/12]

———. *Blue Amberol Cylinders: A Catalogue.* Bournemouth, England: *Talking Machine Review International,* 1978. 130 p.

Carter, Sydney H., Frank Andrews, and Leonard L. Watts. *Sterling.* Bournemouth, England: *Talking Machine Review International,* 1975. 108 p. Contents: "A Catalogue of Sterling Cylinder Records," by Sydney H. Carter; "A History of Their Manufacture," by Frank Andrews; "Sterling Cylinders on Pathé Discs," by Len Watts.

Caruso, Enrico, Jr., and Andrew Farkas. *Enrico Caruso: My Father and My Family.* Amadeus, Oreg.: Amadeus Press, 1990. 850 p. Includes a discography by William R. Moran.

Castleman, Harry, and Walter Podrazik. *All Together Now. The First Complete Beatles Discography, 1961–1975.* Ann Arbor, Mich.: Pierian Press, 1976. 387 p. Two supplementary volumes were issued by the same authors and publisher: *The Beatles Again* (1977; 280 p.) and *The End of the Beatles?* (1985; 553 p.).

Catalogue of Twelve-Inch Monarch Records in March 1904. Gramophone Co., Ltd. London: Gramophone & Typewriter, Ltd., 1904. Reprint Bournemouth, England: Gramophone Co., 1972. 35 p.

Catalogue of Nicole Records, Season 1905–1906. London: Nicole, 1905. Reprint Bournemouth, England: *Talking Machine Review International,* 1971. 25 p.

Celletti, Rodolfo. *Le grandi voci.* Rome: Istituto per la Collaborazione Culturale, 1964. 1,044 columns.

Chambers, Iain. *Urban Rhythms: Pop Music and Popular Culture.* London: Macmillan, 1985. 272 p.

Charosh, Paul. *Berliner Gramophone Records.* Westport, Conn.: Greenwood Press, 1995. 290 p.

Charters, Samuel. "Liner Notes." *Vanguard Collector's Edition* 163 66 (2) (1997).

Charters, Samuel B. "Sears Roebuck Sells the Country Blues." *Record Research* 27 (Mar.–Apr. 1960): 3, 20.

Chew, V. K. *Talking Machines*. 2nd ed. London: Her Majesty's Stationery Office, 1981. 80 p. (1st ed. 1967)

———. "Disc Tinfoil Phonograph." *Hillandale News* 124 (Feb. 1982): 328–329.

Clough, Francis F., and G. J. Cuming. *The World's Encyclopedia of Recorded Music*. London: Sidgwick & Jackson, 1952. 890 p. First supplement (Apr. 1950–May June 1951) bound in Second supplement (1951–1952), 1952. 262 p. Third supplement (1953–1955), 1957. 564 p. Reprint Westport, Conn.: Greenwood Press, 1970. 3 vols. Usually cited as WERM.

———. "Discography." In *Minor Recollections* by Otto Klemperer, translated from the German version by J. Maxwell Brownjohn (London: Dobson, 1964; 124 p.), pp. 103–117.

———. "Myra Hess Discography." *Sound* 24 (Oct. 1966): 104–106.

Cohen, Abraham B. *Hi-Fi Loudspeakers and Enclosures*. 2nd ed. Rochelle Park, N.J.: Hayden Book Co., 1968. 438 p.

Cohen, Norm. "Record Reviews." *Journal of American Folklore* 102 (Apr.–June 1989): 195–198.

Cohen, Ronald, and Dave Samuelson. *Songs for Political Action: Folk Music, Topical Songs, and the American Left, 1926–1953*. Hamburg, Germany: Bear Family Records BCD 15720-JL, 1996.

Cohodas, Nadine. *Spinning Blues into Gold: The Chess Brothers and the Legendary Chess Records*. New York: St. Martin's Press, 2000. 358 p.

Cole, Roger. "The Aeolian Company." *Hillandale News* 57 (Oct. 1970): 161–165.

Collier, James Lincoln. *Louis Armstrong, An American Genius*. New York: Oxford University Press, 1983. 383 p.

Collins, William J., and James F.E. Dennis. 1979. "Giovanni Martinelli." *Record Collector* 25 (7–9) (Oct. 1979): 149–215; 25 (10–12) (Feb. 1980): 221–255; 26 (9, 10) (May 1981): 237–239.

Connor, Russell D. *Benny Goodman: Listen to His Legacy*. Metuchen, N.J.: Scarecrow Press, 1988. 409 p.

Cooper, David E. *International Bibliography of Discographies: Classical Music, and Jazz and Blues, 1962–1972*. Littleton, Colo.: Libraries Unlimited, 1975. 272 p.

Cooper, Reg. "Independent Record Companies." *Talking Maching Review International* 62 (1980): 1,669–1,671.

Copeland, George A. "Understanding the Edison Reproducer." *New Amberola Graphic* 73 (July 1990): 10–14.

Copeland, Peter C. "Playback." *Hillandale News* 172 (Feb. 1990): 336. Comments on this article were made in a letter to *Hillandale News* 174 (June 1990): 52.

Corenthal, Michael G. *Cohen on the Telephone: A History of Jewish Recorded Humor and Popular Music, 1892–1942*. Milwaukee, Wis.: Yesterday's Memories, 1984. 108 p.

———. *Iconography of Recorded Sound, 1886–1986*. Milwaukee, Wis.: Yesterday's Memories, 1986. 243 p.

Cott, Jonathan. *Conversations with Glenn Gould*. Boston: Little, Brown, 1984. Discography pp. 139–150.

Cotter, Dave. "Flexo, San Francisco's Obscure Record Company." *Record Research* 118 (Oct. 1972): 1, 4–7.

———. "National Music Lovers." *New Amberola Graphic* 1 (25) (Fall 1975–Apr. 1988). Series of brief articles.

Creighton, James. *Discopaedia of the Violin, 1889–1971*. Toronto: University of Toronto Press, 1974. 987 p.

Cros, Charles. "Comptes rendus des séances de l'Académie des Sciences ... 3 decembre 1877." Paper deposited with the *Académie* on April 30, 1877.

Croucher, Trevor. *Early Music Discography: From Plainsong to the Sons of Bach*. Phoenix, Ariz.: Oryx, 1981. 2 vols.

Crowhurst, Norman. *The Stereo High Fidelity Handbook*. New York: Crown, 1960. 183 p.

Crutchfield, Will. "Brahms by Those Who Knew Him." *Opus* 2 (5) (Aug. 1956): 12–21, 60.

Culshaw, John. *Ring Resounding: The Recording in Stereo of Der Ring des Nibelungen*. London: Secker & Warburg, 1967. 284 p.

———. *Reflections on Wagner's Ring*. London: Secker & Warburg, 1976. 105 p.

———. *Putting the Record Straight*. New York: Viking, 1981. 362 p.

Cunningham, Agnes "Sis," and Gordon Friesen. *Red Dust and Broadsides: A Joint Autobiography*. Amherst: University of Massachusetts Press, 1999. 371 p.

Curry, Edgar L. *Vogue: The Picture Record*. Everett, Wash.: Author, 1990. 92 p.

Cuscuna, Michael, and Michel Ruppli. *The Blue Note Label: A Discography*. Westport, Conn.: Greenwood Press, 1988. 544 p.

Czada, Peter, and Frans Jansen. "Tefifon." *Hillandale News* 130 (Feb. 1983): 169–171.

Dales, J. S. "Edison Dictation Cylinders." *Talking Machine Review International* 62 (1980): 1,675.

Danca, Vince. *Bunny Berigan: A Bio-Discography*. Rockford, Ill.: Author, 1978. 66 p.

D'Andrea, Renzo. *Tito Schipa nella vita, nell'arte, nel suo tempo*. Fasano di Puglia, Italy: Schena, 1981. 246 p. Discography by Daniele Rubboli, pp. 225–240.

Dangarfield, Jim. "Nina Koshetz." *Sound Record* 7 (4) (June 1991): 154–155.

Daniels, William R. *The American 45 and 78 RPM Record Dating Guide, 1940–1959*. Westport, Conn.: Greenwood Press, 1985. 157 p.

Dannen, Frederick. *Hit Men: Power Brokers and Fast Money Inside the Music Business*. New York: Times Books, 1990. 387 p.

Darrell, R. D. *The Gramophone Shop Encyclopedia of Recorded Music.* Edited by Robert H. Reid. New York: Crown, 1948. 3rd ed. 639 p. Reprint Westport, Conn.: Greenwood Press, 1970. (1st ed., compiled by R. D. Darrell, New York: Gramophone Shop, 1936) 574 p.

Davies, John R. T., and Roy Cooke. *The Music of Fats Waller.* 2nd ed. London: Century Press, 1953. 40 p. (1st ed. 1950)

Davies, John R. T., and Laurie Wright. *Morton's Music.* 2nd ed. Chigwell, Essex, England: Storyville Publications, 1968. 40 p.

Davis C. C., and J. G. Frayne. "The Westrex Stereo Disk System." *IRE Proceedings* 46 (1958): 1,685–1,693. Reprinted in Roys 1978.

Davis, Chester K. "Record Collections, 1960: LJ's Survey of Fact and Opinion." *Library Journal* 85 (Oct. 1, 1960): 3,375–3,380.

Davis, Lenwood G. *A Paul Robeson Research Guide: A Selected, Annotated Bibliography.* Westport, Conn.: Greenwood Press, 1983. 879 p. Discography, pp. 771–795.

Day, Rebecca. "Where's the Rot?" *Stereo Review* 54 (4) (Apr. 1989): 23–24.

Deakins, Duane D. *Comprehensive Cylinder Record Index.* Stockton, Calif.: Author, 1956–1961. Five parts in one volume. Contents in Rust 1980, p. 92.

Dearling, Robert, and Celia Dearling. *The Guinness Book of Recorded Sound.* With assistance from Brian Rust. Enfield, Middlesex, England: Guinness Books, 1984. 225 p.

Debenham, Warren. *Laughter on Record: A Comedy Discography.* Metuchen, N.J.: Scarecrow Press, 1988. 387 p.

Debus, Allen. "Bert Williams on Record." *Hillandale News* 154 (Feb. 1987): 154–157.

De Cock, Alfred. "Maurice Renaud." *Record Collector* 11 (4, 5) (Apr.–May 1957): 74–119; 11 (7) (July 1957): 166–167; 12 (1, 2) (Jan.–Feb. 1958): 37. [De Cock 1957]

Delalande, Jacques, and Tully Potter. "The Busch Brothers: A Discography." *Recorded Sound* 86 (1984): 29–90.

Delaunay, Charles, and George Avakian. *New Hot Discography.* 4th ed. New York: Criterion Books, 1948. 608 p. (1st ed., *Hot Discography*, Paris: Hot Club de France, 1936)

De Lerma, Dominique René. "Philosophy and Practice of Phonorecord Classification at Indiana University." *Library Resources and Technical Services* 13 (Winter 1969): 86–98.

Denisoff, Serge R. *Solid Gold: The Popular Record Industry.* New Brunswick, N.J.: Transaction Books, 1975. 504 p.

———. *Tarnished Gold: The Record Industry Revisited.* New Brunswick, N.J.: Transaction Books, 1986. 487 p.

Dennis, James F. E. "Dating by Labels." *Record Collector* 1 (Aug. 1946): 22–23.

———. "Jean De Reszke." *Record Collector* 5 (1) (Jan. 1950): 3, 6–11. [Dennis 1950/1]

———. "Ernest Van Dyck." *Record Collector* 5 (2) (Feb. 1950): 27–32. [Dennis 1950/2]

———. "Sigrid Onegin." *Record Collector* 5 (10) (Oct. 1950): 223–231; 5 (12) (Dec. 1950): 280–281; 12 (8, 9) (Nov. 1959): 200. [Dennis 1950/10]

———. "Edouard De Reszke." *Record Collector* 6 (5) (May 1951): 99–106. [Dennis 1951/5]

———. "Lillian Nordica." *Record Collector* 6 (9) (Sept. 1951): 195–206. [Dennis 1951/9]

———. "Kirsten Flagstad." *Record Collector* 7 (8) (Aug. 1952): 172–190.

———. "Mattia Battistini." *Record Collector* 8 (11, 12) (Nov.–Dec. 1953): 244–265. [Dennis 1953/11]

———. "Helge Rosvaenge." *Record Collector* 23 (5, 6) (Sept. 1976): 99, 140; 25 (5, 6) (Aug. 1979): 120–122.

Dennis, James F. E., Alfred Frankenstein, and Boris Semeonoff. "Friedrich Schorr." *Record Collector* 19 (11, 12) (Apr. 1971): 243–284; 20 (3) (Oct. 1971): 71.

Dennis, James F. E., and John Stratton. "Lili Lehmann." *Record Collector* 26 (7, 8) (Feb. 1981): 150–190; 26 (9, 10) (May 1981): 199–214. [Dennis 1981/2]

Dennis, Pamela, and James F.E. Dennis. "Jacques Urlus." *Record Collector* 26 (11, 12) (Sept. 1981).

Dethlefson, Ronald. *Edison Blue Amberol Recordings.* Brooklyn: APM Press, 1980–1981. 2 vols.

———. "Dubbing De-Mystified." *Antique Phonograph Monthly* 7 (2) (1983): 3–5.

Dethlefson, Ronald, and Raymond R. Wile. *Edison Disc Artists and Records, 1910–1929.* Brooklyn: APM Press, 1985. 177 p. Revised edition entered at Wile 1990/4.

De Veaux, Scott. "Bebop and the Recording Industry: The 1942 AFM Recording Ban Reconsidered." *Journal of the American Musicological Society* 51 (1) (Spring 1988): 126–165.

Dezettel, Louis M. *Record Changers: How They Work.* Indianapolis: Sams Publishing, 1968. 144 p.

Di Cave, Luciano. "Lina Pagliughi." *Record Collector* 21 (5, 6) (Oct. 1973): 99–125.

Dickason, Vance. *The Loudspeaker Design Cookbook.* 3rd ed. Marshall Jones Co., 1987. 75 p.

Directory of Australian Music Organizations. Compiled by Bill Flemming. Rev. ed. Sydney: Australia Music Center, 1985. 67 p. (1st ed. 1978)

Directory of Member Archives. Compiled by Grace Koch. 2nd ed. Milton Keynes, England: International Association of Sound Archives, 1982. 174 p. (1st ed. 1978)

Directory of Recorded Sound Resources in the United Kingdom. Compiled and edited by Lali Weerasinghe. London: British Library, 1989. 173 p.

Dixon, Robert M. W., and John Godrich. *Recording the Blues.* London: Studio Vista, 1970. 85 p.

Docks, L. R. *American Premium Record Guide.* Florence, Ala.: Books Americana, 1980. 737 p. Includes 500 label illustrations.

Doran, James M. *Erroll Garner: The Most Happy Piano.* Metuchen, N.J.: Scarecrow Press, 1985. 500 p.

Dorgeuille, Claude. *The French Flute School, 1860–1950.* 2nd ed. London: Tony Bingham, 1986. 138 p.

Drummond, H. J. "The Seven Zonophone Records." *Gramophone* (Sept. 1969): 140–143.

Dubal, David. *The Art of the Piano.* New York: Summit Books, 1989. 476 p.

Duckenfield, Bridget. "Sir Landon Ronald and the Gramophone." *Hillandale News* 177 (Dec. 1990): 139–142.

Duckles, Vincent. "Musical Scores and Recordings." *Library Trends* 4 (1955–1956): 164–173.

Dyment, Christopher. "The Recordings of Karl Muck: Some Unresolved Problems." *Association for Recorded Sound Collections Journal* 9 (1) (1977): 66–68. Followed by a discography by Dyment and Jim Cartwright, pp. 69–77.

———. "Misunderstanding Toscanini." *Association for Recorded Sound Collections Journal* 18 (1, 3) (1986): 144–171a.

Eargle, John E. "Loudspeakers." *Journal of the Audio Engineering Society* 10 (11) (1977): 685–688.

Edison Coin-Slot Phonographs. Orange, N.J.: National Phonograph Co., 1906. 20 p. Reprint Brooklyn: Allen Koenigsberg, 1974.

Edison, Musicians, and the Phonograph. Edited and with an introduction by John Harvith and Susan Edwards Harvith. Westport, Conn.: Greenwood Press, 1987. 478 p.

Edison Phonograph. New York: North American Phonograph Co., 1893. Unpaged. Reprint Brooklyn: Allen Koenigsberg, 1974.

Edwards, Ernie, George Hall, and Bill Korst. *Big Bands Discography.* Whittier, Calif.: Erngeobil, 1965–1969. 7 vols. Contents in Cooper 1975.

Einstein, Edwin K., Jr. "Zinka Milanov: A Complete Discography." *Le grand baton* (May 1968): 7–16.

Eke, Bernard T. "Alma Gluck." *Record Collector* 1 (8) (Dec. 1946): 81–88; 6 (2) (Feb. 1951): 27, 33–45; 6 (3) (Mar. 1951): 53.

Elste, Martin R. O. "100 Jahre Schallaufzeichnung: eine Chronologie." *Fonoforum* 5 (May 1977): 434–447.

Enderman, Hans. "Original Dixieland Jazz Band and Its Recreations." *Micrography* 77 (May 1989): 4–10.

Englund, Björn. *Durium: Hit of the Week.* Stockholm: Nationalfonotekets, 1967. 14 p.

———. "Scandinavian Record Labels, No. 2: Grand." *Talking Machine Review International* 4 (June 1970): 101.

———. "Sixty-Five Years of Deutsche Grammophon Gesellschaft, 1898–1963." *Hillandale News* 63 (Oct. 1971): 49–59. Condensed translation of a booklet issued by Deutsche Grammophon Gesellschaft (DGG) in 1963.

Evans, H. "A Hot Performer." *Hillandale News* 168 (June 1989): 214–215. Describes the hot air motor of 1910.

Evans, Roy. "More for Less." *Record Research* 165, 166 (Aug. 1979): 14; 167, 168 (Oct. 1979): 14.

Evensmo, Jan. *The Guitars of Charlie Christian, Robert Normann, Oscar Aleman.* Hosle, Norway: Author, 1976. Unpaged.

———. *The Tenor Saxophone of Ben Webster, 1931–1943.* Hosle, Norway: Author, 1978. 52 p.

Fabrizio, T.C. "Disc Records of the Talking Machine Companies of Chicago." *Talking Machine Review International* 20, 21 (Feb.–Apr. 1973): 118–120.

———. "Survey of American Talking Machines Employing Unusual Methods of Reproduction." *Talking Machine Review International* 42 (Oct. 1976): 787–791.

———. "The Chicago Companies." *Talking Machine Review International* 48 (1977): 1,085–1,089.

———. "The Twilight of the O'Neill-James and Aretino Companies of Chicago, 1910–1914." *Talking Machine Review International* 56, 57 (Feb.–Apr. 1979): 1,480–1,481.

———. "The Disc Records of Turn-of-the-Century Chicago and the Companies Which Sold Them." *Association for Recorded Sound Collections Journal* 12 (1, 2) (1980): 18–25.

Fagan, Ted. "Pre-LP Recordings of RCA at 33 1/3 RPM, 1931 to 1934." *Association for Recorded Sound Collections Journal* 13 (1) (1981): 20–42; 14 (3) (1982): 41–61; 15 (1) (1983): 25–68.

Fagan, Ted, and William R. Moran. *The Encyclopedic Discography of Victor Recordings.* Westport, Conn.: Greenwood Press, 1983, 1986. 2 vols. Vol. 1 includes a reprint of Aldridge 1964.

Farkas, Andrew. *Opera and Concert Singers: An Annotated International Bibliography of Books and Pamphlets.* New York: Garland, 1985. 363 p. Includes comments by William R. Moran on the discographical components of many biographies.

Farmer, John. "The Reproducing Piano." *Recorded Sound* 25 (Jan. 1967): 131–134; 26 (Apr. 1967): 172–180; 28 (Oct. 1967): 249–254.

Favia-Artsay, Aida. "Frances Alda." *Record Collector* 6 (10) (Oct. 1951): 219–233.

———. "The Speeds of DeLuca's Acoustical Victors." *Hobbies* (Feb. 1955): 24–25. [Favia-Artsay 1955/2]

———. "Bettini Catalogs." *Hobbies* (Dec. 1955): 26–27; (Feb. 1956): 28–31; (Mar. 1956): 26–29, 35. Contents of Bettini catalogs of May 1897, June 1898, and 1899. [Favia-Artsay 1955/12]

———. *Caruso on Records: Pitch, Speed, and Comments.* Valhalla, N.Y.: The Historic Record, 1965. 218 p.

Favia-Artsay, Aida, and Gordon Whelan. "Amelita Galli-Curci." *Record Collector* 4 (10) (Oct. 1949): 162–179.

Favia-Artsay, Aida, and John Freestone. "Francesco Tamagno." *Record Collector* 7 (2) (Feb. 1952): 26, 29–39.

Federal Cylinder Project. U.S. Library of Congress. Washington, D.C.: Government Printing Office, 1984. Vol. 1, Vol. 8. Included in Vol. 8 is a list of 101 cylinders made at the World's Columbian Exposition, Chicago, 1893.

Feinstein, Robert. "Caruso and Bettini: The Eternal Youths." *Antique Phonograph Monthly* 8 (2) (1985): 5.

Fellers, Frederick P. *The Metropolitan Opera on Record: A Discography of the Commercial Recordings* Westport, Conn.: Greenwood Press, 1984. 101 p.

Fellers, Frederick P., and Betty Meyers. *Discographies of Commercial Recordings of the Cleveland Orchestra (1924–1977) and the Cincinnati Symphony Orchestra (1917–1977)*. Westport, Conn.: Greenwood Press, 1978. 224 p.

Fenton, Alasdair. "Where Have All the Big Bands Gone?" *Talking Machine Review International* 11 (Aug. 1971): 67–70.

Ferrara, D.E. "The Legacy of Early Recordings by Pupils of Liszt." *Piano Quarterly* 23 (1975): 42–44.

———. "Virginia Rea (A.K.A. Olive Palmer)." *New Amberola Graphic* 63 (Jan. 1988): 10–11. [Ferrara 1988/1]

———. "A Spalding Centenary." *New Amberola Graphic* 65 (July 1988): 12–15. [Ferrara 1988/7]

Ferrara, Dennis E. "Charles W. Harrison: An Edison Retrospect." *New Amberola Graphic* 77 (July 1991): 4–6. [Ferrara 1991/7]

Fewkes, Jesse W. "A Contribution to Passamaquoddy Folk-Lore." *Journal of American Folklore* 3 (1890): 257–280. [Fewkes 1890/1]

———. "On the Use of the Phonograph among Zuni Indians." *American Naturalist* 24 (1890): 687–691. [Fewkes 1890/2]

Field, Mike. "The Bell-Tainter Graphophone." *Hillandale News* 161 (Apr. 1988): 12–15.

Fitterling, Thomas. *Thelonious Monk: sein Leben, seine Musik, seine Schallplatten.* Waakirchen, Germany: OREOS, 1987. 175 p.

Flower, John. *Moonlight Serenade: A Bio-Discography of the Glenn Miller Civilian Band.* New Rochelle, N.Y.: Arlington House, 1972. 554 p.

Foerster, Try, ed. *Elvis Just for You: A Special Goldmine Anthology.* Iola, Wis.: Krause Publications, 1987. 128 p.

Foote, Robert. "The Labels of the U.S. Black and Silver Columbia Records of 1902–1908." *Talking Machine Review International* 4 (June 1970): 97–99.

Ford, Peter. "History of Sound Recording." *Recorded Sound* 1 (7) (Summer 1962): 221–229; "The Age of Empiricism" 1 (8) (Autumn 1962): 266–276; "The Evolution of the Microphone, and Electrical Disc Recording" 1 (10, 11) (Apr.–July 1963): 115–223; "The Evolution of Magnetic Recording" 1 (12) (Oct. 1963): 146–154; "Motion Picture and Television Sound Recording" 2 (1) (Jan. 1964): 181–188; "Evolution of Stereophonic Sound Techniques."

Foreman, Lewis. *Systematic Discography.* Hamden, Conn.: Linnet Books, 1974. 144 p.

Francis, John W.N. "The Gilbert & Sullivan Operettas on 78s." *Association for Recorded Sound Collections Journal* 20 (1) (Spring 1989): 24–81.

Frankenstein, Alfred, D. Brew, Tom Kaufman, and James F.E. Dennis. "Maria Ivoguen." *Record Collector* 20 (5) (Jan. 1972): 98–119; 20–12 (Dec. 1972): 283–284.

Frankenstein, Alfred, and Carl Bruun. "Kerstin Thorberg." *Record Collector* 24 (9, 10) (Oct. 1978): 196–215.

Frankenstein, Alfred, and James F.E. Dennis. "Alexander Kipnis." *Record Collector* 22 (3, 4) (July 1974): 51–79; 23 (7, 8) (Dec. 1976): 166–171.

———. "Jarmila Novotna." *Record Collector* 25 (5, 6) (Aug. 1979): 101–140.

Frederick, H.A. "Recent Fundamental Advances in Mechanical Records on 'Wax'." *Society of Motion Picture Engineers Journal* 18 (Feb. 1932): 141–152. Reprinted in Roys 1978.

Frow, George. "Some Notes on the World Record, and Its Inventor Noel Pemberton Billing." *Hillandale News* 54 (Apr. 1970): 69–71.

———. *The Edison Disc Phonographs and the Diamond Discs: A History with Illustrations.* Sevenoaks, England: Author, 1982. 286 p.

Frow, George L., and Al Sefl. *Edison Cylinder Phonographs, 1877–1929.* West Orange, N.J.: Edison National Historical Site, 1978. 207 p.

Gaeddert, Barbara Knisely. *The Classification and Cataloging of Sound Recordings: An Annotated Bibliography.* Ann Arbor, Mich.: Music Library Association, 1977. 32 p.

Gaisberg, Frederick W. *The Music Goes Round.* New York: Macmillan, 1943. 273 p. British edition titled *Music on Record*.

Galo, Gary. "Transmission Line Loudspeakers. Part I: Theory." *Speaker Builder* (Feb. 1982).

———. "Caruso: The 'Unpublished' Recordings of ARM4-0302 and the Question of Authenticity." *Antique Phonograph Monthly* 7 (9) (1984): 6–8.

———. Review of "The Bayer Complete Caruso" sound recording. *Association for Recorded Sound Collections Journal* 21 (2) (1990): 283–289.

———. Review of "The Complete Caruso" and "The Caruso Edition, I, II" sound recordings. *Association for Recorded Sound Collections Journal* 22 (1) (Spring 1991): 118–125.

Gambaccini, Paul. *Paul McCartney in His Own Words.* New York: Flash Books, 1976. 111 p.

Garlick, Lewis. "The Graphic Arts and the Record Industry." *Journal of the Audio Engineering Society* 25 (10, 11) (Sept.–Oct. 1977): 779–784.

Garrod, Charles. *Larry Clinton and His Orchestra.* Zephyrhills, Fla.: Joyce Record Club, 1984. 30 p. [Garrod 1984/1]

———. *Stan Kenton and His Orchestra (1940–1951).* Zephyrhills, Fla.: Joyce Record Club, 1984. 64 p. [Garrod 1984/2]

———. *Stan Kenton and His Orchestra (1952–1959).* Zephyrhills, Fla.: Joyce Record Club, 1984. 64 p. [Garrod 1984/3]

———. *Claude Thornhill and His Orchestra.* Zephyrhills, Fla.: Joyce Record Club, 1985. 35 p.

———. *Woody Herman,* Vol. 1 (1936–1947). Zephyrhills, Fla.: Joyce Record Club, 1985. 60 p. [Garrod 1985/1]

———. *Harry James and His Orchestra (1937–1945).* Zephyrhills, Fla.: Joyce Record Club, 1985. 66 p. [Garrod 1985/2]

———. *Harry James and His Orchestra (1946–1954).* Zephyrhills, Fla.: Joyce Record Club, 1985. 70 p. [Garrod 1985/3]

———. *Harry James and His Orchestra (1955–1982).* Zephyrhills, Fla.: Joyce Record Club, 1985. 65 p. [Garrod 1985/4]

———. *Woody Herman,* Vol. 2 (1948–1957). Zephyrhills, Fla.: Joyce Record Club, 1986. 64 p.

———. *Charlie Spivak and His Orchestra.* Zephyrhills, Fla.: Joyce Record Club, 1986. 38 p. [Garrod 1986/4]

———. *Jimmy Dorsey and His Orchestra.* Rev. ed. Zephyrhills, Fla.: Joyce Record Club, 1988. 65 p.

———. *Tommy Dorsey and His Orchestra (1928–1945).* Rev. ed. Zephyrhills, Fla.: Joyce Record Club, 1988. 93 p. [Garrod 1988/1]

———. *Tommy Dorsey and His Orchestra (1946–1956).* Rev. ed. Zephyrhills, Fla.: Joyce Record Club, 1988. 80 p. [Garrod 1988/3]

———. *Woody Herman,* Vol. 3 (1958–1987). Zephyrhills, Fla.: Joyce Record Club, 1988. 57 p. [Garrod 1988/4]

———. *Dick Jurgens and His Orchestra.* Zephyrhills, Fla.: Joyce Record Club, 1988. 35 p. [Garrod 1988/5]

———. *Sammy Kaye and His Orchestra.* Zephyrhills, Fla.: Joyce Record Club, 1988. 71 p. [Garrod 1988/6]

———. *Eddy Duchin and His Orchestra.* Zephyrhills, Fla.: Joyce Record Club, 1989. 28 p.

———. *Shep Fields and His Orchestra.* Zephyrhills, Fla.: Joyce Record Club, 1989. 36 p. [Garrod 1989/1]

———. *Spike Jones and the City Slickers.* Zephyrhills, Fla.: Joyce Record Club, 1989. 39 p. [Garrod 1989/2]

Garrod, Charles, and Bill Korst. *Charlie Barnet and His Orchestra.* Zephyrhills, Fla.: Joyce Record Club, 1984. 79 p.

———. *Gene Krupa and His Orchestra (1935–1946).* Zephyrhills, Fla.: Joyce Record Club, 1984. 51 p. [Garrod and Korst 1984/4]

———. *Gene Krupa and His Orchestra (1947–1973).* Zephyrhills, Fla.: Joyce Record Club, 1984. 63 p. [Garrod and Korst 1984/5]

———. *Kay Kyser and His Orchestra.* Zephyrhills, Fla.: Joyce Record Club, 1986. 51 p. [Garrod and Korst 1986/2]

———. *Artie Shaw and His Orchestra.* Zephyrhills, Fla.: Joyce Record Club, 1986. 64 p. [Garrod and Korst 1986/3]

———. *Nat King Cole: His Voice and Piano.* Zephyrhills, Fla.: Joyce Record Club, 1987. 70 p.

———. *Bob Crosby and His Orchestra.* Zephyrhills, Fla.: Joyce Record Club, 1987. 59 p. [Garrod and Korst 1987/1]

———. *Glen Gray and the Casa Loma Orchestra.* Zephyrhills, Fla.: Joyce Record Club, 1987. 45 p. [Garrod and Korst 1987/2]

Gart, Galen. *ARLD: The American Record Label Directory and Dating Guide, 1940–1959.* Milford, N.H.: Big Nickel Publications, 1989. 259 p.

Geduld, Harry M. *The Birth of the Talkies: From Edison to Jolson.* Bloomington, Ind.: Indiana University Press, 1975. 337 p.

Gelatt, Ronald. *The Fabulous Phonograph, 1877–1977.* 2nd rev. ed. Also 3rd ed. New York: Macmillan, 1977. 349 p. (1st ed. 1955)

Geller, Sidney B. *Care and Handling of Computer Magnetic Storage Media.* Washington, D.C.: National Bureau of Standards, 1983. 128 p. (NBS Special Publication, 500-101; SuDoc no. C 13.10:500-101).

George, Nelson. *The Death of Rhythm and Blues.* New York: E.P. Dutton, 1989.

Gibson, Gerald. "Preservation and Conservation of Sound Recordings." In *Conserving and Preserving Library Materials in Nonbook Formats.* Edited by Kathryn Luther Henderson and William T. Henderson. Urbana, Ill.: University of Illinois, Graduate School of Library and Information Science, 1991, pp. 27–44. (Allerton Park Institute series, 30.)

Giese, Hannes. *Art Blakey: sein Leben, seine Musik, seine Schallplatten.* Schaftlach, Germany: OREOS, 1990. 217 p.

Gillett, Charlie. *The Sound of the City: The Rise of Rock and Roll.* New York: Outerbridge & Dienstfrey, distr. by E.P. Dutton, 1970.

Ginell, Gary. *The Decca Hillbilly Discography, 1927–1945.* Westport, Conn.: Greenwood Press, 1989. 402 p.

Girard, Victor, and Harold M. Barnes. *Vertical Cut Cylinders and Discs: A Catalogue of All "Hill-and-dale" Recordings of Serious Worth Made and Issued between 1887–1932 Circa.* London: British Institute of Recorded Sound, 1964. 196 p.

Glazer, Joe. *Labor's Troubadour.* Urbana: University of Illinois Press, 2001. 299 p.

Goddard, Steve. "The Beatles Sessions, CDs, VHS and FDS." *Discoveries* 2 (3) (Mar. 1989): 34–35.

Godrich, John, and Rober M.W. Dixon. *Blues and Gospel Records, 1902–1942.* Rev. ed. London: Storyville Publications, 1969. 912 p. Additions and corrections by Carl Kendziora appeared in issues of *Record Research* from 86 (Sept. 1967).

Goldmark, Peter, Rene Snepvangers, and William S. Bachman. "The Columbia Long-Playing Microgroove Recording System." *IRE Proceedings* 37, 8 (1949): 923–927. Reprinted in Roys 1978.

Goldsmith, Peter. *Making People's Music: Moe Asch and Folkways Records.* Washington, D.C.: Smithsonian Institution Press, 1998. 468 p.

Goldstein, Kenneth. "A Future Folklorist in the Record Business." In *Transforming Tradition: Folk Music Revivals Examined,* edited by Neil V. Rosenberg. Urbana: University of Illinois Press, 1993, pp. 107–121.

Goslin, John G. "Revolving Thoughts." *Talking Machine Review International* 65 (2) (1983): 1,778.

Gottlieb, R. E. M. "Waring's Pennsylvanians." *Record Research* 116 (May 1972): 3–8; 119, 120 (Dec. 1972–Jan. 1973): 8–9; 121 (Mar. 1973): 8–9; 122 (June 1973): 4–5.

Grable, Ronald J. "Mr. Edison's Right Hand Man: Ernest L. Stevens." *Record Research* 161, 162

(Feb.–Mar. 1979): 4–5; 163, 164 (May–June 1979): 10–11.

Grainger, Percy. "Collecting with the Phonograph." *Journal of the Folk-Song Society* 12 (May 1908): 147–169.

Gray, Judith A., ed. *The Federal Cylinder Project.* Vol. 3: Great Basin Plateau Indian Catalog, Northwest Coast Arctic Indian Catalog. Washington, D.C.: American Folklife Center, Library of Congress, 1988.

Gray, Judith A., and Edwin J. Schupman Jr., eds. *The Federal Cylinder Project.* Vol. 5: California Indian Catalogue, Middle and South American Indian Catalogue, Southwestern Indian Catalogue-I. Washington, D.C.: American Folklife Center, Library of Congress, 1990.

Gray, Michael H. "The Arturo Toscanini Society." *Association for Recorded Sound Collections Journal* 5 (1) (1973): 26–29.

———. "The 'World's Greatest Music' and 'World's Greatest Opera' Records: A Discography." *Association for Recorded Sound Collections Journal* 7 (1, 2) (1975): 33–55.

———. *Beecham: A Centenary Discography.* New York: Holmes & Meier, 1979. 129 p.

———. *Popular Music.* New York: Bowker, 1983. 205 p. (Bibliography of Discographies series, 3)

———. "The Birth of Decca Stereo." *Association for Recorded Sound Collections Journal* 18 (1, 3) (1986): 4–19.

———. *Classical Music Discographies, 1976–1988.* New York: Greenwood, 1989. 334 p. Continues from Gray and Gibson 1977.

Gray, Michael H., and Gerald D. Gibson. *Bibliography of Discographies.* Vol. 1: Classical Music, 1925–1975. New York: Bowker, 1977. 164 p. Continued in Gray 1989.

Green, Stanley. *Encyclopedia of the Musical Theatre.* New York: Dodd, Mead, 1976. 492 p. Reprint New York: Da Capo Press, 1980.

———. *Broadway Musicals, Show by Show.* London: Faber, 1987. 361 p. (Originally published in Milwaukee, Wis.: H. Leonard Books, 1985.)

Greenfield, Edward, Robert Layton, and Ivan March. *The New Penguin Guide to Compact Discs and Cassettes.* Harmondsworth, England: Penguin Books, 1989. 1,366 p.

Greenfield, Mark, and Tony Middleton. *Dinah Shore: An Exploratory Discography.* London: Authors, 1982. 24 p.

Greenway, John. *American Folk Songs of Protest.* Philadelphia: University of Pennsylvania Press, 1953. 348 p.

Griffin, Marie P. "Preservation of Rare and Unique Materials at the Institute of Jazz Studies." *Association for Recorded Sound Collections Journal* 17 (1, 3) (1985): 11–17.

Griffiths, Peter H. "Composers' Recordings of Their Own Music." *Audiovisual Librarian* 3 (2) (Autumn 1976): 48–55.

Gronow, Pekka. "American Columbia Finnish Language 3000 Series." *Record Research* 101 (Oct. 1969): 8–9; 102 (Nov. 1969): 10.

———. *American Columbia Scandinavian E and F Series.* Helsinki: Finnish Institute of Recorded Sound, 1974. 113 p.

———. *The Columbia 33000-F Irish Series: A Numerical Listing.* Los Angeles: John Edwards Memorial Foundation, University of California at Los Angeles, 1979. 78 p. (JEMF Special Series, 10)

———. "Sources for the History of the Record Industry." *Phonographic Bulletin* 34 (Nov. 1982): 50–54.

———. "Early Gramophone Periodicals in Russia." *Talking Machine Review International* 65, 66 (Feb. 1983): 1,784–1,785.

Gronow, Pekka, and Ilpo Saunio. *An International History of the Recording Industry.* London: Casell, 1998. 230 p.

Guralnick, Peter. *Sweet Soul Music: Rhythm and Blues and the Southern Dream of Freedom.* Boston: Little, Brown, 1999.

Guy, P. J. "Disc Recording and Reproduction." In *Encyclopedia of High Fidelity,* Vol. 3. New York and London: Focal Press, 1964. 232 p.

Haggin, B. H. *Music on Records.* 4th ed. New York: Oxford University Press, 1946. 279 p. (1st ed. 1938)

Haines, D. E. "The British 'Toy' Gramophone Records of the 1920s." *Talking Machine Review International* 20, 21 (Feb.–Apr. 1973): 111–118.

Halban, Desi, and Arthur E. Knight. "Selma Kurz." *Record Collector* 13 (3) (May 1960): 51–56; 17 (1, 3) (Oct. 1968): 46.

Hall, David. *The Record Book.* New York: Smith and Durrell, 1940. 771 p. Subsequent editions: *The Record Book: International Edition,* by David Hall (New York: Smith and Durrell, 1948), 1,394 p.; *Records: 1950 Edition,* by David Hall (New York: Knopf, 1950), 524 + 20 p.; *The Disc Book,* by David Hall and Abner Levin (New York: Long Player Publications, 1955), 471 p. + unpaged addenda and index.

———. "The Rodgers and Hammerstein Archives of Recorded Sound History and Current Operation." *Association for Recorded Sound Collections Journal* 6 (2) (1974): 17–31.

———. "An Era's End." *Association for Recorded Sound Collections Journal* 12 (1, 2) (1980): 2–5.

———. "The Mapleson Cylinder Project." *Association for Recorded Sound Collections Journal* 13 (3) (1981): 5–20.

———. "A Provisional Mapleson Cylinder Chronology." *Association for Recorded Sound Collections Journal* 13 (3) (1981): 14.20. [Hall 1981/2]

———. "A Mapleson Afterword." *Association for Recorded Sound Collections Journal* 14 (1) (1982): 5–10. [Hall 1982/1]

———. "The Mapleson Cylinder Project." *Recorded Sound* 82 (July 1982): 39–60; 83 (Jan. 1983): 21–56. [Hall 1982/7]

———. "New Music Quarterly Recordings—A Discography." *Association for Recorded Sound Collections Journal* 16 (1, 2) (1984): 10–27. [Hall 1984/1]

———. "Recordings: Live at the Met, 1901–1903." *Ovation* (Oct. 1984): 26–33; (Nov. 1984): 19–21, 34. [Hall 1984/10]

———. "Discography: A Chronological Survey." In *Modern* 1989, pp. 173–184.

Hall, George. *Jan Savitt and His Orchestra.* Zephyrhills, Fla.: Joyce Record Club, 1985. 32 p.

Hamilton, Chris. "Hines—Not 57 Varieties." *Hillandale News* 150 (June 1986): 46–49.

Hamilton, David. *Listener's Guide to the Great Instrumentalists.* New York: Facts on File, 1982. 137 p.

———. Review of "The Metropolitan Opera on Record by Frederick P. Fellers. *Association for Recorded Sound Collections Journal* 16 (3) (1984): 57–62.

Hammond, John, with Irving Townsend. *John Hammond on Record: An Autobiography.* New York: Ridge Press; 1977. 416 p.

Hanna, John. "The Gramophone Company, 1898–1925." *Journal of the Phonograph Society of New South Wales* 6 (4) (July 1990): 6–11. Continues in the *Sound Record* (new name of the journal), 7 (1) (Sept. 1990): 16–19 (covering 1925–1952).

Hansen, Hans. *Lauritz Melchior: A Discography.* Rev. ed. Copenhagen: Nationaldiskoteket, 1972. 40 p. (1st ed. 1965)

Harman, Carter. "Composers Recordings, Inc." *Association for Recorded Sound Collections Journal* 6 (1) (1974): 26–29.

Harris, Steve. *Jazz on Compact Disc: A Critical Guide to the Best Recordings.* New York: Harmony Books, 1987. 176 p.

Harrison, Max, et al. *Modern Jazz: The Essential Records.* London: Aquarius Books, 1975. 131 p.

Harrison, Max, Charles Fox, and Eric Thacker. *The Essential Jazz Records.* Vol. 1: Ragtime to Swing. Westport, Conn.: Greenwood Press, 1984. 595 p.

Hart, Mary L., Brenda M. Eagles, and Lisa N. Woworth. *The Blues: A Bibliographical Guide.* New York: Garland, 1989. 636 p.

Hart, Philip. "Towards a Reiner Discography." *Association for Recorded Sound Collections Journal* 19 (1) (1987): 63–70.

Hartel, Harold H. "The H3 Chrono-Matrix File." *Record Research* 175, 176 (Sept. 1980): 5–10. A series that had reached 36 parts, with 247, 248 (Sept. 1991). It is a chronological list of the jazz, blues, and gospel recordings that appeared in Rust 1961 (1969 ed.) and Godrich 1969. Artist, matrix, label number, title, and references are given for each disc. The time period covered is Feb. 1922 to Aug. 1933 (as of *Record Research* 247, 248).

Harvey, Hugh H. "Nellie Melba." *Record Collector* 4 (12) (Dec. 1949): 202–215.

Hasse, John Edward. *Ragtime: Its History, Composers, and Music.* New York: Schirmer Books, 1985. 460 p.

Hayes, Cedric J. "Imperial Matrix Listing (IM 1 to IM 2000)." *Record Research* 235 236 (June 1988): 8; 237, 238 (Nov. 1988): 8; 239, 240 (Apr. 1989):

8; 241 242 (Oct.–Nov. 1989): 9; 243, 244 (May–June 1990): 9; 245, 246 (Jan. 1991): 9; 247, 248 (Sept. 1991): 10. A continuing series that extends Rotante 1985.

Hayes, Jim. "Sherlock Holmes? No, It's 'Shellac Hayes'." *Talking Machine Review International* 10 (June 1971): 42, 44–45.

Hayes, Jim G. *Panachord and Rex.* Liverpool: Author, 1974. 23 p.

Hayes, Richard K. *Kate Smith Discography.* Cranston, R.I.: Author, 1977.

Hazelcorn, Howard. *A Collector's Guide to the Columbia Spring-Wound Cylinder Graphophone.* Brooklyn: Antique Phonograph Monthly (APM), 1976. 36 p. (APM Monographs series, 2.)

Hedberg, Tom. "Rescuing the Voices of the Dead—A Laser-Read Sound Reproducing System." *Antique Phonograph Monthly* 5 (8) (1978): 7–8.

Heintze, James R. *Scholars Guide to Washington, D.C., for Audio Resources.* Washington, D.C.: Smithsonian Institution Press, 1985. 395 p.

Helmbrecht, Arthur J., Jr. *Fritz Reiner: The Comprehensive Discography of His Recordings* Novelty, Ohio: Fritz Reiner Society, 1978. 79 p. Supplement, Apr. 1981, 9 p.; and Addenda, Apr. 1991, 4 p. (Madison, N.J.: Author, 1981).

Helmholtz, Hermann L. *On the Sensations of Tone as a Physiological Basis for the Theory of Music.* Reprint of the 2nd English ed., trans. and rev. by Alexander J. Ellis, based on the 4th German ed. (1887); with a new introduction by Henry Margenau. New York: Dover, 1954. 576 p.

Hemphill, Paul H. *The Nashville Sound.* New York: Simon & Schuster, 1970. 289 p.

Henriksen, Henry. "Gennett Research." *Record Research* 94 (Dec. 1968): 3–5.

———. "Herschel Gold Seal." *Record Research* 131 (Jan. 1975): 1, 5.

———. "Autograph." *Record Research* 153, 154 (Apr. 1978): 4–7.

———. "Black Patti." *Record Research* 165, 166 (Aug. 1979): 4–8; 167, 168 (Oct. 1979): 4–8; 171, 172 (Mar. 1980): 4–5, 24; 173, 174 (June 1980): 9; 177, 178 (Nov. 1980): 8; 181, 182 (Apr. 1981): 10; 183, 184 (July 1981): 9; 185, 186 (Oct. 1981): 8; 187, 188 (Dec 1981): 8. At this point, a label list begins: 189, 190 (Mar.–Apr. 1982): 8; 191, 192 (July 1982): 8; 193, 194 (Oct. 1982): 9; 195, 196 (Jan. 1983): 13; 197, 198 (Mar.–Apr. 1983): 9.

Henrysson, Harald, and Jack W. Porter. *A Jussi Björling Phonography.* Stockholm: Svenskt Musikhistoriskt Arkiv, 1984. 269 p.

Henstock, Michael. *Fernando De Lucia.* London: Duckworth, 1991. 505 p. Discography, pp. 437–482.

Hernon, Michael. *French Horn Discography.* Westport, Conn.: Greenwood Press, 1986. 292 p.

Hervingham-Root, Laurie. "David Bispham: Quaker Baritone." *Talking Machine Review International* 7 (Dec. 1970): 197–199. Continued in *Talking Machine Review International* 8, 9, 10, 12, 13, and 14.

Hervingham-Root, Laurie, and James F.E. Dennis. "Pol Plançon." *Record Collector* 8 (7, 8) (July–Aug. 1953): 148–191; 8 (10) (Oct. 1953): 236–237; 10 (12) (Nov. 1956): 277; 12 (7) (Oct. 1959): 165.

Heyworth, Peter. *Otto Klemperer: His Life and Times.* Cambridge, England: Cambridge University Press, 1983. Discography by Michael H. Gray, pp. 444–452.

Hillman, Peter E. "Symmetrical Speaker System with Dual Transmission Lines." *Speaker Builder* (Sept. 1989): 10.

Hinze, Michael. "Medallion Revisited." *Record Research* 144, 145 (Mar. 1977): 12–13.

Hirsch, Julian. "Feelin' Groovy: Head to Head Lab and Listening Tests of Five Leading Phono Cartridges." *Stereo Review* (Jan. 1988): 74–79.

Hirshey, Gerri. *Nowhere to Run: The Story of Soul Music.* New York: Da Capo Press, 1994.

Hoffmann, Frank. *The Development of Library Collections of Sound Recordings.* New York: Dekker, 1979. 169 p.

———. *The Literature of Rock, 1954–1978.* Metuchen, N.J.: Scarecrow Press, 1981. 349 p. Continued by Hoffmann, Cooper, and Hoffmann 1986/2.

Hoffman, Frank, and George Albert. *The Cash Box Country Singles Charts, 1958–1982.* Metuchen, N.J.: Scarecrow Press, 1984. 605 p.

———. *The Cash Box Country Album Charts, 1964–1988.* Metuchen, N.J.: Scarecrow Press, 1989. 300 p. [Hoffmann and Albert 1989/2]

———. *The Cash Box Black Contemporary Album Charts, 1975-1987.* Metuchen, N.J.:Scarecrow Press, 1989. 249. p. [Hoffman and Albert 1989/1]

Hoffman, Frank, George Albert, and Lee Ann Hoffmann. *The Cash Box Album Charts, 1955–1974.* Metuchen, N.J.: Scarecrow Press, 1988. 528 p.

———. *The Cash Box Album Charts, 1975–1985.* Metuchen, N.J.: Scarecrow Press, 1987. 556 p.

———. *The Cash Box Black Contemporary Singles Charts, 1960–1984.* Metuchen, N.J.: Scarecrow Press, 1986. 704 p. [Hoffmann, Albert, and Hoffmann 1986/1]

Hoffmann, Frank, B. Lee Cooper, and Lee Ann Hoffman. *The Literature of Rock II.* Metuchen, N.J.: Scarecrow Press, 1986. 2 vols. Continues from Hoffmann 1981. [Hoffmann, Cooper, and Hoffmann 1986/2]

Hoffman, Frank, and Lee Ann Hoffmann. *The Cash Box Singles Charts, 1950–1981.* Metuchen, N.J.: Scarecrow Press, 1983. 876 p.

Hogarth, Will H. "Nellie Melba." *Record Collector* 27 (3, 4) (Mar. 1982): 72–87.

Hogarth, Will, and R. T. See. "Marjorie Lawrence Discography." *Record Collector* 32 (1, 2) (Jan. 1987): 7–18; 33 (11, 12) (Nov. 1988): 300–303.

Hoggard, Stuart. *Bob Dylan: An Illustrated Discography.* Oxford, England: Transmedia Express, 1978. 108, 23 p.

Holcman, Jan. "The Honor Roll of Recorded Chopin, 1906–1960." *Saturday Review* (Feb. 27, 1960): 44–45, 61–62.

———. "Liszt: Piano Recordings." *Music Magazine* (Nov. 1961): 14–16, 48. [Holcman 1961/11]

———. "Liszt in the Records of His Pupils." *Saturday Review* (Dec. 23, 1961): 45–46, 57. [Holcman 1961/12]

———. "Liszt Records: Part Two." *Music Magazine* (Dec. 1961): 24–25, 60. [Holcman 1961/12]

———. "Debussy on Disc: 1912–1962." *Saturday Review* (Aug. 25, 1962): 34–35.

Holdridge, Lawrence F. "Charles Hackett." *Record Collector* 22 (8, 9) (Feb. 1975): 171–214; 22 (10, 11) (Apr. 1975): 257.

Holmes, John L. *Conductors on Record.* London: Gollancz; Westport, Conn.: Greenwood Press, 1982. 734 p.

Holzman, Jac, and Gavan Daws. *Follow the Music: The Life and Times of Elektra Records in the Great Years of American Pop Culture.* Santa Monica, Calif.: First Media Books, 1998. 441 p.

Hoover, Cynthia A. *Music Machines American Style: A Catalog of the Exhibition.* Washington, D.C.: Smithsonian Institution Press, 1971. 140, 15 p.

Horn, Geoffrey. "Geoffrey Horn Visits Celestion." *Gramophone* 66 (Nov. 1988): 896–898.

Hounsome, Terry, and Tim Chambre. *Rock Record.* 3rd ed. New York: Facts on File, 1981. 526 p. (Published in Britain as *New Rock Record*, 1981. 1st ed. titled *Rockmaster*, 1978; revised as *Rock Record*, 1979.)

Hume, Martha. *You're So Cold I'm Turnin' Blue.* New York: Viking, 1982. 202 p.

Hummel, David. *Collector's Guide to the American Musical Theatre.* Metuchen, N.J.: Scarecrow Press, 1984. 2 vols.

Humphreys, Ivor. "ARCAM." *Gramophone* (Oct. 1990): 857–862.

Hunt, John. *The Furtwängler Sound.* 2nd ed. London: Furtwängler Society, 1985. Apparently superseded by a later edition, cited in *Gramophone* (May 1990): 1,935.

———. *From Adam to Webern: The Recordings of Von Karajan.* London: Author, 1987. 130 p. (Bound with *Philharmonia Orchestra: Complete Discography 1945–1987*, by Stephen J. Pettitt.)

Hurd, Daniel. "35 Shades of Black: The Johnny Cash Story." *Discoveries* (Aug. 1990): 94–97. Includes a discography of LPs.

Hurst, P. G. *The Golden Age Recorded.* 2nd ed. Lingfield, Surrey, England: Oakwood, 1963. 187 p. (1st ed. 1947)

Hutchinson, Tom. "Alessandro Bonci." *Record Collector* 11 (7) (July 1957): 148–162; 11 (9, 10) (Sept.–Oct. 1957): 234–235; 12 (4, 5) (Feb.–Mar. 1959): 108, 116; 18 (1, 2) (Oct. 1968): 47.

———. "Tito Schipa." *Record Collector* 13 (4, 5) (June–July 1960): 75–109.

Hutchinson, Tom, and Clifford Williams. "Giovanni Zenatello." *Record Collector* 14 (5, 6) (1961): 100–143; 14 (7, 8) (1961): 170–171. Copies examined did not have dates.

International Piano Archives at Maryland. *Catalog of the Reproducing Piano Roll Collection.* College Park, Md.: Author, 1983. 281 p.

Isom, Warren Rex. "How to Prevent and Cure Record Warping." *High Fidelity* 22 (Sept. 1972): 50–53.

———. "Evolution of the Disc Talking Machine." *Journal of the Audio Engineering Society* 25 (10, 11) (Sept.–Oct. 1977): 718–723.

Jackson, John. *Big Beat Heat: Alan Freed and the Early Years of Rock and Roll.* New York: Schirmer Books, 1994. 400 p.

———. *American Bandstand: Dick Clark and the Making of a Rock 'n' Roll Empire.* New York: Oxford University Press, 1998. 336 p.

Jackson, Paul T. *Collectors' Contact Guide.* Rev. ed. Springfield, Ill.: Recorded Sound Research, 1975. 58 p. (1st ed. 1973)

Jansen, F.A. "Non-Magnetic Sound Recording on Tape." *Hillandale News* 133 (Aug. 1983): 239–241.

Jasen, David. "Zez Confrey, Creator of the Novelty Rag: Preparatory Research." *Record Research* 111 (July 1971): 5, 10.

———. *Recorded Ragtime, 1897–1958.* Hamden, Conn.: Archon Books, 1973. 155 p.

Jefferson, Alan. *Lotte Lehmann, 1888–1976.* London: Julia MacRae Books, 1988. 333 p. Discography on pp. 243–322.

Jepsen, Jorgen Grunnet. *A Discography of Stan Kenton.* Brande, Denmark: Debut Records, 1962. 2 vols.

———. *Jazz Records 1942–1962.* Holte, Denmark: Knudsen, 1963–1969. 12 vols.

———. *A Discography of Dizzy Gillespie, 1937–1952.* Copenhagen: Karl Knudsen, 1969. 39 p.

———. *A Discography of Dizzy Gillespie, 1953–1968.* Copenhagen: Karl Knudsen, 1969. 30 p.

———. *A Discography of John Coltrane.* Rev. ed. Copenhagen: Karl Knudsen, 1969. 35 p.

Jewell, Brian. *Veteran Talking Machines.* Tunbridge Wells, England: Midas, 1977. 128 p.

Johnson, Colin. "The Oldest Person to Record?" *Hillandale News* 130 (Feb. 1983): 167.

Johnston, Brian Fawcett. *Count John McCormack.* Bournemouth, England: *Talking Machine Review International,* 1988. 57 p. Errata noted in *Hillandale News* 165 (Dec. 1988): 126–127.

Jorgensen, Finn. *The Complete Handbook of Magnetic Recording.* 3rd ed. Blue Ridge Summit, Penn.: Tab Books, 1988. 740 p.

Kallman, Helmut, Gilles Potvin, and Kenneth Winters, eds. "A & M Records of Canada, Ltd." (p. 1); "Ed Archambault, Inc." (p. 27); "Arc Records" (p. 30); "Beaver Records, Ltd." (p. 70); "Berliner Gramophone Company" (p. 80); "Bernadol Music Limited" (p. 79); "Boot Records, Ltd." (p. 99); "Brunswick" (p. 126); "Canada Baroque Records, Ltd." (p. 137); "Canadian Academy of Recording Arts and Sciences" (p. 140); "Canadian Recording Industry Association" (p. 154); "Canadian Talent Library" (p. 155); "Canadian Vitaphone Company" (p. 155); "CAPAC" (pp. 156–157); "Capitol Records-EMI of Canada, Ltd." (p. 157); "CBC Recordings" (p. 167); "CBS Records Canada, Ltd." (pp. 169–170); "Compo Company, Ltd." (p. 212); "CRTC" (p. 246); "Gamma Records, Ltd." (pp. 364–365); "GRT of Canada, Ltd." (p. 395); "Hallmark Recordings, Ltd." (p. 406); "Juno Awards" (p. 487); "Kébec-Disk, Inc." (p. 492); "London Records of Canada (1967), Ltd." (p. 561); "Pathé Frères" (p. 729); "Polydor, Ltd." (p. 769); "Quality Records, Ltd." (p. 784); "RCA Limited" (p. 795); "Recorded Sound" (pp. 796–800); "Rococo Records" (p. 816); "Rodeo Records, Ltd." (pp. 816–817); "Sparton of Canada, Ltd." (p. 888); "Starr" (p. 891); "Gordon V. Thompson, Ltd." (p. 914); "True North Records" (p. 936); "Waterloo Music Company, Ltd." (p. 988). *Encyclopedia of Music in Canada.* Toronto: University of Toronto Press, 1981. 1,108 p. French version published in Montreal: Fides, 1982.

Kastlemusick Directory for Collectors of Recordings. 1981–1982 ed. Wilmington, Del.: Kastlemusick, 1981. 84 p. (1st ed. 1977)

Kaufman, Tom, and James F. E. Dennis. "Leo Slezak." *Record Collector* 15 (9, 10) (1964): 195–235.

Kay, George W. "Those Fabulous Gennetts." *Record Changer* 12 (June 1953): 4–13.

———. "The Superior Catalog." *Record Research* 37 (Aug. 1961): 1–4; 38 (Oct. 1961): 10–11; 41 (Feb. 1962): 11; 42 (Mar.–Apr. 1962): 2, 20.

Kelly, Alan. *His Master's Voice/La voce del padrone. The Italian Catalogue ... 1898–1929* Westport, Conn.: Greenwood Press, 1988. 462 p.

———. *His Master's Voice/La voix de son maitre. The French Catalogue ... 1898–1929* Westport, Conn.: Greenwood Press, 1990. 679 p.

Kelly, Alan, John F. Perkins, and John Ward. "Selma Kurz: A Discography." *Recorded Sound* 73 (Jan. 1979): 2–5.

Kelly, Alan, and Vladimir Gurvich. "Discography." In *Chaliapin: A Critical Biography, by Victor Borovsky.* New York: Knopf, 1988, pp. 541–587.

Kendziora, Carl. "Behind the Cobwebs" columns. *Record Research* 1949–1986. Cited by date only.

———. "Problems of Dating Recorded Performances." In Allen 1971, pp. 8–18.

Kennedy, Michael. *Barbirolli, Conductor Laureate.* London: Hart-Davis, 1973. 416 p. Reprint New York: Da Capo Press, 1982. Discography on pp. 341–402.

Kenyon, Percy, Clifford Williams, and William R. Moran. "Pasquale Amato." *Record Collector* 21 (1, 2) (Mar. 1973): 3–47; 21 (5, 6) (Oct. 1973): 128–132.

Khanna, S. K. "Vinyl Compound for the Phonographic Industry." *Journal of the Audio Engineering Society* 25 (10, 11) (Sept.–Oct. 1977): 724–728.

Kiner, Larry F. *The Al Jolson Discography.* Westport, Conn.: Greenwood Press, 1983. 194 p.

———. *The Rudy Vallee Discography.* Westport, Conn.: Greenwood Press, 1985. 190 p.

———. *The Cliff Edwards Discography.* Westport, Conn.: Greenwood Press, 1987. 260 p.

Kinkle, Roger D. *The Complete Encyclopedia of Popular Music and Jazz, 1900–1950*. New Rochelle, N.Y.: Arlington House, 1974. 4 vols.

Kirvine, John. *Jukebox Saturday Night*. London: New English Library, Times-Mirror, 1977. 160 p.

Klee, Joe. "From the Golden Age of Opera Recordings." *Antique Phonograph Monthly* 7 (1) (1981): 8–9.

———. "From the Golden Age: Caruso Reissues." *Antique Phonograph Monthly* 7 (6) (1983): 6–7.

———. "From the Golden Age ... Caruso on Compact Disc." *Antique Phonograph Monthly* 8 (6) (1987): 15–16.

———. "In the Beginning ... From Berliner to World War I." *Antique Phonograph Monthly* 9 (3) (1990): 13–15.

Klein, Andrew. "A History of the Starr Piano Factory." *Talking Machine Review International* 65, 66 (Feb. 1983): 1,787–1,789, 1,818.

Klein, Larry. "Amplifier Damping Factor: How Important Is It?" *Radio Electronics* 60 (1) (Jan. 1989): 78–79.

Kline, Pete. "The Capitol Years" *Discoveries* 2 (7) (July 1989): 18–21. Discography of Frank Sinatra's Capitol records, 1953–1962.

Klinger, Bill. "The Short-Lived Harris Everlasting Record." *Antique Phonograph Monthly* 10 (1 (1991): 3–4.

Knight, Arthur E. "Roland Hayes." *Record Collector* 10 (2) (July 1955): 27–45; 12 (3, 4) (Feb.–Mar. 1959): 116; 12 (8, 9) (Nov.–Dec. 1959): 215.

Knight, G.A. "Factors Relating to the Long-Term Storage of Magnetic Tape." *Phonographic Bulletin* 18 (July 1977): 16–35.

Koeningsberg, Allen. "In the Pink: A Lambert Discography." *Antique Phonograph Monthly* 6 (8) (1980): 4–10; 6 (9) (1980): 8–9.

———. *Edison Cylinder Records, 1889–1912: With an Illustrated History of the Phonograph*. 2nd ed. Brooklyn: APM Press, 1987. 42 + 172 p. (1st ed. 1969)

———. *The Patent History of the Phonograph, 1877–1912*. Brooklyn: APM Press, 1990. 72 + 87 p.

Kogen, James H. "Gramophone Record Reproduction: Development, Performance and Potential of the Stereo Pickup." *Proceedings of the IEE* (Aug. 1968): 116–118.

———. "Record Changers, Turntables, and Tone Arms—A Brief Technical History." *Journal of the Audio Engineering Society* 25 (10, 11) (Sept.–Oct. 1977): 749–758.

Korenhof, Paul. "Maria Callas discographie." *Luister* 302 (Nov. 1977): 197–122.

Koster, Piet, and Dick M. Bakker. *Charlie Parker Discography*. Amsterdam: Micrography, 1974–1976. 4 vols. Covers 1940–1955.

Koster, Piet, and Chris Sellars. *Dizzy Gillespie*, Volume I, 1937–1953. Amsterdam: Micrography, 1985. 68 p.

Kressley, David. "Catalog of World Transcriptions (1933–1963)." *Record Research* 89 (Mar. 1968): 1–8; 90 (May 1968): 6–7; 91 (July 1968): 5; 92 (Sept.

1968): 5; 93 (Nov. 1968): 8–10; 94 (Dec. 1968): 7; 98 (May 1969): 7–9.

———. "The Frederic W. Ziv Company." *Record Research* 201, 202 (Sept. 1983): 4–6 on Wayne King.; 203, 204 (Dec. 1983): 1–2; 205, 206 (Mar. 1984): 8; 207, 208 (June 1984): 8; 209, 210 (Oct. 1984): 9; 211, 212 (Feb. 1985): 11.

Kunstadt, Len. "The Lucille Hegamin Story." *Record Research* 40 (Jan. 1962): 3, 19.

———. "The Labels behind Black Swan." *Record Research* 229, 230 (June 1987): 1, 4–5. Continues a compilation that began in *Record Research* 221, 222 under Carl Kendziora's name. The Kendziora articles were reprinted from *Record Changer*, but the Kunstadt continuation is new material.

———. "Unmasking the Associated's." *Record Research* 235, 236 (June 1988): 1, 4; 237, 238 (Nov. 1988): 1, 4; 239, 240 (Apr. 1989): 5–9; 241, 242 (Oct.–Nov. 1989): 6.

Kweskin, Jim. "Woody Guthrie." *Record Research* 161, 162 (Feb.–Mar. 1979): 13; 163, 164 (May–June 1979): 13.

Lambert, M. J. "Decca Records, 1929–1980." *Hillandale News* 130 (Feb. 1983): 156–161; 131 (Apr. 1983): 176–181.

Lambert, Ruth L. "Needle Tins." *Talking Machine Review International* 70 (Dec. 1985): 1,945–1,947, 1,997–1,999.

Lane, Michael R. "Equalization and Equalizers." *Association for Recorded Sound Collections Journal* 14 (2 (1982): 29–36.

———. "Sonic Restoration of Historical Recordings." *Audio* (June 1991): 35–44; (July 1991): 26–37.

Lane, Michael, and Richard C. Burns. "On 'Fifty Questions on Audio Restoration and Transfer Technology'." *Association for Recorded Sound Collections Journal* 16 (3) (1984): 5–11. A response to Owen 1983. Owen replied; then Lane and Owen had further comments in *Association for Recorded Sound Collections Journal* 17 (1985): 1–3.

Langwill, Lyndesay. *The Bassoon and Contrabassoon*. New York: Norton, 1965. 269 p. Discography on pp. 223–258.

Laubich, Arnold, and Ray Spencer. *Art Tatum: A Guide to His Recorded Music*. Metuchen, N.J.: Scarecrow Press, 1982. 359 p.

Lawrence, A. F. R., and Steve Smolian. "Emma Eames." *American Record Guide* 29 (1962): 210.

Leder, Jan. *Women in Jazz: A Discography of Instrumentalists, 1913–1968*. Westport, Conn.: Greenwood Press, 1985. 310 p.

Lee, Dorothy Sara. *Native North American Music and Oral Data: A Catalogue of Sound Recordings, 1893–1976*. Bloomington, Ind.: Indiana University Press, 1979. 479 p.

Lenoir, Abbe. "Procédé d'enregistrement et de reproduction des phénomènes perçus par l'ovie." *Semaine du clergé* (Oct. 10, 1877).

Léon, J.A., and Alusio R. Guimaraes. "Bidu Sayao." *Record Collector* 13 (6) (Aug. 1960): 123–133; 16 (2) (Sept. 1964): 46–47.

Leonard, William Torbert. *Masquerade in Black.* Metuchen, N.J.: Scarecrow Press, 1986. 431 p.

Levarie, Siegmund. "Noise." *Critical Inquiry* 4 (1) (Autumn 1977): 21–31.

Levarie, Siegmund, and Ernst Levy. *Tone: A Study in Musical Acoustics.* 2nd ed. Kent, Ohio: Kent State University Press, 1980. 248 p. Reprint Westport, Conn.: Greenwood Press, 1981. (1st ed. 1968)

———. *Musical Morphology: A Discourse and a Dictionary.* Kent, Ohio: Kent State University Press, 1983. 344 p.

Lewine, Richard, and Alfred Simon. *Songs of the Theater.* New York: H.W. Wilson, 1984. 897 p. Replaces their *Songs of the American Theater and Encyclopedia of Theater Music.*

Lewis, Gareth H. "Evan Williams." *Record Collector* 24 (11, 12) (Dec. 1978): 242–277.

Lewis, John Sam. "Fritz Kreisler: The First Hundred Years (1987–1975)." *Record Research* 139, 140 (May–June 1976): 8–10.

———. "Stokowski: The Centenary." *Record Research* 149, 150 (Oct. 1977): 4–5, 12.

———. "Early Violinists." *Record Research* 167, 168 (Oct. 1979): 12.

———. "First Lady of the Keyboard: Wanda Landowska." *Record Research* 163, 164 (May 1979): 9; 165, 166 (Aug. 1979): 13.

———. "The Beecham Celebration." *Record Research* 171, 172 (Mar. 1980): 12; 173, 174 (June 1980): 12; 175, 176 (Sept. 1980): 11.

———. "Jan Kubelik and Jacques Thibaud." *Record Research* 179, 180 (Feb. 1981): 9, 23 about Kubelik; *Record Research* 181, 182 (Apr. 1981): 11, 24 about Thibaud.

———. "The Violinists: Samuel Gardner." *Record Research* 213, 214 (May 1985): 11–12.

———. "Efrem Zimbalist (1889–1985)." *Record Research* 221, 222 (Apr. 1986): 8–9; 223, 224 (Aug. 1986): 9; 225, 226 (Nov. 1986): 2.

———. "The Pupils of Franz Liszt." *Record Research* 235, 236 (June 1988): 5; 237, 238 (Nov. 1988): 5; 239, 240 (Apr. 1989): 7; 241, 242 (Oct.–Nov. 1989): 8.

Lewis, Ted. "Our Society." *Hillandale News* 18 (Apr. 1964): 24–25. About the City of London Phonograph and Gramophone Society.

Lieb, Sandra R. *Mother of the Blues: A Study of Ma Rainey.* Amherst, Mass.: University of Massachusetts Press, 1983. 226 p.

Liliedahl, Karleric. "Swedish Record Labels: Dacapo." *Talking Machine Review International* 10 (June 1971): 35–36.

———. *Dixi-Silverton.* Trelleborg, Sweden: Author, 1973. 93 p.

———. *Comprehensive Discography of Swedish Acoustic Recordings, 1903–1928.* Stockholm: Arkivet för Ljud och Bild, 1987. 800 p. Lists 10,000 titles on 52 labels; excluding Gramophone Co.

Lindsay, Joe. "Vogue, the Original Picture Disc Label." *Discoveries* 2 (3) (Mar. 1989): 24–27.

Lindsay, Joe, Peter Bukoski, and Marc Grobman. *Picture Discs of the World: Price Guide and International Reference Book.* Scottsdale, Ariz.: Biodisc, 1990. 205 p.

Linkwitz, Siegfried H. "Active Crossover Networks for Noncoincident Drivers." *Journal of the Audio Engineering Society* 1 (2) (1976).

Litchfield, Jack. *Canadian Jazz Discography: 1916–1980.* Toronto: University of Toronto Press, 1982. 945 p.

Little, Donald C. "Discography of Tuba Solo Literature." *NACWPI Journal* 26 (Winter 1977–1978): 43–44.

Long, Edward M. "SME V Tonearm and Talisman Virtuoso DTi Cartridge." *Audio* (June 1986): 88–96.

———. "Mats & Clamps by the Numbers." *Audio* (Apr. 1988): 45–52. Discusses mats for turntables.

Lonstein, Albert L. *The Revised Compleat [sic] Sinatra.* Ellenville, N.Y.: S.M. Lonstein, 1979. 702 p.

Lorcey, Jacques. *Maria Callas: d'art et d'amour.* Rev. ed. Paris: Editions PAC, 1983. 615p. Discography on pp. 537–585, 609–612. (1st ed. 1977)

Lorenz, Kenneth M. *Two-Minute Brown Wax and XP Cylinder Records of the Columbia Phonograph Company: Numerical Catalog, August 1896–ca. March 1909.* Wilmington, Del.: Kastlemusick, 1981. 75 p.

Lowery, Alvin L. *Lowery's International Trumpet Discography.* Baltimore: Camden House, 1990. 2 vols.

Lumpe, Ernst A. "Pseudonymous Performers on Early LP Records: Rumors, Facts, and Finds." *Association for Recorded Sound Collections Journal* 21 (2) (Fall 1990): 226–231.

Lustig, Larry, and Clifford Williams. "Giuseppe Anselmi." *Record Collector* 32 (3–5) (Apr. 1987): 51–85.

Lyle, G. R., and Rose Krauskopf. "Phonograph Collection in Antioch College Library." *Library Journal* 59 (15 Mar. 1934): 266–267.

Lynch, Richard Chigley. *Broadway on Record: A Directory of New York Cast Recordings of Musical Shows, 1931–1986.* Westport, Conn.: Greenwood Press, 1987. 357 p.

MacDonald, J. Fred. *Don't Touch That Dial: Radio Programming in American Life, 1920–1960.* Chicago: Nelson-Hall, 1982. 412 p.

MacKenzie, John R., and John Godrich. "The Broadway Race Series." *Matrix* 48 (Aug. 1963): 3–13.

Magnetic Tape Recording for the Eighties. Edited by Ford Kalil. Washington, D.C.: National Aeronautics and Space Administration, 1982. 170 p. (NASA Reference Publications 1075)

Magnusson, Tor. "The Gene Austin Recordings." *Skivsamlaren* 15 (Feb. 1983): 1–82.

Malone, Bill. *Don't Get Above Your Raisin': Country Music and the Southern Working Class.* Urbana: University of Illinois Press, 2002. 392 p.

Malone, Bill C. *Country Music U.S.A.: A Fifty-Year History.* Rev. ed. Austin, Tex.: University of Texas Press, 1985. 562 p. (1st ed. 1968)

Manildi, Donald. "The Rubinstein Discography." *Le grand baton* 20 (56) (Dec. 1983): 56–100.

Manzo, J. R. "A Lambert Sampler." *New Amberola Graphic* 32 (Spring 1980): 4–7.

Marco, Guy A. "Bibliographic Control of Sound Recordings: An International View." *Audiovisual Librarian* 15 (Feb. 1989): 19–24.

Margoschis, Richard M. *Recording Natural History Sounds.* Barnet, England: Print & Press Services, 1977. 110 p.

Marsh, Robert C. "Solti in Chicago: A Critical Discography." *Harmonie-panorama-musique, new series* 20 (46) (Oct. 1984): 26–29, 35.

Martel, Joseph. "Roger Harding—A Forgotten Recording Pioneer." *New Amberola Graphic* 65 (July 1988): 3–8.

Martland, Peter. "Colonel Gouraud's Present." *Hillandale News* 162 (June 1988): 30–32.

———. "Theodore Birnbaum." *Hillandale News* 168 (June 1989): 225.

Marty, Daniel. *Illustrated History of Talking Machines.* New York: Dorset Press, 1979. 193 p. Originally in French: *Histoire illustrée du phonographe.* Lausanne: Edita-Vilo, 1979.

Mason, David. "Aviation on Records." *Talking Machine Review International* 68 (June 1984): 1,843–1,848.

Masters, Ian. "The Demon Room." *Stereo Review* (Apr. 1990): 23–25.

———. "The Basics." *Stereo Review* (Jan. 1990–Feb. 1991). A series covering various components of the home audio system.

Mathews, Emrys G. *John McCormack: Centenary Discography, 1904–1942.* Llandeilo, Wales: Author, 1986. 72 p.

Matthews, Denis. "Cadenzas in Piano Concertos." *Recorded Sound* 68 (Oct. 1977): 723–727.

Mauerer, Hans J. *Sidney Bechet Discography.* Rev. ed. Copenhagen: Knudsen, 1970. 86 p.

Mawhinney, Paul C. *Music Master: The 45 RPM Record Directory. 35 Years of Recorded Music, 1947 to 1982.* Allison Park, Penn.: Record-Rama, 1983. 2 vols.

McCarthy, Albert J. "Discography." In *Big Bill Blue, William Broonzy's Story as Told to Yannick Bruynoghe.* New York: Oak Publications, 1964, pp. 153–173.

McCormick, Don, and Seth Winner. "The Toscanini Legacy." *Association for Recorded Sound Collection Journal* 20 (2) (1989): 182–190.

McCoy, William, and Mitchell McGeary. *Every Little Thing: The Definitive Guide to Beatles Recording Variations, Rare Mixes & Other Musical Oddities, 1958–1986.* Ann Arbor, Mich.: Popular Culture, 1990. 368 p.

McCulloh, Judith. *Ethnic Recordings in America—A Neglected Heritage.* Washington, D.C.: Library of Congress, 1982. 269 p.

McDonough, Jack. *San Francisco Rock: The Illustrated History of San Francisco Rock Music.* Introduction by Paul Kantner. San Francisco: Chronicle Books, 1985.

McKee, Elwood. "ARSC AAA: Fifteen Years of Cooperative Research." *Association for Recorded Sound Collection Journal* 20 (1) (Spring 1989): 3–13.

McPherson, J., and William R. Moran. "Ernestine Schumann-Heink." *Record Collector* 17 (5, 6) (June 1967): 98–144; 17 (7) (Aug. 1967): 154–159; 20 (6, 7) (May 1972): 165; 25 (3, 4) (June 1979): 75–77.

———. "Jeanne Gerville-Réache." *Record Collector* 21 (3, 4) (July 1973): 51–79; 21 (7, 8) (Dec. 1973): 190–191.

McWilliams, A. A. "Tape Recording and Reproduction." *Encyclopedia of High Fidelity*, Vol. 4. New York and London: Focal Press, 1964. 287 p.

McWilliams, Jerry. *The Preservation and Restoration of Sound Recordings.* Nashville, Tenn.: American Association for State and Local History, 1979. 138 p.

———. "Sound Recordings." In *Conservation in the Library: A Handbook of Use and Care of Traditional and Nontraditional Materials.* Edited by Susan G. Swartzburg. Westport, Conn.: Greenwood Press, 1983, pp. 163–184.

Melville-Mason, Graham. "Re-scoring for Recording." In *Phonographs and Gramophones,* Edinburgh: Royal Scottish Museum, 1977, pp. 95–96.

Merriman, H. O. "Sound Recording by Electricity, 1919–1924." *Talking Machine Review International* 40 (June 1976): 666–681.

Methuen-Campbell, James. *Chopin Playing: From the Composer to the Present Day.* New York: Taplinger, 1981. 289 p.

———. "Early Soviet Pianists and Their Recordings." *Recorded Sound* 83 (Jan. 1983): 1–16.

———. *Catalogue of Recordings by Classical Pianists. Vol. 1. Pianists Born before 1872.* Chipping Norton, England: Disco Epsom, 1984. 66 p.

Migliorini, Louis, and James F.E. Dennis. "Olive Fremstad." *Record Collector* 7 (3) (Mar. 1952): 51–65.

———. "Emma Eames." *Record Collector* 8 (4) (Apr. 1953): 74–96.

Migliorini, Louis, and Nicholas Ridley. "Johanna Gadski." *Record Collector* 11 (9, 10) (Sept.–Oct. 1957): 196–231; 11 (11, 12) (Nov.–Dec. 1957): 257–285; 12 (1, 2) (Jan.–Feb. 1958): 36.

Miller, Jim, ed. *The Rolling Stone Illustrated History of Rock and Roll.* Rev. and updated. New York: Rolling Stone, 1980.

Miller, Philip L. "In Memory of the Carnegie Set." *Association for Recorded Sound Collections Journal* 4 (1972): 21–28.

———. "Margarete Matzenauer." *Record Collector* 23 (1, 2) (Jan. 1976): 3–47.

Mitchell, Peter W. "Which Tracks Best, a Pivoted or a Radial Tonearm?" *Audio* (June 1982): 25–29.

Mitchell, Ray. "Panachord Label." *Matrix* 68 (Dec. 1966) through 91 (Feb. 1971). A series listing issues of 1931–1939.

Modern Music Librarianship: Essays in Honor of Ruth Watanabe. Edited by Alfred Mann. Stuyvesant, N.Y.: Pendragon Press, 1989. 252 p. (Festschrift Series, 8).

Montgomery, Michael. "Piano Rollography of Adrian Rollini." *Record Research* 135, 136 (Nov.–Dec. 1975): 5–7.

———. "Eubie Blake Piano Rollography." *Record Research* 159, 160 (Dec. 1978): 4–5.

Moogk, Edward B. *Roll Back the Years: History of Canadian Recorded Sound and Its Legacy: Genesis to 1930.* Ottawa: National Library of Canada, 1975. 443 p.; phonodisc in pocket. Parker 1988 is a title index to Canadian works cited.

Moon, Robert, and Micheal Gray. *Full Frequency Stereophonic Sound: A Discography and History of Early London Decca Stereo Classical Instrumental and Chamber Music Recordings (1956–1963) on Records and Compact Discs.* San Francisco: Robert Moon, 1990. 83 p.

Moore, Jerrold N. "Yale University Historical Sound Recordings Program: Its Purpose and Scope." *Recorded Sound* 16 (Oct. 1964): 270–279.

———. *A Voice in Time: The Gramophone of Fred Gaisberg, 1873–1951.* London: Hamilton, 1976. 248 p.

Moran, William R. "Geraldine Farrar." *Record Collector* 13 (9, 10) (1960–1961): 194–240; 13 (11, 12) (Apr. 1961): 279–280; 14 (7, 8) (1961): 172–174; 20 (6, 7) (May 1972): 163–164.

———. "Discography." In *Yankee Diva: Lillian Nordica and the Golden Days of Opera,* by Ira Glackens. New York: Coleridge Press, 1963, pp. 285–300.

———. "Mario Ancona." *Record Collector* 16 (5, 6) (Apr. 1965): 100–139; 16 (7, 8) (Sept. 1965): 188; 20 (6, 7) (May 1972): 164.

———. "Bettini Cylinders." *Record Collector* 16 (7, 8) (Sept. 1965): 148–185.

———. "Discography." In *Forty Years of Song,* by Emma Albani. New York: Arno Press, 1977, pp. i–v.

———. "Discography." In *The Glory Road,* by Lawrence Tibbett. New York: Arno Press, 1977, pp. i–xxii.

———. "The Recordings of Emma Calvé." In *My Life,* by Emma Calvé. New York: Arno Press, 1977, pp. i–viii.

———. "Discography." In *Nellie Melba, a Contemporary Review.* Westport, Conn.: Greenwood Press, 1984, pp. 447–472.

———. "The Recordings of Emma Eames." In *Some Memories and Reflections,* by Emma Eames. New York: Arno Press, 1977, pp. 313–320.

———. "The Recordings of Olive Fremstad." In *The Rainbow Bridge,* by Mary Watkins Cushing. New York: Arno Press, 1977, pp. i–iv.

———. "The Recordings of Sir Charles Santley." In *Reminiscences of My Life,* by Charles Santley. New York: Arno Press, 1977, pp. i–ii.

———. "The Recordings of Ernestine Schumann-Heink." In *Schumann-Heink, the Last of the Titans,* by Mary Lawton. New York: Arno, 1977, pp. 339–428.

———. "The Recordings of Francesco Tamagno." In *Tamagno,* by Mario Corsi. New York: Arno Press, 1977, pp. 215–218.

———. "Discography." In *Mattia Battistini: il re dei baritoni,* by Francesco Palmegiani. New York: Arno Press, 1977, unpaged.

———. "Discography." In *Titta Ruffo: An Anthology.* Westport, Conn.: Greenwood Press, 1984, pp. 251–269.

Morby, Paul. "Aureliano Pertile." *Record Collector* 7 (11) (Nov. 1952): 244–260; 7 (12) (Dec. 1952): 267–277; 8 (1) (Jan. 1953): 37–41; 10 (12) (Nov. 1956): 277.

Morgan, Charles I. "John Charles Thomas." *Record Collector* 25 (1, 2) (Mar. 1979): 5–31.

Morgenstern, Dan. "A New Standard for Reissues." *Downbeat* (Dec. 1983).

Morin, Philippe. *Conversations avec Pablo Casals.* Paris: A. Michel, 1982. 455 p. Discography on pp. 417–444.

Morritt, Robert D. "Carson J. Robison." *New Ambrola Graphic* 29 (Summer 1979): 4–8.

Moses, Julian Morton. *Collector's Guide to American Recordings, 1895–1925.* New York: American Record Collectors' Exchange, 1949. 200 p. Reprint New York: Dover, 1977.

Mulholland, Pauline. *The Music Recording Industry in Australia.* Fitzroy, Victoria, Australia: Victorian Commercial Teachers Association and Victoria Education Department, 1989. 27 p.

Music Recording Industry in Australia, The. Industries Assistance Commission. Canberra: The Commission, 1978. 79 p.

Musical Instruments at the World's Columbian Exposition. Chicago: Presto Co., 1895. 328 p.

Myers, Kurth, ed. *Index to Record Reviews: Based on Material Originally Published in Notes, the Quarterly Journal of the Music Library Association, between 1949 and 1977.* Boston: G.K. Hall, 1978–1980. 5 vols. Supplements 1985, 1989. Supersedes *Record Ratings.* New York: Crown, 1956.

Narvaez, Peter. "A Tribute: Kenneth S. Goldstein, Record Producer." *Journal of American Folklore* 109 (Fall 1996): 450–463.

New Grove Dictionary of American Music. Edited by H. Wiley Hitchcock and Stanley Sadie. London: Macmillan, 1986. 4 vols.

Newsom, Iris, ed. *Wonderful Inventions: Motion Pictures, Broadcasting, and Recorded Sound at the Library of Congress.* With an introduction by Erik Barnouw. Washington, D.C.: Library of Congress, 1985. 384 p.; two 12-inch LP records included. A collection of articles, including three of interest to sound recording: "A Sound Idea: Music for Animated Films," by Jon Newsom; "Emile Berliner and Nineteenth-Century Disc Recording," by James R. Smart; and "Cartoons for the Record: The Jack Kapp Collection," by Samuel Brylawski.

Newville, Leslie J. "Development of the Phonograph at Alexander Graham Bell's Volta Laboratory." In *Contributions from the Museum of History and Technology.* Washington, D.C.: Smithsonian Institution, 1959, pp. 69–79.

Nolden, Rainer. *Count Basie: sein Leben, seine Musik, seine Schallplatten.* Schaftlach, Germany: OREOS, 1990. 184 p.

Novitsky, Ed. "The Mercury 5000 Series." *Record Research* 233, 234 (Feb. 1988): 4–5; 235, 236 (June 1988): 9; 237, 238 (Nov. 1988): 9; 239, 240 (Apr. 1989): 9; 241, 242 (Oct.–Nov. 1989): 9; 243, 244 (May–June 1990): 9; 245, 246 (Jan. 1991): 9; 247, 248 (Sept. 1991): 9. The 5000 series appeared in 1946–1952.

O'Brien, Ed, and Scott P. Sayers. *Sinatra: The Man and His Music—The Recording Artistry of Francis Albert Sinatra, 1939–1992.* Austin, Tex.: TSD Press, 1992. 303 p.

O'Dair, Barbara. *The Rolling Stone Book of Women in Rock: Trouble Girls.* New York: Random House, 1997. 608 p.

Odell, L Brevoort. "The Edison Diamond Disc Phonograph—Perfect Fidelity 60 Years Ago!" *Association for Recorded Sound Collections Journal* 6 (1974): 3–12.

Olcott, Evan. "Audio Reversal in Popular Culture." Retrieved from www.triplo.com ev reversal. Dec. 13, 2001.

Olson, Harry. *Elements of Acoustical Engineering.* 2nd ed. New York: Van Nostrand, 1947. 539 p.

———. "The RCA Victor Dynagroove System." *Journal of the Audio Engineering Society* 12 (2) (1964): 98–114. Reprinted in Roys 1978.

———. "Microphones for Recording." *Journal of the Audio Engineering Society* 25 (10, 11) (Oct.–Nov. 1977): 676–684.

Olson, Harry, John Preston, and Everett G. May. "Recent Developments in Direct-Radiator High-Fidelity Loudspeakers." *Journal of the Audio Engineering Society* 2 (October 1954): 219.

Olson, Robert C. "The Grey Gull 4000 Series." *New Amberola Graphic* 56 (Spring 1986): 3–10.

Oprisko, Peter Paul. "Frank Sinatra 7-inch Collectibles." *Discoveries* (Sept. 1990): 24–32.

Ord-Hume, Arthur W. J. G. *Pianola: The History of the Self-Playing Piano.* London: Allen & Unwin, 1984. 394 p.

Owen, H. G. "Elisabeth Schumann." *Record Collector* 7 (10) (Oct. 1952): 220–239.

Owen, H. G., and William R. Moran. "Marcella Sembrich." *Record Collector* 18 (5, 6) (May 1969): 99–138; 20 (6, 7) (May 1972): 165.

Owen, Tom. "Electrical Reproduction of Acoustically Recorded Discs and Cylinders." *Association for Recorded Sound Collections Journal* 14 (1) (1982): 11–18.

———. "Fifty Questions on Audio Restoration and Transfer Technology." *Association for Recorded Sound Collections Journal* 15 (2, 3) (1983): 38–45. Comments noted at Lane and Burns 1984.

Palmer, Robert, and Mary Shanahan. *The Rolling Stones.* Garden City, N.Y.: Rolling Stones Press, Doubleday, 1983. 253 p.

Palmieri, Robert. *Sergei Vasil'evich Rachmaninoff: A Guide to Research.* New York: Garland, 1985. 335 p. (Garland Composer Resource Manuals, 3) Discography on pp. 93–118.

Park, Bill. "Lily Pons." *Record Collector* 13 (11, 12) (Apr. 1960): 243–271, 283.

———. "Discography." In *Ponselle, a Singer's Life,* by Rosa Ponselle and James A. Drake. Garden City, N.Y.: Doubleday, 1982, pp. 248–307.

Parker, C. P., and David Emerson. "Title Index to Canadian Works Listed in Edward B. Moogk's Roll Back the Years." Ottawa: Canadian Association of Music Libraries, 1988. 13 p.

Paul, George. "The Kalamazoo Duplex." *New Amberola Graphic* 48 (Spring 1984): 6–7.

———. "The Metaphone Echophone." *New Amberola Graphic* 51 (Winter 1985): 4.

———. "Phonograph Forum." *New Amberola Graphic* 66 (Oct. 1988): 6–6.

———. "Step on It! Dance on It! A Wonder Record Surfaces." *Antique Phonograph Monthly* 10 (1) (1991): 5.

———. "The First Spring-Motor Gram-O-Phone." *New Amberola Graphic* 77 (July 1991): 3.

Pavarotti, Luciano. *Pavarotti: My Own Story.* Garden City, N.Y.: Doubleday, 1981. 316 p. Discography on pp. 291–308.

Pearmain, M. D. J., and R. P. Seemungal. "Miliza Korjus." *Record Collector* 16 (2) (Sept. 1964): 28–45; 16 (7, 8) (Sept. 1965): 188–189.

Peel, Tom, and John Holohan. "Beniamino Gigli." *Record Collector* 35 (8–10) (Aug.–Oct. 1990): 191–240.

Peel, Tom, and Cliff Williams. "Riccardo Stracciari." *Record Collector* 30 (1, 2) (Feb. 1985): 39–53; 31 (8, 10) (Sept. 1986): 239.

Perkins, John F., and Alan Kelly. "The Gramophone & Typewriter Ltd. Records of Camille Saint-Saens (1835–1921)." *Recorded Sound* 79 (Jan. 1981): 25–27.

Perone, James. *Songs of the Vietnam Conflict.* Westport, Conn.: Greenwood Press, 2001. 168 p.

Petersen, Phillip. "The Origin of the I.C.S. Language Cylinders." *Antique Phonograph Monthly* 1 (4) (Apr. 1973): 3–4.

———. "Amberol: A Word Study." *Talking Machine Review International* 33 (Apr. 1975): 316–322.

Petts, Leonard. "A Host of Angels." *Talking Machine Review International* 23 (Aug. 1973): 210–211. Descriptions and illustrations of labels with the Angel trademark.

———. *The Story of "Nipper" and the "His Master's Voice" Picture Painted by Francis Barraud.* Introduction by Frank Andrews. 2nd ed. Bournemouth, England: Talking Machine Review, 1983. 68 p.

———. "Berliner's Compact Disc." *Hillandale News* 165 (Dec. 1988): 114–119.

Petty, John A. "A Look at a Phenomenal Recording Schedule: Cal Stewart's 1919 Columbia Matrices." *New Amberola Graphic* 16 (Winter 1976): 3–5.

———. "Kalamazoo Discs." *New Amberola Graphic* 48 (Spring 1984): 10–11.

———. "Busy Bee Labels." *Hillandale News* 163 (Aug. 1988): 68–70.

Phillips, Ronald. "Mattia Battistini." *Record Collector* 2 (9) (Sept. 1947): 129–133; 3 (May 1948): 73.

"The Phonograph and Sound Recording after One Hundred Years." Edited by Warren Rex Isom. *Journal of the Audio Engineering Society* 25 (Oct.–Nov. 1977). Centennial issue of the journal. Individual articles cited separately in this Bibliography are Burt 1977, Isom 1977, Khanna 1977, Kogen 1977, and Olson, H. 1977.

"Phonographs in Libraries." *Library Journal* 34 (July 1909): 324.

Pickett, A. G., and M. M. Lemcoe. *Preservation and Storage of Sound Recordings.* Washington, D.C.: Library of Congress, 1959. 74 p.

Pinne, Peter. "Australian Theatre on Disc." In Hummel 1984, pp. xxvii–xxxiii.

Pinta, Emil R. *A Chronologic Jan Peerce Discography, 1932–1980.* Worthington, Ohio: Author, 1987. 29 p.

Pitts, Michael R. *Radio Soundtracks: A Reference Guide.* 2nd ed. Metuchen, N.J.: Scarecrow Press, 1986. 349 p.

———. *Kate Smith, a Bio-Bibliography.* Westport, Conn.: Greenwood Press, 1988. 320 p.

Place, Jeff, and Ronald D. Cohen. *The Best of Broadside, 1962–1988: Anthems of the American Underground from the Pages of Broadside Magazine.* Washington, D.C.: Smithsonian Folkways Records, SFW CD 40130, 2000.

Pohlmann, Ken C. *The Compact Disc: A Handbook of Theory and Use.* Madison, Wis.: A-R Editions, 1989. 288 p.

Polic, Edward F. *The Glenn Miller Army Air Force Band.* Metuchen, N.J.: Scarecrow Press, 1989. 2 vols.

Poole, Louis. "Louise Homer." *Record Collector* 2 (7) (July 1947): 96–98.

Popa, Jay. *Cab Calloway and His Orchestra, 1925–1958.* Rev. by Charles Garrod. Zephyrhills, Fla.: Joyce Record Club, 1987. 38 p. (First published in 1976.)

Porter, Bob. "National Records." *Record Research* 149, 150 (Oct. 1977): 8–9; 151, 152 (Jan. 1978): 15; 153, 154 (Apr. 1978): 11–12; 155, 156 (July 1978): 13, 16. [Porter 1978/7]

———. "Majestic Masters Listing." *Record Research* 157, 158 (Sept. 1978): 8–9; 159, 160 (Dec. 1978): 12; 161, 162 (Feb.–Mar. 1979): 12; 163, 164 (May–June 1979): 12; 165, 166 (Aug. 1979): 12; 167, 168 (Oct. 1979): 9. [Porter 1978/12]

———. "List of Signature Masters." *Record Research* 171, 172 (Mar. 1980): 11; 173, 174 (June 1980): 11; 177, 178 (Nov. 1980): 14; 179, 180 (Feb. 1981): 12; 181, 182 (Apr. 1981): 9.

Porterfield, Nolan. *Jimmie Rodgers: The Life and Times of America's Blue Yodeler.* Champaign: University of Illinois Press, 1992. 460 p.

Potter, Tully. *Adolf Busch: The Life of an Honest Man.* Billericay, Essex, England: Author, 1985. Vol. 1. Discography on pp. 59–135.

Potterton, Robert, and James F. E. Dennis. "Zélie de Lussan." *Record Collector* 17 (8) (Dec. 1967): 171–182.

Poundstone, William. *Big Secrets.* New York: William Morrow & Company, 1983. 228 p.

Powell, James R., Jr. "Audiophile's Guide to Phonorecord Playback Equalizer Settings." *Association for Recorded Sound Collections Journal* 20 (1) (Spring 1989): 14–23.

Proceedings of the 1890 Convention of Local Phonograph Companies. Introduction by Raymond R. Wile. Reprint ed. Nashville, Tenn.: Country Music Foundation Press, 1974. 210 p.

Proudfoot, Christopher. *Collecting Phonographs and Gramophones.* New York: Mayflower Books; London: Studio Vista, 1980. 119 p.

Randel, Don Michael, ed. *The New Harvard Dictionary of Music.* Cambridge, Mass.: Harvard University Press, 1986. 942 p.

Raymond, Jack. "A Numerical Listing of Liberty Music Shop Records." *Record Research* 181, 182 (Apr. 1981): 8; continued by Len Kunstadt: 185, 186 (Oct. 1981): 9; 187, 188 (Dec. 1981): 9; 189, 190 (Mar.–Apr. 1982): 10; 191, 192 (July 1982): 10; 195, 196 (Jan. 1983): 12; 197, 198 (Mar.–Apr. 1983): 8; 201, 202 (Sept. 1983): 11; 203–204 (Dec. 1983): 9; 205, 206 (Mar. 1984): 12; 207, 208 (June 1984): 11; 209, 210 (Oct. 1984): 12; 215, 216 (July 1985): 11; 217, 218 (Oct. 1985): 2; 219, 220 (Jan. 1986): 5; 221, 222 (Apr. 1986): 4; 227, 228 (Mar. 1987): 10; 229, 230 (June 1987): 14; 231, 232 (Oct. 1987): 12; 233, 234 (Feb. 1988): 6.

———. *Show Music on Record from the 1890s to the 1980s.* New York: Ungar, 1982. 253 p.

Read, Oliver, and Walter L. Welch. *From Tin Foil to Stereo: Evolution of the Phonograph.* 2nd ed. Indianapolis: H.W. Sams, 1976. 550 p. (1st ed. 1959)

Record Tape Collector's Directory. 2nd ed. Santa Monica, Calif.: Rare Record Tape Collector's Directory, 1978. 47 p. (1st ed. 1976)

Reed, Peter Hugh. "Frieda Hempel." *Record Collector* 10 (3) (Aug. 1955): 51–71.

Reid, Gordon. "CEDAR." *Hillandale News* 172 (Feb. 1990): 314–319.

Reinhard, Kurt. "The Berlin Phonogramm-Archiv." *Recorded Sound* 1 (2) (June 1961): 44–45.

Reiss, Eric L. *The Compleat Talking Machine: A Guide to the Restoration of Antique Phonographs.* Vestal, N.Y.: Vestal Press, 1986. 184 p.

Rektorys, Artus, and James F. E. Dennis. "Emmy Destinn." *Record Collector* 20 (1, 2) (July 1971): 3–47; 20 (4) (Dec. 1971): 93–94.

Renton, Arthur. "Toti dal Monte." *Record Collector* 4 (9) (Sept. 1949): 142, 147–150.

Reuss, Richard A., and JoAnne Reuss. *American Folk Music and Left-Wing Politics, 1927–1957.* Lanham, Md.: Scarecrow Press, 2000. 297 p.

Richards, John B. "Elisabeth Rethberg." *Record Collector* 3 (2) (Feb. 1948): 26–30; 3 (4) (Apr. 1948):

51–56; 4 (11) (Nov. 1949): 192–196; 5 (1) (Jan. 1950): 11–16; 8 (1) (Jan. 1953): 4–19. [Richards 1948/2]

———. "Lucrezia Bori." *Record Collector* 3 (10) (Oct. 1948): 161–166; 4 (1) (Jan. 1949): 2–12; 4 (5) (May 1949): 98–99; 9 (5) (1954): 104–123; 21 (7, 8) (Dec. 1973): 147–168. [Richards 1948/10]

———. "Elisabeth Rethberg." *Hobbies* (Mar. 1950): 18–19; (Apr. 1950): 18; (May 1950): 18–19.

———. "Eva Turner." *Record Collector* 11 (2, 3) (Feb.–Mar. 1957): 28–57, 71; 11 (8) (Aug. 1957): 183–184; 11 (9, 10) (Sept.–Oct. 1957): 231–233.

———. "Hipolito Lazaro." *Record Collector* 16 (3, 4) (Nov.–Dec. 1964): 52–94; 16 (9, 10) (Jan. 1966): 226–228; 18 (11, 12) (Dec. 1969): 280–281.

———. "Gemma Bellincioni." *Record Collector* 16 (9, 10) (Jan. 1966): 196–219; 18 (5, 6) (May 1969): 139–140.

———. "Claudia Muzio." *Record Collector* 17 (9, 10) (Feb. 1968): 197–237; 17 (11) (Apr. 1968): 256–263; 28 (5, 6) (Oct. 1983): 120–128.

———. "Lucrezia Bori." *Record Collector* 21 (7, 8) (Dec. 1973): 147–168.

Richards. John B., and J. P. Kenyon. "Ezio Pinza." *Record Collector* 26 (3, 4) (Aug. 1980): 51–95; 26 (5, 6) (Dec. 1980): 101–137.

Richards, John B., and Phillip Wade. "Luisa Tetrazzini." *Record Collector* 4 (8) (Aug. 1949): 122–139.

Ridley, Nicholas A. "Emma Albani." *Record Collector* 12 (4, 5) (Feb.–Mar. 1959): 76–101; 12 (8, 9) (Nov.–Dec. 1959): 197–198; 14 (9, 10) (1961): 236.

Riemens, Leo. "Julia Culp." *Record Collector* 2 (7) (July 1947): 100–104.

———. "Irene Abendroth." *Record Collector* 6 (4) (Apr. 1951): 75–85.

Riggs, Quentin. "The Revelers." *Talking Machine Review International* 6 (Oct. 1970): 158–163.

Roach, Helen. "Two Women of Caedmon." *Association for Recorded Sound Collections Journal* 19 (1) (May 1988): 21–24.

Robertson, Alex. "Canadian Gennett and Starr-Gennett 9000 Numerical." *Record Research* 195, 196 (Jan. 1983): 1–7; 197, 198 (Mar.–Apr. 1983): 7; 199, 200 (June 1983): 10–11; 201, 202 (Sept. 1983): 10; 203, 204 (Dec. 1983): 4.

———. "The Rare Canadian Aurora Label from Victor Masters." *Record Research* 219, 220 (Jan. 1986): 1, 3–8.

Robertson, John, and James F. E. Dennis. "Leonid Sobinoff." *Record Collector* 24 (7, 8) (Sept. 1978): 147–190.

Robinson, Earl, and Eric A. Gordon. *Ballad of an American: The Autobiography of Earl Robinson.* Lanham, Md.: Scarecrow Press, 1998. 477 p.

Rolling Stone Record Guide. Edited by Dave Marsh and John Swenson. New York: Random House, 1979. 631 p.

Romanowski, Patricia and Holly George Warren, eds. *The New Rolling Stone Encyclopedia of Rock.* New York: *Rolling Stone* Press/Simon and Schuster, 1995.

Ronin, Ro. *Have Gun, Will Travel: The Spectacular Rise and Violent Fall of Death Row Records.* New York: Main Street Books, 1999. 372 p.

Rose, Al. *Eubie Blake.* New York: Schirmer, 1979. 214 p. Discography on pp. 174–188.

Rosenberg, Kenyon C. *A Basic Classical and Operatic Recordings Collection for Libraries.* Metuchen, N.J.: Scarecrow Press, 1987. 255 p.

———. *A Basic Classical and Operatic Recordings Collection on Compact Discs for Libraries.* Metuchen, N.J.: Scarecrow Press, 1990. 395 p.

Rosenberg, Kenyon C., and Paul T. Feinstein. *Dictionary of Library and Educational Technology.* 2nd ed. Littleton, Colo.: Libraries Unlimited, 1983. 185 p. (1st ed. 1976: *Media Equipment: A Guide and Dictionary,* by Kenyon C. Rosenberg and John S. Deskey.)

Rosenberg, Neil V. *Bill Monroe and His Blue Grass Boys: An Illustrated Discography.* Nashville, Tenn.: Country Music Foundation Press, 1974. 120 p.

Rotante, Anthony. "The 'King' of R & B Labels." *Record Research* 22 (Apr.–May 1959), 24, 25, 27, 29, 30, 87, 90, 91–94, 98 (1969). A serial label list, with background on the firm, is included in issue 87. Title varies.

———. "Bluesville." Anthony Rotante. *Record Research* 73 (Jan. 1966): 5.

———. "Federal; The Federal 12000 Series." *Record Research* 111 (July 1971), 113–117, 119–122 (June 1973).

———. "De Luxe 6000 Series." *Record Research* 124 (Nov. 1973): 10; 125, 126 (Feb. 1974): 14.

———. "Maurice Chevalier on Pathé Salabert Labels." *Record Research* 135, 136 (Nov.–Dec. 1975): 4.

———. "Edith Piaf the Early Years, Polydor Records 1936–1944." *Record Research* 199, 200 (June 1983): 4; 201, 202 (Sept. 1983): 10; 203, 204 (Dec. 1983): 8.

———. "Imperial." *Record Research* 215, 216 (July 1985): 1, 3–4; 217, 218 (Oct. 1985): 6–7; 219, 220 (Jan. 1986): 12; 221, 222 (Apr. 1986): 10–11; 223, 224 (Aug. 1986): 12; 225, 226 (Nov. 1986): 10; 227, 228 (Mar. 1987): 8; 229, 230 (June 1987): 11; 231, 232 (Oct. 1987): 8–9; 233, 234 (Feb. 1988): 10–11. Continues as Hayes, C. 1988.

Royal Scottish Museum. *Phonograph and Gramophone Symposium, 2 July 1977.* Edinburgh: The Museum, 1977. 142 p.

Roys, Henry Edward, ed. *Disc Recording and Reproduction.* Stroudsburg, Penn.: Dowden, Hutchenson and Ross, 1978. 394 p. Consists of 42 papers, reprinted from technical journals.

Rules for Archival Cataloging of Sound Recordings. Association for Recorded Sound Collections, Associated Audio Archives Committee. Silver Spring, Md.: The Association, 1978. 72 p.

Ruppli, Michel. *Atlantic Records: A Discography.* Westport, Conn.: Greenwood Press, 1979. 4 vols.

———. *Charles Mingus Discography.* Frankfurt: Norbert Ruecker, 1981. 47 p. (Jazz Index Reference series, 1)

———. *The Chess Labels: A Discography.* Westport, Conn.: Greenwood Press, 1983. 2 vols.

———. *The Clef Verve Labels: A Discography.* Westport, Conn.: Greenwood Press, 1986. 2 vols.

Ruppli, Michel, and Bob Porter. *The Prestige Label: A Discography.* Westport, Conn.: Greenwood Press, 1980. 378 p.

———. *The Savoy Label: A Discography.* Westport, Conn.: Greenwood Press, 1980. 443 p.

Rust, Brian. *The Victor Master Book, II (1925–1936).* Stanhope, N.J.: Allen, 1970. 776 p. Covers Victor black label issues and Bluebird issues of 1933–1936. Vol. I was not published.

———. *The Complete Entertainment Discography, 1897–1942.* 2nd ed. New York: Da Capo Press, 1989. 794 p. An updated and expanded reprint of the 1st ed. (New Rochelle, N.Y.: Arlington House, 1973).

———. *The American Dance Band Discography, 1917–1942.* New Rochelle, N.Y.: Arlington House, 1975. 2 vols. A series of additions and corrections has been appearing in issues of *Record Research* since vols. 157, 158 (Sept. 1978).

———. *The American Record Label Book.* New Rochelle, N.Y.: Arlington House, 1978. 336 p.

———. *British Music Hall on Record.* Harrow, England: General Gramophone Publications, 1979a. 301 p.

———. *Discography of Historical Records on Cylinders and 78s.* Westport, Conn.: Greenwood Press, 1979b. 327 p.

———. *Brian Rust's Guide to Discography.* Westport, Conn.: Greenwood Press, 1980. 133 p.

———. "(British) Berliner, G & T and Zonophone 7-inch Records." *Talking Machine Review International* 63, 64 (Autumn 1981): 1,726–1,758. Adamson 1983 has useful comments on this list.

———. *Jazz Records, 1897–1942.* 5th ed. Chigwell, England: Storyville, 1982. 2 vols. (1st ed. 1961)

Rust, Brian, and Rex Bunnett. *London Musical Shows on Record, 1897–1976.* Rev. ed. London: British Institute of Recorded Sound, 1977. 672 p. (1st ed. 1958, with Supplement 1959.) A revised edition is Seeley and Bunnett 1989.

Rust, Brian, and Sandy Forber. *British Dance Bands on Record, 1911 to 1945, and Supplement.* Harrow, England: General Gramophone Publications, 1989. 1,496 p. A reprint of the original (1986) edition, with a 72 p. supplement.

Sackville-West, Edward, and Desmond Shaw-Taylor. *The Record Guide.* London: Colins, 1951. 763 p.

Salewicz, Chris. *McCartney.* New York: St. Martin's, 1986. 263 p.

Samuels, Jon. "A Complete Discography of the Recordings of Emanuel Feuermann." *Association for Recorded Sound Collections Journal* 12 (1, 2) (1980): 33–77.

———. "A Complete Discography of the Recordings of the Flonzaley Quartet." *Association for Recorded Sound Collections Journal* 19 (1) (1987): 25–62.

Sanders, Alan. *Sir Adrian Boult: A Discography.* Harrow, England: General Gramophone Publications, 1981. 37 p.

———. *Walter Legge: A Discography.* Westport, Conn.: Greenwood Press, 1984. 452 p.

Sarnoff, David. *Edison (1847–1931).* New York: Newcomen Society, 1948. 24 p.

Schuller, Gunther. *Early Jazz: Its Roots and Musical Development.* New York: Oxford University Press, 1968. 401 p. (History of Jazz series, 1).

———. *The Swing Era: The Development of Jazz, 1930–1945.* New York: Oxford University Press, 1989. 919 p. (History of Jazz series, 2).

Schwartz, Leonard. "The Coon-Sanders Orchestra." *Talking Machine Review International* 69 (Dec. 1984): 1,898–1,902.

Schwarzkopf, Elisabeth. *On and Off the Record: A Memoir of Walter Legge.* New York: Scribner's Sons, 1982. 292 p.

Scott, Michael. *The Record of Singing to 1914.* London: Duckworth, 1978. 243 p. Issued with the EMI record series, *The Record of Singing* (EMI no. RLS 724). Continued by Scott 1979.

———. *The Record of Singing: Volume Two, 1914–1925.* London: Duckworth; New York: Holmes & Meier, 1979. 262 p. Continues Scott 1977.

———. *The Great Caruso.* New York: Knopf, 1988. 322 p. "A Chronology of Caruso's Appearances," by Thomas G. Kaufman, pp. 201–264; "A Caruso Discography," by John R. Bolig, pp. 265–293.

Sears, Richard S. *V-Discs: A History and Discography.* Westport, Conn.: Greenwood Press, 1980. 1,166 p. (ARSC Reference Series). 1st Supplement, 1986 (272 p.).

Seeliger, Ronald, and Bill Park. "Tiana Lemnitz." *Record Collector* 15 (2) (1963): 28–43.

Seeger, Anthony, and Louise S. Spear. *Early Field Recordings: A Catalogue of Cylinder Collections at the Indiana University Archives of Traditional Music.* Bloomington, Ind.: Indiana University Press, 1987. 198 p.

Seeley, Robert, and Rex Bunnett. *London Musical Shows on Record, 1889–1989.* Harrow, England: General Gramophone Publications, 1989. 457 p. A revision of Rust 1977.

Segond, André. *Renata Tebaldi.* Lyon, France: Laffont, 1981. 260 p. Discography on pp. 237–253.

Semeonoff, Boris, and Alan Kelly. "New Complete Discography of Feodor Chaliapin." *Record Collector* 20 (8–10) (Aug. 1972): 171–230.

Seymour, Henry. *The Reproduction of Sound.* London: W.B. Tattersall, 1918. 324 p.

Shaman, William. "The Operatic Vitaphone Shorts." *Association for Recorded Sound Collections Journal* 22 (1) (Spring 1991): 35–94.

Shaw, Arnold. *The Rockin' 50s.* New York: Hawthorne, 1974. 296 p. Reprint New York: Da Capo Press, 1987.

Shawe-Taylor, Desmond, and E. Hughes. "Arthur Nikisch." *Recorded Sound* 4 (Oct. 1961): 114–115.

Sheridan, Chris. *Count Basie: A Bio-Discography.* Westport, Conn.: Greenwood Press, 1986. 1,350 p.

Sherman, Michael. "The First Commercial Berliner Records Made in America." *Antique Phonograph Monthly* 9 (3) (1990): 3–7.

Sherman, Michael W. *The Paper Dog: An Illustrated Guide to 78 RPM Victor Record Labels, 1900–1958.* Brooklyn: APM Press, 1987. 43 p.

Shipton, Alyn. *Groovin' High: The Life of Dizzy Gillespie.* New York: Oxford University Press, 1999. 422 p.

Shipway, E. L. M. "Getting the Best Results from 78 RPM Records in 1984." *Talking Machine Review International* 65, 66 (Feb. 1983): 1,888–1,889.

Sieben, Hansfried. "Vox and Successor." *Talking Machine Review International* 70 (Dec. 1985): 2,000–2,001.

Simms, Eric. *Wildlife Sounds and Their Recording.* London: Elek, 1979. 144 p.

Simon, George T. *The Big Bands.* Rev. ed. New York: Macmillan, 1974. 584 p. (1st ed. 1967)

Sitsky, Larry. *Busoni and the Piano.* Westport, Conn.: Greenwood Press, 1985. 409 p. Discography on pp. 326–333.

———. *The Classical Reproducing Roll: A Catalogue-Index.* Westport, Conn.: Greenwood Press, 1990. 2 vols.

Slide, Anthony. *Great Radio Personalities in Historic Photographs.* New York: Dover, 1982. 117 p.

Slonimsky, Nicholas. *Baker's Biographical Dictionary of Musicians.* 7th ed. New York: Schirmer, 1984. 2,577 p.

Small, Richard H. "Closed-Box Loudspeaker Systems." *Journal of the Audio Engineering Society* (Dec. 1972): 798–808; (Jan.–Feb. 1973): 11–18.

Smart, James R. *The Sousa Band: A Discography.* Washington, D.C.: Library of Congress, 1970. 123 p.

———. *Radio Broadcasts in the Library of Congress, 1924–1941: A Catalog of Recordings.* Washington, D.C.: Library of Congress, 1982. 149 + 14 p.

———. "Carl Engel and the Library of Congress's First Acquisitions of Recordings." *Association for Recorded Sound Collections Journal* 15 (2, 3) (1983): 6–18.

Smart, James R., and Jon W. Newsom. *"A Wonderful Invention": A Brief History of the Phonograph from Tinfoil to the LP.* Washington, D.C.: Library of Congress, 1977. 40 p.

Smiraglia, Richard P. *Music Cataloging.* Englewood, Colo.: Libraries Unlimited, 1989. 222 p.

Smith, John L. *The Johnny Cash Discography.* Westport, Conn.: Greenwood Press, 1985. 203 p.

Smithson, Roger. *The Recordings of Edwin Fischer.* Rev. ed. London: Author, 1990. 25 p. (1st ed. 1983)

Smolian, Steven. *Handbook of Film, Theatre and Television Music on Records, 1948–1969.* New York: Record Undertaker, 1970. 2 vols. in 1; 64 p.

———. "Four Decades of the Budapest Quartet." *American Record Guide* 37 (Dec. 1970): 220–224.

———. "Standards for the Review of Discographic Works." *Association for Recorded Sound Collections Journal* 7 (3) (1976): 47–55.

———. "Preservation, Deterioration and Restoration of Recording Tape." *Association for Recorded Sound Collections Journal* 19 (2, 3) (1987): 37–53.

Soames, Victoria, ed. *The Clarinet Historical Recordings,* Volume I. Clarinet Classics, CC no. 0005, 1993.

———. *The Clarinet Historical Recordings,* Volume II. Clarinet Classics, CC no. 0010, 1994.

Southall, Brian. *Abbey Road: The Story of the World's Most Famous Recording Studios.* Cambridge, England: Patrick Stephens, 1982. 217 p.

Special Collections in the Library of Congress: A Selective Guide. Washington, D.C.: Library of Congress, 1980. 464 p.

Spottswood, Richard K. *Ethnic Music on Records: A Discography of Ethnic Recordings Produced in the United States, 1893–1942.* Urbana, Ill.: University of Illinois Press, 1991. 7 vols.

Stambler, Irwin. *Encyclopedia of Pop, Rock and Soul.* 2nd ed. New York: St. Martin's, 1989. 881 p. (1st ed. 1974)

Stambler, Irwin, and Grelun Landon. *Encyclopedia of Folk, Country and Western Music.* 2nd ed. New York: St. Martin's, 1983. 396 p. (1st ed. 1969)

Stanford, Stan, ed. *The Acoustic Era Clarinet Recordings, 1898–1918.* Stan Stanford, 1998.

Stark, Craig. "Dolby S: A New Standard for Cassette Recording?" *Stereo Review* (May 1990): 78–79.

Steane, J. B. *The Grand Tradition: Seventy Years of Singing on Record.* London: Duckworth, 1974. 628 p.

Steane, John. "Discography." In *My Life,* by Tito Gobbi. London: Macdonald and James, 1979, pp. 201–210.

Stephenson, Tom. "The Impressive Dominion Autophone." *Hillandale News* 135 (Dec. 1983): 288–289.

Sterling, Christopher H., and John M. Kittross. *Stay Tuned: A Concise History of American Broadcasting.* Belmont, Calif.: Wadsworth, 1978. 562 p.

Stevens, S. S., and Fred Warshofsky. *Sound and Hearing.* 2nd ed. New York: Time-Life Books, 1969. 200 p.

Stevenson, Gordon. "Discography: Scientific, Analytical, Historical and Systematic." *Library Trends* 21 (1) (July 1972): 101–135.

Stover, Suzanne. "The 'Fair Use' of Sound Recordings: A Summary of Existing Practices and Concerns." *Association for Recorded Sound Collections Journal* 21 (2) (1990): 232–240.

Stratton, John. "The Recordings of Jean de Reszke." *Recorded Sound* 27 (July 1967): 209–213.

———. "Dmitri Smirnov." *Record Collector* 14 (11, 12) (July 1973): 244–247.

———. "Florence Eaton." *Record Collector* 21 (9, 10) (Jan. 1974): 195–239; 21 (11, 12) (Mar. 1974): 256.

Stroff, Stephen. "Django's Dream: The Life of Django Reinhardt." *Antiques and Collecting Hobbies* (May 1988); (June 1988): 57–59. [Stroff 1988/5]

———. "Young Jussi Björling." *Antiques and Collecting Hobbies* (Oct. 1988): 59–64.

———. "Gennett Records: The Label That Changed History." *Antiques and Collecting Hobbies* (June 1989): 66.

Summers, Harrison B. *A Thirty-Year History of Programs Carried on National Radio Networks in the United States, 1926–1956.* Columbus, Ohio: Department of Speech, The Ohio State University, 1958. 228 p. Reprints New York: Arno Press, 1971; Salem, N.H.: Ayer, 1986.

Sunier, John. "A History of Binaural Sound." *Audio* (Mar. 1986): 36–44.

Sutton, Allan. *A.K.A.: Pseudonyms on American Records, 1900–1932.* Baltimore: Author, 1991. 16 p.

Swartz, Jon D., and Robert C. Reinehr. *Handbook of Old-Time Radio: A Comprehensive Guide to Golden Age Radio Listening and Collecting.* Metuchen, N.J.: Scarecrow Press, 1993.

Swartzburg, Susan G. *Preserving Library Materials.* 2nd ed. Metuchen, N.J.: Scarecrow Press, 1991. 503 p. (1st ed. 1980)

Taylor, George. "Dating Gramophone Co. London Recordings, 1908–1925." *Hillandale News* 132 (June 1983): 204–206.

———. "Vitaphone." *Hillandale News* 144 (June 1985): 218–222; 146 (Oct. 1985): 257–260; 149 (Apr. 1986): 19–22.

———. "Opera on Bettini." *Hillandale News* 155 (Apr. 1987): 174–185.

———. "The Mapleson Cylinders." *Hillandale News* 157 (Aug. 1987): 228–236.

———. "The Recorded Legacy of Jean de Reszke." *Record Collector* 33 (1, 2) (Jan. 1988): 22–25.

———. "Berliner at the Opera." *Hillandale News* 173 (Apr. 1990): 2–4. Comments by P. G. Adamson in *Hillandale News* 174 (June 1990): 36.

Tesoriero, Michael. "Beniamino Giglithe One and Only." *Journal of the Phonograph Society of New South Wales* 6 (3) (Apr. 1990): 20–26; 6 (4) (July 1990): 21–29.

Thielcke, Gerhard. *Bird Sounds.* Ann Arbor, Mich.: University of Michigan Press, 1976. 190 p.

Thiele, A. N. "Loudspeakers in Vented Boxes." *Journal of the Audio Engineering Society* (May 1971): 382–392; (June 1971): 471–483.

Thorgerson, Storm, and Roger Dean. *Album Cover Album.* New York: A & W Visual Library, 1977. 160 p.

Thorgerson, Storm, Roger Dean, and David Howells. *Album Cover Album: The Second Volume.* New York: A & W Visual Library, 1982. 159 p.

Thorin, Suzanne E., and Carole Vidali Franklin. *The Acquisition and Cataloging of Music and Sound Recordings: A Glossary.* Washington, D.C.: Music Library Association, 1984. 40 p. (Technical Reports series, 11).

Timner, W. E. *Ellingtonia: The Recorded Music of Duke Ellington and His Sidemen.* 3rd ed. Metuchen, N.J.: Scarecrow Press, 1988. 554 p.

Toborg, D. "Tex Ritter Collection." *Record Research* 108 (Dec. 1970): 139–140; (May–June 1976). A series of label lists that appeared in most issues of *Record Research* in the period shown.

———. "Tex Ritter: The Complete Capitol Discography." *Record Research* 163, 164 (May–June 1979): 217–218; (Oct. 1985). A series of listings that appeared in most issues of *Record Research* in the period shown.

Treichel, James. *Woody Herman's Second Herd, 1947–1949.* Zephyrhills, Fla.: Joyce Record Club, 1978. 56 p.

Tron, David. "Recordings of Maggie Teyte." In *Star on the Door,* by Maggie Teyte. New York: Arno Press, 1977, pp. 188–192.

Tron, David, and James F. E. Dennis. "Maggie Teyte." *Record Collector* 9 (6) (Nov. 1954): 128–138; 9 (11, 12) (Apr.–May 1955): 270–271.

Tuddenham, Adrian, and Peter Copeland. "Record Processing for Improved Sound." *Hillandale News* 162 (June 1988): 34–39; 163 (Aug. 1988): 72–77; 164 (Oct. 1988): 89–97.

Tudor, Dean. *Popular Music: An Annotated Guide to Recordings.* Littleton, Colo.: Libraries Unlimited, 1983. 647 p. Supersedes Tudor's 1979 books *Jazz, Black Music, Grass Roots Music,* and *Contemporary Pop Music.*

Turner, Patricia. *Dictionary of Afro-American Performers.* New York: Garland, 1990. 433 p.

Turner, Rufus P., and Stan Gibilisco. *The Illustrated Dictionary of Electronics.* 4th ed. Blue Ridge Summit, Penn.: Tab Books, 1988. 648 p. (1st ed. 1985)

Usill, Harley. "A History of Argo." *Recorded Sound* 78 (July 1980): 31–44.

Vaché, Warren W. *This Horn for Hire: The Life and Career of Pee Wee Erwin.* Metuchen, N.J.: Scarecrow Press, 1987. 441 p.

Variety's Directory of Major Show Business Awards. Edited by Mike Kaplan. 2nd ed. New York: Bowker, 1989. 750 p. (1st ed. 1985)

Villchur, Edgar M. *The Reproduction of Sound in High Fidelity and Stereo Phonographs.* New York: Dover, 1965. 92 p.

Villetard, Jean François. "Coleman Hawkins, 1922–1944." In *Micrography,* Amsterdam: 1984. 80 p. Continued by "Coleman Hawkins, 1945–1957" (1985; 80 p.) and "Coleman Hawkins, 1958–1969" (1987; 80 p.).

Dictionary Catalog of the G. Robert Vincent Voice Library at Michigan State University. Edited by Leonard E. Cluley and Pamela N. Engelbrecht. Boston: G.K. Hall, 1975. 677 p. [Vincent 1975].

Voices of the Past. John R. Bennett et al. Lingfield, Surrey, England: Oakwood Press, 1955–1970. Facsimile typescript listings of vocal records on labels issued by the Gramophone Co. and affiliates. Coverage by volume (full titles of the volumes are in Rust 1980):

1. HMV English catalogues, 1898–1925 (1955)
2. HMV Italian catalogues, 1898–1925 (1958)
3. Dischi Fonotipia (1964?)
4. International red label catalogues (1961)
5. HMV black label catalogues, D and E series (1960)
6. International red label catalogues (1963)
7. German catalogues (1967)

8. Columbia catalogue of English celebrity issues (1972)

9. French catalogues (1971?)

10. Plum label C series

11. Russian catalogues, 1899–1915 (1977)

12. (Vol. LP1) Columbia blue and green labels, 1952–1962 (1975)

13. (Vol. LP2) HMV red label, 1952–1962 (1975)

14. (Vol. LP3) HMV plum label, 1952–1962 (1975)

Von Békésy, Georg. *Experiments in Hearing.* New York: McGraw-Hill, 1960. 745 p. Reprint Huntington, N.Y.: Robert E. Krieger, 1980.

Vreede, Max E. *Paramount 12000/13000.* London: Storyville Publications, 1971. Unpaged.

Wachhorst, Wyn. *Thomas Alva Edison: An American Myth.* Boston: Massachusetts Institute of Technology Press, 1981. 328 p.

Wade, Graham. *Segovia, a Celebration of the Man and His Music.* London: Allison & Busby; New York: Schocken Books, 1983. 153 p. Discography on pp. 121–132.

Wallman, James. "The Berne Convention and Recent Changes in U.S. Copyright Law." *Cum notis variorum* 132 (May 1989): 8–10.

Walsh, Jim. "Favorite Pioneer Recording Artists" columns. *Hobbies,* 1942–1985. Cited by date only.

Waltrip, Bob. "Function and Restoration of Edison Rice Paper Diaphragms." *New Amberola Graphic* 73 (July 1990): 9–10.

Want, John. "The Great Beka Expedition, 1905–06." *Talking Machine Review International* 41 (Aug. 1976): 729–733.

Ward, Alan. *A Manual of Sound Archive Administration.* Aldershot, England; Brookfield, Vermont: Gower, 1990. 288 p.

Ward, Andrew. *Dark Midnight When I Rise: The Story of the Jubilee Singers Who Introduced the World to the Music of Black America.* New York: Farrar Straus & Giroux, 2000. 493 p.

Warner, Larry. "Researching the Pre-LP Original Cast Recording." In Hummel 1984, pp. xli–xliv.

Warren, Richard, Jr. "A Preliminary Bibliography of Published Basic Source Materials and Guides to Dates of Recording for Pre-LP Classical Music and Spoken Word Sound Recordings." *Association for Recorded Sound Collections Journal* 10 (2, 3) (1979): 163–166.

Waters, Howard J. "The Hit-of-the-Week Record: A History and Discography." *Record Research* 26 (Jan.–Feb. 1960): 2–18.

Watts, Len, and Frank Andrews. "The Vertical-Cut Disc Record." *Hillandale News* 108 (June 1979): 249–255.

———. "Pathé Records in Britain." *Hillandale News* 170 (Oct. 1989): 258–263; 171 (Dec. 1989): 289–295; 172 (Feb. 1990): 320–325; 173 (Apr. 1990): 8–11.

Welch, Walter L. *Charles Batchelor: Edison's Chief Partner.* Syracuse, N.Y.: Syracuse University Press, 1972. 128 p.

Weston, Pamela. *Clarinet Virtuosi of the Past.* London: Hale, 1971. 292 p.

———. *More Clarinet Virtuosi of the Past.* London: Author, 1977. 392 p.

Whisler, John A. *Elvis Presley: Reference Guide and Discography.* Metuchen, N.J.: Scarecrow Press, 1981. 265 p.

Whitaker, Donald W. "Brass Recordings." *Instrumentalist* 20 (June 1966): 73–78.

Whitburn, Joel. *The Billboard Book of Top 40 Country Hits.* New York: Billboard Books, 1996.

———. *The Billboard Book of Top 40 Hits,* 7th ed. New York: Billboard Books, 2000.

———. *Joel Whitburn's Top R & B Singles, 1942–1988.* Compiled from Billboard's Rhythm & Blues Charts, 1942–1988. Menomonee Falls, Wisconsin: Record Research, 1988.

White, Don, and William Hogarth. "Florence Austral." *Record Collector* 14 (1, 2) (1962): 4–29; 14 (7, 8) (1962): 168–169.

White, Glenn D. *The Audio Dictionary.* Seattle: University of Washington Press, 1987. 291 p.

Whittington, Jennifer. *Literary Recordings: A Checklist of the Archive of Recorded Poetry and Literature in the Library of Congress.* Rev. ed. Washington, D.C.: Library of Congress, 1981. 299 p. (1st ed. 1966)

Whyte, Bert. "Shure Things." *Audio* (Apr. 1986): 26–27. [Whyte 1986/4]

———. "Fingering Prints." *Audio* (Aug. 1986): 16–18. [Whyte 1986/8]

———. "Put on Your Happy Feet." *Audio* (July 1989): 36–40. Discusses tweaking.

Wile, Ray. "The First Electrics." *Record Research* 85 (Aug. 1967): 5.

———. "The Edison Long-playing Record: Complete List of Issued and Unissued Masters." *Record Research* 88 (Jan. 1968): 8; 90 (May 1968): 9.

———. "How Well Did Edison Records Sell?" *Association for Recorded Sound Collections Journal* 3 (2, 3) (1971): 59–78. [Wile 1971/1]

———. "The First Martinelli Recordings." *Association for Recorded Sound Collections Journal* 3 (2, 3) (Fall 1971): 25–45. [Wile 1971/2]

———. "The Edison Discs of Frieda Hempel." *Association for Recorded Sound Collections Journal* 3 (2, 3) (Fall 1971): 47–51. [Wile 1971/3]

———. "The Edison Recordings of Gladys Rice." *Record Research* 143 (Dec. 1976): 5–7.

———. "Edisonia Local Phonograph Companies (1890–1893)." *Record Research* 115 (Feb. 1972): 8; 116 (May 1972): 9; 117 (Aug. 1972): 10.

———. "The Rise and Fall of the Edison Speaking Phonograph Company, 1877–1880." *Association for Recorded Sound Collections Journal* 7 (3) (1976): 4–31, with 9 plates.

———. "The Edison Recordings of Edna White, Trumpet." *Record Research* 144, 145 (Mar. 1977): 5. [Wile 1977/3]

———. *Edison Disc Recordings.* Philadelphia: Eastern National Park and Monument Association, 1978. 427 p.

———. "The Edison Recordings of Anna Case." *Association for Recorded Sound Collections Journal* 10 (2, 3) (1979): 167–184. [Wile 1979/1]

———. "Berliner Sales Figures." *Association for Recorded Sound Collections Journal* 11 (2, 3) (1979): 139–143. [Wile 1979/2]

———. "The Edison Invention of the Phonograph." *Association for Recorded Sound Collections Journal* 14 (2) (1982): 5–28.

———. "Record Piracy." *Association for Recorded Sound Collections Journal* 17 (1, 3) (1985): 18–40. [Wile 1985/1]

———. "The Last Years of Edison Recording Activities Day by Day, January 1928 to October 1929." *Record Research* 213, 214 (May 1985): 1, 3–10; 215, 216 (July 1985): 8–9; 217, 218 (Oct. 1985): 1, 12–13; 219, 220 (Jan. 1986): 13; 223, 224 (Aug. 1986): 10–11. [Wile 1985/2]

———. "Jack Fell Down and Broke His Crown: The Fate of the Edison Phonograph Toy Manufacturing Company." *Association for Recorded Sound Collections Journal* 19 (2, 3) (Feb. 1989): 5–36.

———. "Etching the Human Voice: The Berliner Invention of the Gramophone." *Association for Recorded Sound Collections Journal* 21 (1) (Spring 1990): 2–22. [Wile 1990/1]

———. "The Development of Sound Recording at the Volta Laboratory." *Association for Recorded Sound Collections Journal* 21 (2) (Fall 1990): 208–225. [Wile 1990/2]

———. "From the Edison Vault: Edison Blue Amberol 28100 Series." *New Amberola Graphic* 74 (Oct. 1990): 3–13. Lists 189 records in the "Concert" or "Grand Opera" series. [Wile 1990/3]

———. "Edison and Growing Hostilities." *Association for Recorded Sound Collections Journal* 22 (1) (Spring 1991): 8–34.

Wile, Raymond R., and Ronald Dethlefson. *Edison Disc Artists and Records, 1910–1929.* 2nd ed. Brooklyn: APM Press, 1990. 187 p. (1st ed., see Dethlefson and Wile 1985) [Wile 1990/4]

Williams, Clifford, and Edward Hain. "Giuseppe De Luca." *Record Collector* 11 (6) (June 1957): 124–140; 11 (7) (July 1957): 184–185; 12 (8, 9) (Nov.–Dec. 1959): 199.

Williams, C., and T. Hutchinson. "Giacomo Lauri-Volpi." *Record Collector* 11 (11, 12) (Nov.–Dec. 1957): 233–272; 12 (1, 2) (Jan.–Feb. 1958): 34–35; 12 (3) (Mar. 1958): 66–67; 12 (4, 5) (Feb.–Mar. 1959): 108; 20 (8, 10) (Aug. 1972): 239.

Williams, Clifford, and William R. Moran. "Adelina Patti." *Record Collector* 10 (8, 9) (July–Aug. 1956): 168–196.

Williams, Clifford, and John B. Richards. "Celestina Boninsegna." *Record Collector* 12 (1, 2) (Jan.–Feb. 1958): 4–33; 12 (8, 9) (Nov.–Dec. 1959): 200 (by Rodolfo Celletti); 12 (10, 11) (Dec. 1959): 257–258 (by C. de Villiers); 12 (12) (Feb. 1958): 267–283 (by William R. Moran).

Williams, Frederick P. "The Times as Reflected in the Victor Black Label Military Band Recordings from 1900 to 1927." *Association for Recorded Sound Collections Journal* 4 (1–3) (1972): 33–46; 8 (1) (1976): 4–14; 13 (3) (1981): 21–59.

———. "Eugene Ormandy Meets the Dorsey Brothers." *New Amberola Graphic* 52 (Spring 1985): 4–6.

Williamson, B. A. "Electrical Reproduction of Acoustical Records." *Talking Machine Review International* 10 (June 1971): 45, 48.

Wilson, Percy. *The Gramophone Handbook.* London: Methuen, 1957. 227 p.

Wodehouse, Artis Stiffey. "Early Recorded Pianists: A Bibliography." Ph.D. dissertation, Stanford University, 1977. 221 p.

Wolf, Robert. "Mengelberg Recordings: A Discography." *Le grand baton* (Aug.–Nov. 1971): 40–54.

Wolfe, Charles. *A Good-Natured Riot: The Birth of the Grand Ole Opry.* Nashville, Tenn.: University of Tennessee Press, Country Music Foundation, 1999. 312 p.

Wölfer, Jürgen. *Dizzy Gillespie: sein Leben, seine Musik, seine Schallplatten.* Waakirchen, Germany: OREOS, 1987. 195 p.

Woods, Robin. "Report on National Program Archives." *Association for Recorded Sound Collections Journal* 2 (2, 3) (Spring–Summer 1970): 3–21.

World Wide Record Collectors' Directory. Los Angeles: Hollywood Premium Record Guide, 1970. 46 p. (Possibly a revision of *World Wide Collectors' Directory*, by Will Roy Hearne, 1957.)

Worth, Paul W., and Jim Cartwright. *John McCormack: A Comprehensive Discography* Westport, Conn.: Greenwood Press, 1986. 185 p.

Yankovsky, M. O. "Nikolai Figner." Translated by John W. Robertson; revised and edited by Boris Semeonoff. *Record Collector* 35 (1, 2) (Jan.–Feb. 1990): 3–21.

Young, Edward D. "Serge Koussevitzky: A Complete Discography." *Association for Recorded Sound Collections Journal* 21 (1) (Spring 1990): 45–129; 21 (2) (Fall 1990): 241–265.

Young, Jordon R. *Spike Jones and His City Slickers.* Beverly Hills, Calif.: Moonstone Press, 1984. 192 p. Includes a 35-page discography.

Visual Index

VISUAL INDEX: COIN-OP PLAYERS

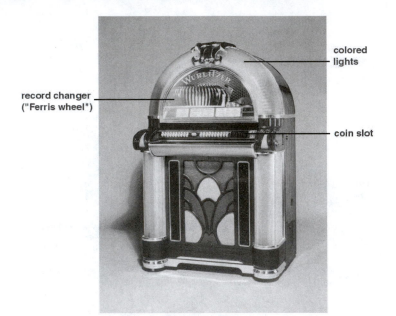

colored
lights

record changer
("Ferris wheel")

coin slot

History

Ampliphone
Autophone
coin-op
Dance Master
Hexaphone
Illustraphone
John Gabel's Automatic Entertainer
Multinola
Multiphone
Orchestrope
patents
Picturized Phonographs
Symphonola
Wurlitzer (Rudolph) Co.

Features

cylinders
jukebox
loudspeaker
record
record changer

VISUAL INDEX: LOUDSPEAKERS

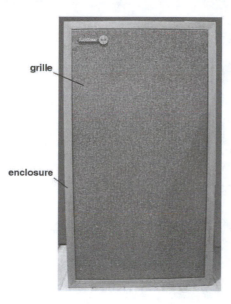

grille

enclosure

baffle
(plywood facing)

tweeter

woofer

History	Features
Amar Bose	acoustic suspension
amplifier	acoustical labyrinth
Joseph D'Appolito	baffle
Rudolph Thomas Bozak	balance
Cary L. Christie	bass
John Dunlavy	bass reflex baffle
horn	bass reflex system
Henry Kloss	
loudspeaker	
Edgar M. Villchur	

VISUAL INDEX: CYLINDER PLAYERS

horn

cylinder

hand crank

History		Features
Acoustic recording	Walter Miller	Amberol
Autophone	Multiplex Grand	Blue Amberol
Chichester A. Bell	oldest records	Combination phonograph
Gianni Bettini	Patents	Cylinder
Columbia Record Players	Phonogram	diaphragm
Concert	Phonograph	dictating machines
Deuxphone	Premier	Edison horns
Eagle	Skelly Manufacturing Co.	Edison repeating attachments
Ebonoid	Charles Sumner Tainter	Edison reproducers
Echophone	Tinfloil Phonograph	groove
Thomas Alva Edison	U.S. Phonograph Co.	horn
Edison Record Players	Voicewriter	matrix number
Indestructible Phonograph		recorder
Record Co.		shaver
Thomas Bennett Lambert		vertical cut
Long Playing Record		wax

VISUAL INDEX: TURNTABLES

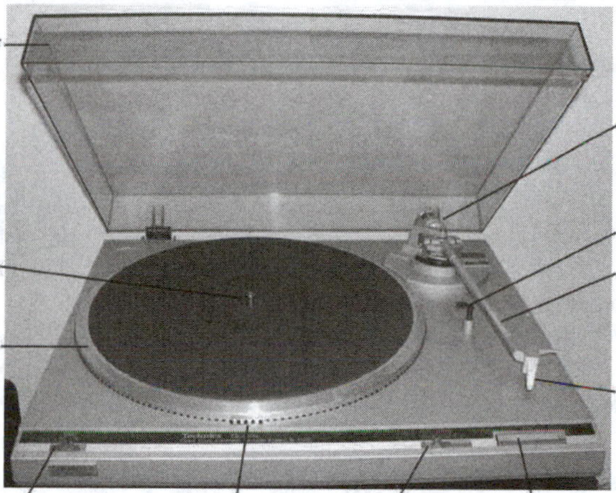

dust cover

counterweight

tone arm lock

spindle

tone arm

platter

magnetic cartridge
and stylus

speed
select

strobe

cuing
control

start/stop
switch

History	Features
American Gramophone Co. (AGC)	automatic stop
Auxetophone	cartridge
Emile Berliner	controls
Berliner Gramophone Co.	flower horn
Alfred C. Clark	flutter
disc	horn
Duplex Phonograph Co.	pitch
Thomas Elva Edison	record changer
Peter Carl Goldmark	skating force
gramophone	soundbox
Gramophone Co.	speeds
laser turntable	spindle
patents	surface speed
Roger Russell	tangential tone arm
Charles Sumner Tainter	tone arm
turntable	wow

VISUAL INDEX: TAPE RECORDERS

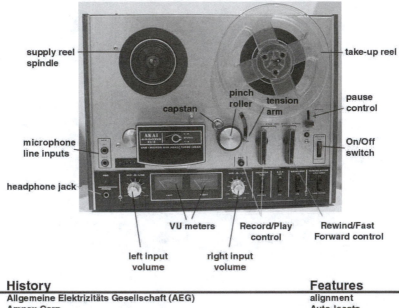

supply reel spindle

take-up reel

pinch roller

tension arm

pause control

capstan

microphone line inputs

On/Off switch

headphone jack

VU meters

Record/Play control

Rewind/Fast Forward control

left input volume

right input volume

History

Allgemeine Elektrizitäts Gesellschaft (AEG)
Ampex Corp.
cassette
Raymond M. Dolby
Max Grundig
Japanese Victor Co. (JVC)
magnetic recording
Magnetophone
Minnesota Mining and Manufacturing Co. (3M)
John T. Mullin
Nagra
Harry Olson
Alexander Mathew Poniatoff
preservation of sound recordings
reel to reel tape
sonic restoration of sound recordings
Sony Corp.
tape
tape composition
tape recording
walkman

Features

alignment
Auto-locate
automatic reverse
automatic search
Azimuth
capstan
DAT
Dolby Noise Reduction System
erase head
layering
multitracking recording
playback head
preamplifier
record head
recording head
rotating head recorder
tape deck
tape guides
tape leader
tape pack
VU meter

VISUAL INDEX: MICROPHONES

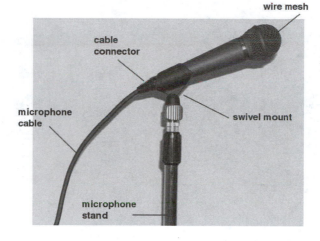

wire mesh

cable
connector

microphone
cable

swivel mount

microphone
stand

History	**Features**
Ben Bauer	atmosphere microphone
Emile Berliner	automatic microphone mixer
Alan Dower Blumlein	Decca tree
British Broadcasting Corp. (BBC)	dynamic
John Eargle	gun microphone
electrical recording	NOS recording technique
Electrovoice	ORTF recording technique
Heitaro Nakajima	parabolic reflector
Georg Newmann	patents
Harry Olson	polar response: microphones
microphone	separation
recording practice	separation recording
Schoeps	spaced array microphone recording
Sennheiser	
Stanley N. Shure	

VISUAL INDEX: AUDIO RESTORATION

78 RPM disc   **magnetic tape**

History & Practice

VISUAL INDEX: DIGITAL MUSIC

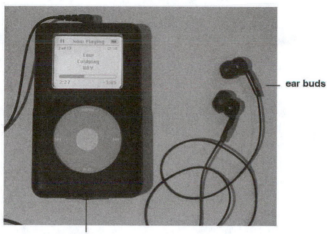

ear buds

iPod

History	Features
Barry Blesser	Advanced Audio Codec
Donald Buchla	aliasing
Compact Disc	analog to digital converter
DAT	byte
Digital Audio Player	Codec
Digital Compact Disc	DAC (digital to analog converter)
Digital Recording	iPod
Internet Music	
Heitaro Nakijima	
Napster, Inc.	
Ken C. Pohlmann	
Recording Practice	
David Rich	